TALKS ON SANKARA'S VIVEKACHOODAMANI

TEXT WITH TRANSLATION
AND COMMENTARY

SWAMI CHINMAYANANDA

CENTRAL CHINMAYA MISSION TRUST
MUMBAI.

Reprint		1989	-	5000 copies
Reprint		1993	-	3000 copies
Reprint		1995	-	3000 copies
Reprint		2003	-	2000 copies
Reprint		2004	-	2000 copies
Reprint	February	2006	-	2000 copies

Published by:
CENTRAL CHINMAYA MISSION TRUST
Sandeepany Sadhanalaya
Saki Vihar Road,
Mumbai - 400 072, INDIA.
Tel: 91-22-28572367 / 28575806
Fax: 91-22-28573065
Email: ccmt@vsnl.com
Website: www.chinmayamission.com

Distribution Centre in USA:
CHINMAYA MISSION WEST
Publications Division,
560 Bridgetown Pike,
Langhorne, PA 19053, USA.
Tel: (215) 396-0390
Fax: (215) 396-9710
Email: publications@chinmaya.org
Website: www.chinmayapublications.org

Printed by
SAGAR UNLIMITED
28-B, Nand-Deep Industrial Estate,
Kondivita Lane, Andheri Kurla Road,
Mumbai-400 059.
Tel.: 28362777 / 28227699

Price: Rs. 125=00

ISBN 81-7597-140-1

INTRODUCTION

The study of any science cannot be undertaken without a preliminary understanding of the exact definitions of the terms and terminologies employed in it. The fundamental beliefs, the accepted theories, the observed modes of behaviour, are all necessary data with which a modern scientist freely launches his new adventure into the realm of science. Similarly, in philosophy also, a fundamental knowledge of the terms used and the correct connotations in which various terms have been employed, is an unavoidable preliminary before a student can start the study of Vedanta.

Vedanta is truly the "Science of Life". Sankara, the great interpreter of Vedanta, not only gave us his commentaries on the Upnishads, the Brahma Sutras and the Bhagavad Geeta, but also many primary texts which introduce the seeker into the joys of Vedanta. One of the greatest texts he has written as an introduction to Vedanta, is the *Vivekachoodamani means,* "The Crest-Jewel of Discrimination".

A careful study of these verses with the full freedom to enquire will give any student a correct understanding of the entire theory of Vedanta and he can, even without a very serious study of the scriptures, start his daily practices with tremendous benefit.

There are hundreds of seekers who, without understanding the fundamentals, are aimlessly struggling along a so-called spiritual path. Naturally, they suffer agonies of painful disappointment, although they have behind them, years of painstaking practices. An exhaustive and careful study of this text helps to avoid all pitfalls on the way to progress. It is my intention to bring forth from every verse not only its obvious meaning, but also it hidden import which gives out a wealth of information and helpful suggestions to ensure a steady progress. Along with the Sanskrit verse I have given a free translation and a running commentary wherein I have not confined myself to the direct bearings upon the words of the verse. These verses have great suggestive wealth which, when made available, can profitably be made use of even in our day to day market place activities.

A word of advice : The seeker should carefully read three or four verses every day, and cogitate over them while pursuing his mundane activities. Only guide-lines are given here. Deep, independent thought by the reader is a must. Only then will there be satisfactory results.

It has been a painful ecstasy, all through the preparation of this manuscript. Painful because the commentaries were written during a confusingly long period of the last three or four years. I had first brought out the opening hundred verses in a volume but thereafter, the pressure of work being so great I could not find the necessary leisure for cogently expressing the pregnant suggestions of these brilliant verses of Acharya Sankara.

In order to drive home the philosophic meaning of these subtle verses, while talking to my students, in Sandeepany Sadhanalaya, I often had to repeat, and at moments I had even indulged myself in lengthy digressions. These lectures were taped.

All these furlongs of tapes were carefully and laboriously taken by Miss Kanta (Hawaii) with her tape-recorder and they were all industriously transcribed by two diligent members of the Mission-Sri Bhatia (Godrej) and Sri Radhakrishnan (Railways). These voluminous manuscripts were sent to Utterkasi when I was last there and to chop and slice them into shape was in fact more laborious than dictating the entire lot afresh.

In the final editing and preparation of the manuscript, Miss Bharathi Naik helped with great devotion.

I am conscious that there are very many jerks along the march of the commentaries upon these verses. Very often the style has conspicuously changed, and the treatment of the verses differs at more than one places in the text. I am conscious of these weaknesses, but I cannot help them as I had to take up the work between long intervals of suffocating work of the Yagnasalas.

However, when at Mysore I was flattened to my bed by the Cardiac Infraction, and when my rehabilitation in Bombay was slow, those tedious months were employed in shaping, out of the confused mass, this humble attempt. No doubt, it looks *very* beautiful to me; but can there ever be a mother who can see the ugliness of her own child?

It is a general courtesy to thank all those who helped us to bring out the book. I cannot follow this courtesy because if I have to thank, I must thank the thousands of students who assembled every morning to inspire me to express all I have recorded here. The first 100 verses that were brought out earlier, have been reedited and incorporated here into this volume.

To the student who is planning to read from the opening verse to the concluding verse 581, I have an apology to make. Such a student will find, at many places, ideas and thoughts repeated time and again deliberately. This is not a defect by oversight. This book is coneived and planned to help the Chinmaya Mission study-group-members, and repetition is the only method by which I can help them to reflect again and again upon the salient features of this great philosophy.

Secondly, every verse has been laboriously made complete in its commentary, as I feel that the majority of my reading a verse here and a verse there. If once they understand exhaustively any single verse at random, I know my work is done. Thereafter, the magic of Sankara will enchant such readers to take up an exhaustive study of the book.

Vivekachoodamani is the cream of the Upanishads and the Bhagavad Geeta. It re-educates the student, in a systematic way, to provide him with a new vision of life. The Goal and the Path are both exhaustively dealt with, in this elaborate treatment of Vedanta, by Acharya Sankara. To one, who is making a deep study of Vivekachoodamani, no other help is needed for leading him to a spiritual life and guiding him to his self improvemnet.

Sandeepany Sadhanalaya,
Powai-Park-Drive,
Bombay-72.

Chinmayananda

18-7-1970
(Guru Pournima Day).

CONTENTS

CONTENTS

॥ ॐ ॥

1. Devoted Dedication

सर्ववेदान्तसिद्धान्तगोचरं तमगोचरम् ।
गोविन्दं परमानन्दं सद्गुरुं प्रणतोऽस्म्यहम् ॥१॥

1. My salutations to Sri Sad-Guru Govinda who is of the nature of Bliss Absolute, who can be known only through the import of the essence of Vedanta and who is beyond the reach of the known instrument of perception.

It is very well-known that Sri Sankaracharya was a disciple of Sri Govindapada, who is traditionally believed to have been the disciple of Sri Gaudapada of the *Karika* fame. Here, in the opening verse, Sankara prostrates to his Master, Acharya Govindapada.

The verse can be interpreted in two possible ways. As a mortal's physical act of prostration unto a finite Guru, it was already been interpreted. It can also be understood to mean the "spiritual salutation" of a man of wisdom to the supreme Truth. When thus interpreted, the word *aham* meaning I, should indicate the subject as dis-associated with the body, mind and intellect. This ego centre in the seeker comes to seek its indentity with the Real and discovers for itself that the supreme Govinda, the essence in all Vedantic literature, beyond the perception of the sense organs, human emotions and reasoning intellect, can be experienced as the ego's own Real Nature when contemplation takes place along the lines of discussion indicated in the scriptures.

2. Glory of Spiritual Life

जन्तूनां नरजन्म दुर्लभमतः पुंस्त्वं ततो विप्रता
तस्माद्वैदिकधर्ममार्गपरता विद्वत्त्वमस्मात्परम् ।
आत्मानात्मविवेचनं स्वनुभवो ब्रह्मात्मना संस्थिति-
र्मुक्तिर्नो शतजन्मकोटिसुकृतैः पुण्यैर्विना लभ्यते ॥२॥

2. For all living creatures, a human birth is indeed rare; much more difficult it is to attain full manhood; rarer than this is a Sattwic attitude in life. Even after gaining all these rare chances, to have steadfastness on the path of spiritual activity as explained in Vedic literature is yet rarer; much more so to have a correct knowledge of the deep significances of the scriptures. Discrimination between the Real and the unreal, a personal experience of spiritual Glory and ultimately to get fully established in the living consciousness that the Self in me is the Self in all---these come only later on, and culminate in one's liberation. This kind of a perfect liberation cannot be had without earned merits of a hundred crores of lives lived intellingently.

In the very beginning of the text-book, Sankara is emphasising the difficulty of awakening ourselves to the real communion of the Divine in us. In fact, there are innumerable specimens of living creatures in the universe. Truth is the substratum of all and therefore, the real nature of all creation, even the inert and the insentient.

In stone life too, Truth exhibits Itself as Existence, but unfortunately, the stone is not aware of it. A little more evolved is plant life which seem to be more aware of the world outside and so the plant compared to the stone is a higher evolved specimen in the world of beings. When we come to animal life, we find that different species exhibit different degrees of awareness not only of their external worlds of stimuli but also of their emotions and feelings.

Of them all, man seems to be the only living creature in the universe who is independent for his rational conquests and is the sacred being which, through intellectual conviction, can gain a firm control over the emotions of the mind and apply this regulated and controlled energy for purposes of transcending psychological existence and thereby, peep into the boundless realms of bliss and beauty, love and perfection. It is in this sense that the Hindu Rishis considered man as the supreme being, while in this modern day and age man is considered great since he has developed technology and can build machines. If one were to follow this argument, the monkey world would take it as a great insult when it hears modern man declaring himself to be a descendent of the ape!.

Here Sankara seems to emphasise that this text is meant only for evolved human beings since it explains and expounds a theory of spiritual perfection which can be understood, practised, pursued and perfected only by men of certain mental calibre and moral character. Such perfect ones who are ripe for a sudden and immediate spiritual self-development are always rare in the world at any given period of its history. Thus the Acharya says that to get a human birth is rare: having got a human birth to have a masculine temperament is rarer still.

In the interpretation of this verse a lot of misunderstanding has crept in and some even glorify their misunderstanding on the score of a Vedic sanction. Thus *pundits* jump to a hasty conclusion and interpret this statement as a direct condemnation of women. According to such a thoughtless reading, women are not considered fit for Vedantic contemplation or Self-realisation. It is indeed strange how such fantastic ideas gained currency in the country of the great Rishis, for more than half our scriptural declarations have been either given out by the divine mothers or were addressed to them directly by the Rishis!

Then why this special preference shown to the masculine sex? At this juncture we must bring our discriminative capacity to understand that when these qualifications were given out, they were not given out with reference to the body. With the body, no Vedantic *sadhana* can be undertaken. The main practices in Vedanta are reflection and meditation which are to be undertaken by a healthy mind and a keen intellect. So it means that feminine qualities of mind and intellect are to be eschewed. A masculine inner personality full of courage, discrimination, detachment, equilibrium, peace and cheer, is the fittest instrument for a quick march to the Goal indicated by Vedanta.

When applications are invited by a government, say, for the police force and for the engineering department, the qualifications required by the two categories will be different from each other. An applicant for the police force will be rejected if his height is less than the prescribed minimum; but an engineer, if fully qualified and experienced, will be accepted even if he looks unhealthy, lean and pale! In the former category what is wanted is a good physique while in the latter, the candidate is expected to fulfil a subtler demand, the required intellectual quality. An expansive chest and a pair of strong biceps are not needed to design a bridge or to plan a power project for the nation; while not much intelligence or calculation is needed in making a successful *lathi* charge!

What is meant is, qualifications are declared according to the functions required of the applicant. A seeker in Vedanta is expected to carry out daring intellectual flights to the Unknown through a process of deep study, vigorous reflections and tireless meditations. So here, when it is said that, according to the *Sastras*, he must be a "he-man", it must necessarily mean that he should have a special quality of the head and heart.

Woman is the symbol of softness, attachment, sentiments, and anxieties; she is essentially a mother. Wherever these qualities predominate, there we have a "woman". In this sense there are many "women" among bearded ones and if firmness of determination, detachment, intellectual hardiness and steadiness of composure are signs of a better evolution, these masculine tendencies of head and heart are amply seen in many women. Therefore, the verse refuses none that chance to study the scriptures and seek through Vedanta one's self-development, simply because one happens to have a feminine body.

Viprata : This again is a term upon which the orthodoxy built up an absurd interpretation that Self-realisation is available only for those who are, (by sheer accident of birth), worthy or unworthy sons of Brahmins. This misunderstanding has been glorified to the status of wisdom and the amount of devastation it has brought to Hinduism looks almost irreparable now. As before, we must consider this qualification also as indicating a special quality of head and heart.

Santosh (contentment), *samadhana* (spirit of self surrender) and *santi* (peace arising from right knowledge) are the special qualities (Sattwic temperaments) of a well-evolved man. Man in any generation, when observed closely, can be classified into three distinct categories: the animal-man, the man-man and the God-man. He who is ever a victim of his gross instincts and a hopeless slave to his emotions and impulses is classified as an animal-man. When he has disciplined these instincts in himself, he is considered a full-grown, mature he-man. Such a *Vipra,* meaning a man-man has the necessary *viprata* to strive rightly and grow steadily into the last stage of his evolution --- the supermanhood or Godhood, when he becomes a God-man.

Vaidika dharma marga parata : When one has a human body along with the serener qualities of the heart and the Sattwic attitude of the intellect, one is indeed blessed with all the preliminaries for his evolution. But all these can run to waste if not properly harnessed and intellingently applied. So Sankara declares that even after gaining all the above qualifications, rarer still are those who will find the energy to apply themselves faithfully to the methods of integration as suggested in Vedic literature.

Self-less *karma,* rituals and practices of devotion, *japa, puja,* etc., alone can purify the inner personality and bring more and more integration to it. Concentration increases through desireless actions, and a person who has greater concentration *(ekagrata)*, has necessarily a finer *antah karana*. So a steady concentration must be the initial attempt of all seekers, especially those on the path of knowledge.

Vidvattwam : When such a man-man has developed a high power of concentration, he becomes fit for a profitable sudy of the scriptures. But without the true knowledge of the "whys" and the "wherefores" of the techniques, he will not be able to keep up his enthusiasm for *Sadhana* because of his limited understanding. Therefore, the study of the scripture is indicated here. And the literature that shows the Goal, declares the path, and gives the rational arguments for both is the Upanishads.

When a man-man, having developed his powers of concentration through selfless actions, studies the scriptures properly, he gains in discrimination between spirit and matter, the Real and the unreal. Soon he comes to realise that the Self in him is the Self in all, and ere long he gets established in his experience of god-hood.

Sankara in enumerating these stages of self-development, gives us in a nut-shell the unwritten chapters in Darwin's half declared theory of evolution. Here we have all the various stages through which man consciously, by right living and self-progress climbs on to the lap of the Lord, there to merge with Him, there to become Siva. This is called *mukti* ---the full and final liberation of a mortal from all his limitations.

The last line is not a cry of pessimistic despair; it is the call of hope, urging man to wake up and act, to grow and achieve the highest gain. No reader of this verse should consider himself as standing low down in this upward procession. One who feels charmed by the call of Vedanta, who can appreciate its arguments, who feels a sympathetic understanding of the ideal indicated, is indeed at the fag-end of his transmigrations, the product of an entire evolutionary past. If he makes use of his present chance with diligent and careful application, success is guarnateed to him by Vedanta. This is a call to man to throw off his lethargy, his dejections, his sentiments of self-pity and to wake up to face life and through understanding, to grow fast to reach the Goal---*here and now*.

3. Unique Graces in Life

दुर्लभं त्रयमेवैतद्देवानुग्रहहेतुकम् ।
मनुष्यत्वं मुमुक्षुत्वं महापुरुषसंश्रयः ॥३॥

3. Manhood, burning desire for liberation, the capacity to surrender completely to a man of wisdom---these three things are rare indeed, and wherever they are found, they are due to the Lord's own Grace.

Earlier we were told how rare is the human birth and the necessary qualifications one must have for a vital and positive living by which one can grow in one's inner evolution. In order to emphasise to the seeker the importance of the qualities which he should have when going to a great man of learning, seeking spiritual knowledge, these qualifications are here stressed.

Sankara says that to be born as a human being is a sign of Lord's Grace. After this, to employ in life a deep discriminative understanding and to perceive the ultimate futility of all the ordinary mundane pursuits of life and thereby discover an enthusiasm to seek a nobler path of self-redemption is rarer still. Lastly, when a creature is born as a man, when he feels a gnawing sense of impatience at his own limitations, for him to find the right Master to guide him across the thorny paths of his imperfections into the soft meadows of limitless joy and bliss is the rarest. Sankara attributes all these three rounds of seeming luck to the Grace of the Almighty.

The Grace of the Almighty as expressed in Vedanta is not to be understood as the blessings of a God, a Sultan of the sky sitting amidst the clouds showering special packets of Grace on chosen individuals. What is meant here by God's Grace is only the sum total of reactions gained through the healthy and intelligent way in which the individual has lived through his many previous lives of great and noble cultural pursuits.

4. Miseries of the Unspiritual Man. (4-7)

लब्ध्वा कथंचिन्नरजन्म दुर्लभं
तत्रापि पुंस्त्वं श्रुतिपारदर्शनम् ।
यस्त्वात्ममुक्तौ न यतेत मूढधी :
स ह्यात्महा स्वं विनिहन्त्यसद्ग्रहात् ॥४॥

4. Is there a man who, having somehow gained a human embodiment, and there having a masculine temperament and also a complete knowledge of the scriptures, is foolish enough not to strive hard for Self-realisation? He verily commits suicide, clinging to things unreal.

This verse declares that having been born in a human form, and possessed of the necessary masculine qualities of the head and heart, when such an individual has also made a through study of the deep significances of scriptural techniques, if he has not the enthusiasm to walk the sacred path and reach the divine Goal of self-perfection---such an individual, alas, commits suicide. Having got such a rare chance, a chance in a million, if he is not ready to take hold of it and use it in a profitable manner, he is indeed committing *hara kiri* and such a squanderer of human birth is very fittingly termed by Sankara as a dull fool---*mudhadhihi.*

How does a person commit this senseless suicide? By his false attachments with the objects of the world as he looks out from the parapets of his body and his mind. Forgetting his own Real Nature, which is all-pervading Consciousness, he comes to misunderstand himself to be the matter envelopments which are nothing but thought-created encrustations around the Divine in him. Perceiving through the prism of the body, mind and intellect, he sees the Truth splashed and splintered into endless plurality and the objects give a delusory enchantment to the senses and the mind. To satisfy these urges of his body and his mind, the individual runs after the objects. Necessarily, such a deluded person, having misunderstood his Real Nature, becomes the *samsaric* ego-centre,a victim of his own ignorance. This fall of the Self to be the selfish ego is spiritual suicide.

There is no real suicide possible to the Atman. No danger can come to me simply because I dream the greatest of dangers, even though the dreamer in me suffers all the dangers of my dream. The moment I wake up I realise that the dangers as well as the dreamer who suffered them were all my own mental creations only in an unsubstantial dream world.

So, from the standpoint of Reality there is no suicide; but Sankara comes down to our level to help us discriminate between the Real and the unreal, in and through our day to day life and it is in this sense that he says we commit suicide. It is not the destiny of the Self to suffer, but it is the lot of the ego, the ego that strives in this world to be the sacred and the divine.

इतः कोन्वस्ति मूढात्मा यस्तु स्वार्थे प्रमाद्यति ।
दुर्लभं मानुषं देहं प्राप्य तत्रापि पौरुषम् ॥५॥

5. Is there a greater fool than the man who, having got the rare chance of a human birth and there too, the masculine qualities of the head and heart, falls short in his efforts to rediscover himself?

All creatures must wait for millions and trillions of years until nature takes them up step by step and moulds them into greater evolutionary equipments. In all the lower strata of existence, evolution is not a conscious development on the part of the individual but an involuntary thrust up received by him from the course of nature.

Millennia of growth, change and decay must pass before a rock becomes soil, the soil anchors a tree, the tree bears fruit and the fruit contributes towards the making of a human being. Millions and trillions of spermatozoa and ova are produced but only a few of them are united to create a human being. Of all the countless possibilities, to be born a human is a rare chance, indeed. And having thus got a human form, what do we do with it? Man because of his mind and intellect equipment is, to an extent, free from nature in evolving himself. Man alone, of all the species of the living kingdoms, can hasten his own evolution by co-operating with the great eternal scheme of things around him. Physically, he has evolved to perfection and nature has nothing more to improve him.His next lap of evolution awaits him at the level of his mind and intellect and this is a process in which nature cannot help him at all

With this *Sastric* conclusion in mind when the Acharya takes up his pen to guide the generation, he must necessarily exclaim and conclude that there can never be a greater fool than the one who, being blessed with a human birth and the necessary mental and intellectual capacities, does not intelligently invest them for the higher purpose of self-redemption and Self-rediscovery.

वदन्तु शास्त्राणि यजन्तु देवान्
कुर्वन्तु कर्माणि भजन्तु देवताः ।
आत्मैक्यबोधेन विना विमुक्ति-
र्न सिध्यति ब्रह्मशतान्तरेऽपि. ॥६॥

6. Let erudite scholars quote all the scripture, let gods be invoked through sacrifices, let elaborate rituals be performed, let personal gods be propitiated---yet, without the experience of one's identity with the Self, there shall be no liberation for the individual, not even in the lifetime of a hundred Brahmas put together.

A disciple who has come to the feet of a Master of Vedanta, is expected to know already some of the traditional technique of the religious world wherein, for purposes of training the animal-man into the man-man, various methods of discipline have been advised such as study of the scriptures, performing sacrifices, making offerings, worship of a personal god and even selfless *seva.* Here the Master is addressing those few, who, having practised all these with sincerity and diligence for a number of years, have come to feel poignantly their limitations and in their growing dissatisfaction with ritualistic religion, have rushed to the Master's feet, seeking guidance along their path for self redemption. To such a student the Master has to tell the naked truth and all of it, keeping nothing back. So here is a passage which reads like an out and out condemnation of the ritualistic aspects of all religions.

There is a type of dull seekers who have become so addicted to their method of spiritual practices that they would rather claim a dreary patience with life and its pains, with their disappointments in *sadhana* and faith, than dare take up a more satisfying and advanced practice. This is in fact, an expression of their superstitious fear at leaving the path which they have been practising for so long. A devotee who has been through *kirtan, puja, japa and dhyana,* developing his devotion for a personal god for a number of years, will not dare to drop for a short time even an iota of his daily routine, even if he were asked to do so by the greatest living Master in the world. Just as one gets addicted to a false way of living, so one can easily become habituated to whatever is accepted as a good way of living. To live in a routine will never yield the secret of living in inspiration. To get habituated to any method is to get into a rut and balk all progress. We must have the freedom, at every moment, to change our pattern of living and seek new methods of keeping the mind and intellect occupied in a lively warmth of love and cheer. Else even our worship becomes mechanical and in the end, stultifying.

In this sense Vedanta is heretical and revolutionary. The attitude with which one should do the "hearing" *(sravana),* of the scriptures is totally different from the attitude with which one is asked to do "reflection" *(manana)* upon what one has heard. Again, neither the *sraddha nor sravana nor* the intellectual freedom of *manana* are permitted to poison the deep serenity of the thought-less meditation hours. Thus, a Vedantic student is taught, from the very beginning, to be original at every moment and to live ever in the white heat of inspiration, at once thrilling, divine, ennobling.

Here, as soon as the student reaches the Master, he is washed clean of all his tradional beliefs. This is, indeed, a kind of shock therapy by which the student is brutally shaken out of the deep ruts into which he may have fallen and shown new dimensions of thought along the right, the straight path.

His wrong notions about religion, his confirmed belief in rituals, his blind faith in hearsay, are all shown here as having nothing to do with true and permanent liberation. Learning the *Sastras*, invoking gods through sacrifices self-less work and even devotion to a personal god have been denied as having any capacity to give us *mukti* ---"even in the life-time of a hundred Brahmas" ---which is, according to our mythology, equivalent to 311,040,000,000,000 years ! ! This is not at all a statement of despair but a a way of self-discovery the secret of which is for the seeker to realise that the Self in him is the Self in all, as prescribed here. The method of this discovery, the meaning of the Self, etc., are all the theme of this text.

अमृतत्वस्य नाशास्ति वित्तेनेत्येव हि श्रुतिः ।
ब्रवीति कर्मणो मुक्तेरहेतुत्वं स्फुटं यतः ॥७॥

7. It is clear that liberation cannot be the effect of good works, for *Sruti* herself declares that there is no hope for immortality by means of wealth.

Amritattwam is the goal indicated in all the Upanishads. When it is translated as merely *immortality*, readers are apt to misunderstand it to be a profit that can accrue to man only after his death. This misunderstanding then must take away the edge from religion and dry up all enthusiasm for spiritual living, especially from the modern man who wants immediate gains. He is not ready to invest even a thought in a proposition that will yield to him a great profit only at a future time. Even if we promise him a great existence after death, the modern educated youth will not be interested, since what he seeks is immediate joy and perfection, here and now.

At this healthy insistence of the sons of the land, the old orthodox pundit despairs and brands them as atheists. This is an unfair conclusion. Correctly interpreted, the "immortality" promised by the *Srutis* is not a state or condition that comes to us after our departure from this world. It is a perfection that can be lived *here* and *now*. By the term "immortality" the Rishis indicate a state of continuous existence which has in it no experience of finitude. The disturbances caused by the multiple experiences that rise and fall in us are the causes for all our sorrows and man, knowingly or unknowingly, is struggling hard to continue his experiences. It is very well known that even in deep sorrow, if the experiences are continuos, the experiencer must come to smile in his sorrow, else we would not have had even one peal of laughter from our slum areas.

The rich man wants to stretch continuously his experience of joy in his wealth but, alas, it diminishes with the passage of time. All over the world, modern man is struggling to increase his joy in life, to maintain his virulence, to lengthen his life-span and in a thousand and one other activities.

There is an anxious impatience with law of finitude that seems to whip man from all sides. The word "immortality" in Vedanta indicates not a continuous and monotonous living in joy in a hazy *yonder there*, but a perfection *here within* ourselves by which we can, irrespective of the circumstances that play around us, come to live a continuous experience of tranquillity and peace.

This mental equilibrium which refuses to entertain any revolting or choking disturbances from without---this mental poise and intellectual dexterity which make it possible for the mind to rise in revolt against itself, this endless peace cannot be gained, says Sankara, through the wealth *(vittam)* of sense-objects. *Vittam*, though it generally means "wealth", here means the "wealth" that gives us immediate experiences and indeed, it is the sense-objects that directly convey experiences to us from the external world. So a continuous and infinite experience of peace and tranquillity, joy and perfection, cannot be had through the satisfaction of our animal urges by procuring, maintaining and enjoying these ephemeral sense-objects.

In this sense, this verse throws a flood of light on the previous one. No number of sense-objects, be they as sacred as the Vedic texts, no amount of activities, be they as sacred as *yagnas* or worship, can by themselves take us to that mental poise.

All Acharyas, irrespective of their philosophical beliefs, accept the declaration of the scriptures as absolute and as having unquestionable authority. This attitude is not acceptable to the modern youth, who, in his colossal ignorance thinks himself daring enough to question even the Rishis. He may not dare to question in his Physics class-room and will silently and satisfactorily swallow a statement such as, that electrons and protons are moving with a terrific frequency around a neutron in every atom. His spirit of enquiry and courage of understanding seem to freeze when it comes to modern science but the moment he hears the declarations in ancient texts, he finds in himself the audacity to question but unfortunately has not the courage to examine or the stamina to experiment with those ideas. What a let-down !

The great Acharyas of yore were not the senile or idiotic dreamers we are prone to label them. This is not only an insult to their intelligence, but also to our own and that of our ancestors who believed and followed them with benefit.

The Acharyas accepted the declarations of the *Srutis* because of the bonafide character and temperament of the

Rishis who declared them. They did not, like politicians, go to the public to thrust their ideas down the throats of the listeners. They lived in complete contenment and happiness in their Self-discovery and it was for the seekers to make a foot path and reach them with their questions and doubts upon life and its meaning, the goal and the path. To those seekers, out of sheer kindness, these men of Realisation declared the Truth of their own experiences, in a burning spirit of inspiration and love. They had no intentions to misguide these precious young hearts of the generation.

These Rishis had no *ashramas* to build or missions to run so they wanted no agents to hood-wink people and collect funds. They desired nothing, they asked for nothing, they demanded nothing. Physically, as far as they were concerned, they were dead and wanted the world to accept them as such. To such men of wisdom who had divorced themselves so completly from the world of desires and demands, to impute low motives for misguiding their generation would reflect only upon our lack of understanding of the literature. When we study a Shakespearean drama, we go to great lenghts to understand the life of the dramatist and the Engalnd of Elizabethan times. But these scientific methods of study are totally ignored when we come to the scriptures where we do not even try to understand the mental attitude, the intellectual accomplishments, the physical environments etc., under which the great Rishis served, worked and lived.

The Acharya accepted the *Sruti* declarations as eternal aspects of the One Truth. Later on, for those who want more logic and reason, we have a number of verses which support the assertion that work, no matter how noble or divine, cannot by itself tune the individual perfectly to that equanimous and peaceful mental attitude wherein he can come to experience, in this variegated world of pluralistic experiences, a continuous and unbroken peace of perfection.

5. Means of Wisdom. (8-13)

अतो विमुक्त्यै प्रयतेत विद्वान्
सन्न्यस्तबाह्यार्थसुखस्पृहः सन् ।
सन्तं महान्तं समुपेत्य देशिकं
तेनोपदिष्टार्थसमाहितात्मा ॥८॥

8. Therefore, the learned seeker who is striving to gain this freedom within and who has renounced all his desires for pleasures in the sense-objects, should duly approach a good and generous Master and must live attuned to the true significances of the words of the Master.

If *Sruti* declares that a man cannot achieve victory over his lower self and inner weaknesses through actions, however glorious and noble they may be, one is apt to conclude that there is no method by which one can redeem oneself. This despair, perhaps, the Master noted on the face of the disciple and so hastened to console him. We have here a positive declaration of what exactly a seeker should do in order that he may be well-established on the path of Truth.

A seeker in Vedanta is not a non entity who has walked into the sanctum of a temple or has casually thought of sitting in prayer or visiting a sacred place. These constitute but the very primary steps in spiritual life. A student entering the Halls of Wisdom can gain admission only when he has had a good education, not only in the market place but also in the great works discussing the theory and meaning of life. Hence the word *Vidwan* is used here to indicate a true seeker. When therefore, a student having had a cursory knowledge of life and its meaning realises the futility of running after sense-objects, he comes to a certain amount of renunciation of desires and thus he approaches his Master. Sankara in this verse also lists the special qualifications necessary for a seeker on the spiritual path.

Santam : The word *santa* is often used in the vernacular to indicate a Sannyasin, but rarely does one realise what exactly the term means. He is a *santa* who is firmly established in the consciousness of pure existance *(Sat.)* A Guru must not only be a man of full Realisation and experience but he should be a *Mahantam*, a large-hearted, sympathetic, kind person. Without these qualifications of the heart, he will not be able to come down from the high seat of his experience and mingle with the imperfect seekers who come to him and fully understand their difficulties on the path. One can be a Guru only if one has the required magnanimity, intimate personal experience of the Divine and great familiarity with the scriptures.

A thorough study of the scriptures gives the Teacher the necessary language of expression and also the required intellectual arguments to resolve a student's doubts into abiding convictions. There are innumerable great sants who have been sitting silently in their caves, brimful with their experiences and yet unable to communicate to the world of seekers. There are on the other hand many among us who have the music in them but no flute to transform it into a melody. Therefore, the word *desikam*---well read in the scriptures---is of special importance.

Even if a seeker discovers such a perfect Master, he will not be able to react favourably in the Master's presence or even to his discussions if he has not the necessary mental attitude, denoted by the word *samupetya*. The manner of approaching a Master is not merely a prescription for a sapless formality. It specifies, mainly, a mental attitude. If we approach a Master with the objective of judging him or evaluating his knowledge, certainly we are not going to benefit. There are some who approach a man of wisdom to make him understand how far they are men of wisdom themselves. This exhibitionism of their laboriously gathered second hand informations will choke their hearts and they will not be able to gain anything from the Master's words which rise from his own first hand experiences. Water flows only from a higher level to a lower level; so too it is with the flow of knowledge. Unless we have the meekness and the spirit of surrender, knowledge cannot reach us.

The divine attitude of full receptivity is the aroma of a heart which has reverence for and surrender to, faith in and love for, the Guru. These are, therefore, insisted upon in the *Sastras*, but they may seem to the modern man as arrangements set up by a team of social criminals to loot and plunder the credulous public. Such an opinion reflects the level of decadence into which modern man has fallen.

Again, even with all the prescribed qualifications if a seeker were to reach the feet of a perfect Master, the transferred knowledge cannot take root in the student unless he is himself ready to strive along the path. The instructions given here explaining how he should conduct himself in the presence of the Master are very significant indeed, especially so in our times when we are all labouring under terrible misunderstandings about this Guru-shishya relationship.

After all, a Master can only explain truths and give sufficient logic to give the seeker intellectual conviction. These ideas are, at best, prescriptions for certain values of life which cannot yield any benefit unless they are taken up and made a part of the entire scheme of our evolution. The major part of the work depends upon our own efforts to rehabilitate ourselves. Thus, it is said, the individual should try to live the deep significances of the precepts of the Master.

More often than not, we find that we try to follow what the Master *did* and not what he *said*. Here it is definitely pointed out that we have nothing to do with what the Master does. Else we should have to applaud the traders in *bhakti* who conveniently declare that theirs is only the fifth marriage while their Lord had 16,008 ! There can be, indeed, very interesting varieties even in the methods of self-destruction!

उद्धरेदात्मनात्मानं मग्नं संसारवारिधौ
योगारूढत्वमासाद्य सम्यग्दर्शननिष्ठया ॥९॥

9. Having attained the state of *Yogarudha* through continuous and well-established discrimination, one should lift oneself from the ocean of change and finitude wherein one has come to be drowned.

When an individual has realised his limitations and feels that he must by some means redeem himself from his weaknesses and gain mastery over himself, it is not sufficient that he surrenders to his Master no matter how great, or runs away from the world into a quiet jungle or even makes a thorough and complete study of all the *Scriptures*. Practices such as these may somewhat help the individual but he can lift himself from the mire of his inner weakness only by dint of sustained self-effort.

Through study, following of *Sastraic* instruction, practices of self-control and various other spiritual *sadhanas*, generally undertaken in the name of religion, one can expect to develop the subtlety of one's inner instruments for experiencing the world as it is, uncoloured by any personal prejudices, attachments or hatreds. This perception of the world as it is, in perfect detachment and discrimination is called *samyag darsana*. *Darsana* in Sanskrit also means "philosophy" and, therefore, the term can also be interpreted as the vision of the world through the eye of philosophy.

When one views life from this angle and with a right mode of perception, slowly and steadily one gains the state of a *Yogarudha*.[1] *When desires are not murmuring, thoughts cannot* arise; and when thoughts do not rise, there will be a complete cessation of actions. When an individual through study, *satsang* and intelligent thinking has come to observe life and its happenings with the right attitude and intellectual poise, he automatically gets established in *Yoga*.

---

1. *In Geeta VI--4, we have a description of the Yogarudha* State. "When a man is not attached to sense-objects or to actions and has renounced all thoughts, then he is said to have attained to *Yoga*." In this verse, Sri Krishna explains that state of living as the state of establishment in *Yoga* in which an individual's mind is neither wandering into the sense-objects; nor is gurgling out towards its desires.

The word *Yoga* has come to be associated with so many unnecessary trappings, that a student is apt to miss his grip on its import here. *Yoga* in its right sense is only that state of mind in which the mind having recognised its weaknesses attunes itself to a greater and more perfect ideal which the intellect has shown it. Any attempt of the mind to rise from the low values of its present existence to a healthier and diviner scheme of living is *Yoga*. To get established in *Yoga* is to make it a habit to strive sincerely to rise above one's known weaknesses in order to attain the ideal.

संन्यस्य सर्वकर्माणि भवबन्धविमुक्तये ।
यत्यतां पण्डितैर्धीरैरात्माभ्यास उपस्थितैः ॥१०॥

10. May the wise and learned man give up all actions which are motivated by desires and start the practice of rediscovering the Self and thereby attain freedom from the bondage of birth and death.

Here is a piece of advice given to a man who has all the necessary theoretical knowledge of the science of self perfection. He is told to renounce all activities motivated by self-aggrandising hopes or disintegrating desires.

This renunciation of the activities of the world is not to be over-emphasised and misunderstood, as is generally done, to mean that Vedanta is calling man to a life of lotus-eating. It is only asking us to reduce over excitement in life and to curb the wasteful expenditure of our mental and intellectual energies born out of our unintelligent desires and lofty expectations. That good and sincere work will yield noble fruits should be a sufficient direction to guarantee us a peaceful passage for our pilgrimage here. But we expect the impossible, a noble return from a vicious or ill-planned action instead of the painful returns of sorrow, that will yield to us many a terrible hour of unproductive anxiety and suicidal worry. A seeker who is striving to integrate himself is advised to walk the path of intelligent living.

The renunciation of false values is only a negative aspect of self-making. Man-making fulfils itself in God-discovery and this spiritual art of perfection is not to be gained by a negative endeavour. Sankara specifies the positive aspect by saying, "Let him practise the various means of Self-discovery."

चित्तस्य शुद्धये कर्म न तु वस्तूपलब्धये ।
वस्तुसिद्धिर्विचारेण न किंचित्कर्मकोटिभिः ॥११॥

11. Self-less work and charitable acts help to purify the mind but they do not, by themselves, contribute to the perception of Reality. The discovery of the Self is brought about only by discriminative analysis and never by any number of actions.

This verse may give a novice the impression that Vedanta is decrying all the orthodox and accepted methods of religious practice. A child is told by his parents to revise his arithmetic tables every day. The obedient child soon gets into the habit of starting his day with a reading of the tables. But if the child continues his habit as a dull and unintelligent routine even in his post-graduate classes, it is but natural for his professor to laugh at his stupidity.

Similarly, in the halls of Vedanta, the seeker is laughed at because of the time-worn techniques of self-development to which he has become habituated. But that does not mean that Sankara or the Vedantins are against them. The paths of *karma, bhakti* etc., have certainly a place in the scheme of self-development and they are unavoidable in hauling up an animal man through the various stage of self development to the pinnacle of perfection.

Here Sankara points out that *karma* when undertaken with a pure *nishkama bhava* purifies the inner instruments of feeling and understanding. The word *suddhi* used in connection with the mind is to be understood as a greater degree of integration. The purer mind has a greater capacity to concentrate. When an action is undertaken with a motive, the individual must necessarily be shattered and fatigued under its persecution. On the other hand when an act of charity or kindness is done in a spirit of dedication and love, with no ulterior motive, the mind cosily settles down, and the peace that rises within the *sadhak* increases automatically and his personality becomes more and more integrated.

Selfless actions do not help a seeker directly in his flights of Self-discovery. But they certainly have a place in one's *sadhana* in as much as they prepare the individual to transcend the ego and give him the wings for the last flight to the Beyond.

Sankara is uncompromisingly severe when he declares in his irrevocable statements that the Self is not produced nor knowledge created as a result of finite actions, however noble, divine and great they may be.

सम्यग्विचारतः सिद्धा रज्जुतत्त्वावधारणा ।
भ्रान्त्योदितमहासर्पभयदुःखविनाशिनी ॥१२॥

12. The fear and sorrow created by the delusory serpent on the rope can be ended only after fully ascertaining the truth of the rope which is available for recognition only through steady and balanced thinking.

Why the discovery of the Self is not possible through *karma* and how this is possible by means of right thinking is being explained here by the famous analogy of the serpent and the rope. In Vedanta, this example is often quoted to make the student understand how the names and forms created through the ignorance of Reality can end with the rediscovery of the Truth underlying them. It is never possible that one who has seen the rope as a rope will ever have the fear and sorrow of a snake-bite. But in the gathering darkness of dusk a traveller mistakes an innocent rope to be a snake. The serpent-delusion is created in the mind of the traveller because of his ignorance of the rope-reality.

Having thus been bitten by a delusory serpent, the individual, so long as he is under the delusion, suffers the agony of a snake-bite and, if left alone, will exhibit symptoms of blood-poisoning too. But the traveller is advised to make an enquiry into his delusion. Faithful friends or near and dear ones will approach the deluded one and exclaim, "Oh, it is only a length of rope". He will accept this statement as a possibility because of his faith in his friends.

But however much he may try, he will not enjoy complete peace of mind unless he himself sees the rope as a rope. The moment he is led to the place of the incident and in a clear light, he discovers the rope for himself, the fear and anxiety, and the delusory snake and its bite all end. No amount of beating the rope in the darkness can kill the snake or finally bring peace, happiness and cheer to the individual. Even if the rope is burnt, he cannot find his balance again and take his mind away from the thoughts of fear and pain caused by the snake-bite, for he may still believe that he was bitten by a snake and it was the snake which was burnt to ashes.

So through *karmas* performed even for thousands of years, one cannot come to that joy of Self-discovery, the only method for which is to treat the path of discriminative analysis. This example, famous in Vedantic literature, is given by Sankara only to remind us how and in what way correct thinking can blot out the miseries of life, which are only the outcome of our misunderstanding and ignorance of Reality.

अर्थस्य निश्चयो दृष्टो विचारेण हितोक्तितः ।
न स्नानेन न दानेन प्राणायामशतेन वा ॥१३॥

13. Neither sacred baths nor any amount of charity nor even hundreds of *pranayamas* can give us the knowledge about our own Self but a firm experience of the nature of the Self can be gained when we send our thoughts along the rails of argument laid down in the salutory advices of the wise.

Here again we find the superficial methods of easy religious practices condemned. Since the student is a Vedantin, Ṣankara's efforts are to show him the right and direct path. In thus indicating to the student the correct path every Master has to be very severe in his criticism of the by-lanes of religion. No doubt they too can help in the progress of the individual, but they are all primary lessons.

Techniques followed in the kindergarten are not applied in the university. A teacher must pluck out the seeker from his flounderings in the muck and mire of marshes and put him on the firm metalled road to truth. Therefore, external methods of self-purification such as baths at the sacred confluences of rivers, visits to various temples and other sacred places,desire-prompted or even unselfish charities, exercises such as breath-control as *asanas* are wholly condemned.

The hasty convert to Vedanta suddenly finds it very convenient to give up every religious practice and call himself an accomplished Vedantin. This attitude also has no sanction in the Master's advice. While condemning these preliminaries, he is, at the same time, very strict and severe in prescribing the more subtle and intense practices of Vedanta. For a Vendantin, he prescribes correct thinking and continuous self-analysis. Merely giving up the usual methods of religious discipline is not the Vedanta prescribed by the Acharya. If at all they are to be given up, it is only for a greater *abhyasa* called *vichar.* This *atma-vichar* is not to be done in any manner that pleases the individual. There is an exact method of correct and intense thinking and this method is advised in the scriptures. Therefore, *vichar*, undertaken as taught by the Rishis *(hitoktitah)*, alone can take us ultimately to our redemption.

6. The Fit Student. (14-17)

अधिकारिणमाशास्ते फलसिद्धिर्विशेषतः ।
उपाया देशकालाद्याः सन्त्यस्मिन्सहकारिणः ॥१४॥

14. Ultimate success in spiritual endeavours depends entirely upon the degree of fundamental qualifications in the seeker. Auxiliary conveniences such as time and place all have a place indeed, but they are essentially secondary.

Here is a suggestion to seekers who generally get disappointed at having to encounter obstacles at the very outset of their *sadhana.* When a team of students is working under the instructions of the same Master, it is always observed that some of them progress faster than others. Those who lag behind soon reach a state of despair and they complain about the hollowness of the *Sastras.* Such students are advised to attribute their lack of development to some intrinsic subjective maladjustments in their psychological and intellectual make-up.

Adhikari is a word which has been much misinterpreted by hasty pundits, who in their loftiness often rejected sincere seekers on the assertion that they were not properly qualified for Vedantic *sadhana.* This is absurd. No living man can conclusively judge another especially upon these points. The qualifications necessary for a successful spiritual pilgrimage have been enumerated here by the *Acharya* only for the self-scoring of the seekers themselves.

That is, if success on the spiritual path has been slow or unsatisfactory, the seeker himself is to blame. It is invariably because of some clogs of the heart. All that he has to do in order to achieve more progress in his efforts is to remove these clogs and apply himself more intensely to self-development.

This is true even in our everyday life. A brand new car, let us say, with a tank-full of petrol is on the road and it stalls for no conceivable reason. Few owner-drivers know anything about what lies under the bonnet of their cars. Sitting in the driver's seat they wrench out all the switches and labour with all the handles and when they find that there is no reponse from the engine, they leave it on the kerb and go home.

But if in their place there were a professional driver, he is at once able to sense out the trouble spot. He gets out of his seat, raises the bonnet and checks all possible points of engine trouble. After making the necessary adjustments, he resumes his seat and the machine responds to his demands.

Similarly, when in meditation a *sadhak* finds his mental avenues blocked, it is meaningless for him to sit in the *asana* and rave in disappointment, cursing the entire hierarchy of Rishis or the science of Vedanta. He must at once lift the bonnet of his bosom and look within to see if the necessary adjustments are all properly maintained therein. The description of the necessary qualifications is for our guidance, that we may know what are the common troubles that arise in the inner vehicle during our flight to the Beyond.

There are some seekers who wait for better circumstances to do their *sadhana*, a more suitable time or a greater Master to initiate them. No doubt, time, place etc., are important, but not unduly so, for they are only subsidiary requirements. Without the needful inner adjustments even if a *sadhak* is placed under the best conditions of time and place he will not be able to make use of them. On the other hand, a true seeker even under adverse conditions will turn them to the best advantage and will progress steadily, unhampered. These prerequisites are described in detail in verses 16 and 17.

अतो विचारः कर्तव्यो जिज्ञासोरात्मवस्तुनः
समासाद्य दयासिंधुं गुरुं ब्रह्मविदुत्तमम् ॥१५॥

15. Therefore, a true seeker of the Self should learn to enquire and meditate after duly approaching a Guru who is himself established in the experience of the Self and who is an ocean of kindness.

For the reasons so far given, it should be the endeavour of a true seeker to find a true Master and approach him duly to get initiated into the methods of enquiry through the process of meditation.

Here a true *Guru* is described. Just as there are essential qualifications for a true disciple, there are those also which are essential to make a man of wisdom a true and efficient *Guru*. It is not every man of Realisation who can efficiently take up the work of directing others on the path towards the Goal.

A *Guru* should be not only a man of Self-experience, but he should also have a large heart full of kindness and sympathy for all types of seekers. This is an indispensable requisite, for without it the Master will not be able to go down to the level of the disciples and sympathetically appreciate their difficulties in understanding the *Sastras* and in living up to the high discipline that is expected of them by the *Srutis*.

The word *samasadya*[1]--by duly aproaching--is a simple word full of suggestions. It pin-points the mental attitude with which a seeker should approach the Master in order that he may derive the maximum benefit during his intercourse with the Teacher.[2]

मेधावी पुरुषो विद्वानूहापोहविचक्षणः ।
अधिकार्यात्मविद्यायामुक्तलक्षणलक्षितः ॥१६॥

16. He who has a keen memory with enough knowledge of the world outside and understanding of the world within, who can argue for the scriptures and refute arguments against them, is fit for receiving *Atma-vidya*

Here are mentioned some essential qualities in a student before he can successfully undertake a study of the *Upanishadas*. The power of memory *(medha)*, is not merely a prodigious capacity that some have to memorise an impossible number of scriptures in a very short time. Among the men of letters in England, there was once a mania to memorise long poems and, we are told, many could recite the whole of Milton's Paradise Lost or an entire Shakespearean drama! This sort of mechanical memorising is not what is meant by *medha*--memory power--here.

By "memory" Sankara means a capacity on the part of the student to react intensely to an experience at the time of its occurrence so that, later on, it automatically, without any effort, springs forth into the level of memorised

1. Earlier the term used is *Samupetya*.
2. Refer Verse 8.

experiences. In this sense, none of us lacks the power of memory. Even those who cannot memorise a single stanza or a paragraph can remember some incidents of their childhood. This clearly shows that they have, generally, a good memory.

A student attending the discourses given by a Master is therefore required to react intensely to his words and thus make the ideas and theories explained his own at the very time of listening to them. There is no question of writing down notes and learning them later on as modern college students do. The study of Vedanta insists on an immediate understanding. He who has this capacity is fit for a study of Vedanta. If there be a student who could not understand what the Master said on a previous occasion, then as the lessons proceed, the Master will not be able to give his discourses freely since the student, at every moment, will have to speak out his misunderstandings, doubts, and confusions. Every time the Teacher will have to go back to the chapters finished earlier and that would necessarily mean no progress at all. Such a dull-headed, wool-gathering mind is not a fit instrument for the study of the science of Vedanta.

Vidwan : learned or well-informed. This does not mean a man who is already well-versed in the scriptures because without listening to the teachings of a Master, no amount of self study in the scriptures will make one a true *vidwan.* What is meant here is that the student must have a fairly good general knowledge of the world outside and also a certain amount of insight into his own psychological and intellectual composition. The more general knowledge an aspirant has, the easier it will be for the Master to make him understand the subtle Truth through a variety of examples, and metaphors.

An argumentative spirit of enquiry and understanding is also absolutely necessary for walking the path of knowledge. In the other paths of Self-discovery, this spirit of independent enquiry is not so much emphasised because the seekers walking them do not demand an explanation for personal conviction. But, for the man who wants to walk the path of knowledge, neither a blind faith in the scriptures nor in the Teacher can supply a sufficient motive force. He needs a conviction that rises from within himself, born out of his own intelligent thinking and intellectual absorption of ideas.

Similarily, a student of Vedanta must be a man of receptive and agile intellect, ready to catch every subtle idea thrown out by the Master and through a process of intellectual assimilation, get at its true significance. If this agility of the head and heart is lacking, he cannot hope to have a steady and unobstructed progress in meditation. In the following verses Sankara gives details of the qualities which are prerequisites for a student of Vedanta.

विवेकिनो विरक्तस्य शमादिगुणशालिनः ।
मुमुक्षोरेव हि ब्रह्मजिज्ञासायोग्यता मता ॥१७॥

17. He alone is considered qualified to enquire after the supreme Reality, who has discrimination, detachment, qualities of calmness etc., and a burning desire for liberation.

If the former verse gives us the broad characteristics of those who are fit receptacles for Knowledge, here we have more clearly etched specifications.

These terms have often been found to frighten away the students since their othodox interpretations have been rather severe and relentless. But on a closer analysis, they are found to be very healthy instincts present in every bosom. Only a very few of us, however, are conscious of them and even fewer consciously develop these qualities in themselves.

Viveka is the capacity to discriminate between the Real and the unreal, between the true and the false, between the permanent and the impermanent. It is a faculty which we employ in almost all our day to day decisions but when it is brought to play into the inner constitution of the individual it is called *Viveka*.

Vairagya is commonly translated as detachment. For many, it holds an uncanny fear, for it seems to point more to a condition of a living death than to a state of a better and fuller living. The *vairagya* of Vedanta is only a fullfilment of *viveka.* Having discriminated between the Real and the unreal, it should not at all be agonising to pluck ourselves away from the false.

When, through discrimination, we are intellectually convinced of the fallacy of our way of thinking, detachment is the fructification of that discrimination. Accordingly, it manifests to the degree to which we have been convinced by our discrimination. When I am convinced that my shadow is not really me, it does not take an iota of my energy to rid myself of the sorrows of my shadow. Even if ten thousand elephants pass over it, I shall still smile and be happy for I know that no matter how much my shadow is trampled upon, it cannot bring me any pain.

Sama : calmness. This and associated qualities will be taken up by Sankara in the coming verses and we shall be going into them at length there. For the time being, suffice it to understand that these are the mental values in life which should be cultivated by a healthy man with an evolutionary urge. Success in any creative thinking will be directly proportional to the amount of these qualities in an individual. Even in the material world an individual's success can be increased if only he develops these qualities in himself.

Last but not the least of four qualifications mentioned here is *mumuksutva*--a burning desire for liberation. This, in its old drapery, may have the ugly look of an impracticable idea. Liberation is, by and large, understood to be a gain, *post-mortem,* which the seeker will enjoy only after his death. This is not a sufficient inducement to the modern man, full of impatience and with an unquenchable thirst for practical gains.

These are days when we want immediate gains. No one is ready to invest anything in the expection of an immense gain promised in the future. This being the attitude of the age, we find that this promise of Vedanta, in its obsolete explanation, does not appeal to us. In its subtler implications, *mumuksutva* indicates an immediate benefit which is directly proportional to the amount of effort invested.

Mumuksutva is a deep desire to rid oneself of one's limitations, felt and experienced during one's intercourse with the world, whether it be through one's body, mind or intellect. A true seeker gets impatient with these physical, mental and intellectual limitations in living a full life and he who has come to protest vehemently against life's limitations and who is struggling earnestly to overcome them, is the *mumuksu.* The spirit of revolt against one's self-shackling weaknesses is the spirit absolutley necessary in order set forth in seeking new powers and gaining new strength.

7. The Four Qualifications. (18-30)

साधनान्यत्र चत्वारि कथितानि मनीषिभिः ।
येषु सत्स्वेव सन्निष्ठा यदभावे न सिध्यति ॥१८॥

18. Great sages have spoken of four qualifications for attainment which, when present, succeed in the realisation of Brahman and in the absence of which the Goal is not gained.

The four prerequisites described in the previous verses are the determining factors in a seeker which ensure success. To the degree in which these four are present in a *sadhak*, to that degree his success in spiritual endeavours is assured. Whenever a seeker struggling on the path does not make a definite progress, he should look within himself for the absence of these qualifications.

Sankara is emphasising that a seeker must, first of all, try to see that he is fully equipped with these qualifications; and at all periodcial reverses in spiritual progress, the *sadhak*, instead of despairing, must intelligently evaluate himself and detect his own deficiencies.

When a patient looks pale, the doctor will immediately examine him for deficiencies. To make up the deficiency, he will supply him with the necessary ingredients. Similarly, when a spiritual seeker is fagged out, it is never due to an external obstacle as people generally complain, but always because of a serious deficiency in his spiritual constitution.

आदौ नित्यानित्यवस्तुविवेकः परिगण्यते
इहामुत्रफलभोगविरागस्तदनन्तरम् ।
शमादिषट्कसम्पत्तिर्मुमुक्षुत्वमिती स्फुटम् ॥१९॥

19. (While enumerating the qualifications), first we count the ability to discriminate between the Real and the unreal; next comes a spirit of detachment from the enjoyment of the fruits of actions here and hereafter; after that is the groups of six essentials such as *sama;* and last is undoubtedly a burning desire for liberation.

Here, in sequence, the *Acharya* repeats the necessary attributes for a student who wants sure success on the spiritual path. While giving a rough outline of these he elaborates upon the theme of *viveka* and *vairagya.*

Though potentially there, *viveka* is not generally awakened in all men. However actually intelligent the generation might be, it is the special privilege of a few to have the subtlety of intellect to delve deep into things and happenings and discriminate between the true and the false. Those who are sufficiently evolved, exhibit a greater keenness of intellect but those who do not have it, should not despair. For, it is not a God given bonus which comes to us from the heavens but it is the aroma of a well-developed and integrated mind and intellect. Where there is a large amount of *viveka,* it is safe to presume that the individual has a fairly well-integrated personality.

Running away from life in cowardice, retiring to a jungle in languor of intellect, unappreciation of things around and about us, denial of the bare necessities of the body---these are not *vairagya.* Many educated pundits too, tell us that detachment means a life of complete mourning and bereavement, an unnatural existence which has nothing to do with the life lived by others in society. This interepretation is quite wrong and harmful.

As a result of one's discriminative capacity when one differentiates between the Real and the unreal in the world outside or in the world within, all false values automatically drop off. When once a thing is understood to be full of bitterness, pain and imperfection, rare is the man who will continue to court it.

Invariably, we run after a thing only when we hope to get out of it a greater fulfilment of joy or peace. Once we come to the intellectual appreciation that the object is riddled with sorrow, our immediate attempt would be to get rid of it.

Thus *vairagya* born out of *viveka* is what is meant by detachment. In fact, *vairagya* is the fulfilment of *viveka* and wherever the former is strong, the latter gains in essence and efficiency.

Therefore, when Sankara defines *vairagya*, in the vocabulory of his times, as detachment from all the fruits of one's actions here and hereafter, he only means that a spiritual seeker must come to a sufficiently strong intellectual conviction that fruits born as a result of actions cannot be infinite,. Hence he must, of necessity, be totally detached from them. These results of action reach us in the form of circumstances in the outer world and mental conditions within and when *that* mind reacts to *those* circumstances, we gain our day to day experiences.

The other two requisites mentioned in verse 17 are repeated here---the six qualifications such as *sama* and a passion to redeem oneself *(mumuksutvam)*.

ब्रह्म सत्यं जगन्मिथ्येत्येवंरुपो विनिश्चयः ।
सोऽयं नित्यानित्यवस्तुविवेकः समुदाहृतः ॥२०॥

20. A firm conviction of the intellect that Brahman alone is Real and the phenomenal world is unreal is known as discrimination between the Real and the unreal.

Here is a complete and exhaustive definition of the faculty of discrimination. In its application to a student of *Vedanta*, discrimination is the capacity to know the Real from the unreal from a mixture of things, for Truth or Reality is that which is changeless and ever-present.

Just as scientists enquire about the basis of life by an analysis of the things of the outer world, so too, the scientists of the inner world, the Rishis, tried to understand the fundamental of life in us. This "fundamental" is that Truth which is changeless and omnipresent. So, when we enquire into life and try to understand it in its pure essence, we come to experience that Life which is present everywhere at all times. This universal Factor, the Substratum is what is meant by the word *"Brahman"* in *Vedanta.*

To come to a logical understanding and arrive at a complete intellectual appreciation of the fact that this Permanent Substratum alone is ever-existent, changeless formless and therefore immortal, is to understand that *Brahman* alone is Real and the world of plurality that we now cognise is unreal and imperfect, although it be Its magnificent and wondrous manifestation, changeable, impermanent and joyless. To build up life in this correct perspective and to order our existence on the basis of this value is called *viveka* in *Vedanta.*

तद्वैराग्यं जिहासा या दर्शनश्रवणादिभिः ।
देहादिब्रह्मपर्यन्तेह्यनित्ये भोगवस्तुनि ॥२१॥

21. That desire to give up all transitory enjoyments gained through seeing, hearing, etc., and also experiences gained through equipments ranging from a mortal body to the form of Brahma is called "detachment".

A complete and exhaustive explanation of *vairagya* is given here. It is not only a detachment from external objects and circumstances that are conducive to joyous experiences. but it is a mental condition in which the mind no longer runs after the phenomenal world in the hope of gaining peace or joy. The idea is that through discrimination when one has come to, at least, intellectually appreciate that sense objects have not in themselves any intrinsic value for joy and that they are ephemeral, naturally the mind will never take wandering flights into the realm of the objects with a craving for them

It has been logically concluded in our *Sastras* that a man's mind will constantly hover around and land on objects only when it is convinced that there are three desirable qualities in them They are, a sense of reality *(satyattwam)* of the objects, a belief in their permanency *(nityattwam)* and a faith that they contain potentialities for satisfying our craving for joy *(samahitatwam)*. When we understand through discrimination that the objects perceived through the senses are all, in fact, unreal *(asat)*, ephemeral *(anitya)*, and that they have no real capacity to give us joy, riddled with sorrow as they are, our minds will not pant after them.

In Sri Gyaneswara's commentary on the Geeta, the *Yogiraja* beautifully brings out this idea in a series of inimitable similes. Describing the attitude of a man of detachment towards sense objects, he gives some examples which are very striking and effective. He says that a man of true detachment will run towards sense objects with as much enthusiasm as one would rush out to embrace a dead queen's rotting body; with as much satisfaction as one would decide to quench one's thirst by drinking the pus flowing out from a leper's wound and with as much readiness as one would enter a boiling cauldron of molten iron to take a refreshing bath. It is a very powerful way of expressing the idea that where the intellect has come to a firm conviction about the hollowness of sense objects, the mind will not gush forth towards them with hopes and expectations of satisfaction therein. This sense of detachment that arises from a full application of one's discriminative faculty is called true *vairagya.*

विरज्य विषयव्राताद्दोषदृष्ट्या मुहुर्मुहुः ।
स्वलक्ष्ये नियतावस्था मनसः शम उच्यते ॥२२॥

22. The peaceful state of the mind when it rests constantly upon the contemplation of the Goal after having again and again detached itself from the chaos of the sense objects through a process of continuous observation of their defects, is called *sama*.

Sankara now enters into a discussion of the six qualities which are essential in the constitution of a mind and intellect for making a pilgrimage to their fulfilment in *Jnana*. These are not enumerated to frighten away the unqualified. I have already emphasised that a discussion of the necessary qualifications in *Vedanta* is more for a self-analysis and adjustment than for exercising a tyranny upon the seeker.

The first among the six qualifications is *sama*---calmness of mind. This calmness descends upon the mind when it comes to rest in its meditations, free from the agitations created by its continuous desire for sense objects. But when the mind is thus taken away from the sense objects, it cannot be relieved of its sense-thoughts, all at once.

It is the nature of the mind to entertain thoughts and if it has nothing better to do, it will dwell on one or the other object of the world. Therefore, it is enjoined in all the *yogas* that the mind should be soaked some way or the other, with an idea, greater, nobler and diviner than sense objects. Unless we train the mind to revel in a subtler and diviner field, it cannot redeem itself from the field of ordinary pursuits. In *bhakti*, the devotee employs his mind constantly in the meditation of his beloved Lord and therefore, the mind is automatically drawn away from its pursuits of sense objects.

In the path of knowledge, in the early stages, the mind is to be given an alternative field for occupation. Therefore, a mind basking in the contemplation of the all-pervading

Consciousness of Awareness, *Brahman*, alone is the mind that can successfully detach itself from sense objects.

Not only should the mind steep and maintain and steep itself in *Brahman* by meditating upon the glories of the Goal, but it should be whipped away from its mischievous fields of false entertainments by making it constantly aware of the weaknesses and imperfections of the field of objects. The more we gain control over the mind and through that control withdraw it from its revellings in the field of finite objects, the more will it become equanimous, peaceful and serene, and this condition of "calmness in the mind" consciously brought about by a lived discipline is meant by the word, *sama*.

विषयेभ्यः परावर्त्य स्थापनं स्वस्वगोलके ।
उभयेषामिन्द्रियाणां स दमः परिकीर्तितः ॥
बाह्यानालम्बनं वृत्तेरेषोपरतिरुत्तमा ॥२३॥

23. Steering both kinds of sense organs (of knowledge and action), away from their sense objects and placing them in their respective centres of activity is called *dama* (self-control). The best *uparati* (self-withdrawal) is that condition of the thought-waves in which they are free from the influences of external objects.

In this verse we have the explanations of two more requirements of the mind and intellect which are essential in an aspirant. They are *dama* and *uparati*.

Compared with *sama*, *dama* is a system of discipline concerned with a relatively outer field since it prescribes a control for the sense organs. To withdraw our mental rays that shoot out through the sense organs for the perception of their respective sets of objects and to absorb those rays of perception within the sense organs is *dama* or self-control. That is, *dama* is the control of the sense organs while *sama* is a condition experienced by the mind when it does not function in wordly activities, but is quietly settled upon the contemplation of the supreme Goal.

When one has gained a degree of proficiency in *sama* and *dama*, *uparati* (self-withdrawal) automatically takes place, wherein the seeker's mental condition is such that it no longer gets affected by any disturbances created by external objects.

When we think of these requirements, it is possible that we think of them as very delicate, difficult and distressing feats, but in fact, the more we practise them, the more easily will we understand that after all this is but a verbal explanation of the state of mind of anyone who is trying to achieve or execute any great work. Even on a material plane, we find these qualifications are essential for a person who wants unqualified success in his activities. In any successful business man too, we observe a certain amount of self-control within as well as without, and also *uparati,* at least while he is at his desk. Of course, the comparison of these qualities with the qualities exhibited by the materialist or the money-hunter is not fair, because a seeker needs a subtlety a million times more than the materialist. Yet, to a large extent, we can appreciate and understand these qualifications within ourselves when we watch for them and experience them as available in our work-a-day world.

सहनं सर्वदुःखानामप्रतीकारपूर्वकम् ।
चिन्ताविलापरहितं सा तितिक्षा निगद्यते ॥२४॥

24. *Titiksa* is the capacity to endure all sorrows and sufferings without struggling for redress or for revenge, being always free from anxiety or lament over them.

Describing the fourth psychological qualification in a man of true spiritual stamina, Sankara gives a full and scientific definition of the quality of silent endurance which is glorified in all the religions of the world. Meek surrender and silent suffering are the watchwords in all religious disciplines. This quality to endure and to suffer for a cause which has been accepted by the individual as the ideal and the perfect, finds a place in every great philosophy whether it is religious or secular. In order to bring about a revolution even in the world outside, the revolutionaries are called upon to make silent sacrifices in order to establish it in life. How much more essential is it then, in the inner revolution of an individual who is trying to free himself from his psychological and intellectual confines? This spirit of *titiksa* is to be cultivated and pursued to ensure success in all schemes of subjective rehabilitation.

It is a great pity that many people indulge in acts of perversion in the name of *titiksa*. I have met a number of unintelligent people who, in the name of spiritual seeking, persecute themselves physically and mentally and as a result of their self-persecution, all they gain at the end of years of suffeing is a crooked, ugly deformed mind! They do not ever achieve the least amount of inward beauty or perfection.

Discarding clothes or starving oneself to a skinny existence, denying the body its bare necessities or giving unnecessary pain to the mind, running away from life or preserving oneself on inhuman diets in solitary caves, living an animal's life open to a brutal climate or breaking the body in an effort to make it endure more discomforts---none of these is true *titiksa*. And yet, how many a blind seeker has foundered on this rock of ignorance!

Titiksa (forbearance), is that faculty of the mind which it maintains when intellectually it is governed by a tempo and a conviction which is complete and self-ordained, divine and noble. When the intellect is fully convinced of its accepted values of life, of the sacredness of its Goal, thereafter in trying to gain it, the mind smilingly faces all difficulties and obstacles. This capacity of the mind to accomodate cheerfully all its vicissitudes and patiently ignore any obstacles that might come its way is *titiksa*.

शास्त्रस्यगुरुवाक्यस्य सत्यबुद्ध्यावधारणा ।
सा श्रद्धा कथिता सद्भिर्यया वस्तूपलभ्यते ॥२५॥

25. That by which one understands the exact import of the scriptures as well as the pregnant words of advice of the preceptor is called *sraddha* by the wise; by this alone does Reality become manifestly clear.

Sraddha is the fifth of the qualifications found necessary in an aspirant. Perhaps no other spiritual term has been so badly mauled by the priest-class and so profitably polluted by the laity in Hinduism.

In the name of *sraddha*, a perverted set of priests start trading upon the highly credulous but extremely ignorant community, shamelessly but successfully. *Sraddha* is not blind faith as it is generally understood. It is very clear in the definition of the *Acharya* that *sraddha* is a healthy attempt at a clear intellectual appreciation of the secret depths of the significances underlying the words of the scriptures and the Teacher.

Indeed, this is an essential requisite for anyone trying to master the truths of the scriptures. The scriptures give us, through a technique of suggestions, as clear a decription of the infinite Truth as is possible through finite sounds and words. As such, the pure Consciousness which is the core of Reality cannot be defined or expressed in words and this supreme point of human evolution can only be indicated by the scriptures. So, an honest and sincere effort on the part of the readers and students is absolutely necessary if the words indicating the Truth are to be correctly interpreted, understood and efficiently made use of. This capacity through effort to realise the words of the scriptures in all their suggestiveness is termed as *sraddha*.

We need a certain amount of *sraddha* even in our every day life. When my friend narrates to me how he fell in love or how he was insulted by someone, in his narration it is not so much the words that give me a complete idea of what he experienced, but it is my *sraddha* in his words that illumines for me in all vividness his experiences. If in the material world it is my *sraddha* in the words of the poet that makest me see the face of beauty, if it is my *sraddha* in the strokes and colours of the canvas that makes me realise the experience of the artist, if it is my *sraddha* in a given prospect that gives me a glimpse of its message of beauty and innocence, if in the gross outer world *sraddha* is so essential, how much more should it be so in my attmept to understand the suggestive beauty, the indicative message and the implied meanings of the pregnant words of the scriptures and of the Teacher ?

सर्वदा स्थापनं बुद्धेः शुद्धे ब्रह्मणि सर्वथा ।
तत्समाधानमित्युक्तं न तु चित्तस्य लालनम् ॥२६॥

26. *Samaadhana* (tranquillity) is that condition when the mind is constantly engaged in the total contemplation of the supreme Reality; and it is not gained through any amount of intellectual oscillations.

In any country, generally the atheists or the vehement critics of the scriptures attract the people towards an independent enquiry into the main texts, and there is nothing basically wrong in this. But when we find that our men of culture supposedly living the values that have been advised, behave as low despicable creatures with crumbling values, necessarily, the man of average intelligence immediately comes to the conclusion that there is something fundamentally wrong with the tradition. It is the lip-Vedantins and pseudo seekers who have damaged our sacred edifice of Perfection and Truth more than a Ghazni or an Aurangzeb. It is these half-baked Vedantins and *bhaktas* who have dealt mortal wounds upon the revered body of our society.

As we look around, we find that society falls into two groups ---the "believers" and the "non-believers". Even among the believers there are those who, in their cowardice, dare not face life squarely and have, therefore, come to blindly accept some superstitious ideas of religion. They live their lives aimlessly in undefined fears and vague tremblings. Such ineffectual beings, roaming about in languorous idleness are only procreating more and more non-believers in a healthy society. Those who are alive to the beauties of life, and the dignity of human existence, who believe in the noble things of life, such educated and healthy men do not subscribe to a faith that parades itself as self-suppression and a frog-like existence in their mental and intellectual lives.

Samaadhana,as it is understood today, is an indifferent attitude towards both good and bad, especially towards insults and failures, threats and despairs. It is believed that *samaadhana* is the mental attitude of an individual who has completely hardened himself and has grown to be insensible to the lashes of failures and the arrows of insults.

The *Acharya's* definition does not sanction such a superstitious belief. Sankara is quite emphatic when he defines *samaadhana* as a state of poise and tranquillity that the mind gains when it is trained sufficiently to revel continuously in the concept of a perfect ideal at once universal and omnipotent.

Samaadhana is not state of the mind where in cowardice, the individual sits quietly, not daring to face life and its challenges, but, at the same time, in the secret of his bosom, goes on lamenting against the scheme of destiny that he has to face in life. The tossings of the mind created by passive revolts against life are his only gains. And if physically and intellectually he accepts them all silently, in consummate cowardice, it is not *samaadhana. Samaadhana* is the state of mental equilibrium which comes to one when intellectually one has unshakeable foundations and mentally when one soars to the highest pinnacles of greater visions.

When we are on the ground our neighbours may be a nuisance to us. There may even be bitter hatred between us, say, because of a land dispute. But when we have taken off in a plane, these bickerings seem to have no meaning; from those tremendous heights, my property and my neighbours's property seem to merge into one unbroken expanse of beauty. In an aerial view of the world, there are no disquieting mental agitations, because in that vision of oneness, the little differences of opinion about a boundary line pale into insignificance.

Similarly, when a spiritual aspirant raises himself into greater ambits of spiritual vision, his mind can no longer entertain any agitations at the ordinary levels of likes and dislikes. This poise gained as a result of constant contemplation on the Supreme and the Divine is termed as *samaadhana.* And naturally this becomes a special qualification for every seeker on the path.

So then, these are the six great qualifications that are essential psychological traits in a fully evolved man who alone can walk the last lap of this journey with hope and success.

अहंकारादिदेहान्तान् बन्धानज्ञानकल्पितान् ।
स्वस्वरूपावबोधेन मोक्तुमिच्छा मुमुक्षुता ॥२७॥

27. *Mumuksutva* is the impatient and burning desire to release oneself, by realising the Real Nature of One's Self, from all bondages of egoism to the body etc., which are bondages created by ignorance.

In this discussion, we have spoken of (1) discriminative capacity to separate the Real from the unreal, (2)capacity to detach ourselves completely from the false which we have now rightly understood as unreal, (3) calmness, self-control, inner peace, forbearance, faith and self-settledness, which are the positive qualities of the head and heart to be consciously developed. Now, last in the series, (4) a complete definition of the spirit of seeking that is essential in every neophyte is given.

The burning aspiration of a seeker should not be an idle enthusiasm to gain some unknown goal through some mysterious intervention of a God or a Teacher. He should definetely know what are his limitations and also the causes for them. He must be clear about his Goal and the various techniques and paths by which he can attain it. All these points are hinted at in this small, pithy verse.

Because of the non-apprehension of our Real Nature, misapprehensions about ourselves arise in our mind. The identification with the body, mind and intellect, together called the 'ego', is what gives us our sense of limitations. The limitations do not belong to the Self, for It is Infinite and

Absolute. It is Perfection. While forgetting our Real Nature we come to look upon ourselves to be something other than what we actually are and this misconstrued personality is the sufferer, the finite, the mortal. To rediscover ourselves is to end all our sorrows. This is the consummate point of evolution.

A Lalaji after a substantial meal retires to a comfortable bed with his wife and children to take rest. There he dreams that he is a destitute into a wide world where, in a jungle, famished and broken of spirit, he is looking for safety and shelter. He is pursued relentlessly by a hungry lion. The Lalaji pants and runs to save himself and consequently jumps into the Ganges and the touch of the cold water wakes him up---only to find that he is profusely perspiring in his own little room.

The dreamer in Lalaji forgetting his own real identity in which he was in all security sleeping with his wife and children, came to identify himself with his own mental creation and thus became the destitute of his dream. The moment he woke up, he rediscovered his real identity. He need not then run to the closet to take his gun, open the door and walk out into the darkness, if not to kill, at least to frighten the lion. The moment he woke up he understood that he had never been famished and that he was never in a jungle and that the lion was nothing but a creation of his own mind.

In the ignorance of our Real Nature, we start indentifying with our ego-centric concepts such as, "I am the body", "I am the mind" and "I am the intellect" --and thereafter the conditions of the body, mind and intellect, in my stupidity, become my conditions. To end this ignorance is to gain the wisdom of Reality.

He who has understood the logic of the true philosophical concept of the Self and the Vedantic explanation of his seeming sense of finitude and limitations is the true seeker. Therefore, it is evident that a *mumuksu* is not a blind-seeker vaguely wanting some unknown pleasure or development within himself by the practice of some pseudo spiritual activities, pursed only at a given time during the day. To be a seeker only for half an hour in the morning and another half an hour in the evening is not to be a right pursuer of knowledge.

To rediscover ourselves is to invite into our life the cognition of a greater Intellect and a divine Consciousness. In order to turn the entire beam of my consciousness upon myself, I need to purify my mind and intellect and then slowly and steadily give them a turn so that they may come to contemplate upon themselves. This inner revolution cannot be accomplished as a half-hearted hobby but it can only be the result of a life-long dedication and a full-time endeavour. Such a true seeker who is ready to live every moment of his life in a diligent pursuit of the Real is a *mumuksu.*

मन्दमध्यमरूपापि वैराग्येण शमादिना ।
प्रसादेन गुरोः सेयं प्रवृद्धा सूयते फलम् ॥२८॥

28. Half-hearted and mediocre aspirations in a seeker may also come to bear fruit, being increased by the Grace of the Guru and by means of renunciation, calmness etc.

The burning desire for redemption from one's known weak-nesses and limitations can be increased and kept at its highest tempo when through slow but steady pursuits of the six qualities enumerated above and through detachment one develops them. By developing a capacity to discriminate between the Real and the unreal, when one has gained an easy control over oneself in renouncing that which is unreal, when one has psychologically cultivated by steady and conscious effort the qualities of self-control, tranquillity of mind, inward peace, endurance, faith and mental poise, then one's aspirations gain an edge and an irresistible effectiveness.

These four great qualities have among themselves such a relationship that having developed one, the others too come to flourish in the personality . So even if one has only half-hearted or mediocre aspirations, one need not despair. If one assiduously cultivates any one of these qualities, one will definitely feel a greater longing for the Highest.

The "*Guru*-Grace trick" has been a very lucrative profession in our country in recent years. The credulous public demanding cheap methods for the highest gains becomes an easy prey for the self-appointed *Gurus.* Without any investment, if a young man wants immense and quick gains, there can be no better way than to become one of these unscrupulous *Gurus*. The "trade" has fallen to such depths that now there are *Gurus* available who can, through the nation's postal service, send to their distant disciples packets of Grace and Glory of curative strength, failure-proof talismans, child-bearing seeds or even packets of God's own vermilion Glory. All these, mind you, at a reasonable rate quoted ex-godown! Sankara's statement here does not of course advocate such a free trade in ignominy.

A true Teacher of innei vision and perfect life cannot, by any logic, come to dispense a greater share of his Grace on people of his choice nor can he withhold his Grace from some others. In fact, the distribution of Grace is not controlled by the *Guru* but depends upon the capacity of the recipient.

The perfected man, living abosorbed in the Self, equally disseminates joyous perfection, cheer and bliss to all, at all times. It depends upon the equipments that approach him to take a greater or a lesser share of it.

The ocean does not put a ban upon the quantity of water that you can carry from it; the limitations are the limitations of your own pot. The sun does not ration its light from house to house or from room to room but it is the walls that deny the entry of sunlight into a room. The river flows; everything depends upon the canals that you can cut to take its waters to your land.

Smililarly, the Guru, living in perfection, gives out knowledge in the language of his own intimate experience and it is up to the individual seekers to get for themselves as much benefit as they can.

This shows that when a seeker has developed in himself *viveka, vairagya* and *shad sampatti*, his *mumuksutva* increases automatically and he who has these four qualities can come in contact with the *Guru* more profitably. The greater the degree to which they manifest in an individual, the more will he be in tune with the Master and he will be able to understand the significance of the Teacher's words completely and exhaustively.

वैराग्यं च मुमुक्षुत्वं तीव्रं यस्य तु विद्यते ।
तस्मिन्नेवार्थवन्तः स्युः फलवन्तः शमादयः ॥२९॥

29. Calmness and other practices have their meaning and they bear fruit, indeed, only in him who has an intense spirit of renunciation and yearning for liberation.

There are many seekers who, having practised for long the six requirements such as calmness etc., complain that they have not progressed at all. Vedantic practices are not a training in ethics or morality. These great qualities are mainly to create an ethical and moral atmosphere in the pschological field of the neophyte. There are many spiritual cowards who ask, "Merely by living an honest life can we not reach the Perfection which is explained as Godhood?" This question has become very common these days and people in confusion and perhaps intellectual fatigue refuse to make a thorough study of the *Sastras*.

Such people claim for themselves a "true living" in their honest endeavours in life. They say , "I am very dutiful. I earn honestly, I look after my home and my dependants, and to the extent I can afford it, I share my wealth with others in a spirit of charity. I believe that I am a nobler soul than those who practise the so-called spiritual discipline".

This wrong notion has been blasted by Sankara in his statement that the qualities of self-restraint, self-control, purity, etc., can bear fruit only when they are in an individual who has a complete sense of detachment born out of discrimination and a burning aspiration to surmount the limitations of his mortal existence. The destiny of some of those I have met who were living an "honest life" all the time is indeed heart-rending. They live in the world in sensuous excesses, running after the mirage of wealth, power, popularity, enjoyments, etc., and though their means are fair, their goal has always been low and finite. So in their pilgrimage through life whenever they come across a ditch of hatred or a mount of challenge, they sit back fatigued and weary and blame religion and their own philosophy based upon hollow and meaningless ethical living. Since spiritual evolution is not the outcome of their "pure" living, whenever the scheme of things around them changes, they find themselves lost. Without spiritual stamina, no one can stand up to the threats and onslaughts of circumstances in life. It is therefore that *sama* etc., cannot bear fruit unless they grow in a heart watered by detachment and ploughed by an intense wish for liberation.

एतयोर्मन्दता यत्र विरक्तत्वमुमुक्षयोः ।
मरौ सलिलवत्तत्र शमादेर्भानमात्रता ॥३०॥

30. *Sama* etc., become as ineffectual as the mirage in the desert in him who has a weak detachment and yearning for freedom.

The idea expressed in the previous verse is now reinforced with another statement. Sankara says that *sama* etc., cannot even effervesce in a bosom where detachment is weak and the yearning for liberation brittle, spasmodic and eccentric. Seekers,who are now facing a blind alley in their progress may very well look back upon their own wasteful days and re-equip themselves for a surer and faster flight to success. A correct understanding about themselves will certainly give them the secret key to the halls of success.

In those who have neither the spirit of detachment from the unreal, nor a consistent aspiration to evolve, true calmness etc., cannot flourish. The *Acharya* says that in such people self-control, self-restraint, joy and happiness are all mere delusion; they are only a similitude of Reality; they do not thrive well and flower forth to bear fruits. This we can observe even among many of our present-day *Mahatmas* who, by their dress and profession, declare their detachment and *mumuksutva* and yet, in their life, they seem to enjoy no calmness etc., to experience no joy, to practise no self-control. In such individuals where true *vairagya* and *mumuksutva* are absent, *sama* etc., can never bear fruit or grow or even germinate.

8. Bhakti---Firm and Deep. (31)

मोक्षकारणसामग्रयां भक्तिरेव गरीयसी ।
स्वस्वरुपानुसन्धानं भक्तिरित्याभिधीयते ॥३१॥

31. Among the instruments and conditions necessary for liberation, bhakti alone is supreme. A constant attempt to live up to one's own Real Nature is called single-pointed devotion.

Assuming that the seeker has a large share of intelligent detachment, a conspicuous amount of anxiety to liberate himself from his inborn weaknesses and also a fully developed moral and ethical life, the question comes to one's mind, "What practice should one adopt in order to integrate oneself into a proportionately beautiful, divine existence?"

According to *Vedanta*, the means of self-integration on the path of knowledge is *atma-vichar* or constant meditation upon the nature of the eternal Self. But Sankara makes use of a popular word to indicate the subtle practice of meditation. For this, there are critics who complain that the *Prachhanna Bouddha* (the "veiled Buddhist" as they sometimes call Sankara), is playing upon the credulity of the people and luring them into his own den. There are *dwaitins* who criticise this verse and say that the *Acharya* is deceiving true seekers by the word *bhakti*, misinterpreted and misconceived as pure meditation.

Sankara says that *bhakti* is the path, but he adds codicil explaining the term *bhakti*. According to him *bhakti* is not a practice of beggary at the feet of a noble ideal, however transcendental it may be, but he defines it openly as a constant and consistent effort at raising the ego-centre from the welter of its false values to the memory and dignity of Self-hood.

In thus defining *bhakti*, Sankara cannot be criticised, at least not by those who understand what he says. *Bhakti* as it has come down to us to day, represents almost a superstitious conception, stinking in its decadence, a moral dread, a disgusting intellectual slavery, a crawling mental attitude, a blind dependence upon a supreme God to take us away from all our self-created mischiefs. So we find a self-ruined society being faithfully courted by a profit-seeking priest-class, functioning generally from spiritually polluted centres which have come to be called temples. Those who visit temples with seeming symptoms of devotion, after psycho-analysis, are found to be a set of helpless personalities with neither the courage to face life nor the conviction to renounce, neither the mental stamina to live nor the intellectual vigour to enquire, neither the imagination to believe nor the daring to disbelieve--they are mainly a crowd of men flocking towards the sanctum--half in fear and half in deluded hopes.

Such a devotee in the presence of his brimstone-raining God who will be angry at every weakness of the mortal, but can be a convenient abettor of the devotee's own criminal intentions in society and life, cannot be expected to grow spiritually or to gain any satisfaction from his religion. This is an ugly caricature of the great theory of *bhakti* as expounded by Vyasa in his *Narada Bhakti Sutra*. According to the *Bhakti Sutra* God-devotion has been described as *para-anurakti*, the supreme unquestioned, unmotivated love for the Lord which seeks no reward.

As Kahlil Gibran beautifully puts it, "Love gives naught but itself, and takes naught but itself; Love possesses naught, nor would it be possessed; for love is sufficient unto love". This being so, the best of love is in the lover's atunement with the beloved. The attunement is successful to the degree the lover indentifies himself with the beloved.

Thus, identification is the measuring rod of love. When the identificattion is complete, love is fulfilled. Identification of the little ego, with all its weaknesses, imperfections and limitations, with the absolute Reality, Perfection, Bliss, Knowledge, is achieved through a constant remembrance of the nature of the Self. When the finite ego gets released from its false notions of limitations, it discovers itself to be nothing other than the Supreme, and in this self-discovery, it experiences complete identification with the Self. Then alone is love entirely fulfilled.

This process is accomplished through a constant awareness of the Divine in us, which can be maintained only if we maintain in ourselves an unbroken stream of divine thoughts. So *anusandhan* when it is unbroken, increases the frequency of divine thoughts in us, and when the frequency of such thoughts comes to the degree of frequency with which the ego idea now persists in our hearts, we shall be able to experience the Divine as intimately and freely as we experience now our ego-centric life.

Therefore, when we re-read the verse with a correct understanding of the practical implication of *atma-vichar* and the suggestions of *bhakti marga*, we find that Sankara is only too right when he says that for those who want to walk the path of knowledge and reach the Ultimate, the most efficient technique is *bhakti*, restated in its correct meaning.

9. Courtesy of Approach and Questioning.

(32-40)

स्वात्मतत्त्वानुसन्धानं भक्तिरित्यपरे जगुः ।
उक्तसाधनसंपन्नस्तत्त्वजिज्ञासुरात्मनः ।

उपसीदेद्गुरुं प्राज्ञं यस्माद्बन्धविमोक्षणम् ॥३२॥

32. Others say that *bhakti* means a constant enquiry into the Real Nature of one's own Self---one who has the above mentioned qualifications and is anxious to know the Self must, therefore, devotedly serve a Teacher, well-established in knowledge, for redeeming himself from bondage.

Continuing the definition of *bhakti*, Sankara quotes some other great writers who had declared before him that true devotion lies in a constant awareness of one's Real Nature. There is a subtle difference between the previous definition and the present. The previous definition prescribes the *path* by which devotion is gained, and this one declares *love as its own goal*. One is said to be devoted to his profession when he is constantly aware of his duties in his profession. A full-time dedicated life towards any activity is called, even in everyday life, as devotion. Examples of devoted wife, devoted son, devoted husband, devoted student, etc., are not uncommon usages in our language.

To live as the Self and to meet others in life, standing upon this solid foundation of the true nature of the Self, is the culmination of knowledge and this is termed by sankara as *bhakti*. That is, he defines *bhakti* both as the means and the end; love is the means to gain love. The path of the seeker is through love to Love.

In thus hinting at the Glory of devotion, the author continues prescribing other practices necessary for a Vedantic seeker during his evolution. A seeker who has the necessary qualifications, in order that he may be redeemed from his inner weaknesses, attachments, animalisms and false values, is advised to serve with devotion a Teacher who is well-established in the experience of the Self.

We have already the *Guru*-trick in India[1], which has made a credulous society fall so precipitously into the depths

1. See commentary on verse 28.

of utter decadence. As without an instructor we cannot learn even a simple thing like opening the door of a car, or typing, or even the art of eating, we cannot deny the need of a teacher for instructing us to live intelligently. The difficulty nowadays is to find the right type of Teacher whom the scriptures call the *Guru* Sankara indicates the qualities of the *Guru* by the pregnant expression, *Pragnyam*, meaning, one who is established in the intimate experience of the divine Consciousness in himself.

Upasana of the *Guru* is not a mere servile attendance upon him in an attitude of growing disgust, or in a mood of melancholy dissatisfaction. The disciple, out of sheer love and reverence for the Master, forgets himself and serves him at all times and in all possible ways; thereby the student is made to remember, constantly, the glories and the noble qualities of the Master. This constant mental awareness of the Ideal through the person of the *Guru* slowly and steadily raises the moral tempo and ethical goodness in the neophyte who finds himself well established in his inner purity which would otherwise have taken him painfully long years to develop.

Again, this sort of "love-making" with the *Guru*, not through the heart and its sentiments, but through the intellect and its idealisation, makes the disciple efficient to set himself in unison with the Master which is essential for the student if he is to really benefit by the Master's original ideas, minted in the seer's own inner experiences. When suggestive words of deep import are given out by a Teacher in his moments of inspiration, the student at once understands the Teacher. It is for this reason that Sankara is compelled to declare that as a result of *Guru* upasana, the disciple becomes capable of liberating himself from his limitations.

श्रोत्रियोऽवृजिनोऽकामहतो यो ब्रह्मवित्तमः
ब्रह्मण्युपरतः शान्तो निरिन्धन इवानलः ।
अहेतुकदयासिन्धुर्बन्धुरानमतां सताम् ॥३३॥

33. He, who is well-versed in the scriptures, sinless, unafflicted by desires, a full knower of the Supreme, who has retired into the Supreme, who is as calm as the fire that has burnt up its fuel, who is a boundless ocean of mercy that needs no cause for its expression and who is an intimate friend of those who have surrendered unto him.

Sankara exhausts his list of adjectives in enumerating the qualities of the true *Guru* to supplement his declaration that the Master should be well-established in the supreme Consciousness. He adds here certain qualities which, on a closer observation, reveal that every man of realisation and wisdom cannot aspire to and become an efficient Teacher of spirituality. To guide and instruct a deluded soul and help him to unwind himself and unravel the knotty traits in him, one must have something more than a perfect experience. The Teacher must, no doubt have full realisation but he must also have a complete grasp of the great scriptures. Without the study of the scriptures even the Self-realised Master will not have the language or the technique of expression to convey his profound knowledge to his disciples.

Apart from spiritual knowledge and erudition, the Guru must also have great self-control and the immense riches of a well-developed heart. He must have an irresistible flow of mercy which demands no special cause for its manifestation, especially when it descends upon those who have surrendered themselves to him, having reached his feet as spiritual refugees.

It is well-known that in all constitutions, laws are prescribed both for the governors and the governed. Since this is a text laying down the rules for spiritual progress, Sankara is as vehement in prescribing specificatios for a true and honest Teacher as he is in describing the prerequisites for a spiritual aspirant.

तमाराध्य गुरुं भक्त्या प्रह्वप्रश्रयसेवनैः ।
प्रसन्नं तमनुप्राप्य पृच्छेज्ज्ञातव्यमात्मनः ॥३४॥

34. Worshipping that *Guru* with deep devotion, when he is pleased with your surrender, humility and service, approach him and ask him to explain what you must know.

It is clear that no amount of enquiring into or discussing with a Teacher is of any avail unless the student has taken enough time to tune himself up to the Teacher. The essence of *satsang* lies in perfect attunement (at-one-ment).

Spirituality is not something that we can start discussing and arguing among ourselves to while away an idle hour. It is to be understood in an atmosphere of peace and tranquillity for this understanding is an attempt at comprehending the deep experiences of the Master expressed not so much through his words as perhaps, through the ring of sincerity that the words carry when they come from his heart throbbing with his own *nishtha.*Therefore, Sankara here explains how a seeker should approach the Teacher and learn, first of all, to love him, trust him and later on, through love-inspired acts of service, become receptive and establish an intimate rapport filled with reverence. Such a relationship alone will yield results. Therefore, *Vedanta* is almost over-emphasising the method of approaching the Teacher. These days, unfortunately, we find seekers who think nothing about calling over the phone to enquire form the Teacher at the other end of the city about the goal of life, the path, the means and so on. Such a telephone-tuition is not possible in spirituality and the seeker of a spiritual life and religious truths is asked to approach the Master in an attitude of reverence and surrender. Then alone can the Teacher acquaint the disciple with the knowledge of the Self.

In this verse it has been indicated very clearly that seekers should not misuse the Teacher and discuss with him secular questions or domestic problems. It is almost prohibited. He should be asked only about the special knowledge of the Self in which he is perfect.

स्वामिन्नमस्ते नतलोकबन्धो
कारुण्यसिन्धो पतितं भवाब्धौ ।

मामुद्धरात्मीयकटाक्षदृष्ट्या
ऋज्व्यातिकारुण्यसुधाभिवृष्ट्या ॥३५॥

35. O Master, O friend of those who reverentially surrender to thee, thou ocean of mercy, I salute thee; save me, fallen as I am into this sea of change, with a direct glance from thy eyes which rain nectarine Grace supreme.

Characteristically oriental in style, the poet in Sankara here extends himself beyond the pale of the philosopher in him. Any estimate of Sankara as a philosopher cannot be complete without recognising the poet in him for there are moments when, even while writing his commentaries upon the Upanishads, he forgets that he is a philosopher to whom economy of words and precision of expression should be a religion. At times, the poet Sankara outranks the philosopher Sankara. This verse is an example where he uses expressions full of hyperbole. The modern news-paper-reading-generation may not easily appreciate the poetic beauty of the verse unless it is hauled up and made to notice it.

This is a verse that provides the seekers with a perfect prayer addressed to the *Guru*. Prayer is not begging, although in all the religions of the world today, it has come to gather almost a scandalous and painful meaning of beggary. To beg of the Lord for something or the other for the sake of which we chant and sing glorified words of praise along with offering sweets and candles, is an act of pulling down the edifice of the Immortal and the Perfect to the level of desire-ridden human creatures. God in His own Glory needs none of our glorifications; nor has He any desire to partake of the objects that the devotee in his love can offer Him, He being the giver of all and ever the perfectly satisfied.

Yet, how is it that every prophet, irrespective of the place and the period of his manifestation has invariably advised his devotees to approach the Lord with offerings and prayers? In the sayings of these prophets, the eternal Masters of the World, we invariably notice that they have emphasised the idea that God is not purchasable nor is He available for one's persuasions to be an ally in one's animalistic activities. But a true devotee is advised to surrender himself at the feet of the Lord through prayer, love, and devotion in order that during the surrender, the nobler and the diviner in him now laying dormant may come to manifest itself.

Here is a trick of "stooping to conquer"! While the loving devotee prostrates to the idol, he also surrenders his ego, the vanities of false values in him and his attachments to his body, mind and intellect.

It is these false attachments that lower one to the level of an animal and effictively screen one away from one's true divine nature.The surrender of the ego is the unveiling of the Divine in oneself and the degree to which the Divine is manifest, to that degree the individual raises himself in his potency to face life and to remain equanimous in all circumstances.

Here a Vedantic student is asked to surrender himself to the *Guru* and to praise him in *kirtan* and serve him with meek surrender. This prescription is not meant to make the student, intellectually, a slave to the Teacher. But these practices, when pursued for some time, easily make the student fully turned up to the Teacher's heart. What the Teacher has to convey is the experience of the Transcendental and as the Infinite cannot be defined in finite words, the words of the Master can echo their message only in a bosom that has been stilled in complete love.

Any discordant notes arising in the bosom of the disciple create disturbances which molest, rape and disturb the true significance of the scriptural words used by the Master during his discourses. In order that we ourselves may not create any discordant notes and destroy the harmony, we as students are asked to serve and surrender, to pray and worship at the Master's feet.

दुर्वारसंसारदवाग्नितप्तं
दोधूयमानं दुरदृष्टवातैः ।

भीतं प्रपन्नं परिपाहि मृत्योः
शरण्यमन्यद्यदहं न जाने ॥३६॥

36. I am being roasted in the blazing infernal fire of change; I am being tossed by the cruel storms of misfortune; I am terrified (without and within)--- O Lord ! save me from death; I seek refuge in thee, for I do not know of any other harbour wherein to seek shelter.

A comparison of the rhyme and rhythm of this verse with those of the previous one gives us an idea of the mastery of Sankara's pen in poetry. If the former is a melodious flow of peaceful tranquillity, a flow that removes all the clogs of the heart and allows it to move freely into molten love and liquid surrender, this verse, in its brisk trot, exhibits in its very rhythm and sound an irresistible impatience and pressing urgency.

The first line in the verse explains the dangers to which the seeker is exposed while in the second line we have an indication of the dangers that he realises are besetting him from within. In the outer world of contact with things he is overwhelmed by sorrows of an ever-changing pattern, while in himself he recognises an endless storm caused by his likes and dislikes, his loves and hatreds, his hopes and disappointments. These two lines beautifully summarise the experience of finitude which is the lot of every seeker before he enters the hall of Wisdom.

It is only when an individual develops his sensibility, subtle enough to recognise these weaknesses in life that he comes to feel such a pressing urgency for liberation. When he experiences this, he comes to demand of the *Guru*, safety and shelter from the threatening cries of death with their poisoning evil experiences in life. We should not construe death to mean only the experience of dying which is the lot of all beings, but it is to be understood in its broadest sense as the poison of finitude. Every moment there is death, as each experience dies away, and out of its ashes springs the next circumstances to be experienced. The disciple is aksing for guidance to the realms beyond death--a state of living in which the experience of life is the continuous, homogeneous, Bliss Absolute.

This verse again is a prayer addressed to the *Guru* coming from the bottom of the student's heart, thereby making his attunement with the *Guru* perfect and complete.

शान्ता महान्तो निवसन्ति सन्तो
वसन्तवल्लोकहितं चरन्तः ।
तीर्णाः स्वयं भीमभवार्णवं जना-
नहेतुनान्यानपि तारयन्तः ॥३७॥

37. There are peaceful and magnanimous saints who live---like the spring season --for the good of humanity. They have crossed the dreadful ocean of finitude through their own efforts and with no ulterior motives, they also help others to cross it.

A man of full realisation instinctively becomes a lover of the whole universe. Like spring, his is a love which demands no cause to flower into a wealth of blossoms. He who has discovered that the Self within himself is none other than the All-pervading Consciousness which is non-dual, he instantaneously discovers It to be in the core of all pluralistic forms around him.

Living as he does in this intimate understanding of Oneness, he cannot but love others as his very own Self. In his case, universal love is not an art to be practised, not a formality to be followed, nor a goal to be reached; it is his very life breath. This can be brought within the understanding of the laity through a comparison.

There can be no occasion for you to feel a constant hatred for any part of your own body. Even if your hand or your leg gives you a dose of pain, your anger towards them cools down when you realise that they are but your own hand or leg. For instance, if the finger of your right hand accidentally pokes your right eye, it is a case of one part of your body giving pain to another part of it. These can be moments of terrible protest of anger mixed with pain. But almost immediately you realise that it is your own forefinger that is the culprit and you cool down to a spirit of mercy and tolerance and paternally ignore both the offender and the offended. It would be foolish to punish the finger for, the pain to it would be more pain to yourself only. Similiraly, when one has realised that the Reality within him is the pith and substance that constitute all others in the universe, love and kindness are natural and continuous in his bosom for all in the world.

On understanding the essence of Truth in ourselves, we gain a freedom from the sense of finitude which was ours so long as we identified ourselves with the body, mind and intelect. Since these disturbances can no longer affect a man of Perfection, it is one of the surest symptoms of knowledge and saintliness if we can observe an individual who is, under all provocative circumstances, infinitely at peace with himself and with the world. Therefore a *Sant* is a man of true broadmindedness which is the natural outcome of kindness tolerance etc. This is the Flag of Realisation.

To say that a *Mahapurusha* after Realisation, casting off his desires, will retire, totally, to a dark cave in the Himalayas, to count his days of forced existence in this corporeal form is fallacious. He may dwell in the cave or may walk about in the market-place; where he lives is a matter of no concern to him. Wherever he be, whether in a jail among criminals or among devotees in a temple, irresistibly, instinctively, he will spread around him an aura of knowledge, light, cheer, jay and peace. It is his very nature. Just as heat is the nature of fire and we cannot say that fire creates or generates heat.

Sankara gives us an inimitable example when he compares the *Mahatmas* and the touch of joy they lend to the world with the spring season. When spring comes, it does not court every tree to bring forth its flowers, nor does it reach the world and canvass the moon to be brighter, the sky to be clearer and cleaner, the grass to be thicker and every heart to be more joyous. "The presence of spring and the concomitant conditions are complementary. The one cannot be without the other.

Similarly, it is for the *Mahtma* to spread knowledge and cheer around him and whenever true seekers reach him, they are irresistibly drawn into his orbit to bask in the warmth of his personality.

The poetic suggestion is that he, travelling in his own experience, is one who, unasked, helps others to cross the shores of delusion and sorrow. Therefore, to surrender to such a one, requesting him to save us from our misunderstandings is to assure for ourselves a true liberation---almost a luxury liner to Truth !

अयं स्वभावः स्वतः एव यत्पर-
श्रमापनोदप्रवणं महात्मनाम् ।
सुधांशुरेष स्वयमर्ककर्कश-
प्रभाभितप्तामवति क्षितिं किल ॥३८॥

38. Indeed, it is the nature of the magnanimous to help remove the troubles of others, even as the moon of its own accord cools the earth scorched by the flaming rays of the sun.

This is another mellifuous verse to emphasise that the noble qualities of magnanimity, cheerfulness etc., in a perfect Master are natural and not the products of a self-tutored habit.

Sankara compares a Seer with the moon, and directs our attention to the fact that the moon alone can, and with effortless ease does, cool the parched earth which gets baked in the burning rays of the sun. Nothing else can cool the earth so satisfactorily as moonlight. Also, there is no chance ever of the moonlight adding a single calorie of heat to the earth.

The company of the wise is the surest remedy to cool down the bosom to a state of complete peace and happiness when it is in conflagration, fed by desires and hatreds, attachments and yearnings.

In verse 34, we have been told that a disciple should, having approached a true Master, please him with his service, humility and surrender. Sankara has so far used four verses in praise of the Masters to express the attitude of total surrender of the disciple to the Teacher. In the following verses, we hear a definite and pointed request to the Master to answer the seeker's doubts , so that through his inspired discourses and explanations, the seeker may be lifted out of the ruts of wrong thinking. It is an elaborate metaphor, so beautifully executed that its finish and grace remind us of some fo the classical works in Sanskrit.

ब्रह्मानन्दरसानुभूतिकलितैः पूतैः सुशीतैर्युतै-
र्युष्मद्वाक्कलशोज्झितैः श्रुतिसुखैर्वाक्यामृतैः सेचय ।
संतप्तं भवतापदावदहनज्वालाभिरेनं प्रभो
धन्यास्ते भवदीक्षणक्षणगतेः पात्रीकृताः स्वीकृताः ॥३९॥

39. O Lord, thy nectarine speech, honeyed by the elixiric Bliss of Brahman, pure, cooling, issuing in streams from thy lips as from a water-jug, and pleasing to the ear---do thou shower upon me who am tormented by earthly afflictions as by the tongues of a forest fire. Blessed are those who have received even a passing glance from thy eyes, accepting them under thy protection.

Sanskrit metaphors cannot be contained in the embrace of the English vocabulary and however much we try to translate them, they read as a confused jumble of words.

In this instance Sankara, the philosopher, has taken up his pen to write in the style of a *Kavya*,a chiselled poem of exquisite beauty, depth and serenity, both in diction and cadence.

When we carefully open up the various metaphors and discard the literary embellishments, all it says is, "Have pity on me, Master, and teach me the method of transcending the world and its sorrows."

कथं तरेयं भवसिन्धुमेतं
का वा गतिर्मे कतमोऽस्त्युपायः ।
जाने न किन्चित्कृपयाऽव मां प्रभो
संसारदुःखक्षतिमातनुष्व ॥४०॥

40. How to cross this ocean of relative existence? What is to be my ultimate destination? Which of the many means should I adopt? I know nothing of these. O Lord! Save me and describe in all detail how to end the misery of this life in the finite.

This is the type of question the student should ask when he is approching the Master after having served him long enough and perfectly tuned up to him. These questions in themselves speak volumes of clear thinking and logical conclusions which the student has reached of his own accord. He has lived intelligently his life of varied expriences and has evaluated it correctly. He has neither despaired because of the unsurmountable difficulties experienced by him nor is he ready to make any compromise with Truth. He has analysed his experiences in life and has come to the conclusion that finite objects cannot give him anything but finite satisfaction. He has looked within himself and has estimated correctly his own demands in life as nothing short of infinite Perfection, which alone can yield to him infinite Happiness. He wants to know from the Master how he can come to experience the Infinite and thereby gain a complete transcendence of the finite. Hence he asks, "How can I cross this ocean of relative existence?"

Unless one somehow or the other fulfils this self-evolution and reaches the portals of the Infinite and experiences the Real, one wonders as to what would be his "ultimate destination". The question, therefore, does not necessarily mean that he is ignorant of what the destination would be. In fact, it is a dreadful premonition of the consequences of getting entangled in the finite world of desires, excitements and endless responsibilities of satisfying each nerve-tickling, unless he experiences the Transcendental.

Though he has come to an independent conclusion about the life he is living and though he knows the Goal, yet he feels unsure as to what exactly is the method by which he can end his delusions and reach the Goal. The student has already read a lot of the science of life as expounded in the literature on religion and he finds therein different methods of self-perfection prescribed. He wants to know from the *Guru* What exactly should be the path for him. Through a process of trial and error one can, for oneself, find the right path but it is more convenient, and indeed, a sacred blessing if one can have a true Teacher to show the correct path of self development Therefore, the student asks, "Which of the means should I adopt?"

The expression, "I know nothing", is not the student's dullwitted confession of ignorance but it is an expression of modesty, and devotion and reverence for the Teacher.

10. Loving Advice of the Guru. (41-47)

तथा वदन्तं शरणागतं स्वं
संसारदावानलतापतप्तम् ।
निरीक्ष्य कारुण्यरसार्द्रदृष्ट्या
दद्यादभीतिं सहसा महात्मा ॥४१॥

41. As he speaks, afflicted by and seeking protection from the conflagration of the fire of *samsar*--the noble Teacher looks at him in all pity and kindness and spontaneously bestows upon him protection from fear.

Just as the *Sastra* lays down a code of behaviour for the student, with equal emphasis does it formulate laws for the Teacher. There is a school of thinkers in Vedanta which

belives that a perfect Master is beyond laws, that he is a law unto himself, that not even the Vedas dare lay down codes of morlity or rules of behaviour for the perfect Master. This does not mean that he is free form all moral obligations and ethical norms of behaviour. No laws are applicable to him in the sense that because of his perfection whatever he does will automatically become the code of perfect action. He cannot go wrong because his actions can never be low and ego-centric. He has surrendered himself completely to the Supreme, and as such, the only music that can emanate from his action is the music of the spirit. The very *Sastras* and Vedas are the codified expressions of the perfect behaviour of such Masters. Therefore, such critics who would object to the interpretation that the verse lay down codes for the *Gurus* would be right.

What is meant here by "laws prescribed for the Teachers"? It is merely a re-statement of what they would do under given circumstances. If they are true to their full experience of perfect tranquillity, they will not run away form sincere seekers, but unquestioningly oblige them with their vast experience and knowledge. To him who has approached the Master with infinite fear, he (the Master), should immediately give a message of hope, assuring him that there is nothing for him to fear, nor is there cause for despair.

Later on, we shall find that when the student crystallises his thoughts into definite questions, the Master also uses less sweeping generalisations and gives more and more definite and pointed answers.

विद्वान् स तस्मा उपसत्तिमीयुषे
मुमुक्षवे साधु यथोक्तकारिणे ।
प्रशान्तचित्ताय शमान्विताय
तत्वोपदेशं कृपयैव कुर्यात् ॥४२॥

42. To him, who, in his anxiety for liberation, has sought the protection of the Teacher, who abides by (scriptural) injunctions, who has a serene mind

and who is endowed with tranquillity, the Master should pour out his knowledge with utmost kindness.

The Teacher is advised to initiate the student only after testing wheter the knowledge given out will take root in his heart. This testing of the student and the qualities for a spiritual seeker are enumerated in *Vedanta* not for the purpose of denying this benefit to any single individual. It is out of sheer kindness that *Sruti* prescribes these qualifications, for unless an individual has these metnal and intellectual qualities, it will be a sheer waste of the Teacher's energy to impart knowledge to the undeserving.Also, spiritual knowledge and its concomitant strength will be misplaced in an imperfect student as he will make use of it for his own annihilation as well as the annihilation of the world. When an unscrupulous man comes to power in any country, we know what a menace he can be to society.

If the student has a burning anxiety for liberation from his known weaknesses, if he is meek and ready to follow the prescribed path and the necessary discipline, then the Teacher is asked to initiate him into the path of Knowledge.

These qualities are, no doubt, quite essential but we must also note that they are all external attributes of daring and readiness to act. Since spiritual seeking is not the march of an army, a mere outward discipline in itself will not suffice. It requires of the student some mental and intellectual qualities and therefore, it is insisted that he must be well-disciplined in his sense-impulses and equally well-balanced in his mental make-up.

Even if a man well-restrained and his mind does not get agitated with low thoughts of sensuousness, the philosophy being so subtle, it is not possible for a lay man to understand it immediately, in all its deep significance. If the Teacher is impatient and has not the kindness to repeat even for the hundredth time, if need be, with equal love and consideration, the student will not be benefited by the Teacher. So the

Teacher should take up the job of initiating the student with extreme kindness. He should not forget that he himself was once a seeker and had his own quota of doubts and difficulties. If the Teacher is not divinely kind and godly in his sympathies, the relationship between the Teacher and the taught will be strained and the student will never find proper guidance for his progress on the spiritual path.

The word *kripa* has, unfortunately, no corresponding word in English. It is not merely "kindness" nor is it a superficial sympathy. At best we can say that it is an attitude of sympathy cooked in kindness, honeyed with love and served on golden platters of understanding. A man of bad temper and extreme impatience, lacking in sympathy, tolerance and kindness cannot ever become a true Teacher, no matter what his claims to nobility and depth of experience are.

(श्री गुरुरुवाच)
मा भैष्ट विद्वंस्तव नास्त्यपायः
संसारसिन्धोस्तरणेऽस्त्युपायः ।
येनैव याता यतयोऽस्य पारं
तमेव मार्गं तव निर्दिशामि ॥४३॥

43. (The Guru said:)
Fear not, O learned one! There is no danger for you. There is a way to cross over this ocean of change. I shall instruct you in the very path by which the ancient Rishis walked to the Beyond.

The perfect disciple, having duly reached the Master's feet, expresses his fears that he will never be able to grow out of the distrubing concepts of time and space which provide for him experiences of unending sorrows of finitude. Things change in their relationship both to time and place. Objects remaining the same, they, with reference to different conditions of time and place, react upon the same individual differently. These pluralistic experiences produce agitations in the mind and that is indicated in verse 40 by the word, *samsara dukha.* When the student reached the Master, he despairingly requested him, "Condescend to save me, O Lord! and describe in full how to put an end to the misery of this relative existence".

The Teacher now gives the answer to the student's question. Psychologically, when a questioner is extremely upset because of some fear or agitation in his mind, he is not in a mood to receive any philosophical idea, even when elaborately explained. Therefore, a sympathetic Teacher, if he knows what he is about, will, first of all, pacify the student and give him hope and spiritual solace. Then alone would he become fit to receive the logical conclusions arrived at by a fully rational philosophy. Most fittingly then, the Master with paternal consideration and love, here assures the student that what he fears is only a myth.

This, however, is not a false assurance, an idle hope given to the student just to save him from imaginary fears. The Master can clearly see the spiritual destiny and the divine perfection which lie in the innermost core of the disciple. Change is only at the level of the mind and intellect. But when the pure Consciousness, eternal and infinite, functions through these equipments, it gathers into itself a delusive vision which interprets a world in terms of change and plurality. Therefore, danger or death are not the phenomena of the Spirit but only the hallucinations of the mind. Therefore, with all confidence, the Teacher assures the student, "There is no death for you."

The theory may be quite consoling and the assertion hopeful, but, if there is no practical method to realise it in life, it would be futile and hence there would be no place for it in Hindu philosophy. But the Teacher asserts here, "There IS a way of crossing this sorrowful ocean of *samsar.*"

Now this is not the theory born out of the Teacher's own intellect, but it is the Path hallowed by the foot-prints of the ancient Seers, who had themselves crossed over from the finite to the Infinite. We are assured that what is to follow now in the Teacher's discourse is an exhaustive discussion upon this sacred path of Self-realisation, the authenticity of which has been proclaimed by an endless array of brillant Rishis of yore.

अस्त्युपायो महान्कश्चित्संसारभयनाशनः ।
तेन तीर्त्वा भवाम्भोधिं परमानन्दमाप्स्यसि ॥४४॥

44. There is a supreme means by which you can put an end to the fear of relative existence; by that you will cross the sea of *samsar* and attain supreme Bliss.

A psychological assurance is again given here in a flood of love that pours out from the heart of the Teacher. The repetition is not merely for the sake of emphasis, but also to clearly reveal the infinite consideration and divine sympathy which the Teacher has for the student.

It is the one most important insistence of Vedanta that there is a sovereign means by which our misunderstanding and consequent false evaluation of life can be completely crushed, culminating in right understanding. This method is explained in the following verse.

वेदान्तार्थविचारेण जायते ज्ञानमुत्तमम् ।
तेनात्यन्तिकसंसारदुःखनाशो भवत्यनु ॥४५॥

45. The highest knowledge arises from the sincere contemplation upon the meaning of the *Upanishad mantras*. By this knowledge, immediately a total annihilation of all sorrows born of the "perception of change" takes place.

The previous verse assured us of a sovereign means by which we could cross over the world of our finite experiences. Now we are given a definition in the form of a clear declaration of what exactly that is.

Constant *vichara* upon the meaning of Vedantic truths leads one to true knowledge. *Vichara* is a term which has no corresponding word in English. Words like thinking, contemplating, reasoning, analysing etc., do not fully express the meaning of technique of *vichara. Vichara* comprises all these in synthesis, along with certain essential mental and intellectual discipline. With a mind and intellect trained and made steady, a seeker rips open the Upanishad declarations one by one, and comes to experience the implications and the deeper suggestiveness of each *mantra.* This process is called *vichara.*

The nectar in a flower is always secreted in its innermost chambers. Its enchanted lover, the honey-bee, which courts it with ardour and adoration, alone can scent the nectar and groping through its dusty exterior reach the honey treasured in the blossom.

Similarly, in the garden of Vedanta are the flower of the Upanishad *mantras.* The sweetness of each is secreted not in its outer words, fascinating though they be, but lies hidden in the pulsating, bosom where its immortal heart throbs with the thrilling ecstasy of Love fulfilled and Perfection experienced. This divine secret can reach this meaning only through his prepared mind and intellect.

The process by which the acutely intellectual and the divinely sympathetic head and heart of a seeker come to live in their subjective experience, the strangely enchanting voice-less cadence rising from the *Rishi's* heart, is called *vichara.*

During moments of meditation[1] when we strive hard to experience the meaning Upanishad *mantras* we are in the realm of *vichara.* Through *vichara* our misunderstandings about ourselves, which are the expressions of our ignorance, are removed, and when ignorance is banished, knowledge shines forth. With this right knowledge, instantaneously, all

1. For theoretical explanations, practical suggestions and graded lessons in the art of meditation, study Swamiji's MEDITATION and LIFE

the delusive sorrows of *samsar* end. After waking up from our dream, the moment we realise our waking-state identity, all the sorrows created in us due to our dream-identification and the dream world, end instantaneously. On the rediscovery that our spiritual nature is pure Knowledge, uncontaminated by any trace of ignorance, we come to enjoy our divine heritage of Perfection and Bliss-- ever beyond even the penumbra of any misery thereafter.

श्रद्धाभक्तिध्यानयोगान्मुमुक्षो-
र्मुक्तेर्हेतून्वक्ति साक्षाच्छ्रुतेर्गीः ।
यो वा एतेष्वेव तिष्ठत्यमुष्य
मोक्षोऽविद्याकल्पिताद्देहबन्धात् ॥४६॥

46. Faith, devotion and the practice of meditation---these are mentioned in the songs of *Sruti* as the chief factors that help a seeker to attain liberation. Whoever pursues these is liberated from the bondage of the body which is a projection mysteriously accomplished by his spiritual ignorance.

The technique of *vichara* has been exhastively analysed and insisted upon. The power to do *vichara* is the very fuel which helps the spiritual vehical to maintain its motion. What constitutes *vichara* has also been explained. Here we are told of the practices we must follow, strictly and sincerely, so that our capacity to do *vichara* may be increased and the *Vichara* itself be rendered most efficient.

Sraddha and *bhakti* encourage and increase *dhyana*, one's meditative poise, and these three together constitute the entire technique of self development as visualised by the *Rishis*. It is interesting to note how each preceding factor strengthens and nourishes the succeeding factor. Faith increases devotion, meditation is easily accomplished. Here we must clearly understand faith in the same sense as has been described earlier.[1] So also we must not identify *bhakti* with the cheap decadent meaning which we, in our ignorance, have given it. It is to be rightly understood[2] as our identification with our concept of our Ideal.

When thus we are truly aided by faith and devotion, we are able to meditate properly, and through meditation we come to realise our true nature. Having experienced our Divine Glory we shall no more misconceive ourselves to be the limited creatures identifying with our matter vestures.

False identifications are created by the ignorance of our spiritual Glory. The body, mind and intellect are all superimpostions upon the glorious Self, and yet, we consider them to be real and permanent. These superimpositions are the real bondages upon us and because of them we feel the limitations of the mortal. He who abides in faith, devotion and meditation in his inner experience comes to re-cognise his infinite nature of Bliss and Perfection, and thus gets released from the bondage of matter.

अज्ञानयोगात्परमात्मनस्तव
ह्यनात्मबन्धस्तत एव संसृतिः ।
तयोर्विवेकोदितबोधवह्नि-
रज्ञानकार्यं प्रदहेत्समूलम् ॥४७॥

47. It is indeed, through contact with ignorance that you, who are the supreme Self, experience yourself to be under the bondage of the not-Self. From this misunderstanding alone proceed the worlds of births and deaths. All the effects of ignorance, root and branch, are burnt down by the blaze of knowledge, which arises from discrimination between these two--the Self and the not-Self.

What causes us, the supreme Self that we really are, to suffer these bondages, and what exactly is that which compels

1. My belief in what I do not know so that I may come to know what I believe in is my *sraddha*. Cf. *sloka* 25.

2. The seeking for one's own Real Nature as the eternal Atman is true devotion. Cf. *sloka* 31 & 32.

us thereafter to struggle hard to regain our true Divine Glory through the delicate process of Self re-discovery is explained here.

Just as a ghost-vision is possible on a way-side post when there is ignorance of the post, so too, it is the ignorance of the Self in us that gives birth to the "thought-flow" called the mind. The mind projects the sense-organs at the level of the body and beyond them it gives us the apparent perception of the five great elements (Pancha Mahabhoota) and world of sense-objects. The pure Consciousness or Life gets reflected in the pool of thoughts and in our preoccupation with our mental life we take ourselves to be this ego-centric (jeeva), which is nothing but life conditioned by our own thoughts in a given pattern of time and place.

The sorrows of life, the limitations of the equipments, the imperfections of the world, the concept of likes and dislikes, the pulls of pleasures and pains, the shattering concepts of merit and sin--all these are effected by this ego.

The ego ends upon its own funeral pyre lit by itself, which blazes into a conflagration of knowledge. The fire arising from a constant discrimination between and Real and the unreal, between the Self and the not-Self, between the Spirit and matter, is fanned into a blazing brilliance through steady *vichara* in which all the effects of ignorance are burnt down. When ego ends, we realise our real nature to be intrinsically divine, eternally free and absolute Bliss. This is immortality.

Where there is light, darkness cannot be; where knowledge has come to rule, ignorance must quit. Where the cause has been eliminated, the effect cannot remain. Where ignorance has ended, all its effects--the five *Kosas* constituting the three bodies, the three planes of Consciousness, the realms of pains made up of sense-objects, feelings and ideas--must end instantaneously, totally.

11. Questions of the Disciple. (48-49)

शिष्य उवाच ।
कृपया श्रूयतां स्वामिन्प्रश्नोऽयं क्रियते मया ।
यदुत्तरमहं श्रुत्वा कृतार्थः स्यां भवन्मुखात् ॥४८।

48. The *sishya* said:

Kindly listen, O Master, to the questions that I now raise. Hearing their answers from your lips, I shall feel entirely satisfied.

The entire *Vivekachoodamani* has, by now, changed from being a text-book into an outstanding poem, a literaby masterpiece because, while writing this great work, Sankara often excels the philosopher in him and becomes a poet to splash the entire work with brilliant colours of pure literary genius. Anyone with a poetic temperament and a taste for music cannot but feel enchanted by the ring of the mellifluous words used in the construction of each verse. There is a perfect mastery in this literary artistic garland of beauty and rhythm.

In his *Bhasya*, Sankara was too preoccupied with his philosophical theory, depicting his vision of Oneness. But when he took up, leisurely, his experienced pen to produce this work, indeed a crest-jewel, both in style and substance--Sankara the poet blended with Sankara the philosopher. He has a special niche in the "poet's corner" and will perhaps be remembered as the noblest poet who ever wielded a pen to bring about a cultural revival.

The very conversational style of this verse relieves the monotony of the philosophy and brings into its arid fields the touch of the human heart and the thrills of a warm, pulsating life. Here, an ignorant student reaches a Seer, who is the fountain of knowledge, and through a process of discussion, tries to attune himself to his Teacher for walking out of the dark ignorance into the Master's brilliant domain.

It is evident that a student silently sitting like a statue even before the greatest of Teachers and for an endless period of time, can have no benefit of any spiritual evolution. The student has to rub his ideas and thoughts against the experienced head and heart of the Teacher, and gain for himself a polish and a fragrance, at once Divine and Perfect. Discussion is the heart of *Satsang.*

The *Rudraksamala* remained nearest to the heart of Sankara all through his life, for a period much longer than his disciples, Totaka and Sureswara remained with him. But both these disciples have been immortalised and as long as we remember *Acharya* Sankara, we shall, with equal devotion and reverence, remember these two, not only as his great disciples, but as God-men themselves. The poor *Rudraksamala!*

The stones in the inner walls of the *sanctum sanctorum* of even the greatest temple, that have faced the Lord for years, have remained stones even after a thousand years. Hundreds of devotees, on the other hand, who have stood, even for a few moments, before the altar, have reacted to the divine atmoshere and have been lifted from their sense of finitude. They have left the temple enveloped in the joys of a fuller existence lived in the process of a greater evolution.

Mentally and intellectually, it is necessary that we come to wrestle with the mind and intellect of the Master in order to develop inner health and beauty and vitality. That is why this text has a great message for the world of seekers.

को नाम बन्धः कथमेष आगतः
कथं प्रतिष्ठास्य कथं विमोक्षः ।
कोऽसावनात्मा परमः क आत्मा
तयोर्विवेकः कथमेतदुच्यताम् ॥४९॥

49. What is bondage? How has it come? How does it continue to exist? How can one get out of it completely? What is the not-Self? Who is the

supreme Self? And what is the process of discrimination between these two (Self and not-Self)? Please explain all these to me.

This is series of seven questions which the student asks the Teacher, who will now take them up one by one and answer them exhaustively.

These questions exhaust almost the entire field of ignorance and ignorance-created confusions. Therefore, they are not to be treated as a set of questions just casually asked by some individual; they are questions that would be asked by sincere seekers who are intellectually curious to know, to understand, to evaluate and to have explained the confusing world of endless plurality. Thus, these questions give us an inkling into the type of questions to be asked and the spirit in which to open our discussion when we approach a divine Master.

To go to a Saint with flowers and camphor, fruits and sweets, is not the correct way of approaching one's spiritual *Guru*. This tradition, though with the best of intentions, has only created a set of fruit-gatherers as *Gurus*,and flower-offerers as disciples, and together the two have dug deep the grave of sacred *Vedanta* and have there hoisted the skeleton of Hinduism!

These thirsty questions, demanding an explanation for the sense of limitation and confusion experienced by us are, each in itself, an exhaustive declaration of the student's observations on life, as it is available to him within and without.

Again, they show the perspicacity with which the student has followed what the Master has said so far. In all the previous verses, the Teacher spoke in terms of 'bondages', 'liberation', 'not-Self', 'supreme Self', and the 'discrimination between the Self and the not-Self' till now these terms were freely used; but the student is not satisfied with a mere understanding of the theories of *Vedanta*. He wants to live them in life. So he is now holding the Teacher by the collar, as it were, and is pointedly asking him to explain more clearly. Naturally, the Teacher catches the contagion of the body's enthusiasm, and we shall see how beautifully he warms up to the discussion.

12. Intelligent Disciple--Appreciated. (50)

श्री गुरुरुवाच ।
धन्योऽसि कृतकृत्योऽसि पावितं ते कुलं त्वया ।
यदविद्याबन्धमुक्त्या ब्रह्मीभवितुमिच्छसि ॥५०॥

50. The *Guru* replied:
Blessed you are. For you wish to attain the absolute Brahman by freeing yourself from the bondage of ignorance. Indeed, you have fulfilled your life and have glorified your clan.

The Teacher's face now beams with a smile of satisfaction, and soon, words expressing his joy at meeting such a perfect student flow out of him. The very fact that the boy has decided that he wants to be free from all his weaknesses, that he wishes to walk out into the boundless fiedls of perfection, has made him blessed. Not only has he glorified himself but he has even sanctified his entire clan *(kulam)*.

The word *kulam* is not merely the family. It connotes all the ancestors and the future descendents, while "family" means only the present living members and the immediate forefathers.

This is not a hyperbole. It has already been said that rare indeed are those who come to exhibit such a burning thirst for liberation among living creatures at any period of human history. Evidently, the boy is a highly evolved being and hence he feels an acute impatience for liberation.*

In ordinary life too, we use expression such as "baking the bread", when we know that bread need not be baked. In

* "It is not to be attained except through the well-earned merits of a hundred crores of births." Cf. *sloka* 2.

such cases, we generally use the immediate *future* fulfilment to indicate the *present* activity. Similarly, the enquiry into life and its relationship with its cause, with a burning desire to live and accomplish the ultimate Perfection in one's own Self, is the present activity which will, in a short time, end in the final consummation of the purpose of life. Therefore, the Teacher in anticipation, declares that the boy has fulfilled the purpose of his life. Very rarely do we say, "the foetus in the womb", we invariable use the term, "the child in the womb", although in its pre-natal condition it is not yet a child.

To release ourselves from the shackes of ignorance is not merely to have knowledge but, transcending the ignorance-created projection of the body, mind and intellect, it is to live and experience Reality in Itself. Therefore, the Teacher says, "You wish to attain *Brahman*-hood i.e. Good-hood."

13. Glory of Self-Effort. (51-55)

ऋणमोचनकर्तारः पितुः सन्ति सुतादयः ।
बन्धमोचनकर्ता तु स्वस्मादन्यो न कश्चन ॥५१॥

51. A father has his sons and others to save him from his financial debts, but to redeem himself from his delusions, there is none but himself.

मस्तकन्यस्तभारादेर्दुःखमन्यैर्निवार्यते ।
क्षुधादिकृतदुःखं तु विना स्वेन न केनचित् ॥५२॥

52. Exhaustion and fatigue caused by carrying a load on the head can be relieved by others coming to one's help. But none save one's own self can end the pangs caused by hunger etc.

पथ्यमौषधसेवा च क्रियते येन रोगिणा ।
आरोग्यसिद्धिर्दृष्टाऽस्य नान्यानुष्ठितकर्मणा ॥५३॥

53. The patient who faithfully follows the right diet and takes the proper medicine alone is perceived to recover from his illness; no one recovers because another undergoes the treatment.

In these three verses, the Master is trying to drive home the student. Any amount of hearing, study, intellectual thinking and logical discussion cannot by themselves bring about liberation from our misconceptions and false evaluations in life. Text-books on culture and tradition and missives on religion are not talismans which can keep the Satan away. In order to impress this idea upon the student, the Teacher gives three verse with three different examples. These homely analogies which fall within the experience of everyone are given to remove any possible misunderstanding of the student regarding the technique of Self-realisation.

All the objective sciences in the world can be mastered by merely studying them. The man who studies the law of the country with all its implications can become a lawyer; he who studies the symptoms of diseases and their cures can become a doctor. An advocate of criminal law need not be a criminal himself; a doctor need not himself be a patient to know the science of medicine. But *Atma vidya* is gained only when it has brought about a complete regeneration of the individual who studies it. After gaining the objective knowledge there must also be a subjective achievement. You may learn to play an instrument and be able to do so faultlessly, but it is inspiration alone which makes an artist. Your painting might be exactly like a photograph but unless you have grasped the essence of what you are painting and are able to express it--you will only be a craftsman and not an artist.

It is, therefore, that no Teacher, however great he may be, can impart the subjective knowledge to a student. All that the Teacher can supply is a clear vision of what is involved, a glimpse of the Goal to be achieved and logical arguments to convince the student of the blessedness and perfection of both the Goal and the Path.

The examples given in the three verses are very telling. A father may be suffering agony and mental agitations due to his debts. In such a case, his children, dutiful and sympathetic, can certainly relieve him from his debts by their co-operation and help. But the sorrows and agitations which are due to his spiritual delusion can be relieved only by himself; none else can do it.

If a traveller is fatigued and exhausted because of the extremely heavy load he is carrying on his head, he can be helped and relieved by fellow-travellers, nay, even an inanimate load-rest can relieve the man. But the pangs he suffers from hunger, which is an inner disturbance, cannot be removed by somebody else eating a sumptuous dinner on his behalf. To remove hunger, his own stomach must receive the food and be appeased.

The Teacher, not satisfied with these two striking examples, adds yet another verse to drive home to the student the necessity for conscious personal effort. He says, only those patients are cured of their ailments who faithfully follow the prescribed diet and take the right medicines themselves. A person suffers because of some mal-adjustments in *his* physical system, and the medicine must be assimilated and absorbed by *his* body, so that it may remove the causes of *his* illness. One cannot cure one's illness by the medicines another has taken.

In fact, health is the natural condition of man. Some causes enter the system which obstruct the experience of the body's true vitality, and the person suffers. The medicine does not create health; it only removes the causes of ill-health. Similarly, the misunderstandings created by ignorance can be removed and the conditions required for a fuller expression of the Reality can be brought about in him only by his own efforts. In short, each one of us must walk the path by himself but properly guided by the instruction of the Teacher and the scriptures.

वस्तुस्वरूपं स्फुटबोधचक्षुषा स्वेनैव वेद्यं न तु पण्डितेन।
चन्द्रस्वरुपं निजचक्षुषैव ज्ञातव्यमन्यैरवगम्यते किम् ॥५४॥

54. The actuality of things is to be known by a first-hand personal experience through the eye of clear understanding, and not through the report of learned men. The beauty of the moon is enjoyed through one's own eyes. Can one appreciate it through the description by others?

Sankara reinforces the idea in the above three examples with yet another verse, hammering, as it were, the last nail on the coffin of our doubts.

The beauty, the brilliance, the soft glory, the queenly dignity, the serene consolation, the message of love and leisure, of peace and quietude, which the moon sheds as it glides across the spring-time skies cannot, indeed, be captured in words but are experiences to be enjoyed subjectively only. The vision of its majesty is to be perceived by one's own eyes and experienced in satisfying suggestive silence. A blind man cannot enjoy the love messages of a moonlit night.

When the Self rises in the dark bosom of our ignorance and glides across the horizon of our experiences, that experience cannot be described fully to us by another even though he may have experienced it himself. Each must experience it for himself, in himself. This analogy of moon-rise is indeed the most poetic, and by far the most appropriate example to indicate the soft silvery light of knowledge that illumines, with its sublime peace and perfection, the dark atmosphere in the bosom of the ignorant.

अविद्याकामकर्मादिपाशबन्धं विमोचितुम्।
कः शक्नुयाद्विनात्मानं कल्पकोटिशतैरपि ॥५५॥

55. Who else, but oneself can help rid oneself of the bondage caused by the chains of ignorance, desire, action, etc. ---even in a hundred crore of *kalpas*?

The bondage felt by the mortal is caused by the ignorance of his own real nature. This ignorance of his own All-fullness in his spiritual personality creates in his intellect waves of desires with which he expects to make himself full. Desires create in his mind thought-wave, and thoughts express themselves as action. These three---ignorance, desire and action are together called in *Vedanta Sastra* as the "heart knots" *(hridaya granthi)*. These are the cords that bind the ego *(Jeeva)* to the finitude and sorrows of a mortal. In this enumeration of ignorance, desire, action when Sankara adds "and the like", he means, the residual impressions *(vasanas)* that are left on the mind when a desire-prompted activity is consciously undertaken. These *vasanas* thicken the ignorance by darkening desires, agitating thoughts, and propelling us into a world of frenzied activity.

The *Acharya*, naturally asks, who can save a man from the chaos in his mind and intellect which is responsible for his rabid activities in the world of objects and his painful confusions in his relationships with his fellow beings? The answer is contained in the question itself; none but he himself.

The term *Kalpa* is used to indicate the entire duration of one Universe from its day of creation to its day of doom. It has been calculated that the life of the Universe is one day of the Creator which is equivalent to 432 million years, in terms of calculation of time, possible with our finite and limited time.

14. Knowledge of the Self---Its Beauty. (56-61)

न योगेन न सांख्येन कर्मणा नो न विद्यया ।
ब्रह्मात्मैकत्वबोधेनमोक्षः सिध्यति नान्यथा ॥५६॥

56. Neither by *Yoga*, nor by *Sankhya*, nor by ritual, nor by learning, is liberation possible. Only by the realisation of one's identity with Brahman is liberation possible, not by any other means.

None of the paths enumerated in this verse can take the student to his goal if he only mechanically follows it without an ardent and sincere co-operation.

Altogether, there are six schools of philosophical thought in India; only some of them are mentioned here. Not that the others are positively against Self-realisation, against its principles. The few mentioned here include the rest. By the term *"Yoga"*, Sankara means the path of mysticism developed an maintained through the exercises of *Hatha-Yoga.* The *Sankhyan* philosophy is one of the main fountain-heads of *Vedanta. Vedanta* has sprung from its early roots and has ultimately reached a greater precision of thought and perfection of detail from what was only an elaborate philosophy.

According to the Sankhyan philosophy---essentially dualisitc---the world is constituted of two intrinsic factor---*Purusha* and *Prakriti :* Spirit and matter. Spirit is the sentient, intelligent, Knowing Principle, the vital factor, the source of all life that expresses through physical forms. Matter is insentient, unintelligent and lifeless in itself, but it comes to exhibit the characteristic of life when it is blessed with a close proximity with the Spirit. *Purusha* by itself, cannot achieve or execute but when matter comes in contact with it, it is charged with dyanamism. The spring in the watch is inert---then what makes the watch work ? The tension in the spring. That is not an activity; all activities of life take place when *Purusha* has no activity; all activities of life take place when *Purusha* dons the robe of matter.

Prakriti herself is inert; *Purusha* by himself has no activity. But when they are wedded to each other, both seem to gather divinity, might and power, as a result of each blessing the other. In this philosophical concept the logic of thinking took the *Sankhyans* to a natural conclusion that *Purusha* revelling within one sample of matter is different from the *Purusha* in all others. Liberation from the entanglements of *Prakriti* is gained by *Purusha* when there is discrimination on all occasions and in all conditions, recognising the eternal Spirit as separate from finite matter. One step ahead of *Sankhya* is *Vedanta.* It explains that when one gains the true knowledge of the *Purusha*, the *Atman*, the *Yogi* experiences that *Prakriti* is only a super imposition upon the *Purusha*, that there is, in fact, no such distinction---the Supreme alone is, One-without-a-second, revelling everywhere, the subtlest of the subtle, the pure Principle of Consciousness.

The term *karma* is here used to include and incorporate the *Mimamsakas* who believe that ritualistic activity, divine and sacre, yields for them merits, to enjoy which they will be shifted to other realms of intense pleasure. When these merits are exhausted through enjoyment, they will return to physical forms for another period to earn more merits to enjoy another round of utmost pleasure. This for them, is *Moksa*. This is their ultimate concept of life. This, they consider *Amritatwam!*

The term vidya may be taken both in its Vedic connotation and in its literal dictionary meaning. In its Vedic application, *vidya* means *upasana*--concentrated and devoted meditation wherein the intellect tries to get away from its circumscribing vanities through a deliberate identification with a vaster concept as --"I am *Prana*, the All-pervading", or "I am the Sun, the Almighty" or "I am Fire, the Effulgent" or "I am Indra, the Omnipotent", ect. *Vidya*, in its other sense, means mere learning or book-knowledge.

All these are in themselves only techniques of self-development, but are not the goal. The Calcutta route is not Calcutta, the Bombay route is not Bombay. Of course, they both, if consistently pursued, will certainly take us to Culcutta or to Bombay. Having reached in neither of the cities will we find the stretches of the roads we travelled in order to reach them. *Yoga*, *vidya*, etc., are all means; they do not represent the end.

The Goal is in realising that the Self in us is the same Self in every thing and being. This realisation of the divine nature of man, individually experienced, each for himself, is the only method by which we can be liberated from the bondages of intellectual restlessness, mental agitations and physical cravings.

viveka = discrimination sense between what is real and unreal

To avoid any trace of doubt that might still linger in the mind of the student that there is, perhaps, some mehtods other than *Yoga, Sankhya,* etc., which has not been described by the Teacher, Sankara says point-blank, "and by no other means". Realisation of the Self is the only method; there are no other means by which our present experiences of finitude and limitations can be destroyed, root and branch.

वीणाया रुपसौन्दर्यं तन्त्रीवादनसौष्ठवम् ।
प्रजारञ्जनमात्रं तन्न साम्राज्याय कल्पते ॥५७॥

57. The beauty of the *veena* and the proficiency of one playing on its chords serve but to please an audience; they do not, by themselves, ever prove sufficient to confer full sovereignty.

In using analogies, nobody has yet come to the field of philosophy who can rival Sankara's efficiency and perfection. According to him, the schools of philosophy which argue emphatically, describe beautifully and enunciate exhaustively, discussions that give clear intellectual pictures of the why and wherefore of this universe, are all nothing but the beauty of the words or the eloquence of the speaker. The player of an instrument with his proficiency may entertain the largest conceivable audience, and for the time being, the listeners may even consider him the king of artistes. Yet, in effect, he can never gain so vereignty, permanent and complete, over the audience through the instrument.

Similarly, the various schools of philosophy are intellectual entertainments no doubt; yet the seeker cannot gain the status of God-hood by merely dabbling in philosophy. A king might entertain himself and his friends by playing the *veena.* But his empire is not consolidated, nor is order maintained among the people nor is royal dignity nourished throuth his proficiency in the instrument.

Acharya Sankara wants to emphasise that any amount of philosophical studies, even a mastery over all the six schools of philosophy cannot bring about a complete evolutionary fulfilment.

The term *Samrajya* has a reminiscent Upanishadic flavour; in ancient literature this term is used for the kingdom of God within, in the heart of every individual.

वाग्वैखरी शब्दझरी शास्त्रव्याख्यानकौशलम् ।
वैदुष्यं विदुषां तद्वद्भुक्तये न तु मुक्तये ॥५८॥

58. Loud speech in a steam of words, the efficiency in expounding or commenting upon the *Sastras*, erudition, ---these bring only a little joyous, material satisfaction to the scholar; but they are insufficient to liberate him completely.

The *Yoga Sastra* gives us the various subtle stages of metamorphosis of a thought or a desire before it is expressed in the form of sounds and words. Altogether it describes four distinct stages in a thoughts manifestation as an expression in words. First of all, the thought arises from or has contact with the Reality of Life in us, and at this stage, it is called *Para*. When it manifests sufficiently for the ego in us to be conscious of it, it is in a state grosser than the previous one and at this stage of its perceptible existence it is called *Pasyanti*. A thought of which we have become conscious, passes through a state of inner moulding in the crucible of language and this state of transcribing thought into a series of symbolical sounds for the purpose of conveying it to another is called *Madhyama*. And through expressed audible sounds, the thought in its grossest manifestation is called *Vaikhari*.

By the term *Vaikhari*, Sankara means the unproductive and noisy discussions on philosophy which some students of Vedenta engage in. These gabblers are laughed at, condemned, and quite ignored by all the great *Acharyas* like Sankara. To the Rishis an ounce of practice is more sacred than tons of discussion around a table.

According to Sankara, mere knowledge of philosophical thoughts can be used only for purposes of eking out a profit for one's own livelihood, or for gaining some insignificant popularity or short-lived glory.

अविज्ञाते परे तत्त्वे शास्त्राधीतिस्तु निष्फला ।
विज्ञातेऽपि परे तत्त्वे शास्त्राधीतिस्तु निष्फला ॥५९॥

59. Without knowing the supreme Reality, the study of the *Sastras* is futile. Having known the supreme Reality, the study of the *Sastras* is again futile.

Here is an exquisite example of the use of a deliberate statement of contradiction, to hammer a point into a student while creating in him a sense of wonderment. The verse, even in its tenth reading, leaves a staggering sense of amazement and confusion. Wonder is an emotion in which there is a dizzy pause in thinking and at such a moment of intellectual arrest, the verse filters through. When one realises the meaning fully, it goes straight into the deepest vaults of one's heart-cave.

The paradox is resolved when we give a little conscious application of purified intellect on the word "knowing" in both the lines of the verse,---"without knowing" in the first and "having known" in the second. In both cases "knowing" connotes a different meaning, the literal and the indicative. In the first line it means "intellectually understanding" and in the second line it means "realising".

In the light of these interpretations, the verse becomes a clear statement of Truth. As long as we have "no right intellectual appreciation" of what the *Vedanta* texts indicate, all study of the scriptures is futile. Again, when we "have realised the Truth," study of the scriptures is redundant.

Elsewhere in *Vedantic* literature, it is said* that the efforts of all the *Vedas* is, ultimately, to deny the existence of plurality which is a sorrowful dream projected by the individual mind, a delusion superimposed upon the *Atman*, the substratum. All arguments that we can marshal to convince a deluded friend that what he perceives is not a ghost but only a harmless post, constitute the "scriptures" indicating the post. Naturally therefore, any man of

* "All *Sastras* endeavour to explain what is not, and deny the delusion."

Realisation, reading even the best of scriptures must laugh indulgently at the colossal inefficiency of Mother *Sruti.*

And those, who have no conception of Reality, to them no scriptural study can give even a trace of thrill. We read in *Vedanta* that to such immature intellects the *Upanishads* are empty words. Just as children can never understand the physical thrill of married life, so too, poor things, they have not the instruments to understand, or the maturity to comprehend the Truth. Then, as they grow, even if it is not taught, they will instinctively learn to feel or to know.

शब्दजालं महारण्यं चित्तभ्रमणकारणम् ।
अतः प्रयत्नाज्ज्ञातव्यं तत्त्वज्ञैस्तत्त्वमात्मनः ॥६०॥

60. Commentaries on philosophies constitute a thick jungle in which a roaming mind may easily get lost, in its own delusion. Therefore, true seekers of *Brahman* should, through right efforts, come to experience the Real Nature of the Self.

In this brilliant metaphor the *Acharya* woos both poetry and philosophy with the ardour and fevour of a true and noble lover, handling the philosophy and dandling the poetry, as it were.

Here he conveys to us the idea that mere philosophical discussion is a dangerous jungle, dark and dreary, with luxuriously growing poisonous weeds and prowling beasts lying in ambush, ready to pounce upon innocent, unsuspecting piligrims. No better description of the dialectics could be given of the endless arguments of the six schools of Indian philosophy each trying to disporve the others to establish its own point of view.

Into this jungle infested with dangerous flora and fauna, if an unprepared or innocent mind frail in strength, carelessly enters, it might get attacked or destroyed by the lurking dangers. Even an intellectual Master, of great erudition and perfect scholarship can, now and then, tumble down into unseen pot-holes and suffer mental repercussions. So the warning given here by the benevolent *Acharya* is of extreme service to initiates entering the portals of *Vedanta*.

Let not the new seekers enter with hasty enthusiasm into such jungles of noisy confusion. The chances are that their minds will get over-burdened with contradictory assertions of the great champions of the different philosophical view-points, and they will ultimately get lost in the blind alleys of wordy arguments. Therefore, a seeker should set about only after knowing the true nature of the Self, through the method of *Atma Vichara*, when he has fully acquired the necessary qualifications for it through *upasanas* and meditations.

अज्ञानसर्पदष्टस्य ब्रह्मज्ञानौषधं विना ।
किमु वेदैश्च शास्त्रैश्च किमु मन्त्रैः किमौषधैः ॥६१॥

61. For him who has been stung by the cobra of ignorance, the only remedy is the knowledge of *Brahman*. Of what use are the *Vedas* and the scriptures, *mantras* and medicines to such a victim of poison?

The Supreme, poisoned, as it were, by Self-forgetfulness has come to suffer the burning agony of limitations and sorrows. It has forgotten its divine nature and identifying with the matter envelopments, it sobs at its mortality, its sorrows, its imperfections. To one who has realised these and has come to feel a choking impatience to be relieved from the tyranny of pain, nothing short of Self rediscovery can be satisfying. A victim of the snake-bite of ignorance can be relieved of his painful delirium only by Self-realisation. Only then can he live as the spirit, the Reality in every thing and being.

It is natural that when a person realises that he has been bitten by a cobra,he will have none of the ordinary prejudices of faith, creed, position, status, time, or place; any help that reaches him from any quarter, offered in any attitude will be most welcome. In that moment of dire sorrow, in the magnitude of his tragedy, he realises the urgency of the situation, and his only demand is for some antidote to the poison, which can restore him to natural health and vitality.

Similarly, no sooner a seeker realises that he has been bitten by ignorance, the most dangerous of all serpents in the wild jungles of uncultured and uncultivated hearts, than he will take the best from the *Sastras* and will try to imbibe immediately the specific cure for ignorance, the knowledge of the Real. To such a one, of what avail then are the slower though more comfortable means of study of the *Vedas and Sastras*, repetition of *mantras* and dizzy philosophical arguments?

15. Direct Experience; Liberation. (62-66)

न गच्छति विना पानं व्याधिरोषधशब्दतः ।
विनाऽपरोक्षानुभवं ब्रह्मशब्दैर्न मुच्यते ॥६२॥

62. A disease is not cured by merely repeating the name of the medicine and without taking it; without direct realisation, by a mere utterance of the word, *"Brahman"*, none can be liberated.

How and why mere chanting of a *mantra* is by itself, considered impotent is explained here. Any person suffering from ignorance cannot expect to be cured by merely repeating the word *"Brahman"*, the name of the absolute Reality. Repeated utterances of *Aham Brahmaasmi* or a mechanical murmuring of endles *Sivohams* cannot by themselves produce any cure. However effective the medicine may be, no patient is known to have been cured only by repeatedly reading a prescription.

By merely repeating for hours the word "Aspirin", when one is suffering from headache, one can only increase it. The only cure is to take the medicine and assimilate it till it becomes one with the patient. By this alone can he get complete relief.

Similarly, a mere repetation of the sacred truths of *Vedanta* is futile without the struggle to raise ourselves to the subtler joys of a higher culture and a divine way of living, by individually assimilating the Truth of the Upanishads and becoming one with It by intimate personal experience. Subjective Realisation, most intimate and immediate, total and permanent, is called *aparoksa anubhava* of the Self. No doubt, this must be preceded by an intellectual understading of the Truth called in Sanskrit *paroksa jnanam*

intellectual appreciation is the *way* to reach Truth and a full subjective apprehension of the self is the *Goal*. Liberation from our delusions can come only when they have ended in pure Knowledge. Darkness can end only in the presence of light.

अकृत्वा दृश्यविलयमज्ञात्वा तत्त्वमात्मनः ।
ब्रह्मशब्दैः कुतो मुक्तिरुक्तिमात्रफलैर्नृणाम् ॥६३॥

63. Without achieving the disappearance of the entire pluralistic world and without realising the Real Nature of the Self, how can one achieve full liberation by a mere repetation of the word, *"Brahman"*? Surely it will end only in a wasteful effort of speech.

The, conditions preceding the full state of liberation are explained here. In the white heat of intense meditation, when the mental rays of the individual have been made single-pointed and turned completely inwards to *recognise* the Self within, the world of perceptions gets eliminated in the experience; just as the world of the dream naturally rolls away from the waker's comprehension. We perceive the pluralistic world from the levels of the body, the plains of the mind and the peaks of the intellect. With the body we recognise the waking-state-world of names and forms, with the mind we perceive the world of feelings and emotions and with the intellect we recognise and experience our world of ideas which has no declared boundary.

On transcending our identifications with the body, mind and intellect, the world of plurality filtering into our consciousness through the sense-organs gets absorbed, as it were, into what unfolds Itself as the pure Self, the Truth. On waking from a dream it cannot be said that the dream has rolled away into some other point of time and place. We will have to accept that the dreamer in us arose only because of our complete forgetfulness of real self as the waker. On waking, the dream is considered to have vanished. Similarly, on awakening to the full spiritual Consciousness of God-hood, the world of change and finitude is experienced as having totally "vanished".

Without coming to this state of total Self-realisation, even though for only a fleeting moment, there is no liberation possible from the instinctive weakneses that one suffers because of one's false identifications. This is the way shown by our scriptures. This is the path by which an endless caravan of perfect men travelled to gain their Goal in life. And in our own times also, many a noble soul has enjoyed the fulfilment of his mission in life, walking the very same path and attaining the very same Goal.

Lip-*Vedanta* has never helped any one to gain perfection. Mere discussion, idle repetition, boisterous argument---these have never brought to anyone any substantial blessing, except the exhaustion of over-talking. Sankara urges the seeker to talk less and practive more.

अकृत्वा शत्रुसंहारमगत्वाखिलभूश्रियम् ।
राजाहमिति शब्दान्नो राजा भवितुमर्हति ॥६४॥

64. Without eliminating his enemies and without bringing the entire land of his kingdom under his sway, by merely repeating, "I am the Emperor", one can not become an emperor.

It is necessary to fulfil all the required conditions in one's inner life before one can experience the Infinite, the Divine. Self-mastery is a reward one comes to gain when one has conquered all the inner enemies and has come to rule over all the different matter-provinces in one's personality.

In this verse the *Acharya* is throwing a flood of light on the previous declaration. By an apt example, he is trying to make us understand that by mere verbal repetition nothing will be accomplished. A fool who, without annihilating his enemies and without bringing with his own might and power all the provinces under his sway, just repeats that he is the emperor, can never become one for all his loud claims. Certain necessary conditions must be fulfilled before he can hope to gain the Sceptre and the Crown and be recognised as the Emperor. An emperor has no enemies within his own empire, and everyone living in his empire is directly under his will command. If these conditions are accomplished, he need not even announce or declare that he is the emperor; the world will do it for him. Similarly, if a seeker has successfully destroyed all his inner enemies---of desires and thoughts, physical demands, mental appetites and intellectual wanderings---and if he has established mastery over the vast province of the waking, dream and deep-sleep states of consciousness, he need not thereafter repeat "I am *Brahman*". For every cell in him, every thought and every idea that rises in him will sing in chorus his sovereignty over all, at all times and in all conditions.

The idea that man's self-effort in the right direction alone can make him rediscover for himself the spiritual essence in him to be divine and all-powerful, is vividly brought out by the following exquisite verse, pregnant with suggestion, rich in melody, perfect in flow and rhythm.

आप्तोक्तिं खननं तथोपरि शिलाद्युत्कर्षणं स्वीकृतिम्
निक्षेपः समपेक्षते नहि बहिः शब्दैस्तु निर्गच्छति ।
तद्वद्ब्रह्मविदोपदेशमननध्यानादिभिर्लभ्यते ।
मायाकार्यतिरोहितं स्वममलं तत्त्वं न दुर्युक्तिभिः ॥६५॥

65. A treasure hidden deep below under the earth can be found only when the exact site is known, excavations carried out and the earth, stones, etc., hiding it are removed; never can it come out if merely called by name. Similarly, the pure Truth of the Self which lies hidden beneath our delusion and its effects can be attained through the instructions of one who is a knower of *Brahman*, followed by reflection, meditation, etc. But never can the Self emerge and manifest Itself as a result of repeating perverted arguments.

In the course of the last several verses, Sankara has been trying to bring home to us the utter necessity and urgency for self-effort undertaken in the right direction. That no amount of study and philosophical dialectics can take one, even by a fraction of an inch, nearer to the divine experience which is life's fulfilment, has already been eleborately discussed. The same idea has been brought out here which, we may consider, is the summary of a library of books on spiritual literature.

In order to explain this idea, Sankara pints the picture of one digging for a treasure. One may wonder how the treasure-hunters' activities can be a theme by which spiritual technique can be explained; but a poet always sees much more meaning in a factual happening than an ordinary matter-of-fact observer does.

A treasure-hunt can be successful only when the digger has correct information of the place where the treasure is hidden. He must also have the enthusiasm and energy to dig and find the treasure. He must slowly and steadily, with hopeful patience and perseverence, continue digging and remove all obstacles that he may meet with till he reaches the goal of his seeking---the treasure trove. At last, when he comes to the rich vaults he must be level-headed and calm enough not to lose his balance so that he is in a position to gather the treasure and make use of it.

In the same fashion, the infinitely rich treasure of Perfection that lies unseen beneath the outer crude layers of matter envelopments in the bosom of man is to be discovered as his own Self. The seeker must have the assiduity, industry, hope and patience to dig in the right place, in the right fashion, constantly and continuously with unabated enthusiasm, in the face of even the greatest obstacles, until at last he comes not only to see the treasure but to gather it, possesss it and enjoy it, as its sole proprietor. The seeker must not dig just anywhere; he must start his endeavour in the right direction as advised by those who know the Truth *(apta-vakyam)* as declared in the scriptures.

In the spiritual treasure-hunt, the endeavour of digging is made with the pick-axe of thought and the spade of discrimination. With these we remove the earth---the attachments with the body, mind and intellect, which are the effects of the ignorance of the Self. *Aditya* creates in us various misunderstandings and it is these agitations of the mind and negative thought-veilings of the intellect that conceal the Treasure Divine---the Self. These can be removed by reflection and meditation.

Manana and *dhyana*, reflection and meditation, prepare the mind for a single-pointed application by bringing it to the state of least agitation. This is the condition of the mind and intellect fit for *vichara*, the highest spiritual *sadhana* known to man. This is exhaustively indicated only in *Vedanta*.

Faithful to his arguments, honest in his convictions and obedient to his experiences, *Acharya* Sankara cries out that this is the *only* path for complete and permanent liberation from the chaotic confusions created by our ignorance of the underlying divinity in ourselves. Naturally, he points out the hollowness of all other methods and the immaturity of all other techniques which are, according to him, putrified logic, sourced reason, distorted vision and false assertion compared with the perfect philosophy and detailed practicality of *Vedanta*.

तस्मात्सर्वप्रयत्नेन भवबन्धविमुक्तये ।
स्वैरेव यत्नः कर्तव्यो रोगादाविव पण्डितैः ॥६६॥

66. Therefore, an intelligent seeker should, as in the case of illness etc. strive hard by all the means at his disposal to be free from the bondage of births and deaths.

The ideas in the preceding nine verses are now being concluded with this tenth *sloka*. Naturally the term, "therefore", with which this verse opens is a sequel to all the reasons shown and explained in the previous verses.

In verse 56 Sankara started this discussion. All through he has emphasised that self-effort is essential and said that, compared to it, mere *sastraic* studies and the capacity to discourse upon them were not sufficient. Because of these reasons, it can be logically understood that each seeker must, for himself, strive with all sincerity and regularity in the right direction, so that he may come to realise in himself the eternal God-hood of his spiritual nature.

The simile used here is very significant. Like a sick patient, we are to consider ourselves as infected with the microbes of ignorance. Health is the real nature of all living beings. Illness is the unnatural condition of the body, when it has, for reasons known or unknown, fallen away from its essential health. Therefore, health is not to be created, but all our efforts should be to remove the causes that created the disease. A body rid of its disease-germs comes to manifest full health and vigour. Similarly, ignorance creates in us all the maladjustments through which spiritual dynamism, divine Glory and supreme Perfection are veiled from us.

No two patients suffering from the same disease can be cured with the same dosage of the same medicine. The same medicine can be the cure for the disease, but dosage and application will differ from person to person depending upon the degree of infection. Similarly, though Vedanta *sadhana* is the same for all seekers, in its application, individually, each seeker must take his own right dose. Merely taking the medicine does not assure a cure. It depends upon a dozen other factors, of which *tapas* is the most essential. The patient may be tempted to enjoy things denied him by his doctor. But he must avoid them scrupulously, else the medicine instead of curing him might even kill him.

16. Discussion on Question Raised. (67-71)

यस्त्वयाद्य कृतः प्रश्नो वरीयांछास्त्रविन्मतः ।
सूत्रप्रायो निगूढार्थो ज्ञातव्यश्च मुमुक्षुभिः ॥६७॥

67. The questions which you raised today are excellent, accepted by those well-versed in the *Sastras*, aphoristic, full of hidden meaning and such that they are fit to be known by all seekers.

When the student asked his questions* the Teacher, instead of replying directly and immediately, indulged in a long and exhaustive discourse upon the futility of mere discussion if it were not accompanied by an all-out enthiusiastic effort at straightening oneself from one's inner deformities. This was nò idle digression on the part of the Teacher, but it expressed his deep concern that his disciple should not misunderstand and misuse the freedom given him to ask questions to get his doubts cleared. There are always in society, a set of wise-looking foolish disciples who misuse the freedom given to them and abuse the privilege of discussing with their Teacher.

They, poor foik, have so fallen in love with their own questions, that they repeat them with a passion amounting to sheer lunacy. To ensure the student does not fall into this intellectual ditch and obstruct his own evolution,Sankara with ten explicit verses warns the world of seekers. After concluding the digression, he now pointedly answers all seven questions raised by the diciple.

In this verse, the Master once again, compliments the student on the intelligence of his questions and the beauty and precision that graces the very form in which they are framed. The glories that are enumerated here by the *Guru* are the perfections that come about,when a chiseled thought is packed in appropriate language and offered at the feet of true Wisdom. When a true disciple reaches his Master's feet, he

---

* Ibid verse 49.

feels so choked with admiration, revernce, devotion and love for him that he dares not disturb the divine atmosphere of tranquility around the Teacher with thoughtless blabberings and empty talk.

A fit student has got his ideas crystallised and after logical self-analysis, has come across certain insurmountable obstacles for the removal of which he has approached the Teacher. Since the doubt was really felt and thoroughly digested by him, the student could present it in the fewest number of words, indicating at once the logic of his thought.

If on a dark night you fall into a wayside well, indeed, your condition is unenviable. You are extremely anxious to extricate yourself from the situation. At this moment you hear approaching foot-steps and you cry out for help. The benevolent person reaches the well. Would you then, from the bottom of the well, begin the narration of the entire story of how you came upon the well at that late hour, how you fell, what thoughts kept you company in the sandy bottom of the well, ect., besides giving him details of your name, details of your family, position status, etc.? No. At such critical moments you will only cry, "I am here in the well. Save me, O please save me. Help me, save me, save me." Any other cry will be unnatural. Similarly, a student who has understood that in the darkness of ignorance he has fallen into dry well of limitations and sorrows, when he sees Master, he will have no stories to tell, no idle discussion to indulge in. His one heart-rending cry is, "Save me, O Master, save me."

Sankara, through his compliments to the disciple, is advising generations of seekers not to be too wordy when they approach a Master. This does not take away from us our liberty to talk to the Master in our attempt to evaluate him. Sankara only means that having accepted him as your Teacher, when you approach him for correct initiation into the subtle truths of Vedanta, you should not destroy the sanctity of the atmosphere by an exhibition of your knowledge or sentiments.

The questions asked by the student were all couched in a precise aphoristic style, indicative of his independant attempts at understanding the preliminary thoughts in the philosophy. These questions are pregnant with secret thoughts which are not obvious in their literal word-meanings. Also, there discussions are not just Sunday magazine themes, written to entertain the vulgar tastes and cheap demands of an idle hoilday crowd. They rake up the innermost depths of investigations undertaken in all tranquility, possible only for a human intellect blessed with acute reasoning capacity. These topics are of interest only to those who wish to get away from their limitations to experience the essential freedom of their own pure nature as the Self.

श्रुणुष्वावहितो विद्वन्यन्मया समुदीर्यते ।
तदेतच्छ्रवणात्सद्यो भवबन्धाद्विमोक्ष्यसे ॥६८॥

68. Listen attentively, O learned one, to what I shall now tell you. Listening to it you shall immediately gain a thorough liberation from the bondages of *samsar.*

The *Acharya* gives the student full assurance that if he listens attentively and looks for the subtle meaning in the words of the Teacher, he shall attain a sence of complete fulfilment in life.

"Indeed, this *Vedanta* is cheap. A seeker of liberation has only to discover a great Teacher and listen carefully to his words and immediately he shall experience a total release from all physical imperfections, mental debilities and intellectual weaknesses created by his own spiritual ignorance. How easy! Just listen and you will be liberated. Can there be an easier path? *Vedanta* is truly cheap" --thus one may be tempted to exclaim.

Here is a clear example which amply illuatrates that literal word-meanings do not convey the right philosophical implications in Vedantic literature. If, by listening, one could liberate oneself, *moksa* would have been so cheap that it could be easily dispensed universally. But the scripture cannot be false; and mere listening cannot be the path for a total spiritual redemption. Therefore, we must understand that the word, "listening" is used here in a sense much more ample and accomodative than its dictionary meaning.

From what you have been told so far, you know how essestial it is for a student to be completely attuned to the Master. The student already has, through a process of self-discipline, made his inner kingdom clean and peaceful, wherein he stands in all devotion and meekness, receptivity and alertness. When he 'listens' to the inspired words of the Master, full of subtle suggestions, he within himself, starts living the unworded implications coursing through the words.

As the tongue of the temple bell strikes the bell-cup, there is a harsh metallic sound. But as we listen to it, it warbles out a lingering melody before it slowly dies out into the very silence in which it was born. Simiarly, the words of the scriptures have a harsh sound but a lingering ringing music. The harsh sounds are caught in a web of language and preserved in text-books; but the warbling notes are to be produced in the secret cave of the seeker's heart.

This preparation is indicated by the practices of reflection and meditation, concentration and devotion, self-control and celibacy, moral purity and ethical goodness advised for the *sadhaks*...

A student, thus prepared, when he comes to 'hear' a discourse from the Master, not only hears the words but spiritually lives the Truth; this is called 'listening'. Unlike the other techniques of self-perfection like devotion, and *Yoga*, in *Vedanta* the student has nothing to do or gain save to 'hear' and truly 'listen'. In the other paths, techniques are advised and explained and the experience comes to the student when he gain a certain amount of perfection in quiet and steady practice of them.

In *Vedanta* it is a scriptural discussion between a saint of inner experience and a student of inner purity. It is a *Guru-sishya samvada,* and the experience of Reality which is the theme of discussion is brought within the experience of the student, immediately and instantaneously, if the student is ready to receive it. Therefore, Sankara is perfectly orthodox when he declares that the disciple shall experience liberation if only he knows the 'art of listening' to the spiritual voice that sings through the Master's words.

मोक्षस्य हेतुः प्रथमो निगद्यते
वैराग्यमत्यन्तमनित्यवस्तुषु ।
ततः शमश्चापि दमस्तितिक्षा
न्यासः प्रसक्ताखिलकर्मणां भृशम् ॥६९॥

69. For liberation, first comes extreme detachment from finite objects of sensual satisfaction. Then follow calmness, self-control, forbearance and complete renunciation of all selfish actions.

This is a text which not only expounds *Vedanta,* but is also full of practical instructions to a real seeker who wishes to be fully established on the path of spirituality and maintain his progress in his programme of self-development. Any true seeker will be impatient, not only to understand the nature of liberation but also to get a detailed discussion on the specific cause and conditions under which final liberation from the pains of mortality and the sorrows of finitude can be had. Here the *Acharya* enumerates the conditions of the mind in which true wisdom can blaze forth.

Among them, the capacity to be completely detached from the craving for things known to be finite and perishable is considered most important. A discriminative intellect *(viveka)* can grow and fulfil itself only when there is full detachment *(vairagya).* Without developing sufficient disinterest in the acquisition, possession and enjoyment of the sense-objects of the world, we cannot enter the portals of true Wisdom. When we become acutely conscious of the finite and impermanent nature of the world of objects, our minds, which are always athirst for stability, continuity and perfection, will immediately be repelled from their usual playgrounds, the by-lanes of sensuousness, where we spend a large amount of our vital energy and disciplining, conserving and rightly applying this newfound energy to raise ourselves from the state of bondage to one of inner freedom and spiritual suzerainty.

Sama, dama and *titiksa* are again qualities[1] to be developed by the seeker himself so that he may discipline and train the newly released energies for right application in a concentrated, single-pointed meditation.

When there is detachment as a result of pure discriminative perception of a better balanced intellect, and when this mental condition is reinforced by self-control, calmness and forbearance, the individual entertains no more egoistic, desire-prompted schemes of activity. He relinquishes them all, sacred or secular, ritualistic or otherwise.[2] All these contribute to the true preparedness of the intellect for the higher flights to the brilliant peaks of transcendental Glory and Perfection.

ततः श्रुतिस्तन्मननं सतत्त्व -
ध्यानं चिरं नित्यनिरंतरं मुनेः ।
ततोऽविकल्पं परमेत्य विद्वा -
निहैव निर्वाणसुखं समृच्छति ॥ ७० ॥

70. Thereafter comes "hearing", then reflection on what has been heard and, lastly, long, constant and continuous meditation on the Truth, for the *Muni*. Ultimately, that learned one attains the supreme *Nirvikalpa* state and realises the Blisss of *Nirvana* in this very life.

---

1. Defined earlier in verses 20-24. In Brihadaranyaka Upanishad, IV, iv. 23 there is a famous reference to these qualities of clamness, self-control, forbearance, etc.

2. The idea of renunciation of all activities is not to be misunderstood as amounting to an existence as inert as the rocks on the Ganges banks. Cf. discourse on verse 10.

Sankara has already started an enumeration of the various techniques to be followed by a person on his march towards realising the eternal Freedom of the soul. In this *sloka* the *Acharya* is outlining the different stages of practices which one must follow when one has renounced all pursuits of ego-prompted, desire-ridden activities contributing to a life of sensuousness.

An individual who has enough detachment from the enjoyment of finite objects, who has cultivated the four great qualities and who has renounced all self-motivated activities, is fit for the process called in *Vedanta*, 'hearing' the scriptures. Scriptures have to explain life as we perceive and live it now and indicate the Truth, the Goal, only through finite words. Therefore, a direct approach to the text may misguide the seeker if he has wrong understanding.

It is imperative, that one must 'listen' to the exposition of at least one scriptural text from a true Teacher. In this transaction of wisdom, the Master also uses but finite words to explain the Absolute; there is no magic formula involved. Therefore, the student must be fully tuned to the Teacher so that the latter's experiences may, in resonance, be amplified and conveyed to echo in the heart-chambers of the student.

This 'listening' to the discourses *(sravana)*, is to be followed by inner arguments and final assimilation by the intellect in a process called reflection *(manana)*, by which alone the ideas in the text can become the student's own philosophy. Even this intellectual conviction is not sufficient, for Vedanta seeks a fulfillment not in merely propounding a theory to explain the happenings of the world and the destinies of mankind, but to lift man to the highest pinnacle of evolution of cultural purity, that he may thereafter revel as a God-man on earth.

Therefore, a person must attain Truth through a process of re-discovery of his real Self by detaching himself from his wrong and false identifications with matter. This technique of detaching oneself fom the false, -and rediscovering one's identity with the Self through disciplined currents of constant thought-flow is called meditation *(dhyana)*. It is indicated here that when *dhyana* is practised for a long period daily and constantly ---every word is important ---for a long period of years *(chiram)*,daily *(nityam)* and constantly *(nirantaram)* --one gets established in God-consciousness and attains *Nirvana* in this very life.

The word *Nirvana* means "blown out". Modern physics tells us that the tip of a candle flame, though apparently whole and steady, is constituted of independent flickerings at a greate frequency. Just as when a fan whirls at a great speed, its blades are not distinguishable but only one continuous whirling movement is observed. A movie is constituted of a number of individual pictures projected on the screen, but because of the speed and high frequency of the change, the movie gives us a continuous experience. So too, the "wholeness" of the candle flame is only apparent. This example is often quoted in the *Yoga Sastra* to explain the mind in man which seems to be a substantial factor, though created by the frequency of the flow of thought-waves. In one who has realised his own Self and has transcended the mind, there is no more rising of thoughts. This state is indicated by the term, *Nirvana*,the state of Self-realisation.

This *moksa* condition is possible in two stages, just as before sleep, there is a period of dozing followed by the deep-sleep state. During dozing, we are conscious that we are "going to world are slowly and steadily becoming obscure. But the deep-sleep state is a period when we are neither conscious of the outer world nor even of ourselves.

Similarly, in meditation also there is a hazy period of awareness, wherein we are conscious of ourselves nearing the Transcendental, and that state of *Samadhi* where there is still a vestige of the ego is called *Savikalpa Samadhi*. The ego-less moment *Yogi* experiences the infinite Bliss of pure existence, that state is called *Nirvikalpa Samadhi*. That is the experience of God-hood, and after this *Iswara darsana*, there is no falling back into the values and impulses of the lower, worldly life any more.

Not only does Sankara explain the various states *en route* this divine pilgrimage and describe exhaustively the Goal with its experiences, but he also insists that this is not a *post mortem* experience to be gained in some future embodiment, after the death of this body, in a special are called heaven or in another world. He insists that a *Muni* experiences the Bliss of *Nirvana* even here and now. *Muni* in Sanskrit, in its etymological meaning, has an import equivalent to "a man of discriminative reflection".

यद्बोद्धव्यं तवेदानीमात्मानात्मविवेचनम् ।
तदुच्यते मया सम्यक् श्रुत्वात्मन्यवधारय ॥ ७१ ॥

71. Now I am going to describe the discrimination between the Self and the not-Self most elaborately---it is what you ought to know. Listen to it properly and receive it well in you mind.

Earlier the student had asked the Master about the discrimination between the Self and the not-Self.* This verse onwards, Sankara gives an elaborate description of the various layers of matter envelopments which together constitute the not-Self, identifying with which the Self behaves as though it is limited, bound and conditioned to suffer as the *samsarin*. A mere repetion that *viveka* means discrimination between the Self and the not-Self will not in itself be very helpful to a seeker unless he is able to realise the exact meaning of the Self as contrasted with the perceived world of plurality.

The *Acharya* stresses the importance of this theme of discussion by saying that each student should not just listen, but must come through a process of independent, discriminative self-analysis, to a firm conviction of the truth of what is discussed hereunder.

---

* Verse 49.

17. Gross Body.(72-75)

मज्जास्थिमेदः पलरक्तचर्म -
त्वगाह्वयैर्धातुभिरेभिन्वितम् ।
पादोरुवक्षो भुजपृष्ठमस्तकैः -
रङ्‌गैरुपाङ्‌गैरुपयुक्तमेतत् ॥ ७२ ॥

72. Composed of the seven ingredients---marrow, bones, fat, flesh, blood, dermis and epidermis, and consisting of the following parts---legs, things, chest, arms, back and the head......

अहं ममेति प्रथितं शरिरं
मोहास्पदं स्थूलमितीर्यते बुधैः ।
नभोनभस्वद्दहनाम्बुभूमयः
सूक्ष्माणि भूतानि भवन्ति तानि ॥ ७३ ॥

73. This body, the seat of delusion, expressing in terms of "I" and "mine", is termed by reputed sages as the gross body. Sky, air, fire, water and earth are the subtle elements.

In these two verses, Sankara describes the gross body. In biology, we frequently find that an organ is discussed by describing its anatomy by an explanation of its cross-sections. This methods does not seem unfamiliar to our ancient tradition, since it is used quite freely and liberally even in the realm of philosophy, when a philosopher explains such subtle things as the "layers" of a human being. Sankara too, makes free use of this technique of explaining through a cross-section examination. In verse 72 we have a beautiful description, layer by layer, of a cross-section of the physical body.

Let us examine the contents of the body by studying the transverse section of, say, the upper arm. Therein we shall find at its centre, a pulpy white matter called the marrow *(majja)*, bone *(asthi)*, and still external, a layer of fat *(medah)*, envoloped by the flesh *(pala)*. On the outer layers of the flesh are conspicuously the blood *(rakta)* vessels and all these are packed beautifully with two layers of skin of which the inner cream-coloured tissue is called the dermis *(charma)* and the outer thicker layer which we see is called the epidermis *(twak)*. These seven items then, form the bulk of the body in a transverse section of any part of it.

Gathered together in the above squence and moulded into a human form, they form the most beautiful physical structure * fashioned in matter, consisting of various parts such as hands, legs etc., enumerated in verse 73.

In the following verse we are told how this body, the harem of all our egocentric assertions and misunderstandings is the very seat of our vanities and possessiveness. All our *I-ness* and *my-ness* function from the headquarters of the physical body. This seat of all painful activities and ego-prompted criminalities against our own divine nature, consisting of the filth of flesh and fat with its various appendages is described by the *Rishis* as the gross body.

The five great elements are described as first created in their subtle form and then through a process of combinations among themselves they become the gross elements which we are able to perceive with our sense-organs. The process by which the subtle elements become the perceivable gross elements is described in the next verse.

परस्परांशैर्मिलितानि भूत्वा
स्थूलानि च स्थूलशरीरहेतवः ।
मात्रास्तदीया विषया भवन्ति
शब्दादयः पञ्च सुखाय भोक्तुः ॥ ७४ ॥

*** It has been declared by the greatest artists in the world, time without number, that the human male form outshines in beauty everything else under the sun.**

74. Having united with parts of one another, they become gross, and become the cause for the formation of the gross body. Their subtle essence constitutes the sense-objects, five in number, such as sound etc., which contribute to the enjoyment of the experiencer, the individual ego.

A mention has already been made of the subtle elements and now we are told how they by a process of mutual combination, condense to a grossness sufficient to become perceptible to the sense-organs. The process by which the subtle elements become the five gross elements which are accepted even by modern scientists as the unit of matter in the world, is called in Sanskrit, *Panchikaranam*, a pentamerous self-duplication and mutual combination.

This process is explained in *Vedanta* as taking place in four distinct stages of self-division and mutual combinations. The rudimentary subtle elements are constituted of units

PANCHIKARANA

The process of Pentamerous Self-division and Mutual Combination.

Stage	Ether 1	Air 2	Fire 3	Water 4	Earth 5	Description
I						Tanmatras : each in itself.
II						Tendency to divide into two equal parts.
III						The split is complete.
IV						One half remaining intact, the others split into four.
V						Each half married to four bits borrowed from all others

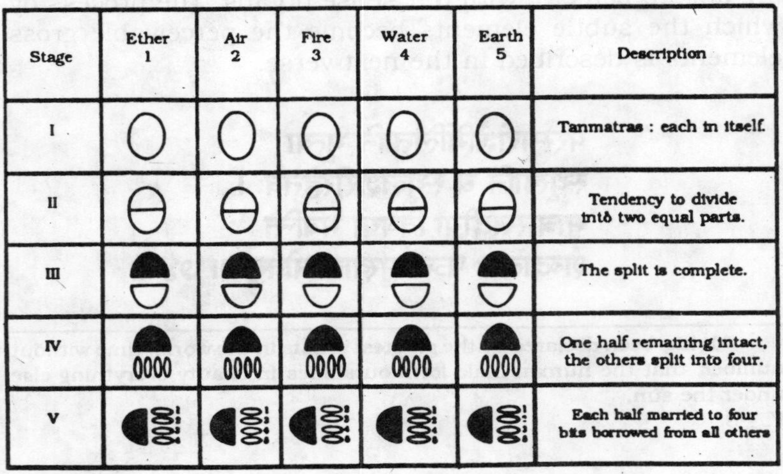

called *tanmatras.* There are five distinct *tanmatras* each for the five great elements---Ether, Air, Fire Water and Earth. Each *tanmatra* (unit of each of the five elements), in the first stage of its grossification, shows a tendency to divide itself into two halves. In the second stage, each *tanmatra* of the five elements bifurcates and separates into two equal parts.

In the third stage, one half of all the five elements remains intact* while the other half (of each element) gets divided into four equal parts. Thus under the column 'Ether', we have in its third stage, half a *tanmatra* remaining intact (the dark half), and the other half divided into four equal parts, each constituting therefore, 1/8th of the original *tanmatra.*

In the fourth stage of its development, each half *tanmatra* combines with 1/8th *tanmatra* of all the other elements, constituting one unit of the gross element. Thus, in the accompanying chart, one half of Ether joins with four 1/8th bits borrowed from the other four elements (i.e. 1/2 Ether + 1/8th Air + 1/8th Fire + 1/8th Water + 1/8th Earth), which then constitute one unit of the gross *Akasa* (Ether). Similarly, half of Air plus 1/8th bits borrowed form Ether, Fire, Water and Earth, becomes one unit of gross Air. Thus is the combination in each of the five elements.

This process is called *Panchikarana*, the pentamerous self-division and combination process. Out of the gross elements the physical body is formed. But the sense-objects of sound, touch, forms, taste and smell are constituted of nothing other than the subtle *tanmatras* of the rudimentary elements. The gross elements provide the instrument for the enjoyment of the subtle elements. All these arrangements are made so that the ego-centre may experience a life of happiness or misery as directed by the store-house of his *vasanas.*

The enjoyer or sufferer (ego) is the Self conditioned by the mind and the intellect. This conditioning can never bring

* Refer Swamiji's commentary on Atma Bodha.

about any real bondage to the Self just as any harm done to my reflection in the mirror can never harm me.

य एषु मूढा विषयेषु बद्धा
रागोरुपाशेन सुदुर्दमेन ।
आयान्ति निर्यान्त्यध ऊर्ध्वमुच्चैः
स्वकर्मदूतेन जवेन नीताः ॥ ७५ ॥

75. Those thoughtless ones who are bound to these sense-objects by the stout ropes of attachment so very difficult to cut asunder, come and go, up and down, carried by the compelling force of the envoy of the reactions of their own past actions.

We know that the sense-objects are innocent *tanmatras* which, in another form, become the sence-organs and the gross body. Steam cannot bind water both being but the same element in its subtle or gross form.

A *samsarin* is under the persecution of sense-objects because of his attachment to them. These attachments are so strong that they become almost unbreakable. Thus bound to the gross, the ego ekes out its experiences and yearns for more. Every moment it perpetrates endless activities each providing its own reactions to be enjoyed or suffered by the same ego. Thus repeatedly, the same ego visits different fields of activities and in a variety of environments. It again and again enters and leaves the arena of existence, reaping its reaction, and sowing new seeds through desire-prompted activities, which, in their turn, compel it to come again to reap the fruits of the new harvest.

In the last line of this verse are two innoncent looking phrases which, in an aphoristic form, give us the theory of *karma* as understood by the *Vedantin.*

According to the *Mimamsakas*, God is the Almighty Power Omniscient and Omnipotent, Just and True, who distributes the fruits of actions according to the purity of motives, clarity of conscience, sincerity of application, faithfulness and obedience to the eternal prescriptions laid down in the immortal *Vedas.* But according to *Vedanta*, much more intellectually satisfying is the theory that the reaction of an action is not anything different from the action itself.

An action performed in a particular time and place may fulfil itself, perhaps, in another place and in a future period of time. A bud fulfils itself in its fruit and there is no need for a supreme power's intervention for the petals to fall off and the fruit to mature. The life history of a thought expressed (action), is the immediate action which is finally concluded only in its reaction. "Action and reaction are equal and opposite", one of Newton's laws, is perhaps true even in philosophy.

So, actions undertaken and performed at the instance of its delusory attachment with the sense-objects, guide each ego-centre to its self-dictated destinies of enjoyment or sorrow. Thought by thought, wading through actions, the ego orders for itself a future world wherein it can enjoy its demand, be it the life of a pig or the life of a God-man. This is the burden of the term 'carried up and down' the ladder of evolution and devolution. Through right activity and discrimination when we develop detachment, the sense-objects cannot bind us and our activities become oriented to end ignorance through discovery and knowledge of the eternal and true Principle of Divinity in us.

In *Vedanta Sastra*, the possible wombs for taking births from fall under two distinct groups, the higher and the lower. In the higher *yonis*,--- we are born only to enjoy the ethereal sense-objects which can provide, through the necessary instruments of perception and enjoyment, a greater share of finite joys for a longer period of existence. This is called the experience of "heaven". The other type is called the lower *yonis* which comprise existence in the form of animals and birds, plants and trees. These lower wombs intorduce us to a plane of consciousness wherein the individual egos, with their different degrees of dullness come to experience and immense amount of concentrated sorrow'. These two groups exhaust all possible future births and are indicated by the term, carried up and down'.

When the reactions of the past actions neither tend towards too much enjoyment, nor too much suffering, that is, they are almost equibalanced, then such an ego-centre, with its slightly predominant tendencies to be either good or bad, presents itself in a human form. Every man in his life-time has occasions to smile and to sob, to enjoy success and to suffer failures but he is also provided with a discriminative intellect with which he can distinguish between the Real and the unreal. In this world, neither are we dead drunk with happiness nor fully drowned in sorrow. Thus a chance is given to every one to consciously move either up or down, or towards the infinite Freedom of pure God-hood. Spiritual endeavour however, is possible neither in the heavenly planes of experiences indicated by the term 'up' nor in the fields of sorrows covered by the term 'down'.

Each of us comes to gain the required field, appropriate and forming a perfectly logical sequence with the motives, thoughts and desires entertained in the past. Guided by the very instincts created in us as a result of our past *karmas*, that is, ordered by our own *karma-duta*, we reach our destinations sought by ourselves. They are nothing but frozen past intentions now beginning to thaw.

18. Sense-objects a Trap : Man Bound. (76-82)

शब्ददिभिः पञ्चभिरेव पञ्च
पञ्चत्वमापुः स्वगुणेन बद्धाः ।
कुरङ्.गमातङ्.गपतङ्.गमीन -
भृङ्.गा नरः पञ्चभिरञ्चितः किम् ॥ ७६ ॥

76. The deer, the elephant, the moth, the fish and the honey-bee---these five are annihilated because of their slavery to one or the other of the senses such as sound etc., through their own attachment. What then is the condition of a man who is attached to all these five?

We are now discussing how attachment to the senses bind, enslave and destroy the peace of mind and freedom of true living. At this moment Sankara is, very appropriately, reminded of the various examples provided by nature where certain species meet their death due to extreme attachment to one or the other of the five senses.

These examples clearly show that Sankara was not living in the state of a "Ganges-stone *Samadhi*". He was very much alive to the world of beauties and thrills, the world of incidents and happenings around him.

The deer is always fascinated by melodious sound and the deer hunter sings to charm the deer. Attracted by the melody of sound, the deer has no awareness of the danger it is in, and turns in the direction of the music; the hunter soon makes it his target. The elephants, especially in the mating season, become extremely attached to the sense of touch; rubbing against each other and walking without caution, they fall into the pits got ready to catch them. The moth is enchanted by form and attracted by the brilliance of the flame. It flutters towards it with an agonising impatience and gets burnt. The fish, ravenously hungry at all times, in its gluttony, swallows the bait, is caught and thus meets its end in the stomach of fish-eaters. The poor honey-bee, attracted by the fragrant smell of flowers, pursues its industrious vocation, collects honey from the flowers and hoards it in its hive, unil at last, heartless man sets fire to the hive in order to loot the honey-wealth of the bee.

Thus, Sankara gives us five typical examples wherein each has met its doom because of its attachment to one or the other of the five senses. Most dramatic it becomes when Sankara concludes with the exclamation, "What then is in store for man who is attached to all these five?"

When a man of ignorance, having neither discrimination nor detachment, vulgarly runs after sense-objects for his temporary nerve-ticklings, he becomes a sad victim of his delusion, and meets a calamitous end for he has allowed himself to be bound by the five strong ropes.

दोषेण तीव्रो विषयः कृष्णसर्पविषादपि ।
विषं निहन्ति भोक्तारं द्रष्टारं चक्षुषाप्ययम् ॥ ७७ ॥

77. Sence-objects are even more venomous in their tragic effects than cobra poison. Poison is fatal to one who swallows it, but the sense-objects kill him who even looks at them with his eyes.

At this juncture, Sankara discusses how dangerous it is for a seeker to be attached to the enjoyment of sense-objects. He has already told us how tragic is the end of those living beings who have but a single sense appetite. In order to emphasise the virulence of sense-poison, Sankara gives yet another verse, which is very famous in as much as we often here it being quoted from all pulpits.

Explaining the dangerous intensity of this poison, the Acharya compares it with the venom of the cobra. If there is some distance between a cobra and an individual, the poison in the cobra cannot affect him. Nobody is known to have died of poison because he merely saw a cobra in a zoo. The venom can be fatal to a person only when he is bitten by a cobra. Compared with this, sense-objects are more virulent because they can annihilate the individual who just looks at them. 'The organ of vision' *(chaksusa api)*, mentioned in the verse, represents all the other four sense organs and indicates a similar end when all other sense-organs, individually or collectively, run after their sense-objects, bringing about a total annihilation.

विषयाशामहापाशाद्यो विमुक्तः सुदुस्त्यजात् ।
स एव कल्पते मुक्त्यै नान्यः षट्शास्त्रवेद्यपि ॥ ७८ ॥

---

* The Sanskrit word Guna has two meanings, (1) rope and (2) mental tendency.

78. He who has liberated himself from the terrible bonds of desires for sense-objects, (indeed), very difficult to renounce, is alone fit for liberation; none else, even if he is well-versed in all the six schools of philosophy.

We have been told again and again that *vairagya* is an essential and salient factor in the study of Vedana. So, without total and complete *vairagya*,the energy in us which is being spent in wrong pursuits will not be conserved for greater purposes of self-culture and ultimately of Self-rediscovery.

Indeed the *Vedantic* Masters were not impractical men, ignorant of the ordinary man's sense-attachment. They certainly realised that to control the sense-organs and to avoid their gushing forth into their respective sense-objects is very difficult for an ordinary man. And yet, where *viveka* has come, *vairagya* is natural, and he who has gained a certain amount of freedom from the charms of sense-objects is fit for liberation. The idea is that so long as the individual thirsts after anything, his entire energy will be consumed in its acqusition and possession, and there will be nothing left in him to supply him with the required dynamism for listening, reflecting and meditating upon the contents of the scriptures.

That 'such a one alone is fit for liberation' is a very positive statement denying sensuous people any hope of success in spiritual life. Not even men who are erudite scholars in all the six schools of Indian philosophy are recognised by the *Sastras* as fit for total liberation from ignorance and ignorance-created misunderstandings in themselves. With mere book-learning, without the heart's purity, mind's tranquillity, intellect's application and body's self-denial, no progress in spiritual life, which can take us towards complete liberation from our limitations is ever possible.

आपातवैराग्यवतो मुमुक्षून्
भवाब्धिपारं प्रतियातुमुद्यतान् ।

आशाग्रहो मज्जयतेऽन्तराले
निगृह्य कण्ठे विनिवर्त्य वेगात् ॥ ७९ ॥

79. Those who have only an apparent dispassion and are trying to cross the ocean of change are caught by their throats by the shark of desire which violently dragging them along, drowns them in the middle of the ocean.

In the last verse, we noticed how Sankara, with an enthusiasm almost amounting to fanaticism, insisted that spiritual life can be claimed as a birthright only by those who have a true spirit of dispassion. Here the *Acharya* warns us that false *vairagya* cannot sustain us for long.

A spirit of detachment and a craving for dispassion may be generated in us as a result of repeated tragedies. A tragic bereavement, a shocking disappointment, a painful failure, an agonising physical pain, all these have been found, either individually or collectively, capable of creating a temporary sense of *vairagya*, termed in Sanskrit as *smasana vairagya*,---an aversion to life and its finutude which is usually generated when one has occasion to visit a cremation ground. This passing phase and temporary mood is not a solid capital upon which a person can build his entire future in the spiritual world. No doubt, these temporary mental moods may be capitalised in training the mind and intelect to generate more and more sense of discrimination, which will ultimately increase the intensity of true *vairagya*.

True dispassion is a wise condition of the ego created from a deep intellectual conviction which in its turn, has its roots in perfect discrimination. Only in the maturity of an individual's spiritual florescence, can one hope to gather the fruits of wisdom.

False *vairagya* has ruined more men than even atheism has ever done. Hundreds and thousands of indiscriminate people, in almost all the religions of the world, reach the sanctuaries of their respective monasteries. In the long run, however, they discover that they are not fit for a life of total renunciation and perfect self-control. Many of them who find sufficient moral courage return to the market place and the world of contentions to fight for and acquire and enjoy material wealth. But many come to live a chiking life of frustrations and sorrows, with neither the capacity to live the life of renunciation nor the daring to return to the world of cut-throat competition. A few, though wearing the apparel of seekers, surely live a sensuous life; they are the leprous ulcers on the world's spiritual body that contaminate the serene atmosphere and vitiate its salubrious climate.

The *Acharya* has briefly pointed out these dangers by comparing men of insincere *vairagya* to those who are ship-wrecked on the 'ocean of change' which is infested with ravenous sharks of sensuous desires. These desires jump at the throats of the poor victims and drag them down and drown them midway on their pilgrimage to the Beyond.

विषयाख्यग्रहो येन सुविरक्त्यसिना हतः ।
स गच्छति भवाम्भोधेः पारं प्रत्यूहवर्जितः ॥ ८० ॥

80. He who has destroyed the shark called "sense-objects" with the sword of mature dispassion crosses the ocean of *samsar* unobstructed.

Continuing the idea, it is said here that he alone who has destroyed the shark of desire lurking in the ocean of *samsar* can safely cross to the other shore. In order to kill the enemy we have no other instrument save the sword of discriminative knowledge. With *viveka* alone can we end our desires. Desires can come and sabotage our happiness only when the discriminative faculties in us have, as it were, gone to sleep. So long as the pure intellect is awake, the whims and fancies of the mind cannot emerge to loot and plunder the peace of the inner kingdom. Only in the darkness of the bosom, when the illuminating intellect has disappeared behind the cloud of ignorance, can the temptations and desires of the heart walk out of their hide-outs to steal the wealth of peace and tranquility which the individual enjoys.

Once in the grasp of these minions of the moon, the person identifying with desires gets choked and drowned in the stormy sea of plurality. To live intelligently with discriminative analysis, ever conscious of the fallacies in each thought and not getting victimised by fanciful desires, is to live in *viveka*. Where *viveka* is steady, the desires, however, strong they be, will not dare to attack. Sankara rightly says that with the sword of discrimination, the seeker must destroy the shark of desire and make his way safely across the ocean of *samsar*.

विषमविषयमार्गैर्गच्छतोऽनच्छबुद्धेः
प्रतिपदमभियातो मृत्युरप्येष विद्धि ।
हितसुजनगुरुक्त्या गच्छतः स्वस्य युक्त्या
प्रभवति फलसिद्धिः सत्यमित्येव विद्धि ॥ ८१ ॥

81. Know that mortality soom overtakes a foolish man who walks the dangerous path of sense-pleasures. Whereas one who sticks to the path of divinity, according to the instructions of well-meaning and noble Gurus, constantly walks the path divine helped by his own reasoning faculty---he achieves the end; know for certain this is true.

In *Vedanta*, meditation is the technique for gaining the final experience of Self-rediscovery : but meditaiton can be successful only when the mind is not agitated by desires. In a sensuous life one is never without some desire or the other. Thus an individual cannot have success both in the life of meditation and in the world of sensuousness. If one is fatigued after a long walk, one cannot recoup if one continues walking. A diabetic cannot bring his sugar down---even by taking saline injection daily--if he is continuously consuming sugar.

The human mind is disintegrated because of its desires and it cannot be brought back to its state of healthy integration without its renouncing the very germs of its present disease. So, in *Vedanta*, great stress has been laid upon the necessity of avoiding the mind's running amok with its uncontrolled appetites.

This idea is explained again in a very powerful style. Sankara crisply repeats what the *Rishis* have been continuously saying in the pages of the scriptures, that the path of sensuousness leads straight to mortality while the path divine leads to Immortality. Physiology also, in a much more limited sense of the term, declares that over-indulgence impoverishes our vitality, bringing the physical structure to doom and death. In Vedanta, however, the term 'death' connotes not only the condition of the body when life has ebbed out from it, but includes the very principle fo change and finitude.

Thus sensuous activities with motives of pleasure and indulgence harden the animal impressions in our minds and thereafter, thoughts begin to flow in that direction more and more powerfully. Such a stupid man becomes increasingly daring in his criminalities, until at last he becomes irredeemable and slips down the ladder of evolution to be ultimately destroyed.

On the other hand, the way up the evolutionary ladder is also open to man by climbing which he can slowly ascend to the very pinnacles of total fulfilment. This path has been beautifully described in the third line of the verse which insists that he must follow the instructions given by reliable guides, the *Gurus*, on the path of spirituality.

The *Gurus* must be well-meaning and worthy. These epithets speak volumes of suggestions. They must be well-meaning in the sense that they should not be mere gramophone records repeating what the *Sastras* say, but must be men so well established in their own experiences and so familiar with the path, that they can interpret it to different types of students belonging to different climes and of different ages.

Also, the Teacher must be a worthy man*(Sujana)*. There are many *Gurus* all over the world who are scriptural in word but cruel in actions.Like a tape-recorder,they repeat what the

Rishis have said, but in their daily activities they follow faithfully what the *rakshasas* did. Such ones are not worthy to be guides for true seekers on the path of God-seeking. The guru must be perfect in all his conduct; there is no excuse for him to be vulgar in any aspect of his living.

Even if there be a sacred *Guru*, and the disciples surrender unto him, this in itself cannot bear any fruit unless they are ready to actively co-operate with the Teacher and cultivate for themselves the Perfection indicated to them by him.

Each of the disciples must, all through his contact with his *Guru*, bring into his field of enquiry his entire powers of reasoning, bright and intelligent, independent and orginal. He should not, on any score, allow himself to be overwhelmed by the Master. No Teacher worth the name will allow the disciple to choke his independent reasoning faculty. The best of Teachers have always endeavoured to cultivate a better crop of reasoning in the intellect of their disciples.

A student who has turned away from the tragic path of sensuousness and has stepped on to the glorious highway of the Divine, who is prepared to go forward under the guidance of a true Teacher, with nothing but his independent discriminative reasoning to supply him with mental agility and strength, will surely reach his Goal. In order to prove the validity of these declarations, the last line ends with a powerful rejoinder, an emphatic assertion--- *'Know this to be true.'*

मोक्षस्य कांक्षा यदि वै तवास्ति
त्यजातिदूराद्विषयान्विषं यथा ।
पीयूषवत्तोषदयाक्षमार्जव -
प्रशान्तिदान्तीर्भज नित्यमादरात् ॥ ८२ ॥

82. If you have indeed a craving for liberation, avoid sense-objects from a distance, just as you avoid things known to be poisonous; and with

respectful reverence, daily cultivate the nectarine virtues --contentment, forgiveness, straightforwardness, calmness and self-control.

So far, Sankara (through the *Guru)* was advising the seekers in *Vedanta* on what they should do in order to realise the Self, and thus end their misunderstandings and sorrows in life. He has, so far, insisted upon the importance of *viveka* and *vairagya.* Now he is slowly coming to a discussion to encourage the development of the noble qualities of the head and heart which, as we have earlier discussed, is the third item of adjustments to be made by a student before a guranteed success in Self-realisation is assured to him.

Having known a thing to be poisonous, however thirsty you may be you will not be tempted to drink it: so too, however tempting the sense-objects may look, an individual who seeks liberation should totally renounce the idea that they contain even a trace of potency to supply joy.

By withdrawing the sense-organs from their field of activity, we conserve a tremendous amount of energy which would otherwise be wasted. If this new-found energy is not immediately harnessed to do special work, the chances are that we will spend this dynamism in mentally dreaming of sense-indulgance. This brings about an ugly deformity in our personality. To remain physically inert but mentally sensuous develops a distorted personality, drained of all brilliance and beauty through suppressed desires and unseen mental dissipations.

It is to avoid such dangerous consequences at the mental plane that we should have the guidance of the Teacher. Fresh fields have been discovered where the energy so conserved could be used up to raise smiling crops of beauty and profit. We are told how an individual who has learnt to shun sense-objects must immediately take up the constructive scheme of developing the positive qualities such as, contentment, compassion, forgiveness, straightforwardness, calmness and self-control. When we analyse them we find that each one of these qualities is in itself an attitude of the mind which will not suffer even the least disturbance in itself. As we diligently practise them, necessarily will we seek and establish our identity with our fellow-beings and enjoy the intimate brotherhood of man and the divine fraternity of the soul.

19. Fascination for Body Criticised (83-86)

अनुक्षणं यत्परिहृत्य कृत्य -
मनाद्यविद्याकृतबन्धमोक्षणम् ।
देहः परार्थोऽयममुष्य पोषणे
यः सज्जते स स्वमनेन हन्ति ॥ ८३ ॥

83. This body is essentially an instrument for realising the *Paramatman*. He who does not constantly use it for liberating himself from the bondage born of beginningless ignorance but struggles to nourish it, is destroying himself.

Every physical sheath, be it in the human, plant, or animal life, is an instrument for its "mind and intellect" to eke out from the world of situations a definite quota of experiences. The body provides for the time being, as it were, a locus for the mind and intellect to function from. Identifying one's self with the body because of ignorance, one may behave as if one was the doer and the enjoyer and use the physical body to its own damnation.

A drunken driver, identifying himself with his drunken hallucinations, may use his vehicle to drive recklessly and crash into a wayside tree.

The very same physical body could be made use of properly by a discriminating intellect when it serves the ego as a vehicle to take it to its supreme Goal.

A sensible driver with his wits about him can drive his vehicle easily with speed and comfort, straight to his destination.

Sankara thus reminds the students that the body is not meant merly for gross activities and indulgence in sensuous enjoyments but, having experienced the imperfections of the world, it is also meant for striving hard for self-redemption. Having gained this wondrous instrument, if a person does not make use of it properly, he is, in effect, committing suicide.

The meaning of the verse pivots around the crucial word, *pararthah.* This word can be milked to yield two different and distinct meaning of which the nobler and more spiritual has already been discussed. From the same word we can coax out another meaning-- "an object that is meant for others to enjoy", is also *pararthah.* In this sense, we get in the single term, a beautiful summary of the biography of the body.

In the womb the body grew, nourished by the mother's assimilated food; the body born in the world was fed by the milk of the mother and it grew to childhood. Till its death it is being fed, from within and without, with various nutritive diets and oil massages. But after death the very same body, so laboriously tended, so carefully nourished, so lovingly fattened, becomes a substantial meal for the worms of the earth, if it is lucky to be buried deep enough! Else it becomes food for the wolves and dogs, the vultures and crows. This is a timely reminder for discriminative spiritual students to realise the futility of paying court to their bodies and living a life dedicated to the health and comforts of this disgusting bundle of matter.

शरीर पोषणार्थी सन् य आत्मानं दिदृक्षति ।
ग्राहं दारुधिया धृत्वा नदीं तर्तुं स गच्छति ॥८४॥

84. Whoever seeks to rediscover the Self by devoting himself to the care of the body, is like one who proceeds to cross a river, holding on to a shark which one has mistaken for a log of wood.

Sankara here strikingly brings out how dangerous and suicidal is the attempt of the individual to perfect himself through physical indulgences and enjoyments. Anxiety for the body is an expression of our identification with it. This can come only when, in our delusion, we have totally forgotten our essentially divine nature.

Ignorance and knowledge cannot exist at the same place and the same time. Where the ghost is recognised there the post, is non-existent; and one who recognises the post, to him the ghost is not available at all. Similarly, one's beloved in a dream in non-existent in the waking state.

So, he who is attached to his body and is wasting his time and energy nourishing and fattening it, is indeed a fool. He is as far removed from the Goal as the recognition of the rope is from one who is dying in delusion of being bitten by a serpent.

मोह एव महामृत्युर्मुमुक्षोर्वपुरादिषु ।
मोहो विनिर्जितो येन स मुक्तिपदमर्हति ॥८५॥

85. For a student seeking liberation, infatuation with the body etc. is a 'tragic death'. He who has totally conquered this attachment deserves the state of liberation.

To him who is aspiring to rise above the fascination of the sense-organs for the sense-objects and the calamitous confusions of emotions and thoughts, it is indeed a dire tragedy, if he were to allow himself to be tempted, by the fields of immediate pleasures which the body experiences in the midst of objects. To turn our attention away from the sense-world and to seek diligently the experience of the Transcendental is the path by which the Higher can be unfolded. Prompted by his *vasanas*, the individual might meet situations and moments when he is irresistibly jerked out of his contemplative moods to fulfil the demands of the world around him. This will destroy the equipoise of the seeker and so Sankara characterises it as a "dire death" *(maha mrityu)*.

On the other hand, he who has won a victory over his own delusory misconceptions *(moha)*, and is not tempted by the outer world, discovers in himself a steadiness of contemplation with which he can certainly learn to withdraw himself from the whirlpools of matter and come to experience the pure Self. This is the condition of utter liberation from the entanglements and fascinations of one's matter vestures.

मोहं जहि महामृत्युं देहदारसुतादिषु ।
यं जित्वा मुनयो यान्ति तद्विष्णोः परमं पदम् ॥८६॥

86. Conquer this great infatuation for your body, wife, children etc. By conquering these, sages reach the supreme State of Lord Vishnu.

Explaining the great 'tragic death' of the seeker, Sankara pinpoints what exactly this death is. Infatuation with the body, no doubt, makes the seeker constantly search for more and more sense-objects in the world outside, so that he may discover a greater fulfilment and happiness in life. The body here may be considered as indicating all the layers of man's gross as well as subtle personality.

Wife *(dara)*, is to be understood as not only the wedded partner in life. In philosophy, the word often indicates all those on whom you depend for your happiness and sons *(suta)* stand for all those who depend on you. In the world of mutual relationships, each individual is but a link, holding all the other parts of the chain in position. As an individual I exist in society looking up to people who make me happy and look after those who are looking up to me for their comforts. In the language of the spiritual Masters, 'wife and children' is an idiom that includes all these relationships.

In the midst of all these webs of relationships an individual exists, maintaining different types of intimate attachments which have a knack of expanding their thraldom. Suffocated by these, he gets exhausted. This is the death of all spiritual aspirations of the seeker.

Men of reflection *(munayah)* conquer this meaningless infatuation, victoriously rise, above the hungers of the flesh and come to experience the Bliss of the supreme State. Here the word *Vishnu*--the 'Long-strident' --stands for the 'All-pervading'.

A spiritual seeker has a healthy attitude towards things and he keeps a balanced relationship with every thing around him in life. He loves all and he fulfils his duties towards them. But he never allows the world of relationships around to bind him and loot him of his freedom to grow. He keeps ample elbow room to wage war against his own lower nature. Such an individual, intelligently orgainsing his connections with the world will certainly run fleet-footed towards the Goal to enter the state of freedom and experience supreme *Vishnu-hood.*

20. Gross Body Condemned. (87-91)

त्वङ्मांसरुधिरस्नायुमेदोमज्जास्थिसंकुलम् ।
पूर्णं मूत्रपुरीषाभ्यां स्थूलं निन्द्यमिदं वपुः ॥८७॥

87. This gross body is most offensive as it is composed of skin, flesh, blood vessels, fat, marrow and bones and also it is everfilled with urine and faecal matter.

In order to create the necessary sense of detachment from and in order to wean the mind from all its infatuation with the body, Sankara brings the seeker's scientific attention to focus completely on the composition of his own physical body. Infatuation can arise only through hasty, immature observations but when the nature of the thing becomes fully evident through close scientific study, this infatuation must lift and right understanding dawn. For this purpose, the human physical body is fully dissected in its biological composition in this verse.

The body is made up of unholy things which by themselves cannot engender any fascination in a thoughtful man. Sometimes it happens that the container may be ugly yet the contents can enrich it. Even this is not the case for our physical body-- a filthy container containing nothing but gallons of filth. It is this filth packet that man hugs to himself, panting to experience peace and happiness through it. When we realise the folly of loving a thing which is so abominable, our endless attachment and attraction for it will cease.

In the following verse the body is analysed in more detail for the purpose of observing closely its contribution to the total experience of the individual.

पञ्चीकृतेभ्यो भूतेभ्यः स्थूलेभ्यः पूर्वकर्मणा ।
समुत्पन्नमिदं स्थूलं भोगायतनमात्मनः ।
अवस्था जागरस्तस्य स्थूलार्थानुभवो यतः ॥८८॥

88. Made up of the gross elements formed by the combination of the subtle elements and ordered by past actions, this gross body is the seat of experience for the Self. The state in which it perceives gross objects is its waking condition.

Anything gross must necessarily rise from a previous condition of subtle existence. The five gross elements that can be perceived by the sense-organs must have risen from their previous condition of subtlety in which they were not perceivable. In this, their nascent state, they are called *tanmatras*. The theory that explains how these five subtle elements from their nascent condition have grossified is called *Panchikarana*, as has already been explained.

The five elements that have undergone this process are the very material with which all gross bodies are made. They are fashioned out according to he result of the actions done in the past by the "indweller" of a given body. The gross body so formed is the hutment of experiences, the temple of joy and sorrow. The indweller of the body experiences his joys and sorrows only through his physical body. The state in which the ego making use of its physical body comes in contact with the world of objects and ekes out its joys and sorrows in the 'waking' condition of the *jeeva*.

बाह्येन्द्रियैः स्थूलपदार्थसेवां
स्त्रक्चन्दनस्त्र्यादिविचित्ररूपाम् ।
करोति जीवः स्वयमेतदात्मना
तस्मात्प्रशस्तिर्वपुषोऽस्य जागरे ॥८९॥

89. The individualised ego identifying itself with this body, enjoys gross objects such as garlands, sandal-paste, women, etc., of an endless variety by means of the sense-organs. Therefore this body has the greatest play in the waking state.

The Self identifying with the gross body expresses itself as the perceiver and therafter recognises the world of objects as being other than Itself. Expressing through the physical body and its sense-organs, the *jeeva* gathers its quota of pleasures by indulging in sense-objects. The endless varieties of objects that cater to man's sense gratifications are comprehended by the idiom, "garland, sandal-paste, woman" *(srak-chandana-stree)*, and even these are enjoyed by the individual according to his whim and fancy in a thousand variegated combinations and arrangements.

Thus to the *jeeva*, the gross physical body is the vehicle by which it comes in contact with and indulges in the world of objects. When a person is not conscious of the physical body, he cannot perceive the world of objects around him. The world of waking experiences is available only when we are conscious of the physical body and when we express ourselves through its sense-organs. Therefore it is that the 'waking'-condition is the fullest expression of the gross body.

सर्वोऽपि बाह्यसंसारः पुरुषस्य यदाश्रयः ।
विद्धि देहमिदं स्थूलं गृहवद्गृहमेधिनः ॥९०॥

90. Know this gross body to be the "shelter" for the individual to conduct all his dealings with the world outside just as a house is to a householder.

Man dwells in his house and goes out daily into the world to strive for his livelihood. After earning his means of existence, he returns home to enjoy what he has earned and to rest awhile. Rested and refreshed under the security of his house, he moves out again the following day, full of energy, to meet the challenges of a new day. In the same way, the ego moves out of the physical body to contact the sense-objects and returns to it to savour its joys and sorrows.

The joy or sorrow resulting from conducive or unconducive environments is not felt outisde ourselves. They are always felt within, though indeed the objects are always outside. Therfore, the mind has to go out to contact the objects, but having contacted them, it returns to the individual's own heart to experience the consequent joy and sorrow.

Thus the physical body is not only an instrument for experiencing the world outside but also it is a shelter for the experiencer to return to.

स्थूलस्य सम्भवजरामरणानि धर्माः
स्थौल्यादयो बहुविधाः शिशुताद्यवस्थाः ।
वर्णाश्रमादिनियमा बहुधाऽमयाः स्युः
पूजावमानबहुमानमुखा विशेषाः ॥९१॥

91. Birth, decay and death are the essential properties of the gross body; fatness etc., childhood etc., are its different conditions; it has rules of caste and orders of life; it is subject to a variety of diseases and it is this body that meets with different kinds of treatment such as worship, dishonour, honour, etc.

In order to make the student focus his entire attention on the physical body, the author enumerates the characteristics, the various conditions, the different rules of conduct etc., of the gross body. Change is the characteristic of all things finite and the body has its essential property *(dharma)*, of undergoing modifications such as birth, growth, decay, disease and death. It is again the nature of the body to express itself as stout, lean, tall or short. The human form goes through stages of growth such as childhood, youth and old-age, when the body gathers to itself new dimensions and looks.

It is with reference to the physical body and its relations with the world around that the social codes of behaviour are prescribed and strictly followed in society. The various regulations of communal living and standards of behaviour laid down for the various orders of life *(ashramas)*, are all prescribed for the discipline of the body and they have a sanction only with reference to the embodied. The body is the seat of the diseases. To the body, indeed, is all worship *(puja)* offered, all honour *(mana)* given, all dishonour *(apamana)* shown.

These are all indicative strokes which bring the student's mind to focus upon the gross physical body which is the abode of the ego, the seat of all its experiences in the world.

21. Organs of Perception and Action. (92)

बुध्धीन्द्रियाणि श्रवणं त्वगक्षि
घ्राणं च जिह्वा विषयावबोधनात् ।
वाक्पाणिपादा गुदमप्युपस्थः
कर्मेन्द्रियाणि प्रवणेन कर्मसु ॥९२॥

92. The ears, skin, eyes, nose and tongue are organs of knowledge, for they help us to gain knowledge of objects (stimuli, *vishayas*). The organ of speech, hands, legs, the anus and the genital organ are the organs of action since they have a tendency for work.

Here the Teacher undertakes to enumerate the different faculties of our personality that together constitute the subtle body. These faculties, in their aggregate, express through the gross body and establish the individual's contact with the world of objects around from where he gains his own experiences of the world. The Teacher points out the five organs-of-knowledge *(jnana indriyas)*, and the five organs-of-action *(karma indriyas)*. To perceive the stimuli reaching us and to respond to them, together constitute the expression of life through us.

The inlets that allow the stimuli to reach us are called the organs-of-knowledge because they perceive the world around us. These, the sense-organs, are the ears, skin, eyes, nose and tongue.

When the stimuli are received, we respond to them through our motor-organs which are also five in number. These are called the organs-of-action, as our responses expressed at the body level are our own reactions to the stimuli received. They are, the organ of speech, the hands, the legs, the anus and the genital organ. Since these are are points at which the individual explodes into action while expressing his responses, they are called the organs of function or action.

22. Inner Instruments. (93-94)

निगद्यतेऽन्तःकरणं मनोधी -
रहंकृतिश्चित्तमिति स्ववृत्तिभिः ।
मनस्तु संकल्पविकल्पनादिभि -
र्बुद्धिः पदार्थाध्यवसायधर्मतः ॥९३॥

अत्राभिमानादहमित्यहंकृतिः ।
स्वार्थानुसन्धानगुणेन चित्तम् ॥९४॥

93, 94. The "inner organs" are called, according to their functions as mind, intellect, ego and *chitta;* mind, from its doubts and hesitations; intellect from its function of determining the truth of thing; the ego in its identification with both these and *chitta* from its function of constantly illumining the things of its interest.

After the description of the instruments of perception and action, we logically proceed to the subtle factors that constitute the "inner-equipment" *(antahkarana).* It is evident that the eyes do not see by themselves: the eyes are the instruments of seeing for the "inner" person. The inner-equipment has different names, but they indicate only functional differences. In fact, one and the same mental stuff, the inner-equipment, has different functions and so different names. Of course, they are all constituted of thoughts-only.

When the thoughts are in a state of chaos and agitation, with doubts and despairs, they constitute the 'mind'. When the mind has determined its perceptions with reference to its memories of similar or dissimilar experiences in the past, in that condition of relative quietitude caused by such determination, it is called the 'intellect'. Willing, wishing, desiring, judging, etc., are the functions of the intellect.

To have a doubt regarding any outer phenomenal factor and to come to a decision about it are the two equal yoke-fellows in the process of intelligent living. The continuous process of this dual function gives us the experience of intelligent living which man alone is capable of. In this process, it is not very difficult for us to detect that the doubts and the decisions must belong to one and the same individual in order to create in him the experience of intelligent living. That is, the doubt must be mine and the ultimate understanding must also be mine so that I may experience the disappearance of my doubt. This vanity of the individual that arrogates to itself both the doubts and the decisions as its own is called "the ego" which expresses in terms of 'I' and 'mine'.

Our doubts and our decisions constantly singing their breathless duet constitute an unbroken experience of intelligent living and this is not possible unless we are continuously aware of our *doubts*, conscious of our *decisions* and unless we fully experience them as *our* doubts and *our* decisions. In short, we must be aware of the mind,the intellect and the ego. This Awareness or Consciousness playing upon the mind-intellect-ego, is called *'chitta'*. In its pure state, unconditioned by these three, the *chitta* becomes the pure Consciousness, the Infinite *(Chit)*. *Chitta* is that which constantly illumines my personality constituted of my ego, my mind and my intellect *(swarthanusandhana)*.

These four factors, *manas*, *buddhi*, *ahmkara* and *chitta* constitute the inner equipment whose play through the organs of perception and action makes it possible for a person to come in contact with the world around him. Therefore, as a contrast to the outer equipments *(bahir karana)*, these are called the inner equipment *(antah karana)*.

23. The Five Pranas. (95)

प्राणापानव्यानोदानसमाना भवत्यसौ प्राणः ।
स्वयमेव वृत्तिभेदाद्विकृतिभेदात्सुवर्णसलिलादिवत् ॥९५॥

95. One and the same *Prana* becomes *Prana, Apana, Vyana, Udana,* and *Samana,* according to its funcions and modifactions, like gold, water, etc.

Prana is very often misunderstood as breath. In philosophical terminology, *Prana* stands for the manifested Life Energy which expresses itself in the various physiological functions such as perception *(Prana)*, excretion *(Apana)*, digestion *(Vyana)*, circulation *(Samana)*, and the thinking of thoughts *(Udana)*. These varying names are given to one and the same Vital Energy of Life only because they are its various modifications. They are only functional names.

As an individual grows older we find that these departments of activities become weak and shattered and ultimately, at the time of death, all of them cease. For easy comprehension, we can recommend the reader to consider these five as constituting the physiological systems in the body.

The *Prana* layer of the personality is that which holds the gross physical body and the inner subtle body together. The sense-organs must be in contact with the inner equipment and it is the *Prana* that maintains this vital connection. Since the *Prana* holds the gross and the subtle together, some commentators consider it to belong to the gross body while others, to the subtle body. Both are right since one aspect of *Prana* has intimate connection with the gross while the other aspect of it has an equally intimate relationship with the subtle. Just as the same gold is called bangle, chain, ear-ring, etc. depending upon its function and the same water as ice, steam, foam, bubble, etc., so too, the same Life is called by different names according to its manifestation in the world.

24. Subtle Body: Effects. (96-101)

वागादि पञ्च श्रवणादि पञ्च
प्राणादि पञ्चाभ्रमुखानि पञ्च ।
बुध्याद्यविद्यापि च कामकर्मणी
पुर्यष्टकं सूक्ष्मशरीरमाहुः ॥९६॥

96: (1) The five organs-of-action such as speech etc., (2) the five organs-of-perception such as ears etc., (3) the five *Pranas*, (4) the five elements starting with space along with (5) the discriminative intellect etc., and also (6) ignorance, (7) desire and (8) action---these eight 'cities' together constitute the subtle body.

Sankara here sums up all the factors that constitute the subtle body. The organs of perceptionl the organs of action and the five *Pranas* have already been discussed. The five elements in their mutual combination become the material cause for the world of objects and, in their subtle form, the very same elements form the subtle body.

The 'discriminative intellect' is the term used to include all the factors constituting the inner-equipment. All these can express themselves only when there is non-apprehension of Reality and this ignorance of the spiritual Truth in the subjective personality is called *avidya.*

When the true nature of a thing is not known, the human mind imagines things which are not there and an individualised ego sense arises when the universal oneness is not cognised. This individuality experiencing its own limitations comes to suffer a gnawing sense of restlessness and discontent. The human intellect conceives and plans various possibilities by which the confused ego can experience its unlimited true nature of Perfection. These plans suggested by the intellect are called 'desires'.

Thus *avidya* generates desires and desires expressed at the body level are called actions. these eight factors called here the 'eight cities', in their totality, constitute the subtle bodv.

इदं शरीरं श्रुणु सूक्ष्मसंज्ञितं
लिङ्गं त्वपञ्चीकृतभूत सम्भवम् ।
सवासनं कर्मफलानुभावकं
स्वाज्ञानतोऽनादिरुपाधिरात्मनः ॥९७॥

97. This subtle body, listen carefully, also called the *Linga Sarira*, produced from the subtle elements is possessed of the inclinations *(vasanas)*, and it causes the individual to experience the fruits of his past actions. It is the beginningless conditioning on the Self brought about by its own 'ignorance'.

The body described earlier as consisting of the 'eight cities' constitutes the subtle body which is also called the *Linga body*. *Linga* is a symbol of "something that is not yet revealed". the subtle body contains the latent urges in an individual and is therefore called the *Linga sarira*. This body made up of thoughts and their functions is composed of the five subtle elements which have not yet undergone the process of division and combination.

The subtle body along with its *vasanas* becomes the conditioning on the Self to create the sense of an imperfect individualised ego. *Vasanas* are the foot-prints of past thoughts and actions left upon the personality. These impressions of the past provide the conditioning for our present thoughts by giving them their specific texture, quality and fragrance.

The *vasanas* erupt thoughts similar to the very thoughts that created them which, flowing out from us, prompt our endless activities. Along with the *vasanas*, the subtle body causes the *jeeva* to experience the joys and sorrows of the world which are the rewards or punishments of actions good or bad, right or wrong, performed in the past.

Time itself is a concept of the *antahkarana*---of the intellect. The intellect express itself only when thoughts are flowing in a continuous unbroken chain. Therefore, when the 'first thought' arose in the Infinite, there was no concept of 'time'. Identifying with the first thought, the Self allowed the second, third and fourth thoughts in a continuous procession, thus generating the concept of the intellect and its perception of 'time' and 'space'. It is quite evident that in the nascent intellect, i.e. at the time when the first thought arose, time was not yet born. So it is said that the conditioning of thoughts upon the Self is *before* time, is without beginning *(anadi)*.

स्वप्नो भवत्यस्य विभक्त्यवस्था
स्वमात्रशेषेण विभाति यत्र ।
स्वप्ने तु बुद्धिः स्वयमेव जाग्र -
त्कालीननानाविधवासनाभिः ॥९८॥

कर्त्रादिभावं प्रतिपद्य राजते
यत्र स्वयं भाति ह्ययं परात्मा ।
धीमात्रकोपाधिरशेषसाक्षी
न लिप्यते तत्कृतकर्मलेशैः ।
यस्मादसङ्गस्तत एव कर्मभि -
र्न लिप्यते किञ्चिदुपाधिना कृतैः ॥९९॥

98, 99. Dream is the state when this (subtle body) is distinctly in expression, where is expresses all by itself. In dream, the intellect by itself revels as the agent of experiences etc., due to the various impressions gathered by it in its waking, state. In this condition, the supreme Self shines in Its own glory, with the intellect as its only conditioning, witness of everything, and It is not contaminated in the least by the activities of the intellect. Since It is entirely unattached, It is not tained by any action that It apparent conditionings may perform.

Dream is the state of Consciousness when the Self functions exclusively through the subtle body. In the waking condition, Consciousness expresses through the gross and the subtle bodies. But the subtle body has its exclusive expression in the dream state of Consciousness, i.e.. it is the body in which we are when we dream.

Describing the dream, the *acharya* says that it is the mind recognising its own agitations at a time when the discriminating intellect is partially doped with fatigue and sleep. What we see in our dreams is the expression of the latent impressions *(vasanas)*, gathered by suppressions and repressions during our waking condition and the vivid experiences lived by us.

In this great inner drama, the mind tickled by its own memories, projects a world of objects wherein the dreamer lives his joys and sorrows and the Self, the pure consciousness, stands apart, a mere Witness, illumining everything. This Light of Consciousness apparently conditioned by the intellect is the dreamer, seeing its own dream. Since It is ever a Witness, It is not contaminated by the activities and agitations of the mind intellect equipment.

The *Atman* is thus untouched in all states of our experiences. In all the three, the waking, dream and deep-sleep conditions, the Consciousness is an unattached Witness of all that is happening within and without us. Since it is a mere onlooker, It is not involved in the joys and sorrows of any one of It's these three levels of experiences.

To summarise, none of the activities of the equipments of body, mind and intellect can ever bring about any contamination upon the immaculate Reality, the Self. The *Atman*, though It lends Its Existence and Energy to the whirls of matter around it for their activities, is never itself involved in the imperfect pantings of the inert matter-conditionings.

सर्वव्यापृतिकरणं लिङ्गमिदं स्याच्चिदात्मनः पुंसः ।
वास्यादिकमिव तक्ष्णस्तेनैवात्मा भवत्यसङ्गोऽयम् ॥१००॥

100. As the tools of a carpenter are his instruments, so this subtle body is an instrument for all activities of the Atman, which is Knowledge Absolute. This Atman, therefore, is perfectly un-attached.

Here the description of the subtle body is being continued. Consciousness indentifies with the instrument of the subtle

body when It, as it were, comes in contact with the objects of the world outside. The ego gathers to itself all its daily experiences of joy and sorrow. The mind-intellect equipment has no capacity, all by itself, to contact the world outside since it is inert in itself. Only when presided over by the Life Principle, the Consciousness, does it function in the manifested world.

The mind and intellect which constitute the subtle body can be compared with the instruments of a carpenter---the chisel, pliers, hammer etc. These instruments have no capacity to do any work unless the carpenter uses them. But the carpenter himself is not an instrument. Similarly, the Consciousness is something other than Its instruments---the mind and the intellect. Again, the wear and tear caused by their use affect the instruments only and not the carpenter. Similarly, all the activities fo perceiving, feeling and thinking belong to the subtle body and not to the *Atman*, the Self. The Self has neither enjoyments nor activities.

अन्धत्वमन्दत्वपटुत्वधर्माः
सौगुण्यवैगुण्यवशाद्धि चक्षुषः ।
बाधिर्यमूकत्वमुखास्तथैव
श्रोत्रादिधर्मा न तु वेत्तुरात्मनः ॥१०१॥

101. Blindness, weakness, or keenness of the eye are conditions merely due to its defect or fitness. So too, deafness, dumbness etc., belong to the ear etc. These attributes can never belong to the Atman, the All-Knowing Principle the Consciousness.

The gross imperfections of the organs belong to the respective parts of the gross body. The*Atman*, the Self is not involved in the imperfections, because It is immaculate and Absolute in Itself.

If an instrument is defective, one cannot use it eficiently. But the defect belongs to the instrument and not to the man. If the eye is defective, he cannot see clearly. If it is keen, he can see even minute things. Similarly, if the ear is deaf, one cannot hear anything. If a man be dumb, he cannot talk. These are conditions of the respective organs of the gross body in which the *Atman* the Self, who is the Knower of all these imperfections, dwells. The *Atman* is perfect everywhere and is the Knower of everything. The *Atman* is behind the eye, ear, tongue, etc., as the Awareness that illumines all the conditions of these instruments. It is present at all times, without being affected by any of the things It illumines.

So far, the construction of the gross and subtle bodies and their *dharmas* have been discussed. Now the Acharya says that the conditions and arrangements of your different sense organs belong to the gross and sublte bodies only. Your are unaffected by them. "Thou art the Self".

The development of thought leads us to analyse and discriminate between the Self and the not-Self, and to know their respective dharmas. This discriminative analysis *(viveka)*, is in fact, the theme of this work of Sankara's, so aptly entitled *"vivekachoodamani"*.

25. Functions of Prana. (102)

उच्छ्वासनिःश्वासविजृम्भणक्षु -
त्प्रस्पन्दनाद्युत्क्रमणादिकाः क्रियाः ।
प्राणादिकर्माणि वदन्ति तज्ज्ञाः
प्राणस्य धर्मावशनापिपासे ॥१०२॥

102. Experts call inhalation, exhalation, yawning, sneezing, secretion, death etc. as functions of the *Pranas*, while hunger and thirst are the *dharmas* of the main *Prana*.

Experts, who have an exhaustive knowledge of physiological activities in the anatomical structure, say that inhalation, exhalation, yawning, sneezing, secretion and death are functional properties of the *Pranas*, meaning, they are merely physiological functions. They are called the ten

upa-pranas ---subsidiary *pranas.* So too, hunger and thirst belong to the *Prana.*

You are the illuminator of all the conditions of the *Pranas.* You say, "I am conscious of my hunger and thirst. I am aware of the demands of my body." The *Pranas* function in the body so that the anatomical structure may continue to exist and act. The Atman illumines their conditions, their demands and their functions. Therefore, It is something other than the *Prana.* It is ever-present and can never be affected by the *Pranas.* It is the changeless Awareness.

26. Ego Discussed. (103-105)

अन्तःकरणमेतेषु चक्षुरादिषु वर्ष्मणि ।
अहमित्यभिमानेन तिष्ठत्याभासतेजसा ॥१०३॥

103. The inner equipment has its seat of expression in the sense-organs such as the eye etc. Identifying with them, it exists, clothed in just the reflection of the Atman.

The mind functions through the five organs of perception. When the mind is controlled, the sense-organs are controlled. The sensee-organs are the platforms upon which the mind functions, and they can only functions when the mind enlivens them. When I say, "I am seeing," what exactly happens within me? The light of Consciousness functioning in the mind is 'I'. This mind, thrilled by the Consciousness and functioning through the senseorgans, becomes the seer. Therefore, the Atman is not Itself the seer, nor the hearer, nor the smeller, nor the taster , nor the toucher. Only when It functions through the mind, does It become the Illuminator of what the senses are doing. For, in the pure Consciousness there are no objects at all. It is One-without-a-second.

It is just like the play of sunlight. Only when it is reflected upon an object it is perceived. Pure light is not perceptible. Similarly, when Consciousness is reflected upon a thing, one becomes conscious *of* the thing.

If a dark room is found to be illumined by a reflected beam of light from a bucket of water in the verandah, the illumination in the room will remain as long as the bucket of water remains in the verandah. When the reflecting medium is removed, the light in the room too, must depart. If the reflecting medium is disturbed, the light in the room is also disturbed and the intensity of the illumination gets reduced. Thus, the water in the bucket is the source of light for the dark room. Similarly, when the mind is agitated, the light of intelligence in an individual becomes dull. When the mind is quiet, the intellect is bright and efficient. Quieter the mind, brighter the intellect. Hence, the Self remaining the same, the 'light of intelligence' in an individual is directly proportional to the quietude of his mind. The sun and its illumination remaining the same, the illumination in the dark room depends upon the stillness and clarity of the water in the bucket.

It is not the Self, the pure Consciousness, which is functioning as I (Aham), but it is Its reflection (Abhasa Chaitanya), otherwise called the ego which functions as 'I-I-I', at all moments of the waking and dreaming states of our expression.

अहंकारः स विज्ञेयः कर्त्ता भोक्ताभिमान्ययम् ।
सत्त्वादिगुणयोगेन चावस्थात्रयमश्नुते ॥१०४॥

104. Know that it is the ego which, identifying with the body, becomes the doer or the experiencer, and in union with the Gunas such as Sattwa, this ego assumes the three different states (of waking, dreaming and deep-sleep.)

In each one of us, the vanity of feeling that 'I am the doer, I am the enjoyer',---that 'I am the seer, the hearer and the smeller', ---that 'I am the feeler and the thinker', --is called the individuality, the ego*(jeeva)*, the perceiver-feeler-thinker entity. He who arrogates actions to himself by saying, 'I am the doer *(Karta)*' and 'I am the enjoyer *(bhokta)*', he is the experiencer of joys and sorrows---the little ego.

This sense of individuality, when it identifies with the three Gunas-Sattwa, Rajas and Tamas, which are the three modes of the mind, comes to express itself in the three states of Consciousness--- waking, dream and deep-sleep. Thus, roughly we may say, the ego conditioned by Sattwa is the 'waker'; conditioned by Rajas is the 'dreamer'; and conditioned by Tamas is the 'deep-sleeper'. The same ego, according to the condition of the mind, experiences itself as the waker, the dreamer and the deep-sleeper, and in all these states, naturally, it claims to be the 'doer' and the 'experiencer'.

विषयाणामानुकूल्ये सुखी दुःखी विपर्यये ।
सुखं दुःखं च तद्धर्मः सदानन्दस्य नात्मनः ॥१०५॥

105. When the sense-objects are conducive, the situation is happy. When they are non-conducive, it is miserable. Happiness and misery are, therefore the *dharmas* of the ego and do not belong to the Atman, which is ever-blissful.

Each individual is attracted to those patterns in the world around, which are conducive to his own existing *vasanas*. As long as your wife and children are in harmony with you, you are happy. But if they misbehave, you become miserable. Happiness is often born of self-gratification. A drunkard feels happy in the dirty toddy-shop. Others may feel miserable there, because of the difference in their attitudes or *vasanas*. When in the outer world, things happen against one's intentions and purposes, one becomes unhappy. Therefore, as long as one has *vasanas*, one has to experience joys and sorrows in the world, since the world is ever changing and things and their arrangements will never remain the same. If the *vasanas* are ended, one is in harmony with whatever conditions are available outside. So it is wrong to say that happiness is in the outer world. It is not. Happiness is withing and solely depends upon the mental condition of the experiencer.

If a person knows the secret of finding his balance in what ever conditions that arise. He becomes totally independent of the outer world for his inner happiness.

Thus happiness and sorrow are conditions of the ego. When the ego is in a conducive atmosphere it is happy, when it is not it is sorrowful. I am the illuminator of these joys and sorrows at all times as I am not the ego. But when I, the Self, function through my mind, I apparently appear as an ego *(Abhasa matram).* My reflection in the mirror depends upon the curvature of the reflecting surface. If it is concave, my reflection, is short; if it is convex, it is long, and if it is plain, it is my normal, natural shape and size. The reflected image in a pond is steady when the waters are undisturbed. When they are disturbed, the image becomes distorted. But I myself am unchanged. The shortness or the longness, the clarity or the crookedness are of the image, not mine at all. Similarly, happiness and sorrow do not belong to the *Atman,* the Self. The nature of the Self is ever-blissful *(sadananda).* So happiness and sorrow belong to the 'reflection'--the ego alone.

Thus, when you identify with matter, the ego arises, and then you, as the ego, feel happy or unhappy. The Spirit, the Self, is ever-blissful, joyous. Indeed, perfection is your Real Nature; but as an ego, you delude yourself that you are imperfect and unhappy.

27. Infinite Love---the Self. (106-107)

आत्मार्थत्वेन हि प्रेयान्विषयो न स्वतः प्रियः ।
स्वत एव हि सर्वेषामात्मा प्रियतमो यतः
तत आत्मा सदानन्दो नास्य दुःखं कदाचन ॥१०६॥

106. Sense-objects are pleasure-giving only because of the Self which manifests through them, and not independently, for the Self is, by Its very nature, the most beloved of all. The Self, therefore, is ever-blissful and can never suffer any grief or misery.

The sense-objects of the world are pleasurable, no doubt, but only when they are illumined by the Atman---the Life. Things are pleasurable only when I am *alive.* If I am dead, nothing is pleasurable. A thing in itself has no joy. the happiness that we seem to gain from the objects outside, is, in fact due to the nature of the *Atman*, which is happiness itself. The most enjoyable thing in every one of us is our own *Atman*.

A man learning that his house is on fire runs to the house. When he comes to know that his only child is sleeping inside the house, he announces a large cash award for whoever will go and bring the child out to safety. When there is no response, he increases the sum of his award, and at last he offers all his, wealth for his child. But he himself does not risk the blazing fire and the burning rafters to bring the child out. This is because he loves himself more than anything else--his wealth and even his only child.

'The wife is dear to a man not for the sake of the wife, but for the sake of the Self*' Man loves himself only. His attitude universally is, 'So long as you contribute to my happiness, I love you'. When a father chides his son and asks him to get out of his house, he only means to say, 'you are bringing more sorrow to me. Therefore I do not want you in the house'.

The *Atman*, at all times, is indeed blissful *(Sadananda)*. Never is there any sorrow in the Self. When I have a *vasana* for smoking, the agitations created in my mind due to that *vasana* are temporarily quietened by smoking and therefore, I say, "I feel happy when I smoke". I foolishly consider that the happiness is in the cigarette, and I run after such objects of pleasure in order to repeat the experience of happiness. A dog gnawing at a bone enjoys it more and more, not because there is any meat on it. It is because the sharp ends of the bone scratching its lips, tongue and inner mouth, draw out its own blood. The dog sucks it and feel that the enjoyment is in the bone. Thereafter, its mouth gets lacerated and it cannot eat for days together. Again, a camel often runs after a kind of thorny grass. The sharp grass cuts the mouth of the camel and it enjoys its own blood. The result is that its mouth gets scratched and it cannot eat for months

* Brihadaranyaka Upanishad II. 4-V.

afterwards. That is why the drivers prevent their camels from running after this particular kind of desert grass.

Similarly, the human mind runs after sense-objects like the dog after the dry bone. In fact, the joy content is not in the object. It is the Consciousness, the *Atman*, the pure Bliss of the Self, arising in us when the object is acquired and the mental agitation for that object ceases. You may consider a thing to be pleasant but if it does not bring me an expansion of myself, I would not consider it so.

This great joy of the Self is not readily available because of mental agitations at all times. These become, as it were, a wall between the happiness which is inherent in the Self, and the world outside. The acquisition of a desired object ends the disturbances created by the desire, and the Light of Consciousness beams out from behind the mind. In our lack of discrimination we understand that the joy is in the object secured. In fact, the joy is not in the object at all. But it makes me joyful if it brings me a contact with myself. It is only because of the *Atman*, the Self that each one of us ekes out for himself the maximum joy.

Universally, everybody wants joy, but nobody seems to know wher exactly is the source of happiness. Hence, everyone runs after sense-objects. Here the Teacher is asking us to pause for a moment, and to reflect upon the location of the fountainhead of joy. Indeed, the Atman is of the nature of Bliss and Beatitude, and there is not even a trace of sorrow ever to veil the Face of the Atman.

यत्सुषुप्तौ निर्विषय आत्मानन्दोऽनुभूयते ।
श्रुतिः प्रत्यक्षमैतिह्यमनुमानं च जाग्रति ॥१०७॥

107. Scriptural declarations, direct experience, tradition and inference clearly say that in deep-sleep, we experience the Bliss of the Atman independent of sense-objects.

In the state of deep-sleep, where there are no objects, the joy experienced is the Bliss of the Self. We are not able to experience this joy during deep-sleep because at that moment, we are in a state of *non-apprehension.* All that we experience at that moment is the 'absence of all sorrows'. Sorrows are created by the sense-organs, the mind and the intellect. These equipments are not available in deep-sleep, hence the sorrows that could be created by them are absent. There is a common experience of happiness by everyone even though there are no objects. 'Objectless-Awareness' is the nature of Brahman. In deep-sleep 'objectlessness' is there, but there is no 'awareness' if the Divine.

The equipments of the body, mind and intellect do not function in deep-sleep and at that time we burrow into our *vasanas.* Though the equipments of experience have been left behind, we are in the causal-body-*Avidya.* That is why we are not able to experience what Om, the pure Self, is. The absence of sorrow which is experienced then is called joy. This joy experienced during deep-sleep is not because of the pillow, nor the cool atmosphere, nor the achievements of yesterday. It is *Atmananda.* The *Srutis* declare so. It is also evident that such is the direct experience of all people. It has become a tradition among men to accept it. It can also be ascertained by observation and inference. *(anumana).*

All this evidence compels us to accept that the joy experiened during the deep-sleep state is nothing but the distant splendour of pure Consciousness and Its spotlesss brilliance. Before I slept, I was a miserable creature. When I woke up, I found myself equally miserable. But after I slept and before I awoke, I had no miseries and I was in a state of happiness. This joy was distrubed when the equipments of the body, mind and intellect came into play. Thus it is established through the words of the scriptures, through direct perception, through tradition and through inference that joy is not in the objects outside, but it is only in the Self within us.

So far, the gross-body, the subtle-body and the *Pranas* have been described and it has been said that these are the vestures of the *Atman.* Now the causal-body is being explained. In Atma-Bodha, it is described as, "the indescribable, beginningless ignorance of the spiritual essence."*

The causal-body is beginningless, meaning, beyond the pale of time. It is also 'non-apprehension' --the cause because of which all 'misapprehensions' arise. When a post is not seen as a post, the misapprehension that it is a ghost arises. Non-apprehension of Reality gives rise to misapprehension of the same. When truth is known, all misapprehensions end. The cause for all misapprehensions is non-apprehension. All misapprehensions--'I am the body', 'I am the mind', 'I am the intellect', --arise out of some cause. This cause is called the causal-body. The non-apprehension of Reality is constituted of *vasanas.* The causal-body is also called *avidya.* Nescience, lack of wisdom, lack of correct apprehension, *Maya* lack of knowledge,-- are all the various names of the same dark, dreary state of non-apprehension. It is called differently by different *Acharyas* when they used it in different contexts.

Now the causal body is being described.

28. Maya---**Pointed Out .** (108-110)

अव्यक्तनाम्नी परमेशशक्ति -
रनाद्यविद्या त्रिगुणात्मिका परा ।
कार्यानुमेया सुधियैव माया
यया जगत्सर्वमिदं प्रसूयते ॥१०८॥

108. Nescience *(Avidya),* or *Maya,* is also called the "Unmanifest", and is the power of the Lord. It is without beginning; it comprises the three Gunas and is superior to their effects. It is to be inferred only by one who has a clear intellect, from the effects it produces. It is this *avidya* which projects the entire universe.

---

* Atma-Bodha 14.
(अनाद्यविद्यानिर्वाच्या कारणोपाधिरुच्यते)

One of the powers of the omnipotent Lord *Parameswara* is the power to delude Himself! This Power Divine is called "the Unmanifest" and is the causal-body. The Lord can play through any of His powers: the Power to Discriminate *(Jnana sakti)*, the Power to Desire *(Ichha-sakti)*, or the Power to Strive *(Kriya-sakti)*. All are His powers-divine. This unmanifest power is otherwise called Nescience *(Avidya)*. It is a solid mass of Ignorance. In deep-sleep, one experiences only one thing-- ' I don't know'. 'I don't know', is the one's nature in deep-sleep. This substance of deep sleep falls under the influence of three *Gunas--Sattwa, Rajas* and *Tamas*.

Sattwa, Rajas and *Tamas* are three 'climatic' conditions, as it were, under which thought functions. From these alone various manifestations arise. This *Maya-sakti* consisting of the three Gunas is beyond sense perceptions *(Para)*. Only its effects can be perceived, just as we do not know what electricity is except through its manifestation. When a particular tendency manifests in an individual, then only can it be said that his *vasanas* are of a particular type. Hence from the effects only, *Maya-sakti* can be inferred by those who have the necessary subtle intellect.

This finite, mortal, ever-changing world that we see around us, is born out of *Maya* alone. Due to the non-apprehension of Reality, man recognises the world of objects, emotions and thoughts. Through the body, mind and intellect he contacts the world and creates more and more *vasanas*. These *vasanas* make one act more and more, and in the end, man becomes co-cooned in them and gains permanently for himself the sense of a separate individuality, the *jeevabhava*. All these are created by this *avidya*, this non-apprehension of Reality.

Avidya is the *vasanas* in the microcosm. The *avidya* of all individuals put together is its macrocosmic form and is called *Maya*. This is the vehicle of the Supreme when He functions as *Iswara*. When the Supreme functions through *jeeva*--the individual ego. When the Supreme functions through macrocosmic *Avidya (Maya)*, He is *Iswara*.

Each individual creates his own world around himself due to his ignorance *(Avidya)*, through his mind. The sum of each one's world put together is the total world which we call the universe, the *jagat*. Therefore, the total world the universe, is created by the total mind when expressing through the total *vasanas*, otherwise called *Maya*. Thus the Supreme functioning through total *avidya* is God, *Iswara*, and the Supreme expressing through the total mind is the Creator *(Brahmaji)* who creates the universe.

From the above, it becomes clear that the question, "Is there a God?" is as foolish as one asking, "Have I a father?" The very fact that you exist is enough proof that you must have had a father. Without a father, you cannot be, even if that father be unknown. Without a cause an effect can never arise.

सन्नाप्यसन्नाप्युभयात्मिका नो
भिन्नाप्यभिन्नाप्युभयात्मिका नो ।
साङ्गाप्यनङ्गा ह्युभयात्मिका नो
महाद्भुताऽनिर्वचनीयरुपा ॥१०९॥

109. It *(Maya)*, ia niether existent nor non-existent, nor both; neither same nor different nor both; neither made up of parts nor whole nor both. Most wonderful it is and beyond description in words.

This *avidya* cannot be said to have a separate existence from Brahman. Nor can it be said that it exists not. Because we are both enjoying and suffering it. It cannot also be said that it "exists as well as does not exist", because a non-existent thing can never become existent, nor can an existent thing express as non-existent. We cannot say that the ghost in the post 'exists'. Nor can we say, 'It exists not', because we sweat and perspire when we 'see' it. To say that it 'exists as well as exists not', is a clumsy contradiction in terms.

Also, it cannot be said that this great *Maya* exists and is other than *Brahman*, because *Brahman* is one-without-a-second. To say that this *Maya* is 'with the Lord as well as without the Lord', is again a contradiction in terms. We cannot say that the ghost came from the post at any time. Neither can we say, 'It is with parts and without parts', because it is again a contradition that cancels itself and becomes utterly meaningless, for ignorance can never be known.

Then what is this *avidya?*

All that we can say about it is that it is a 'great wonder!' It can only be said to be indescribable *(Anirvachaneeya)*. There is wonder when the intellect is not able to comprehend a thing. Anything that I see and my intellect cannot explain, I say is a 'wonder'. The more I think about this *avidya*, the more my intellect fails, because this *avidya* is the very cause for the intellect. The intellect cannot comprehend its own cause because it is the child born out of Maya, and a child cannot go back to look for the womb. This *Maya* when it manifests, becomes the intellect. Therefore, the intellect cannot comprehend the unmanifest which it its own cause. the effect cannot, by itself, comprehend its own cause. *Maya* is also called a "delusion", and a delusion can never be explained. There cannot be a biography of the ghost I saw on the post, nor can I grow rich by extracting the 'silver' from the mother-of-pearl. This *Maya-sakti*, we can only say, is an indescribable, mightly, inscurtable power of the Lord. Strange, for by his own inscrutable power a person deludes himself and says, "Tell me, tell me what is this power? Where is it?"

A Brahmin boy, one day, went to meet, his friends in a students' hostel. That being the festival day of Holi, the boy's friends were preparing *Thandai*--a cool drink in which a bit of opium is also added.In order to tease him they gave him a strong dose of the opium drink. The boy not being used to it, gulped it down somehow, unable to refuse his friends' offer.

As the opium started having effect on him, he thought of going home. He felt that he could not go alone, so he started shouting, "Take me home! Take me home!" Now he was under the full influence of the intoxicant, and he shouted even more loudly, "Take me home! Take me home!"

Then one of his friends took pity on him. He led him home and made him lie down on his bed. Not realising where he was,the boy continued shouting, "Take me home!" Hearing his meaningless, shouts, his parents rushed to his bedside. they tried to tell him that he was already at home. But the boy would bot stop his blabbering. Suspecting some mischief, the father questioned his friend and found out that he was under the intoxicating influence of opium. He then fetched some butter-milk which is an antidote and made him drink it. When he had drunk the butter-milk, the boy, in time, started coming to his senses. But he continued shouting, "Take me home"!. After some time, he became fully conscious that he was reclining in his own bed, shouting, "Take me home"! In a flash he realised how foolish he was, that there was no need for him to shout, for he was already home. So he stopped shouting and thereafter, slept peacefully.

Similarly, we, at the moment, under the influence of the opium of *avidya*--non-apprehension of Reality, consider ourselves to be the body-mind-intellect and are supremely confused by the objects perceived, emotions felt and thoughts entertained. We cry out, "O Lord!" O Teacher! Take me home. give me peace. Make me happy!" Take you where? Give you what? In reality you are the Self, but due to *avidya*, you live and behave as though you are an ego.

Take me to myself. Give me my own Self. You are already in Om, which is your home. Your home is really Om. Never were you out of Om, your home. Hurry home! Hari Om!

You ask, "Then why am I suffering?" All on account of this opium, the *avidya*, which is within you. The Guru, the Teacher, will give you the butter-milk of the 'study of the

Sastras', 'spiritual discipline', etc. All these for what? To take you home which is Om, where you already are.

Lack of correct thinking produces misconceptions. Think rightly: All misery will end. The text that teaches us to think correctly and discriminate properly is the Vivekachoodamani, *the Crest-jeewl-of-Discrimination.*

शुद्धाद्वयब्रह्मविबोधनाश्या
सर्पभ्रमो रज्जुविवेकतो यथा ।
रजस्तमःसत्त्वमिति प्रसिद्धा
गुणास्तदीयाः प्रथितैः स्वकार्यैः ॥११०॥

110. By realisation of the pure, non-dual Brahman, Maya can be destroyed, just as the illusion of the snake is removed by the discriminative knowledge of the rope. Its *Gunas* are *Rajas*, *Tamas* and *Sattwa*, distinguished by their respective functions.

The mighty power of delusion can be destrcyed through the direct experience of the pure *Brahman*, the One-without-a-second, just as the illusion of the serpent can be destoryed by the knowledge of the rope, which is the reality behind the delusion. When the *non-apprehension* of the real substratum ends, the objects of illusory perceptions created by it called *mis-apprehension*, also end.

When the Reality, the *Brahman*, is realised, the confusions that 'I am the body', 'I am the mind', 'I am the intellect', also end, just as the illusory serpent disappears totally on cognition of the rope.

This great avidya *or non-apprehension, has Sattwa, Rajas and Tamas as its Gunas or properties. They are so named after their functions. The functions of* Maya-sakti *fall under these three kinds. The Gunas determine the landscapes of the mind and appear different, as in summer and winter and landscape appears different. What will be the indivudual landscape under the influence of the Gunas is described in the following verse.*

29. Rajoguna--Nature and Effect. (111-112)

विक्षेपशक्ती रजसः क्रियात्मिका
यतः प्रवृत्तिः प्रसृता पुराणी।
रागादयोऽस्याः प्रभवन्ति नित्यं
दुःखादयो ये मनसो विकाराः ॥१११॥

111. Rajas has projecting power *(Vikshepasakti)*. Activity is its very nature. From it the initial flow of activity has originated. From it, mental modifications such as attachment and grief are also continuously produced.

The Rajas attitude of *Maya* creates the agitations of the mind*(Vikshepa)*. *Maya* expressed at the mental level manifests in the fom of mental agitations. The *Maya* which creates restlessness in the mind is called *Rajoguna*, from which all activities are born.

When the mind is active, we act in the world outside. When the mind is quiet, all actions end. During deep-sleep, the mind is at rest and is calm, therefore, no activity is taking place. Activities are only possible when the mind is active. A mental picture exists before every activity. Our association with objects and beings creates more and more attachment. We see a possibility--until it becomes an agitation. Then desires and passions arise in the mind. To satisfy them, man has to act in the world outside. For it takes less exertion to yield to them than to fight them. From this activity alone the mind's various attitudes are born. Thus the mind gains its experiences of joys and sorrows. The nature of *Avidya* when expressed in a given personality is called Rajoguna.

Rajoguna *creates agitations in the mind. Due to these mental agitations, objectively we act in the world and subjectively we experience desires, passions, lust and consequently, joys and sorrows.*

कामः क्रोधो लोभदम्भाद्यसूयाऽ
हंकारेर्ष्यामत्सराद्यास्तु घोराः।

धर्मा एते राजसाः पुम्प्रवृत्ति -
र्यस्मादेषा तद्रजो बन्धहेतुः ॥११२॥

112. Desire, anger, greed, hypocricy, arrogance, jealousy, egoism, envy, etc.-- these are the dreadful attributes of Rajas, from which the wordly tendencies of man are produced. Rajas is therefore the cause for bondage in life.

Objectively, all actions arise out of the Rajoguna aspect of *Maya.* Reactions arising subjectively in the human personality are explained in this verse.

Desire, anger, avarice, hypocricy, arrogance, jealousy, egoism, envy etc., all of them manifest because of Rajoguna. They are the lower types of emotions created by Rajoguna in the psychological layer of the personality. These reactions created by the agitations of the mind are terrible because they multiply the agitations and man gets totally shackled by them. Since all worldly activities arise from *Rajoguna,* it is said to cause all bondages in life. For under the forces of Rajas, man becomes limited by his own lower impulses.

Rajas *generates agitations* (Vikshepa), *and these very agitations of the mind veil* (Avarana) *the Self in us. When a* Rajasic *man gets exhausted due to his own over-exertion, he gets tired and feels sleepy--a state when he is about to enter* Tamas. *That is,* Rajas *must necessarily lapse into* Tamas. *Once the higher Awareness is "veiled", we are apt to act foolishly and get more and more entangled in the mad pursuit of obects of pleasure.*

30. Tamoguna--Nature and Effects. (113-116)

एषाऽऽवृतिर्नाम तमोगुणस्य
शक्तिर्यया वस्त्ववभासतेऽन्यथा ।
सैषा निदानं पुरुषस्य संसृते -
र्विक्षेपशक्तेः प्रवणस्य हेतुः ॥११३॥

113. The veiling power *(Avriti)*, is the power of *Tamas*, which makes things appear to be other than what they actually are. It causes man's repeated transmigration and initiates the action of the projecting power (Vikshepa).

Maya, in its Tamoguna nature, acts in our personality as the 'power of veiling', by which Reality is veiled from our cognition, and things are observed as something other than what they actually are. *Tamas* veils Reality and *Rajas* creates agitations in the mind. As the result of a combination of these two, we see things which are not really there.

Things as they are, are veiled by *Tamas* and the mind projects its imaginations upon them. Objects are not perceived in their right perspective when the inner personality is poisoned by *Rajas* and *Tamas*. This *Tamas* is the spring-board for man's repeated transmigration. Considering myself to be the body, the mind and the intellect, I function in the world of objects, emotions and thoughts, creating more and more *vasanas* for myself. In order to exhaust these *vasanas*, I must necessarily search for another physical body when the present one drops off. The cycle of birth and death goes on until all the *vasanas* have been exhausted. All this is only because Reality is not clearly apprehended. Reality is veiled because of *Tamas*. This *Tamasic* aspect of *Maya* is actually the cause for all the agitations of the mind.

So far, it has been described how man comes to suffer the persecutions of the world. The *Tamasic* aspect of *Maya* veils the intellect, and so the intellect cannot have the right judgement of things. When the intellect is veiled by *Tamas*, (the mind under the influence of) Rajas, *projects a wrong idea* of things perceived by the sense-organs. The individual then gets excited.

When the rope is not recognised as a rope, man suffers from the misconceptions projected by his own mind that it is a serpent.

Similarly, due to the *Tamas* in me, I am not able subjectively to realise the nature of *Brahman*, the *Atman* in me. In Its place I recognise the subject-object world of experiences caused by the *Rajas* in me. Not only do I not know that I am the Self, the *Atman*, but in Its place I experience the limitations of the equipment of the body, mind and intellect, and their experiences.

So Maya *palys in two ways--through her* Avarana-sakti *(veiling power), and through her* Vikshepa-sakti *(projecting power), which are due to* Tamas *and* Rajas *respectively.*

प्रज्ञावानापि पण्डितोऽपि चतुरोऽप्यत्यन्तसूक्ष्मार्थदृग् -
व्यालीढस्तमसा न वेत्ति बहुधा संबोधितोऽपि स्फुटम् ।
भ्रान्त्यारोपितमेव साधु कलयत्यालम्बते तद्गुणान्
हन्तासौ प्रबला दुरन्ततमसः शक्तिर्महत्यावृत्तिः ॥११४॥

114. Even the wise and the learned, and those who are proficient in the vision of the supremely subtle meaning of the scriptures, are overpowered by Tamas and cannot comprehend Truth, even though It is clearly explained in various ways. They consider as real what is simply superimposed by delusion and attach themselves to its effects. Alas! How powerful is the veiling power of dire *Tamas!*

Even a man who is very clever, exceedingly capable of seeing the subtle meaning of things, and endowed with great intelligence and genius, is overpowered by the influence of Tamas and becomes incapable of understanding Reality though it is clearly explained in different ways, with many references and examples. Not only does he not understand Truth, but he also insists that what has been falsely projected by him alone is real. Even after reading all the *Upanishads*, he says that the existence in the body, mind and intellect and their activities of perceiving, feeling and thinking constitute the only Reality. His intellect cannot comprehend the truth because of the thickness of Tamas that has come to cover it. By insisting upon his projections alone as Truth, he becomes victimised by their properties. When the properties of his projected misconceptions change, he too changes. When the body is a little ill, he says, "I am ill". If the mind is worried, he complains, "I am worried". Thus the *Gunas* of the body, mind and intellect become his *Gunas*. Alas! This endless *Tamas* is very powerful.

The *Tamasic* aspect of *Maya* has such a mighty power, that even a brilliant intellect, when under the influence of *Tamas*, cannot understand the Reality though It is pointed out in a thousand clear ways by the *Sastras*.

अभावना वा विपरीतभावना ऽ-
संभावना विप्रतिपत्तिरस्याः ।
संसर्गयुक्तं न विमुञ्चति ध्रुवं
विक्षेपशक्तिः क्षपयत्यजस्त्रम् ॥११५॥

115. Absence of correct judgement, or contrary jugement, lack of definite belief and doubt--certainly these never leave one who has any connection with this veiling power; also, the projecting power gives endless trouble.

Tamas is connected with: (1) absence of right judgement *(Abhavana)*, (2) contrary judgement *(Vipareeta-bhavana)*, (3) want of definite belief in the existence of a thing, even though there may be a vague notion of it *(Asambhavana)*, and (4) doubt *(Vipratipatti)*. As long as there is *Tamas*, these are present. They are all effects of the influence of *Tamas* in one's personality. When the intellect is veiled, *Rajas* comes to play its pranks; the mind starts projecting ceaselessly, and the individual suffers.

अज्ञानमालस्यजडत्वनिद्रा -
प्रमादमूढत्वमुखास्तमोगुणाः ।
एतैः प्रयुक्तो नहि वेत्ति किंचि -
न्निद्रालुवत्स्तम्भवदेव तिष्ठति ॥११६॥

116. Ignorance, laziness, dullness, sleep, inadvertance, stupidity etc., are the attributes of *Tamas*. One tied up with these cannot comprehend anything, but remains like one asleep, or like a stump of wood or a block of stone.

Ignorance or Reality, inability to act rightly, incapacity to comprehend properly, excessive sleep, doing things for the sake of doing them, colossal stupidity, and all other such attributes are the effects of *Tamoguna.*

When one is under the influence of Tamoguna, *the above qualities are seen in him. These defects in the functioning of the personality layers in us are like parasitic growths on the intellect which make it dull and inert. Man, with such a maladjusted intellect moves in the world as though asleep, and lives like an inert telegraph post, a dead pillar or an insentient statue. It is all due to the manifestation of concentrated* Tamas *in the bosom of the individual.*

31. Sattwa-guna--Nature and Effects. (117-119)

सत्त्वं विशुद्धं जलवत्तथापि
ताभ्यां मिलित्वा सरणाय कल्पते ।
यत्रात्मबिम्बः प्रतिबिम्बितः सन्
प्रकाशयत्यर्क इवाखिलं जडम् ॥११७॥

117. Pure *Sattwa* is like clear water, yet in combination with *Rajas* and *Tamas*, it provides for transmigration. But when the light of the Self gets reflected in *Sattwa* alone, then, like the sun, It reveals the entire world of matter.

Having explained *Rajoguna* and *Tamoguna*, Sankara now gives an explanation of *Sattwa-guna.* Sattwa is ever pure like water. Like water it can get mixed up with many things, but not as a compound of its own nature.Water as water is ever pure. When we say 'dirty water', we mean that a sample of pure water has something other than it, in it. When we say 'stinky water and muddy water', we mean a specimen of pure water in which the stink and the mud are held in suspension. If the stink and the dirt are removed, the water again becomes pure. Similarly, *Sattwa* is always present, evenin a *Tamasic* man. When pure *Sattwa* in an individual is in conjuntion with *Rajas* and *Tamas*, it becomes the cause for his transmigration. If he is in pure *Sattwa*, i.e. if he has eliminated *Rajas* and *Tamas*, then for him there can be no transmigration. Only when *Sattwa* is muddied with *Rajoguna* and *Tamoguna* does it cause transmigration.

When there is pure *Satwa*, the intellect works steadily. There is no veiling and there are no agitations. The mind then becomes steady in utter meditation. It is face to face with Divinity, with Reality.

When this state is veiled by *Tamas* and disturbed by *Rajas*, the mind starts seeing things other than Reality. The body, mind and intellect turned towards objects, emotions and thoughts create *vasanas*. To exhaust these *vasanas* fresh bodies have to be taken. This going and coming *(Samsar)*, of the individuality from one equipment to another, from one time to another, from one place to another, is called transmigration.

When the consciousness gets reflected in the *Sattwa*-mode of the mind. It illumines the inert; insentient world around, just as the sun illumines them during the day. The light of the sun itself is imperceptible. If there is light on this book, and if it is coming from the window, there must be light between the window and this book. This light bewteen the window and the book cannot be perceived. Light itself is imperceptible. When it falls on an object and gets reflected, the reflected light alone can be seen.

The *Atman*, cannot see anything, nor know any object, nor illumine anything--because in *Brahman*, there is nothing for It to illumine. It is One-without-a-second. We generally recognise the things in the world with our intelligence. Intelligence is the light of consciousness reflected in the intellect. Therefore, when the intellect is agitated, the intelligence is less. Since the reflecting surface is not steady, the reflection of Consciousness gets shaky and so Its brilliance becomes dimmed. If the reflecting surface is unclean, the reflected beam must be dim. When the intellect is under the influence of *Tamas*, it is rendered dull (as when he is under chloroform). He cannot understand anything within or without him.

Therefore when *Rajas* and *Tamas* are mixed with *Sattwa*, there is little intelligence in an individual. But when *Rajas* and *Tamas* are reduced in one's personality, the proportion of *Sattwa* increases. The light of Consciousness reflected in the intellect becomes more and more clear. Thus out of the stupid personality of today, a great brilliance of intelligence can be produced when the personality gets purified.

Upasana, *japa*, and *meditation* and other such spiritual disciplines are all meant for the prufication of the personality. When the mind becomes more and more *Sattwic*, it starts apprehending things it could not apprehend before. By such spiritual practices the mind becomes calm, and the clarity of the light of consciousness reflecting in the intellect becomes more and more. Man's devotion to the Higher and his burning aspiration for liberation becomes greater and greater and noble virtues come to shine forth in him.

As a result, one's capacity to apprehend things increases. This extra-brilliant capacity is called *INTUITION*. In Sanskrit it is called *jnana-chakshu* otherwise called the power of Divine Vision, or Revelation--Trans-experience. All these indicate a mind in a fully Sattwic condition. The whole process is like an ascending spiral--it gathers momentum and carries itself.

Consciousness being the same in all beings, the intelligence of individuals differ on account of the proportion of Rajas and Tamas functioning in their personalities.

मिश्रस्य सत्त्वस्य भवन्ति धर्मा -
स्त्वमानिताद्या नियमा यमाद्याः ।

श्रद्धा च भक्तिश्च मुमुक्षुता च
दैवी च सम्पत्तिरसन्निवृत्तिः ॥११८॥

118. The characteristics of mixed Sattwa are, utter absence of pride etc., *Niyama, Yama* etc., and also faith, devotion, yearning for liberation, the divine tendencies and a natural turning away from everything unreal.

In the above verse, the consequences of the preponderance of *Sattwa* with the presence of *Rajas* and *Tamas* in the intellect have been explained. An individual is already on the path to Realisation if the proportion of *Rajas* and *Tamas* is very little, and the intellect is predominantly of a *Sattwa*, nature. Because of the predominance of *Sattwa*, the individual's yearning for liberation will be great. When this anxiety for liberating one's personality increases, pride etc., which belong to the nature of a *Rajasic* personality, will totally disapper from the seeker's heart.

The qualities of a *Sattwic* personality have been explained in the Geeta.* They are called the Divine qualities. A man of *Sattwic* temperament is divinely good. It is in the nature of such an individual to turn away from the unreal *(Asannivritti)*, and progess towards liberation.

All the qualifications of a fit student (Adhikari), *are present in such an individual. The qualities leading to the supreme good, i.e. absence of pride etc.*[1] *qualities that add tempo to the spiritual practices such as Yama, Niyama etc.*[2] *and the*

---

* *Geeta XVI--1,2,3.*

Fearlessness, purity of heart, steadfastness in the yoga of knowledge; alms-giving, control of the senses, sacrifice, study of the Sastras, **austerity and straightforwardness;**

Harmlessness, truth, absence of anger, renunciation, peacefulness, absence of crookedness, compassion to beings, uncovetousness gentleness, modesty, absense of fickleness.

sixfold wealth consisting of Sama, Dama *etc, with sufficient devotion to the Ideal, are all the indications of mixed* Sattwaguna, *where* Rajas *and* Tamas *are less and* Sattwa *is preponderant.*

विशुध्धसत्त्वस्य गुणाः प्रसादः
स्वात्मानुभूतिः परमा प्रशान्तिः ।
तृप्तिः प्रहर्षः परमात्मनिष्ठा
यया सदानन्दरसं समृच्छति ॥११९॥

119. The characteristics of pure Sattwa are cheerfulness, the experience of one's own Self, supreme peace, contentment, bliss, and constant devotion to the supreme Self, by which the aspirant comes to enjoy everlasting bliss.

When the last traces of dirt *(Rajas* and *Tamas)*, are removed, the personality becomes completely pure. Such an inner equipment is full of uncontaminated *Sattwa.* When such a state is attained, the aspirant realises the supreme Self and gains everlasting bliss. It is everlasting because having gained this state, no sorrow can ever affect a

---

1. Geeta XIII-7-11.

Humility, unpretentiousness, non-injury, forebearance, uprightness, service to the Teacher, purity, steadiness, self-control,

The renunciation of sense-objects, and also absence of egoism; reflection on the evils of birth, death, old age, sickness and pain;

Non-attachment, non-identification of self with son, wife, home and the rest, and constant even-mindedness in the occurrence of the desirable and the undesirable;

Unswerving devotion to Me, by the yoga of non-separation, resort to sequestered places, distate for the society of men;

Constant application to spiritual knowledge, understanding of the end of true knowledge: this is declared to be knowledge, and what is opposed to it is ignorance.

2. Sama--control of inner mind, Dama--control of the sense organs Uparati--self-withdrawal, Titeeksha--capacity to suffer silently the little pinpricks of life, Sraddha--deep faith, Samadhana--peace of mind etc.

person.[1] Some of the traits of this transcendental state of experience are indicated by some very choice expressions in this verse.

Experience of one's own Self : *(Swaatma-anubhooti)*--- *Rajas*, the cause for all misapprehensions and *Tamas*, the cause for non-apprehensions are totally absent in pure *Swattwa*. Therefore, the Self is apprehended when the intellect becomes immaculately pure.

Supreme peace : *(Parama prasanti)*--- There is no *Rajas*--- the cause for agitations---in that spiritual state of Divine experience. When the Self is apprehended, all agitations end. Hence there can only be perfect peace.

Contentment : *(Tripti)*---Because of the absence of all desires, the seeker feels a sense of supreme contentment. Presence of desire is the indication of a sense of incompletness. Attainment of perfect peace, must end all sense of incompleteness. This is the state of desirelessness, the state of perfection or God-hood.

Bliss :*(Praharsha)*--- This is not the bliss of ignorance, but dynamic Bliss of Realisation. This bliss springs from a source transcending all our known concepts of joys and sorrows which ooze out from the filthy marsh-lands of our minds.

Firm devotion to the supreme Self: *(Paramatma-nishtha)*--- Because of non-apprehension of Reality, our individuality[2] is entirely engaged in seeking its joys among the objects, emotions and thoughts, through the equipments of the body,

---

1. Geeta XV-6.

Nor does the sun shine there, nor the moon, nor fire; to which having gone they return not; that is My Supreme Abode.

and

Geeta VIII-21.

That which has been called Unmanifest and Imperishable, has been described as the Supreme Goal. That is My highest state, having attained which, there is no return.

2. The perceiver-feeler-thinker entity in us.

mind and intellect. When these equipments are transcended, the objective and subjective worlds are no more. When the *vasanas* of *Rajas* and *Tamas* are removed, the ego rediscovers itself as the supreme Reality and becomes one with It. Thereafter, there is no slipping back into the state of body identification. Unwavering, steady and deep devotion to the Supreme becomes natural to such a seeker. Thus, by making the intellect completely pure, the aspirant enjoys the essence of everlasting Bliss.

32. The Causal-body---Its Nature. (120-121)

अव्यक्तमेतत्त्रिगुणैर्निरुक्तं
तत्कारणं नाम शरीरमात्मनः ।
सुषुप्तिरेतस्य विभक्त्यवस्था
प्रलीनसर्वेन्द्रियबुद्धिवृत्तिः ॥१२०॥

120. This "Unimanifest", described as a combination of all three' Gunas, is the causal-body of the individual. Its special state is deep-sleep, in which all the functions of the mind-intellect and the sense-organs are totally suspended.

सर्वप्रकारप्रमितिप्रशान्ति -
र्बीजात्मनावस्थितिरेव बुद्धेः ।
सुषुप्तिरेतस्य किल प्रतीतिः
किंचिन्न वेद्मीति जगत्प्रसिद्धेः ॥१२१॥

121. The mind remains in a subtle seed-like form in deep-sleep, which is the state of complete cessation of all kinds of perceptions. Indeed, the universal experience in this state is, "I did not know anything".

So for the three Gunas have been explained exhaustively by Acharya Sankara.* Now the causal-body, called the Unimanifest, is taken up for a detailed discussion.

---

* From verses 111 to 119.

The causal-body consists of the three *Gunas*---*Sattwa, Rajas* and *Tamas*---in their unmanifest state. When the individual withdraws himself from the waking and dream states of Consciousness, he is said to be in the deep-sleep state. The waking state and dream state experiences are present in the deep-sleep state in the unmanifest or the seed form. The seeds when manifested at the subtle and gross levels give rise to the dream state and the waking state respectively. In deep-sleep it is like the seed going back to the seed.

When a man is in deep-sleep, all the activities of his intellect, mind and sense-organs are temporarily at rest. This state is known as the state of the unmanifest *(Avyakta)*, because neither Reality nor the world of objects-emotions-thoughts is manifest and available for his cognition. In short, it is the state of non-apprehension of Reality. The experience of the individual in this state is, "I do not know" Complete ignorance is the characteristic of this state. For where the intellect is arrested, the intellect-projected objective world will not be there. The total absence of all kinds of knowledge is directly experienced in deep-sleep by all creatures, everywhere. This level of pure and complete ignorance, and total non-apprehension, is the causal-body.

33. Not-Self---Description. (122)-123)

देहेन्द्रियप्राणमनोऽहमादयः
सर्वे विकारा विषयाः सुखादयः ।
व्योमादिभूतान्यखिलं च विश्व -
मव्यक्तपर्यन्तमिदं ह्यनात्मा ॥१२२॥

122. The body, sense-organs, *Pranas*, mind and ego etc. and all their modifications; the sense-objects and their pleasures etc; the gross elements such as ether etc; the whole universe up to the Unmanifest---these constitute the not-Self.

माया मायाकार्यं सर्वं महदादिदेहपर्यन्तम् ।
असदिदमनात्मतत्त्वं विद्धि त्वं मरुमरीचिकाकल्पम् ॥१२३॥

123. Everything is due to the effect of *Maya*--- from *Mahat* down to the gross body. Know thou, that these and *Maya* itself are the not-Self---therefore, they are unreal, like the mirage-waters in desert.

So far, all that constitutes the *An-atman* (not-Self), has been explained. All equipments---body *(Deha)*, sense-organs *(Indriya)*, physiological functions *(Prana)*, mind *(Mana)*, and the ego*(Aham)*; all modifications *(Vikara)*, like pain and pleasure etc. *(Sukhadayah)*, all sense-objects *(Vishaya)*, the gross elements *(Bhootani)*, and the perceptible world of objects, emotions and thoughts *(Vishwa)*, upto the Unmanifest *(Avyakta*--- all are the not-Self *(An-atman)*.*

The entire world within and around, up to the *vasanas*, i.e. the world of matter which is other than the Self, the Atman, is *An-atman*. This *An-atman* is the creation of *Maya* due to non-apprehension of Reality. *Maya* is "that which is *not*". All things created out of a thing which exists not must be unreal, entirely non-existent. Though they are all non-existent, for the time being they are perceptible to us in our own delusion. Hence they are mere illusions.

Though the Mirage in the desert can be 'seen', it has no reality. Similarly, the entire range of things consisting of *An-atman* are unreal, mere whiffs of the mind's imagination.

In order to know the Reality, all that is unreal has to be rejected, and so transcended. The next verse onwards, Sankara explains the nature of the Self, the Atman, which is to be known and attained.

---

* Geeta enumerates them as the *"kshetra"* and gives the following list: Geeta XIII-5 & 6. The great elements, the ego, the intellect, and also the Unmanifest; the ten senses, the mind, the five objects of the senses; desire, hatred, pleasure, pain, the aggregate, intelligence, fortitude---the Kshetra with its modifications has thus been briefly described.

34. The Self---Its Nature. (124-135)

अथ ते संप्रवक्ष्यामि स्वरूपं परमात्मनः ।
यद्विज्ञाय नरो बन्धान्मुक्तः कैवल्यमश्नुते ॥१२४॥

124. Now I will tell you of the Real Nature of the supreme Self, realising which, man is freed from all his personality encumbrances (bondages), and attains liberation.

To mark the conclusion of the previous idea and to inaugurate a new theme of discussion, Sankara says, "I shall now very clearly explain to you the nature of the supreme Self (having explained the not-Self)." Once this Self is fully apprehended subjectively, man's personality will be released from all persecutions of matter with its low demands. He will be released from the bondages created by his own unintelligent and pain-giving identifications. Not only will he be liberated from his unnecessary sorrows, but he will also come to experience the pure One-ness of his own Self.

Kaivalya is the state of liberation from the BMI, PFT & OET.* When one is released from all the equipments and their objects, pure Knowledge is experienced. According to the Rishis this is *Kaivalya.*

Sitting on a rock you can see the movement of a river but if you are on the river itself you will see no movement. The observer must be motionless in order to observe movement---no mutation can be recognised without reference to an immutable factor.

As the Pure Subject, no more are there any limitations in one. Such a person is called a "Seer". We must note, very carefully, that he is not "seeing" anything---he is a mere "Seer". There is nothing for him to see. This state is being described in great detail in the following verses.

---

* Body-Mind-Intellect (BMI); Perceiver-Feeler-Thinker (PFT); and other Objects-Emotions-Thoughts (OET). Hereafter we shall often be using the abbreviations BMI, PFT, OET, in our discussions. Please note them carefully.

अस्ति कश्चित्स्वयं नित्यमहंप्रत्ययलम्बनः ।
अवस्थात्रयसाक्षी सन्पञ्चकोशविलक्षणः ॥१२५॥

125. Something there is, which is the Absolute Entity, the Eternal Substratum for the very awareness of the Ego. It is the Witness of the three states and it is distinct from all the five sheaths.

When I say, "I am happy", "I am unhappy", "I am joyful", "I am sorrowful", "I am educated", "I am worried", --in these conditions, the external world around me has changed. The conditions of the body, of the mind, of the intellect, and of the external world of objects have changed. But all through these changes the subjective sense of I-ness has remained changeless. In all conditions good, bad or indifferent, this 'something' in our life---within us---has remained unchanged, and this is generally indicated by the word 'I'. The subject 'I' remains a changeless entity, common in all changes, experiencing them all. In each one of us it takes up different attitudes, at different places and at different times, such as child-hood, youth and old-age; waking, dream and deep-sleep; happy, unhappy, etc. In all such conditions, behind the very subject 'I', there is a common changeless factor, the Consciousness. This factor is by its own nature, formless and changeless, depending upon which we have the constant experience of I....I....I....our individuality.

This subject in each one of us is a mere witness of the three states of Consciousness---the waking, dream and deep-sleep states. In the waking state, it is 'I the waker'; in dream it is again 'I the dreamer'; and when fast asleep too, it is 'I' the deep-sleeper'. In these states of Consciousness, the 'I' remains a mere witness. It neither undergoes any changes characteristic of these states, nor does it have any share in them. This I-ness gains vivid experiences of all the three different states. Let me give you an example to clarify the idea.

I, the individual, going to Surat, Ahmedabad and Bomaby, gather to myself three different experiences at the three different places. let us say, at Surat I was loved, at

Ahmedabad I was honoured and at Bombay I was insulted. Surat is not Ahmedabad. Surat and Ahmedabad are not Bombay. I was not at Surat, Ahmedabad and Bombay at one and the same time. The experiences of three different places. at the three different times are different, yet all these experiences are mine, because I was the common factor in all the three places and at all the three times. This is so in the waking, dream and deep-sleep states also. The waker himself becomes the dreamer and the deep-sleeper and gains the experience of the dream and the deep-sleep. But during these changes in the states of consciousness, he himself never undergoes any change, but remains as mere witness.

Atman *being the witness of the three states of consciousness, It is, indeed, something other than the five-sheaths---the food-sheath, the vital-air-sheath, the mental-sheath, the intellectual-sheath and the bliss-sheath. The* Atman *is not identified with, and therefore is never limited by, any of these sheaths. It is something other than them, knowing them and their individual involvements in the world around and within.*

यो विजानाति सकलं जाग्रत्स्वप्नसुषुप्तिषु ।
बुद्धितद्वृत्तिसद्भावमभावमहमित्ययम् ॥१२६॥

126. That which knows everything that happens in the waking, dream and deep-sleep states, That which is aware of the presence or absence of the mind and its functions, That which is the essence behind the ego, That is "This".

This verse expresses the import of some of the famous *Sruti* passages such as those found in the Kena and

Brihadaranyaka Upanishads.* That faculty in me because of which I am able to know, constantly, all my experiences of waking, dream and deep-sleep is called the *Atman* or self. By this faculty I am not only aware of the world of objects around me, but I am also equally aware of the equipments of knowledge within me and their main functions.

I know my intellect, the instrument with which I know other things. All my inner equipments *(antah karana)*, are also objects of my experience from the stand-point of the Self. In my mind and intellect, where all activities are disturbances *(vrittis)*, I am equally aware of the absence of all *(vrittis)*, as in deep-sleep. The agitations and also the absence of agitations are known. I am aware of not only my intellect and the thoughts in it, but also of the absence of thoughts. This knower, I, is "This"---the great Consciousness to be realised as the subjective Essence.

In each one of us, it is this Consciousness alone which knows constantly the world of objects around us, as well as the intelect and its thoughts, nay, even the absence of thoughts. Remember, the intellect can investigate only the presence of things; Consciousness can illumine their absence as well. This grand Knowing Principle constantly enlivens us. It is the Self we talk of as "This", the subject.

---

* Kenopanishad I-6.

That which cannot be seen by the eye, but by which the eyes are able to see.... know That alone as Brahman and not this, which people worship here.

Brihadaranyakopanishad III-4, 2.

न दृष्टेर्द्रष्टारं पश्येः, न श्रुतेः श्रोतारं श्रृणुयात्, न मतेर्मन्तारं मन्वीयाः, न विज्ञातेर्विज्ञातारं विजानीयाः । एष त आत्मा सर्वान्तरः, अतोऽन्यदार्तम् ॥

"You cannot see that which is the witness of vision; you cannot hear that which is the hearer of the hearing; you cannot think that which is the thinker of thought; you cannot know that which is the knower of knowledge. This is your Self that is within all; everything else but this is perishable."

यः पश्यति स्वयं सर्वं यं न पश्यति कश्चन ॥
यश्चेतयति बुद्ध्यादि न तद्यं चेतयत्ययम् ॥१२७॥

127. That which sees all but which no one can see; That which illumines the intellect etc., but which they cannot illumine, That is "This".

That which by Its own light sees everything at all times, is the Knowing Principle. This is the same Truth in all physical bodies, so everybody's experience is the experience of the Divine. Whenever anybody knows anything, he knows it because of the same Knowing Principle. That is why this Principle is also called the All-knower. Consciousness knows through me, my experiences, through you, your experiences, and through her, her experiences. Thus, through every physical body and every mind and intellect, at all times, It illumines everything with Its awareness. But Consciousness* cannot be known through any of these equipments.

The sense-organs, the mind, etc. are all made of matter. Therefore, they are inert. That which gives illumination to these equipments to function in their respective fields, and That which is not illumined by any of these equipments, That is this *Atman*, this Self. Consciousnes is the source of all sentiency. This great Reality lends sentiency to all matter vestures, but the matter vestures have no sentiency of their own to lend to the Consciousness.

*The Upanishad Rishis roar out that "this whole world is illumined with His Light".***

येन विश्वमिदं व्याप्तं यं न व्याप्नोति किञ्चन ॥
आभारूपमिदं सर्वं यं भान्तमनुभात्ययम् ॥१२८॥

---

* Kenopanishad I-6. See foot-note to verse 126.

** Mundakopanishad II-2-10.

There the sun does not shine, nor the moon nor the stars; these lightenings also do not shine---how then (can) this earthly fire? Verily, everything shines after Him Who shines. This whole world is illumined with His Light.

128. That by which this universe is pervaded, but which is not pervaded by anything, which when It shines, the entire universe shines as Its reflection, That is "This".

That by which all this is pervaded, yet nothing pervades It---we are not able to understand That, since our mind is not tuned up to Its frequency. Our mind is tuned up to the frequency of OET. That is why we are not able to recognise It ordinarily, even though It is present everywhere. It is All-pervasive. Pervasiveness is the nature of subtlety. That which is subtler than the subtlest must necessarily be All-pervading. The All-pervading cannot be pervaded by anything else.

All that exists does so only because of Its support. If my ears and eyes have the capacity of hearing and seeing, it is only because of the Consciousness which shines through them.

These verses explain the Atman *and point It out to be the subjective Consciousness in our bosoms. Therefore, these verses end with the chorus, That is "This". "This" indicates nearness. So it has been brought within our bosom, at a point nearest to us: "This".*

यस्य सन्निधिमात्रेण देहेन्द्रियमनोधियः ।
विषयेषु स्यकीयेषु वर्तन्ते प्रेरिता इव ॥१२९॥

129. That by whose very presence the body and the sense-organs, the mind and the intellect perform their respective functions like a team of servants prompted by their master!

The *Atman* is that factor by whose mere presence, the gross, the subtle and the causal bodies function in their respective fields. Here it is to be understood that Om, the Self, is not *doing* anything. It is not the doer. By its mere presence the matter equipments function. *Purusha* only looks at *Prakriti, Prakriti* gets enlivened and does everything. When Krishna is nearby, the Gopis get excited and dance about. The *Sariravritti, indriya-vritti, mano-vritti* are all to be understood as the Gopis. The Gopis look after the cows and tend them.

Similarly, the *vrittis* tend the cattle in us---sense-organs with their sense-objects.

By the mere *presence* of Consciousness, the sense-organs, the *Pranas*, the mind, the intellect, even the *vasanas*---function in their respective fields, without interfering with each other. Had consciousness not been present, none of them would have functioned. Thus it *appears* that the Consciousness prompts the equipments! they function as though prompted by the Self.*

All living creatures consciously or unconsciously draw their energy from the same light, and each one acts according to his own *vasanas*. The sun does not interfere with anyone's activities. It is not even conscious that so many living creatures are drawing their nourishment from it. In the absence of the sun all activities end, but the sun has nothing to do with the activities that go on.

Similarly, the body draws its energy from the Consciousness and the individual according to his vasanas. *Consciousness, which lends its energy, never interferes with the activities of the individual. Yet, in Its absence, no activity would be possible.*

अहङ्कारादिदेहान्ता विषयाश्च सुखादयः ।
वेद्यन्ते घटवद् येन नित्यबोधस्वरुपिणा ॥१३०॥

130. That, because of which everything---the ego, the body, the sense-objects and their pleasures etc., are known, as clearly as a jar, is of the nature of Eternal Knowledge.

From the subtlest, innermost concept of 'I', down to the physical body, its world of objects, and the subtle body and its objects---all these are known by a 'knower'. The gross-

---

* Atma Bodh-20.

Depending upon the energy or vitality of Consciousness *(Atma-chaitanya)*, the body, senses, mind and intellect engage themselves in their respective activities, just as men work depending upon the light of the sun.

body and its objects constituted of the world around, and the subtle-body and its objects consisting of pleasures and pains, attachments and revulsions, are all known just as a pot or a jar is clearly known in our everyday life.

A pot or a jar has not any light of its own. It is only seen because of some other source of light. All pots and jars are illumined by sunlight which is something other than them. Similarly, all things that are cognised as objects are cognised in the Light of Consciousness. This Consciousness is of the nature of Knowledge, which is the nature of the Self.

This is the great Truth * which illumines everything. The instruments of experiences and the experiences themselves are illumined by It at all times.

What is this great Truth?

एषोऽन्तरात्मा पुरुषः पुराणो
निरन्तराखण्डसुखानुभूतिः ।
सदैकरूपः प्रतिबोधमात्रो
येनेषिता वागसवश्चरन्ति ॥१३१॥

---

* *The verse is hinting at the pregnant suggestions found in the Brihadaranyaka Upanishad.*

Brihadaranyaka Upanishad IV-III-23.

यद्वै तन्न पश्यति पश्यन्वै तन्न पश्यति
नहि द्रष्टुर्दृष्टेर्विपरिलोपो विद्यतेऽविनाशित्वात् ।
न तु तद्द्वितीयमस्ति
ततोऽन्यद्विभक्तं यत्पश्येत् ॥

That it does not see in that state is because, though seeing them, it does not see; for the vision of the witness can never be lost, because it is imperishable. But there is not that second thing separate from it which it can see.

131. This (great Truth) is the innermost Self, the ancient *Purusha*, whose essential nature is the constant experience of infinite Bliss, which is ever the same. Yet, It constantly gets reflected through different mental modifications and, commanded by It, the sense-organs and the *Pranas* perform their functions.

All that we can say about this great *Atman*, the *Purusha*, Who dwells in the subtle-body, is, that It is an experience of constant unbroken joy. This is because the sources of sorrows---the body, the mind and the intellect are not there. Lesser the mental agitations, more is the joy. When the body is transcended, no sorrow is experienced. Thus, in terms of the mind, we can only say that this *Atman* is of the nature of constant Bliss. It is a unique transcendental experience because in it there are no mental agitations.

When a tiny little girl asks about marriage, all that can be said to her in terms of her understanding is, that when a little girl gets married, her husband will get her all the dolls in the market so that she could play with them all day long. Only when she grows up will she understand that it is not dolls'-play, that it is life consisting of more serious stuff. Similarly, in terms of the experiences of the students, to enable him to understand, it is said here that the Atman is of the nature of constant Bliss. It is because he is, at that time, so entirely wrapped up in the BMI and all their pains and tragedies.

This *Atman* is also said to be the *innermost* Self. "Inner" in *Vedanta* means "subtle". Therefore, when we say "innermost" we mean "subtlest", that is, All-pervading. This all-prevading Atman is One-without-a-second and is of the nature of Pure Existence. It is not the existence of a thing. It is existence *itself*. It is always of one nature *(Sada-eka-roopah)* ---that of Pure existence only. That which is always of one nature never changes. Hence all the pluralistic phenomena are only delusory misconceptions which we have projected upon It. Due to our misconceptions when we see a ghost on a post, what really exists is the post. The post alone is the only real thing, at all times. Similarly, Pure Existence alone is the only nature of the Self.

Again it is the Consciousness which constantly knows things. Hence knowledge of a thing minus the thing is Pure Knowledge, the Self. Thus Consciousness is subtly indicated as "Objectless Awareness". Prompted by this Consciousness everything functions. This has been explained in an earlier verse.[1] It is that factor, which was even before creations and is still serving as the very substratum for the entire universe of things and beings and their happenings.

अत्रैव सत्त्वात्मनि धीगुहाया
मव्याकृताकाश उशत्प्रकाशः ।
आकाश उच्चै रविवत्प्रकाशते
स्वतेजसा विश्वमिदं प्रकाशयन् ॥१३२॥

132. In this very body, in a mind full of *Sattwa*, in the secret cave of the intellect, in the atmosphere of the Unmanifest, the *Atman*, of captivating glory, shines like the sun, high in the sky, illumining this universe by Its very effulgence.

Here itself, in this very body, not in Kasi or Rameswaram, not in Jerusalem or Mecca, but in one's own mind which is full of *Sattwa*, meaning in a pure and quiet mind,[2] in the cave of the intellect,[3] in the space of the Unmanifest, this Self shines forth.

This Consciousness can be apprehended in the unfathomed depths of one's personality as a splendid Light Divine only when one's mind has been quietened. Since everything is illumined by It is is conceived of as Light---"a Light without properties".

---

1. Ibid verse 129.
2. A mind in which the Rajas and Tamas impulses have been reduced and Sattwa has been increased.
3. In the core of one's personality.

The sun illumines the entire world of plurality from its place high up in the sky. Similarly, the Atman *in the inner space of the heart illumines all the experiences within. When our attention is on the sunlight no objects can be perceived, and if the attention is on the objects the sunlight is not perceived. if our attention is on the* Atman, *the world, of OET is not cognised, but if it is on the OET, Om the Reality is not experienced. When the object is removed, light is not perceived as such. It is only intuitively experienced.*

ज्ञाता मनोऽहंकृतिविक्रियाणां
देहेन्द्रियप्राणकृतक्रियाणाम् ।
अयोऽग्निवत्तानुवर्तमानो
न चेष्टते नो विकरोति किञ्चन ॥१३३॥

133. The knower of the modifications of the mind and the ego, and the activities of the body, the sense-organs and the *Pranas*, which apparently take their forms like the fire in a ball of iron, is the Self, which neither acts nor changes in the least.

The *Atman* is the knower of the experiences within, of all joys and sorrows which are the conditions of the mind and the intellect. It is the Knowing Principle in the absence of which nothing can be known. The ego in the individual is the experiencer-and-doer entity in him. This *ahamkar* is the experiencer of all that happens within, and the doer of all activities without. *Ahamkar*, having the sense of doership and enjoyer-ship is the *jeeva. Brahman* functioning through the BMI expresses as the *jeeva*. In fact, it is not the doer or enjoyer of anything.

When ten pieces of iron of different shapes are put into the fire and removed only when they are red-hot, they appear as the cubical-fire, rectangular fire, elliptical fire, etc. The fire itself has no shape but it takes the shape of the iron pieces. Similarly, the Light of Consciousness *appears* to funtion according to the modifications of the equipments. Sunlight itself has no shape. But it takes the shape of the waves, the ripples and the bubbles in the sea. Its shape depends upon the object it illumines at any given time.

When consciousness illumines the experiences of the mind, It Seems to gather to Itself the attitude of the enjoyer. When It illumines the activities of the world outside, It appears to take the attitude of the doer. In fact, It is not involved in anything. When It appears to be so, it is but an illusion.

न जायते नो म्रियते न वर्धते
न क्षीयते नो विकरोति नित्यः ।
विलीयमानेऽपि वपुष्यमुष्मि -
न्न लीयते कुम्भ इवाम्बरं स्वयम् ॥१३४॥

134. Neither It is born nor does It die; neither does It grow nor does It decay; being eternal, It does not undergo any change. Even when this body is destroyed, It does not cease to exist. It is like the space in the jar that is broken--it is independent of the jar.

This great *Atman* is neither born nor does It die. The bubble is born and the bubble dies. The air in the bubble is neither born nor does it die when the bubble bursts. Similarly, the PFT is born, not the Reality, the Self.

It is meaningless to complain that my Consciousness was dull yesterday and that today it is bright. For Consciousness never increases nor decreases. It is only the rise and the fall of ignorance that causes an apparent veiling of Consciousness and a sudden blaze of Its effulgence. When the mind is full of attachment, hate, anger, greed and delusion, the awareness becomes dull. When these weaknesses are less, more light of Consciousness is manifest in the bosom. Consciousness is the one Reality at all times. When the thickness of *vasanas* is increased, Its splendour in us seems to be dimmed.

The *Atman*, the Self, never gets modified. The feeling of "I" in child-hood, youth and old-age remains the same. The body, the mind and the intellect are modified from time to time but not the *Atman* which quietly illumines all the changes in all the equipments.

The first two lines of this verse contain the definition of the term "eternal" *(Nitya)*. That which is never born nor dies, nor grows nor reduces, nor ever is modified is infinite, eternal *(Nitya)*. Conversely, that which is finite and ephemeral *(Anitya)*, is that which is born, that which grows, decays, and undergoes different modifications.

Thus this Atman *is eternal and even when this body falls off, the Self does not perish. Just like the space in the pot,-- when the pot is broken, the pot-space is not broken. When the walls are pulled down, the room-space becomes the space around. Similarly, when the body (gross, subtle and causal), is destroyed, the* Atman *is not destroyed. That which was the Consciousness in the bosom of the individual, merges back, as it were, into the Consciousness ever-present, everywhere, at all times.*

प्रकृतिविकृतिभिन्नः शुद्धबोधस्वभावः
सदसदिदमशेषं भासयन्निर्विशेषः ।
विलसति परमात्मा जाग्रदादिष्ववस्था -
स्वहमहमिति साक्षात्साक्षिरूपेण बुद्धेः ॥१३५॥

135. Different from *Prakriti* and its modifications is the Supreme Self, of the nature of pure Knowledge. It is Absolute and directly manifests the entire gross and subtle universe as the very essence behind the steady sense-of-egoism. It manifests Itself as the Witness of the intellect, the determining faculty in man.

The Self has been indicated here again as that which is other than *Prakriti* and its modifications. These are constituted of the BMI, PFT, OET. This Supreme Self is of the nature of pure Knowledge.

Consciousness is the illuminator of all that can be said to be 'this, this, this'. All things cognised can be classified as gross and subtle. Gross things are those which can be seen outside--this chair, this room, this money, this sun, this moon, etc. Subtle things are those which are experienced within--subjectively perceived--this perception, this emotion, this thought, etc. Consciousness illumines them all without any exception. But It, Itself, is without any change *(Nirviseshah)*, immutable.

Again, from the stand-point of the ego it can be said that this Consciousness revels in the three states of waking dream and deep-sleep. Meaning, there is no time when, or no place where, Consciousness is not. In the waking and dream states, It illumines the waking and the dream objects, and in the deep-sleep state, It illumines the absence of the entire range of objects known to us in the waking and the dream states.

This Atman, then, revels in all the three states of Consciousness, as the ego, the 'I,I,I'. In the waking state 'I' am conscious of my waking-world, in the dream state, 'I' am conscious of my dream-world, and in the deep-sleep state 'I' am conscious of the absence of everything. So this Consciousness in us, the Paramatman, *expresses at all times in the form of 'I,I,I' but never gets involved in the happenings around. It is the Knowing Principle--the Witness, observing all thoughts and experiences of the mind and the intellect.*

35. Advice for Self-Control. (136)

नियमितमनसामुं त्वं स्वमात्मानमात्म -
न्ययमहमिति साक्षाद्विद्धि बुद्धिप्रसादात् ।
जनिमरणतरंगापारसंसार सिन्धुं
प्रतर भवकृतार्थो ब्रह्मरूपेण संस्थः ॥१३६॥

136. With a regulated mind and a purified intellect, realise your own Self while in this body. Identify yourself with It, and cross the shoreless ocean of *Samsar*, whose waves are births and deaths. Become blessed by getting firmly established in *Brahman* which is your own essence.

In these verses, Sankara the poet and Sankara the philosopher revels together, each outshining the other.

A well-controlled (regulated) mind here indicates a purified mind, i.e. a mind which has withdrawn itself from its involvements with the OET, having accomplished this through worship or meditation *(upasana)*. A pure mind is one made relatively calm by meditation. It is to be remembered here that mind and intellect are the same. (Only in their functions do they differ.) Mental agitations veil the intellect. This veiling is called *Maya, vasana, avidya, Causal-body*, etc. They are all synonymous. Due to *avidya*, the intellect is not able to see the Truth clearly. When Truth is not apprehended, misapprehensions are generated by the unhealthy intellect.

When the mind's agitations *(vikshepa)*, are quietened through *upasana*, the veiling *(Avarana)* of the intellect also lifts and the *buddhi* becomes quiet. As a result of mental quietude, when the intellect becomes bright, it is able to apprehend the Self. The Self is thus apprehended as, 'I am This'. One comes to experience it intimately as the very subjective essence in oneself. He who so long considered himself to be the body, the mind or the intellect, now experiences, 'I am not the body, nor am I the mind, nor the intellect but I am This, the Self, who is the illuminator of all these three equipments and their modifications.' This experience is not through any medium. It is not through the medium of the intellect. It is not a 'mediate-knowledge'. It is apprehended as "immediate-knowledge". For example, nobody needs tell you that you are Mr. So-and-so. You know who you are (Mr./Mrs./Miss...) even when you are in pitch darkness. Thus the Self is realised as an 'immediate-knowledge' as one's own Self.

"Mediate-knowledge" is that which is gained through the instruments of the sense-organs, the mind and the intellect. 'Immediate-knowledge' is that to know for which no instrument is necessary. It is the knowledge of one's own Self.

When you wake up from a dream you do not 'see' the waker, you 'become' the waker. The experience at that time is, 'I am the waker', Mr. So-and-so, and not that fool who was dreaming the horrors of his dreams only a moment ago. Yes,'I am This, not that, which I in my delusion thought myself to be'.

At this moment we all live identified with the BMI, and we have the experience of, 'I am the body, I am the mind, I am the intellect'. Quieten the mind and, transcending its limitations, come to apprehend this great Truth--the Self.

May you feel fulfilled thus. fulfilment *(kritarthah)*, is the joyous feeling of 'having done what was to be done'. When what had to be done has been done, what had to be accomplished has been accomplished, no more is there any tyrant in the form of *vasanas*, who occupies our bosom, making more and more demands upon us. When the *vasanas* are all ended, no more desires are there . Nothing more is needed to contribute to one's happiness. May you thus, become of the nature of *Brahman*, the Reality, by crossing the ocean of change, consisting of the waves of births and deaths. *Buddhi Vritti* in *Vedanta* means, all activities emanating from a living organism.

If we reflect sufficiently upon what we have read so far, one doubt might still linger in us. How does the Infinite Lord, Who is All-knowledge, get into this avidya, *and become an abject slave, a helpless victim of the world of objects and their tragic play? How does one get so strongly BMI-conditioned? This is explained in the following two verses. They are both very very important. Only if you reflect long on these suggestive verses, will you understand them and get the maximum benefit out of them. The more you chew on these verse, the more will you experience the essence of understanding.*

36. What is Bondage--The Reply. (137-142)

अत्रानात्मन्यहमिति मतिर्बंध एषोऽस्य पुसः
प्राप्तोऽज्ञानाज्जननमरणक्लेशसंपातहेतुः ।
येनैवायं वपुरिदमसत्सत्यमित्यात्मबुद्ध्या
पुष्यत्युक्षत्यवति विषयैस्तन्तुभिः कोशकृद्वत् ॥१३७॥

137. Due to his ignorance man identifies the Self with not-Self. This is the bondage of man and brings in its wake, the miseries of birth and death. Through this, he considers his perishable body as real. He identifies himself with it and nourishes, bathes and preserves it with the help of sense-objects. Thereby, he becomes bound like the silk-worm in its cocoon woven by its own threads.

I am what I am, a confused, confounded entity. At one moment I am a sweet little thing, at another, a terrible monster, because of the variety of gratifications of my physical demands of lusts, mental demands for emotional satisfactions and because of my perturbed intellect, tossed by its endless mischievous thoughts. Somehow, I am aware of all this. Yet I cannot get out of it. Why this helpless bondage? All these pernicious sorrows arise because I, the *Atman*, misunderstand myself to be the not-Self *(an-atman)*.

Suppose in a drunken mood you misunderstand yourself to be your own shadow. Terrible suffering must then start for you. You find that you are lying down on the road, and the traffic is incessantly passing over you. Your head is sometimes in the filthy, way-side gutter. You refuse to move because you are being dragged. Thus, all the sufferings of the shadow become your sufferings. A simple misunderstanding that you are your shadow becomes the source of a chain of terrible sufferings.

Similarly, the misunderstanding, "I am the *anatman*", is the spring-board for all bondages and limitations that are suffered in voiceless agony by our personality. To end this misunderstanding would be redeeming at once our personality from the encrustations of matter and its tyranny. One who is released from the tyrannies of matter is God-man on earth--perfect, free, liberated totally from the weaknesses which characterise a mortal.

God, apparently suffering the sorrows of persecuting matter is man.

In the dream when I forget my real nature, I identify with the things projected by me in the dream and suffer the consequences. The sufferings of the dream last only till I wake up. The moment I wake up and realise my real nature, all the sorrows of the dream end. When in a drunken state I forget my real nature, I keep the wrong relationship with the world around me, and consequently, I come to suffer. A mad man, because of some psychological changes in him, forgets himself, and starts behaving wrongly in the world around him. In the same manner I, who am God, the *Paramatman*, the pure Self, not understanding myself, in the non-apprehension of my Real Nature, start creating misapprehensions. Then, identifying myself, with the not-self, which I am not, I come to suffer the pains of existence created by myself for myself.

This identification with the not-Self in each one of us is the cause of our life's sufferings. In a cinema-hall, we identify ourselves with the hero or the heroine on the screen. We feel happy at their happiness and agony at their sorrows.

As a result of this bondage, which is nothing other than our identification with the not-Self, the *Atman*--which is never born nor ever dies, which is ever the same, Eternal, Pure, seems to suffer the pangs of an apparent birth and death. Such a fall to the ever-changing ephemeral state of imperfection is caused by this identification alone.

The 'unreal' is that which was not and that which shall never be, but only apparently exists. This is otherwise called an illusion. The body which was not there before birth and shall not be there after death, but is only temporarily existent, must fall under the category of the 'unreal'. But because of man's spiritual ignorance, and his consequent bondages, this body which is mortal, is considered by him as his real nature.

When this body is not only considered real, but in total identification with it, when a man asserts that the body alone is real, then there can be only one duty in life for him. That duty is to fatten, to nourish, to feed it and to enjoy himself thoroughly. Here we have the true to life picture of what we are.

Think of the tragedy. You must attend to this body constantly, all the twenty-four hours of all the three hundred and sixty-five days of a year, nay, one day more in a leap year. There is no escape. You must be with it all the time, without any holiday. An all-time-servant you become of your own body. You can have a release from your office, home, friends, society,--from everything, but not from this body-catering-mission in life.

Because of this identification you must preserve this body, feed it, clothe it, treat it when ill, and when necessary it must also get a blood transfusion or a heart transplant.

It is not sufficient that we look after and preserve the body, but we must also run after all the objects desired by it--house, car, radio, air-conditioner, television and what not! 'Why am I living so contentedly in this slavery?' 'Because this body is me. My body's happiness is my happiness.'

Once we are under the hallucination that we are worms, we certainly become afraid of all insectivorous birds. This fear will vanish only when we are convinced that we are human beings and not worms. No matter how many times a psychiatrist tells us that we are not worms, it will not help us if we do not realise that we are human beings.

Similarly, however much the Teacher may tell us that we are the *Paramatman*, we may read and study books like the *Vivekachoodamani*, we may attend *satsangs*, and discuss in study-groups, but deep down in ourselves we are convinced that we are this body only. Why? Becasue of the *avidya*, the non-apprehension of our Real, Divine, Spiritual Nature.

The silk-worm spins fine threads from its own saliva and weaves a cocoon around itself. The cocoon becomes stronger and stronger untill at last the worm gets entangled in it and cannot come out. Similarly, once the misunderstanding that, 'I am the body' has arisen, this false notion makes endless demands for the preservation of the body. These demands multiply and they become so strong that the individual gets gagged and bound by them.

Under the circumstances, your personality becomes conditioned by these endless demands and your essential vitalities, capacities, and intelligence fail to bloom and express themselves as they get shackled and conditioned at all times by your past, which you have woven into inescapable patterns around yourself. All this arose from one and the same spring-board--you forgot yourself. You lived all along, misunderstanding yourself to be the matter equipment of BMI, the not-Self (anatman). *In this condition, you come to experience sufferings. This is called bondage* (samsara-dukham).

अतस्मिंस्तद्बुद्धिः प्रभवति विमूढस्य तमसा
विवेकाभावाद्वै स्फुरति भुजगे रज्जुधिषणा ।
ततोऽनर्थव्रातो निपतति समादातुरधिक -
स्ततो योऽसद्ग्राहः स हि भवति बन्धः श्रृणु सखे ॥१३८॥

138. When one is overcome by ignorance one mistakes a thing for what it is not. In the absence of discrimination, the snake is mistaken for a rope, and great danger befalls him who seizes it through this false notion. So listen, my friend, it is mistaking the not-Self for the Self (the unreal for the Real), that creates bondage.

Now *(atah)*, meaning, having forgotten one's real nature, projecting oneself into the not-Self *(anatman)*, considering oneself to be the BMI, tending the body in many different ways, and getting self-bound like a silk-worm in it cocoon---what happens after this is described in this verse.

"In This the idea of That" *(atasmin-tat-buddhi)*.[1] In this body to maintain the feeling that , this is Reality, is --'in This the understanding of That'. Such a wrong idea can come only

1. This is an idiom in *Vedanta*.

to a supremely foolish man. This foolishness is the result of Tamas the non-apprehension of Reality, which overwhelms an individual when the potential discriminative power of his intellect is not available to him under the blinding effect of *Tamas.* Such a thing generally happens in the dream condition. The intellect is slowly overcome by sleep. The hundred per cent discriminative power available during the waking condition, slowly gets clouded, and about ninety percent of it gets veiled by sleep. With ten percent discrimination when I look at my own thoughts, I start living in the dream-world projected by my mind. When I wake up from my dream, the full power of discrimination is available to me, and my dream rolls away. The dream cannot exist in the light of full discrimination.

Much the same thing happens when a respectable man's decency has been swallowed up by half a bottle of whisky or by a couple of LSD pills or by a few puffs of opium. When ninety-five percent of the discrimination hitherto available for him gets clouded by the unconscious in him, then, with the remaining five percent when he moves about he feels 'funny' and starts seeing things which are not there. A stranger, who is walking peacefully on the road, mistakes a lamp-post for his brother, and feels like embracing him. Another man who is standing on the foot-path appears to be a lamp-post, and he feels like leaning on it. Even the gutter looks inviting enough for a nap. If such a drunken fool is given two or three blows on his head, his discrimination suddenly increases and he starts behaving more decently.

Similarly, what we think is one hundred percent discrimination in our waking condition is, in fact, only five percent of the total possibility of discrimination lying dormant in us. If this total potential discriminative power becomes available, meaning, if Tamas has been completely eliminated and the intellect has become pure, then by such Sattwic intellect, one comes to comprehend the Truth all by oneself. To a Sattwic intellect, Truth is self-evident. A foolish man's intellect gets veiled by *Tamas* and he suffers from lack of discrimination. In that tragic condition he comes to understand the *anatman* as the Atman. This misapprehension is explained by Sankara with an illustration.

'In the snake the understanding of a rope'[1]--by a simple twist of the snake-in-the-rope example, the great artist in Sankara has brought home a wealth of understanding necessary to the students of *Vedanta*. If a snake is believed to be an innocent rope when some use is found for the rope, and if a person runs to catch hold of it, imagine the unnecessary agony which the fool is bargaining for! What would be the condition of such a mad one who drags the snake thinking it to be a useful rope!

The *Acharya* indicates that this is precisely what is happening in our lives. The body is misunderstood as the Atman, the Self. That is all. The consequences are--a house, a car, a wife, plenty of money, anxieties of how to procure it, having procured it how to keep it, and having kept it, the responsibility of guarding it day and night, radio, television, air-conditioning, pleasures, parties, entertainments and recreations.... all these can heap unnecessary, meaningless agonies *(anarthavrata)*, upon our heads. The more we identify with the body, the more are our life's botherations. Thus, 'holding on to an unreal thing[2] becomes the essence of all bondage. This is the second definition of bondage. The first definition was in the previous verse where it was declared that considering the *anatman* to be the Self was bondage.[3]

Bondage is nothing other than the identification with the unreal, the perishable, the changeable, the variable, the

---

1. *Bhujagae Rajju Dhishana* --भुजगे रज्जुधिषणा
Note :-This is the opposite of the usual example in Vedanta which is "rope misunderstood as a snake".
2. *Yo asat-grahah sahi bhavati* bandhah--
योऽसद्ग्राहः स हि भवति बन्धः
3. Verse 137, *Anatman -nyaha-miti-matirbandhah*--'
अनात्मन्यहमितिमतिर्बन्धः

mutable---together called the *anatman*, The not-Self. *Adi* Sankara, in this verse, addresses the reader as 'friend'. 'Listen, O friend!' he says. This spirit of *camaraderie* brings the mighty Master to our level. First the Teacher explained what was *anatman*. Then he explained what was *Atman*. Now he is explaining the nature of bondage.

In the unhappy wedlock of Atman and anatman, this ego is created. And in each of us it is this ego which supplies our sense of limitations, the bondages in life.

अखण्डनित्याद्वयबोधशक्त्या
स्फुरन्तमात्मानमनन्तवैभवम् ।
समावृणोत्यावृतिशक्तिरेषा
तमोमयी राहुरिवार्कबिम्बम् ॥१३९॥

139. *Avriti* (the veiling power), is of the nature of *Tamas* (Ignorance). It covers the Self whose glories are infinite, which is Indivisible, Eternal and One-without-a-second just as Rahu covers the sun during a solar eclipse.

In these verses, Sankara revels in the irrepressible surge of his poetry. Though there is not much progress in the flow of ideas, Sankara delights here in his subjective experience of *Brahman*.

This great Self is Immutable, Eternal and One-without-a-second. The glory of the Self is never away from us. It is always present in us, illumining both the inner pulsations of the mind and the outer presence of objects. Even though this Consciousness is always present in us, it is not readily available for our cognition because of the veiling over it created by *Tamas*. How does this great Consciousness come to be covered by Tamas? How can ignorance cover knowledge? Sankara answers this doubt by an illustrative example from nature, just as the sun 'covered' by Rahu during the solar eclipse.[1]

---

1. *Rahu-riva-arka-bimbam*-- राहुरिवार्कबिम्बम् ।

The phenomenon of the solar eclipse is explained with characteristic poetic expression in Hindu mythology. It is said that Rahu, a demon swallows the sun during the eclipse but Rahu is a demon having only a head and no trunk. So when he swallows the sun by the mouth, it emerges out from his neck. Here is science wedded to poetry!

When the moon comes between the sun and the observer (on the earth), the phenomenon is termed as the solar eclipse. In fact, the moon only 'covers' the sun from the vision of the observer. How can the moon really cover the sun? The moon is comparatively smaller than the sun. The moon does not and cannot cover the sun. Since the sun is so far and the moon is nearer, and the observer on the earth is so very much smaller than both, it appears as though the moon has 'covered' the sun. All the same, the moon has obstructed the observer's vision of the sun. From his stand-point, the sun is completely covered. If we could move away even a little from the shadow of the moon we will see that the sun is not covered at all. For those who could rise above the moon there would be no solar eclipse at all. If there were inhabitants on the sun they would not even be conscious of the eclipse.

In Hindu mythology, the moon is the presiding deity of the mind. The sun, the illuminating factor, is equated with the Atman, *the Self. Applying the above example subjectively, as long as there is this mind between me and my Self, the glory of the Self is veiled from me. Mind is the manifestation of* avidya, *the non-apprehension of Reality caused by Tamas. Transcend the mind and there is no pluralistic perception. Realise the Self and all sufferings will end.*

तिरोभूते स्वात्मन्यमलतरतेजोवति पुमा-
ननात्मानं मोहादहमिति शरीरं कलयति ।
ततःकामक्रोधप्रभृतिभिरमुं बन्धनगुणैः
परं विक्षेपाख्या रजस उरुशक्तिर्व्यथयति ॥१४०॥

140. When a man's own Self of purest splendour is hidden from his direct experience, that man, due to ignorance, comes to falsely identify himself with his body which is the not-Self. Then the merciless persecution of *Rajas* (projecting power), binds him down with fetters of lust anger, etc.

When the immaculate divine light of wisdom, the great light of Consciousness is veiled from a man, he comes to consider the body (which is the not-Self), as his real Self. When his power of discrimination gets clouded by the gathering *Tamas* in him, the Self appears to be veiled and he, not knowing his real nature, believes himself to be his own body. (Body, here means, all the three bodies--gross, subtle and causal.) Then the whole gang of negative tendencies--desire, anger, greed, delusion, passion and jealousy, come to bind his personality to his lower ego and as a *samsarin* he lives in pains and agonies.

All the thoughts in the human mind can be classified under the above six categories, and all the six have the quality of binding the individual to the lower, to the baser aspect of his personality. Qualities are called *Gunas*, and in Sanskrit *Guna* also means *'rope'*. 'These *Gunas* (ropes) shackle man', is a statement employing a pleasant pun upon the word *Guna*. When the knowledge of the Self is veiled by *Tamas*, the concept of, 'I am the body', comes first. Then, consequently, the baser agitations arise in the mind and bind the individual. Thereafter he has no freedom at all to live a life of spiritual bliss. There are six types of emotions which arise in the ignorant man: desire *(kama)* anger *(krodha)*, greed *(lobha)*, delusion *(moha)*, passion *(mada)*, and jealousy *(matsarya)*. All these spring from the power of agitations in the mind *(vikshepa)*. When, this power projects the world of likes and dislikes, the individual gets afflicted and suffers the agonies of life in the world. All this suffering is because of *Tamoguna* acting as the veiling and *Rajoguna* acting as the agitations in the mind. *Sattwa*, *Rajas* and *Tamas* are together *Maya*---the *avidya*, the causal-body *(karana-sareera)*, or are indicated as the *vasanas*.

This is the trick by which the mind seduces each individual by its magic of illusions and they sustain their meaningless existence in a world of dire limitations. The way of life by which we can remove them all is spiritual life. Remove them all and know what you are--The Infinite Divine Self. Then come to revel in the world using the vehicle of BMI which has been given to you so that you may play and enjoy the world, and not feel it as a cross to be carried on your shoulders for your own crucifixion.

महामोहग्राहग्रसनगलितात्मावगमनो
धियो नानावस्थां स्वयमभिनयंस्तद्गुणतया ।
अपारे संसारे विषयविषपूरे जलनिधौ
निमज्योन्मथायं भ्रमति कुमतिः कुत्सितगतिः ॥१४१॥

141. An individual who has a perverted intellect, whose knowledge of his Self has been swallowed by the shark of complete ignorance, behaves as though the different states of his intellect were the natures of the Self, and drifts up and down, now rising and now sinking, on the ocean of change, which is full of the poison of sense-pleasures. Indeed, what a calamitous fate!

When an individual's Self-knowledge is swallowed up by the shark of delusion *(Tamas)*, he dances to the tune of his intellect according to the various conditions of its likes and dislikes, just as a drunkard behaves, forgetting that he is a decent, respectable man.

Depending upon the innate individual tendencies *(vasanas)*, various thoughts arise in a man and he is compelled to act according to their dictates. His condition becomes like that of a neglected boat in a stormy ocean. In the ocean of *samsar* which is whipped up by waves of dangerous and poisonous sense enchantments, this neglected boat is tossed about, now rising, now sinking. This ocean of *samsar* is indeed very difficult to cross.

Thus when a man acts in the world outside, his actions accumulate more and more *vasanas* create more and more thoughts. More the thoughts, more is the activity and more are the fresh *vasanas* generated, and entangled in an endless chain of activity, man suffers.

In the study of *Vedanta*, it is not sufficient that a student very seriously reads the text, verse by verse. He must also note the arrangement of ideas, as this in itself has a voiceless content which clears many of his doubts. In this text also, first the qualities of a *Guru* and a disciple were explained. It was dramatised how a perfect Master and a perfect student meet, and when they meet, what were their respective duties.

Then the discrimination between *Atman* and *anatman* was taken up. Next, the *Atman*, the Self was explained, followed by the description of the *anatman*, the not-Self. Here, again Sankara emphasises how the nature of the *Atman* gets veiled from our cognition and how the *Rajas* and *Tamas* qualities condemn an individual.

When so much has been explained, there will still be a vestige of doubt in the minds of the students who have followed the arguments closely. It has been said that in all our sufferings we are not aware of the Reality in us, because It is lying veiled from our vision by avidya. How can this be? How can my ignorance of a thing give me solid, perceptible sorrows? The following verse gives the answer in the form of an example.

भानुप्रभासंजनिताभ्रपङ्क्ति-
र्भानुं तिरोधाय विजृम्भते यथा ।
आत्मोदिताहंकृतिरात्मतत्त्वं
तथा तिरोधाय विजृम्भते स्वयम् ॥१४२॥

142. As the formations of clouds generated by the sun's rays come to veil the very same sun and appear clearly manifest in the sky, so too, the ego arisen from the Self covers the Reality of the Self and expresses itself in full manifestation.

Had there been no sunlight and no sun's heat, there would have been no clouds. The arrays of clouds born out of the sunlight, cover it and vividly manifest themselves. Similarly, the ego, the PFT born out of *Om*, the Reality, says, 'I alone am'. When the Consciousness functions through the equipment of BMI the concept of PFT[1] ---the doer-enjoyer feeling --is born. Thereafter this ego appears and starts saying, 'Where is God? I am the only Truth. What is there besides me?' Out of this psychological phenomenon are born all the sufferings of man.

This is exhaustively explained in the following verse.

37. The Powers: Agitating and Veiling. (143-144)

कवलितदिननाथे दुर्दिन सान्द्रमेघै-
र्व्यथयति हिमझंझावायुरुग्रो यथैतान् ।
अविरततमसात्मन्यावृते मूढबुद्धिं
क्षपयति बहुदुःखैस्तीव्रविक्षेपशक्तिः ॥१४३॥

143. Just as, on a cloudy day, when the sun is swallowed up by dense clouds, cold, shivering blasts persecute man, so too, when the Atman is screened off by utter ignorance, the dreadful projecting power *(Vikshepa-sakti)*, persecutes the foolish man with endless sorrows.

The Lord of the day is the sun *(Dina-nath)*. When it is covered by dense clouds, the day is said to be cloudy. On a sunless wintry day, the terrible ice cold breeze persecutes the living beings on the face of the earth. Those who are not under the shadows of such a miserable cloudy day are happy and are not persecuted. Those who are on the other side of the clouds have no suffering.

Similarly, the fools in whom the knowledge of the Self is veiled by dense *Tamas* (ignorance), come to suffer the endless varieties of persecutions of matter, provided by the dreadful power of agitations *(Vikshepa-sakti)*. But from the point of view of the *Atman* and of those who are Self-realised, the

1. Refer footnote, verse 124.

avidya and *avidya*- created egocentric individuality has no existence at all. When I look as an egocentric, as a PFT, the "ignorance" is very near me. The Self is far away from me. Thus we can say that when the ego looks through *Tamas*, he finds that the *Atman* is not there. He is a fool who lives totally identified with the BMI. He then comes to suffer the imperfections of OET. He is afflicted by the power of agitations. Thereafter, a thousand varieties of sorrows dog his heels wherever he goes.

Just as cold breezes afflict the people when the clouds cover the sun, the power of agitation afflicts the individualised ego when Tamas *covers the* Atman. *It is not only that we do not know the* Atman *but, at the same time, we are afflicted with various kinds of sorrows and agitations equal to shivering in the cold wind.*

एताभ्यामेव शक्तिभ्यां बन्धः पुंसः समागतः ।
याभ्यां विमोहितो देहं मत्वाऽत्मानं भ्रमत्ययम् ॥१४४॥

144. Man's bondage has sprung forth from these two "powers". Deluded by them, he mistakes his body for the Self and wanders from life to life.

Because of these two powers (of veiling and agitations), man has reached his present stage of bondage and has become limited. When an individual allows himself to be confused and beguiled by these two -- *avarna-sakti* and *vikshepa-sakti*, he considers himself to be his body, (gross, subtle and causal bodies). Normally everyone believes himself to be his gross body. An emotional person may consider himself to be an emotional personality. A modern rational man may think of himself as an intellectual. Thus confused they move about, satisfying their physical, emotional and intellectual needs. Each man acts in his peculiar delusion. Thus they move like mad men, from one place to another, from one time to another, from one life to another, from one cradle to one grave, and another cradle to another grave...alas! continuously.

38. Bondage in Action. (145-146)

बीजं संसृतिभूमिजस्य तु तमो देहात्मधीरङ्कुरो
रागः पल्लवमम्बु कर्म तु वपुः स्कन्धोऽसवः शाखिकाः ।
अग्राणीन्द्रियसंहतिश्च विषयाः पुष्पाणि दुःखं फलं
नानाकर्मसमुद्भवं बहुविधं भोक्तात्र जीवः खगः ॥१४५॥

145. Ignorance is the seed for the tree of *samsar.* Body-identification is the sprout, desires are its tender leaves, work is its water, the body is its trunk, the *Pranas* are its branches, the sense-organs are its twigs, the sense-objects are its flowers, different miseries born out of the varieties of actions are the fruits, and the individual *jeeva* is the bird perched upon it.

The picture of the "tree of life" or the "tree of *samsar*" is etched here by Sankara, his philosopher's pen moving with the throbbings of his poetic heart. The "seed" for this "tree of *samsar*" is *Tamas*, which is synonymous with *avidya*, ignorance, *vasanas*, causal-body and "non-apprehension of Reality". If the seed is once roasted in fire, i.e. if the *vasanas* are burnt in the fire of knowledge, there would no more be any tree at all.

The "sprout" is the intellectual conception and strong conviction that this body is the Self, which is of course, the first expression of *avidya.* The first couple of "tender leaves" are the desires. As long as I do not recognise the Self, I consider myself to be the body. When I am the body, I am anxious to preserve it. 'I want this', 'I want that'. Thus all desires start. Desires are expressed in two ways---likes and dislikes (the couple of leaves). The growth of the tree can be arrested even at this level by destroying the sprout, or at least by neglecting to water it.

The "water" is the egocentric activity undertaken to fulfil the desires of the body. At this stage the growth of the tree can be prevented by stopping the supply of water. In case it is not possible to stop the watering, the addition of two drops of nitric acid will do the trick. If in the activities of the ego, two drops of spirit of dedication are added, the tree will soon be destroyed. Therefore, dedicated activity *(Nishkama-karma)*, is advocated here, which will ultimately destroy the *vasanas*, the very seeds.

The "trunk" is the body. If activity is undertaken motivated by desires, the tree grows stronger and becomes the trunk, which is the gross body in each one of us. The "branches" are the *Pranas*. The *Pranas* are five in number ---*Prana, Apana, Samana, Vyana, Udana*. As the five main branches of life's activities, these maintain the body and its functions, just as the branches maintain the trunk of the tree.

The "twigs" are the sense-organs. They depend upon the *Pranas*. If the branches are removed, the twigs cannot remain. When the *Pranas* depart, the sense-organs can no longer function. The sense-organs are of two types---the organs of perception and the organs of aciton. They are so named becaused of their special functions of reception of stimuli and responses in the world outside.

The "flowers" are the sense-objects. They always have the tendency to attract. Each sence-organ has its sense-objects, just as each twig has its flowers. All sense-objects can be classfied under forms and colours, smells, sounds, tastes and touches. The classification depends upon the organs of perception, just as the flowers depend upon the twigs.

The "fruits" are the sorrows created by the endless varieties of actions performed in different modes by the egocentric mind. When an individual is attracted by any sense-object (the information about its enchanting existence is brought by the organ of perception). He, desires first to possess it and then hungers to enjoy it. Here he acts with his organ of action and actions must produce reactions. These are called "fruits of actions" born out of the flowers of sense-objects. The actions are of various kinds depending upon the mode in which they are performed, the triple modes being *Sattwa, Rajas* and *Tamas*. The fruits thus created are always sorrowful, because from the stand point of the Absolute, the state of everlasting happiness, the little ephemeral and short-lived happiness gained through the sense-objects in this welter of change *(samsar)*, is really sorrowful. Also,the fruits always contain seeds. Thus, the fruits of actions are replete with *vasanas*--- the seeds for continuing *samsar*.

The "enjoyer of the fruits" is the individual who moves about, flitting about from one branch to another, like a bird. A fruit-bearing tree is never fulfilled unless there are the enjoyers of the fruits. The *jeeva*, the individuality, is compared to the bird, because it sits on the tree, enjoys its fruits and also, takes shelter in its shade. The moment it finds that the tree is no more useful to its purpose, it flies away and finds yet another tree. Similarly, the individuality in each one of us flies from body to body, from time to time, when each previous body has become useless for the great purpose of its evolution.

The ego is the bird which enjoys the fruits of action born out of different activities performed under the different urges. The fruits are born out of the flowers, the sense-objects. The flowers are born out of the twigs, the sense-organs. The twigs belong to the branches, the Pranas, *the physiological functions. These in turn take place in the trunk, the body. The body has grown because it has been steadily watered by karma. In the beginning, there were only two tender leaves, the desires and attachments. These came from the sprout, from the idea, "I am the body". All this came from the seed of ignorance, the "non-apprehension of Reality" caused by* Tamas.

अज्ञानमूलोऽयनात्मबन्धो
नैसर्गिकोऽनादिरनन्त ईरितः ।
जन्माप्ययव्याधिजरादिदुःख-
प्रवाहपातं जनयत्यमुष्य ॥१४६॥

146. This bondage caused by the not-Self springs from ignorance and is self-caused. It is described as without beginning and without end. It subjects one to the endless flood of miseries---birth, death, disease and senility.

How sorrow is the result of the misconception that the not-Self *(anatman)* is the Self *(Atman)*, is explained in this verse. Non-apprehension of the post creates the illusion that there is a ghost. Non-apprehension of Reality alone creates the mis-apprehension that 'I am this body'.

How and where did this misunderstanding of the *anatman* to be *Atman* arise? When did the Absolute become the relative? Such questions in terms of time and space often arise in our minds.

Ignorance is said to be self-caused. It is not caused by any other cause. It is the nature of the cave to have darkness. Darkness in the cave is created by the cave. If the cave was not there, there would be no darkness. Similarly, when the Self is not known, there is darkness in the bosom. In terms of the intellect all that can be said is that this *avidya* is without beginning and without end, meaning, it is essentially beyond 'time'. As long as there is the concept of time, the *samsar* experiences will be there, because time is the medium in which *samsar* is perceived. The moment time is transcended, *samsar* also must end. 'Beginning' and 'end' are meaningful only in the medium of time.

The sorrows of *samsar* arising out of this identification with the *anatman,* unavoidably manifest as the agonies of birth, the pains of growth, the discomforts of decay, the fears of old age, the pangs of disease and the tragedies of death. The cause for all these is ignorance and the consequent identification with the not-Self.

If all the sorrows are to be removed, the cause for them has to be removed. Ignorance can be removed only by the first-hand experience of the Infinite Reality.

39. Atman and Anatman---Discrimination.

(147-153)

नास्त्रैर्न शस्त्रैरनिलेन वह्निना
छेत्तुं न शक्यो न च कर्मकोटिभिः ।
विवेकविज्ञानमहासिना विना
धातुः प्रसादेन सितेन मञ्जुना ॥१४७॥

147. Neither by weapons, nor by wind, nor by fire, nor by millions of actions can this bondage be destroyed. By nothing save the wonder-sword of Knowledge which comes from discrimination and is sharpened by the purification of the mind and the intellect, can we end this bondage.

All the sorrows of *samsar* arise out of the confusion between the *Atman* and the *anatman*, the Self and the not-Self. In order to end these sorrows, this confusion has to be ended This confusion is called bondage. How can one cut this bondage? How can one destroy and end it?

Weapons of destruction are two types, (1) when it (the weapon) leaves the hand of the wielder, then whether it strikes the target or not, it never comes back, (2) when it leaves the hand of the wielder, it strikes the target and returns, just like the guided missiles of today. The former type of weapon is called the *astra* and the latter is known as the *shastra*. These are the two types of weapons of destruction known to mankind, with which the whole world can be destroyed. But the confusion of the *Atman* with the *anatman*--- the idea that 'I am the body', cannot be destroyed by either of these types of weapons.

Wind and fire are nature's powers of annihilation. Wind dries up things and destroys them. Fire destroys them by burning them. The conviction that 'I am the body', this ignorance, can neither be dried up nor can it be burnt down.

Habits, or even some of the imbecilities can be changed by acting contrary to them. Activity is another instrument with which human beings can put an end to habits, tendencies, urges, etc. but *Avidya* cannot be ended by even millions of activities, because *avidya* is the very cause for all activities.

Thus, this *avidya* cannot be ended by any known scientific instrument of annihilation, nor by any of nature's rupturing reactions resulting in destruction, nor by millions of activities, noble or ignoble. This is precisely the despair of existentialism. The way out is given in the last two lines of this verse.

Mere erudition will never be sufficient. At best it can puncture ignorance---but it cannot cut it down. So this non-apprehension can be ended only by the sword of discrimination, which results in the first-hand experience of the pure Self. This sword has to be sharpened by the cleansing of the inner instruments---the mind and the intellect. *'Dhatu Prasada'*, the term as used here means, 'purification of the inner instrument'. This purification can be done by reducing the *vasanas* for when *vasanas* are reduced, agitations of the mind are reduced. Quieter the mind, the greater is the contemplative power in man. And a developed power of contemplation makes his discrimination sharper.

With this sharpened sword alone can the confusion between the Self and the not-Self be finally removed.

श्रुतिप्रमाणैकमतेः स्वधर्म-
निष्ठा तयैवात्मविशुद्धिरस्य ।
विशुद्धबुद्धेः परमात्मवेदनं
तेनैव संसारसमूलनाशः ॥१४८॥

148. He who has deep devotion to the *Srutis* and who is established in his *Swadharma*-- for these alone contribute to the purity of his mind---and is of pure mind realises the supreme Self. By this knowledge alone is *samsar* destroyed, root and branch.

The man whose intellect is soaked in the knowledge of the Upanishads, whose mind has become single-pointedly devoted to the truths declared in the scriptures *(Srutis)*, that man alone is really able to walk steadily the narrow path of *Swadharma. Swadharma* is, 'the nature *(Dharma)*, of one's own Self *(Swa)*'. He who has knowledge of the Self alone will be able to live the nature of the Self. Else, again and again he will slip into the natural idea, 'I am the body'. When one lives selflessly for a long period of time according to the dictates of *Swadharma*, one's mind and intellect become purer and purer, meaning, calmer and quieter.

When one works in the world dedicatedly, without the ego and the egocentric desires, the existing *vasanas* get exhausted, and no new *vasanas* are created. When there are no *vasanas*, there can be no agitations in the mind. The mind becomes calm and quiet. A calm mind is a pure mind. In the pure mind alone is the experience of the supreme Self possible. An agitated mind cannot apprehend Reality.

Knowledge of the *Srutis* gained through sincere, daily reading and continuous reflection upon them, facilitates selfless and dedicated activitiy, which helps one to quieten the mind. Then, as an irresistible sequence, the experience of the Reality floods the seeker's heart. It is always understood that the experience of Reality is not the result of *sadhana. Sadhana* only purifies the mind and in a pure mind, recognition of the Reality is unavoidable. The ego *disappears into* the Vision Divine.

"Vedana" means right understanding. With a purified intellect alone can one understand the words of the scriptures and the instruction of the *Guru.* Otherwise it will be merely some dry, unproductive book-knowledge. Such knowledge is like writing the word 'sugar' in more than one language on a piece of paper and licking it for gaining the experience of its sweetness.

Thus, if a person has gained an intuitive glimpse of the Reality even for a brief moment, samsar--- *the perception and* persecutions of the ever-changing phenomenal world---is destroyed, root and branch. The root is the non-apprehension of Reality (Avidya). "Ending samsar *along with its root" means, when Truth is apprehended, non-apprehension of Reality vanishes, and the consequent misapprehensions depart from the bosom of a man of true God-realisation.*

कोशैरन्नमयाद्यैः पञ्चभिरात्मा न संवृतो भाति ।
निजशक्तिसमुत्पन्नैः शैवालपटलैरिवाम्बु वापीस्थम् ॥१४९॥

149. Covered by the five sheaths, such as the food-sheath, which are produced by Its own Divine Power, the Self ceases to appear, just as the water in a tank ceases to appear due to the collection of moss, which is born out of itself (Water).

The change in the metre of poetry is generally adopted to shake up the student or the reader to full wakefulness, and to make him understand that the thought which was being discussed so far has ended. This stanza is a typical example.

The *Atman* is covered by the five sheaths and so, at the moment, It is not readily available for our direct cognition. The five sheaths are---the food-sheath, the vital-air-sheath, the mental-sheath, the intellectual-sheath and the bliss-sheath. They apparently cover the *Atman* from direct vision and are born out of the *Atman's* own Power Divine called *Maya.* By Its own power of projection the Self has created these five sheaths and by identifying with them It seems to get covered by them.

There is a kind of moss which grows in still waters. It is a green, granulated plant which covers the surface of the pond water, so completely, that the water can no longer be seen. A completely green surface alone is visible at all times, and from a distance it may look like a lawn . When the moss covers the water, the beauty of the shining sun is no longer reflected in it. If the moss is pushed aside, it will (move away to) reveal the brilliant reflection of the sun but as soon as the hand is removed from the water, the moss returns to cover the reflective surface of the water.

The *vasana - created* agitations and the perceptions of the pluralistic phenomenal world are like the moss in our minds. Because of them the mind is not clear, is not pure enough to reflect the divinity behind it. To remove this moss is to remove the ego is the egocentric desires while acting in the world. The mind which is running towards the OET should be turned in contemplation towards the Reality. When this 'moss' is even slightly removed from the mind, Consciousness, which is always present, gets reflected in the clear waters of the mind's divine thoughts. Children may run and slip into the lawn-like moss-expanse and suffocate and die in it. But an intelligent man who knows that it is only moss covering the waters will not walk into it.

When the moss is pushed aside by the hand, immediately the water manifests itself. But if one removes the hand and sits back even for a moment, thinking that all has been achieved, the moss, the *Maya*, returns and covers the Self again by blanketing the reflective surface of the mind.

The best way to remove the moss is to make the water overflow the tank. Let in more water to flood and flush out the tank. Study, reflection and contemplation will bring new streams of spiritual thought into the mind. When they overflow the mind in devotion and service, what overflows first will be this 'moss' which obstructs the vision of the Self.

तच्छैवालापनये सम्यक् सलिलं प्रतीयते शुद्धम् ।
तृष्णासन्तापहरं सद्यः सौख्यप्रदं परं पुंसः ॥१५०॥

150. when the moss is removed, absolutely pure water, which can quench the pangs of thirst and give immediate joy, becomes visible.

When the moss is removed, pure and clear water can be seen. This moss has the properties of fixing and absorbing all the impurities in the water. Wherever it is present, the water beneath it is supposed to be extremely pure and clean. The sorrow arising from thirst can immediately be removed by this pure water. The thirst can be quenched.

'Thirst' *(Trishna)*, is a word traditionally used in a spiritual lore for 'sense-indulgences'. Indulgence in sense-objects is the cause for all the troubles of the world. Apprehension of Reality ends all the troubles of *samsar*, and the thirst for sense-objects is quenched only when Truth is apprehended.

One cannot quench one's thirst by eating the moss. Drinking water alone can quench thirst. Identification with the sheaths will never give anyone lasting happiness. Realisation of one's true nature alone will give eternal Bliss. The moss is not water, though it is born out of water. The five sheaths (Panchakosa) *are not the Self, though they are born out of the* Atman

पञ्चानामपि कोशानामपवादे विभात्ययं शुद्धः ।
नित्यानन्दैकरसः प्रत्यग्रूपः परः स्वयंज्योतिः ॥१५१॥

151. When all five sheaths have been negated, the Self is apprehended as being the essence of everlasting Bliss, as the indwelling, Self-effulgent Spirit Supreme.

The five *kosas* have apparently arisen from the *Atman*. They have their individual properties and accordingly, their definite sets of experiences. However, their tragedies and comedies do not belong to the *Atman*, the Consciousness.

When I, the conscious entity, withdraws from them all, the Subject illumines Itself, since Consciousness is Self-effulgent. This Consciousness is eternal *(Nitya)*. "Eternal" is that which is not conditioned by the past, present and future. Reality is eternal Bliss *(Nitya-ananda)*--- a bliss that is not conditioned by time. "Time" is a concept of the mind and hence this bliss is an experience transcending the mind. Also, It is of one essence *(Eka-rasah)*, changeless, uncontaminated and eternal.

This Atman is realised subjectively, deep within the heart, and not objectively as something existing somewhere outside. When the dreamer becomes the waker the dreamer ends. Similarly, when I come to apprehend the Paramatman, *I realise how baseless and stupid it was that I had considered myself to be this little* jeevatman.

आत्मानात्मविवेकः कर्तव्यो बन्धमुक्तये विदुषा ।
तेनैवानन्दी भवति स्वं विज्ञाय संचिदानन्दम् ॥१५२॥

152. The wise man should discriminate between the Self and the not-Self, in order to remove the bondage. Only then does he know his own Self to be Absolute Existence-Knowledge-Bliss, only then, does he become happy.

Those who walk this path of *jnana*, have always to distinguish between the *Atman* and the *anatman*. An intelligent person, who is learned in the scriptures should, in order to liberate himself from bondge, constantly discriminate between the Real and the unreal, the Self and the not-Self.

One part of his personality should continuously analyse every experience to find out which part of his personality-layer is springs from. Having ascertained clearly that such and such an experience belongs to the body (or the mind or the intellect), he should direct his attention upon the Self and feel that the experience belongs to the equipment, not to the Self which is his Real Nature.

By this process of discrimination and assertion alone can he release himself from the sorrows of bondage and keep his rendezvous *with this Self and dock himself in everlasting happiness. Thereafter, there is no strife, no stress and no strain for him. By realising that the Self---Existence-Knowledge-Bliss-Absolute---is his Real Nature, he transcends his body-mind-intellect equipment.*

मुञ्जादिषीकामिव दृश्यवर्गा-
त्प्रत्यञ्चमात्मानमसङ्गमक्रियम् ।
विविच्य तत्र प्रविलाप्य सर्वं
तदात्मना तिष्ठति यः स मुक्तः ॥१५३॥

153. He who separates all sense-objects, perceived, felt and thought of, from the subjective, unattached, actionless Self---like the enveloping sheaths separated from the core of the *Munja* grass---he is free, for having merged everything with It, he remains ever identified with It.

Munja is a type of grass which is nothing more than a stock of leaves held together, like the common plantain tree. These sheaths can be removed one by one until the central core is reached. Similarly, the *Atman* which is actionless and unattached can be "taken out" of the enveloping sheaths, but one must be very careful because the inner core is very tender and delicate. All that can be classified as "seen"---which is perceived, felt and thought of---is other than the "subject", covering the *Atman*, which is like the core in the *Munja* grass. The BMI and OET are the objects perceived which veil the Self. Just as the soft, tender core of the *Munja* grass can be reached and revealed by removing sheath after sheath, so too, all the covering of the Self can be "removed" and the *Atman*, which is unattached and actionless can be reached. This *Atman*, which is always inside, revelling as the subject in every bosom *(Pratyak)*, is not available for our cognition now because we remain, ever looking through the coverings of the BMI. When this Consciousness, the Actionless, the state of Objectless Awareness is realised, the entire perceptible, phenomenal world merges into It, just as on waking up, the dreamer and his dream-world merge into the waker. He who thus reaches the Self and merges with It, is a "liberated one". He has no more coming and going into this world of perceptions, feelings and thoughts as a doer-enjoyer ego.

This verse provides us with the definition of a liberated man, a man of God-realisation.

In the following verses the Acharya addresses the seekers directly. The five sheaths (Pancha-kosa), *are taken up one by one and each one is described fully. The universal teacher, Sankara, shows how they can be trascended one by one, and how one can ultimately reach the experience of the subjective Self.*

40. Negation of the Five Kosas.

(a) Annamaya-kosa (Food-sheath). (154-164)

(अ) अन्नमयकोशः

देहोऽयमन्नभवनोऽन्नमयस्तु कोश-
श्चान्नेन जीवति विनश्यति तद्विहीनः ।
त्वक्चर्ममांसरुधिरास्थिपुरीषराशि-
र्नायं स्वयं भवितुमर्हति नित्यशुद्धः ॥१५४॥

154. The body is a product of food. It constitutes the food-sheath. It exists because of food and dies without it. It is a bundle of skin, flesh, blood, bones and filth. Never can it be the Self-existing, the eternally pure *Atman*.

From this verse onwards there is deep reflection on each of the five sheaths of the human personality. One by one they are taken up, exhaustively investigated, reflected upon, and as a result of this deep and unbiased reflection each one is in turn negated. These ten verses[1] discuss the physical body, the food-sheath.

The physical body is the most powerful attraction for the majority of living beings, and most of us are aware of nothing nobler and diviner than the body. For millions and millions of years man has been living in this world mainly as a physical entity. Life after life he has been living and striving under the self-preserving instinct, and to say all of a sudden, "I am not the physical body", is ridiculous, impossible and supremely absurd.

Proper light has been thrown upon the assertions in these verses by the well-known technique of scientific observation and analysis. The constituent parts of the body, their behaviour, how the body gathers its knowledge of the world outside, its relationship with the possessor of the body and with the world around---when all these are analysed and carefully investigated into, we shall readily come to know that we are in fact not the body. With this subjective knowledge

1. From verse 154-163.

alone is it possible for us to learn to withdraw from the body-identifications. The arguments are convincingly marshalled here. To remember these arguments is to help ourselves in our daily independent reflections.

In this verse, the body is brought under the focus of our close observation. This body was born out of the seed in the loins of its father. The seed is formed by the food assimilated by the father. When the seed was in the mother's womb, it was being maintained by the food taken by the mother. After birth it grew because of the food taken and assimilated by it day after day. When it perishes it shall become food for other living creatures like birds, insects and plants. Hence, that which is born out of food, exist in food and goes back to be food for others is appropriately called the food-sheath *(Annamaya-kosa)*.

This body when carefully analysed is found to be constituted of skin, flesh, blood, and marrow. The container made up of the above parts is filled with faecal matter. All these together constitute this fascinating, this enchanting, "my body".

Therfore this filthy, unholy body cannot be the ever-pure and resplendent Atman because the parts that constitute it are finite.

पूर्वं जनेरधिमृतेरपि नायमस्ति
जातक्षणः क्षणगुणोऽनियतस्वभावः ।
नैको जडश्च घटवत्परिदृश्यमानः
स्वात्मा कथं भवति भावविकारवेत्ता ॥१५५॥

155. Before its birth it does not exist, nor does it continue to be after its death. It lasts only for a short period. Its qualities are fleeting and by nature subject to change. It is diversified and inert and like a jar, is a sense-object. How then can it be the Self---the Witness of all changes in all things?

This body came into existence with the birth of the individual. After death it shall perish and decay. Its existence

is only for a short time, from its birth to its death--at the most a span of eighty to a hundred years. From the concept of infinite time, eighty or a hundred years are most insignificant. Indeed, this body is very short-lived.

Psychologists have discovered that no dream can last for more than one-and-a-half minutes. Within this short time-span we dream, sometimes, the experience of many years. From the concept of the waking time, the dream-time is very short. from the vision of infinite time, our life-span too, is very small. The concept of time itself is relative.

During this short period of time while the being resides in the body, the nature of the body changes from moment to moment. Now it is happy, now unhappy, now *Sattwic*, now *Rajasic*, a good man becomes bad and a bad man good. All the time, the *Gunas* are changing. These changes--physical, emotional and intellectual--cannot be stopped; their expressions continuously manifest through the body.

As long as the body is carefully looked after, it lives. If we neglect it, even then it lives. Now it is up to each one to decide whether looking after it is necessary or not. It lives because of its destiny *(Prarabdha)*. The nature of this body is most uncertain and unsteady. It can never be predicted with exactitude. Also, there is not just one body. Each one has his own body, different from all others. How then can this be the *Atman*, which is One-without-a-second?

The body by itself is inert. It is not conscious. My clothes move where I move--but they have no independent movement. When the individuality presiding over the body's activities departs, it perishes. Like a pot or a jar, it is an object of perception. It has no knowledge or consciousness of its own. It is not the perceiver. But as an object of perception, it is the perceived. It merely helps Consciousness to be conscious of the world of objects, through it. It is only an instrument for Consciousness to function through. Just as a telescope by itself cannot see distant objects, but as intelligent observer alone can see them *through* the telescope, similarly, Consciousness functions *through* the body.

How then can this inert body be the Consciousness, which is the knower of all thoughts and thought-modifications? In this verse we have arguments to indicate that the body cannot be the Self, for indeed, it is nothing but a cancerous growth on the Paramatman.

पाणिपादादिमान्देहो नात्मा व्यङ्गेऽपि जीवनात् ।
तत्तच्छक्तेरनाशाच्च न नियम्यो नियामकः ॥१५६॥

156. The body which is made of arms, legs, etc. cannot be the *Atman*, for even if these organs are amputated or removed, it contiunes to function efficiently. It is thus subject to the rule of another and cannot be the *Atman*, the Ruler of all.

This body is constituted of limbs such as the hands the feet. Even if the limbs are amputated, the body continues to live. The life is not hands and legs. The functions of the limbs are specific. Normally one limb cannot perform the function of another. Eating food with the legs, or moving about on the hands is not possible. But the Self it Omnipotent. This body is regulated and controlled by the subtler personalities of man. That which is controlled by other cannot be the *Atman*, the controller of everything.

Here then, are more arugments to reflect upon, to realise that "I cannot be this body".

देहतद्धर्मतत्कर्मतदवस्थादिसाक्षिणः ।
सत एव स्वतःसिद्धं तद्वैलक्षण्यमात्मनः ॥१५७॥

157. It is self-evident that the *Atman* is the enduring Reality, that It is different from the body and its characteristics, its states and activities, that It is a Witness of them all.

The Atman *is the Witness of the body, its nature, its activities, its states etc. That which is the witness of a thing cannot itself be the thing observed. The seer is always something other than the seen. Therefore it becomes clear that the* Atman *is soemthing other than the body, and that the body is NOT the Self--this is yet another argument to prove it.*

शल्यराशिर्मांसलिप्तो मलपूर्णोऽतिकश्मलः ।
कथं भवेदयं वेत्ता स्वयमेतद्विलक्षणः ॥१५८॥

158. How can the Self-existent *Atman*, the Knower, ever be the body which is a packet of bones, covered with flesh, full of filth and extremely impure?--for It is always distinct from it.

This framework of bones, plastered with flesh and filled with faecal matter is at all times most impure and inauspicious. The container and the contained are both filthy. How can this be the ever-pure, All-knowing principle, the *Atman*?

Here is one more argument clearly showing that the filthy body cannot be the pure and divinely holy Self.

त्वङ्मांसमेदोऽस्थिपुरीषराशा-
वहंमतिं मूढजनः करोति ।
विलक्षणं वेत्ति विचारशीलो
निजस्वरूपं परमार्थभूतम् ॥१५९॥

159. The foolish man identifies himself with this skin, flesh, fat, bones and filth. But the man of discrimination knows that his Self is distinct from the body, unique, and the only Reality.

Fools consider themselves to be this packet of filth, consisting of skin, flesh, fat and bones. These are, in themselves, nothing but filth, each one of them. Those who have the habit of correct analysis and right thinking, consider themselves certainly something other than this filthy body, filled with its contents which are equally filthy.

Correct analysis and right thinking will point to us man's Real Nature which is supreme Truth, Pure Consciousness Itself.

It is not the body, as Its nature is distinctly different (Vilakshana), *from the body and its component parts.*

देहोऽहमित्येव जडस्य बुद्धि-
र्देहे च जीवे विदुषस्त्वहंधीः ।
विवेकविज्ञानवतो महात्मनो
ब्रह्माहमित्येव मतिः सदात्मनि ॥१६०॥

160. "I am the body", thus thinks a foolish man. A man of mere book-knowledge considers himself to be a combination of the body and the *jeeva*. *But the realised sage, because of his discrimination, knows that "I am Brahman"*, and looks upon the Eternal *Atman* as his Self.

Fools, who have no discriminative power consider themselves to be the body. They think, "I am the body". Erudite scholars, who read many books, conclude that in addition to the body they have a psychological and intellectual entity in them. But those great souls who have the discriminative power between the Self and the not-Self, they, in their direct experience of Truth, realise themselves to be *Brahman*. Just as a spoon is needed only for eating and need not afterwards be carried about everywhere, similarly, the wise know that the body is necessary only to spoon out their experiences, and subsequently, serves no purpose whatsoever.

This verse explains the three schools of philosophy prevailing in India. The three great Masters--Madhwa, Ramanuja and Sankara--studied the same Upanishads, experienced and explained the same Truth; but while expounding It, they propounded three different schools of philosophy. They are-dualism *(Dwaita)*, qualified non-dualism *(Visishta-adwaita)*, and non-dualism *(Adwaita)*.

These three schools do not differ from each other, except in explaining the relationship of man with God. In everything else they are the same. They all consider that the life of the flesh is not the goal of life. All of them assert that there is a great Reality to be experienced and consider that the life of the flesh is full of *samsaric* sorrows. They hold that the experience of the Reality is the acme of evolution, the state of complete fulfilment. They all accept and base their arguments upon the declarations of the Upanishads, the Brahma Sutras and the Bhagawad Geeta.

Therefore the difference in their explanations should be considered as having been due to the difference in the types of students they addressed during their respective times. Some students, in their total identification with the body consider themselves to be the body. Such students can have but one relationship with the Supreme--that they are entirely different from It. Accordingly, they have been told that they are entirely different from God. Such students are addressed by Acharya Madhwa, and his school of thought is known as *Dwaita* or "Dualism".

The second type of students, slightly more intellectual, insist, "I am a composite being, comprising an anatomical structure with physiological functions and also a psychological entity with intellectual abilities. I am the body as well as the *jeeva*, the individuality, the thinking-feeling entity". The psychological and intellectual entity has the glow of reflected divinity, just as in the achievements of an artist or a scientist, there is certainly a spark of divinity. Such students are addressed by Sri Ramanujacharya. He says, "You are not separate from Truth. You are a part and He is the whole." This school of thought is *Visishta-adwaita* or "Qualified Non-dualism".

The third variety of students, however, are the intellectual giants, who, through *sadhana*, develop a subtle intellect and discriminate between the Real and the unreal. They have the capacity to live up to their convictions by fully accepting what is Real, ever rejecting what is unreal. As a result of their dispassionate discrimination, they consider themselves to be entirely different from their matter-vestures and realise their identity with the Supreme, the *Brahman*. Such students are addressed by Sri Sankara, for he says, "Thou art nothing but *Brahman.*" this school of philosophy is known as *Adwaita* or "Non-dualism".

All three points of view are explained in this verse, now under discussion.

अत्रात्मबुद्धिं त्यज मूढबुद्धे
त्वङ्मांसमेदोऽस्थिपुरीषराशौ ।
सर्वात्मनि ब्रह्मणि निर्विकल्पे
कुरुष्व शान्तिं परमां भजस्व ॥१६१॥

161. Cease to identify yourself with this packet of skin, flesh, fat, bones and filth, O foolish one. Instead, identify yourself with the Absolute *Brahman*, the Self of all, and gain the experience of Supreme Peace.

In this verse, *Acharya* Sankara is advising the students to give up their false and painful identifications with the *anatman.* What is to be renounced is only the idea, "I am the body". Renounce not the house, nor the wife nor the children. Money, position status in society etc. need not be given up. But only the idea, "I am the body", is to be totally renounced. Those who consider themselves to be the body, whose constituents are the skin, flesh, fat, bones and filth are addressed as "fools" by the *Acharya.*

Giving up the the identification with this packet of filth, (Atmabuddhi) the sense of I-ness should be redirected into the right channel--towards the unchanging, eternal self everywhere, the Brahman. Thus, fixing the identification in Brahman, which is the Atman, the Self, come to experience and enjoy Supreme Peace. There is no peace as long as we identify with the body, which is the cause for all our sorrows.

देहेन्द्रियादावसति भ्रमोदिता
विद्वानहंतां न जहाति यावत् ।

तावन्न तस्यास्ति विमुक्तिवार्ता-
प्यस्त्वेष वेदान्तनयान्तदर्शी ॥१६२॥

162. There is no liberation for a man of mere book-knowledge, even if he be very well-read in the philosophy of Vedanta, so long as he does not give up his false identification with the body, sense-organs, etc., which are unreal.

Avidya, or spiritual ignorance, is the cause for one's delusory identification with the matter vestures and the effect of this identifications is bodage. Unless the cause is removed, the effect cannot be removed.

To see a thing as something other than what it actually is, called delusion *(bhrama)*. From the stand-point of *Brahman*, the body and the sense-organs do not exist at all. It is possible to gather from the study of *Vedanta* that there is an *Atman*, which is the Absolute and Ultimate Reality, which is something other than the body, the sense-organs etc. But it is not possible to have the experience of Truth unless one completely, subjectively, ends the identification with the body. Here, neither can there be any help from the sacred scriptures, nor from the Teacher.

At this point, it is to be carefully noted that what is to be given up is the "identification with the body", and not the body itself. As long as this identification remains, there will not only be no experience of the Supreme, but there cannot even be a talk of liberation. One will be nowhere near the Self if this body-identification persists.

छायाशरीरेप्रतिबिम्बगात्रे
यत्स्वप्नदेहे हृदि कल्पिताङ्गे ।
यथात्मबुद्धिस्तव नास्ति काचि-
ज्जीवच्छरीरे च तथैव माऽस्तु ॥१६३॥

163. Just as you would not identify yourself with your shadow, your reflection, your dream-body or the body in your heart's imagination, so too, you should not identify yourself with your living body.

Giving up identification with your body does not mean neglecting it. If it is neglected and not kept clean and healthy, it becomes a problem for you and for the people around you. You will ask, "Then in what way should I keep my body without identifying with it? What should be my relationship with it?"

What is your relationship with your shadow? How much do you identify with your reflected image? How do you keep up your dream-body and look after it? Such should be your relationship with your living body too.

In the shadow-body, the reflected-body, the dream-body and the imagined-body, you do not have the idea, "I am this". While working in the world with this body, let there always be an idea in your mind that, "This body is only an instrument of mine, with which I contact the world outside in order to serve it as much as I can. But I am always something other than the body."

The body should be kept and looked after *only* as an instrument, a vehicle. Always keep it as best as it can be kept. Take out of it as much work as it possible, so that the *vasanas* may get exhausted for if it falls away in death prematurely, without exhausting, the *vasanas*, another body will have to be taken; but do not get attached to it. Free as you are, be free, and use the instrument efficiently, continuosly.

In the last line, with the peculiar usage of the negative maa *("ought not to"), instead of the usual negative* naa *(don't), Sankara implies more of a humble request than a categorical warning. He means, it would be good for the* sadhak *if he were to maintain this mental attitude towards his physical body. This is a classical usage of negation often used in our* sastras.[1] *It has not the force of the imperative; it is a suggestion.*

---

1. मा. शुचः "ought not to worry"--Geeta XVIII-66.

देहात्मधीरेव नृणामसद्धियां
जन्मादिदुःखप्रभवस्य बीजम् ।
यतस्ततस्त्वं जहि तां प्रयत्ना-
त्त्यक्ते तु चित्ते न पुनर्भवाशा ॥१६४॥

164. For those who are attached to the unreal, identification with the body is the seed from which the misery of birth etc. stems forth. Therefore, put in all your efforts to destroy it. There can be no chance of rebirth if this identification caused by the mind is renounced.

This verse concludes the reflection upon the body.[1] The body, like all other objects in the world outside, must undergo the five-fold change--birth, growth, disease, decay and death. Every change has inherent pain and consequent sorrows in it. When identified with the body, one has to undergo all the sorrows which arise from it and its unavoidable modifications. therefore the cause for these sorrows is the identification with the body. The idea that "I am the body", is the seed from which all these sorrows stem forth.

So the only way to get rid of these sorrows is to renounce this devastating identification. Each one of us has been living with this identification for ages, all through our many past lives. Any amount of study and logical arguments will not help us to stop this idetification. At times, no doubt, we may feel that we are not the body, but the very next moment, alas, we fall back into this natural delusion.

Acharya Sankara advises us to give up this identification through effort, practice and exercise of the will *(prayatnat)*. Time and again, we are required to study and reflect, to feel and think, to comtemplate and meditate, that we are not the body and that we are the supreme Reality. When this study and contemplation has taken deep roots in our understanding*(Chitta)*, and when glimpses of Reality are perceived, then there is no more any "becoming". "Becoming"

2. This discussion started with verse 154.

means, getting subject to change. These five-fold changes will not affect the individual who has disengaged himself from the sense of being the body, and has identified himself with the nature of the supreme Self.

When the idea, "I am the body", is removed from the intellect, when the subtler equipment is disengaged from the body, then there are no more any *vasanas* in the inner equipment. The body will go on like a car, for as long as its momentum lasts. Thereafter, since it has no more *vasanas* for taking up another body, the individual crosses all "becoming".

The analysis of the body (Annamaya-kosa), is over with this verse. Next is the Pranamaya-kosa, the vital-air-shearth, also known as the physiological layer of man's personality.

(b) Pranamaya-kosa (Vital-air-sheath) (165-166)

कर्मेन्द्रियैः पञ्चभिरञ्चितोऽयं
प्राणो भवेत्प्राणमयस्तु कोशः ।
येनात्मवानन्नमयोऽनुपूर्णः
प्रवर्ततेऽसौ सकलक्रियासु ॥१६५॥

165. The *Prana* along with the five organs-of-action, constitutes the vital-air-sheath, pervaded by which the food-sheath (physical body), performs all its activities as though it were living.

The manifestation of life in the physical body, which express itself in the gross body as the activities of the five organs of action, is called the vital-air-sheath. The five organs of action are--hands, feet, the organs of speech, the organ of reproduction and the organ of evacuation. The food-sheath which was exlained in the preceding verses is completely pervaded by this vital-air-sheath. There is *Prana* in the toe as well as in the brow. If from some portion the *Prana* is gone, that portion becomes paralysed. Thus, this *Pranamaya-kosa* is the "Atman" of the *Annamaya-kosa.* Owing to the vital-air-sheath and its dynamism alone all the activities of the body take place, hence the *Pranamaya-kosa*--is considered as the "soul" of the *Annamaya-kosa.*

Some text-books consider it along with the gross and some along with the subtle body. Both are right because it is the "glue" which holds the subtle body with the gross body; therefore, one part is in cohesion with the gross and the other part with the subtle body.

नैवात्मापि प्राणमयो वायुविकारो
गन्ताऽऽगन्ता वायुवदन्तर्बहिरेषः ।
यस्मात्किञ्चित्क्वापि न वेत्तीष्टमनिष्टं
स्वं वान्यं वा किञ्चन नित्यं परतन्त्रः ॥१६६॥

166. The vital-air-sheath cannot be the Self because it is a modification of air *(Vayu).* Like air it enters the body and goes out of it, never knowing its joys or sorrows or those of others. It is ever dependent upon the Self.

The *Pranamaya-kosa* is a modification of air *(Vayu).* As long as it is in the body, all the activities of the body go on. But once it leaves the body, all the activities of the body stop. Since it is a modification of air and has the quality of coming in and going out, it cannot be the *Atman.* When this "air" is inside the body, it is called *Prana* and when it is outside, it is called the atmospheric air.

Prana does not know anything, neither its own joys and sorrows nor those of others. It cannot know anything, being inert by itself. The *Atman,* the Self, is Eternal, All-pervasive and Omminiscient. It has no modifications, no movements and It is the "Knower of all." Therefore, the *Pranamaya-kosa* cannot be the *Atman.* This verse is the negation of the vital-air-sheath. In our day-to-day living we are not conscious of the *Pranamaya-kosa.*

---

* Refer Taittireya Upanishad.

Next we take up the mind for discussion. It is called the Manomaya-kosa. Its nature and the secret technique of negating it are given in the following verses.

(c) Manomaya-kosa (Mental-sheath). (167-183)

ज्ञानेन्द्रियाणि च मनश्च मनोमयः स्यात्
कोशो ममाहमिति वस्तुविकल्पहेतुः ।
संज्ञादिभेदकलनाकलितो बलीयां-
स्तत्पूर्वकोशमभिपूर्य विजृम्भते यः ॥१६७॥

167. The organs of perception along with the mind form the mental-sheath which is the sole cause for the "I" and "mine" diversity of things. It has the essential faculty of creating differences of names etc. and it is powerful. It pervades the sheath preceding it-- the vital-air-sheath.

This opening verse on the discussion of the mental-sheath explains what is meant by *Manomaya-kosa* in *Vedanta.* The mind along with its sense-centres constitutes the mental-sheath. The sense-*organs* are in the body, but when the mind is engrossed elsewhere, we do not perceive the things though they are within the range of our senses. This is because the sense-*centres* are in the mind* and if the mind is not available, no perception is possible. The sense-organs by themselves cannot perceive. When the mind flows through the sense-organs and reaches, say, the place where the pot is, the experience of, "this is a pot", is generated. The theory of perception in *Vedanta* is, that the Consciousness riding on the mind as *Chitta* flows out through the sense-organs to reach the pot-place *(Ghatadesa)*, and contacts the existence *(Sat)* of the pot. Thus I become *conscious* of the pot: the consciousness of the pot is the "knowledge of the pot".

"I-ness" and "my-ness" are born in and maintained by this *Manomaya-kosa.* Consisting of the sense-organs and the mind, the mental-sheath creates two distinctions, "me" and "mine". Through them the mind annihilates the peace within.

* Ibid verse 92.

It destroys the inner peace by the sense of "me" *(Aham)*, and the outer peace by the sense of "mine" *(Mama)*.

"My-ness" is nothing but the "I" reflected upon certain objects outside. The extension of the ego upon the world of objects around is called "my-ness". So extension of "I-ness" is "my-ness". This extension spreads to frontiers which can never be well-defined. All this hallucination is caused by the *Manomaya-kosa*.

Manomaya-kosa is that powerful force which creates all the apparent differences in the world of pluralistic experiences. Wherever there is no plurality there is no mind. Hence mind alone is the cause for all plurality--the plurality of names, forms, qualities, activities and utilities. Where the mind is not, nothing is.

Manomaya-kosa fully pervades the preceding *kosa* i.e. the *Pranamaya-kosa*. Mind can only conceive things known. What I do not know, I cannot think about. The moment I get a new knowledge, it becomes a new idea to think about. Inshort, the present boundaries of my knowledge are the outer-most frontiers to which my mind can run and pervade.

पञ्चेन्द्रियैः पञ्चभिरेव होतृभिः
प्रचीयमानो विषयाज्यधारया ।
जाज्वल्यमानो बहुवासनेन्धनै-
र्मनोमयाग्निर्दहति प्रपञ्चम् ॥ १६८॥

168. The five sense-organs act as priests who feed the fuel of numerous desires into the mental-sheath, which is the sacrifical fire. This fire (mental-sheath), brings about and maintains the entire phenomenal world when it is set ablaze by the sense-objects which act as a continuous stream of oblations.

Explaining the *Manomaya-kosa*, Sankara gives us a metaphor from the Vedic rituals. In the Vedic period, when *Yagnas* and *Yagas* were performed, fire was usually invoked first. So a trough was made which was called the Fire-altar. In it, fuel was kept and then the fire was kindled. As the fire blazed up, the priests and house-holders poured their offerings of ghee etc., into it to the chanting of appropriate *mantras.* When into the blazing fire the offerings *(aajya)*, were poured, the flames licked higher. This picture of the *Yagna* is very familiar to all students of ritualism and hence Sankara uses it here to explain the *Manomaya-kosa.*

The priests who perform the *homa* are called the *hotr.* The five organs of perception represent the priests. They bring the offerings to the Fire-alter, *(Kunda).*

The sense-objects are the offerings *(aajya)*, in the subjective Fire-altar within. The sense-organs bring the sense-objects in the form of sense-stimuli to the individual. The eyes bring forms and colours. The ears bring sounds. The tongue brings tastes. The nose brings smells. And the skin brings the sensation of touch. Thus the sense-stimuli are brought by the sense-organs as their oblations into the body which is the trough *(kunda)*, serving as the Fire-altar.

In the sacred trough, fire is already blazing and into this the offerings are poured. The fuel for the fire are the *vasanas* which are already burning in the flames of thought-agitations. When the offerings are poured into the already burning fire, it blazes forth to the very roof of life.

Agni is the lord invoked in this ritual. When the Lord is fully invoked, He manifests and blesses the priests and the householders. Here, as a result of the subjective *Yagna* of the mind, the Lord manifests and blesses to maintain the world of pluralistic phenomena.

The *Manomaya-kosa* is kept blazing because of the fuel of the *vasanas.* Into the fire, the ghee (the sense-stimuli), is poured by the five great priests, the sense-organs. When they pour the offerings, the fire blazes forth. Thoughts are only imaginations *(Sankalpas)* of the mind, expressed in the form of agitations because of its own burning *vasanas.* When the sense-organs bring the stimuli, the mind appears to be more ablaze i.e. the agitations become more and more. These agitations manifest as activities in the world. All this is maintained by the mental-sheath.

न ह्यस्त्यविद्या मनसोऽतिरिक्ता
मनो ह्यविद्या भवबन्धहेतुः ।
तस्मिन्विनष्टे सकलं विनष्टं
विजृम्भितेऽस्मिन्सकलं विजृम्भते ॥१६९॥

169. Apart from the mind there is no ignorance *(avidya).* The mind itself is the ignorance which is the cause for the bondage of rebirth. When the mind is destroyed, everything else is destroyed. When the mind manifests, everything else manifests.

All *avidya* put together is *Maya. Maya* is constituted of the three *Gunas--Sattwa, Rajas* and *Tamas.* These function only in the mind. Therefore, other than the mind, there is no *avidya.* mind alone is *avidya.* It is the cause for all the bondages in the world-of-becoming.

When this mind is destroyed, all pluralistic perception and the sense of mortality end. When it is projected, the entire world gets projected.

Therefore, in order to go beyond the world-of-becoming, the mind has to be controlled and transcended. The mind cannot be controlled unless the sense-organs are controlled. The sense-organs cannot be controlled unless their fields are controlled. So one should first get away from the sense-objects in order to quieten the sense-organs. Then to gain a greater conviction, the seeker must study and reflect upon the scriptures. He should read, study, reflect, contemplate and meditate deeply. When the non-apprehension of Reality

---

* Macrocosmic *avidya*--collective *avidya* in all bosoms=*Maya.* Maya, when expressing in an individual mind is called *avidya,* the "non-apprehension of of Reality."

and the consequent mis-apprehensions of plurality are removed, the mind becomes predominantly filled with *Sattwa (Sattwa-guna-pradhana)*. *Maya* is then dispelled and one comes to apprehend one's own Real Nature.

स्वप्नेऽर्थशून्ये सृजति स्वशक्त्या
भोक्त्रादिविश्वं मन एव सर्वम् ।
तथैव जाग्रत्यपि नो विशेष-
स्तत्सर्वमेतन्मनसो विजृम्भणम् ॥१७०॥

170. In the dream-state, even though there is no contact with the outside world, the mind alone projects the entire dream-universe of enjoyer etc. Similarly, the waking-state is no different. All this (world of pluralistic phenomena), is but a projection of the mind.

During the dream, when there is, in fact, no connection with the waking world, the mind, out of itself, creates the dreamer, the dream-world and the dream-experience. The experiencer, the experienced and the experiencing in the dream are all created by the mind alone. The mind is the dream-subject, the mind is the dream-object and the mind again is the dream-experience of joy and sorrow.

Similarly, in the waking-state also there is no reality at all. Just as, in the dream, the mind creates a world of its own which has an appearance of Reality, so too, the apparent Reality of the universe perceived in the waking world is but a hallucination. All that we see around is a projection of our mind. Stop the mind and the world ends. One may say, "How about the other man seeing it?" But the other man is also the perceiver's own creation only.

So the mind in all of us is the cause which gives rise to the feelings and experiences of the pluralistic world.

Therefore, get out, get out--roll up the the universe, carry it as a seat under your arm. Turn around, turn inside out--step into another dimension. Stop the mind.

सुषुप्तिकाले मनसि प्रलीने
नैवास्ति किञ्चित्सकलप्रसिद्धेः ।
अतो मनःकल्पित एव पुंसः
संसार एतस्य न वस्तुतोऽस्ति ॥१७१॥

171. In deep-sleep, the mind is reduced to its causal-state and nothing perceivable exists as is proved by the universal experience of all people. Therefore, man's world of change is just the creation of his own mind and has no objective Reality.

As has been explained earlier, the mind alone is the cause for the appearance of the whole world. One more argument is added here to what has been already said.

During deep-sleep when the mind is completely dissolved, the experience of the individual is that there is nothing. Such an experience is universally lived by all. Everyone under the spell of deep-sleeep has the same experience. There is no exception to it. Thus when the mind is not there, there is no world perceived. So then, this world of variable experiences *(samsar)* of man, this woeful life of plurality and its sorrows, is projected by man's mind alone. Consequently, this world is of the mind alone, *de facto* it is not there. You are seeing the world because you are looking through your mind. Rise above the mind and look "over" it: world-perception then is not possible, as in the deep-sleep state of Consciousness.

वायुनाऽऽनीयते मेघः पुनस्तेनैव नीयते ।
मनसा कल्प्यते बन्धो मोक्षस्तेनैव कल्प्यते ॥१७२॥

172. The wind gathers the clouds together and the wind itself scatters them. So too, the mind is responsible for bondage and also for liberation.

The clouds are brought together by the wind and they get scattered again by the same agency---the wind. By the mind one considers oneself limited, mortal and bound. When the wind brings the clouds together, the ever brilliant sun is not seen. When the mind brings the storms of its agitations into the bosom, the resplendent *Atman* is not readily recognised. When the agitations are reduced and the same mind is turned towards subjective realisation, all the sense of limitation and bondage ends.

Sankara leaves nothing unsaid, which might create doubts in the immature mind of the beginner in the study of Vedanta. How the mind causes bondages and how the same mind brings about liberation is explained in the following verse.

देहादिसर्वविषये परिकल्प्य रागं
बध्नाति तेन पुरुषं पशुवद्गुणेन ।
वैरस्यमत्र विषवत्सुविधाय पश्चा-
देनं विमोचयति तन्मन एव बन्धात् ॥१७३॥

173. The mind causes man's attachment for the body and the sense-objects. These attachments bind him like an animal that is bound by ropes. Thereafter, the same mind creates a distaste for the very same sense-objects as though they were poison and liberates man from his bondage.

From the stand-point of the mind, the body, the sense-organs and the objects of the world are all "objects". Not only does the mind project all these, but having projected them, it creates an attachment in man for these "objects". By this attachment, he gets bound and becomes limited and sorrowful. Thus the *Atman*, the Self, apparently tied down is the jeeva, the individuality. Its freedom all gone, it lives as an abject slave of the mind.

On account of the attachment for objects thus created, the individual gets bound like cattle with a rope. The properties of *Sattwa, Rajas* and *Tamas* bind the individual.*

Though the infinite heavens invite the bird to fly free and enjoy, it does not leave the mirror in the verandah, because

* Again a pun on the Sanskrit term *"Guna"* which means both, the modes of the mind as well as a "rope". The cattle with rope *(Guna)* and man with his moods *(Gunas)* are tied down.

of the attachment it has created for its own reflection in the mirror. Nobody wants to leave the object of his attachment and liking.

When an animal is tied down with a rope, it has a limited freedom commensurate with the length of the rope. Similarly When the infinite Consciousness is (apparently) bound by the *Gunas*, It seems to have lost Its omnipotency and omnisciency and become and limited *jeeva*, but this individuality also has a limited freedom ordered by the proportion of its *Gunas* (modes). These attachment and bondage are created by the mind alone. The same mind is useful to liberate the *jeeva* from this bondage, that it may revert to its original nature, the pristine glory of divine omnisciency and omnipotency.

After being bound to the world of objects, liberation comes to man only when he gets rid of his meaningless fascination for the sense-objects. Freedom lies in not depending upon the sense-objects for one's inner happiness. This dependency can be overcome only when there is a total dispassion *(vairagya)* for the sense-objects. Dispassion for a thing will develop only when one finds that the object no more gives one any joy. If the idea that the joy-content is not in the object outside is firmly established in one's understanding then one is immediately released from all one's personality bondages. This dispassion *(vairagya)*[1] is brought about by the mind alone.

Nobody in the world has attachment for poison. Nobody longs to take a pinch of potassium-cyanide. When one finds no taste *(rasa)*, in an object, no more is there any attraction *(raga)* towards it.

Lack of "taste" *(rasa)* creates desirelessness *(vairagya)*. So by understanding, that there is no real "taste" in the object, the mind frees us completely from the persecutions of the world of plurality.

1. *Raga* = desire; *Vai-ragya* = state of desirelessness; *Vai-rasya* = tastelessness (for the pleasures of sense-indulgence).

Thus the mind alone causes bondage and it is the mind again that liberates the individual.[1] This play is called *Maya*, which is, in fact our own *avidya*, our non-comprehension of Reality.

तस्मान्मनः कारणमस्य जन्तो-
र्बन्धस्य मोक्षस्य च वा विधाने ।
बन्धस्य हेतुर्मलिनं रजोगुणै-
र्मोक्षस्य शुद्धं विरजस्तमस्कम् ॥१७४॥

174. Therefore, the mind is the cause for both liberation as well as bondage. When it is blemished with the effects of Rajas, it causes bondage. When it is free from the *Rajas* and *Tamas* qualities, it paves the way to liberation.

Therefore, meaning, because of the reasons explained in the above verses, it is now clear that the mind alone is the cause for bondage as well as for liberation. The feeling in man that he is bound or that he is liberated is only a state of his mind.

The *Atman*, which is one's Real Nature is never bound. Then where is the question of release for it? Liberation is only with reference to the bondage. When one is really liberated, there is neither any bondage nor any release. One is just "That".

The conditions of bondage and liberation are only states interpreted with reference to the condition of the mind. Where ever it is in constant agitation, the individual is in bondge *(bandhan)*. *Rajoguna* is the cause for the agitations of the mind. This *Rajoguna* comes into play because of *Tamoguna*, the non-apprehension of Reality. Whenever there is in the mind a preponderance of *Rajas* and *Tamas*, it is agitated and therefore is in bondage. When the taints are removed and it

---

2. Hencee the famous declaration, मन एव मनुष्याणां कारणं बन्धमोक्षयोः mind alone is the cause for both, the bondage *(Bandhana)* and the liberation *(Moksha)*

is quietened, that is, when it becomes predominantly *Sattwic*, one has the experience that one is free and so totally liberated. When the mind is turned inwards towards OM, it is a mind full of *Sattwa* and when it is turned towards the OET, it is a mind impure, being mixed with *Rajas* and*Tamas*.

Both these are tricks of the mind.

विवेकवैराग्यगुणातिरेका-
च्छुद्धत्वमासाद्य मनो विमुक्त्यै ।
भवत्यतो बुद्धिमतो मुमुक्षो-
स्ताभ्यां दृढाभ्यां भवितव्यमग्रे ॥१७५॥

175. When the mind has been made pure due to a predominance of discrimination and dispassion, it turns towards liberation. These two must be strengthened by one who is an intelligent seeker of liberation.

When there is a preponderence of these two qualities of discrimination *(viveka)*, and dispassion *(vairagya)*, in an individual, he can readily attain purity of mind.

Viveka is the power to discriminate between the Real and the unreal, between Spirit and matter, between the Self and the not-Self.

Vairagya is the capacity and heroism to reject the unreal, the matter, the not-Self.

In order to make the mind pure one has to develop these two qualities. By an intelligent self-denial of sense-pleasures dispassion will increase. By study, reflection and contemplation upon the scriptures, discrimination will increase. When discriminative power is developed, it will help in increasing dispassion. When dispassion has increased, there will be a greater power of discrimination. They are both complementary to each other in their development.

When the agitations in the mind are reduced, the veil over the intellect is lifted. *Rajoguna* and *Tamoguna* get eliminated. Such a mind is useful in obtaining total liberation.

The mind is not the instrument with which Reality is comprehended. When the pure mind is in His presence, the dissolution of individuality takes place. The pure mind here acts as a catalytic agent.

That is why intelligent aspirants should strengthen these two qualities in themselves. If one is an intelligent student, wanting to release oneself from the thraldom of matter, one must try to develop discrimination and dispassion in plenty.

मनो नाम महाव्याघ्रो विषयारण्यभूमिषु ।
चरत्यत्र न गच्छन्तु साधवो ये मुमुक्षवः ॥१७६॥

176. A huge tiger called "mind" prowls in the thick jungles of sense-pleasures. Let not those virtuous people who have a deep aspiration for liberation ever wander therein.

For seekers who are on a pilgrimage to the Temple of Liberation, a warning board should be kept on their route. it should read, "Route unsafe---man-eater called MIND at large. Take to diversion ---*here, now*"

Here is an indication to those who do *sadhana*, to be careful with their minds. The mind has the capacity to run out into the sense-objects through some chink in the armour of self-control. Once it so escapes, it will pull you down into the jungles of sense-instincts *(Vishaya-vasana)*, and tear you to pieces. It will make you a victim of sense-pleasures.

Hence, ***sadhaks*** should always stick to the path of discrimination *(viveka)* and dispassion *(vairagya)*, tirelessly, ceaselessly. Never relax. The moment you slip from this path, the mind will take hold of you and you will find yourself helplessly dragged in the jungles of sense-objects and their endless pain-ridden enchantments.

The mind is an instrument provided by the Lord, and it, by its very nature, must continuously run out to the sense-objects. This is its essential function. To cleanse the mind of all its sensuousness is to expect the mind to leave its own *dharma.* This is impossible. Yet we, as *sadhakas* can keep ourselves away from our blind identification with the mind and its roamings. We may meet the man-eater prowling in the deep jungle tracts, but we can avoid rushing at and embracing it. Be warned. The mind is a dangerous threat if we identify with it; let it be in the bosom. Be a "witness" to it and you are safe.

मनः प्रसूते विषयानशेषान्
स्थूलात्मना सूक्ष्मतया च भोक्तुः ।
शरीरवर्णाश्रमजातिभेदात्
गुणक्रियाहेतुफलानि नित्यम् ॥१७७॥

177. The mind continuously delivers for the experiencer, (1) all sense-objects, gross or subtle, without exception, (2) distinctions based upon body, caste, order-of-life and creed, as well as, (3) the difference of qualities, actions, motives and results.

All the sense-objects without any exception are bred by the mind. It goes on creating the gross things of the world outside and the subtle things within. Not only are the objects created by the mind, but the subject, the enjoyer-of-objects, is also created by the mind alone. We may not be in a position to accept the statement that "I" and the "world around me" are the creations of the mind. In the dream-state, the dreamer, the dream-world and the dream-experience are all created by the waker's single mind. The dreamer while dreaming cannot appreciate and understand that the things around him, and he himself playing as the dreamer, are created by his own mind. The waking-state is in no way different from this illusory dream-state.

Gross objects are constituted of forms and colours, sounds and tastes, smells and touch. The subtle objects consist of feelings and thoughts.

In the sense-objects, gross and subtle, we find innumerable varieties and endless differences such as those based upon caste, creed, status, position in life, etc. All such differences are, without an exception, always created by the mind. The differences in qualities activities, causes, and their consequences are all created by the same mind. If the mind is not there, then, as in deep-sleep, none of these is present.

All things perceived in the dream---subtle or gross, objects or beings, thoughts or emotions---all their differences in kinds and moods---in fact, everything created in the dream is in the mind alone. So too, the waking mind creates the waking-world, the individual experiencer and the endless play between them.

असंगचिद्रूपममुं विमोह्य
देहेन्द्रियप्राणगुणैर्निबद्ध्य ।
अहंममेति भ्रमयत्यजस्त्रं
मनः स्वकृत्येषु फलोपभुक्तिषु ॥१७८॥

178. Unattached Pure Intelligence is the essence of the *jeeva*, but the mind beguiles it and binds it by ties of body, sense-organs and *Pranas*. It causes this *jeeva* to wander with the idea of "I" and "mine" in the varied experiences of "results" gathered by itself.

Out of the supreme Reality, *Brahman*, which is ever unattached to the matter vestures and the very nature of which is Absolute Knowledge, a mortal, limited *jeeva* is created by the mind. The mind does this trick by first deluding itself, by forgetting its Real Nature. Having achieved this non-apprehension of Reality, the mind makes man attached to the matter sense-organs and all the physiological functions within him. Thereafter, he gets bound by the *Gunas*--*Sattwa*, *Rajas* and *Tamas*. This is entirely a deliberate trick of the mind.

Really speaking, the Atman is never deluded. The weaker is never confused. In the dream, the waker *apparently* becomes the dreamer. By such identifications, the qualities of the BMI becomes the limited ego, the *jeeva*. This is the bondage, the limitation, the delusion. The mind perpetrates all these and the individual starts behaving like a separate entity and suffers the sorrows of "I" and "mine".

The feeling of "I-ness" in the activities of the mind, and the feeling of "my-ness" in the enjoyments of the mind are delusions created by the *Manomaya-kosa.* When such a feeling arises, it announces the birth of the *jeeva*, and this *jeeva*, exhausted and weary, seeks its liberation.

So, it is this mind with which you have to remove the mind.

अध्यासदोषात्पुरुषस्य संसृति-
रध्यासबन्धस्त्वमुनैव कल्पितः ।
रजस्तमोदोषवतोऽविवेकिनो
जन्मादिदुःखस्य निदानमेतत् ॥१७९॥

179. The evil of superimposition causes man's transmigration and the mind alone is responsible for the bondage of superimposition. For a man who is tainted with *Rajas* and *Tamas* and who lacks discrimination, this causes the misery of birth etc.

The ever-changing phenomena of the world, both outside and within one's self, and its consequent joys and sorrows, is called *samsar.* Invariably, there is inherent sorrow in the phenomenon of change. Where there is change, there is agitation and agitation is the expression of sorrow. The root of all this is the misapprehension arising out of the non-apprehension of Reality. This misapprehension, otherwise called superimposition, is termed as *adhyasa* in *Vedanta.*

When the truth of a thing is not correctly seen as it is, in our error of judgement, we see another object substituted in its place. This trick of the mind is called superimpsition, *adhyasa* or its power of self-projection.

When a rope is not seen as a rope, our error of judgement gives us the misconception that it is a snake, or a streak of water, or a piece of wood or a crack in the earth. When such superimposition starts, the superimposed illusion completerly covers the "reality". When the serpent is seen, the serpent covers the rope completely. When Truth is not recognised as Truth, there is no sorrow; it is only ignorance. But when ignorance breeds misapprehensions, then sorrow arises. Therefore, sorrow is not in the non-apprehension, but is inherent in the misapprehension. In deep-sleep we are in ignorance, pure non-apprehension, and there is no sorrow in it. In fact, there is much in the saying, "Ignorance is bliss"

This theme of superimposition---*adhyasa*---is very exhaustively discussed by Sankara in his introduction to the Brahma sutras. He says, the phenomenon of superimposition is not onesided. Not only is Truth misapprehended as the illusion, but the illusion is firmly understood as the Truth. But the illusion is not without a basis.

When a rope is not seen as a rope, never do we, in delusion, see an elephant, or a cow or a building instead of the rope. Upon a post, a ghost or a man can be superimposed but never a cow or a snake. Hence it is clear that although it be only a superimposition, still it strictly follows certain laws.*

When a snake is seen in place of a rope, the illusory snake form covers the form of the rope and the *dharmas* of the snake are superimposed. The colour, the shape and the rough surface of the rope are not seen, but the colour, the shape and the smooth surface of the snake are seen instead. When these *dharmas* of the snake are seen, we say the snake IS: the snake exists. In fact, the snake IS NOT and the rope IS. but we say the rope IS NOT and the snake IS.

Therefore, it is not just a case of the snake lending its *dharmas* to the rope. But the "existence" in the rope is also

---

*** Hence the scientific laws in the universe. Though an illusion or the mind, there are incontrovertible scientific laws that govern its movements and behavious, actions and reactions.**

temporarily loaned to the snake. Where there is no rope, superimposition of the snake cannot be. Hence the rope lends its "existence" to the snake, and the snake lends its *"dharmas"* to the rope. When we put the two of them together, we say, "This is a snake". This experience of the "existence" of the snake is the cause of sorrow.

Again, if there be any superimposition, it will always be complete: a half-snake-half-rope-vision or a half-ghost-half-post-vision is not possible. Either it is a ghost or it is a post. Even when we have a glimpse of Reality, the continuance of *samsar* ends, as ignorance completely disappears.

When the mind is predominantly *Rajasic* and *Tamasic*, it will create superimpositions and will make a fool of the individual; for he will then start seeing things which are not there. Such a fool is subjected to the sorrows of *samsar*. They are birth, growth, disease, decay and death. Nobody can escape them. He who has been deluded by his own superimpositions will have to undergo these sorrows.

अतः प्राहुर्मनोऽविद्यां पण्डितास्तत्त्वदर्शिनः
येनैव भ्राम्यते विश्वं वायुनेवाभ्रमण्डलम् ॥१८०॥

180. Hence the mind is considered to be *avidya* by sages who have discovered its secret. By this alone the universe of experience is tossed around like the clouds by the wind.

Because of the reasons given,* the learned ones say that the mind alone is *avidya*. It is because of the mind that the world and its activities continue. Purposeless knocking about is *bhramana*--the illusion of purposeless change. *Bhramyate*, means moving about with no aim or goal through a series of profitless changes. Thus the universe and its activities are knocked about by the mind just as the clouds are knocked about by the wind. This jogging alone in the realm of change creates sorrows for man.

---

* In verses 174-179.

तन्मनःशोधनं कार्यं प्रयत्नेन मुमुक्षुणा ।
विशुद्धे सति चैतस्मिन्मुक्तिः करफलायते ॥१८१॥

181. Therefore, the mind must be diligently purified by one who seeks liberation. When the mind has been purified, liberation becomes as readily available as a fruit in one's own hand.

From the above explanation it is evident that for spiritual realisation, the mind has to be purified. "Purification" of the mind means removal of *Rajoguna* and *Tamoguna*, meaning, their resultant agitations and veiling from the personaltiy. This is not an easy job because the psychological "dirt" within has been accumulated by us all through ages past. With great effort and intelligent self-control, purification of the mind can be achieved.

No effort can be consistently put in by anyone unless he has seen an inspiring goal. Such an amount of effort to cleanse one's inner equipment can be put in only by him who is inspired by the goal of liberations from matter-vestures. Those who have a burning desire for liberation should make, at first an all-out effort to cleanse the mind, that is itself spiritual ignorance. When this is done, liberation is not far away at all. It is, like the fruit on your palm, already there, right with you.

मोक्षैकसक्त्या विषयेषु रागं
निर्मूल्य संन्यस्य च सर्वकर्म ।
सच्छ्रद्धया यः श्रवणादिनिष्ठो
रजःस्वभावं स धुनोति बुद्धेः ॥१८२॥

182. With single-pointed devotion for liberation, he who roots out his attachments for sense-objects, renounces all actions and with faith in Truth, constantly hears (the Truth) etc., he can purge the *Rajasic* nature in his intellect.

Relinquishing both, the doer-ship and the enjoyer-ship, one accomplishes the end of the ego. Ego, the *jeeva*, is constituted of these two vanities only. Of them, it is easier to remove the enjoyer-ship. The "I am the enjoyer" attitude from the fruits-of-actions can be removed easily. For this, selfless dedicated service *(Karma Yoga)*, has been recommended. Activities without ego and egocentric desires cleanse the mind. When one works dedicatedly, without the ego and the egocentric desires in the world, the existing *vasanas* get exhausted and no new *vasanas* are created. Then the mind becomes calmer and quieter the mind, greater is its contemplativeness. So one gains a deeper understanding of the scriptures. Through *Sastra*-study, one will be able, ultimately, to eliminate the false vanity, "I am the doer".

So for a person who has cultivated single-pointed devotion for liberation, a way has been suggested here for the purification of his mind. Dedicated activity without the ego and ego-centric desires, study of the scriptures with faith and understanding, and an intelligent removal of the vanity that arrogates all activities to itself, will result in the complete elimination of the *Rajasic* nature of the intellect. When the mind and intellect are purified, liberation is just like the fruit on one's palm---one has only to enjoy it.

मनोमयो नापि भवेत्परात्मा
ह्याद्यन्तवत्त्वात्परिणामिभावात् ।
दुःखात्मकत्वाद्विषयत्वहेतो-
र्द्रष्टा हि दृश्यात्मतया न दृष्टः ॥१८३॥

183. The mental-sheath cannot be the supreme Self either, for it has a beginning and an end. It is subject to modifications; pain and suffering characterise it and it is an "object" of cognition. The subject can never be identified with the "object of knowledge."

Defining and expounding the *Manomaya-kosa*, Sankara has used the largest number of verses,[1] and now with this verse he denies and negates it. So many verses have been

1. 16 verses--from verse 167-182

used to explain it, so that the student may get a precise understanding of the *Mannomaya-kosa*, how it works and what is its nature, structure and function.

After having given explicit information about the *Manomaya-kosa*, the *Acharya* gives us five reasons to prove that the mental-sheath also cannot be the *Atman* the Self: (1) because it has a beginning and an end; (2) it is subject to modifications; (3) it is characterised by pain and sorrow; (4) it is an object of cognition; and (5) it is ever identified with the objects of knowledge.

The mind has a beginning and an end. When one wakes up from sleep, the mind begins to function; when in deep-sleep, it ceases to function. The *Atman*, the Self has neither a beginning nor an end. It is Eternal and Infinite. Hence the mind which is ephemeral and finite cannot be the *Atman*.

Even while it exists, the mind is fickle, ever-changing. At one moment sorrowful, at another it becomes joyful, now peaceful, now agitated. This changing mind cannot be the changeless *Atman*, whose nature is eternal *Bliss*.

The very fabric of the mind is pain and sorrow. Even when it is joyous, its joyful nature is accompanied by the fear of change. From the stand-point of eternal Bliss, our little joys and pleasures are, at their best, comparative sorrows. So the mind cannot be the *Atman* because of the obvious contradiction in its very nature.

The mind is the cause for all the sense-objects.[1] Since the objects constantly change, the mind too must constantly change to become the objects. The effects are nothing else but the cause in another form. The mind cannot be the *Atman* because the *Atman* is neither the cause nor the effect of anything. It is the divine changeless substratum for all changes.

---

1. Verse 177.

The mind is identified with the objects; What we see around us is the "seer" in another form. The subject and the objects are really one and the same. When the subject is projected through the mind, it appears as though it is a pluralistic world. But in fact, it has no reality, in as much as, where the subject is not, the world of objects can never be. Through the world of objects, the mind looks at itself. The subjective-subject looking at the objective-subject is the experience of the world of objects--like the child sucking its own thumb and enjoying it. Remove the thumb, it cries. Remove the object, we cry. The *Atman* does not identify with the objects. It is the Knowing Principle. This being so, the mind cannot be the *Atman*.

With this verse, the explanation and the negation of the *Manomaya-kosa* is over. *Next we take up for discussion, the intellectual-sheath the Vignanamaya-kosa.*

(d) Vignanamaya-kosa (Intellectual-sheath).
(184-188)

बुद्धिर्बुद्धीन्द्रियैः सार्धं सवृत्तिः कर्तृलक्षणः ।
विज्ञानमयकोशः स्यात्पुंसः संसारकारणम् ॥१८४॥

184. The intellect with its modifications along with the organs of perception form the intellectual-sheath *(Vignanamaya-kosa)*. It has the characteristics of "the agent" (or doer), which is the cause for transmigration.

The *Vignanamaya-kosa* (intellectual-sheath), constitutes the intellect, the sense-organs of perception and all the different modifications of the intellect. It controls the organs of perception.

This intellectual-sheath in man veils the Infinite Reality. It is the cause for *samsar*. The modifications of the intellect are the awareness of "doing" and the concept of "I am the doer." This concept creates more and more *vasanas*. In order to exhaust the *vasanas* the individual has to move from one field of enjoyment to another--so there are births and deaths, again and again. How this *Vignanamaya-kosa* is the cause for *samsar* is explained in the following verse.

अनुव्रजच्चित्प्रतिबिम्बशक्ति-
विज्ञानसंज्ञः प्रकृतेर्विकारः ।
ज्ञानक्रियावानहमित्यजस्त्रं
देहेन्द्रियादिष्वभिमन्यते भृशम् ॥१८५॥

185. Accompanied by a reflection of the light of *Chit*, the intellectual-sheath is a modification of *Prakriti*. It is endowed with the function of knowledge and is always completely identified with the body, sense-organs etc.

The *Vignanamaya-kosa* is constantly accompanied by the reflection of the light *Chit*, Consciousness. Consciousness is all-pervasive at all times. The world of plurality floods up within it, as it were. Consciousness reflected in the intellect is *intelligence*, just as the electricity reflected in, or functioning in the bulb is light, in the fan is rotation, in the heater is heat and in the refrigerator is cold. In Sankara's and the Vedic times, there was no electricity So he has taken the example of the sun being reflected in, conditioned by, functioning through, playing in, a bucket of water.

This mighty power of Eternal Consciousness, God which is the spark of life in every one of us, is not confined to the within. It is present everywhere at all times. This Consciousness playing in the pools of thought is the individual, in whom It generates the doer-ship idea. Where the doer-ship has ended, there the individuality has also ended. This idea is explained in the *Upanishads* through the "Reflection theory" *(Pratibimba-vada)*.

The matter-vestures cannot function by themselves in the absence of Consciousness. They are, after all, composed

* *Vraja* means, "roaming about."
Anu-vraja is, "constantly roaming about", "always at the heels of", "constantly accompanied by or followed by".

of inert cells. The intelligence is there only because of the Consciousness playing through the intellect in us. The matter-equipment, the intellect, becomes brilliant because of the light of consciousness. The intellect by itself has no intelligence. It is like a mirror in darkness.

The function of the intelligence, the *Vignanamaya-kosa* is "to-know". *Jnana* is its main function. It gives rise to the concept of, "I, the knower".

The mind projects the world of objects and the intellect illumines them with its intelligence which is reflected in the light of Consciousness, and there arises the notion of, "I know". This process of mental projection and intellectual recognition goes on at all times and the feelings of "I" and "mine" are created. The feeling of "I" is with reference to the body, the sense-organs, *Pranas*, and the mind. The feeling of "mine" is with reference to the world of objects.

This intellect, due to the light of Consciousness playing in it, develops the capacity to illumine things projected by the mind, and as a final result of all these, it comes to identify with the body, the sense-organs etc. It becomes the restless ego, the "I-ness", and identifying with the objects perceived by the sense-organs, it provides the "my-ness". Thereafter starts the "I" and "my" play which we call "samsar".

This great tyrannical power which enters our bosom, loots our discrimination and ties us down to our limitations, is none other than the *Vignanamaya-kosa.* If a person withdraws from this sheath, he shall have neither this "I-ness" nor this "my-ness". Nor will he identify any longer with the body, the sense-organs etc. and have the feeling of "mine" regarding the world of objects around him.

अनादिकालोऽयमहंस्वभावो
जीवः समस्तव्यवहारवोढा ।

करोति कर्माण्यपि पूर्ववासनः
पुण्यान्यपुण्यानि च तत्फलानि ॥१८६॥

भुङ्क्ते विचित्रास्वपि योनिषु व्रज-
न्नायाति निर्यात्यध ऊर्ध्वमेषः॥
अस्यैव विज्ञानमयस्य जाग्रत्-
स्वप्नाद्यवस्थाःसुखदुःखभोगः ॥१८७॥

186/187. It is without beginning, is of the nature of the ego and is called the jeeva, which carries out the entire range of activities on the relative plane. It performs good and evil actions according to its previous *vasanas*, and experiences their results. It comes and goes, up and down, taking birth in various bodies. The waking, dream and other states, and the experiences of joy and sorrow, belong to this intellectual-sheath.

The concept of "I" is beginningless. It started even before the beginning of time. Before one recognises an object, there must already be an "I". If there be an object, and the "I" is not present, there cannot be an experience. For every experience, the I-factor representing the subject is indispensible. I, the ego, myself am the subject. So the first object that emerged at the beginning of creation must have been the first thought at zero time. When I arrogated the first thought to myself, the concept of "I do" arose. Thus the ego is beginning-less *(anadi)*. This I-ness *(Aham-swabhava)*, which is beginningless, is the *jeeva*, the individuality. All activities on the relative plane are carried out by this *jeeva*. The light of Consciousness conditioned by thought carries out all the activities in the world. When the last thought is ended, there is no more an ego and so no more any actions. To realise consciously and dynamically this state of actionlessness is called *Samadhi*.

The *jeeva* carries out the activities of the world in strict adherence to a blue-print provided by itself. This blue-print, the peculiar mode of one's activities, is determined by *vasanas* acquired earlier. The activity may be good, bad or indifferent. It is all ordered by the texture of one's *vasanas*.

Accordingly, when the *jeeva* acts in the world, ordered by the past *vasanas*, the activities produce results. These fruits are enjoyed by the *jeeva* under finite varieties of physical environments. In order to act as per the old *vasanas*, and to enjoy the fruits of actions, the individual has to take birth in various fields of activities, high and low, with reference to this relative existence. The three states of Consciousness, the waking, dream and deep-sleep, are conditionings of this *Vignanamaya-kosa.* The experiencer of joy and sorrow in these three states of Consciousness is this intellectual-sheath. In whatever state there is an experience, the concept of "I" is immanent.

देहादिनिष्ठाश्रमधर्मकर्म-
गुणाभिमानं सततं ममेति ।
विज्ञानकोशोऽयमतिप्रकाशः
प्रकृष्टसान्निध्यवशात्परात्मनः ।
अतो भवत्येष उपाधिरस्य
यदात्मधीः संसरति भ्रमेण ॥१८८॥

188. Identifying with the attributes of the order-of-life, their duties and functions, which actually belong to the body, it considers them as its own. The *Vignanamaya-kosa* is extremely radiant because of its nearness to the supreme Self. It is a superimposition on the Self, which, when It identifies with it, suffers transmigration through delusion.

The intellectual-sheath is subtler than the mental, the vital-air and the food-sheaths. Owing to its subtlety it has the maximum pervasiveness. In the order of sheaths, it is nearest to the *Atman*, the Self. Consequently, it is extremely brilliant. Compared with all other sheaths, it has more reflectiveness. This sheath is the conditioning nearest to Reality.

The term *Atma-Dheehi*, is indicative of the ego *(jeeva)*, at the same time defining the individuality.* The *Atman* conditioned

---

* *Atman* + Dheehi=*Atman*-Dheehi=*jeeva*, ego The light of Consciousness in us, the Atman fuctioning in the thought-springs (Dheehi), is the ego, the jeeva; so *Atman-Dheehi* means, the individuality, the PFT, the ego. (Pratibimba--vada--the theory that the ego is the "reflection" of the Self in the intellect).

in the intellect is the individuality, the ego. This *jeeva* is the factor which undergoes the phenomenon of coming and going, the phenomenon of transmigration. Transmigration is occasioned by the delusion of not knowing the Self as the Reality, and considering the not-Self, the jeeva, to be the Reality.

41. Atman--Unattached. (189-191)

योऽयं विज्ञानमयः प्राणेषु हृदि स्फुरत्ययं ज्योतिः ।
कूटस्थः सन्नात्मा कर्ता भोक्ता भवत्युपाधिस्थः ॥१८९॥

189. The *Atman*, which is Knowledge Absolute, shines within the *Pranas*, in the heart.[1] Though It is immutable, It becomes the doer and the experiencer because of Its superimposition (the intellectual-sheath).

In Vedanta, it has been constantly asserted that the seat of the intellect is in the heart, that in the "cave-of-the-heart" is the intellect and in the midst of the intellect is the shining *Atman*. This is just a poetic expression. A man with noble emotion is called a man of "heart"; and he who is bereft of emotion is called "heart"-less. The mind full of love is called the "heart". When I enter a rocky cave, then above me, below me, to my sides and in front, in fact, every where there is nothing but rock. In the same way, when I enter the heart-cave, all around me there can only be "heart". "Heart" means "love", pure love. In such an atmosphere of universal love the seeker's intellect must function. In the cave-of-the-intellect is *Brahman*, that is, when the intellect is contemplating upon the *Atman* in an atmosphere of universal love, it will be able to recognise the Self as the light illumining its meditative, single-pointed thought. Therefore, the teachers of *Vedanta* say that in the *hridaya* is the *buddhi*.

The heart agitated with likes and dislikes is called the mind. The mind is the choking chord around the neck of the individual, while the heart is the releasing angle that helps one to free oneself from the thraldom of the mind. To achieve

---

1. The earlier part of this verse is a statement from Brihadaranyaka Upanishad--IV-iii-7.

it; one has to bring the mind to a single-pointed thought. This is not possible unless there is love. With love or devotion, when one moves towards the *Atman*, the mind becomes single-pointed with only one thought in it. And He who illumines that thought is *Brahman*. This condition of meditative poise has been indicated in the verse when it says that the intellectual-sheath is in the heart.

Kootasthah, means, that which remains immutable like an anvil. An anvil allows all changes to take place upon it, but itself does not undergo any change. "Immutable", therefore, is the significance of the term, *"kootasthah"*. The *Atman, the Self, as Kootasthah* is immutable, and as conditioned by the BMI (Upadhisthah), It apparently becomes the doer and the enjoyer.

This ego-centric attitude of the ever-changing, sorrowful, miserable individuality and its experiencer-hood comes to the *Atman* because of the conditionings *(upadhis)*, which are themselves only illusory projections due to man's ignorance.

स्वयं परिच्छेदमुपेत्यबुद्धे-
स्तादात्म्यदोषेण परं मृषात्मनः ।
सर्वात्मकः सन्नपि वीक्षते स्वयं
स्वतः पृथक्त्वेन मृदो घटानिव ॥१९०॥

190. This *Atman*, although It is the Self in every existing thing, assumes the limitations of the intellect and wrongly identifying with this entirely false entity, It considers Itself as something different--like the mud-pots from the mud of which they are made.

The nature of the infinite consciousness everywhere is, One-without-a-second. Even then, out of delusion, It comes to accept the conditionings as real and continues to identify with the matter-vestures. Having identified with the conditionings, It suffers from its sense of limitations. Thus, if the body is slightly indiposed, the individual suffers and groans under that indisposition.

Having been conditioned by the intellect, a man becomes identified with it and behaves as though he is the experiencer of the joys and sorrows in life. All this is indeed false. But, because of this identification, he understands himself to be a separate entity and starts seeking Truth--which is his very own nature. He believes that Truth is something other than himself. The fallacy in the notion of God being someone other than the devotee is being brought out here very forcefully,

If the idea that 'Truth is something other than me' is accepted, I should negate my BMI, for they are only my conditionings projected by my imagination. All that I have to negate is the ghost which is not there, so that I may ultimately understand the post.

Just as when the pots made of mud develop individual identities of names and forms, we recognise them as separate from each other. But in truth, they all are in essence, Mud only.

उपाधिसम्बन्धवशात्परात्मा
ह्युपाधिधर्माननुभाति तद्गुणः ।
अयोविकारानविकारिवह्नि-
त्सदेकरूपोऽपि परः स्वभावात् ॥१९१॥

191. Even though the supreme Self is by nature perfect and ever unchanging, due to Its realtionship with the superimpositions, It assumes the characteristics of these superimpositions and *seems* to act just as the equipment do--like the changeless fire assuming the forms of the iron-pieces which it turns red hot.

The supreme Reality, due to Its identification with the conditionings *(upadhis)*,behaves in accordance with the *dharmas* of the conditionings. Life, when it functions through the body, assumes the qualities of the body.

A clean glass near a blue cloth appears blue. If the cloth is red, the glass appears red. As the colour of the cloth, so appears the colour of the glass. The glass has no colour of its own. It borrows the colour of its environments. In the same way, the *Atman* functioning through the *upadhis* acquires the properties of the *upadhis* for the time being.

In this verse, to indicate the same idea, another example is given. Fire has neither shape nor form. Spherical heat, cubical heat, cylindrical heat, rectangular heat, etc, are not possible. Nor has the heat any weight. Ten-ounce heat, one-pound heat, five-pounds heat too, are impossible. But when iron-pieces are put in the fire, the fire assumes their shapes and weights. These are not the properties of the fire, but because of the iron-pieces, the fire is said to have shape and weight.

Paramatman is ever the same *(Sada-eka-roopah).* It is of the nature of Existence. It is pure Is-ness, the *Such-ness* in such-and-such a thing. If that Such-ness is removed from it, the thing will not have existence. Existence alone is Its nature. There is no being or non-being in It. Nothing has even emerged out of It. In Its pure Existence state, It is not even Consciousness. * Consciousness It becomes only when it is illumining objects. It cannot be said to 'be' anything. It is of the nature of Existence. No other description is possible. And you are *That.* Even now you are That. Nobody can say, "I have no existence". "I exist", "I am", is the universal experience of all. That Am-ness is the Truth.

It is of one nature because It transcends all nature. As Consciousness, you cannot use any other definition. It is indescribable. All descriptions only detail the qualities of the thing described. Qualities are not there in the Infinite. The moment properties are seen, It becomes finite. The properties are, what you see, hear, smell, taste, touch, feel and think.It is beyond all properties or characteristic features. To understand that I am Conciousness, and that I have nothing to do with the BMI, is the realisation of the hightest state of Spiritual Perfection.

---

* नान्तःप्रज्ञम् "It is not that which is conscious of the inner' world ...." Mandukya I-7,

42. "What is Liberation?" --Disciple. (192-193)

शिष्य उवाच ।

भ्रमेणाप्यन्यथा वाऽस्तु जीवभावः परात्मनः ।
तदुपाधेरनादित्वान्नानादेर्नाश इष्यते ॥१९२॥
अतोस्य जीवभावोऽपि नित्या भवति संसृतिः ।
न निवर्तेत तन्मोक्षः कथं मे श्रीगुरो वद ॥१९३॥

192 & 193. The *Sishya* asked-- That the supreme Self has come to consider Itself as the *jeeva*, through delusion or otherwise, is a superimposition which is beginningless; that which is beginningless cannotbe said to have an end. So the *jeeva*-hood of the Self must also be without an end, ever subject to transmigratio. Please tell me, O revered Teacher, how then there can be liberation for the Self?

The disciple *(Sishya)*, has understood what the master *(Guru)*, had been explaining so far. Here a doubt arises in the minds of all those who have been closely following the arguments. Naturally, the *Sishya* has his doubt and he puts it to the *Guru*.

Howsoever may it be, by confusion, delusion or whatever else--the *Paramatman*, the supreme Reality, has come to this attitude of a limited ego *(jeeva-bhava)*. The conditioning due to which the *Paramatman* has apparently become the *jeeva*, is said to be *Maya*. *Maya* is beginningless *(An-adi)*. That which is beginningless cannot have an end. Hence *Maya* can never end. It can never be destroyed. Once the *Paramatman* has entered this *Maya*, His *jeeva-bhava* becomes eternal. If the *jeeva-bhava* is eternal, the coming and going, the transmigration *(Samsritti)*, must also be ever-lasting. This birth and death phenomenon for the *Paramatman*, who has once identified with the conditionings, becomes eternal.

"If it be so, dear Sir, how can one get liberation? O *Guro, please tell me." This is the crux of the humbly worded, meeksounding, respectful question put by the Sishya* to the *Guru*.

43. Self-knowledge Gives Liberation. (194-206)

श्रीगुरुरुवाच ।
सम्यक् पृष्टं त्वया विद्वन्सावधानेन तच्छृणु ।
प्रामाणिकी न भवति भ्रान्त्या मोहितकल्पना ॥१९४॥

194. The *Guru* replied--

O learned boy, you have put a proper question. Listen then carefully. Things conjured up by imagination, which is itself a product of delusion can never be accepted as "facts".

Having heard the question asked by the student, the *Guru* replies. While replying, he appreciated the *Sishya's* close observation of the logic and compliments him on the very way the question has been put. He says, "Well put, indeed, is your question, O intelligent boy. Now carefully and attentively listen to my reply."

The imagination created by delusory thinking cannot be accepted as real. The very thought, to begin with, that there are the equipments, is a delusory misconception. Indentification with them is a subsequent delusion. These are all imagined due to one's inner confusions. Whatever has been seen in a dream cannot condition the waker. A sumptuous dinner enjoyed in the dream will not remove any hunger in the waking state. Hence, the imagination conjured up by delusion can never be a fact. "If what you say is a fact, then of course, *moksha* is impossible, because of the logic given by you," admits the *Guru*, and adds, "But the mind itself is a delusion. Through a delusion you have created an imagination."

This *avidya* ends only when *true* wisdom comes. Therefore, my dear boy, the idea that there cannot be any *moksha* is not true. Thus though *avidya* is "beginningless" *(An-adi)*, it can end *(Antavati)*, when Truth is realised.

भ्रान्तिं विना त्वसङ्गस्य निष्क्रियस्य निराकृतेः ।
न घटेतार्थसम्बन्धो नभसो नीलतादिवत् ॥१९५॥

195. For the Self which is unattached, without activity and formless, there can be no connection with the world of objects other than delusion, just like the blueness etc. seen in the sky.

Continuing his reply, the *Guru* adds:

The supreme Reality is unattached, has no actions and no forms. It is One-without-a-second. There is nothing other than It for It to get attached to. The Self has no activity, for It has no limbs to act with. There are no motivations in It egging It on to act. It has no fields to act in, no objectives to gain, no motivation to act. Being all-pervading, It has no form. The concept of any connection between the Self and the objects is a delusory misconception. Without delusory misconceptions and imaginations conjured up by delusion *(avidya)* there cannot be a world of objects. Only when there is a world of objects can we have any relationship and identification with it. Only then can we try to make one thing out of another, that is, perform action.

The idea that the sky is blue, murky, dirty or golden is a delusion. The sky can never be contaminated by colour or dirt. Yet, we "see" the blue colour of the sky and due to lack of correct thinking, conclude that the sky is blue. But if we contemplate we will find that the sky has no colour at all.

Equally so, if a man contemplates upon the Atman, he will find that It is his self, non-dual, without any activity or attachment. But then this *Atman*, through delusion (Maya) starts recognising the various personality layers *(kosas)*, the world of objects, the organs of perception and action, the *pranas*, the mind and intellect. Thus, the Self *(Atman)*, appears to be conditioned by the body, the mind and the intellect and this apparent conditioned Self is called *jeeva*. This ignorance can be ended only by the direct knowledge of the Self.

स्वस्य द्रष्टुर्निर्गुणस्याक्रियस्य
प्रत्यग्बोधानन्दरूपस्य बुद्धेः ।

भ्रान्त्या प्राप्तो जीवभावो न सत्यो
मोहापाये नास्त्यवस्तुस्वभावात् ॥१९६॥

196. The *jeeva*-hood of the *Atman* which is the Witness, which is beyond all qualities and activities, and which is subjectively experienced as Bliss and Knowledge Absolute, is unreal and is but a delusion caused by the intellect. Since by nature it (*jeeva*-hood) is unreal, it ceases to exist once the delusion had been lifed.

By nautre, the Self is without action, without qualities, and is constant Knowledge-Bliss Absolute. It is of the nature of Bliss because it is a state transcending the mind and the intellect which constitute the springs of all sorrows. By delusion, this *Atman* gets identified with the intellect and acquires *jeeva*-hood.

In my dream, when I am jailed, I myself enter the jail and live in it. In fact, I have not really gone to any jail. But due to the misconception in my mind, temporarily, I have the experience of being limited by the jail. When the dream ends, neither is there a jail nor is there a jailor. Similarly, when the delusion is removed, when the *avidya* has ended by the knowledge of *Brahman*, then with regard to the supreme Reality, never is there any *jeeva*-hood. A delusion may give us an experience which is *seemingly* real, but being a mere delusion, it has no existence *(Sat)*.

यावद्भ्रान्तिस्तावदेवास्य सत्ता
मिथ्याज्ञानोज्जृम्भितस्य प्रमादात् ।
रज्ज्वां सर्पो भ्रान्तिकालीन एव
भ्रान्तेर्नाशे नैव सर्पोऽपि तद्वत् ॥१९७॥

197. Having been caused by an error of judgement and false understanding, the *jeeva*-hood can exist only as long as the delusion lasts. The rope is mistaken to be the snake only when there is an illusion. Once the illusion is destroyed, there can be no snake. So too, in this case.

Concluding the argument, Sankara tells the student that as long as there is confusion and delusion, so long there will be the existence of the "individuality", the *jeeva*. The *jeeva*-hood exists only as long as the delusion lasts.

The delusion or non-apprehension of Reality gives rise to the misapprehension that "I am the body", "I am the mind", "I am the intellect". With reference to the world of objects, there arises a feeling, "I am the doer". With reference to the mind and intellect, there arises the feeling, "I am the enjoyer". These feelings in their aggregate constitute the *jeeva*-hood. Since they have arisen out of delusion, they will last only as long as the delusion lasts.

As long as the *nature* of the rope is not understood and as long as the *knowledge* of the rope is not fully realised, so long the delusion continues and the snake-vision persists. In utter mental confusion alone can you have the vision of the serpent. When the mental confusion has ended, the snake cannot be. With the knowledge of the rope, the misconception that it is a snake must necessarily vanish.

Likewise, as long as the *Atman* in us is not experienced, the pluralistic phenomenal world is experienced through the instruments of the body, mind and intellect. There will also be the triple world of the subject, the object and the relationship between them. Once the *Atman* is realised, the entire perceived, pluralistic, phenomenal world will roll away and disappear. The experience of the Self is gained in an immediate knowledge.

This experience comes *not as a result* of any special *sadhana*. All *sadhanas* help the seeker to withdraw from his BMI-preoccupations. Real knowledge comes only through intuition. It is immediate. In *Kathopanishad* it is said, "It is like lightning". It is sudden, quick. Teaching yourself to withdraw from wordly preoccupations takes time. When the mind is withdrawn from all its preoccupations, the experiences of the Infinite is instantaneous. This experience has been explained by hundreds of examples throughout the Upanishads. In Buddhist literature it is called *Pragnana*--

"Instant Consciousness". Intellectual analysis *(Vignana)*, is necessary for certain types of students. Philosophy and religion are only helpful hand-maids to prepare the mind of the seeker for the direct and immediate experience to the Infinite.

This infinite Self is experienced *not because* of religion, *nor because of* philosophy. They are as much help as ourpilgrimages, rituals, vows, *japa*, austerities *(tapa)*, and meditations *(dhyana)*. Experience of the Infinite *Brahman* does not depend upon anything. It is not a *mediate* experience, meaning, it is not gained through the instrument of any equipment. It is not because of the Teacher nor because of the scriptures. However, Teacher, scriptures, *sadhana*, study, all help us to withdraw the mind from its preoccupations. The mind withdraws from its preconceptions and held in attention---in full alertness---is the mind that receives intimations from the Infinite. The Infinite is your essential nature---It is an *immediate* experience.

अनादित्वमविद्यायाः कार्यस्यापि तथेष्यते ।
उत्पन्नायां तु विद्यायामाविद्यकमनाद्यपि ॥१९८॥

प्रबोधे स्वप्नवत्सर्वं सहमूलं विनश्यति ।
अनाद्यपीदं नो नित्यं प्रागभाव इव स्फुटम् ॥१९९॥

198-199. So too, *avidya* and its effects are said to be beginningless. But when there is rise of *vidya*, then *avidya*, even though it is beginningless, is destroyed, root and branch, just as dreams are destroyed on waking up. The phenomenal universe is not eternal, it is evident, like the "former non-existence", *(Prak-abhava)*.

When the cause is beginningless, its effects must also have the same nature. Ignorance, *avidya*, which is beginningless, must necessarily produce effects which are also beginningless. *Avidya* is the cause for the very first thought. Therefore it is beyond time. But when true knowledge of the Self is born, when the right apprehension is born, the non-apprehension will have to end. As long as the cause, the non-apprehension remains, its effects, the misapprehensions must also remain. But there is one solvent for this great cause. The antithesis of ignorance is knowledge. Where there is knowledge, there ignorance cannot be. Where there is light, there darkness cannot be. Light and darkness cannot remain in one and the same place at one and the same time. The moment light is brought into a cave which might have been in darkness from the beginning of time, the darkness, no matter how old or how dense, must immediately vanish. Similarly, when the knowledge of the Self is born, the ignorance with all its effects---non-apprehension with all its misapprehensions---will have to end, though it is "beginningless".

On waking up, the dream ends fully. On realising the nature of the Self, the "misapprehensions" to their very roots---the "non-apprehension" ---must end. Not only are the misapprehensions eliminated but also their very cause, the non-apprehension. In deep-sleep the "effects" end, but the causal-body, the non-apprehension, meaning, the "cause" remains. In the final spiritual experience, the "cause" also ends. Then, never will the fear of "misapprehensions" rise in us.

When Truth is apprehended, the effects along with their cause, the causal-body, end even though the cause is beginningless *(An-adi)* Though ignorance *(avidya)*, is beginningless, it is not eternal.* That which is born must die and that which is unborn cannot die. But there are exceptions. *Avidya*, though it is unborn will end. This peculiar paradox is explained by an example: "It is clear, just as *Prak-abhava*". *Prak-abhava* is a technical term used by the Indian logicians *(Naiyayikas)*. In *Nyaya-sastra* they employ this term freely.

A pot, before it was made, was in the mud. Instead of the pot there was only mud. From the mud the potter cannot make a milch-cow. Nor can he make a succulent apple. He

---

* *Anadyapeedam no nityam*---through beginningless *(Anadi-api)*, this *(edam) Avidya* is not *(no)* eternal *(nityam)*.

cannot create a wife for himself out of mud. He can only create various kinds of pots. The pot he is going to make must be potentially possible in the mud. In the mud is the potential pot. In the mud is the unmanifest pot. The unmanifest pot was in the mud even before the pot was made. When the pot is made, the pot which was hetherto unmanifest is now manifest. Now when was the *potential pot* born in the mud? The possibility of the pot in the mud was beginningless *(Anadi).* The possibility of the pot in the mud was born when the mud was born, nay when the earth was born, nay it was in the very essential nature of the earth. When the pot is made the potential pot has become manifest. When the pot is made the potential pot has become manifest. When a pot has manifested, *Its* beginningless "potential" condition has ended. Before *(Prak)*, its actual manifestation, the manifested pot was not there *(Abhava)*. The moment it manifested, its potential state which was "beginningless, ended. So this "previous non-existence" *(Prak-abhava)*, is an example given to illustrate a beginningless thing coming to an end. Ordinarily, that which is beginningless must be endless. But *Vedanta* says, that it is possible for a beginningless thing to end. How? Like the "previous non-existence" of a pot. When the pot has manifested, its "unmanifest condition" which was beginningless has ended.

"Similarly", says the *Guru*, "even though *avidya* is beginningless, it ends with the apprehension of Reality *(vidya)* Therefore, though your question is beautifully put, please understand that it is not a great question after all".

अनादेरपि विध्वंसः प्रागभावस्य वीक्षितः ।
यद्बुद्ध्युपाधिसम्बन्धात्परिकल्पितमात्मनि ॥२००॥

जीवत्वं न ततोऽन्यत्तु स्वरूपेण विलक्षणः ।
सम्बन्धस्त्वात्मनो बुद्ध्या मिथ्याज्ञानपुरः सरः ॥२०१॥

200-201. Although it is beginningles, "former non-existence" is found to have an end. So too, the *jeeva*-hood which is imagined to be in the *Atman*, through its apparent conditioning in the super-imposed attributes like the

intellect, is not real. But the other, (the Self), is intrinsically different from it (*Jeeva*-hood). The relation between the *Atman* and the intellect is due to the "false knowledge".

The concept of individuality has arisen because of the Consciousness identifying with or reflecting in the intellect. "Intellect" is used here because the mind and the sense-organs are incorporated in the subtle-body. This *jeeva-bhava*, the individuality, in its essential nature, is nothing other than the *Atman*. But because of the conditionings, the Self, the *Om*, appears to be the PFT, the *jeeva*. if I can understand myself to be of the nature of the Self, the sorrows that are supplied to me through the body, the mind and the intellect can be ended. Thus, though this *avidya* is beginningless, it has an end, as in *prak-abhava*, as in the example of the "beginningless non-existence of the pot in the mud ending in the production of the pot from the mud". If this *avidya* has an end, O Teacher, tell us how it can be ended. What is the secret technique?

This *jeeva-Bhavana* has come about because of the intellect, and so through the same intellect it should be ended. The intelledct turned outwards towards the OET creates the *jeeva*-hood. When the same intellect is turned inwards towards the *OM*, the awakening of the *Atman* the Self, takes place. At this moment the intellect is functioning, turned entirely outwards and is fully engaged in its busy preoccupations with the fascinating world of OET. The worlds of experiences in the OET are all delusory misconceptions born out of the non-apprehension of Reality. Hence the intellect at this moment is full of wrong notions, misconceptions and false knowledge *(Mithya-jnana)*. Due to the ignorance of the Self, the misconceptions, "I am the body, I am the mind, I am the intellect", have arisen, and thereafter, considering myself to be the limited ego, and thinking that my happiness depends upon the world of objects, I find no way to gain real and lasting happiness. All this is "false-knowledge", *(Mithya-jnana)*. When the intellect leaves its misconceptions and turns towards the Eternal Self, then even though the *avidya* is beginningless it ends with the dawn of the knowledge of the Self *(Jnana)*.

विनिवृत्तिर्भवेत्तस्य सम्यग्ज्ञानेन नान्यथा ।
ब्रह्मात्मैकत्वविज्ञानं सम्यग्ज्ञानं श्रुतेर्मतम् ॥२०२॥

202. The superimpositions will cease to function at the dawn of right knowledge and in no other way. According to the scriptures, realisation of the identity of the soul and *Brahman* is right knowledge.

When a reality is apprehended, the non-apprehension of it called *avidya* ends. There is no other method by which the confusions of life created by the false ego can end.

At present the intellect is riddled with illusory misconceptions such as, "I am the body", etc. This "false knowledge" is discussed in the previous verse. Now in this verse, "right knowledge" *(Samyak-jnana)*, is being explained.

False knowledge *(Mithya-jnana)*, gives the feelings, "I am a limited mortal, a finite creature", etc. When this intellect now drowned in wrong notions emerges out in right knowledge *(Samyak-jnana)*, this misconception-created, stupid idea, "I am a limited creature" will also end.

Right knowledge is the first-hand knowledge of the identity of *Atman* and *Brahman*.* *Jnanam* means "book-knowledge" *Vijnanam* is the "special knowledge" meaning, a first-hand, direct-knowledge---the first-hand experience that "the *Atman*, the Self, in me, is the one Self everywhere". This *Samyak-jnana* alone can remove *Mithya-jnana*.

तदात्मानात्मनोः सम्यग्विवेकेनैव सिध्यति ।
ततो विवेकः कर्तव्यः प्रत्यगात्मसदात्मनोः ॥२०३॥

203. This realisation comes only through right discrimination made between the Self and the not-Self. That is why one must strive to discriminate between the individual Self within and the Eternal Self everywhere.

---

* *Brahma-atma-ekattwa-vijnanam*, the knowledge rising from the direct experience of the identity of *Atman* and *Brahman*, is right knowledge, *Samyak-jnana*.

Right knowledge *(Samyak-jnana)*, can be gained by diligent discrimination between the Self and the not-Self and this must be continuously done. Because of the past *vasanas*, we strongly identify, again and again, with the matter-vestures in a result of this discrimination, we come to understand the identity of the individual Self within and the Eternal Self present everwhere.

Samyak-jnana is the antidote for *Mithya-jnana:* right knowledge is the specific remedy for false knowledge. Right knowledge can be gained through discrimination. Every seeker should therefore, discriminate continuously between *Atman* and *anatman*, until direct realisation dawns in his heart.

जलं पंकवदत्यन्तं पंकापाये जलं स्फुटम् ।
यथा भाति तथात्मापि दोषाभावे स्फुटप्रभः ॥२०४॥

204. Water which is extremely muddy appears as transparent water when the mud has been removed. So too, the *Atman* manifests Its clear lustre when the impurities have been removed.

Water is clear in its essential nature. When it holds mud in suspension, it is said to be muddy. From a sample of muddied water if all the mud is removed, what remains is the water pure and clear, as it was before it got muddy.

Likewise, the *Atman* is ever Immaculate. When there are impurities such as objects, emotions and thoughts in the *Atman*, they create agitations in the mind and the *Atman* is not cognised in Its essential purity and infinite brilliance. When these agitations and sorrows are removed from one's direct and intimate recognition, the *Atman* shines forth.

These impurities---our false knowledge *(Mithya-jnana)* can be removed by right knowledge *(Samyak-jnana)*, which can be generated only through diligent and constant discrimination. Hence, "discriminate constantly", is the unsaid suggestion of the Acharya to the seekers.

असन्निवृत्तौ तु सदात्मना स्फुटं
प्रतीतिरेतस्य भवेत्प्रतीचः ।
ततो निरासः करणीय एवा -
सदात्मनः साध्वहमादिवस्तुनः ॥२०५॥

205. This very individual Self is clearly realised as the Eternal Self when the unreal ceases to exist. So one must strive to completely remove the ego etc. from the Eternal Self.

The* BMI, PFT and OET are the constituents of the not-Self. At present we are preoccupied with them. When the not-Self is entirely eliminated at the still moment of meditation, this very same PFT or ego will be recognised as the pure Self, the *Sada-Atma.* When all that is the not-Self and its consequent agitations *(vikshepa)* are removed, the ego which is suffering its limitations will cognise itself to be the *Brahman.* Therefore, this negation of the *anatman* should be continued till the point of deep and total realisation is reached.

अतो नायं परात्मा स्याद्विज्ञानमयशब्दभाक् ।
विकारित्वाज्जडत्वाच्च परिच्छिन्नत्वहेतुतः ।
दृश्यत्वाद्व्यभिचारित्वान्नानित्यो नित्य इष्यते ॥२०६॥

206. For the following reasons, the intellectual-sheath which we have so far spoken of, cannot be supreme Self: It is subject to change, it is inert and insentient, it is limited, it is an object of the senses and it is not constant. A mortal, perishable thing, indeed, cannot be said to be the immortal, imperishable *Atman.*

The Vignanamaya-kosa is being negated in this verse. it cannot be the *Atman* because of the following reasons:

(a) *Because it is subject to change (Vikari-ttwad):* The intellectual-sheath is subject to change. Our ideas and ideals are always changing. Our intelligence varies from time to time. Therefore, this cannot be the Self which is ever the same.

---

* Refer foot note verse 124.

(b) *Because it is insentient (Jada-ttwad):* The intellect by itself is inert. When the light of Consciousness touches it, then alone does it become sentient, and shines out of the individual, to think, to rationalise, to discriminate, to judge, etc.

(c) *Because it is limited (Parichhinna-ttwad):* Every intellect has its limitations. A great artist may know everything about art, but he may not know anything about physics. A physician may be a great genius in science, but he may not know anything in politics. Politicians in India need not necessarily know economics. A Vedantin may know his *Vedanta*, but know perhaps nothing of other subjects. So each one may be great in his own field, but not in others. The intellect in everyone is limited. Therefore, the intellectual-sheath cannot be the unlimited infinite Self. The Self is unlimited and undivided. hence the intellect cannot be the *Atman*.

(d) *Because it is perceivable (Drishya-ttwad):* We know our own intellects. We say, "I am dull", "I am intelligent", etc. We are conscious of our intellects. The intellect is an "object" of Consciousness. The object cannot be the subject, the pure Consciousness.

(e) *Because it is not constantly present (Vyabhichari-ttwad):* It is not constantly present, faithfully serving at all times. In deep-sleep, the intellect is not available. In the waking condition it is available. In a perverted condition it slaves in the dream. It does not work at all during deep-sleep, when swooning or when under chloroform. At times it is available, at times we are intelligent and at other times we are dull and unintelligent. Therefore, it cannot be the *Atman*.

(f) *Because it is not eternal (A-nitya-ttwad):* It is mortal, changeable and variable. Hence the intellect cannot be the Self, the Reality, which is eternal.

The next personality layer, the bliss-sheath, is taken up for discussion from the following verse.

44. Anandamaya-kosa (Bliss-sheath). (207-211)

आनन्दप्रतिबिम्बचुम्बिततनुर्वृत्तिस्तमोजृम्भिता
स्यादानन्दमयः प्रियादिगुणकः स्वेष्टार्थलाभोदयः ।
पुण्यस्यानुभवे विभाति कृतिनामानन्दरूपः स्वयं
सर्वो नन्दति यत्र साधु तनुभृन्मात्रः प्रयत्नं विना ॥२०७॥

207. The *Anandamaya-kosa* (bliss-sheath), is that modification of Nescience which is kissed by a reflection of the *Atman*, which is Bliss Absolute. Pleasure, etc. are its attributes and it springs into expression when an object agreeable to it presents itself. The fortunate feel it spontaneously when the fruits of their good actions manifest. Every being, without the least effort, derives great joy from it.

Now the *Anandamaya-kosa* is being described. *Anandamaya-kosa* is also a *vritti*, a mental disturbance. "*Vritti*" means "thought". Even during deep-sleep there are thought-waves. The *prana*, the mind and the intellect are annihilated or transcended. During actual moments of *Samadhi*, there are no physological functions in the physical body. Clinically one is supposed to be dead. Sri Aurobindo's and Swami Paramahansa Yogananda's bodies were kept for some days after their *Maha-samadhi*, with the expectation that they would come back. When the body starts rotting, it is dispossed of. When one is in *Samadhi*, it is God's and nature's job to protect it. If one's *karma* with the body is not finished, it will be protected and preserved by nature for one's future use. *Samadhi* is a state wherein all thought-waves have totally stopped. Deep-sleep is not *Samadhi*. during deep-sleep there are yet subtle *vritties* in the intellect.

These *vritties* can be said to be bliss-thoughts *(Ananda vritti)*. Happiness experienced in a man's bosom is inversely proportional to the amount of agitation in his mind. Ordinarily, we are used to the endless stress and strain in our daily life. That moment in our life when our agitations are comparatively less, is a relatively happy moment. So the happiest moment is that in which there are but negligible agitations in our bosom. These small thought-waves are said to be "bliss-thoughts". At these moments the bliss of Infinitude is tasted a little. Sankara, in his poetic exuberance says, "The ripples of thoughts-waves arising out of Tamas in our mind, kiss the reflection of the bliss of Infinitude. This is the characteristic of the *Anandamaya-kosa."*

From the non-apprehension of Reality, soft ripples of thoughts arise in the mind and when these ripples are kissed by, meaning, illumined by, the light of divine Bliss, it is called *Anandamaya-kosa.* Even during our waking state we some times experience this bliss-sheath. Depending upon our relationship with the object of our liking, we feel different degrees of happiness. They are, *Priya. Moda* and *Pramoda.*

Priya, Moda and *Pramoda* are different degrees of happiness experienced when we come in different degrees of contact with the objects of our liking. When we are near an object of pleasure, or contemplating upon it, we feel happy. A lover sitting in his home and thinking of his beloved feels happy. Though the beloved is far away, to think of the beloved is happiness. In English, we may call this pleasurable emotion felt in the bosom as pleasure *(Priya).*

When the beloved, the object of our liking is in front of us, the pleasure is intensified and that intensified pleasure is called *Moda;* in English let us call it Joy.

And when we are actually indulging in or enjoying, when the object of our pleasure is in our possession, that pleasure is, naturally, most intensified. This maximum intensity of joy is called *Pramoda;* again in English let us call it Ecstasy.

The happiness that is illumined by the light of supreme Bliss, is one of nature of Pleasure, Joy and Ecstasy, ---*Priya, Moda* and *Pramoda.* At such moments we are in the *Anandamaya-kosa.* These joys can be experienced in relation to an object of pleasure, when we consider that the pleasure is in the "object". This is possible only when we are ignorant of *Brahma,* the Reality, that is, when we are in *avidya.*

At times, in our life, we feel happy without any reason. This is due to the noble *vasanas* created in us due to our past meritorious actions. Merit *(Punya)*, and sin*(Papa)*, are determined by the condition and the type of *vasanas* in us. The *vasanas* that create more and more agitation in the bosom are termed as *papa*, and those creating peace and serenity in the mind are called *punya*. When there are more and more such noble *vasanas* in an individual, the condition of his mind will become more and more serene. When there is more calmness in the mind, more joy is sure to be experienced. We see, a *Mahapurusha*, sitting down under some tree, shivering with cold to his very toes, not knowing where his next meal is to come from, yet supremely happy, even hilarious. This joy is from the *punya* in his heart. Whenever such joys are experienced, one is in the *Anandamaya-kosa*.

The bliss-sheath consists of "non-apprehension". There is, therein, no positive experience of joy. What is experienced. in this state is only the absence of sorrow. Very few in the world know what joy is. All that we know is either sorrow or a slight absence of it; either pain or the absence of it. But real joy very few of us know. Real joy is nothing but the experience of Brahman---Ananda-ghana. Real homogenous Bliss *(Ananda)* is the nature of *Brahman*. We do not experience that. At best we experience only a relative absence of agitations. This is called the bliss-sheath.

आनन्दमयकोशस्य सुषुप्तौ स्फूर्तिरुत्कटा ।
स्वप्नजागरयोरीषदिष्टसंदर्शनादिना ॥२०८॥

208. The *Anandamaya-kosa* is fully manifest in the deep-sleep state. While in the dream and waking states it is only partially manifest depending upon the sight of pleasing objects etc.

The *Anandamaya-kosa* is fully manifest in deep-sleep. When we are in dreamless deep-sleep, we are in the bliss-sheath. Our experience in deep-sleep is, "I don't know" "I know nothing", is our only experience in deep-sleep. None of the things that one generally experiences as objects, emotions and thoughts are there. So absence of things and utter ignorance are the nature of this sheath. This is called the non-apprehension condition *(avidya)*. Sleep is a state wherein we neither apprehend the objects nor Reality.It is a state of sheer non-apprehension.

In deep-sleep, this *Anandamaya-kosa* is fully manifest. In the dream and waking conditions, it manifests only a little, whenever one perceives things that are pleasant.

At the body, mind and intellect levels, whenever we are in an environment which is conducive to our *vasanas*, our mental agitations are temporarily quietened. At such moments, we experience a flicker of joy. But this is only a slight expression of the *Anandamaya-kosa*. This joy depends upon the objects and the circumstances around us. It is called *Vishaya-ananda* (sense-pleasure). The joy that we get from sense-pleasures is but a drip-drop from the ocean of infinite Bliss.

नैवायमानन्दमयः परात्मा
सोपाधिकत्वात्प्रकृतेर्विकारात् ॥
कार्यत्वहेतोः सुकृतक्रियाया
विकारसंघातसमाहितत्वात् ॥२०९॥

209. Nor can the *Anandamaya-kosa* be the supreme Self because it has attributes which are ever-changing. It is a modification of *Prakriti*, is created as the result of good actions of the past, and it lies embedded in the other sheaths which are in themselves all modifications.

Even this *Anandamaya-kosa* cannot be the *Atman* for the following reasons:

(a) *Since it has conditionings (So-upadhika-ttwad):* It is limited, conditioned. It is not constant. At certain moment this experience is available and at other moments it is not. So the bliss-sheath cannot be ever-present Self.

(b) *Since it is a modification of nature (Prakriter-vikarat):* It is a subtle expression of matter, the grosser being the desire, the grossest the action. The bliss-sheath consists of the causal-body made up of *vasanas.* They too, are modification of matter as the BMI and so the bliss-sheath also cannot be the modificationless *Atman.*

(c) *It manifests as a result of good and meritorious actions of the past (Karyattwa-hetoh):* Hence it belongs to the realm of the effect, *not* of the cause. It causes the types of desires and actions, but itself is an effect caused by past actions. As an effect, it cannot be the Supreme which is the cause of all.

(d) *This Anandamaya-kosa is the assemblage of matter-modifications (Vikara-samghata-samahita-ttwad): Vasanas* cannot but manifest under conducive circumstances. The tendencies express as thoughts. The *vasanas* can exist only in a medium of matter. So the *Anandamaya-kosa* is always associated with the assemblage of matter. Naturally, therefore, it is held in a mesh of thought-vibrations and this assemblage itself is a modification.

Hence for the reasons given above, the bliss-sheath cannot be the *Atman.* The *Atman* ever is; never is not. It is Immutable. It has an existence even without equipments.

पञ्चानामपि कोशानां निषेधे युक्तितः श्रुतेः ।
तन्निषेधावधि साक्षी बोधरूपोऽवशिष्यते ॥ २१० ॥

210. When the five sheaths have been negated through reasoning based upon authoritative scriptural texts, then at the acme of the process what remains is the Witness, Knowledge Absolute, the Self.

So far we have enquired into and found the activity, nature and functions of the five *kosas,*---the food, the vital-air, the mental, the intellectual and the bliss sheaths. Having enquired into them, we found that none of them could be the Reality and hence we rejected them all.

When all these sheaths are negated, and when an individual crosses the five frontiers, intellectually, with right argument and full understanding, he reaches the culminating point of this negation. The destination reached by thus negating and finding that the five sheaths are hollow, is the "I", the negator. The remainder, the Witness of this negation is of the nature of pure Consciousness.

45. Atman---other than the Five Kosas. (211)

योऽयमात्मा स्वयंज्योतिः पञ्चकोशविलक्षणः ।
अवस्थात्रयसाक्षी सन्निर्विकारो निरञ्जनः ।
सदानन्दः स विज्ञेयः स्वात्मत्वेन विपश्चिता ॥२११॥

211. This Atman is self-effulgent and distinct from the five sheaths. It is the witness of the three states, is Real, is without modifications, is unsullied and bliss everlasting. The wise man should realise It as his own Self.

When we negate all the five sheaths through close observation, intellection and meditation, what remains is the self-effulgent *Atman*. It is known by Itself. The Self-effulgent is something other than the five sheaths. It is that Illuminating Factor whichremains a Witness of the three states of Consciousness---the waking, the dream and the deep-sleep. It is the changeless Substratum for all the changes in the BMI. They are all illumined by the *Atman* which does not Itself undergo any change. The *Atman* is Immaculate, meaning, It is untainted by the qualities of *Sattwa*, *Rajas* and *Tamas*.

This changeless ultimate Truth is to be known. It is to be known not as an object outside, but as one's very own nature *(Atma-ttwena)*. The wise student should not only negate the *Panchakosas*, but must come to realise That which is behind them all, not as an *object yonder*, but as his *own Self*.

46. "What is Atman?" ---Disciple. (212)

शिष्य उवाच ।
मिथ्यात्वेन निषिद्धेषु कोशेष्वेतेषु पञ्चसु ।
सर्वाभावं विना किञ्चिन्न पश्याम्यत्र हे गुरो ।
विज्ञेयं किमु वस्त्वस्ति स्वात्मनाऽऽत्मविपश्चिता ॥२१२॥

212. The *Sishya* asked---
"After negating these five sheaths as unreal, I find nothing but an absence of everything, O revered Teacher. By which entity then, should the wise man, realise his oneness with the *Atman?*"

"On the basis that all the five sheaths are delusions, when I negate them, I find a state of sheer non-entity, a total absence of everything, an empty void," cries out the disciple.

This is the despair of the intellect when spiritual ideas are merely thought of by it. This is where the nihilists among the Buddhists reached and cried out that his experience of total annihilation and complete negation of everything is the Reality. They insisted that pure non-existence is the ultimate Truth.

And yet, in the above verse, the Teacher said, "What remains is to be known by the wise man". The disciple questions here, "O *Guro!* when there is a total negation of everything, then, at the end, I find only a void remaining. I find naught therein. What then is to be known by the wise man?"

The Buddhistic ideology is being taken up here in the form of a question from the disciple. The Teacher answers in the following verses.

47. Nature of the Self---Discussion. (213-225)

श्रीगुरुरुवाच ।
सत्यमुक्तं त्वया विद्वन्निपुणोऽसि विचारणे ।
अहमादिविकारास्ते तदभावोऽयमप्यनु ॥२१३॥

सर्वे येनानुभूयन्ते यः स्वयं नानुभूयते ।
तमात्मानंवेदितारं विद्धि बुद्ध्या सुसूक्ष्मया ॥२१४॥

213-214. The *Guru* answered---
"Rightly have you spoken, O learned one. You are indeed clever in your ability to discriminate. Through an extremely subtle intellect realise the *Atman*, the Knower, to be that by which all modifications like the ego, as well as their absence during deep-sleep are perceived, but which Itself is not perceived."

To those who have been following the arguments so far, and who have reflected sufficiently upon these ideas, one doubt can naturally come. When everything has been negated, then what is to be known? The *Guru* replies encouragingly, complimenting the *Sishya* on his intelligent and reasonable doubt. He says that behind the "naught" is the Knower knowing the "nothingness."

When the mind and its various modifications---the ego etc.---have been totally negated, that which would then remain is THAT, by which all other things are experienced by the ego during its existence.

"When all the five *kosas* have been negated, what remains?" "Nothing." "Right. But who is knowing that there is nothing?" "I". "Who is this I?"

It is this I-factor, the Subject, which the Teacher is trying to indicate. "*That* by which you are able to experience the various emotions and thoughts of the mind and the intellect, but which by Itself cannot be experienced, *That* is to be realised *That*, which you had never experienced while you were entertaining thoughts and feelings, but *because of which* you had all your experiences, *that* is, in fact, your Self who knew them all. *This* is to be experienced and known."

Come to know *that* "Knower" of everything, the "principle of Knowledge", in whose presence all knowledges are rendered possible

"How should I know *that"? Buddhya* ---through intellectual discrimination." " Can I know that with my intellect?" "Certainly," emphasises the Teacher. "How", enquires the *Shishya.* "With an intellect made very subtle ---*Su-sukshmaya buddhya"*---is the confident and precise reply.

With the gross intellect we see gross things. Grosser the intellect, grosser the vision. Our intellect at this moment is so gross, so full of sensuality, that we no more see a woman going along; we only see "lust" moving on legs. When the mind is made a little subtle, you see "beauty" going. A little more subtle and you see a "living being". Make it as subtle as that of a philosopher's and you will see "divinity" on the move.

How do we make our intellect subtle? "Subtle intellect" means that intellect which is not running headlong to crash into sense objects. That intellect which is not functioning under the pressure of its *vasanas*, the intellect which is fully redeemed from their deadening pressures, is a subtle intellect. *Vasanas* are removed through dedicated activity *(Nishkama-karma).*

With such a purified intellect we will be able to recognise that Divine Factor which remains when the five *kosas* have been transcended.

तत्साक्षिकं भवेत्तत्तद्यद्यद्येनानुभूयते ॥
कस्याप्यननुभूतार्थेसाक्षित्वं नोपयुज्यते ॥२१५॥

215. That which is witnessed by something else has the latter as its witness. When there is no entity to witness a thing, we cannot say that it has been witnessed at all.

The student might now think, "Allright then, I am the Witness, i.e., the Consciousness is the Witness of everything that is happening."

So the *Guru* now clarifies the idea already expressed by him for fear that the subtle suggestions hinted at by him could be misconstrued by the not-yet-disciplined intellect of the student.

We can say a thing is a Witness only when it is experiencing something. But when there is no experiences at all, the *Atman* cannot even be called a *sakshi*. A "witness" is with reference to some definite sets of experiences. In the realm of world-Consciousness, when it is having the experience within and without, It can be called as a Witness. Then it can be a Witness of things happening. But when all the happenings are removed, there cannot be any Witness-hood. The "Witness" Itself becomes the Reality.

That which was a "Witness" while things were happening is Itself *re*-cognised as the pure nature of Absolute Truth.

असौ स्वसाक्षिको भावो यतः स्वेनानुभूयते ।
अतः परं स्वयं साक्षात्प्रत्यगात्मा न चेतरः ॥२१६॥

216. This *Atman* is a witness of Itself, for It is realised only by Itself. Hence the *Atman* Itself is the supreme *Brahman* and nothing else.

The Consciousness, the *Atman*, can only be said to be a Self-Witness *(Swa-sakshi)*. We cannot say that It is a Witness, save with reference to the parade of experiences within and without.

As long as there is the world and the sun, one can say that the sun is the illuminator of the world but if the world itself is wiped out by some cosmic convulsion or collision, the sun can no longer be said to be the "illuminator" of the world, the world itself being not there to be illumined by the sun.

Similarly, the Consciousness is a Witness of all that happens at the body, mind and intellect levels. When the body, mind and intellect, as equipments, are no more functioning, there can be neither inner nor outer experiences. Then the Self cannot be the *Sakshi*. What can It withness? All that can be said, is, that It realises Itself *(Swa-sakshi)*.

This *Atman* Itself is the supreme Self. This Life in each one of us is the same Life everywhere in the whole universe.

The realisation that "the Self in me is the Self everywhere", is not a different process of realisation. After experiencing the Self in me, I need not take up another *sadhana* to realise the Self everywhere. When I move towards the Self, the pluralistic, phenomenal world of perceptions suddenly ends, and where it ends, there is the experience of Consciousness alone, which is the Witness of Itself. It is a peculiar experience unlike all other experiences, It can be had *now---here*---in this very body.

With the body, mind and intellect, we get experiences of things other than ourselves, within the web of subject-object relationships. Where the subject and the object have merged to become a homogenous one, a knowledge wherin there is no object for knowing other than the Self, there we have to admit that this knowledge *(jnana)*, knows Itself. Here the subject and the object have become one and the same. What is called the "experience of *Brahman*" is, "becoming" *Brahman*. When a dreamer wakes up, he "becomes" the waker. Similarly, the limited individuality, at that moment, "becomes" *Brahman* and so there is not even the role of a Self-Witness *(Swa-Sakshi)*.

जाग्रत्स्वप्नसुषुप्तिषु स्फुटतरं योऽसौ समुज्जृम्भते
प्रत्यग्रूपतया सदाहमहमित्यन्तः सफुरन्नैकधा ।
नानाकारविकारभागिन इमान् पश्यन्नहंधीमुखान्
नित्यानन्दचिदात्मना सफुरति तं विद्धि स्वमेतं हृदि ॥२१७॥

217. That which clearly manifests Itself in the waking, dream and deep sleep states; that which is perceived inwardly in various forms by the mind as a series of unknown impressions of the ego; which witnesses the ego, the intellect, etc. which are of different forms and modifications, which is felt as Existence-Knowledge-Bliss Absolute, know this *Atman*, within your heart, as you own Self.

"That" is to be realised in one's own heart. The nature of "That" is being explained in this verse.

The *Atman* is clearly manifest in the waking, dream and deep-sleep states. That One, in whose presence all e- periences, at all times, throughout life are taking place, is the Self in us. The Consciousness which illumines the objects of the world in my waking state, and the experiences within during my dream state, and also the "absence of things" during my deep-sleep state, is the Self in me. This self which illumines the experiences in all three planes of consciousness, is to be very clearly known and experienced.

The subject illumines the objects outside. The subject can be recognise inside, in the deeper recesses of the personality, as the ever expressing I-I-I, the individuality. The "I", *(Aham)*, is the factor by whose grace our experiences within and without are made possible. The one Reality illumining the various types of experiences at the various personality levels, and ever expressing Itself as I-I-I, deep within, is one's Real Nature which is to be realised.

The diverse forms and their modifications are cognised through the intellect as the individual's knowledge. We say, "I know", "I experience", etc. It is that consciousness which is experiencing through the intellect, the various types of vicissitudes and their changes. When these differences of objects and their changes are transcended, this great Reality can be cognised in Itself, in Its pure nature as the Self in all.

When I start a sincere enquiry into this great Reality, I am compelled by the very nature of the enquiry, to withdraw from all my perceptions, emotions and thoughts. What then remains is Eternal, Changeless Bliss. This existence-Knowledge-Bliss Absolute *(Sat-chit-ananda)*, is to be realised in one's own heart.

घटोदके बिम्बितमर्कबिम्ब-
मालोक्य मूढो रविमेव मन्यते ।
तथा चिदाभासमुपाधिसंस्थं
भ्रान्त्याहमित्येव जडोऽभिमन्यते ॥ २१८ ॥

218. The fool, on seeing the reflection of the sun in the water in a jar, considers it to be the sun itself. So too, the fool through delusion, identifies himself with the reflection of the *Chit* caught in the intellect and considers it to be the "I"---his own identity.

Anyone who cries out, "The sun has fallen into a bucket of water on the verandah", is indeed, a fool. Those who consider themselves fallen into the PFT are equally foolish. In both cases it is only the reflection. The sun is reflected in the water, and consciousness plays upon the thoughts in the mind.

This "reflection" of Reality upon the thoughts is called *Chitabhasa.* It is the Consciousness playing upon the thoughts, and dancing to their rhythm, just as the reflected sun in the bucket dances when the waters are distrubed. I say, "I am agitated," "I am bad", "I am good". What is this "I"? It is the *Chitabhasa*, the "reflected Consciousness" ---this is the PFT, the Consciousness functioning through my BMI equipments.

Once you understand that the sun is in the heavens, then let the sun in the bucket be broken into a thousand pieces, you are not worried about the future existence of the sun. Only an insentient fool who considers the reflected sun to be the real one, will worry about its safety when he actually "sees" the sun in the bucket shatter to a thousand pieces.

I was looking into a lake and admiring my charming form when suddenly my reflection broke into pieces. Will I be foolish enough to weep and die, saying, "I am broken"? I *understand* that it is my reflection only. If I have not forgotten myself, I can watch the reflection and enjoy whenever the waters are rippled by the breeze and my reflection consequently gets corrugated. I shall laugh at the ugliness of my reflection and still remain unaffected. But if a fool has forgotten himself, and has identified himself with his own reflection, he will suffer when he directly *perceives* himself to be squeezed out of shape in the restless waters by some cruel breeze, created by an unmerciful and blind God.

घटं जलं तद्गतमर्कबिम्बं
विहाय सर्वं विनिरीक्ष्यतेऽर्कः ।
तटस्थ एतत्त्रितयावभासकः
स्वयंप्रकाशो विदुषा यथा तथा ॥ २१९ ॥

219. The intelligent man leaves aside the jar, the water and the reflection of the sun in it and sees the self-luminous sun. So too, The wise realise the Self-luminous Reality which illumines "these three" and reconise It as independent of them all.*

When we perceive the reflected sun in a jar of water, there are three things--the jar, the water in the jar and the reflection of the sun in it. As long as our attention is on the reflection, the *real* sun is not perceivable. In order to see the sun, we will have to lift our eyes *high up* from the jar, the water and the reflection. In the sun there is no jar, no water and no reflection. These three are symbolical examples to help us understand the play of the Self. This is called *Tatastha-lakshana*. You know the sun to be without the jar, the water and the reflection. If you are told, "The house on which the crow is sitting is Sri Gopal's residence", then every time you pass by, you don't look for the crow, do you? Once you know the house, the crow becomes dispensable. In this case, the crow is only a convenient, temporary, extraneous factor which helped in the first instance to distinguish Gopal's house from the array of all other houses. This method is called *"Tatastha-lakshana"*; the crow is no part of the house, but it hepls us to distinguish a particular house. The crow is *tatastha*.

Once you know the sun, you will understand that it is the illuminator of the jar, the water and the reflection. Nobody need illumine the sun. It is self-effulgent. It is its own light. In the light of the sun all other things are illumined.

Similarly, the wise man realises the Self. Apply the analogy subjectively to your own life and contemplate. Jar:

---

* **Swami Tapovan Maharaj used to say that these two verses, (218 & 219), helped him a lot in his *sadhana*.**

the body, water: the thoughts, the reflected sun: the ego. The sun in the heavens: the supreme Reality which illumines all these.

देहं धियं चित्प्रतिबिम्बमेवं
विसृज्य बुद्धौ निहितं गुहायाम् ।
द्रष्टारमात्मानमखण्डबोधं
सर्वप्रकाशं सदसद्विलक्षणम् ॥ २२० ॥

नित्यं विभुँ सर्वगतं सुसूक्ष्म-
मन्तर्बहिःशून्यमनन्यमात्मनः ।
विज्ञाय सम्यङ्.निजरूपमेतत्
पुमान् विपाप्मा विरजो विमृत्युः ॥ २२१ ॥

विशोक आनन्दघनो विपश्चित्
स्वयं कुतश्चिन्न बिभेति कश्चित् ।
नान्योऽस्ति पन्था भवबन्धमुक्ते-
र्विना स्वतत्त्वावगमं मुमुक्षोः ॥ २२२ ॥

220, 221, 222, So too, leaving aside the body, the intellect and the reflection of *Chit* in it, and realising in the cave of the intellect, the Witness, the Self, which is Knowledge Absolute, which is the cause of everything; which is distinct from the gross and the subtle, which is Eternal and Omnipresent, All-pervading and supremely subtle, which is without exterior or interior, which is the one Self; by fully realising this, one becomes free from sin, blemish, death and grief and becomes the ocean of Bliss. Being illumined, he is not afraid of anyone. For him who seeks liberation, there is no other path to break away from the bonds of transmigration than realising the Truth of his own Self.

The analogy given in the previous verse is elaborated in these three verses and exhaustively explained. As said above, the sun in the heavens can only be seen when one's attention is diverted from the pot, the water and the reflection of the sun in it. Similarly, in our subjective life, when the attention is turned away from the BMI we can realise *Brahman*, the Reality.

Diverting the attention from the body, the intellect and the reflection of *chit* in it, come to experience the supreme Reality, which is in the cave of the intellect. "In the cave of the intellect" means, that which is not even the intellect, but that which is the essence in the intellect. Therefore, the Self is that which is the intelligence in the intellect.

"What is to be seen in the cave of the intellect?" *Drashtaram*--the "Seer", not the "seen". The seer without the "objects seen", meaning, that One which illumines everything, which is your very own Self.

Atmanam--in your own Self.

"What is Its nature?" This is exhaustively discussed now.

Of Infinite Knowledge: *(Akhanda-bodham)*--That, because of which, all other knowldeges are possible is called Pure Knowledge. This is the *objectless*-Awareness. It is knowledge which is unbroken *(akhanda)*,--not the knowledge *of* things, but the knowledge which illumines all other knowledges.

Ever-effulgent: *(Sarva-Prakasam)*-Illumining everything and also the absence of things. It ever Is: never is not.

Neither has it form, nor is it formless: *(Sad-asad-vilakshanam)*---Neither gross nor subtle. It is beyond the form and the formless. It is the Knowing Principle of both the gross and the subtle: the knowledge *of* the gross and the subtle, *of* the form and the formless. The "knower" must be something other than the "known".

Eternal: *(Nityam)*--That which is changeless; not conditioned by time, space and causality.*

---

* *Desha-kala-vastu-aparichhinnah*-- (देश काल वस्तु अपरिच्छिन्नः)

All-pervading : (Sarva-gatam)-- Pervasiveness indicates subtlety--the Self pervades all and nothing pervades It--hence the epithet following immediately.

Subtler than the subtlest: *(Su-sookshmam)*--Subtlety is measured by pervasiveness: therefore, the term means, All-pervading.

Devoid of division within and without: *(Antar-bahirsoonya)*--The supreme Reality is All-pervading and Eternal and is One-without-a-second. For such a divine Truth, how can there be a "within" and a "without"? Within and without of what? It is homogenously present everywhere, at all times, in all circumstances.

Not different from yourself: *(Ananyam-atmanah)*--It is not to be recognised as an object existing and functioning somewhere outside. It is not other than the Self. We have to identify ourselves with this supreme Reality.

Having clearly understood this great Truth as one's own self, one becomes rid of all mental agitations. When we understand a thing as we understand ourselves, there will be no trace of doubt about it in us. Even if hundreds of people were to come and tell me that I was Swami Govindananda, will I ever have any doubt as to who I really am? Should such a thing happen, I would say there is definitely something wrong with them all.

If many people say something contradictory about any other thing, I may have doubts about it, but never can there be any doubt about myself. So firmly rooted must become the knowledge of the Self. This is not merely because the Teachers of the Upanishads say so, but because "I know It". We must come to live It, every moment of our lives.

Such a man of merit who has known thus, gets rid of all his "sins" *(papa)*. "Sin" is the negative vasana which creates agitations in the mind. Such a man becomes taintless. Even the good *vasanas* should be got rid of . *Vasanas*, good and bad, both are taints in the personality. In *Brahman*, the Reality, even good *vasanas* are disturbances. From the stand-point of supreme Peace *(Parama-shanti)*, even merit *(punya)* is relatively bad, a "sin" *(papa)*.

He becomes free from death *(vi-mrityuh)*: Death means, "the principle of change". His experiences are, thereafter, not through the body, mind and intellect. These equipments are constantly changing. Therefore, the experience gained through the BMI are not permanent. Every such experience must die. The man of realisation lives not upon these finite experiences-- hence, he is "free from change".

When one has realised the Infinitude, he no more experiences the world through these equipments. So he has no experience of finitude. He is free from all *vasanas*, negative and positive He no more lives in the realm of the mind. Indeed, his experience is of the Infinite alone.

Without any grief *(Vi-sokah)*: Never can any sorrow ever reach him. The body, the mind and the intellect are the three cancerous ulcers that pour forth the pus of sorrow into life. When these three are transcended, there can be no more agitations, or disturbances. The pauseless calm and unbroken serenity of the pure *Brahman*, the Absolute, is no more affected by anything in life.

Not only is there no pain, but there is a positive joy *(Ananda-ghana)*. A passive state of the no-pain condition is not the state of spiritual realisation. In deep-sleep, with a bottle of whiskhy, under chloroform or while swooning also there is no pain. In these cases, neither is there any pain, nor is there any lasting joy. But spiritual realisation is a state in which, not only are you not affected by the imperfections and sorrows of the BMI, but you experience the Infinite as a homogenous mass of everlasting happiness *(Ananda-ghana)*. At the BMI level, experience of a homogenous mass of happieness is not possible. All experiences at our present level of Consciousness are because of some object. The pure Bliss *(Ananda-ghana)*, is object-less. The self-illumined sage *(Vipaschit)* is he who has known all that is to be known. There is nothing more for him to know. He, thereafter has no fear at all. At the BMI level, there will always be a fear for security. Security of ideas and emotions, health and objects of attachment. A man who has transcended the BMI level, has no fear whatsoever, at any time, at any place, under any situation.[1]

Other than knowing the essential Reality which is the core of one's personality, there is no path[2] for liberation from the bondage-of-becoming. There is no other way to get out of the entanglements of change. Those seekers who have a burning desire for liberation, must try to know their real essential nature, through a direct and immediate experience.

ब्रह्माभिन्नत्वविज्ञानं भवमोक्षस्य कारणम् ।
येनाद्वितीयमानन्दं ब्रह्म सम्पद्यते बुधैः ॥ २२३ ॥

223. The cause for liberation from transmigration is the realisation of one's identity with *Brahman*. By means of this, wise men attain *Brahman*, the one-without-a-second, the Bliss Absolute.

Theoretical book-knowledge is called *jnanam*, but a full subjective experience is called direct-knowledge, *vijnanam*. It is not a *mediate* knowledge--it is an *immediate* knowledge.

The personal experience of one's identity with *Brahman*, the experience that "the Self in me is the Self everywhere", is the cause for liberation from the phenomenon-of-becoming. The experience of the merger of the life in me with the Life-Universal alone can remove the bondage of transmigration.

We, at present, have the knowledge *(Jnanam)*, that the life in us is the life manifesting everywhere. We know it from books. We have a vague intellectual appreciation of it; we can

---

1. Brihadaranyaka Upanishad III.8.8.
2. Taittireeya Upanishad II-2.

even convince others. But personal experience *(Vijnanam)*, is not there.

Brahman, the Life-spark in each one of us is One-without-a-second and is of the nature of All-Bliss.

A man of discriminative intellect alone can realise his spiritual identity. A dreamer, only when he wakes up, can realise the non-dual, one-without-a-second waker in him.

A bliss in duality is known to us all. The bliss arising out of the enjoyment of objects other than us (sense-pleasure), is known to us all. But the Bliss of Realisation is not because of any objects. It is *Brahma-ananda*--the very nature of *Brahman*. Wise men, experiencing this Bliss of the Self, which is the Self present everywhere, transcend all possibilities of transmigration.

ब्रह्मभूतस्तु संसृत्यै विद्वान्नावर्तते पुनः ।
विज्ञातव्यमतः सम्यग्ब्रह्माभिन्नत्वमात्मनः ॥ २२४ ॥

224. No more does one return to the world of transmigration after having become of the nature of *Brahman*. One must therefore, strive to realise one's identity with *Brahman*.

Brahma-bhootam is an idiom used in the Geeta: "One who has become of the nature of *Brahman*" At present we are but "masses of matter" *(bhootam)*.

It is a like a river which flows into the ocean and there becomes the ocean itself. When an individual realises his identity with *Brahman*, the jiva-hood *(jiva-bhootam)*, becomes the *Brahman-hood (Brahma-bhootam)*. Such an individual never returns to this world of births-and-deaths. He does not come back to live in the world-of-time, the world-of-change. Even if he does, he knows that they are all in him, not he in them.*

---

* *Na-tu-aham-teshu te-mayee* (न त्वहं तेषु ते मयी)
"I am not in them; they are in Me." Geeta VII-12.

Therefore, this is to be personally experienced. One has to be established in the experience of *Brahman*.

सत्यं ज्ञानमनन्तं ब्रह्म विशुद्धं परं स्वतःसिद्धम् ।
नित्यानन्दैकरसं प्रत्यगभिन्नं निरन्तरं जयति ॥ २२५ ॥

225. *Brahman* is Existence-Konwledge-Absolute, extremely Pure, Transcendental, Self-existing, Eternal, Indivisible-Bliss, not essentially different from the individual *jeeva*, and with no differences within or without. It is ever victorious!

Terms *indicating* Consciousness are given in this verse. They are repeated many times in the text-book. A correct knowledge of these terms helps one in meditation.

Truth or Existence: *(Satyam)*--That which remains the same in the three periods of time--past, present and future--is called Truth.

Knowledge: *(Jnanam)*--That Consciousness because of which all other knowledges are possible. This is "Knowledge" itself--not knowledge-of-a-thing.

Endless: *(Anantam)* --Endless, because it is eternal and because it is the Truth. Also, endless because it is without any beginning: so It is Absolute.

Satyam-jnanam-anantam Brahma--This is the Upanishadic definition of Truth: Truth-Knowledge-absolute. That which is permanent and endless and functions in the intellect as the Knowing Principle is the supreme Reality. It serves only as one blazing Consicousness at all times.

Extremely pure: *(Vi-suddham)*--Transcending all matter-vestures. A thing is said to be "pure" or "dirt free" only when there is no other thing in it than itself. In its subjective application the term comes to mean a person without *vasanas*.

Transcendental: (Param)--meaning,It transcends the BMI, When the BMI is transcended, there is naturally no PFT, and hence no OET also. What remains is Pure, Infinite Consciousness alone, the One-without-a-second.

Self-existing: *(Swatah-siddham)*--No instrument is necessary to know It. It is known by Itself. It is Self-effulgent. It being the Knowledge in the light of which all other knowledges are possible, to know this Knowledge, no other knowledge is necessary.

The nature of *Brahman* is said to be the "essence-of-Bliss-Absolute": *(Nitya-ananda-eka-rasa)*--If asked about the nature of *Brahman*, all that one can say is, It is of the essence-of-Bliss: not "Bliss". The essence-of-Bliss transcends even Bliss. The bliss (joy) arising out of sense-contacts cannot be "bliss" unless the enjoyer is conscious of it. This "bliss" that we ordinarily experience in the midst of objects is not of one homogenous nature *(eka-rasa)*. It is of varying intensities. The Bliss-of-*Brahman* is "of one essence". It is one continuous experience of unbroken, eternal Bliss.

Not different from the individual soul: *(Pratyak-abhinnam)*--*Brahman* is not anything other than the Self. It is the very *Atman*, the Self ever present in every one of us.

Ever victorious: *(Jayati)*---It gloriously lives in the bosoms of all. It wins victories over all other layers of matter which must, in their finitude, decay and perish.

48. All Manifestation Absolute. (226-236)

सदिदं परमाद्वैतं स्वस्मादन्यस्य वस्तुनोऽभावात् ।
न ह्यन्यदस्ति किञ्चित् सम्यक् परमार्थतत्त्वबोध-
दशायाम् ॥ २२६ ॥

226. This Absolute Oneness alone is Real since there is nothing other than the Self. Truly, there is no other independent entity in the state of realisation of the supreme Truth.

This Reality, which is of the nature of the pure Knowledge, is supreme-most and non-dual. There is, in It, no otherness.

Distinctions such as the experiencer and the experienced are not possible in It. When you realise the higher plane of Consciousness, the lower planes and their objects are transcended. It is non-dual because It is one's own Self. In that moment, there is a total absence of all things save the Self. There is only One Infinite *Brahman*. In the moment of Realisation, this supreme-most essence is complete. Complete in Itself, with Itself, there is nothing other than It.

यदिदं सकलं विश्वं नानारूपं प्रतीतमज्ञानात् ।
तत्सर्वं ब्रह्मैव प्रत्यस्ताशेषभावनादोषम् ॥ २२७ ॥

227. This entire universe which, because of ignorance, appears to be of infinite forms, is, in fact, *Brahman* alone, which is free from all limitations of thought.

The world of plurality, with its manifold froms which we see all around, is perceived because of the non-apprehension of *Brahman*, the Reality. Due to the non-apprehension of Reality, all misapprehensions of the pluralistic phenomenal world have arisen.

All that we see is *Brahman*, and *Brahman* alone do we see everywhere as objects and things. When the evil of "imagination" of the mind is destroyed, without an iota of it remaining to defile the Truth, then you shall realise that what you are perceiving is *Brahman* only.

मृत्कार्यभूतोऽपि मृदो न भिन्नः
कुम्भोऽस्ति सर्वत्र तु मृत्स्वरूपात् ।
न कुम्भरूपं पृथगस्ति कुम्भः
कुतो मृषा कल्पितनाममात्रः ॥ २२८ ॥

228. Though a pot is a modification of clay, it is not any different from it. In essence, the pot is the same everywhere. So why call it a pot. It is merely a false and fancied name.

Pots, made out of mud, though named differently, in essence are all nothing but mud. A Ganges-pot, a milk-pot, a honey-pot or a water-pot---they are all different names depending upon the usage of each pot. In essence, they are all mud only.* They have come out of mud, therefore they are all nothing but mud in their true nature.

Similarly, out of *Brahman* the world has come and therefore, it cannot be anything other than *Brahman.* But at the same time, when we are dealing with the world, we forget that it is all *Brahman.* When we see the world-of-change we are apt to forget that it is the changeless *Brahman* everywhere.

Whatever be its name, shape and form, a pot is nothing but mud. Similarly, the BMI and OET are all nothing but different names and forms playing in the same Infinite Consciousness, from which they have arisen.

केनापि मृदभिन्नतया स्वरूपं
घटस्य संदर्शयितुं न शक्यते ।
अतो घटः कल्पित एव मोहा-
न्मृदेव सत्यं परमार्थभूतम् ॥२२९॥

229. No one can show by demonstration that the essence of a mud-pot is other than the mud. Therefore, the pot is merely imagined through delusion, and mud-aspect alone is the enduring Reality in the mud-pot.

A mud-pot can never be proved as made up of anything else. A mud-pot is mud. Whatever be its contents, the mud alone is the pot. The pot has no independent existence apart from the mud. So the pot is the "imagination" of a form and a function in the mud. Similarly, the world has no independent existence from *Brahman.* Among mud-pots, the

---

* वाचारंभणं विकारो नाम धेयं मृत्तिकेत्येव सत्यं ॥छां३॥ Chhandogya Upnishad: "Names are given to the various modifications -- but mud alone is the Truth in all mud-pots......"

ultimate truth is mud alone and there is nothing other than mud. The pot is a superimposition on the mud.

सद्ब्रह्मकार्यं सकलं सदेवं
तन्मात्रमेतन्न ततोऽन्यदस्ति ।
अस्तीति यो वक्ति न तस्य मोहो
विनिर्गतो निद्रितवत्प्रजल्पः ॥२३०॥

230. So too, the entire universe, being the effect of the Real *Brahman*, can be nothing other than It. It is of the essence of That and it cannot exist apart from That. Anyone who says it does, is still under delusion and twaddles like one in deep-sleep.

The effect that has arisen from the cause, the Existence *(Sat)*, can only be the same *Sat*. The effect is nothing but the cause itself in another form. One pot may be called the Ganges-pot and another may be called a water-pot. the difference is in their usage. But in essence they are both nothing but mud.

Similarly, in this world, one can be a saint and another a sinner. People may have varying degrees of goodness and badness, but they are, in their Real Nature, divine, because they are all the effects of the one *Brahman*.

If anyone insists that there is something other than *Brahman*, he is not to be blamed, since he is only crying in delusion. His *vasanas* have not yet left him completely. Any perception of plurality is on account of the *vasanas*. As long as *vasanas* exist, so long the mind functions and the mind can only perceive duality *(dwaita-bhavanā)*. He who says that there is some factor or factors other than *Brahman*, is only prattling meaninglessly.

A man in dream seeing a dream-tiger, cries out in sleep. On waking up he himself understands that his shouting was but senseless drivelling.

Similarly we, asleep to the Supreme State, know only the body and its ego and all our experiences are "meaningless prattlings", says the man of Realisation *(Jnani), Acharya* Sankara.

ब्रह्मैवेदं विश्वमित्येव वाणी
श्रौती ब्रूतेऽथर्वनिष्ठा वरिष्ठा ।
तस्मादेतद्ब्रह्ममात्रं हि विश्वं
नाधिष्ठानाद्भिन्नताऽऽरोपितस्य ॥२३१॥

231. Truly, this entire universe is *Brahman*-- this is the declaration of the *Atharva Veda*. Therefore, this universe is *Brahman* alone, for a superimposition has no existence independent of its substratum.

"*Brahman* alone is this universe" --*(Brahma-eva-idamviswam)*--This is the declaration we find in the *Mundakopanishad** *which belongs to the Atharva Veda.* The entire world of names and froms we preceive is nothing but *Brahman.*

Not only do we find by analogy that the effect is nothing but the cause in another form, but also, this conclusion is supported by the scriptures *(Sruti)*. The *Upanishads* too, declare the same Truth. Therefore, *Brahman* alone is this world of plurality that is around us.

The ultimate reality of a superimposition is its own substratum.The "ghost" cannot be anything other than the post. Nor can the "serpent" be different from the rope. While the delusion lasts, we are subject to the "vision" of the superimposition, and we suffer all the consequences thereof. When Realisation *(bodha)* dawns, we come to know that the substratum alone is real. Not only do we come to know the *reality* of the post, but we also realise that the post had never undergone any change to become the "ghost". There was no modification ever in the post to create the vision of the ghost: it was only a projection of the mind, an illusion of the mind called *vivarta*

सत्यं यदि स्याज्जगदेतदात्मनो-
ऽनंतत्त्वहानिर्निगमाप्रमाणता ।

---

* Mundakopanishad II-2-II.

असत्यवादित्वमपीशितुः स्या-
न्नैतत्त्रयं साधु हितं महात्मनाम् ॥२३२॥

232. If the universe, as it is, is Real, the *Atman* would not be Infinite, the scriptures would not be false, the Lord Himself would be guilty of having spoken an untruth. None of these three is considered either desirable or wholesome by the pure-minded ones.

If you say that the universe, the world as we see it, is *real*, there would be the following contradictions:-

(a) Loss of endlessness : *(anantattwa-hani)*--*Brahman* is said to be All-pervading and Infinite. If the world as we see it is also *real*, it would then condition the Infinite, rendering It limited. The *Atman* will be limited and will no more be Infinite. This is contradictory to the declarations of the *Upanishads*.

(b) Falsification of scriptures: *(nigama-apramanata)*--The scriptures declare that *Brahman* is Real and the world is unreal. If you say that the world is real, the incontrovertibly true declarations of the scriptures would be falsified.

(c) The Lord becomes a liar: *(asatya-vadittwam-api-Isuh)*--The Lord is the Revealer of the Truths of the *Upanishads*. If the Upanishadic declarations are false, so would be the Lord Who revealed them. *Bhagavan* Sri Krishna, in the Geeta, declares more than once that the world is just a projection and in fact, has no reality.

Wise men will not accept these terrible conclusions:-

(a) loss of the *Atman's* Infinitude, (b) falsification of scriptural declarations and (c) the Lord becoming a liar. None of the six schools of philosophy will accept them. So we have to conclude that the world is "unreal".

ईश्वरो वस्तुतत्त्वज्ञो न चाहं तेष्ववस्थितः ।
न च मत्स्थानि भूतानीत्येवमेव व्यचीक्लृपत् ॥२३३॥

233. The Lord, who knows the secret of all things, has expressly supported this view in His words---"But I do not live in them....", "Nor do beings exist in Me."

The Lord is One Who knows the play of plurality and its substratum, *Brahman*. In *Brahman* there is no world, nor is *Brahman* available for direct perception in the world. He who knows both is the All knower, the *Iswara*. He knows that there is *Brahman* and He, in His infinite wisdom, plays with the world of objects. Lord Sri Krishna in the Geeta says,[1], I do not live in them", meaning, I am not in the joys and sorrows of the BMI."They are all in Me"[2]

Again, the Lord says, "Nothing is born out of Me".[3] They are all only apparently there, just as the ghost in the post. The world of plurality has only a relative existence. When you look at Truth through the BMI, the world of OET alone is perceived. When the BMI are transcended, pure Consciousness is experienced, as Full both within and without.

यदि सत्यं भवेद्विश्वं सुषुप्तावुपलभ्यताम् ।
यन्नोपलभ्यते किञ्चिदतोऽसत्स्वप्नवन्मृषा ॥२३४॥

234. If the universe were true, it would have been perceived even in the deep-sleep state. Since it is not at all perceived, it must be, like dreams, false and unreal.

Truth *(Satyam)*, is that which remains unchanged, in all the three periods of "time". The pluralistic phenomenal world is perceptible as long as one is awake. Once the individual enters the bliss-hall of deep-sleep, the pluralistic world at

1. Na cha-aham teshu-avasthitah-- न चाहं तेष्ववस्थितः "But I do not live in them....."
Bhagawat Geeta IX--4

2. In the same verse it is declared, *Mat-sthani sarva-bhootani*--- मत्स्थानि सर्व भूतानि "All beings exist in Me."
Bhagawat Geeta IX--4

3. *Na cha mat-sthani bhootani*--न च मत्स्थानि भूतानि "Nor do beings exist in Me."
Bhagawat Geeta IX--5

once ends. On his waking up, it again manifests itself to him. That which remains at one time but not at another, can never be the Truth. Even when available for cognition during the waking-state, it undergoes change. It never remains the same. Hence the world is only *as true* as is a dream. Both are equally unreal---mere projections of a mind under delusion.

अतः पृथङ्नास्तिजगत्परात्मनः
पृथक्प्रतीतिस्तु मृषा गुणादिवत् ।
आरोपितस्यास्ति किमर्थवत्ताऽ-
धिष्ठानमाभाति तथा भ्रमेण ॥२३५॥

235. Therefore, the world does not exist independent of the Supreme Self and, like "qualities" the notion of its separateness is false. Can a superimposition have any meaning apart from its own substratum? Through delusion, it is the substratum itself which appears like that.

The world has no separate existence from the Supreme Self. In case you see anything other than *Brahman*, it is false, like the "properties" *(gunas)*. The blueness in the summer sky and the horrible grin of the bony ghost-in-the-post have no existence at all. The superimposition has no existence apart from its own substratum, which is seen to be of a different form because of the observer's delusion. The mind and the intellect have delusory misconceptions, hence we see the phenomenal world. It has no existence apart from its "substratum", the Supreme Reality. Any preception of plurality is but a delusion of the mind.

भ्रान्तस्य यद्यद्भ्रमतः प्रतीतं
ब्रह्मैव तत्तद्रजतं हि शुक्तिः ।
इदंतया ब्रह्म सदैव रूप्यते
त्वारोपितं ब्रह्मणि नाममात्रम् ॥२३६॥

236. Through error of judgement whatever a deluded man perceives can only be *Brahman* and *Brahman* alone. The silvery sheen perceived is nothing but a mother-of-pearl. *Brahman* is ever-present as "this" universe and that which is superimposed on *Brahman* can only be a mere name.

A mad man or a lunatic is he whose intellect is not functioning fully and properly. Man generally experiences the world alone which, really speaking, is nothing but *Brahman*. Whatever he experiences is *Brahman* alone. The bright reflecting silvery pieces on the sea-shore are nothing but bits of mother-of-pearl. Similarly, wherever one sees the pluralistic phenomenal world, it is nothing but Consiciousness.

Whatever you can point out as "This", "This", *(idam-taya)*, as an object, or as an emotion or as a thought, is nothing but *Brahman* playing in those forms. *Brahman* playing in conceivable and perceivable forms, is the world we see around us. The name of a thing is because of its form. The names and forms are projected on *Brahman*. In the world that you see around yourself, if from any single object, you remove the name and form, what remains? "That" is the Infinite Reality, "That" is *Brahman*.

Contemplate upon any object. The leaves fluttering in the breeze, the bird perched on the tree---anything---remove the name and form.* What remains is the Existence *(Sat)*, that expresses as the existence-of-the-thing. This is Peace-Auspiciousness-Beauty. *(Santam-Sivam-Sundaram)*.

49. Brahman---Its Nature. (237-240)

अतः परं ब्रह्म सदद्वितीयं
विशुद्धविज्ञानघनं निरञ्जनम् ।
प्रशान्तमाद्यन्तविहीनमक्रियं
निरन्तरानन्दरसस्वरूपम् ॥२३७॥

---

* Thus in the Zen meditation exercises, the teacher advises the student, "meditate upon your face.....as it was just before you were born".

निरस्तमायाकृतसर्वभेदं
नित्यं सुखं निष्कलमप्रमेयम् ।
अरूपमव्यक्तमनाख्यमव्ययं
ज्योतिः स्वयं किञ्चिदिदं चकास्ति ॥२३८॥

237, 238. Therefore, whatever is manifested is the Supreme *Brahman* Itself---Real, Non-dual, extremely pure, the essence of Knowledge-Absolute, taintless, supremely peaceful, without beginning, or end, beyond all activity, always of the nature of Bliss Absolute, transcending all diversities created by *Maya*, Eternal, the essence of joy, Indivisible, Immeasurable, Formless, Unmanifest, Nameless, Immutable and Self-effulgent.

The world of object that we see around is, in itself, by itself, nothing but *Brahman*. *Brahman* misrepresented by our misconception is the world. In these two verses Sankara gives us twenty *adjectival* phrases which *indicate Brahman*.

(1) Transcendental- *(Para)* -the illumining principle behind BMI, PFT, OET is the pure Self the Consciousness which is one-without-a-second upon which the universe of names and forms is an illusory projection. Hence *Brahman* is indicated in Vedantic philosophy as transcendental.

(2) Real: *(Sat)*--- That which remains the same in all the three periods of time---past, present and future---is called "real".

(3) One-without-a-second: *(Adwiteeyam)*--- The One ultimate Eternal Reality, without any otherness to limit or condition It is the Non-dual, the One-without-a-second.

(4) Extremely pure: *(Vi-suddham)*--- A thing is said to be pure when there is nothing other than it, in it. It is non-dual and therefore it is extremely pure, that is, it has no *vasana*--- dirt in it.

(5) Homogenous mass of Pure Knowledge: *(Vigyana ghanam)*--- Knowledge *of* things varies according to the things. This is the Knowledge because of which all other knowledges

are possible. This is objectless-knowledge, Absolute Knowledge.

(6) Without any taint: *(Niranjanam)*--- *Vasanas* are said to be the "taints". The *Atman*, the Self, is beyond all *vasanas* and so is taintless.

(7) Supremely peaceful: *(Pra-santam)*--- There are no agitations in It because the mind and the intellect have been transcended. It is not a temporary cessation of thoughts as in deep-sleep or when swooning. It is the realisation of That which is the Witness of the very condition of peacefulness--- hence supremely peaceful.

(8) Devoid of beginning and end: *(Adi-anta-viheenam)*--- Eternal, Immutable, changeless, Limitless. That which is not conditioned by birth and death: no beginning, no end, no modification.

(9) Beyond activity: *(A-kriyam)*--- Because It is All pervading, it cannot act: there is nothing other than It for It to serve, no field for It to function in. Also, where there are no *vasanas*, there cannot be any desires, and hence there is no activity in the All-full *Brahman*.

(10) Of the nature of Eternal Bliss: *(Nirantar-ananda-rasa-swaroopam)*-- It is not just happiness. Bliss is Its state, because when we are in that plane, we live beyond the tossings of the mind and intellect. Now this Bliss also is to be known. The man in *Samadhi* rises above both his mind and intellect.

(11) Transcending all diversities created by *Maya: (Nirasta-maya-krita-sarva-bhedam)*--- *Maya* means the non-apprehension of Reality. *Maya*-created confusions are the diversities caused by *Maya*. They together constitute the world of plurality. They are the sum total of our *misapprehensions* created by the non-apprehension of Reality.

(12) Eternal: *(Nityam)*--- That is Eternal which is not conditioned by space, time or objects. It is that which is ever unconditioned by the three periods of time.

(13) The essence of pleasure: *(Sukham)*--- Not the pleasure-emotion as such, but that which illumines all sentiments of joy and emotions of pleasure in us.

(14) Without any parts: *(Nish-kalam)*--- Unconditioned, limitless. That which is All-pervading and One-without-a-second cannot have parts.

(15) Immeasurable: *(A-prameyam)*---Incomparable. That which cannot be reached or known through any means of measure *(Prama)*, such as comparison or argument. How can we ever measure or compare the All-pervading, One-without-a-second, Infinite Reality? With what will we measure It? With what else will we compare It?

(16) Formless: *(Aroopam)*--- An unconditioned eternal thing cannot have any form. It is limitless, hence there can be no form for It.

(17) Unmanifest: *(Avyaktam)*--- That which cannot be sensed by the sense-organs, felt by the mind or comprehended by the intellect is "unmanifest".

(18) Nameless: *(An-aakhyam)*--- Since there is no form there can be no name to indicate It. Only That which has form and qualities can have a name to distinguish it from similar things.

(19) Immutable, Irreducible: *(Avyayam)*--- That which is Eternal and Changeless is Immutable too.

(20) Self-lumious or Self-effulgent: *(jyoti-swayam)*--- To know that no other medium, no other light is necessary. It is the light of Consciousness by which the whole world is illumined.

All these twenty terms are *indicative* of the *Atman*, the Self, which is ever present in each one of us. These may be considered as twenty exercises in deep meditation for developed *sadhaks*. None of them, in fact, defines Reality. But each one of them *suggests*, and all of them in their totality, directly point out the essential Self behind the mind and its agitations.

ज्ञातृज्ञेयज्ञानशून्यमनन्तं निर्विकल्पकम् ।
केवलाखण्डचिन्मात्रं परं तत्त्वं विदुर्बुधाः ॥२३९॥

239. Sages realise the Supreme Truth in which there are no distinctions such as the knower, the knowledge and the known, which is Infinite, Transcendental and which is of the essence of Knowledge Absolute.

Truth is beyond the triple factors of the knower, the knowledge and the known. When the individuality has ended there is no instrument of experience separate from the object of experience. As long as the dream lasts, there is a dreamer experiencing the dream objects. The dreamer with the help of his equipments saw, heard, smelt, tasted and touched the dream-world around. On waking up, not only does the dreamer become the waker, but the dream experiences too, become the waker, nay the dream-world-of-objects also becomes the waker.

Today, as an individual entity, the ego, I may recognise the world of plurality through my body, mind and intellect equipments. When I rise above them and spiritually wake up, I become fully awake to the Consciousness. Then I, my equipments of experience and my objects of experience can no longer be separate, but they all merge into the One Supreme Consciousness.

This awakening to the Consciousness is not a *passing* experience. Once it has been experienced, it is endless. It is beyond all doubts and imaginations. It is the unbroken experience of pure Consciousness *(Kevalam-akhandam-chinmatram)*. Wise men come to experience this Supreme

Essence in themselves as their very being. Experience of this great Truth is God-realisation.

अहेयमनुपादेयं मनोवाचामगोचरम् ।
अप्रमेयमनाद्यन्तं ब्रह्म पूर्णमहं महः ॥२४०॥

240. That which can neither be thrown away nor taken up, that which lies beyond the limits of mind and speech, which is Immeasurable, which is without beginning and end, which is whole and one's own Self, which is of outshining glory--- that is the Self.

Indicating this great Truth it is said, "It can never be rejected *(Aheyam)*". The five *kosas* can be rejected. After rejecting the five sheaths we come to a substratum which cannot at all be rejected. That is the Supreme Consciousness.

Nor can it be taken up: *(Anupadeyam)*--- That which is not with you can be taken up by you. This great Truth is your very own Self which is already there. How can it be taken up, accepted, the very one who accepts being the essence accepted?

The ultimate Reality is beyond the comprehension of the sense-organs and the mind. It is not an object which can be experienced. It is the very subject which comprehends all objects. Also, It is Immeasurable and Incomparable. Measurements and comparisons are possible between *two* objects. The One without a beginning and an end, an Infinite Reality, is one's own Self.

In the previous verse the Teacher said that wise men alone realise this great Truth. In this verse he says it is our own Real Nature.

50. "That Thou Art"--- Explanation. (241-249)

तत्त्वंपदाभ्यामभिधीयमानयो-
र्ब्रह्मात्मनोः शोधितयोर्यदीत्थम् ।

श्रुत्या तयोस्तत्त्वमसीति सम्य-
गेकत्वमेव प्रतिपाद्यते मुहुः ॥२४१॥
ऐक्यं तयोर्लक्षितयोर्न वाच्ययो-
र्निगद्यतेन्योन्यविरुद्धधर्मिणोः ।
खद्योतभान्वोरिव राजभृत्ययोः
कूपाम्बुराश्योः परमाणुमेर्वोः ॥२४२॥

241-242. If *Sruti* in her maxim "That Thou Art", repeatedly establishes the identity of *Brahman* and *jeeva*, indicated by the term "That" *(Tat)* and "Thou" *(Twam)* respectively, then stripping these terms of their relative associations, their implied but not literal meanings are to be inculcated. For they are of contradictory attributes---like the sun and the glow-worm, the king and the servant, the ocean and the well, mount Meru and the atom.

Tat and *Twam* are the two words in the famous maxim *(Mahavakya)*, of the Vedas, *Tat Twam Asi*. *Tat* means *"Brahman"* and *Twam* means *"Atman"*. These two are one and the same" *(Asi)*, is the meaning indicated by the *Upanishads*. When the *Mahavakya* says, "You are God", you the body can never be God. Neither can you the mind, nor can you the intellect ever be God. When all the five *kosas* are transcended, the divine Spark of Existence is to be known. In all the previous verses, the *Atman*, the Self functioning in man has been explained.

Brahman, the universal Consciousness functioning in the physical body is called "subjective Self" *(Adhyatma)*. This *Atman* functioning in you is the Self present everywhere *(Brahman)*. This is indicated by this *Mahavakya*, this great declaration of the *Upanishads*.

When the nature of the three bodies is investigated, we come to apprehend that there is a Consciousness which is illumining all our thoughts. That Consciousness in us is the Consciousness everywhere is the meaning of the pregnant statement, *Tat Twam Asi*. This declaration of the *Upanishads* again and again indicates the identity *(Ekattwam)*, of *Atman* and *Brahman*.

According to the literal word-meaning, the identity of man *(Twam)* and God *(Tat)*, is impossible. How can I, a limited. mortal, finite, miserable creature be that Infinite *Satchidananda?* Between the two there is as much difference as there is between a lamb and an elephant. How can they be one and the same?

The identity, of the *Atman* and *Brahman* is derived from the *indicative* meaning or the *implied* meaning;* of the *Mahavakya*. In the declaration, the identity is *implied*. It is trying to explain that the essential core in each one of us is one and the same, and that is god. God is All-pervading, and therefore Omnipresent. Thus, the *Upanishad* is trying to make us understand the oneness of the Essence of the individual and the Essence of the whole universe. The distinction between the two is obvious. Man is "born", God is "unborn". Man is "growing", God is "changeless". Man is "perishable". God is "imperishable". Man is "mortal", God is "immortal". Man's knowledge is "limited", God's knowledge is "unlimited".

Hence the *Mahavakya* is not declaring the literal meaning but suggesting the implied, the indicative meaning. The essence, the core, the very existence in us is the substratum and vitality of the whole universe. The reality behind the universe is the Reality behind each individual also.

When from the universe the names and forms are removed and from the individual the five *kosas* are negated, what is left over in the outer and the inner world is the One Infinite Consciousness which has no such distinctions as outside or inside.

To indicate this obvious distinction between man and God four examples are given here by *Acharya* Sankara :--

(1) The glow-worm and the sun, (2) the servant and the king, (3) the well and the ocean and (4) the atom and mount Meru.

---

* *Vakya-artha*---word-meaning; *Lakshya-artha*---indicative meaning.

In these examples, the limited light of the glow-worm *(jeeva)*, and the unlimited light of the sun *(Iswara)*; the ruled servant *(jeeva)*, and the ruler-king *(Iswara)*; the limited space of the well *(jeeva)*, and the unlimited expanse of the ocean *(Iswara)*; the minute atom *(jeeva)*, and the gigantic Meru *(Iswara)* ---between these, how can there be any identity?

तयोर्विरोधोऽयमुपाधिकल्पितो
न वास्तवः कश्चिदुपाधिरेषः ।
ईशस्य माया महदादिकारणं
जीवस्य कार्यं श्रृणु पञ्चकोशम् ॥२४३॥

243. The difference between them is only created by superimposition and is not real. The conditioning in the case of *Iswara* is *Maya*, or *Mahat* etc. And listen, the conditionings in the case of the *jeeva* are the five sheaths.

The difference between *Iswara*, the Lord, and *jeeva*, the individual entity is indeed great. This is brought out clearly by the examples cited in the previous verse. On a close observation we find that the much talked-about differences between them are all because of each one's conditionings, the *upadhis*--- they do not exist in essence. The equipments are different and so the difference between them due to the equipments is only apparent. In Its essential nature, *Brahman*, the Supreme, has no equipments at all. It is One-without-a-second. This *Brahman* or Reality expresses itself as *Iswara* and *jeeva* because of the difference in conditionings. When the great Rishis of the *Upanishads* declared, "That Thou Art", they did not mean that the expression of the divine Self in the various equipments is one and the same, but they only meant that the Factor which is expressing through all conditionings is one and the same. The Supreme expresses through two different types of vehicles givinig rise to two different types of expressions---*Iswara* and *jeeva*. When the equipments of both are removed, that which expresses through both is experienced as one and the same. In fact, in reality there are no equipments at all.

The supreme Reality functioning through *Maya* is called *Iswara* or God. Vedantic masters call this equipment *Maya, which is called. Mahat* in other schools of philosophy.[1] When the supreme Reality functions through a set of five sheaths, there is an expression of a *jeeva*, an individual entity.

When these equipments the *Maya* or *Mahat* and the five *kosas*[2] are removed from God and Man respectively, what remains is the one and the same Ultimate Reality.[3]

In order to make us clearly understand this, the *Upanishads* explain it employing a set of terms and terminologies evolved by them. Consciousness functioning through an individual entity is called the Microcosm *(Vyashti)*, and that functioning through the totality, the whole cosmos, is called the Macrocosm *(Samashti)*.

The Absolute Reality which functions through the Microcosm and the Macrocosm are transcended, what remains is the Supreme Reality. When the mind and the intellect are transcended, the *jeeva* merges into *Iswara*.

God is the Reality functioning through the total *vasanas*. In Vedanta, the total *vasanas* are called *Maya*.

Brahman, the Reality, functioning through my *vasanas*, thoughts and emotions ordered this physical body in my mother's womb and has appeared in an environment where alone it can find their fulfilment. After taking the physical body, it moves from environment to environment in order to exhaust its most powerful *vasanas*.

Any conscious act---physical, mental, or intellectual---creates *vasanas*. A physical body is not necessary to create *vasanas*. Going Back to the cause of thoughts or the first

1. Ibid verse 123 where *Mahat* is explained as "total intellect".
2. Ibid verse 125.
3. We may in short say that God minus *Maya* is *Brahman*; and *jeeva* minus the five sheaths is also *Brahman*.

cause, is called "meditation". *Vasanas* create the world, and the world around us creates *vasanas* in us.

MICROCOSM *(VYASHTI)*	MACROCOSM *(SAMASHTI)*
1. Represents an individual entity : *jeeva*	Represents the entire world of plurality put together, the cosmos : *Jagat.*
2. The Supreme Consciousness functioning through a given gross body is called *Vishwa*, and because it expresses itself in the waking condition, it is called the "*waker*".	The Supreme Consciousness functioning through the aggregate of all the gross bodies is called *Virat.* This is the cosmic form of the waker.
3. The Supreme Consciousness functioning through the individual subtle body is known as *Taijasa* It expresses itself in the dream condition and so is called the "dreamer"	The Supreme Consciousness functioning through the aggregate of all subtle bodies (the total mind-and-intellect), is called *Hiranya-garbha, the* Creator.
4. The Supreme Self functioning through the causal body, the *Vasanas* (ignorance), the non-apprehension of Reality, the *Avidya*, is called *Prajna.* It expresses itself in the deep-sleep condition and hence is called the "sleeper".	The same *Atman* functioning through the aggregate of all causal bodies (the non-apprehension of Reality), The *Maya*, is called *Iswara*, the Great Lord.

Brahman functioning through the total *vasanas* is called God *(Iswara)*, and functioning through individual *vasanas* is called the *jeeva*. Hence when the individual *vasanas* are exhausted, the individual-concept also ends, the microcosm gets annihilated, the *jeeva* is no more. When *jeeva* is annihilated there is no one to recognise the macrocosm, and so the macrocosm also ends. Thus the oneness of the *jeeva* and *Iswara*--- the individual ego and God---is realised. This is called God realisation.

Maya is termed differently by different philosophers. All of them agree that the cause for the whole universe is the dynamic infinitude functioning through the Total-Cause, but this Total-Cause is denoted by various terms. The cause for the individuality is the Conciousness functioning through the five sheaths, or the three bodies or the three states. *Brahman* has no conditionings but *jeeva* and *Iswara* are the two concepts arising when *Brahman* apparently functions through the illusory equipments.

एतावुपाधी परजीवयोस्तयोः
सम्यङ्निरासे न परो न जीवः ।
राज्यं नरेन्द्रस्य भटस्य खेटक-
स्तयोरपोहे न भटो न राजा ॥२४४॥

244. These two are superimpositions of *Iswara* and *jeeva*, but when they are completely eliminated, there is neither *Iswara* nor *jeeva*. When the kingdom of the king and the shield of the soldier are taken away, there can neither be a king nor a soldier.

When electricity functions through a 1,000 candle-power bulb, its intensity of light is more than when it functions through a 5 candle-power bulb when there is certainly less light. If the 5 candle-power bulb is replaced by a 1,000 candle power bulb, the light in both will be the same. When the bulbs

---

* कार्योपाधिरयम् जीवः कारणोपाधिरीश्वरः

are destroyed, the electricity becomes one and the same energy without its different light-manifestations.

Consciousness functioning through a limited equipment manifests as a limited individual who is at all moment suffering from the passions of his flesh, the agitations of his mind and the limitations of his intellect. Thus the *jeeva* is a sorrowful, miserable creature, suffering more and more in his anxiety to fulfil himself. The same Consciousness functioning through the total equipments is the mighty Presence in the entire cosmos and its Creator, God, is the substratum for and the sole sustainer of everything.

"Now then," the Teacher says, "When I destroy the 5 candle-power bulb with a stick and with the same stick when the 1,000 candle-power bulb is also broken, there is neither less light nor more light; there is no light at all. What remains is electricity". Similarly, when the equipments are removed from both, God and the individual, there is neither a *para*, God, nor a *jeeva*, the individual. Then there is no distinction at all between the essence in God and the presence in the *jeeva*. To the *jeeva*, there is a world of plurality, and to the world of plurality there is a Creator. This is acceptable to the intellect, very satisfying indeed. But the pure Essence behind the world lies beyond the intellect. Therefore the intellect is to be transcended. The intellect cannot be transcended unless the *vasanas* are exhausted. When an individual's *vasanas* are exhausted, he transcends the intellect and directly realises that he, the individual, is no more an individual. He has risen above the individuality, the ego (*jeeva-bhavana*). When one has risen above one's sense of individuality, one has risen above the sense of totality, the God concept also.

Sankara, faithful to his own style of discourse, gives an example here to illustrate the idea. When the kingdom of the kind and the shield of the soldier are both taken away from them, then there can be neither a king nor a soldier.

The king is a king and the soldier is a soldier because of each one's position and status. An officially dismissed

policeman and a politically relieved minister are both common citizens with no distinguishing powers or duties.

Maya is the equipment of *Iswara*, God and the five *kosas* are the equipments of the *jeeva*, the ego. When these equipments are transcended, the essence behind both *Iswara* and *jeeva* will be realised as the One Infinite Reality.

Then how are we to reject these limiting adjuncts that condition the Self and make It play as god and ego? This is explained in the following verse.

अथात आदेश इति श्रुतिः स्वयं
निषेधति ब्रह्मणि कल्पितं द्वयम् ।
श्रुतिप्रमाणानुगृहीतबोधा
त्तयोर्निरासः करणीय एव ॥२४५॥

245. "Now is the injunction' etc.---in these words the scriptures reject the imagined duality in *Brahman*. Supported by the authority of the scriptures one must certainly eliminate these two superimpositions by means of direct Realisation.

In Brihadaranyakopanishad, the *Rishi* starts, "Now then, is the injunction, 'not this', 'not this',* meaning, "Now, therefore, we are giving you the *adesa*, the injunction for the experience of the Reality". Thus the instructions continue and explain how the pluralistic phenomenal world or the equipments are to be transcended and negated. The *Upanishad* negates plurality which is the illusion of the mind. Plurality is only the projection of the mind and intellect. Where the mind and the intellect do not function there is no plurality. In deep-sleep or swooning there is no plurality perceived at all. *Sruti* negates plurality as unreal, and says that behind and beneath it, there is a vital Absolute Reality which is to be experienced. One has to get out of this plurality in order to realise the Reality.

---

* "अथात आदेश नेति नेति" इति श्रुतिः *Brihadaranyaka Upanishad II-3-6.

How can one get out of it? The *Surti* declaration alone is not sufficient. The knowledge gained as a result of scriptural information, confirmed by one's rational independent thinking can help one to negate this plurality. Whenever there is a bodily demand, think, "I am not the mind", etc. Thus by negating all the five *Kosas* and experiencing the Self behind them all as one's own nature, the *jeeva*-hood is transcended and the Supreme is realised.

नेदं नेदं कल्पितत्वान्न सत्यं
रज्जुदृष्टव्यालवत्स्वप्नवच्च ।
इत्थं दृश्यं साधुयुक्त्या व्यपोह्य
ज्ञेयः पश्चादेकभावस्तयोर्यः ॥२४६॥

246. "Neither this (gross), nor this (subtle)"---like the snake seen in the rope and like dreams, are not real, being products of the imagination. By a perfect elimination of the objective world by reasoning, one must realise the oneness underlying the *jeeva* and the *Iswara*.

"Not this, not this"* is the language of the *Upanishads*. I am not the body, the body is mine. I am not the mind, the mind is mine. Not only do the scriptures say so, but also rational thinking makes it clear that what is delusorily projected cannot be an actual fact. Had it been true the world would have been available to me at all times. The body, mind and intellect are not always available. In deep-sleep, I do not gain anything from them, since they are not available. So they cannot be the Truth. "That which was not there in the past and will not be in the future but which is apparent only in the present, is called an illusion."

Thus the conviction that the body, the mind and the intellect are not the *Atman* is held not just because the scriptures say so, but by right thinking it becomes amply clear

* In the Brihadaranyaka Upanishad, this, statement of twice-repeated negation indicates that when *Maya* the conditioning for *Iswara*, and the five *kosas* the conditionings for the *jeeva*, are both eliminated--not this--what remains is *Brahman*.

that truly, they are not "real", but are mere projections like the serpent-in-the-rope or like dreams.

The snake-and-rope example is an objective one and the example of the dream is a subjective one--the delusion outside and the delusion within.

Thus, one who is a *Sadhu*, a spiritual thinker, having eliminated the world within and without by rational thinking *(Yukti)*, will realise that "I, who experienced the objects, emotions and thoughts through the body, mind and intellect, am the One, the Substratum, the pure Consciousness".

ततस्तु तौ लक्षणया सुलक्ष्यौ
तयोरखण्डैकरसत्वसिद्धये ।
नालं जहत्या न तथाऽजहत्या
किन्तूभयार्थात्मिकयैव भाव्यम् ॥२४७॥

247. Therefore, the two terms *(Iswara*-and *jeeva)*, should be carefully considered through their indicative meanings in order to establish their absolute identity. Neither "the method of total rejection", nor "the methods of complete retention" will suffice. One must reason by a combined process of both.

You are you because of the Infinite functioning through the total *vasanas*. When you remove your equipments, there is neither a world for you, nor a concept of God. Then alone will you come to understand that *jeeva* and *Iswara* are one and the same. In order to realise that One is *Brahman*, the Reality, the intellect must be prepared by the study of the scriptures as well as by independent thinking and reflection

By an intellect which has been so prepared for this great flight, you must negate the body, the mind and the intellect and come to apprehend the Truth.

In the profound declaration, "That Thou Art", the implied meaning has to be ascertained and appreciated by an intellect which has already been prepared by the study of the scriptures. The word-meaning, in itself, certainly sounds absurd. One should try to understand the implied meaning of the sacred words of the great *Rishis* which burst forth from them in the white-heat-moments of their Experience-divine.

If you dandle the words, they convey no meaning. They talk directly of an impossibility. Therefore, you have to go deeper, analyse ruthlessly, and understand the secret sacred meaning behind them, in order to get into the very experience of the Oneness--the experience of the common denominator in you and God --the Inifinte Eternal Truth.

The suggestive meaning of a statement is generally appreciated in three ways. Suggestiveness is very often used in our day-to-day talks and discussion. When I say, "My house is right on the sea", you understand that my house is on the sea-shore. The house is not on the water but is on the earth and is located nearest to the sea. Though I say, "Right on the sea", you understand what I mean, by *leaving* the literal meaning of the term, "right on the sea". When you say,"The house on which the crow is sitting is mine", I understand the house without the crow.

When I say,"The red ran", you understand that the red horse ran because of your association with the race course. In this case we *add* something to the spoken words and arrive at an intelligent understanding.

In the third case, we add something as well as *remove* something from the spoken words in order to understand their implied meaning.

The method of deriving the implied meaning of a statement is called *Lakshana* in Sanskrit. The first, where we *leave* some aspects of the direct meaning in order to understand, is called *Jaha-lakshana.* The second where we *add* something to the actual words spoken and arrive at the indicated meaning is called *Ajaha-lakshana.* And the third is where we *leave* some aspects and *add* certain others to reach the indicative meaning. This is called *Jaha-Ajaha-lakshana.**

The third method is useful in understanding the implied meaning of the *Mahavakya*, "That Thou Art". When the equipments, the *upadhis*, of both "That" and "Thou" are removed, what remains is one and the same, the Infinite Reality.

When the intellect has been prepared by the study of the *Sastras* and by correct thinking, when an individual has come to negate his identifications with the body, the mind and the intellect, then he shall come to experience the pure Consciousness, which as the core of his personality expresses as the *jeeva*, and Itself expresses as *Iswara* when functioning through *Maya*.

स देवदत्तोऽयमितीह चैकता
विरुद्धधर्मांशमपास्य कथ्यते ।
यथा तथा तत्त्वमसीति वाक्ये
विरुद्धधर्मानुभयत्र हित्वा ॥२४८॥
संलक्ष्य चिन्मात्रतया सदात्मनो-
रखण्डभावःपरिचीयते बुधैः ।
एवं महावाक्यशतेन कथ्यते
ब्रह्मात्मनोरैक्यमखण्डभावः ॥२४९॥

248-249. "This is that Devadatta"--just as in this sentence the identity expressed is arrived at by eliminating contradictory portions, so too it is in the statement, "That Thou Art". Men of wisdom should give up contradictory elements on both sides and recognise the identity of *Iswara* and *jeeva*, carefully noting that the essence of both is Knowledge Absolute. In such wise, hundreds of scriptures declare the oneness and the identity of *Brahman* and the *jeeva*.

---

* *The Jaha-Ajaha-lakshana* is also *Bhaga-Tyaga-Lakshana* by some *Acharyas*.

When it is said, "God--the Infinite, the All-pervading, the Blissful, the Perfect, is you--the finite the congested, the sorrowful, the imperfect", ---you will have to remove all these imperfections around you to understand this statement. The spark of Consciousness that is behind the thoughts in you, is the same Consciousness that is functioning through God. In order to make us understand this, an example is given.

"This is that Devadatta". "That" and "This" are the pronouns indicating two different things. If the pronoun "that" indicates a thing far off, then "this" indicates a thing which is relatively near. "That John is this man", ---when we say, we mean, "that John" at a different period of time and existing in a different place, and "this man" seen right now, today, at the present time and place, are one and the same person. The time and the place have changed but the individual has remained the same.

Here we remove the contradictory conditionings *(Viruddha dharmah)* and understand correctly that "this" individual and "that"individual are the same:

When we say, "Man is God", we do not mean that the size of man is the size of God, or that the shape of man is the shape of God, or that the imperfections of man are the imperfections of God--we only mean that in man there is a Godly Essence.

Just as in the example, "*That* Devadatta is *this* man", in the *"Tattwamasi"* declaration also when the contradictory conditionings are removed, what remains is the same Infinte Self.

Man is subject to birth, God is unborn. Man is limited, God is unlimited. Man is a perishable being. God is Imperishable. Man is mortal, God is Immortal. Remove all these qualities. Then what remains is Pure Consciousness.

Wise men having understood the One Essence both in man and the God say that the essential core in God is the essential core in man. Thus hundreds of great declarations indicate and glorify the great oneness of *Brahman* and *Atman*.

When I look out through the body I become conscious of objects. When I transcend the body, the world of objects is eliminated, when I transcend the mind, the emotions are eliminated, and when I go beyond the intellect the thought-disturbances are also eliminated. What remains in me at that time is only Consciousness. With that Conciousness when I look out--without the body, the mind and the intellect--I see in the world no objects, no emotions and no thoughts, because they were all interpretations of my BMI only. Where the equipments are removed, the objects that I perceive through the equipments are also removed. At that time, what I see is nothing but Consciousness within and without--everywhere. In this sense, the scriptures say that the *Atman*, the Self in you is *Brahman*, the Reality behind the whole universe.

51. Attitude in Meditation. (250-253)

अस्थूलमित्येतदसन्निरस्य
सिद्धं स्वतो व्योमवदप्रतर्क्यम् ।
अतो मृषामात्रमिदं प्रतीतं
जहीहि यत्स्वात्मया गृहीतम् ।
ब्रह्माहमित्येव विशुद्धबुद्ध्या
विद्धि स्वमात्मानमखण्डबोधम् ॥२५०॥

250. Discarding the not-Self, in the light of passages such as "It is not gross etc.", one realises the Self, which is Self-established, unattached like the sky and beyond the pale of thought. So negate this illusory body which you are perceiving and have accepted as your own Self. With a purified understanding that "I am *Brahman*", realise your own Self which is Knowledge Absolute.

Whenever the *Upanishad Rishis* want to indicate the *Atman*, this essential Divine Existence to us, they cry out, "Brahman is not gross, not short, not long etc." By saying that

Brahman is not gross, all that is the not-Self is eliminated. That which is the not-Self is gross. Gross is that which is perceived. The world of objects is perceived by the sense-organs; the world of emotions by the mind; and the world of thoughts by the intellect. Since we perceive them, they are all objects of our perception. The subject, the essentia. Reality, must be something other than an object. In such wise, the not-Self is negated by saying that the *Atman* is "not gross".

When the gross has been transcended, you come to apprehend the Self-established *Atman*, like space, which can never be described. The *Atman* is Self-existent. Its existence is not because of anything else. When the equipments are all negated, what remains is that because of which the equipments were able to experience.

All that is perceived as "this, this, this"--as objects, emotions and thoughts *(idam-prateetam)*, are mere illusions--- things that do not really exist. Now you are holding on to them as your real nature. Holding on to things that are not really there is called delusion. Ergo leave, renounce, remove, destroy the false. This removal cannot be done easily. The identification has to be removed by the pure understanding *(Visuddha-buddhi)*, of one's real nature as Pure Consciousness *(Brahma-aham-iti)*. All these equipments are one's own play, but their nature is not one's subjective nature.

Such a direct and full understanding of one's Real Nature should not be a passing experience. It should be a constant knowledge *(Akhanda-bodham)*. At present, we have the constant knowledge that "I am the body" or "I am the intellect". This constant knowledge that "I am the Pure Consciousness" *(Brahma-aham)*.

मृत्कार्यं सकलं घटादि सततं मृन्मात्रमेवाहितं
तद्वत्सज्जनितं सदात्मकमिदं सन्मात्रमेवाखिलम् ।

यस्मान्नास्ति सतः परं किमपि तत्सत्यं स आत्मा स्वयं
तस्मात्तत्त्वमसि प्रशान्तममलं ब्रह्माद्वयं यत्परम् ॥२५१॥

251. All modifications of mud such as the pot are accepted by the mind as real but are, in fact, mud alone. So too, the entire universe which comes from *Brahman* is *Brahman* alone and nothing other than *Brahman*, the Self-existent Reality, one's very own Self, Thou art That, the Serene, the Pure, the Supreme *Brahman*, the Non-dual.

All things made of mud, being the effects of mud, are nothing but mud. Mud in one form is a pot, in another form, a jar and in yet another form, a cup. Everything born out of mud is mud alone. Just as everything born out of gold is gold alone. Whatever be the names given to the objects, in essence, they are the material from which they are made. Equally so, all things that are born out of Pure consciousness *(Sat)* are, in essence, nothing but *Sat*. The whole universe, the subject-object world in which we experience our joys and sorrows is, in essence, nothing but Concsiousness. That alone is the Reality, the Self-existent *Atman*. Thou art That Reality alone.

निद्राकल्पितदेशकालविषयज्ञात्रादि सर्वं यथा
मिथ्या तद्वदिहापि जाग्रति जगत्स्वाज्ञानकार्यत्वतः ।
यस्मादेवमिदं शरीरकरणप्राणाहमाद्यप्यसत्
तस्मात्तत्त्वमसि प्रशान्तममलं ब्रह्माद्वयं यत्परम् ॥२५२॥

252. Just as the place, time, objects, knower etc. in a dream are unreal. so too is the world we experience in our waking-state, which is due to our own ignorance. Since the body, the organs, the *Pranas*, the ego etc., are unreal, Thou art That, the Serene, the Pure, the Supreme *Brahman*, the Non-dual.

The time, space, objects and their knower projected in a dream are all cognised as unreal when the dreamer reviews them after fully waking up. Similar is the case of the world-of-waking which is created by the ignorance of the Self.

There can be no dream once you are awake. You dream when you do not know your waking condition. The moment you come to apprehend your waking condition, the dream ends. In the same way, because of the ignorance of the Self, because we have no experience of the fourth, the higher plane of Consciousness, we regard the waking world as real.

On waking up, the dreamer, the dream-world, the dream equipments and the dream-experiences are all unreal to the waker. So too, the waking-world will be unreal if we look at it from a higher plane of Consciousness. Hence, the body, the equipments such as the mind, intellect, ego and *Chitta*--all of them are unreal. For when one realise the Spiritual Essence, none of these is available.

Therefore, Thou art That, the Serene, the Pure, the Supreme *Brahman*, the one-without-a-second.

यत्र भ्रान्त्या कल्पितं तद्विवेके
तत्तन्मात्रं नैव तस्माद्विभिन्नम् ।
स्वप्ने नष्टं स्वप्नविश्वं विचित्रं
स्वस्माद्भिन्नं किन्नु दृष्टं प्रबोधे ॥२५३॥

253. That which is wrongly supposed to exist in something,, is, when the truth about it is known, recognised as nothing other than the "substratum" and not at all different from it. The pluralistic dream-universe appears and subsides in the dream itself. On waking, does it appear as something different from one's own mind?

A *thing* "perceived" in delusion, disappears on discrimination when its substratum is seen. The ghost-in-the-post, the serpent-in-the-rope, the silver-in-the-shell, all disappear when the perceived things are approached discriminatingly and scientifically. Hasty observation may lead me to a wrong conclusion regarding a certain *thing;* but when I think clearly and contemplate upon it, the *thing* disappears and I come to apprehend the *truth* of the *thing.* The post alone is the reality. Whatever other than the post is seen is delusion and has no existence at all. It is only a play of the mind. When the mind has been transcended, then no more is there a cause for any such delusion at any time whatsoever.

When the dream has ended, the dream-world also ends. Where discrimination *(viveka)* comes, there the delusion *(bhranti)*, vanishes. Reality-alone is then available for experience. On waking-up the dream never appears as anything other than the waker's own mind. Similarly, in the world projected by your own unintelligent perceptions you may see *things* which are not there. But when you discriminate, the delusion ends and the illusory perceptions disappear.

When the individual has experienced the Highest, how can there be any experience of the illusory pluralistic world perceived during the state of delusion?

52. Aids to Meditation. (254-266)

जातिनीतिकुलगोत्रदूरगम्
नामरूपगुणदोषवर्जितम् ।
देशकालविषयातिवर्ति यद्
ब्रह्म तत्त्वमसि भावयात्मनि ॥२५४॥

254. That which has no caste, creed, family or lineage, which is without name and form, merit and demerit, which is beyond space, time and sense-objects-- "That *Brahman* Though Art"......meditate on this in your mind.

From this verse onwards for ten verses, there are ideas to help the meditator at his seat of contemplation. You would do well to learn them by heart and employ them continuously for reflection and daily contemplation.

"That *Brahman* Thou Art"--keep this attitude constantly in your bosom. Understanding or knowing is the function of the intellect, while feeling is the function of the mind. Knowing

Truth alone will never take you to Truth nor is Feeling truth sufficient to realise It. Knowing is developed through the study of the scriptures and feeling for God is increased by *bhakti* or devotion.

Thus, knowledge and devotion are the methods and techniques by which the understanding of the Lord's nature and devotion for the Lord are enhanced. Neither of them, by itself, is capable of realising the Truth, because It is beyond the mind and the intellect. But where the mind and the intellect merge, the instrument so forged is called the "heart" in all scriptural literature.

Just as understanding *(jnana)*, is the funtion of the intellect, and feeling *(bhakti)*, is the function of the mind, contemplation *(bhavana)*, is the function of the "heart". Since the heart is the combination of the mind and the intellect, its function too must be a combination of the two. Therefore, contemplation is feeling fully what you have understood and understanding fully what you have felt. "Feelingful understanding" or "understandingly feeling", is *bhavana or contemplation.*

Not merely understand the sacred text which any professor can, and not merely feel which any purblind man, can, but within yourself, try to *feel* what you have understood and to *understand* what your own strange feelings confirm. Thus contemplate. Constantly meditate in your own heart, "That *Brahman* I am". Contemplate steadily upon it. Any amount of study will not help you. Come to apprehend it as your innermost Self. "That *Brahman* art Thou".

The Truth which is beyond caste, creed, family and lineage is *Brahman*. Whether an Indian or a foreigner, a Christian or a Muslim, a man or a woman, whether Brahmin, Kshatriya, Vaishya or Sudra, the Self is beyond all such distinctions.

Brahman is beyond all names and forms, merits and demerits, and consequently is not a substance. *Brahman* is that which is not conditioned by time, space or objects.

This set of ten verses is an inspiring guide for meditiation. While repeating them in your meditation, do not think that you are telling them to somebody else. You are only advising yourself. Your higher intellect is advising your own lower intellect. Keep this *bhavana* always as a holy and divine attitude in yourself.

The burial ground is creeping towards you every moment. There is no time to waste on regretting your past or being anxious for your future. Contemplate upon these ideas, from now onwards. Let your hands and legs function---but let a part of your mind steadily hold on to the idea of the divine essence in you.

यत्परं सकलवागगोचरं
गोचरं विमलबोधचक्षुषः ।
शुद्धचिद्घनमनादिवस्तु यद्
ब्रह्म तत्त्वमसि भावयात्मनि ॥२५५॥

255. The Supreme Brahman which is beyond the expression of speech, which is only for the eye of "pure-illumination", which is pure mass of Consciousness, which is a beginningless entity,---"That *Brahman* Thou Art".....meditate on this in your mind.

That which is beyond all speech: *(Sakala-vak-agocharam)*-In no language, by no method of expression can it ever be expressed. That which will never come within the embrace of any language, any word, or any combination of words is the Reality. That great Truth cannot be thought of and hence cannot be expressed by speech.

Yet it can be experienced by one with "the eye of clear knowledge"* By the purified intellect alone you will be able to perceive it. A purified intellect is an intellect which is not oscillating. Oscillations of the intellect are due to the *vasanas*.Therefore, one in whom the *vasanas* have been

* विमलबोधचक्षुषः (VIMALA-BODHA-CHAKSUṢHAH).

reduced---the sub-conscious and the un-conscious have been eliminated---such an individual can bring his intellect into quietude and equipoise. With such a pure intellect, which has a subtle power of perception, the *Atman* can be perceived. It is not perceivable by any other instrument.

Pure mass of Consciousness: *(suddha-chit-ghanam)*--- It is not the Consciousness *of* objects. It is Pure Consciousness. It is without beginning. Everything that is born has a beginning The world of plurality is born, therefore, it has a beginning. *Brahman* is that from which everything else is born. Therefore, it is beginningless *(Anadi)*. That great *Brahman* Thou Art. Contemplate upon this Truth.

षड्भिरूर्मिभिरयोगि योगिहृद् -
भावितं न करणैर्विभावितम् ।
बुद्ध्यवेद्यमनवद्यमस्ति यद् -
ब्रह्म तत्त्वमसि भावयात्मनि ॥२५६॥

256. That which is untouched by the "Six waves of sorrow", which the *yogi*'s heart meditates upon but which is not grasped by the sense-organs, that which the intellect cannot know, which is unimpeachable---"That *Brahman* Thou Art".....mediate on this in your mind.

The six enemies: *(Shad-urmi)** ---They are the six sorrows common to all men which rise one above the other, like waves, and toss man about on the waters of their tumultuous restlessness. They are: (1) hunger, (2)thirst, (3) revulsion for objects producing sorrow, (4) delusoiy fascination for pleasurable objects, (5) old age, and (6) death. That which is not conquered by, which has no contact whith (A-yogi) these six waves of sorrow in life, is the Infinite Consciousness.

**Shad*--six-fold; Urmi--waves: enemies; "क्षुत्पिपासे शोकमोहौ जरामृत्यू उर्मिवत् तरंगवत उपर्युपरि सम्भवन्तीती एते षडूर्मय इति कथ्यन्ते ॥ "
Hunger and thirst, grief and delusion, decay and -death--these are the "six-fold waves" of sorrow that irresistibly rise in every bosom, against which there is no known insurance in the material world of wealth and power, law and authority.

Brahman, the Reality, is that which is not conditioned by, conquered by, the above six waves of sorrow, and is that which is constantly contemplated upon by the meditators *(yogis)*. *Yogis*, who are not persecuted by these enemies contemplate upon *Brahman* in their own hearts, with a quietened mind. The quiet mind gathers to itself a new power of perception with which the infinite Truth is perceived.

That unimpeachable Truth which the intellect cannot know, "That *Brahman* Thou Art". Contemplate upon this great Truth---Sankara repeatedly advises.

भ्रान्तिकल्पितजगत्कलाश्रयं
स्वाश्रयं च सदसद्विलक्षणम् ।
निष्कलं निरुपमानवद्धि यद्
ब्रह्म तत्त्वमसि भावयात्मनि ॥२५७॥

257. That which is the "substratum" for the universe and its various aspects which are all due to delusion, which supports Itself, which is other than the gross and the subtle, which has no parts and truly has no comparison---"That *Brahman* Thou Art".....mediate on this in you mind.

The world-of-plurality is a mere projection of our delusion. All that we project must have a substratum upon which alone we can project our imaginations. If you see a snake in your delusion there must be a rope to hold your projection. Without a substratum a delusion can never be. The substratum for the world-of-plurality is *Brahman* alone It serves as the changeless substratum for the entire world-of-change projected by us because of our lack of discrimination. At the same time, It ever is Its own substratum.

Gross things are perceived by the sense-organs and subtle things by the mind and the intellect. *Atman*, the Self, is neither perceived by the sense-organs nor by the mind and intellect. Hence It is neither gross nor subtle. It is the Consciousness by which one becomes aware of things gross and subtle.

Consciousness is the subject which illumines both the gross and the subtle experiences of all creatures. It is without any parts. It is the One, All-pervading, Homogenous Entity.

Incomparable : *(Nirupamana)*---All objects of comparison are absent in the Self because no objects, emotions or thoughts exist in It. Hence It is Incomparable. That *Brahman* Thou Art..... Contemplate upon this great Truth within yourself---with true anxiety, Sankara hastens us.

जन्मवृद्धिपरिणत्यपक्षय-
व्याधिनाशनविहीनमव्ययम् ।
विश्वसृष्ट्यवविघातकारणं
ब्रह्म तत्त्वमसि भावयात्मनि ॥२५८॥

258. That which is changeless and so free from birth, growth, development, waste, disease and death; which is indestructible and the cause for the creation, maintenance and dissolution of the universe---"That *Brahman* Thou Art".....meditate on this in you mind.

Every organism must go through these six modifications ---birth, growth, change, decay, disease and death. Every modification is a source of pain. *Brahman*, the *Atman* is without any modifications. That which is subject to the above modifications is called changeable, variable or mutable.

In *Brahman*, the Reality, none of these changes takes place. Therefore, It is *Avyaya*:[1] Immutable. Mutation can take place only by these six processes.

The world that we see around us heaves under three movements: creation, maintenance[2] and dissolution. *Brahman*, the Reality, is the cause for all these three.[3]

---

1. न व्येतीत्यव्ययं = never reduces hence Immutable, changeless: स्वतो वा परतो वा नाशरहितं नित्यं
2. Refer Rise and Fall of Man-Kindle Life.
3. यतो वा इमानि भूतानि जायन्ते येन जातानि जीवन्ति यत्प्रयन्त्यभिसंविशन्ति

Taitireeya- Upanishad III

That *Brahman* Thou Art. Contemplate upon this Truth as you own Self, urges Sankara.

अस्तभेदमनपास्तलक्षणं
निस्तरङ्गजलराशिनिश्चलम् ।
नित्यमुक्तमविभक्तमूर्ति यद
ब्रह्म तत्त्वमसि भावयात्मनि ॥२५९॥

259. That which is free from all distinctions, which is never of the nature of non-existence, which is calm like an ocean without waves, which is ever free and is of indivisible form---"That *Brahman* Thou Art".....mediate on this in you mind.

Set: *(asta)*---differences or distinctions: *(bheda)*---"All differences set"---*asta-bheda.* All differences of plurality are completely at rest in the Self. When everything is "set", the nature of the Self is still "unset" in all Its shining effulgence. That which never decays, that which is never non-existent---are the suggestions of the eloquent term used by the philosopher-poet, Sankara. When the BMI are transcended, when the OET are no more perceived, then what is left over is the Consciousness which illumined the OET when they were in delusion, experienced by the illusory PFT.

That experience of the divine is indicated by an ordinary example. Watch the heaving bosom of the sea. Then imagine, that, as though by the wave of a magic wand, all the waves have frozen suddenly. The student's mind halts.....he is pushed into a voiceless state of awe-ful joy and inexplicable peace. Try.

When you see the undulating waves of the ocean, your mind too moves with them. Imagine then, that the rising wave has suddenly frozen and the wave behind it too, has come to an immediate halt. If you can imagine this, you will come to experience a peculiar peace and silence. Just as the waveless sea is without any movement, so too is the ever-free, individual form of the One, Infinite, Homogenous mass of

Motionlessness. Constantly away from the sorrows of the world, ever liberated from the thraldom of BMI---"That Thou Art".

एकमेव सदनेक्कारणं
कारणान्तरनिरासकारणम् ।
कार्यकारणविलक्षणं स्वयं
ब्रह्म तत्त्वमसि भावयात्मनि ॥२६०॥

260. That which, even though It is One Existence, is the cause for the many, which refutes all other causes but Itself is without cause, which is distinct from cause and effect and is independent---"That *Brahman* Thou Art".....meditate on this in your mind.

Consciousness, though uniformly one, is the cause for the entire pluralistic phenomenal world of the BMI, PFT and OET. It alone is the material, the efficient and the instrumental cause for the universe. The pluralistic world is our own projection which has sprung from our delusion. The substratum for this delusion is the Consciousness without which the delusion itself would have been impossible. Since, because of the Consciousness, the world has been possible, Consciousness alone is the cause for the universe of happenings.

It is Its own substratum; It is Its own cause; It is the uncaused cause for the entire pluralistic world. With reference to the world, Consciousness is the cause. By Itself, It is something other than both cause and effect. Cause and effect are concepts of the intellect. The *Atman* is beyond the intellect. In this respect, it can also be said that where the effect is the world of plurality, its cause is the non-apprehension of Reality, i.e. *Maya*.

Consciousness is beyond *Maya*, the cause, and its effects "That *Brahman* Thou Art"---contemplate upon this great causeless cause as your own Self.

निर्विकल्पकमनल्पमक्षरं
यत्क्षराक्षरविलक्षणं परम् ।
नित्यमव्ययसुखं निरञ्जनं
ब्रह्म तत्त्वमसि भावयात्मनि ॥२६१॥

261. That which is free from *Maya,* which is Infinite and Indestructible, which is other than the world of change, which is Supreme and Eternal, which is permanent and indivisible Bliss, Untainted,---"That *Brahman* Thou Art".....meditate on this in your mind.

That which is not made of *Maya: (Nirvikalpakam)*--Beyond all agitations of the mind and the intellect which are created by the *vasanas:* that is, the Self is behind the *vasanas* but Itself is uncontaminated, Immaculate.

Infinite: *(Analpam)*--- *Alpam* means finite, limited. *Analpam,* therefore, means, Infinite, unconditioned. In Chhandogya-Upanishad the *Rishi* defines the Infinite-- *(Yo-vai-bhooma),* "that which is Infinite *(Bhooma)* is eternal"; *(Yad-alpam-tat-mritam),* "Whatever is finite *(Alpam)* is mortal".

Reducible, changeable: *(Kshara)*---The world of plurality which is in a state of constant flux.

The changeless: *(A-kshara)*---Refers to *Maya.* That which is other than *(vilakshanam),* both *Kshara* and *A-kshara,* is the Consciousness with which the changing and the changeless are illumined.

Undying Bliss: *(Nitya-avyaya-sukham)*---Not the joy of sense-objects which are fleeting and variable in their intensity. This is the Supreme, Permanent Bliss experienced on transcending the mind-intellect equipment. The Upanishad seers are only employing the term to give us, who live in the mental arena, some measure of what the experience is when the mind is transcended. Literally, it is *not* Bliss in the sense we now understand it to be.

Taintless: *(Niranjanam)*--- Without the imperfections of *Tamas* means, beyond the *vasanas*, beyond the great delusory power of *Maya*.

"That *Brahman* Thou Art"---thus assert yourself and realise It in a direct experience in your own life.

यद्विभाति सदनेकधा भ्रमा-
न्नामरूपगुणविक्रियात्मना ।
हेमवत्स्वयमविक्रियं सदा
ब्रह्म तत्त्वमसि भावयात्मनि ॥२६२॥

262. That One Reality, which appears variously because of delusion---though Itself always unchanged---and assumes names and forms, qualities and changes, like gold through all its modifications---"That *Brahman* Thou Art".....meditate on this in your mind.

The supreme Reality though One, appears as many. This is due to the delusion of the perceiver. Such a trick of the mind is called "illusion", *(bhrama)*.

The multiplicity that we see around us is only in the form of names, forms, qualities and activities. If you look at the world by removing these four, what you would see is nothing but *Brahman*. Such a subtle perception is required to discover the true essense in the life around us.

Ordinarily, we do not *perceive* the objects: we only *look* at them. At best we only *see* what is projected by our minds. We fail to *perceive* the Truth. Through an alert spiritual perception alone is Truth* revealed to us and not by seeing what is but an illusion.

When we look at an object we do so through our outer instruments of sense-organs and inner instruments of the mind and intellect.

* Bhaja Govindam--14: पश्यन्नपि च न पश्यति मूढः "Though "seeing", the fool is not "perceiving

They can report to us only the sense-stimuli and the feelings and thoughts. Altogether, they may give us the name, form, nature, function, qualifying properties of things and their relationships.*

Thus, when we look at a flower, we only *see* it, we never *perceive* it. "Ah! Ah! This is a wonderful flower! It is called.....It is.....in colour. It has a fragrance like.....I saw it first in the Fiji Islands. There of course, it was much bigger. This is a smaller variety" etc. etc. Now, what have you "seen"? you have not seen this *flower*, you have seen *that* flower, in *that* environment---a flower called by *that* name, with *those* properties, shape, smell, colour etc. All these you have seen projected on *this* flower. Similarly, this world is nothing to most of us, but so many names and forms.

Names, forms, qualities and activities are all the blabbering of the mind. Therefore, *mind-less seeing* is perception of Truth; *mind-ful-perception* of Truth is the world. So then, if we were to *perceive* the world outside without any attempt at verbalisation, without any blabberings of the mind, what we would see is *Brahman* alone.

Like gold: *(Hemavat)*---Gold does not want to be on your neck, or to clasp your hand or to cling to your finger. It is you who mould it into various shapes, use it for various purposes and thereafter call it by various names. Name, form, property and activity are all projected on to gold, and we "see" the world of ornaments, oblivious of the fact that they are all nothing but gold. Similarly, the world is nothing but *Brahman*. Understand that *Brahman* to be your own Self.

यच्चकास्त्यनपरं परात्परं
प्रत्यगेकरसमात्मलक्षणम् ।

---

* नाम, रुप, गुण, क्रिया विशेष सम्बन्धः these together constitute the world perceived.

सत्यचित्सुखमनन्तमव्ययं
ब्रह्म तत्त्वमसि भावयात्मनि ॥२६३॥

263. That beyond which there is nothing, which is above *Maya* which is superior to its effects---the universe, which is the innermost subjective Self, which is of one essence, which is continuous Existence-Knowledge-Bliss, which is Infinite and Immutable---"That *Brahman* Thou Art"---meditate on this in your mind.

Anaparam is an expressive term used in the Chhandogyopanishad. It means, "there is nothing other than It"

The most supreme: *(Paratpara)*---*Para* means supreme. Supreme here means, subtle. Subtle is used to denote the "cause", the "effect" being gross. So *para* means, the cause for all effects. The effect is the world, the BMI, PFT and OET, which are caused by the *vasanas*. So *para*, the cause, is *Maya*. Therefore, *paratpara* is that which is the "cause" for *Maya*. That whose manifestation is *Iswara* Himself. That supreme Reality beyond which there is nothing and that which is the cause for the very cause of the whole universe. Thus the Self is defined as "beyond-the-beyond".

Within: *(Pratyag)*---means subjective; that which lies in the depth of the personality, ever functioning from behind the very mind.

Of one essence: *(Ekarasa)*---It's essence does not change; permanent is the infinite nature of the blissful Self.

Continuous Existence-Knowledge-Bliss: *(Sat-chit-sukham-anantam)*---The Self is indicated in the *Upanishads* as Existence *(Sat)*, pure Knowledge *(Chit)*, and Bliss *(Sukham)*, which is endless, infinite *(Anantam)*.

Undecaying *(Avyayam)*---There is no decay for this Bliss of *Brahman*.

---

* तदेतद् ब्रह्मापूर्व - अनपरं -- chhandogyopanishad
न विद्यते परं कार्यं यस्य = अनपरं

All these terms are as many arrow marks pointing the direction of our attention in meditation towards the Supreme; they are not "definition" of Truth. They are only guide-posts enroute to Truth, to help the human mind reach It.

This Reality Thou Art. These ten verses are a greate help to meditation. All serious students of *Vedanta* make them their own and grow in their meditation.

उक्तमर्थमिममात्मनि स्वयं
भावयेत्प्रथितयुक्तिभिर्धिया ।
संशयादिरहितं कराम्बुवत्
तेन तत्त्वनिगमो भाविष्यति ॥२६४॥

264. One must meditate with the intellect in one's heart on the Truth inculcated above by means of scriptural arguments. By these means, one will realise Truth without any doubts and the like, just like water in the hollow of one's hand.

The deeper significance of what has been declared earlier in the set of meditative verses is to be contemplated upon in the heart. "Thoughtfully feel" within yourself to experience it, with an intellect that has been trained to argue and discuss in the line of the great scriptures. Hence the term, "recognised arguments". *(prathita-yuktibhih)*, has been used here.

Every science has its own technique of analysis, and a student of that science alone knows how to analyse the theme. A doctor knows the technique of analysing the symptoms and diagnosing the disease. Similarly, at the beginning of his career, a lawyer will have to practise with other proficient lawyers and achieve mastery over thinking in line with the existing laws of the land. In all professions, there is a way-of-thinking. The intellect that has been trained in the technology of logical thinking in the Science of Reality, alone can come to experience this Truth without a trace of doubt. Just as, if one is holding a spoonful of water in the hollow of one's palm, one have no possible doubt about it.

By such a direct experience, reach the state of Realisation of the Self, which is beyond all doubts and despairs, says *Acharya* Sankara.

स्वबोधमात्रं परिशुद्धतत्त्वं
विज्ञाय संघे नृपवच्च सैन्ये ।
तदाश्रयः स्वात्मनि सर्वदा स्थितो
विलापय ब्रह्मणि विश्वजातम् ॥२६५॥

265. In this cause-effect bundle, realising Knowledge-Absolute free from ignorance and its effects, like the king in an army, and resting in that Knowledge, ever established in your own Self, merge the universe into *Brahman*.

Brahman is pure Consciousness; not the consciousness-*of*- things but objectless-Awareness, (Bodha-matram).[1] It is to be realised as pure objectless-Awareness in this assemblage of not-Self, the cause-effect bundle,[2] the body.

The king in any State is well-protected, and every soldier draws his inspiration from his king. Everyone does his allotted duty because of the king. Similarly, the *Atman*, though Itself not doing anything, It lends Its sentiency to the insentient matter-layers, gets into their midst and is ever established in them.

When you move away from the apparent functions and the consequent agitations of the BMI created in the field of OET, then in the sequestered quietude of meditation you will move towards It. Take It as your shelter *(Asraya)*. Move under the shelter of the Divine. Be ever-established in It. Merge all the pluralistic experiences born out of this world into *Brahman*, just as the dreamer, and the dream-experiences born out of the dream all merge into the waker.

---

1. स्व = आत्मानं ; बोधमात्रं = सर्वावभासकज्ञानमात्रं दृश्यसंबंधरहितं
2. संघे = शरीरेन्द्रियप्राणाहंकार - रूपकार्यकारण संघाते

बुद्धौ गुहायां सदसद्विलक्षणं
ब्रह्मास्ति सत्यं परमद्वितीयम् ।
तदात्मना योऽत्र वसेद्गुहायां
पुनर्न तस्याङ्गगुहाप्रवेशः ॥२६६॥

266. In the cave of the intellect is *Brahman*, other than the gross and the subtle, Existence, Supreme and Non-dual. He no more enters the mother's womb who dwells in this cave as *Brahman*.

In the very opening verse of *Vivekachoodamani*, three stages were explained for Self-realisation.

1. Discrimination between the Self and the not-Self. *(Atma-anatma-vivechanam)*
2. Subjective experience of the Self within *(Swa-anubhava)*
3. Getting established in the oneness of *Brahman* and *Atman (Brahmatmana-samsthitih)*.

Of these the first---the discrimination between *Atman* and *anatman* is over. From this verse onwards, the subjective experience is being indicated.

In the cave-of-the-intellect is the "heart" and in the "heart" the *Atman* is apprehended. The idea of being, in an atmosphere of love, when an individual starts thinking regularly, he will arrive at the experience of the *Atman*. This Self which is in the cave-of-the-heart is something other than the subtle and the gross. It is the supreme *Brahman* and is non-dual. He who enters this "cave" through meditation and comes to apprehend that he himself is the pure Consciousness, to him there is no re-entry into a fresh body. "Cave-of-the-body" *(guha)*, means the wormb of the mother, i.e., he will have no more births.

At present we are caught up in the cave-of-the-body. Once you are engaged with *Brahman*, there are no more engagements with the flesh.

As a result of your *sadhana* and courtship---the engagement is announced. Thereafter, there are no more births, since there are no residual *vasanas* to conjure up a fit body and environment for them to play out.

53. Give up Vasanas---the Method. (267-276)

ज्ञाते वस्तुन्यपि बलवती वासनाऽनादिरेषा
कर्ता भोक्ताप्यहमिती दृढा याऽस्य संसारहेतुः
प्रत्यग्दृष्ट्याऽऽत्मनि निवसता सापनेया प्रयत्ना-
न्मुक्तिं प्राहुस्तदिह मुनयो वासनातानवं यत् ॥२६७॥

267. Even after the Realisation of Truth, there remains a powerful beginningless, deep impression that one is the doer and the enjoyer, which is the cause for re-birth. By living in a subjective state of steady identification with the Self, it has to be conscientiously removed. That which is the annihilation of the *vasanas*, here and now, is called liberation by the sages.

Sankara is trying to define what liberation *(Mukti)*, is. The sudden change of metre in the poetry is to arrest the attention of the student. The teacher enters the realms of ecstasy and dances to the heavenly rhythm set in his own depths.

Even if, as student, through the study or the *Sastras*, one has known that there is a Reality, one will not be able to live the dictates of the scriptures because of the pressure of the *vasanas*. Lust, anger, likes, dislikes etc. will not easily leave one just because one has book-knowledge of the Reality.

By studying the *Sastras* and learning to argue, you may have a very good opinion of yourself, but the people around you will understand you exactly as you are. The *vasanas* are very powerful. Even though you have studied the *Sastras*, you will not be able to express the Perfection that you know yourself to be. It will always be sullied by the stink of your *vasanas*. As a result, the identification with the mind and the intellect will continue and the attitudes of doership *(kartrittwam)*, and enjoyership *(bhoktrittwam)*, will maintain themselves in your bosom. Identification with the mind will give rise to a sense of enjoyership and with the intellect to a sense of doership. These two put together constitute the *jeeva* the PFT, the individuality. This vanity of agency and enjoyership is the essence of the ego. The ego is thus the final manifestation of the subtle and powerful *vasanas* in each personality.

The feeling that I am the not-Self, I am the PFT, I am the ego, is the cause for all *samsar* and its transmigrations. Birth and death are for the ego. It is the ego which goes from one body to another.

Thus, even though one has studied the *Sastras*, there will be transmigration because of the play of powerful *Vasanas*.

The subjective state: *(Pratyak-drishtya)*---*Pratyak* means subjective, inner. At this moment our entire attention is dissipated by the endless varieties of objects, emotions and thoughts. We are extroverts. So "introvertedness" is the state of complete withdrawal from the BMI and the OET and turning the mind towards that great Reality. In order to turn inwards towards the *Atman*, we must make an effort and learn to give up the "I-do" mentality. Nobody can help us do it. Each one must struggle for himself. Getting rid of the idea, "I-do" and "I-enjoy", takes us to "liberation". This liberation is not afterwards, somewhere, at some distant time. It is right here and now. In this very world; in this very body. This liberation is gained by the contemplative seer *(Muni)*.

He who gets away from the bonds of the *vasanas* is the liberated one. So "liberation" means, "release from the *vasanas*"---which create desires, passions, lusts, greeds--- which in their turn drive the individual out-of his Real Nature into the world of objects seeking gratifications.

अहं ममेति यो भावो देहाक्षादावनात्मनि
अध्यासोऽयं निरस्तव्यो विदुषा स्वात्मनिष्ठया ॥२६८॥

268. "I" and "mine" ---this notion in the body, sense-organs, etc., which are the not-Self---this superimposition the wise man must end by identification with his own Self.

Various obstacles may come in one's attempt to release one-self from one's *vasanas*. How to remove these one by one is explained here.

The sense of "I" and "my" is the main obstacle. The ego within the physical structure is called "I". The extension of "I" projected into the world of objects is called "my". This "my" is nothing but "objectified I". "I" projected and reflected in the objects is "my".

At present, there is the feeling of I-ness in matter, gross and subtle-body, the sense-organs, the mind and the intellect. The totality of all these is "me". Thereafter, I spread out "me" into things around, and claim them to be "mine".

The superimposition, "I am this, this, this", must be rejected: *(nirastavyah)*. A wise man can raise himself above these misconceptions by constantly holding on to the idea, "I am the Consciousness because of which the body, the sense-organs, the mind and the intellect are functioning. I am the mere Witness of their function". By this Self-assertion, "I am *Brahman*", the wise man should get out of the superimposition *(adhyasa)*, that he is the body, the mind and the intellect.

ज्ञात्वां स्वं प्रत्यगात्मानं बुद्धितद्वृत्तिसाक्षिणम् ।
सोऽहमित्येव सद्वृत्त्याऽनात्मन्यात्ममतिं जहिं ॥२६९॥

269. Realising your innermost Self, as the Witness of the intellect, and its disturbances and ever maintaining the thought, "That I am", shed your identification with the not-Self.

Jnanam here means book-knowledge, a mere intellectual appreciation of the texts. Having gained this ineffectual book-knowledge: *jnattwa*.

The Self within is to be known as the Witness of the intellect and its thoughts. Having known and understood Its nature, one should move towards it. To step towards the Self is to assert, "I am That" ---*(Hamsa)*; "He alone am I" --*(Soham)*. Start living as a mere Witness of all the pulsations of the body, mind and intellect. By this practice, the idea, "I am the Self", becomes rooted in our understanding. At present we have this understanding rooted only in the BMI. This should be renounced and the feeling, "I am the Self", should be cultivated.

Earlier, we were told how to remove the obstacle of the ego-sense made up of "I" and "my" the constant pursuit of the idea of the Self, ---*Swa-atma-nishtha.*

The egocentric idea of the PFT in the assemblage of the equipments has to be renounced by realising the Consciousness, which is the Witness of the intellect and its modifications. The subject that knows the thought procession in the bosom is the Consciousness. Having *known* the Consciousness, one has to move towards It. This moving towards It is possible only when one has identified one-self with It. In order to indentify with Reality, one must dissociate one-self from one's involvement with the body, mind and intellect. "I am not this assemblage of equipments. I am That, the Consciousness, the Witness of equipments and their function." This idea *(Brahma-akaravritti)*, should be kept alive during the entire period of our waking state. This too, is a "thought". The understanding arising out of this "thought" is also a "limited knowledge" *(Vritti-jnanam)*. But with this "right thought" *(Sad-vritti)*, in the intellect, the "wrong thought" *(asad-vritti)*, is removed. When thus you practise on, ere long, the feeling, "I am the body, mind and intellect", is destroyed. Here again, you are replacing one "thought" with another "thought". But even this "limited knowledge" *(vritti-jnanam)*, removes the false assumption that the not-Self is the Self *(An-atmani-atma-mati)*.

लोकानुवर्तनं त्यक्त्वा त्यक्त्वा देहानुवर्तनम् ।
शास्त्रानुवर्तनं त्यक्त्वा स्वाध्यासापनयं कुरु ॥ २७० ॥

270. Leaving your involvement with social formalities, leaving all ideas of beautifying the body, leaving aside unnecessary study of the *Sastras*, banish the superimposition which has crept up on the Self.

Always following, blindly following: *(Anu-vartanam)*--At this moment we all, as members of society, are fully engaged in the standard way of doing things, the standard methods everywhere adopted by others according to the fashion of the times --this is termed here as *loka-anu-vartanam.* Since we live as we are living, we are what we are. If you want to lift your life into a greater ambit, you have to change your ways of living.

A girl after marriage suddenly becomes more responsible, and her old way of life undergoes a change. A boy becomes a middle-aged man and then an old man, and at each stage, the old ways of life change yielding place to new. So too, if you want to gain a hold on the spiritual path.....change. Without changing the old *values of life* and *ways of life*, a new dimension of life and living cannot be achieved.

You have to give up imitating the false values of others around you, meaning, stop living blindly a stamped-blue-print of life, supplied by the fashions of the times or by the sensuous men who seek their fulfilment in sense-indulgences. Just living the routine life of unintelligent imitation of others in society is the surest way to a life of sensuality. For spiritual purposes, a most intelligently re-planned way of life is to be followed. If you want to take up sincere *sadhana*, you will have to redirect your life's flow. Hence the first thing to be renounced is the "blind following of the patterns of the time" --*loka-anuvartanam.*

Deha-anu-vartanam--to live obeying implicitly the impulses of the flesh. Till now we have been slaves to the physical body. Feeding it, looking after it, fattening it, taking it to hospital when ill, when healthy squandering its vitality in sensual living-- thus we live, always at its service. This should also be given up. Renounce living in the flesh as the flesh.

The next thing to be left is "the blind following of the scriptures, without understanding their deeper implications"--*Sastra-anu-vartanam.* Some commentators, however, interpret this term as, "leaving the study of all books other than texts on spiritual ideals and religious ways of living.*

Leaving these three, what should one do?

In your own Self *(Swa);* the misconception that I am the body, the mind and the intellect *(adhyasa);* end or do away with *(apanayanam);* do, accomplish *(kuru).* In short, end the misconceptions created by the superimpositions upon your divine Self.

We cannot do away with the shortcomings in our personality without the world, the body and the scriptures. This verse, read as a whole means: make use of the world! Be of healthy body. Make intelligent use of the *Sastras,* instead of following them blindly. How modern, how progressively fresh is this denuded idea!

We are tempted to follow the world, we are egged on to live a life of the flesh, we are whipped to pursue the study of secular things only because of the three kinds of *vasanas* in us.** They are also called the triple appetites *(eshanas).* These breed the respective blind following of the body, the texts and the world. In order to get over these, their respective *vasanas* are to be eliminated.

The existence of these *vasanas* is symptomatically proved by the manifestation of the aping tendency in their respective

---

* शास्त्रानुवर्तनं नाम मोक्षप्रयोजक - ग्रन्थपरिशीलनं विना इतर ग्रन्थाध्ययनादिकं .... शास्त्रपदं कर्मशास्त्रपरं वा ॥

** *deha-vasana; sastra-vasana: loka-vasana.*

fields, *(anu-vartanam)*. When these three *vasanas* are removed, many other *vasanas* get associated with these. The "symptomatic treatment" by which the disease germs are ultimately removed, is indicated in this verse.

लोकवासनया जन्तोः शास्त्रवासनयापि च ।
देहवासनया ज्ञानं यथावन्नैव जायते ॥ २७१ ॥

271. People cannot attain Realisation because of their desire to run after the world, their thirst for unnecessary study of the *Sastras* and their anxiety to pamper the body.

That which has taken birth: *(jantu)*--A living creature. In our day-to-day experiences of life, many a time we do not view things in their right perspective. This is normally due to some pre-conceived notions we entertain regarding things and beings around us. It is the predicament of man that his vision of the world around him is dictated by his personal bias of the moment.

The equipment of understanding, the intellect, always tries to apprehend the things of the world in sympathy with its own existing *vasanas*, the "ultimate propensities". If I dislike you intensely, even if I see you performing a good deed, I lable all your actions as vile and vicious. When you are my enemy, the "enemy idea" will be in my mind whenever I see you doing anything. Even if your work is most selfless and highly dedicated, I will interpret it only in the light of my *vasanas*.

Thus, when your mind is not prepared and you study the *Sastras*, you will invariably miss their moot point. The *Sastra* statements will get distorted to yield you an understanding which will readily cater to all your existing urges. These urges will not allow you to understand things as they should be understood. A polluted mind renders us incapable of knowing things as they really are.

The total urges in our bosom can be broadly classified under three categories. They are, "the social urges" *(loka-*

vasana), "the bodily or physical urges" *(deha-vasana)*, and the "urge to know" *(Sastra-vasana)*. These are the three tragic shackles upon the human personality.

How these shackles bind us is explained in the following verse.

संसारकारागृहमोक्षमिच्छो-
रयोमयं पादनिबन्धशृंखलम् ।
वदन्ति तज्ज्ञाः पटु वासनात्रयं
योऽस्माद्विमुक्तः समुपैति मुक्तिम् ॥२७२॥

272. The wise have spoken of the three kinds of *vasanas* as iron chains shackling the feet, for him who wishes to be liberated from the prison-house of this world. He who is free from them, attains liberation.

These three types of desires *loka-vasana, deha-vasana* and *sastra-vasana* perpetrate the utmost cruelty towards a human being. They bind him down to *samsar*, as the strong iron chains binding a prisoner to the prison-house. So say the wise men who have broken these chains and come out of the *samsar*-prison.

In order to be free you will first have to break these shackles. Only then can the prisoner come out of the confining walls of the prison. Our identification with the body, mind and intellect constitutes the prison walls and the iron bars that we have built around ourselves. In this subjective jail, we are tied down by the shackles of the triple hungers. Only he can be the liberated one who has come out of this ever-changing world of limitations.

जलादिसंसर्गवशात्प्रभूत-
दुर्गन्धधूताऽगरुदिव्यवासना ।
संघर्षणेनैव विभाति सम्य-
ग्विधूयमाने सति बाह्यगन्धे ॥२७३॥

273. The captivating fragrance of the *Agaru* (agolochum)---which gets enveloped by an insufferable stink created by its contact with water---again manifest itself as soon as the enveloping smell is entirely removed by scrubbing.

अन्तःश्चितानन्तदुरन्तवासना-
धूलीविलिप्ता परमात्मवासना ।
प्रज्ञातिसंघर्षणतो विशुद्धा
प्रतीयते चन्दनगन्धवत् स्फुटा ॥२७४॥

274. The fragrance of the supreme Self, like the fragrance of sandal-wood, is covered by the dust of unending *vasanas* deeply ingrained in the mind, and is again clearly perceived when it is purified by a continuous scouring with Knowledge.

Because of the *vasanas*, the human personality putrefies and gathers the stinking smell of lust, greed, anger, delusion etc. The smell of flesh and its sensuality are the very characteristics of our personality at present. It does not have the beautiful fragrance of our essential nature. Instead of being useful to other members of society, we are ready to disturb them at all times. Indicating this, Sankara gives an example.

Sandal-wood, when put in water and allowed to remain in it for a long time, emanates an obnoxious odour from the rotting wood. Ordinarily, it has the most heavenly fragrance *(divya-vasana)*. But when it remains in contact with water for a long time it starts stinking. If the wood is taken out and rubbed against a stone, the fragrance slowly emerges to waft pleasant satisfaction to all.

Similarly, even though you are the *Atman*, because of your identification with the body, the stink of your *vasanas* is coming out at the moment. Lust, anger, greed, etc., contribute their stink at all times. Love, mercy and kindness have no accommodation in the heart. To gain its original status, the personality needs a little "rubbing". It should be rubbed against the "greater knowledge" in meditation. The filth and the stink will go away and one's real nature will then be revealed.

By rubbing, we are not giving the smell to the sandal-wood. Its fragrance is already in it. It was not available, that is all. Similarly, divinity is not to be given to you from somewhere else. The *Upanishad* thunders, "That Thou Art".

The inner essentially divine fragrance is convered by the dust of the dirty *vasanas* at present. The dirty *Vasanas (are the social, the physical and the) vasanas* for acquiring know-ledge. Because of these ultimate propensities, the divinity in us is not able to express itself. Hence emanates the stink of our personality

Under such circumstances the personality needs some "rubbing", a little "scraping" with the "right knowledge". By meditation when the "right knowledge" is poured into the mind, it leaves its filthy, unworthy *vasanas*. Then the real nature of the Self manifests Itself, just as the sandal-wood on scraping wafts its refreshing fragrance.

अनात्मवासनाजालैस्तिरोभूतात्मवासना ।
नित्यात्मनिष्ठया तेषां नाशे भाति स्वयं स्फुटा ॥२७५॥

275. Innumerable desires for things that are the not-Self cloud the desire for Self-realisation. When these have been destroyed by being constantly established in the Self, the *Atman* manifests all by Itself.

The real fragrance of the Self is veiled by the cobwebs of our preoccupations with the hungers to enjoy the not-Self *(anatma-vasana)*. It is like the dusty cobweb at the window which obscures the beauty beyond the window. The wordly *vasanas*, meaning the irresistible urges of the lower---the BMI, PFT & OET---cloud the higher urges in us.

By constant meditation upon the Self *(nitya-atma-nishthaya)*, alone can one remove these cobwebs. Study of the scriptures, practice of meditations, sincere devotion to the Lord and selfless dedicated activity in the world---these will bring religion and spirituality into everv minute of our lives.

When the *vasanas* are removed, the Self manifests of Its own accord. The *Atman* is clearly perceived by Its own brilliance.

यथा यथा प्रत्यगवस्थितं मन-
स्तथा तथा मुञ्चति बाह्यवासनाः ।
निःशेषमोक्षे सति वासनाना-
मात्मानुभूतिः प्रतिबन्धशून्या ॥२७६॥

276. To the extent the mind becomes steadily established in the subjective Self, to that extent it leaves its desires for the objects of the world. When all such desires completely end, then there is the clear, unimpeached realisation of the Self.

To the extent the mind becomes introvert, to that extent extrovertedness ends. As the mind gets establsihed in the Self within, the extrovert *vasanas (bahya-vasana)*, for the objects of the world get reduced. Thus when the mind becomes totally introvert, completely established in the Self, that is the state when there are no *vasanas* at all for objects of pleasure. All the *vasanas* are removed. That is the moment of a continuous experience of the *Atman* within and without with no obstacle whatsoever.

Lesser the *vasanas*, lesser are the agitations of the mind; lesser the agitations of the mind, more contemplative is the intellect. No vasanas, no mental turmoil---complete contemplation---then the experience of the Divine is effortless, natural.

54. End Superimposition---the Means. (277-292)

स्वात्मन्येव सदा स्थित्वा मनो नश्यति योगिनः ।
वासनानां क्षयश्चातः स्वाध्यासापनयं कुरु ॥२७७॥

277. Being ever fixed on his own Self, the meditator's mind ends. Then there is a complete cessation of *vasanas*. So negate entirely your superimposition.

In this section, with these sixteen verses Sankara exhaustively indicates how our timeless projections can be ultimately removed and the pure Infinite Self in all Its holiness rediscovered as the essential nature in each one of us.

Without identifying with our body, mind and intellect, let us steadily contemplate upon the Self as our own Divine, Infinite Nature. A *Yogi*, who has yoked his mind to this higher ideal gains mastery over his mind. He alone can annihilate his mind. The annihilation of the mind *(mano-nasa)*, is not possible unless all the *vasanas* in it have been exhausted. Without annihilating the cause the effect cannot end. When the mind becomes quiet, then as a result of our sincere and repeated attempts at meditation all the existing *vasanas* get roasted in the fire of contemplation. Though they give the impression of being there they can never more sprout into desires, thoughts and actions. Ending your misconceptions that you are the body, the mind and the intellect, practise on deligently. End your superimpositions and experience the essential Self which is behind all your personality layers.

तमो द्वाभ्यां रजः सत्त्वात्सत्त्वं शुद्धेन नश्यति ।
तस्मात्सत्त्वमवष्टभ्य स्वाध्यासापनयं कुरु ॥२७८॥

278. Tamas is destroyed both by *Rajas* and *Sattwa; Rajas* by *Sattwa* and *Sattwa* is destroyed on "purification". Therefore, solely depending upon *Sattwa*, deny entirely your superimposition.

The *vasanas* of every individual fall under the three categories of *Tamas*, *Rajas* and *Sattwa*. When these *vasanas* are totally exhausted, the divine Self within us shines forth vividly for our direct experience. How to get rid of these *vasanas?*

Tamasic *vasanas* can be removed by cultivating *Rajasic* and *Sattwic vasanas. Rajasic vasanas* can be ended by replacing them with *Sattwic* ones. When the mind becomes purer, the *Sattwic vasanas* too get exhausted.

Tamasic *vasanas*, the urges of lust and rest, indolence and slumber, are the typical motivational urges in the majority of us. There is no anxiety to do anything. Lethargy, sleep etc. are the sings of *Tamasic vasanas*. These low, devolutionary *vasanas* are removed by instilling into the individual, more and more Rajasic *vasanas*. *Rajas* is activity and dynamism. By injecting into a *Tamasic* man more and more desires, he becomes active. He acts vigourously, so that he may earn more and enjoy more elaborately. Such an individual will act constantly for selfish ends for he is prompted by low desires for cheap and dissipating sense gratifications.

When thus he has started working from morning till evening, exhausting himself, only for the chance to relax from evening till midnight, that he can thoroughly enjoy a life of sensuality, a time soon comes when he starts feeling the hollowness of life. He feels, "Money I have. A good wife I have. Everything I have. But what is the use? There is no peace of mind." Thus when he works at a tremendous tempo and reaches this state of dissatisfaction, his *Rajoguna vasanas* can be curbed, directed and finally transcended by instilling into him more and more *Sattwic vasanas*. Advise him, "Brother, go on working at the same tempo. Work you have to do. There is no other go. Through work we have got ourselves entangled and through work alone we can disentangle ourselves. But do no desire the fruits of your actions. Desire for the fruits of our actions entangles us, and desireless, dedicated activity disentangles our personality." Thus he has to be led from selfish, lusty acts into a field of selfless, dedicated activity.

Selfless dedication comes only as a result of devotion at a higher altar---the Lord, or the *Guru* (Teacher). In such an inspired spirit of dedication, sincerely and lovingly work on in the same cheerful tempo. Instead of working under the whip of your arrogant ego, start acting, inspired by your accepted ideal and your faith in it.

When one starts working without ego and egocentric desires, the existing *vasanas* are exhausted, and no new *vasanas* are created. When Rajoguna *vasanas* get purged, *Sattwic vasanas* alone will linger in such a personality. Devotion to the Lord, anxiety to realise etc. will gather a new momentum. But *Sattwa-guna vasana* is also a *vasana.* Shackles made of gold also bind. How to remove them? The best method is to steadily increase the *Sattwic vasanas.*

When the *Sattwic vasanas* increase, your devotion to your ideal grows more and more. You are no longer satisfied by mere dedication to It. You want to experience It. The more you try to experience It with your mind and intellect, the quieter your mind becomes. Quieter the mind, lesser the turmoil, which means greater is the purity of the inner equipment. When the mind becomes absolutely pure, the *Sattwic vasanas* also get exhausted and at last, it completely transcends *Sattwa* also *(Sattwa-ateeta).* When an individual has gone beyond *Sattwa,* it is the auspicious moment of his direct experience of the Self within.

"Therefore, increase Sattwa", says Sankara, advising those who are heaving under the lashes of the Rajasic *vasanas.* Develop a *Sattwic* nature and reject entirely your superimpositions.

प्रारब्धं पुष्यति वपुरिति निश्चित्य निश्चलः ।
धैर्यमालम्ब्य यत्नेन स्वाध्यासापनयं कुरु ॥२७९॥

279. Knowing for certain that your *prarabdha* will nourish this body, remain undisturbed, and with courage, deny entirely your superimposition.

Those who have taken to *sadhana* as their sole purpose in life may renounce everything and remain in jungles with no security etc., yet one feeling still lingers in their bosom: the anxiety for the maintenance and nourishment of the body---food. When once this worry has started, the *sadhak* has already started another *samsar.* It would have been better then, had he remained with his family, performing his worldly duties.

Even when all other worries are over, it is but natural that the one regarding the preservation of the body will still linger. Once you yield to that physical anxiety, it will multiply by leaps and bounds. The resulting storms of the mind will destroy all the *sadhana* that you might have done for years. Dire then, is the fall.

This body is what it is because of its *prarabdha*. Because of your *vasanas* you have taken this body. Today, the body moves, every minute, expressing its powerful *vasanas*. The body will drop off once the *vasanas* are exhausted. Till then, it will continue to exist, food or no food. It will be looked after by its own *prarabdha*. If my body is not getting food, I become anxious for it. However, when this body was born, it was born without consulting me. That mighty Law by which it was born will keep it going for the purpose for which it was born. If it falls off, never mind, let it go. Understanding this well, strengthen your mind and protect it from all such agitations.

Muster up courage. Reach a discriminative conclusion through intelligent reflections. Put in true effort. With unseen perspiration, with invisible panting, with secret effort, remove the misconception within yourself.

नाहं जीवः परं ब्रह्मेत्येतद्व्यावृत्तिपूर्वकम् ।
वासनावेगतः प्राप्तस्वाध्यासापनयं कुरु ॥२८०॥

280. "I am not the *jeeva*, I am the supreme *Brahman*"---thus by eliminating all that is the not-Self, deny entirely your superimpositions which manifest through the propulsion of your past "urges".

"I am not the *jeeva*, the PFT. I am not limited or conditioned by the body, mind and intellect. I am the supreme *Brahman*, without any entanglements with, or limitations of the body, the mind and the intellect. The All-pervading and Eternal Reality am "I". Let such thoughts always be in your mind as a subdued but clear background music.

With such positive thoughts, the negative ideas gathered by the flood of *vasanas* can be eliminated. These negative thoughts of, "I am the limited. I am the body, the mind, the intellect," etc. have been with us due to the expressions of the *vasanas* in our bosom. They have to be replaced by positive *vasanas* and the misconceptions have to be totally removed.

"Deny entirely all your superimpositions."

श्रुत्या युक्त्या स्वानुभूत्या ज्ञात्वा सार्वात्म्यमात्मनः ।
क्वचिदाभासतः प्राप्तस्वाध्यासापनयं कुरु ॥२८१॥

281. Having realised your own Self to be the "Self-in-all" through scriptures, by reasoning and from your own direct experience, deny entirely your superimpositions, even when a slight trace appears.

By means of what has been read and understood from the *Upanishads (srutya);* by intelligent argumentation *(yuktya);* by your own first-hand experience *(swa-anubhootya),* ---by means of these three methods having apprehended the Truth, a *sadhak* must get fully released from all his superimpositions. The three processes constitute the listening *(sravana),* reflections upon the ideas listened to *(manana),* and meditation upon them for direct personal experience *(nididhyasana),* respectively.* Come to apprehend the *Atman*, the Self in you as the Self everywhere, by listening to the scriptures, by reflecting upon the ideas through intelligent argumentation and come to experience It through contemplation.

While doing *sadhana* whenever the ego and egocentric vulgarities such as lust, greed, anger and passion appear even a little, destroy them immediately. The mind will rush out into sense-objects again and again, since for millions of lives we have been asserting and living at the ego-level. It is necessary that we guard aginst the mind running out again hunting after its sense gratifications.

---

* The term *srutya* is reminiscent of the *Vedantic sadhana* of *sravana;* Sankara's expression here yuktya reminds us of the method of manana; and the *Acharya's* lyrical phrase, *swa-anubhootya* recalls to our mind the advice for *nididhyasana.*

Continue this triple-path of spiritual living and end all your misconceptions. How much you have studied is not the question; how much you have moved towards It is what matters. "Ultimately come to deny entirely all your superimpositions", is the repeated advice of *Acharya* Sankara.

अन्नादानविसर्गाभ्यामीषन्नास्ति क्रिया मुनेः ।
तदेकनिष्ठया नित्यं स्वाध्यासापनयं कुरु ॥२८२॥

282. Since he has no idea of eating or evacuating, the sage has no relationship with action. Therefore, through continuous involvement in the contemplation of *Brahaman*, deny entirely all your superimpositions.

"Eating" is not only putting food into the mouth and swallowing it, but also the anxiety for it, plans for its preparation, all the excitement for it, the sweet expectation of its taste, its mouth-watering smell and ultimately eating it--all these are not there to distract him who is engrossed in the study and reflection of the scriptures. Food *(annam)* in the *Upanishads* also means, "all sense-objects eaten by the sense-organs". So eating food *(anna-adaana)*, means "reception of sense-objects". Our responses to the stimuli received represent excretion or expulsion *(visarga)*. Receiving stimuli from the world of objects and responding to them with egocentric identification are not done by a man of reflection *(muni)*.

One who is striving to learn the art of meditation must slowly and carefully develop in himself an attitude of holding himself neutral in all receptions of stimuli and in his responses to them. A man of reflection does not identify with these. They may go on at the physical level because of the *prarabdha* of the body, but he is not involved in them. He is otherwise busy. This Truth has a universal applicability. Even in ordinary life we find, a man of reflection, a serious thinker, is not normally available for petty reflexes. When the examinations are near, students are very busy with their studies---no movies, no picnics---vigorously studying. When the mind has taken up any idea seriously, it gets engrossed in it. The absent-mindedness of great scientists and aritsts is attributed to their devotion to the theme of their deep contemplation and pursuit.

Always contemplating upon the one ideal *(tat-eka-nishthya),** act on in the world. Get engaged---be wedded---to the theme of *Brahman*, the supreme Self, and deny entirely all your superimpositions.

तत्त्वमस्यादिवाक्योत्थब्रह्मात्मैकत्वबोधतः।
ब्रह्मण्यात्मत्वदार्ढ्याय स्वाध्यासापनयं कुरु ॥२८३॥

283. By means of the realised Knowledge of the identity of *Brahman* and *Atman*, arising from such great maxims of the Vedas as "That Thou Art", deny entirely your superimpositions in order to strengthen you identification with *Brahman*.

The great declarations of the *Upanishads* point out the identity of the individual Self with the Self present everywhere. The substratum for my life is the very substratum for the whole universe. In order to gain intimate experience of this great declaration, end your suprimpositions. In order to be firmly established in *Brahman*, end all misconceptions about yourself.

For deep confirmed experience *(daardyaya)*,---the spiritual experience of the Sef should not be a passing fancy or some super sensuous experience only. It must be a firm and deep experience---as firm as our experience today that we are this body-bundle and as deep as our daily experiences of the world around us.

अहंभावस्य देहेऽस्मिन्निःशेषविलयावधि।
सावधानेन युक्तात्मा स्वाध्यासापनयं कुरु ॥२८४॥

284. Till the identification with the body is completely rooted out, with vigilance and concentration, deny entirely all your superimpositions.

---

* निष्ठा = नितरां स्थितिः ॥

"How long should this practice be continued"? This doubt assails all beginners in *Vedanta* study. Sankara categorically answers this illogical and idle question and says, "Till the attitude 'I am this body', ends totally with no trace remaining". The superimposition has to be done away with very carefully, with all vigilance *(savadhanena)*:

Try to remove this misconception with great concentration and care, through study, reflection and meditation--slowly and calmly.

प्रतीतिर्जीवजगतोः स्वप्नवद्भाति यावता ।
तावन्निरन्तरं विद्वन्स्वाध्यासापनयं कुरु ॥२८५॥

285. O learned one, as long as even a dream-like perception of the world of objects and of the experiencing ego *(jeeva)* persists, continuosly strive to deny entirely all your superimpositions.

There are two interpretations to this verse:

One school of commentators emphasises that till the *jeeva* and *jagat* distinctions--the subject-object relationship--appear even as a dream, the practice of self-withdrawal has to be continued. According to this school, the practice stops when everything around, including the *sadhak's* very individuality appears as a vision in a dream.

The other school says, even if there is a dream-like perception of the subject-object relationship, the practice of self-withdrawal has to be continued till the *sadhak* enters completely into *Samadhi*.

Two types of men-of-Realisation are revered and respected in Hinduism. The first type are those who even after Realisation come to work in society.* They work because they see the world around them and even while they are working, they are fully aware that the world of plurality is

* They are called the *Karaka Purushas*.

unreal, like a dream. Sri Ramchandra, Sri Krishna, *Acharya* Sankara, King Janaka are examples of this type.

There are the others who turn completely to meditation. They do not experience anything of the world outside. Whenever the perception of plurality occurs, they immediately withdraw their minds and try to remain fixed in *Brahman*. Both these types are indicated in the sensitivity of this verse.

निद्राया लोकवार्तायाः शब्दादेरपि विस्मृतेः
क्वचिन्नावसरं दत्त्वा चिन्तयात्मानमात्मनि ॥२८६॥

286. Without giving even the slightest chance to forget the *Atman* because of sleep (unawareness), matters of the world or sense-objects, reflect steadily upon the Self in the mind.

Two forces from within distract men from pursuing their ideal: (a) unawareness and (b) concern for worldly things. It is generally observed that when a man is fired with enthusiasm to dedicate himself to an ideal, the less intelligent and unenthusiastic people around him try to dissuade him. If he yields to this pressure, his enthusiasm will ebb away and consequently, his efforts will weaken miserably.

While at work, if you allow your mind to slip into unawareness and inadvertence, your efficiency suffers. *Sadhaks* should be very alert and should never allow these forces to pollute their *sadhana*. Even for a moment,* do not get distracted. Constantly comtemplate upon the nature of the Self in the mind.

मातापित्रोर्मलोद्भूतं मलमांसमयं वपुः ।
त्यक्त्वा चाण्डालवद्दूरं ब्रह्मीभूय कृती भव ॥२८७॥

287. Shunning to a safe distance, like an outcast, this body which has come from the impurities of the parents, and which itself is constituted of flesh and its impurities, assert your divine *Brahmic* nature and realise the fulfilment of your life.

---

*क्वचित् – कदाचिदपि – *Never--not even for a moment.

This physical body is fashioned from the excretory material of the father and the mother; and itself is flesh and impurities only. To the needs of this we cater so much: we soap it, powder it, perfume it and dress it up in the most modern clothes. This unholy packet of filth should be kept far away from our identifications. Unfortunately, we have to carry it with us wherever we go . So we must not identify with it to such an extent that we are busy dancing attention to it, being full-time slaves to our own abominable flesh.

All that is asked of us is the giving up of our identification with the body. The moment we accomplish this full detachment, we become of the nature of *Brahman (Brahmibhoota)*. Today we are not able to understand Reality because of our flesh-identification and our subsequent slavish catering to its endless demands.

Kritakrityata: It is the feeling that "whatever had to be done has been done": *(Kriti)*--may you become That *(Brahmibhava)*; after experiencing that Infinitude which is free from all sorrows. All our sorrows are contributed by our awareness of our body, mind and intellect. Transcending them all is the experience of the Infinite Beatitude.

Once this is experienced, all our seekings come to an end. We will no more be anxious to acquire, to posses or to aggrandise. All these anxieties arise only at the BMI level. We are asked to give up our identification with our BMI, our packet of filth.* The reward for this sacrifice is Infinite Bliss and a sense of complete satisfaction, a sense of fulfilment, perfect in its totally satisfying joys.

घटाकाशं महाकाश इवात्मानं परात्मनि ।
विलाप्याखण्डभावेन तूष्णीं भव सदा मुने ॥२८८॥

288. Merging the finite ego in the supreme Self, like the pot-space in the infinite space, by meditating on their identity, be for ever peaceful, O Sage.

---

* *Mala-mamsa-mayam vapuh:* मलमांसमयं वपुः

The "pot-space" example is well-known in *Vedanta*. Pot-space *(ghata-akasa)*, means the space enclosed by the pot. Infinite space *(maha-akasa)*, means the total space of the universe.

In the total space, the sun, the moon, the stars and the earth etc., are all moving. Space is all-pervading and is one-without-a-second. It allows other things to exist in it, but is never itself affected by them. This infinite space conditioned by the pot becomes the pot-space. The pot-space is limited, while the total space is unlimited. The pot-space is conditioned by the pot; the total space is conditioned by nothing. If the pot is broken the pot-space becomes one with the total space.

In fact, the pot-space was never separate from the total space, even while the pot was existing. The existence of pot-space was only an illusion created by the mud walls of the pot.

Similarly, Consciousness conditioned by the physical body appears as the *jeeva*. "The concept of individuality has arisen because of the Consciousness identifying with the physical body."* When this identification is removed the limited Consciousness is experienced as the Consciousness present everywhere, Absolute and Infinite.

Thus gain the quietude of mind and intellect *(tooshnibhava)*. May the individual who is reflecting upon the Upanishadic Truth become quiet and serene, having experienced the merger directly in his own heart.**

स्वप्रकाशमधिष्ठानं स्वयंभूय सदात्मना ।
ब्रह्माण्डमपि पिण्डाण्डं त्यज्यतां मलभाण्डवत् ॥२८९॥

* बुद्ध्याद्युपाधिना परात्मा जीव उच्यते ।

** The same idea is repeated in the Bhagavad Geeta XV. 20.

एतद् बुद्ध्वा बुद्धिमान्स्यात्कृतकृत्यश्च भारत ।
Knowing this, one attains the highest intelligence and becomes one who has accomplished all one's duties, O Bharata.

289. Yourself becoming the Self-luminous *Brahman*, the sole substratum of all things, reject the macrocosm and microcosm, like two unclean parcels.

The causal, the subtle and the physical bodies function because of the Consciousness in us. When It is not expressing,the physical body is dead. Hence this Life Principle, this Spark of Existence is considered the Ground, the Substratum which holds them all together. This Substratum is Self-effulgent because It is the divine Consciousness. Come to apprehend this Truth in yourself.

In Sanskrit, the term used to indicate the macrocosmic universe, the totality, is *Brahma-andam;* that used to indicate the microcosmic individuality is *Pinda-andam.* The Great Womb in which grows the entire universe of living creatures and lifeless things is called the macrocosm, the *Brahma-anda.* The microcosm constituted of the individual physical body, its passions, emotions and thoughts is called the *Pinda-anda.* Transcend these two--*Brahma-anda* and *Pinda-anda*--and experience the supreme Reality.[1]

To throw away a bundle of filth we should have no regrets. With no regrets, therefore, renounce, the macrocosm and the microcosm--the concepts of universality and individuality--like two bundles of foul-smelling, abhorrent, filth.

चिदात्मनि सदानन्दे देहारूढामहंधियम् ।
निवेश्य लिङ्गमुत्सृज्य केवलो भव सर्वदा ॥२९०॥

290. Shifting your identification which is now fixed in the body to the *Atman* which is Existence-Knowledge-Bliss Absolute, rejecting the subtle body, may you become, ever the pure Self alone.

Our identification with the body is so deep-rooted today, that we consider ourselves to be the body. This identification should be totally shifted to the *Atman.* Everyone of us

---

1. "अधिष्ठानावशेषो हि नाशः कल्पितवस्तुनः" इति प्रमाणात् -
"by the dictum proof that where the substratum alone remains, all superimpositions lift themselves." When the rope alone is seen, the illusory snake ends.

considers himself to be either the gross body, or the subtle body or the causal body. Each one of us should therefore, replace our body-identification with Self-identification, for the nature of the Self is pure Consciouness, Absolute Knowledge, and Ever-blissful.

When you wake up, your identification with your dream body ends. When the dreamer with his dream body makes a pilgrimage to the waking state then in the waking mind and body, the dream mind and body merge. In much the same way at this moment we have the firm belief that we are the body. Through study, reflection, contemplation and sincere meditation, rise above the subtle body[1] and become the One-without-a-second at all times.[2]

The Infinite One: *(Kevala)*--That which is not limited by time or space or any other conditioning, the homogenous non-dual Self.[3]

यत्रैष जगदाभासो दर्पणान्तः पुरं यथा ।
तद्ब्रह्माहमिति ज्ञात्वा कृतकृत्यो भविष्यसि ॥२९१॥

291. That in which there is the "illusion" of the universe, just as the "city in the mirror", that *Brahman* you are. Knowing this, you will experience that fulfilment of your life.

During *sadhana*, when the merger with the Supreme is not complete, the perception of the world of objects will distract and disturb the *sadhak*, though in fact, it has no existence whatever. Its existence is as real as that of the "reflection" of a city in a mirror.

The reflection in the mirror looks exactly like the object reflected, but there is a lateral inversion of the object, i.e., the right side looks as if it is left side. Also, if you are facing east and looking at the mirror, your image will be facing west.

---

1. *Linga-sareera = Sukshma-sareera = subtle body.*
2. *Kevalo-bhava-sarvada=Asango-bhava.*
3. *Sajateeya-vijateeya-swagata-bheda-rahita KEVALOBHAVA.*

Whenever your attention is drawn towards the world of objects, think of its unreal nature. The world is nothing but the reflection of *Brahman*, having no reality apart from It. The difference between *Brahman* and the world of objects is the lateral inversion. Consciousness is Infinite; the world is finit. It is all-Bliss; the world is all-pain. It is all-Perfect; the world is extremely imperfect. But for these differences, in fact, It is the world.

Thus having apprehended, "I am *Brahman*," in which there is but the illusion of the universe, come to enjoy the sense of supreme fulfilment in life.

यत्सत्यभूतं निजरूपमाद्यं
चिदद्वयानन्दमरूपमक्रियम् ।
तदेत्य मिथ्यावपुरुत्सृजेत
शैलूषवद्वेषमुपात्तमात्मनः ॥२९२॥

292. Attaining that which is intrinsically one's Essence, which is Absolute Knowledge and Bliss, Non-dual, which is beyond all forms and activities, one should cease identifying with the false body, like the actor who relinquishes his dress and make-up.

All joys known to me in my daily life are because of me and the objects of my liking. The supreme Self is Infinite Joy which is the very natture of the Self, not arising from any other object *(Adwaya-ananda)*. This Consciousness is formless, unlimited and unconditioned by anything. It is All-pervading and without any activity for activity is not possible in the All-pervading. Where will He act? With what will He act? What is there to be acted upon? In the Perfect, where are desires, the impulses behind every action? The All-full has no sense of imperfection, and hence there is no desire to be fulfilled through actions.

Having reached this Great Goal, rise above the false notion, "I am the body", like an actor in a drama. When an actor plays the role of a king on the stage, he wears a crown on his head, a false beard and moustache, and orders everyone about. But when the make-up is removed, he emerges from back-stage, free and relaxed. He is now his own self and not the king whose part he played on the stage.

Before he came on to the stage, he was Mr. So-and-so. After going away from the stage, when the make-up is removed, he is again himself, the Mr. So-and so. On stage too, he was the same Mr. So-and-so, but with the make-up, he acted the part of the character he was to play in the drama. Similarly, *Atman*, the Self, you are. But because of the "dress" of the body, you identify with it and play the part of the stupid fool in the world and behave like one. And you act your part so beautifully, that you forget your Real Nature. And then a *Guru* has to come and advise you, "you are not this". Now in true, meditation, you undress yourself and come to live your original nature as the Pure Infinite Self.

55. The Perceived "I" --Factor....False. (293-297)

सर्वात्मना दृश्यमिदं मृषैव
नैवाहमर्थः क्षणिकत्वदर्शनात् ।
जानाम्यहं सर्वमिति प्रतीतिः
कुतोऽहमादेः क्षणिकस्य सिध्येत् ॥२९३॥

293. The objective world is quite unreal. Neither is the ego real, for it is seen to be fleeting. How then can the apparent "I know all" be true of the ego etc. which are momentary?

From the stand-point of the Absolute, all that we see and experience--the entire OET --is false. From the stand-point of the waker, all that he saw in the dream is false. Not only is the world unreal, but even the ego, the "I", is unreal. They are unreal because they are momentary. The concept of "I" changes every moment--in childhood, youth, middle-age and old-age; in the dreamer, waker and deep-sleeper--every moment there is a different concept of "I". The objective and subjective worlds too are constantly changing. Yet we say, "I know", "I have the experience", etc. This can only be a false delusory notion with respect to the ego etc.

If there be a set of continuous experiences, then there must be a changeless Factor in you which knows all changes. The world of the '20s, the '30s, the '40s, the '50s and the '60s has changed. You as an individual of 20, 30, 40, 50 and 60 have also changed. Yet you say, *"I Know"*.Which is the Factor in you which as a child experienced your childhood, as a young man experienced your youth and as an old man is now experiencing your old age?

Childhood, youth, middle-age and old-age are the different vicissitudes of life. What is that great Truth, which, functioning through all these, has the experience of all of them! It is the Self. It is in Its play that we cry out, "I have experienced all these".

अहंपदार्थस्त्वहमादिसाक्षी
नित्यं सुषुप्तावपि भावदर्शनात् ।
ब्रूते ह्यजो नित्य इति श्रुतिः स्वयं
तत्प्रत्यगात्मा सदसद्विलक्षणः ॥२९४॥

294. But the real "I" witnesses the ego etc. It is always there, even in deep-sleep. "It is unborn, Eternal", says *Sruti* herself. Different, therefore, from the gross and the subtle is *Paramatman*.

The real sense of "I": *(Aham-pada-artha)*--is the one which is the Witness of the ego and the objects and their changes. The subject and the objects, both are recognised by the Consciousness which is one's Real Nature.

When I say, "I was unhappy when my wife died" , I am conscious of my sorrow *now*, of the wife's death some time back, and also that it was me who was unhappy. I am conscious of the "I", of its environments, and of its experiences. The subject, the objects and the experiences are all known by *ME*.

This Consciousness in me is Eternal and Real *(Nitya)*. Never is there a time when It is not. Even in deep-sleep, we are conscious of the nothing-ness. The Upanishad says, "This great Truth is Unborn, Eternal."*

This great Reality which is the inner Self is something other than the subtle and the gross: come to apprehend It. This is the anxious exhortation of Sankara to his students.

विकारिणां सर्वविकारवेत्ता
नित्याविकारो भवितुं समर्हति ।
मनोरथस्वप्नसुषुप्तिषु स्फुटं
पुनः पुनर्दृष्टमसत्त्वमेतयोः ॥२९५॥

295. That which is the Knower of all changes in all things which are liable to change, must doubtless be Eternal and Changeless. Again and again, the unreality of the gross and the subtle bodies is clearly perceived in one's fancy, dream and deep-sleep.

The Knower of all changes must Itself be Changeless. The Knowledge of all modifications must be beyond all modifications. The BMI are subject to change. The only changeless factor is the subject, who is the knower of all changes. The knowledge of the change must be something other than the changes. This Changeless Factor is constantly with us, even in deep-sleep, hence It is Eternal.

The gross and the subtle bodies are always the "known" as they are constantly seen and experienced. Therefore, they are *not* real. Their unreality can be clearly understood by analysing our own experiences of imagination, dream and deep-sleep. The moment I start dreaming, my waking body is not available. In my dream, my enemies torture me. They drag me all over on my back. When the fifth hot plate is being placed on my back, in that terrible agony I wake up, only to realise that the hot-water bag in my bed is leaking!** When I

* Kathopanishad I ii-18. अजो नित्यः शाश्वतोऽयं पुराणो ॥

** In Kaivalyopanishad: स्वप्नेर्थशून्ये सृजति स्वशक्त्या भोक्तादिविश्वं मन एव सर्वं ।-

"In the empty void of the dream are created a world of experiencer-experienced etc. --for which the mind alone is the sole cause."

was dreaming, *this* body was not true. When I wake up, *that* body is not true. "Is any one of the bodies true?" "No. Both the bodies are unreal because in deep-sleep, none is available to me."

Thus when you analyse your experiences, honest to your scientific observation, you must come to the conclusion that all that changes is unreal. When you analyse your waking, dream and deep-sleep experiences, it will be instantly clear, to you that the subtle and gross bodies are not real at all--here the term *"real"* means "That which remains the same without change in all three periods of time."

Therefore.....

अतोऽभिमानं त्यज मांसपिण्डे
पिण्डाभिमानिन्यपि बुद्धिकल्पिते ।
कालत्रयाबाध्यमखण्डबोधं
ज्ञात्वा स्वमात्मानमुपैहि शान्तिम् ॥२९६॥

296. Therefore, reject your identification with this mass of flesh and with the ego or the subtle body, of which are the imaginations of the intellect. By realising your own Self which is Absolute Knowledge, which cannot be denied in the three periods of time, attain to the state of supreme Peace.

"Do away with your superimpositions" --this has been repeated in many of the previous verses. How does one deny these entirely?

"Now, therefore", says Sankara. "Renounce your identification with this mass of flesh". Renounce here means, give up your vanity *(abhimana)*,[1] that "I am this". You need not renounce money or house or wife or position or status. Even if you have renounced all these and yet you are anxious about this body, all your renunciations are useless; they will return to you in a very short time, wherever you are.

---

1. **अभिमान – आत्मबुद्धि** – "Vanity" means, the misconception that "I am this", when actually you are not it.

The ego which has the vanity, "I am this body", is nothing but an individual's intellectual estimation of himself. Renounce both--the body, and the idea, "I am this body" --then the ego will be eliminated.

Having renounced thus, come to experience the unbroken Knowledge which is unconditioned by the three periods of time. This unbroken Knowledge *(Akhanada-bodham)*, is always present in the past, present and future. Understand this eternal Reality as your own Self and come to experience the supreme peace.[1]

त्यजाभिमानं कुलगोत्रनाम-
रूपाश्रमेष्वार्द्रशवाश्रितेषु ।
लिङ्गस्य धर्मानपि कर्तृतादीं-
स्त्यक्त्वा भवाखण्डसुखस्वरूपः ॥२९७॥

297. Renounce your identification with family, lineage, name, form and order in life--attributes of the body which is like a foul corpse. So too, renounce your ideas of agency etc. ---attributes of the subtle body. Thus become the very essence of Absolute Bliss.

The vanities (अभिमान) of family, lineage, name, form and order in life etc. belong to the body, which is perishable and rotten.[2] The vanities of *doership* and *enjoyership* belong to the subtle-body which is always changing.

Renounce these vanities and experience the nature of the unbroken Bliss which is the Eternal Self.

Here, the main obstacle in leading a spiritual life has been indicated and the strategy of how to meet efficiently this obstacle has been pointed out. In the following verses, Sankara points out other minor obstacles and shows how each one of them can be avoided by an intelligent readjustment of our ideas and actions.

---

2. Realise the supreme peace =शान्तिं=आत्यन्तिकदुःखनिवृत्तिं=मुक्तिं लभस्व ॥

* आर्द्रशवाश्रितेषु=स्थूलदेहाश्रितेषु ।

56. Condemnation of the Ego. (298-309)

सन्त्यन्ये प्रतिबन्धाः पुंसः संसारहेतवो दृष्टाः ।
तेषामेकं मूलं प्रथमविकारो भवत्यहंकारः ॥२९८॥

298. It is observed that there are other obstacles also which hurl man into a whirl of births and deaths. Their one root---for the reasons given above---is the ego---the first modification of ignorance.

The superimpositions of the not-Self on the pure and then a firm identification with the gross and subtle bodies are not the only obstructions in man's attempt to realise his peaceful Self. There are other causes too, like desires etc., which bring about mental agitations causing the perception of the pluralistic phenomenal world. Desires, passions, lust, greed, jealousy etc, are all causes for more and more sorrows of man. They tie him firmly to the rack of change, to the wheel of births and deaths.

The root cause of all these is the ignorance of Reality. The very first modification of spiritual ignorance is the ego-sense in us. Had "I" not been there, there would not have been any sorrow. If "I" am not there, nothing else can be. As long as this "I" exists, everything else exists. This "I" is the very first effect of ignorance, most appropriately called "ne-science".

Ignorance expressed in the body and mind is called "I". Therefore, the renunciation of this "I" is insisted upon. Then the individual is liberated from the bondage of his *vasanas*. There are no more any "fruits of actions"[1] affecting the individual. If there be effective fruits of actions, there must be somebody who has performed the actions and is the enjoyer of their fruits. When the ego[2] is not there, then what is bondage? Bondage where? Who did the actions? Who enjoys or suffers the results or reactions?

---

1. The fruits of actions linger in us as *vasanas*. These *vasanas* can act only through the ego. Where the ego is not, there the *vasanas* become impotent and cannot express themselves.

2. Ego =doership + enjoyship: the *karta* + *bhokta* entity.

If I have committed murder and a warrant of arrest has been issued, the policeman comes up to my door to execute the warrant. But to whom will he serve the warrant if I have died last night? For the crime perpetrated by me, I must be hung. Admitted. But when I am dead, what can the State do? At best, the authorities can only note on the warrant, "The criminal is deceased and, therefore, the file is closed." What else can anyone do?

Smilarly, if the ego is not there, what can the fruits of action do? All the fruits of actions that have not been enjoyed become burnt in the fire of knowledge, say the *Vedanta* Textbooks.

यावत्स्यात्स्वस्य सम्बन्धोऽहंकारेण दुरात्मना ।
तावन्न लेशमात्रापि मुक्तिवार्ता विलक्षणा ॥२९९॥

299. As long as there is any relationship with this vile ego, so long there should not be even the slightest talk about liberation, which is unparalleled.

As long as there is even a slight identification with the wicked ego, there cannot be even a talk of liberation.

Liberation is so unique *(vilakshana)*, that it will not suffer even an iota of any other mental preoccupation. It must be everything or nothing. If it is sought with a total mind, it is gained forever. If the mind is not turned towards It totally, it can never be experienced.

अहंकारग्रहान्मुक्तः स्वरुपमुपपद्यते ॥
चन्द्रवद्विमलः पूर्णः सदानन्दः स्वयंप्रभः ॥३००॥

300. Freed from the shackles of the ego, like the moon freed from the eclipse, man gains his true nature and becomes Untainted, Infinite, Everblissful and Self-effulgent.

He who is liberated from his ego attains his true nature.

Sankara uses a simile of suggestive words to remind us of the idea of Rahu.* The physical body and its identifications

---

* Refer commentary on verse 139.

are shadows thrown upon the Supreme. When this identification is withdrawn, the Supreme stands revealed in Its own Self-effulgent glory.

यो वा पुरे सोऽहमिति प्रतीतो
बुद्ध्या प्रक्लृप्तस्तमसाऽतिमूढया।
तस्यैव निःशेषतया विनाशे
ब्रह्मात्मभावः प्रतिबन्धशून्य : ॥३०१॥

301. The ego is that which has been produced by the intellect, which is deluded by "nescience" and which is perceived in this body as "I am-so-and-so" --when this ego-sense is totally annihilated, one attains an unobstructed identity with *Brahman*.

The identification with the gross is a powerful imagination of the intellect, which is rendered supremely foolish by the "veil of *Tamas*" *(Avidya)*. This deluded intellect, which cannot see the Reality, imagines and projects the concept of "I am-so-and-so". Based upon this fanciful stupidity one builds up one's ego-sense. This ego has to be destroyed until not even a trace remains.

When this ego-centric concept that "I am-so-and-so" is completely annihilated, there is the realisation, "the Self in me is the Self present everywhere *(Brahma-Atma-Bhav)*". That feelingful understanding without any trace of doubt that, *"the Self in me is the One Self everywhere"*, is called realisation of the Supreme Self.

So long as the ego-sense persists, prompted by its natural personal bias *(Dwandwa)*, suffering under its "ultimate propensities" *(Vasanas)*, it lingers, interpreting a world of its own and confusing itself with the multiplicity perceived around. When the ego ends, ego-centred and society-centred drives no longer affect the individual, and this state is the Experience Divine. Such a *Realised-one* testifies to a depth-dimension in experience, that defies speech and thought and yet provides a more realistic experience than any sense-impressions.

This is the State of Realisation when the "veil of *Tamas*" *(Avidya)* is lifted to reveal the Truth Eternal, the "Self in all".

ब्रह्मानन्दनिधिर्महाबलवताऽहंकारघोराहिना
संवेष्ट्यात्मनि रक्ष्यते गुणमयैश्चण्डैस्त्रिभिर्मस्तकैः ।
विज्ञानाख्यमहासिना श्रुतिमता विच्छिद्य शीर्षत्रयं
निर्मूल्याहिमिमं निधिं सुखकरं धीरोऽनुभोक्तुं क्षमः ॥३०२॥

302. The treasure of the Bliss-of-*Brahman* is enwrapped by the mighty and dreadful serpent of the ego-sense, and jealously guarded for its selfish use, by its three fierce hoods, the three *Gunas*. The wise man who destroys it by severing its three heads with the great sword of Realisation, in accordance with the teachings of the scriptures, alone can enjoy this treasure which brings Bliss.

In the serenade of his poetry, Sankara brings in the refrain of what has already been said.

The treasure of the "Infinite Bliss-of-*Brahman*" is kept secret in the undisturbed cave of the physical body. This treasure is being guarded by a serpent, the ego-sense, the individuality. Individuality is represented by a serpent upon which Shri Krishna danced and destroyed--the serpent in the holds of the peacock, the vehicle of Lord Subramanya--the serpent that is worn as an ornament by Lord Siva--all these represent the ego-sense, which is the stock-pile of all our stupidities. This powerful, terrible, serpent, the ego, protects the treasure-trove of Blissful *Brahman (Brahma-ananda)*. For its own selfish ends, this ego coils round the treasure and protects it. This ego *(Ahamkar)* in us will not allow us to realise the State of *Brahmananda*. It expresses itself at all times through one agitation or another.

A triple-headed serpent is this ego. Its terrible hoods[1] are the gunas *Sattwa, Rajas* and *Tamas*. This serpent can be destroyed only by the sword of direct perception *(Vigyana)*.

---

1. चण्डैः= भीकरैः मस्तकैः = terrible hoods.

By no other means can we end the ego. The ego can be ended by the Sword of Knowledge, forged by direct perception, which is gained through a sincere and intelligent study of the scriptures.

The *Sruti* says, "The Self in you is the Self everywhere". That experience alone will end the ego. There is no other instrument--no other way to achieve this. With such an instrument,[1] let us cut off the three hoods of this fearful serpent. *Tamas* can be ended with *Rajas; Rajas* by *Sattwa* and *Sattwa* finally ends by *itself.* The ego has to be thus annihilated, plucked by its very root *(Moola).* Make it rootless *(Nir-moola).*

Men with discriminative intellect, having destroyed the very root of the ego by the Sword of Knowledge, gained by the study of *sastras*, enjoy the treasure of the Bliss Absolute.

यावद्वा यत्किन्चिद्विषदोषस्फूर्तिरस्ति चेद्देहे ।
कथमारोग्याय भवेत्तद्वदहन्तापि योगिनो मुक्त्यै ॥३०३॥

303. As long as there is even a trace of poison left in the body, how can one hope for complete recovery? Such too is the effect of the ego-sense upon the meditator's liberation.

If there is even a little bit of poison in a man's blood criculation, how can that man be healthy? The ego-sense *(Ahamkar)* is the poison in spritual existence. How can the meditator *(Yogi)*, who is striving for liberation gain it, if the ego-sense of the body is still persistingly lingering in him?

Therefore, this ego must be completely rooted out and annihilated.

अहमोऽत्यन्तनिवृत्या तत्कृतनानाविकल्पसंहृत्या ।
प्रत्यक्तत्त्वविवेकादिदमहमस्मीति विन्दते तत्त्वम् ॥३०४॥

---

1. विज्ञानाख्यमहासिना = निदिध्यासजन्यानुभव नाम्ना ॥

304. By the complete cessation of the ego-sense, gained by restraining the diverse mental waves, created by the ego itself, and through the discrimination of the Innermost Reality, one experiences Reality as "I am This".

When you are living as the ego, it cannot but create various mental agitations of endless varieties of vanities of family, race, name, form, wealth learning etc. When this ego is totally ended the vanities arising from it also end. The ending of the ego is the Realisation of the Supreme State. This Supreme State is not realised as something other than the meditator himself. It is realised as one's own Self. *"I am this Self"*, will be the nature of this total realisation. When the dreamer realises the waker, the experience is, *"I am this waker"*.

The final spiritual experience is subjective, personal, direct and full, always as one's own "Real Nature".

अहंकारे कर्त्र्यहमिति मतिं मुञ्च सहसा
विकारात्मन्यात्मप्रतिफलजुषि स्वस्थितिमुषि ।
यदध्यासात्प्राप्ता जनिमृतिजरादुःखबहुला
प्रतीचश्चिन्मूर्तेस्तव सुखतनोः संसृतिरियम् ॥३०५॥

305. Renounce immediately your identification with the ego-sense, the "sense of agency" which is by its very nature a modification and is lit up by a "reflection" of the Self. It diverts one from being established in the Self. Identifying yourself with this (false sense), you have reached this relative-existence, full of the miseries of birth, decay, death--although you are the Witness, the Essense of Knowledge-Bliss-Absolute.

"I am the dore" *(Karta)*, "I am the experiencer" *(Bhokta)* are both the expressions of the ego *(Ahamkara)*. This constant feeling of "I am the ego" has to be dropped immediately. This *Ahamkara* consists only of the various thought-disturbances *(mano-vrittis)*. When the Light of Consciousness illumines the thought-waves, you become Conscious-of-the-thoughts. Those Conscious-thought-bundles in their totality constitute the ego. The-ego is "the Consciousness relfected in the thoughts" *(Chid-abhasa)*. Therefore, when the thoughts cease, the ego also comes to an end. Because of this identification with the thoughts, and the consequent ego-sense, one has to chance to experience the "Infinite Beatitude" even for a moment. The Infinite Beatitude *(Chin-moorty)*[1] is your own nature; yet, you are not able to recognize It; you are an embodiment of this Bliss-form *(Sukha-tanu)*.[2]

All these confusions arose from the mind's projections. When you assert that you are the mind, all the imperfections of the mind become your imperfections. Birth, death, old age etc., and sorrows of endless varieties, come to you. This is called *samsar*. "I" identified with the ego gets blinded, and hence has no experience of the Self, which is of the form of the Light-of-Consciousness *(Chin-moorty)*. I, identified with my physical body, and the attitudes of my mind, superimpose upon myself various sorrows and imperfections such as birth, growth, decay, disease and death and then, due to them suffer endlessly. This is called the miserable "life" *(Samsrithi)*, which is the lot of all. "You are not this", "You are That Infinite Consciousness", "Come to apprehend It yourself " ....so, the *Upansishads* thunder forth.

सदैकरूपस्य चिदात्मनो विभो-
रानन्दमूर्तेरनवद्यकीर्तेः ।
नैवान्यथा क्वाप्यविकारिणस्ते
विनाहमध्यासममुष्य संसृतिः ॥३०६॥

306. But for Your identification with the ego-sense there is no transmigration for You, who are Immutable and Eternally the Same, Knowledge-Absolute, Omni-present, Bliss-Absolute and of unsullied glory.

For transmigration, repeated births and deaths, there is no other cause than the "ego-sense". Your essential nature is Consciousness. Bliss *(Ananda)* is your birth-right. Yours

---

1. चिन्मूर्तेः = ज्ञानशरीरस्य ॥
2. सुखतनोः = आनन्दघनस्य ॥

is the Untarnished Glory. * You are the One, at all times, without any modification. There is no reason why You should stupidly suffer so much and so continuously.

Sankara is advising the disciples here, *"You are That "*. You are suffering because of your own agitations. The agitations are caused by the ego in you. In the gross and subtle projections, the idea *"I am this"*, is the only cause that makes you suffer. Hence, give up this tragic and ruinous ego-sense *(Ahamkar)*.

What is to be done next, is advised in the following verse.

तस्मादहंकारमिमं स्वशत्रुं
भोक्तुर्गले कण्टकवत्प्रतीतम् ।
विच्छिद्य विज्ञानमहासिना स्फुटं
भुङ्क्ष्वात्मसाम्राज्यसुखं यथेष्टम् ॥३०७॥

307. Therefore, with the great sword of Realisation, destroying this ego-sense, your enemy--which is like a thorn in the throat of a man who is eating-enjoy directly and freely the Bliss of Your own Domain, the Majesty of the *Atman*.

The teacher is now suggesting a simple throat operation. If a thorn is sticking in the throat, one cannot appreciate any food, which otherwise one could have enjoyed. The ego is like a thorn in the throat of an eater. Hunger is there, Food is also ready. But the hungry-one cannot eat. Because the painful thorn is in the throat.

Similarly, the Bliss of the Infinitude is everywhere present. We fail to enjoy It, simply becasue of the ego-sense in us. To remove this ego, an "operation" has to be done. This surgery can be done with the instrument of the "experience-of-Reality" alone. Once this sense of ego is removed, we are at liberty to enjoy the Empire of the Self** as we like. All we

* अनवद्यकीर्ति --Untarnished Glory: Ever-Effulgent.

** आत्मसाम्राज्यसुखं = अनन्याधीनं - निरंतराखण्डानन्द - अनुभव ॥

have to do is remove this little ego, the misconception that *"I am this body, a bundle-of-filth"*.

At this moment in all our experience of life this "thorn" sticks in our throat and makes it difficult for us to enjoy the Bliss of the *Atman*.

Therefore, all our enjoyable experiences reach us as sorrowful ones only.

ततोऽहमादेर्विनिवर्त्य वृत्तिं
संत्यक्तरागः परमार्थलाभात् ।
तूष्णीं समास्स्वात्मसुखानुभूत्या
पूर्णात्मना ब्रह्मणि निर्विकल्पः ॥३०८॥

308. Checking the acitivities of the ego-and renouncing all attachments, through the experience of the Supreme Reality, be free from duality through the enjoyment of the Bliss of the Self, and remain serene in *Brahman*. For, then you have attained your Infinite Nature.

It is advised in this verse that all the thoughts connected with *ahamkara* are to be given up. The vanity of race, caste, creed, learning, status-in-life etc. are all connected with the ego-sense. Renounce all desires and gain the Supreme Goal. The price to be paid for the experience of the Reality is a total renunciation of the entire range of all desires.

Having given up the desires, keep quiet. Not physically. The mind and intellect are to be quietened. If the mind and intellect blabber, it is only because of the ego and its ego-centric desires.

When the ego and ego-based thoughts have been withdrawn, the desires end. When desires are no more throttling the mind, it becomes quiet. The thoughtless mind *itself*. is *Brahman*. This is the experience of Supreme Truth *(Parama artha)*. This is the gaining of the Supreme Self.

Thereafter, the mind and intellect will have no more desires to be fulfilled through selfish actions. The *sadhak* reaches the "State of Quietude" *(Tushni-Bhava)*. There he experiences Infinitude, which is his own Nature Divine. Come to realise this quietude

Why does Sankara repeat his advices and instruction? He himself answers in the following:

समूलकृत्तोपि महानहं पुन-
र्व्युल्लेखितः स्याद्यदि चेतसा क्षणम् ।
संजीव्य विक्षेपशतं करोति
नभस्वता प्रावृषि वारिदो यथा ॥३०९॥

309. Even though completely rooted out, this terrible ego-sense, if revived in the mind *(Vyullekhitah)* even for a moment, returns to life and creates hundreds of mischiefs, like a cloud ushered in by the wind during the rainy season.

People bemoan, 'I was much better last year. This year I don't know why I have again "fallen" in my spiritual *"Sadhana"* '. Such complaints we hear everyday, everywhere from almost all seekers.

This is all due to the play of the *vasanas* and the ego-sense. Sankara warns us here: "Even though you have ended the ego, along with its roots, the *vasanas*, again it can revive and rise up to tyrannize over you. If you allow your mind this freedom, then the play of the ego-sense will start aggain. Therefore, beware!"

When the ego is reborn, revived from its burial ground, and starts reasserting itself, a thousand varieties of agitations will immediately rise up. As long as you have the ego, the world of objects-emotions-thoughts can never be satisfactory by itself. A thousand varieties of agitating desires and worries

* व्युल्लेखितः - प्रबुद्धेन पुरुषेण भीकरस्वप्नइव स्मृतःस्यात्॥

must necessarily come up to dance in the mind. The ego will create storms in the bosom: thereby the peace will be lost.

In the rainy season the clouds are all driven away in a moment, and yet, the next moment, we may find the sky cloudy again. The breeze that removed the existing clouds, brings in it next windy dash a hoard of new ones. The sun shines brightly at one moment and the next moment, it is hidden again behind the newly gathered clouds.

So too the mind is at one moment steady in prayerful meditation. Next moment, there is a gush of thoughts which, dashing the brilliant poise of the mind-at-meditation, make it full of agitations. Generally you feel more distracted when you come out of the Pooja-room, than when you went in. All this is because of the devastating play of the ego. Therefore, "Beware"! Conquer the ego and continue with the alert vigilance of a successful conqueror. Never think that the ego has left you permanently. It must have only receded to the background--it can come up again if you slacken your diligence.

57. Actions, Thoughts and Vasanas--Renounce. (310-319)

निगृह्य शत्रोरहमोऽवकाशः
क्वचिन्न देयो विषयानुचिन्तया ।
स एव संजीवनहेतुरस्य
प्रक्षीणजम्बीरतरोरिवाम्बु ॥३१०॥

310. Having once overpowered this enemy, the ego, not a single moment's rest should be given to it to ruminate over sense-objects. That is verily the cause of its returning to life, just like water is the cause for the flowering of a citron tree, that has dried up before.

If a chance is given to the mind and its passions to express themselves, there will be no end to their destructive floods. Therefore, having destroyed the ego, which is our sole enemy, never give the mind the slightest chance to think of the objective-world. Attachment for even the most innocent-looking insignificant thing will pull you down to endless bondage.

A *Sadhu* having attachment for his loin-cloth could not tolerate the rat-trouble. He brought a cat to keep away the rats. The rats, no doubt, disappeared but the cat had to be fed, and hence, he brought a cow to his humble hut-of-study. The cow had to be looked after; hence, he decided to have a wife to look after the needs of the cow. After some time, they had children--their naming ceremony--nourishing and educating them--marriage of each--Endless!--Disastrous!

Therefore, never give a chance to the mind to ruminate over the sense-objects *(Vishaya-anu-chinta)*.[1] Sense-objects will come your way with all their irresistable enchantments. It is absurd to say that they will not come into your mind. They will-and they should; it is but natural. But let us not encourage them and commit ourselves to their thoughts. Mind is essentially of the nature of lust, anger etc. The six-fold emotions are, in their aggregate, called the "mind". You cannot have the mind without these qualities. Any thoughts arising in the mind will belong to one or the other of these six groups. The best way to control and end them is to direct them towards Narayana.[2]

"Desire to possess" when directed towards Narayana becomes the "burning spiritual anxiety of devotion for the Lord". Therefore, turn all attitudes of the mind towards Him. When sense-thoughts come, let us repeat the divine name of the Lord, *"Narayana"*. When you try to maintain the

---

1. When a man thinks of objects, "attachment" for them arises; from attachment "desire" is born; from desire arises "anger".

From anger comes "delusion"; from delusion "loss of memory", from loss of memory, the "destruction of discrimination"; from destruction of discrimination, he "perishes". (Geeta II 62-63)

2. "Having dedicated all activities unto Him, one should turn all one's desires, anger, pride etc. towards Him alone." (Narada Bhakti Sutra-Sutra 65).

thought of Lord Narayana, you unconsciously drive your thoughts away from the fascinating charms of the distracting sensuality all around you.

These sensuous thoughts are the elixir *(sanjeevany)* that revives the once-annihilated mind. This is the miracle that revives the dead "ego". An *apparently* dried up citron-tree, when regulrly watered for a few days revives and flowers again. The tree which *looked* dead, gets revived by a little water. Similarly, the *apparently* dead ego revives, the moment you take an active interest in manintaining sense-thoughts. Discourage extrovert thoughts; as they arise, immediately sublimate them by substitution of Narayana thoughts. Thoughts when oriented towards the Lord become spiritual thoughts capable of bringing about one's personality unfoldment.

देहात्मना संस्थित एव कामी
विलक्षणः कामयिता कथं स्यात्।
अतोऽर्थसन्धानपरत्वमेव
भेदप्रसक्त्या भवबन्धहेतुः ॥३११॥

311. He alone, who has identified himself with the body, is greedy of sense-pleasures. How can one, devoid of the body-idea be greedy? Hence, the tendency to ruminate over sense-objects is, indeed, the cause for the "bondage of becoming", and the idea of distinction or duality.

Now Sankara argues to make the students clearly understand a subtle philosophical truth. *Kama* is "desire"; *Kamee* a "desirer" --a sensuous man. A sensuous man is defined in this verse as one who permanently remains in the idea that "I am the body". As long as one has the feeling, "I am the body", the body's demands for sense-gratifications become imperative and one becomes shamelessly sensuous. Such an individual, starts seeking sense-gratifications, for the body, as a body.

In contrast to the sensuous-man, a Realised man is indicated as being just the opposite. A *Kamee* is one who runs after the objects-emotions-thoughts while the Realised man is one who gets away from these to reach the Self and Its Infinitude. The Man-of-Realisation and desires cannot go together. "Desiring" is the mind gushing towards objects-emotions-thoughts gratifications, while "Perfection" is the mind turned totally away from all objects, both within and without. Just as light and darkness, day and night, cannot co-exist, so too, "ignorance" and "knowledge" can never co-exist. They are at opposite poles, each the antithesis of the other.

"Perception of plurality"[1] is "Constant contemplation of the world-of-objects.[2] This is the cause for bondage; the reason for all conflicts in life; the source of all struggles in existence.

If this be so, then, how can ego-sense once annihilated, ever arise?

Sankara explains in the following verse the secret logic of the ego's return:

कार्यप्रवर्धनाद्बीजप्रवृद्धिः परिदृश्यते
कार्यनाशाद्बीजनाशस्तस्मात्कार्यं निरोधयेत् ॥३१२॥

312. When the "effects" are flourishing, the "seeds" also are observed to increase. When the "effects" are destroyed, the "seeds" also are destroyed. Therefore, the "effect" must be subdued.

When a seed is allowed to grow into a tree, the tree will produce millions of seeds. A thriving tree will yearly bring forth a huge crop of seeds. If the tree is destroyed, there will be no crop of seeds emerging from it. Stop the "effect", and the "cause" also ends.

We all have sense-*vasanas* in us. If these are given a favourable chance, watered by our ego-centric thoughts, the

1. *Bhedaprasakti* (भेदप्रसक्ति)
2. *Artha-Sandhana-Parattwam* (अर्थसन्धानपरत्वम्)

seeds, the urges for sense-gratifications, the *vasanas,*[1] increse, grow, flourish and multiply. Then the individual helplessly confesses : I cannot get out of it". therefore, when the low, base, extrovert *vasanas* spring forth to expression, curb them---crush them---do not allow them to stem forth and yield more of such poisonous *vasanas.*

Even though the ego has been apparently annihilated, the *vasanas* which are the cause for the ego, lie dormant and so, if we allow the sense-thoughts *(Vishayaanu-Chintanam)* a free play in the mind, those *vasanas* will revive and then the ego will necessarily manifest. Therefore, by constant meditation upon the "Self-in-All", turn the mind away from sense-thoughts, and allow no chance for the return of the ego-sense.[2]

वासनावृद्धितः कार्यं कार्यवृद्ध्या च वासना ।
वर्धते सर्वथा पुंसः संसारो न निवर्तते ॥३१३॥

313. Through the increase of *Vasanas*, egocentric "work", increases, and when there is an increase of egocentric "work", there is an increase of *Vasanas* also. Thus, man's transmigration never comes to an end.

In the previous verse, the *cause* and *effect* have been discussed. If the "effect" increases, the "cause" also increases. There, the example of a tree was given to demonstrate the truth of the cause-effect phenomenon.

The "results" come to manifest because of *vasanas.* The *"results"* are egocentric "thoughts", and sensuous "actions". When the actions have manifested, they in their turn, create more and more *vasanas.* From *vasanas* spring forth more actions-- again and again, this endless chain of sorrows continues. Thus, "cause" and "effect" are interchangeable. The "cause" can become an "effect" and this *"effect"* become the next *"cause".*

---

1. The sub-level urges, that determine the emotional profile of an individual, are called *Vasanas:* the channels of thought.

2. तस्मात्कार्यं निरोधयेत् - बिषयानुचिन्तनम् न कुर्यात् ॥

This cause-effect chain is never-ending. When this body becomes incapable of expressing the *vasanas*, another body has to be taken up and there too, man indiscriminately accumulates fresh *vasanas*, and moves on to yet another body. This is called transmigration *(Samsritti)*. To break this vicious circle you can do nothing directly with the *vasanas*. They are already there. Their manifestation alone can be controlled and stopped, by redirecting them into fresh channels of newly discovered, healthier attitudes and nobler urges.

The weeds were in the garden before I purchased the plot. Now I can only try to remove the existing weeds. If I allow the weeds to exist, every year they will multiply. So the moment the weeds sprout, I pluck them off and throw them away.No doubt, fresh ones do grow but I pluck them too. Pluck, pluck, pluck. I do not allow them to thrive in my garden. Every time, the weeds sprout, I pluck them off and throw them away. No After removing them I do not allow them to lie about in my garden grounds. I collect them carefully and throw them far away. Even after weeding the whole garden, I should expect at least some of them to come up again, because there must be some seeds ungrown still lying scattered. They had not grown only because they had no chance to grow and flourish. They were all lying dormant. But I shall never relax. I will go on plucking and throwing them away as they grow, until at last there will be no more "seeds" remaining to germinate more weeds anywhere in my garden. I must then prepare different flowerbeds; thus, my hands must be constantly working on the plot not only for plucking the weeds, but for plucking the flowers also.

Similarly, the mind also must be well-set and diligently attended to, as a gardner with his faithful efforts, ever keeps his garden trim and gay. All sense-thoughts are to be weeded out, and spiritual ideals must be planted. When the sense-thoughts rise up, immediately pluck them out. This attention to the garden-of-thoughts must be a continuous job. There should not be any break in it until you realise the Infinitude.

Destroy this ego completely. There is no time for any slackening anywhere during this precious, though limited, span of life.

संसारबन्धविच्छित्त्यै तद्द्वयं प्रदहेद्यतिः ।
वासनावृद्धिरेताभ्यां चिन्तया क्रियया बहिः ॥३१४॥

314. In order to snap the chain-of-transmigration, one should burn to ashes these two; for, thinking of sense-objects and doing selfish action lead to increase of *Vasanas*.

There are two main causes for the increase in *vasanas:* (1) continuous thinking of the sense-objects *(Chinta-ya);* and (2) acting upon the sense-objects in the world outside *(Kriyaya-Bahih)*.

He who subjectively comtemplates upon the sense-objects, but apparently restricts his sense-indulgence is called a "hypocrite" by the Geeta-*acharya.* Character consists, no doubt, in right acts, but they are built with right-thoughts. Subjective-thoughts and objective-actions both create *vasanas*-limitations, which drag the ego into new births and deaths. These two are to be cut asunder, in order to end the tragedy of transmigration.

These two forces prompt each individual to take up again and again an appropriate physical body, to continue the stupidity of living for sheer sense-gratifications. He who wants to cut off this endless stream of sorrow, the non-stop dash from stupidity to stupidity, has to end these two prompting forces. *Chinta* and *Kriya* are themselves, no doubt, the "effects" of powerful *vasanas*, and they create a fresh crop of more powerful *vasanas.* If you want to get away from these powerful *vasanas*, you must destroy these two.

In the spiritual path there are moments when one has the feeling, in fact a hallucination, that one has reached "somewhere". These are, no doubt, great peaks, but in those apparent heights, we cannot permanently remain in perfect safety. We may slip again, if we "look back" even once. "Back" means towards the object-emotion-thought-world. When the mind-and-intellect have turned towards Reality, never again look back. Once you become an extrovert, the ego at once precipitates; the sense-objects crowd around you for attention, and terrible *vasanas* are created. You fall again into *Samsar*. All *Sadhana* become impotent, futile, a great waste. So, without looking back, go ahead--with a constant forward gaze.

Sometimes, the seeker feels very lustful. This is caused by himself; there is no other cause. He himself allows a lustful thought to rise up in him and encourages it. Then this thought forces you into lustful activity, and the two together create lustful *vasanas*. Tying you down, they blockade your march and you get helplessly stranded. When a lustful thought comes, do not encourage it. Maintain the attitude of a "witness" towards it. Be fully conscious of it, and chant ardently--"Narayana Narayana".

Seeing the pure body and serene face of Lord Buddha, a prostitute felt tremendous attachment. She went to the place where Buddha was resting for the night, with fruits and other offerings. As she knocked at the door, Lord Buddha opened it and stepped out. He saw a beautiful richly dressed girl, standing with offerings of fruits at that untimely hour. Obviously, she had come to offer them to the Lord ....but at midnight? There was no hesitation. Gautama said, "Mother! What can your son do for you?" ....Poor woman, who came with burning passion, froze to the spot.....

Similarly, a lustful thought might rise up in your mind. Do not encourage it. Cry *Hari Om....Hari Om*, with confidence and faith.

Beware of the low thoughts at all times; carefully sublimate them with divine thoughts.

ताभ्यां प्रवर्धमाना सा सूते संसृतिमात्मनः ।
त्रयाणां च क्षयोपायः सर्वावस्थासु सर्वदा ॥३१५॥
सर्वत्र सर्वतः सर्वब्रह्ममात्रावलोकनैः ।
सद्भाववासनादार्ढ्यात्तत्त्रयं लयमश्नुते ॥३१६॥

315-316. Augmented by these two, the *vasanas* produce one's transmigration. These three however, are destroyed by looking upon everything, under all circumstances, always, everywhere, and in all respects, as *Brahman* and *Brahman* alone. Through the strengthening of the longing to be one with *Brahman*, those three will be annihilated.

Vasanas, increased by "thoughts" and "action" cause transmigration. The Pure *Atman*, in delusion, apparently comes to feel the pangs of both births and deaths: just as one suffers the agonies of drowning in one's dream.

The only mehtod of destroying these three---thoughts, actions and *vasanas*---is to recognise nothing but Brahman everywhere under all conditions, at all times, in all circumstances.

"Oh, that thing is beautiful," thus when the mind craves for it, immediately tell it that its "beauty" is because of "Narayana". "How beautiful the Lord must be Himself to impart this much of His beauty to this insignificant thing?" Passionate lust transforms itself by such a divine attitude into pure devotion. The "lustful-love" for the world-of-objects when turned sincerely towards Narayana, is called devotion *(Bhakti)*.

Those who are doing Sadhana will understand this. Others will not understand *now*. "Seeing *Brahman* everywhere" (Brahma-avalokanam) is not merely saying, "everything is Narayana". It is much more serious than a vocal declaration. "All this is nothing but *Brahman*. This play of body-mind-intelect is the play of the "five sheaths" *(Panchakosas)*. As a result of the *Panchakosas*, the *Atman*, the self in me is experienced as being limited and ineffectual all the time. It is all my own consciousness playing in eternal variety, as objects." Such a feeling and understanding will come as a result of developed and deepened spiritual *vasana (Adhyatma-vasana)*.

By this process of constant thinking of Narayana, the "Narayana-*vasana*" becomes stronger than the urges for sense objects *("vishaya-vasanas")*. *Vasanas* generated by our devotion for *Brahman*, the Reality *(Sat-Bhava-Vasana)* can annihilate all our sense-hunger. Therefore, continue practising it diligently.

This *"Brahma-gazing (Brahma-matra-avalokanam)* is to reflect upon the *Upanishad* statements like,[1] "When he becomes one-with-*Brahman*, then with what and whom will he see? etc.", and upon the Geeta declarations as[2] "Having 'seen' the Highest, even the taste for the sense-objects retires". etc. to meditate upon these, and to become aware of the Upanishadic roar "all this is but this Self"[3] is to annihilate the triple-cause for transmigration, *"vasanas"*, *"thoughts"* and *"action"*.

क्रियानाशे भवेच्चिन्तानाशोऽस्माद्वासनाक्षयः ।
वासनाप्रक्षयो मोक्षः सा जीवन्मुक्तिरिष्यते ॥३१७॥

317. With the end of selfish actions, brooding over sense-objects ends, which is followed by destruction of *vasanas*. The destruction of *vasanas* is liberation, and this is considered as Liberation-in-Life.

These three, *vasana*, *chinta* and *karma* are factors closely interconnected. This represents the chain of causation; the one is the cause for the one following. When sensuous actions are not performed, many ethical and moral principles are obeyed implicitly at the body level. If sensuous thoughts are not allowed to express themselves as actions, sensuous

---

1. "यत्रत्वस्य सर्वमात्मैवाभूत् तत्केनकं पश्येत् . . . ."
2. रमोप्यस्य परं दृष्ट्वा निर्वर्तते
3. इदं सर्वं यदयमात्मा ॥

vasanas will also end. Thus, we are trying to end the *vasanas* by attacking their grosser expressions in the form of actions and thoughts. We strive to control the grosser in order to finally come to control the subtler. This is real *Pranayama*---" control of the *Prana*".

Through a process of intelligent control* of the "effect", *Vedanta* advises us to control and annihilate the "cause" for the sorrows of life---the *vasanas.*

Regulate all activities so that *fresh channels of wrong thoughts* (negative *Vasanas)* are not formed. When sensuous thoughts cease to rise in the mind, formation of sensous *vasanas* is automatically controlled. When the *vasanas* have ended, there is "Liberation". Absence of *vasanas* is "Liberation" from the thraldom of desires and actions---*Moksha.* An individual, who has thus eliminated all his entanglements with "thoughts" --as a result of his freedom from *Vasanas*---achieved by controlling his "actions", is considered as "Liberated-even-while-living", *(Jeewan-Muktah).*

सद्वासनास्फूर्तिविजृम्भणे सति
ह्यसौ विलीनाप्यहमादिवासना ।
अतिप्रकृष्टाप्यरुणप्रभायां
विलीयते साधु यथा तमिस्रा ॥३१८॥

318. When the longing to be one with *Brahman* has vividly risen to expression, the ego-centric *vasanas* will readily disappear, as the most intense darkness completely disappears in the glow of the rising sun.

The last line of an earlier verse** declared, *"by the increase of spiritual vasanas, these three will get annihilated".* Here we have a lucid annotation for this daring declaration. When the Narayana-*vasana* becomes stronger, the sensuous

* कार्यनिरोधेन कारणं निरोधव्यं इत्यर्थः ॥
** *Ibid:* Verse No. 316.

"vasanas", "thoughts" and "actions" will autonmatically get annihilated.

The *"vasana* for the Reality" *(Sad-Vasana)* is cultivated more and more when the seeker lives a life engaged in his *sadhana* of hearing, reflection and meditation. When the *Sad-Vasana* has started expressing itself, a total change will come about in all his physical, mental and intellectual relationships. When we recognise only one Narayana, ever-present everywhere, we will have no likes or dislikes. Love, kindness, tolerance, and mercy will thereafter come to express automatically, through all our relationships in the world around us. The ego and ego-prompted *vasanas*, the selfish, arrogant misappropriating attitudes, at the body-mind-intellect levels will get dissolved, to be replaced by the new *vasanas* that have been now generated. So, *Asat-vasanas* are eliminated by "tendencies created in the mind by constant remembrance of the Reality" *(Sat-vasanas)*.

At present we are living a life of identification with the unreal, and hence *Asat-vasanas* are predominant in our hearts. Therefore, we madly behave the way we do. They can be eliminated, and a brilliant spiritual life of beauty and joy can be substituted, by the newly cultivated *vasanas* for the Reality.

"Aruna" is the charioteer of the Lord Sun. Aruna is the "early dawn", the beautiful silent glow that heralds the morn, when the sun has not actually risen above the horizon. Like the Pilot-car of the President, Aruna comes first, and then, soon, the Sun emerges. The pitch darkness of the night, however dreadful it might have been, gets dispelled with the advent of the "light of the dawn" *(Aruna)*. The entire darkness is dissolved effectively and totally. Then the Sun rises; the sun never sees darkness. The Sun cannot be where light is not, light being its very existence.

The *Atman*, the Pure Knowledge, can never be compatible with ignorance. There is no ignorance in *Atman*, the Self.

when the Sun emerges, there is no darkness. The President of a country, as long as he is the President can never experience a traffic-jam in any town.

At the moment of the experience of *Brahman*, there is no more any "ignorance" to be removed. Ignorance gets removed during the *Sadhana* itself. When positive-*vasanas (Sad-Vasanas)* have removed negative-*vasanas (Asad-Vasanas)*, where "ignorance" has been already removed, "Knowledge" dawns. *Vasanas*, incessantly weaving the ego-centric individuality, constitute the "darkness". Selfish and arrogant ideas, are the "darkness" that brings about all the sorrows of existence. They are all lifted at the very presence of the thoughts of the Higher.

Sat-vasanas remove the *Asatvasanas*. When the *Asatvasanas* are all removed, one is ready for the reception of the Great Lord. Therefore, the moral preparation and ethical adjustments for the resurrection of the individuality from its ego and egocentric assumptions, is the very beginning of spirituality---nay, it is also the very culmination of all efforts. This is all that you can accomplish. More than that is not for you to achieve: it will automatically come to you. With such a prepared bosom, sit in a thrilled patience of ecstatic expectancy, like a lover waiting for the promised visit of his beloved. This hopeful and expectant waiting for Awareness to reveal Itself is called "Meditation".

तमस्तमःकार्यमनर्थजालं
न दृश्यते सत्युदिते दिनेशे ।
तथाऽद्वयानन्दरसानुभूतौ
न वास्ति बन्धो न च दुःखगन्धः ॥३१९॥

319. Darkness and its resultant evils are not noticed when the sun rises. So too, on realisation of Bliss Absolute, there is neither bondage nor the least trace of misery.

"Tamas" is darkness; night, and things that are born out of darkness are called *Tamah-karyam.* Fear, actually missing the road, toppling over some stone, falling down and wounding oneself, the treacherous dagger of a hidden enemy--all these are the concomitants of darkness. *Tamas* loots away our peace. When the Lord-of-the-day* (Sun) rises, both the darkness and its effects are totally lifted.

When the sun rises, not only the darkness but the entire bundle of sorrows created by darkness, disappear immediately. Similarly, in the presence of God, every step becomes correct. Not knowing Him, in utter ignorance, we generate ego-centric stupidity in ourselves and bump against everything, whether existing and not-existing. Existing things we fail to see. Non-existing things we imagine and fancifully create. Thus we create for ourselves an entire world of confusions--a most sorrowful, miserable and tragic destiny, indeed.

For him who has experienced Supreme Bliss, there is not even a whiff of sorrow *(Dukhagandha)*. He has no bondage and hence the conditionings of the body-mind-intellect are not there; naturally, there cannot be any more sorrow for him.

That blissful condition of perfect release and joy is indicated in the following verse.

58. Total Vigilance---Its Price. (320-329)

दृश्यं प्रतीतं प्रविलापयन्सन्
सन्मात्रमानन्दघनं विभावयन् ।
समाहितः सन्बहिरन्तरं वा
कालं नयेथाः सति कर्मबन्धे ॥३२०॥

---

* दिनेश --Din-Esa-Lord of the Day. One who regulates, commands and orders the day is called Din-Esa........the Sun.

320. Causing the perceived Universe, both external and internal to vanish, and meditating upon the Reality, the Bliss-Embodied, one should pass one's time watchfully for any residual *Prarabdha*.

All this can happen only when all the three factors---the *"vasanas", "thoughts"* and *"actions"*---get eliminated. If, after all our efforts, the *vasanas* are not totally exhausted, then the balance that remains to trouble us is called "destiny" *(Prarabdha-Karma)*. This is very powerful..... each one will have to live out his *Prarabdha*. When it is strong, it cannot be ended with self-effort *(Purushartha)*. One may try one's best---yet, *vasanas* will assert and insist on inducing their results. They have to be lived through and acted upon. There is no other go. When we thus live through our *Prarabdha*, what must be our strategy to go through it safely, bringing the least wear and tear to our spiritual dimensions which have been acquired by our sincere and long *sadhana?*

In case an individual, even after years of *sadhana*, considers this pluralistic phenomenal world as true, he is still a seeker *(sadhaka)* and not a "perfected-one" *(siddha)*. Then he must go through it all, constantly remembering the Lord. To encourage others, and to sustain himself let him keep smiling---even through the most gruesome experiences. Thus, let him spend his time, constantly, with one hand let him hold on to His Feet, and with the other hand continue working. There is no other way. Insulated with loving contemplation of Him and His Glory, let him go through life, meeting bravely and efficiently all the problems that stand crowding around him---they are all expressions of his "residual *Prarabdha*".

He cannot escape them..... he must live through them.

प्रमादो ब्रह्मनिष्ठायां न कर्तव्यः कदाचन ।
प्रमादो मृत्युरित्याह भगवान्ब्रह्मणः सुतः ॥३२१॥

321. One should never neglect one's steady attunement with *Brahman*. *Bhagwan* Sanatkumara, the Creator's own son, has called inadvertance death itself.

The continuous attempt to hold on to Brahmic-Consciousness is *Brahma-Nishta*. Let not this constant "awareness", this remembrance of the Lord, ever fall away from your memory, even for a short time. Then there shall be no forgetfulness *(Pramada)*. Remember Him constantly. "Him" does not mean "the One who is worshipped in the temples"; He is your *Awareness*, this brilliant *Light of Wisdom* expressing in all creatures. This "Life" in your bosom, which is *Life-everywhere*, is He, the Supreme. Let there not be any carelessness, and consequent forgetfulness and oversight in the constant practice of contemplation, called *Brahma-Nishta*. In no circumstance, in no place, at no time, should you ever forget this Great Reality. Constantly remember Him in your own heart. Just as you never forget that you are an Ego, that you are a man, so continuously and constantly assert that your real nature is the Self.

The forgetfulness *(Pramada)* of the essential divinity in us, and our sense of holiness, is itself death. In fact, this is real *death*. Living in the forgetfulness of one's own divinity is "spiritual death". Because, thereafter, that man can live only as a biped "animal". So said Brahmaji's own son, Sanatkumara.*

न प्रमादादनर्थोऽन्यो ज्ञानिनः स्वस्वरूपतः ।
ततो मोहस्ततोऽहंधीस्ततो बन्धस्ततो व्यथा ॥३२२॥

322. No greater danger is there for the man-of-wisdom than carelessness about his own Real Nature. From this comes delusion, thence egoism, this is followed by bondage and then by misery.

To a spiritual-seeker there is nothing more tragic than this "forgetfulness of his own Real Nature" *(Pramada)*. Inadvertance erupts the volcano of all other sorrows.

---

* In the celebrated *Sanat-sujata-samvada*, the conversation between Sanatkumara and King Dhritarashtra comprising chapters 40-45 of *Udyoga Parva of Mahabharata*, there occur the words (प्रमाद वै मृत्युरहं ब्रवीमि) "I call inadvertance itself "death","

Forgetting our Real Nature means "non-apprehension of the Reality". We have already seen how "non-apprehension of Reality" can create "mis-apprehensions". For a wise-man there can never be any other tragedy greater than this Self-forgetfulness, as this can breed a chain of terrible consequences, each replete with insufferable agonies.

From Self-forgetfulnes starts delusion *(Moha)*. From delusion comes the ego *(Aham-Dhee)*. This ego-sense leads to bondage *(bandha)*. And bondage breeds misery *(Vyatha)*.*

When one forgets one's own Real Nature, the Infinite *Brahman*, one deludes oneself to be the limited ego *(jeeva)*. This delusion gives birth to the concept "I am" *(Aham-Dhee)*. Then one starts considering oneself to be one's own body, mind, and intellect. Naturally, conditioned thus by the body-mind-intellect, one comes to suffer limitations---bondages *(Bandha)*. In order to release oneself from it, one runs after the world of object-emotion-thought; this exertion is sorrow *(Vyatha)*.

Then desires crop up and in order to fulfil the desires, we strive; the desiring produces more sorrow and sweating agony. When the desires are fulfilled, there are even more worries---the struggles required to preserve the objects gained, permanently, with us. But the finite worldly objects must definitely perish in time and, therefore, produce more agony. If our desires are not fulfilled, certainly we are unhappy; if we get them, we certainly want more. This is how the fall comes. For all this, the initial cause is the Self-forgetfulness---the "non-apprehension of Reality". Therefore, do not forget *It*. Remember *It* constantly as you own Self.

विषयाभिमुखं दृष्ट्वा विद्वांसमपि विस्मृतिः ।
विक्षेपयति धीदोषैर्योषा जारमिव प्रियम् ॥३२३॥

---

* जरामरणादिजन्य व्यथा = *misery in the fields of time and space.

323. Finding even a wise-man hankering after the sense-objects, forgetfulness torments him through the evil propensities of the intellect, as a woman torments her doting paramour.

The forgetfulness of the divine within is natural to any ignorant, deluded man. But, how can a wise-man forget his Real Nature? How is it that we can remember everything else so easily? Why is it so very difficult to remember *Bhagawan?* How is it that the Lord made us so?

The truth is that the Lord never makes you forget your Real Nature. When the mind is turned outward *(Vishaya-Abhi-Mukham)*, then you forget your own divine nature and then you come to play the fool, a limited ego.

The Lord has created* the sense-organs turned "outward" and, therefore, the foolish ones forget the Divine Presence of the Consciousness that shines from behind every sense, act and thought. They forget because of their complete identifications with their body vestures. The sense-organs are turned outwards, and they come to gaze on and see only the objects of the world-outside, and never the Consciousness, which is behind the sense-organs vitalising them all, always. Some wise, discriminative men wanting to realise that Immutable Eternal Reality, turn their attention away from OET and realise the Infinitude in their own Self.

This idea of the Kathaka *Rishi* is expressed here by Sankara. Even if a man, well-versed in the book-knowledge *(Vidwan)*, has his attention turned towards the sense-objects, he will forget his Divine Real Nature of Bliss. When he forgets his Real Nature, the imperfections of his intellect make him agitated. *Vasanas*, desires, passions, jealousies, greeds are the ulcerations of the intellect, which then bleed out the pus and blood of sorrows. The poor fellow is led to disaster by the

---

* "The Self-existent (Brahman) created the senses with outgoing tendencies; therefore, man beholds the external universe and not the internal Self *(Atman)*. But some wise man with eyes averted (with his senses turned away) from sensual objects, desirous of Immortality, sees the *Atman* within. (Kathopanishad II-IV-1).

imperfections of his own intellect, just as a paramour tempts and spoils his beloved.

A paramour *(Jara)* is a "secret-lover". He uses his partner *(Priya)* for his own satisfaction. When one is secretly in love but the beloved is beyond reach, the memory of the sweetheart haunts the *Jara* and makes him (or her) miserable.

Similarly, you are wedded to the Self the *Brahman;* but you have also a private, secret love with the matter equipments and the world-of-objects You are constantly fascinated by the innumerable objects of the world. Every one of it deals out more and more disastrous vitrolic sorrows. Normal sorrows could be borne and some sympathy from others could be expected. But these are sorrows one cannot even tell another, or expect any sympathy from anyone. Hence, once you start acting disloyal to your own Divine Nature, you become miserable, like the beloved, haunted by the memory of the secret-lover.

यथापकृष्टं शैवालं क्षणमात्रं न तिष्ठति ।
आवृणोति तथा माया प्राज्ञं वापि पराङ्मुखम् ॥३२४॥

324. As moss, even if removed, does not stay away for a moment, but closes up to cover the water again, so also *Maya*, or Nescience, covers even a wise-man, if he ever gets extrovert.

What had been discussed in the previous verse is, here, with an appropriate example, more clearly brought out, so that even a dull student may fully grasp the idea.

A kind of moss grows in the stagnant waters of neglected ponds. It floats on the surface of the water and spreads out so completely that from a distance the pond appears as a green pasture-land. Due to this covering the waters of the lake will not reflect the blue sky, the passing clouds, or the blazing sun. If you stir the water with your hand, the moss moves away---easily, immediately. You can at once see the reflection of the sky in the water therein. But when you remove your hand, the moss again closes in to cover the waters, and the green spread veils the reflection of the infinite sky.

Similarly, into our mind, *Maya* comes and covers our vision of the Infinite, till It is no more reflected in our bosom. *"Vasanas"* or *"thoughts"* cover up our experience of the Infinite when our attention is turned owtward. Even if a man be very wise, if he becomes extrovert, he ceases immediately to experience Reality.

Therefore, extrovertedness must be annihilated by continuously remembering the Supreme as the Effulgent Consciouness ever shining in our heart.

लक्ष्यच्युतं चेद्यदि चित्तमीषद्
बहिर्मुखं सन्निपतेत्ततस्ततः ।
प्रमादतः प्रच्युतकेलिकन्दुकः
सोपानपङ्क्तौ पतितो यथा तथा ॥३२५॥

325. If the mind ever so slightly strays from the ideal and becomes outgoing, then it goes down and down, just like a ball, inadvertently dropped on a flight-of-stairs, bounces down from one step to another.

The reason for the fall even of wise-men, Sankara says, is the falling away of their attention from their Goal Divine. If the attention is diverted, even a little, the mind tends to become extrovert. If the mind is not turned inward, it will turn outwards; it has nowhere else to go and it cannot keep quiet. If our thoughts turn away from our goal, which is the "altar of our total dedication" even a little, the thoughts shall then run towards sense-objects. When the thoughts are turned outward, stage by stage,* we shall soon reach an utter state of sorrow.

To drive home the idea, an example is given: *As though, when a rubber ball slips from the hand, inadvertertly,* due to

* The stages of its fall were indicated in verse 322.

inattentiveness--meaning not deliberately, but only accidentally--*or due to forgetfulness.* Whatever be the cause, if the ball falls down on the top of a flight of steps--say from the top of Kutub Minar--it bumps down, and we can recover it only on the ground down below. The first drop may be on the first step, the second can be on the 10th ... third on the 40th, and the next bump perhaps on the 98th--it bumps down in leaps and bounds until at last it reaches the bottom--and there knocks about on the walls, right and left, forward and backward, madly, for some time. Only when its momentum is lost, will it remain motionless.

विषयेष्वाविशच्चेतः संकल्पयति तद्गुणान् ।
सम्यक्संकल्पनात्कामः कामात्पुंसः प्रवर्तनम् ॥३२६॥

326. When the mind enters the sense-objects it reflects upon their qualities. From mature reflection arises desire. After desiring, a man sets about to gain that thing, and thus fulfil his desire.

"When the mind enters the sense-objects", meaning, "when the mind entertains the sense-objects", troubles start. If the objects come to the mind by themselves, nothing untoward happens. If your mind goes to the objects, you are a victim. Note the difference. It is like someone coming to your house-then you are the master. He may be seeking a favour form you. But when you go to another's house, you are a guest, and, he is the master.

Similarly, when the "mind enters the objects", it starts imagining their joy-contents. When the joy-contents in an object have been contemplated upon for long, you come to believe, that there is some great joy therein. Therefore, your mind starts seeking that object in order to get at that illusory joy! If the mind is seeking an object, it is always prompted by a desire, which can be fulfilled only by its possession and initmate enjoyment.

When the illusion of an expected joy is maintained in the mind, the mind continuously contemplates upon that object.

Then the desire for possessing the object arises. Because of the desire man starts acting to obtain the desired-object for according to one's *desire* will be one's actions.

But when the sense-objects come to the mind and if the mind has got the desire or *Raga* for it, it will become the victim. Controlling the mind from running after sense-objects, is called *"Sama"* and controlling the sense-organs, so that the sense-objects may not enter the mind is *"Dama"*. More important than controlling the sense-organs *(Dama)* is the control of the mind *(Sama)*. If there is no *Dama*, the mind runs after objects, and it slowly crystallises into a *desire*. And the irrevocable law is: "as the desire so the action". If the mind is continuously going towards Narayana, desire for Narayana will increase. Desire for Narayana is the burning aspiration for the Reality. Therefore, through *Dama* and *Sama*, your actions will themselves become a powerful path, a spiritual *Sadhana*.

ततः स्वरूपविभ्रंशो विभ्रष्टस्तु पतत्यधः ।
पतितस्य विना नाशं पुनर्नारोह ईक्ष्यते ॥३२७॥

संकल्पं वर्जयेत्तस्मात्सर्वानर्थस्य कारणम् ।
अपथ्यानि हि वस्तूनिव्याधिग्रस्तो यथोत्सृजेत् ॥३२८॥

327-328. Through inadvertence, a man may deviate from his Real Nature. The man, who has thus deviated, falls. The fallen comes to ruin, and is rarely seen to rise again. Therefore, just, as the eatables, prohibited by the doctor, are not taken by the victim of the disease, one should totally give up the habit of relfecting upon the sense-objects, which is the root-cause for all the mischief.

Once fallen from our own Essential Nature, there is *no* question of our ever easily understanding the nature of the

---

* "When a man thinks of objects, "attachment" for them arises. From attachment, "desire" is born; from desire arises "anger". From anger comes "delusion"; from delusion "loss-of-memory": from loss of memory the "destruction-of-discrimination", from destruction of discrimination, he perishes."...(Geeta II-62-63)

Self. Man, thereafter, identified with the body, mind and intellect, jumps to reach the world-of-objects, and clings on to one object after another. When our Real Nature is forgotten, there is a deep and precipitous fall. He who has thus fallen goes down to a sad death, miserable destruction, an empty end. It is the tragic and total destruction of his spiritual personality. Such a fallen individual is rarely found to rise again. Therefore, *"don't fall"* is the only logical advice.

In order not to fall, renounce idle thinking of the world-of-objects. Refuse to entertain them. Contemplating upon the objects-of-pleasure is the cause for all sorrows and tragedies in life and for all difficulties and falls in *Sadhana.* Renounce, reject, and refuse all the idle ramblings of the mind. Cry "halt" to the wandering mind.

When the patient renounces the objects which his doctor has advised him not to eat, he will get cured of his illness. When the objects are in front of us, ordinarily we would love to take them. But in order to come out of the disease, we must reject them. Similarly, let the mind, which is now suffering from sensuality, reject its tendency to comtemplate upon sense-objects. Reject and rise above the senses. When the sensuous ideas come, positively let us turn our thoughts to the higher, and learn to rise above the cheap sensuousness of our thought.

अतः प्रमादान्न परोऽस्ति मृत्यु -
र्विवेकिनो ब्रह्मविदः समाधौ ।
समाहितः सिद्धिमुपैति सम्यक्
समाहितात्मा भव सावधानः ॥३२९॥

329. Therefore, to the discriminating knower of *Brahman* there is no greater death than inadvertence to meditation. But the man who meditates regularly attains complete success. (Therefore) carefully meditate (upon *Brahman)* in your mind.

"One should never be careless in one's steadfastness to *Brahman.* Diligently escape from all forgetfulness." The moment you fall into forgetfulness you start considering yourself as the body-mind-intellect equipment, and start seeking through them some ephemeral gains in the field of objects-emotions-thoughts. As you start seeking these, your desires multiply. "As the desires, so the thoughts and as the thoughts, so the action". Actions create more and more *vasanas.* It will all then end in such a great fall, that there will be no more any chance of ever gaining back the lost sense of the Self--the *Paramatman.* Once fallen to such depths, there is no getting up for that seeker.

Thus inadvertence *(Pramada)* itself is death *(Mrityu).* Forgetfulness of your Real Nature is death: the "living death" --so said Sanatkumara.[1] The rest of the verses[2] piled up arguments to come to the conclusion that "indeed Forgetfulness of our 'real nature' is death." Marshalling of the above arguments was done only to explain this statement of Sanatkumara vividly and impress its inevitability on the seeker's understanding.

Having given these arguments, Sankara says: "*Therefore, there is no death other than forgetfulness. This forgetfulness of our Real Nature alone is living death.*" Forgetfulness can come only when one identifies oneself with the sense-objects. This is death; death to all aspirations of any spiritual seeker. To the spiritual seeker who is trying to quieten himself, who has got the spiritual knowledge and who has got the knowledge of the five-kosas, and the required discrimative power, "forgetfulness" is death indeed.

"Forgetfulness" is death because it immediately breeds imaginations, and they bring forth desires. Desires give birth to activity. Activity precipitates more and more *vasanas,* which bring more and more thoughts--more the thoughts, more is the activity. In order to exhaust the new-found-*vasanas,* a fresh body has to be taken up...thus, the

---

1. *Ibid* Verse 321.
2. *Ibid* Verses 322-328.

individual falls into the whirling wheel of births-and-deaths. Indeed other than forgetfulness, there is no death *(Pramadat Na Parosti Mrityuh)*.

"When the mind is withdrawn from the object-emotion-thought world, and when it starts contemplating upon Brahman, refuse to initiate any new *Sankalpas*. In the Geeta,* we are similarly advised: "having set the mind upon That, thereafter never initiate any new line of thought". Similarly here we are told how when the mind has been withdrawn from its outer wanderings and held in abeyance *(Samchita)*, at the chosen point-of-contemplation on Brahman, one gains the goal truly. Then what are we to do? We must ourselves become quiet---without projecting any thoughts *(Samahita-Atma-Bhava)*. Let us try to withdraw our minds from objects, emotions and thoughts, and contemplate upon our own Real Nature, the "One Self in All". Withdrawing from the external activities of the physical, mental, and intellectual imaginations, let us teach ourselves to bring our entire attention to the Consciousness within.

Contemplate upon the Self, "with great care"--meaning slowly *(Savadhana)*. You cannot force open a bud and make it a flower. It must take its own time. A forcibly opened up flower will not have real beauty, or true fragrance. Never hurry up. Let it take its own time. All that we have to do is to put ourselves on the rails, on the right track, running in the right direction. We shall reach in time our coveted destination.

Therefore, very very carefully and slowly, may you gain a State of inner peace, fully abiding in the Self.

59. In the One, No Plurality (330-338)

जीवतो यस्य कैवल्यं विदेहे स च केवलः ।
यत्किञ्चित्पश्यतो भेदं भयं ब्रूते यजुःश्रुतिः ॥३३०॥

---

* Shri Krishna says: "Little by little let him attain quietude by the intellect held in firmness; having made the mind established in the Self, let him not think of anything." (Geeta VI-25)

330. He who is completely aloof, even while living, is alone really aloof after the dissolution of the body. The Yajurveda declares that there is fear for one who sees even the least bit of distinction.

That great Master, who experiences the State of Oneness, while living in the physical body, becomes Himself the One when his body falls off. Even when we see the Master living in the world outside, not only has he already had the experience, but he is continuously experiencing the Infinite Oneness of the Pure Self. When his body falls off, he no more *experiences* the Oneness; but he *becomes* the Oneness. *With the body* he experiences the State of Oneness; *with the fall of the body*, he becomes the One.

This is Truth. But anyone recognising anything other than the Self comes to fear. If you recognize plurality--any distinction between you and the world, any* single thing or being other than you--there is fear for you. He who, in the experience of *Brahman* creates, or feels the existence of, even the minutest distinction--between the subject and object--to him comes fear *(Tasya Bhayam Bhavathi)*.

"Fear" is always born of the recongnition of the "other". You are never afraid of yourself. To protect yourself from your own "fear", you build imaginary fortresses around you and yours, generally with more money, better position, a large house etc.

"Why all these?", if anyone asks, our reply must necessarily start with: "I am afraid"...! "Afraid of what?" The answer can be only: "Of something other than myself!"

So wherever there is the concept of the "other", there is fear, restlessness, agitation, worry, anxiety, each following the

---

* The Taittiriyopanishad which belongs to the Yajurveda says-- तस्मिन्ह्युदरमंतरं कुरुते तस्यभयं भवति - उत = even; अरं = अल्पं; उत +अरं = उदरं; अन्तरं = भेदं = distinction; कुरुते = पश्यति = perceives; उदरमंतरं कुरुते = sees but even a bit of distinctions in it; तस्य भयं भवति = to him comes fear.

other. So, anyone who recognises, or cognises, something other than his own Self, the *Brahman*, will be afraid of the "other".

यदा कदा वापि विपश्चिदेष
ब्रह्मण्यनन्तेऽप्यणुमात्रभेदम् ।
पश्यत्यथामुष्य भयं तदेव
यद्वीक्षितं भिन्नतया प्रमादात् ॥३३१॥

331. Whenever the wise man recognises even the least difference in the Infinite *Brahman*, at once, that which he sees as different through mistake, becomes a source of fear to him.

The same idea as in the previous verse, is being elaborated. Whenever, at any time, even for so much as a fleeting moment, you recognise the least difference in the Infinite *Brahman*, fear starts. The very object that you "see" as other, becomes the source of all your fear.

श्रुतिस्मृतिन्यायशतैर्निषिद्धे
दृश्येऽत्र यः स्वात्ममतिं करोति ।
उपैति दुःखोपरि दुःखजातं
निषिद्धकर्ता स मलिम्लुचो यथा ॥३३२॥

332. He who identifies himself with the objective Universe, which has been denied by hundreds of *Srutis*, *Smritis* and reasonings, suffers one misery after another, like a thief--for he indulges in something forbidden.

The Scriptural lore, time and again, declares that the objective phenomenal world is an illusion. The Upanishads *(Sruti)*, and the books-of-traditions *(Smriti)* advise us, in hundreds of passages, to withdraw our identifications from all our delusory misconceptions. Yet, if anyone identifies with

---

3. द्वितीयाद्वै भयं भवति— "From plurality indeed all fear arises"-- thunders the *Brihadaranyaka Upnishad*.

the perceived objective-world, he comes to live sorrow after sorrow, each one competing in its poignancy with the earlier one.

Man is subjected to such misery only because he is disobeying the law-of-life as discovered and described in the scriptures. Scriptures are the reference books to know the right way-of-life. He who disobeys them must end in misery. He comes to suffer not only sorrows in the outer world, but also the disappointments, dejections, regrets, and agonies of the mind--like one who has defiled himself by an ignoble act.

One who has demeaned himself by a self-insulting act, not only suffers the chastising whip of the neighbours; but even when he is not kicked by others, he sits in his own chair and kicks himself, regretting: "Tut, Tut, why did I do it? I should not have done that"; similar self-criticisms knife him from all sides.

Just as an individual who has committed an ignoble act suffers the physical consequences of the act, as well as his own mental regrets, he who has misunderstood the essence of life and has come to identify with the world of plurality, suffers hundreds of sorrows, consisting of both the physical pains and the mental agonies.

सत्याभिसन्धानरतो विमुक्तो
महत्त्वमात्मीयमुपैति नित्यम् ।
मिथ्याभिसन्धानरतस्तु नश्येद्
दृष्टं तदेतद्यदचौरचौरयोः ॥३३३॥

333. He who devotes himself to meditation on the Reality, and is free from Nescience, attains to the eternal glory of the *Atman*. But he who dwells on the "unreal", is destroyed. That this is so is illustrated in the case of one who is not a thief and one who is a thief.

Contrasting pictures of two individuals, both devoted to constant relfection, but one on the "Real" and the other on the "unreal", are given in this verse.

Truth is that which remains unchanged in all the three periods of time. One who revels in the constant reflection upon Truth, naturally, withdraws his attention from the ever-changing phenomenal world, comprising the body-mind-intellect equipments and their objects-emotions-thoughts world. One who has withdrawn from all his identifications with the equipments is "liberated" from the persecutions of the world-of-objects. Such an individual comes to experience the Eternal glory of the Self.

When one gets liberated from the thraldom of the "equipments", the ego--perceiver-feeler-thinker-"I"--becomes extinct. Naturally, therefore, one thereby reaches the higher climbs of Truth, where one lives the Eternal glory that is the Self.

On the other hand he who is revelling in the constant reflection upon the untruth, the "equipments" and "objects", comes to destruction. He is pushed into more and more confusions and sorrows, passions and lusts, together creating for himself a painful life of tensions, stresses and strains.

An honest man *(A-chor)* and a dishonest cheat *(Chor)* are the examples for both the above cases. An honest man does honest things and therefore he is happy. The dishonest fellow who has, no doubt, acquired plenty, but by dishonest means, is constantly afraid of others. He lives a miserable life in the world. Even though both honest and dishonest men live in the same world, or under the same roof, one is happy and the other is miserable, because of each one's mental identifications and his particular healthy or unhealthy way-of-life.

यतिरसदनुसन्धिं बन्धहेतुं विहाय
स्वयमयमहमस्मीत्यात्मदृष्ट्येव तिष्ठेत् ।
सुखयति ननु निष्ठा ब्रह्मणि स्वानुभूत्या
हरति परमविद्याकार्यदुःखं प्रतीतम् ॥३३४॥

334. The *Sadhak*, should give up dwelling on the unreal, which causes bondage, and should always fix his thoughts on the *Atman* as *"This, I myself am"*. For, steadfastness in *Brahman* gained through the realisation of one's

identity with It, gives rise to bliss and thoroughly removes the misery born of Nescience, which one experiences in the state of ignorance.

Constant contemplation upon sense-objects *(Asad)* is the cause for bondage. When lust and passions cloud the mind's vision, they cloud the higher pruposes in life, and muddy the enduring values of honest living. This drives us to compromise. Therefore, one who is striving to live up to the spiritual values *(Yati)*, the *Sadhak*, should give up the habit of constant reflections upon the "unreal" --the finite objects and ephemeral experiences.

When this is achieved, he starts recognising his Self, to be the Self present everywhere. The first-hand-experience of the Self wipes away all pangs and pains of life, which are the products of ignorance of the Reality.

Then he comes to live the peace "that passeth all understanding".

बाह्यानुसन्धिः परिवर्धयेत्फलं
दुर्वासनामेव ततस्ततोऽधिकाम् ।
ज्ञात्वा विवेकैः परिहृत्य बाह्यं
स्वात्मानुसन्धिंविदधीत नित्यम् ॥३३५॥

335. Constant contemplation upon the external objects will only gather up its fruits, viz., enhancing the evil propensities, which grow from bad to worse. Knowing this, through discrimination, one should leave the thoughts of external objects and constantly apply oneself to meditation on the Self.

If you are, through constant yearning, continuously in contact with the outer-world, the dire results will multiply. What are these natural dire results? The results of contacting the world outside are *vasanas*, which are to manifest as desires and agitations. The more you turn outward, the more the inner entanglements will increase. When you are turned outward, the agitations *(Vikshepa)* get multiplied, and hence, *vasanas* and desires multiply in leaps and bounds within. Thereafter, prompted by your own *vasanas*, more and more desires arise--which create more and more agitations, and which in their turn prompt more and more activities. This chain-reaction continues until at last your entire attention becomes so much engaged with them that you dive into the fields of endless conflict and the individuality in you gets pounded into an unrecognisable pulp of ugliness.

Those who get the discriminative power *(Viveka)*, and the scientific spirit of detachment from the not-self *(Vairagya)*, understand how they have earned and why they have reached this chaotic condition in life. Such individuals, having thus understood, leave all the outer contacts, meaning, withdraw their Consciousness as much as possible, through practice, from the body, mind, and intellect. Not perceiving the objects, not feeling the emotions, and not contacting the world even as thoughts, in such quiet moments, their entire attention turns inward.

So far, the mind had been constantly "contacting" the world-of-objects. Now, turned away from them, the same mind learns to "contact" *Brahman*, as the seat of Pure Consciousness within. With the finite mind, no doubt, we cannot contact the Infinite Brahman. But keep on trying. That "attempt" at contacting the Infinite *Brahman* with the finite mind itself is *Brahma-anu-sandhih--Brahma-anu-chintanam.*

The attempt of our mind to conceive and comprehend the Spirit, the Divine, alone can successfully turn it away from the realm of objects, emotions and thoughts. Or else, it will be impossible. Divine Grace is invoked by our honest and sincere attempts at meditation.

Unless you give the mind another point-of-contact, it cannot heave itself away from its present fields-of-attention. A divine altar of devotion and reverence is needed at which alone you can surrender your world-craving mind in a spirit of utter dedication.

Thus, through constant practice, you will come to experience this "contact with the Higher". An individual, who has with discrimination thus understood the cause for all his pit-falls and sorrows, must strive to withdraw himself from all his mental entanglements, and be released from its usual conditionings. Then he can feel himself ushered into a greater ambit of freedom, a greater fullness-of-existence.

बाह्ये निरुद्धे मनसः प्रसन्नता
मनःप्रसादे परमात्मदर्शनम् ।
तस्मिन्सुदृष्टे भवबन्धनाशो
बहिर्निरोधः पदवी विमुक्तेः ॥३३६॥

336. When the objective world is shut out, the mind becomes quiet, and in the quiet mind arises the vision of the *Paramatman*. When "that" is perfectly realised, the chain of births-and-deaths is broken. Hence the shutting out of the external world is the initial step for reaching liberation.

This is an answer to a possible doubt in the minds of the students; the students may feel: "Why are you insisting upon withdrawal from the outer-world? What is wrong with it? Can we not enjoy the good things of the world, and perform also our *Sadhana?* Why this negative advice to withdraw from the world? If by deliberately withdrawing from the outer-world-of-objects and by contemplating upon the Self, we reach *Paramatman*, then that *Paramatman* will be "caused by" *Sadhana*. So from a finite activity we must expect Infinite results! Absurd! With the finite activity, how can we achieve the Infinite? By an action initiated by us how can we gain the Truth? Even if by this effort we reach any truth it must also be finite, because finite activity can create only finite results. Therefore, O *Vedantin*, your logic is not acceptable to us. Besides it is very inconvenient to "withdraw", for we don't want to withdraw completely from the sense-objects, as they have got an enchanting store of pleasure, all of their own......"

Now the Vedantic Teacher answers: "This withdrawal is not the *direct* cause for the realisation of the Supreme Infinite.

It sets in motion a series of consequences which ultimately lead the seeker to liberation."

"The Earth revolves around the sun, and therefore there are the rains"--this statement may look illogical, but it is true in its sequence. The Earth is going round the sun, and therefore, the waters of its oceans come under the sunlight. Sunlight has got heat, and with the heat the water evaporates. The evaporated water goes up, and as it goes up, it cools. As it gets cooler and cooler it condenses. The condensation increases and hence it becomes more and more dense. The denser drops come down and hence there is rain.

Now, supposing the Earth was not going round the sun, there would not be any rain. Because the portion of the Earth facing the sun would have scorched itself to be a desert, and on the other side there would not have been any sunlight at all, and so it would have become an eerie land of barren snow. Rain is therefore possible only because of the earth revolving round the sun. Thus, as a series of consequences, the statement becomes true.

Here in this verse, the sequence of thought development for the Vedantic assertion is exhaustively enumerated.

When the mind is held back from rushing into the world-of-objects, it becomes calm and serene *(Mana-Prasada)*. Mind is agitated because of its instinctive habit of gushing into the world-of-objects. When the mind is constantly contemplating upon the "Profits not yet gained" or "Profits that it might lose", or "the objects and pleasures that can be gained", or "the pleasures that might have been" --meaning, when the mind is constantly agitated in such high-frequency, how can it experience any peace? To the extent the mind's wanderings into the sensuous objects are arrested, to that extent the mind becomes calm *(Prasanna)*. The Reality can be perceived clearly reflected in such a calm mind *(Mana-Prasadae)*.*

---

* *"In that peace all pains are destroyed; for the intellect of the tranquil-minded soon becomes steady" (Geeta II-65).*

When the mind has become pure, calm, serene and quiet-- when it is not consciously going out into the world outside, it becomes agitationless. Agitationless or thoughtless mind is not a mind. This is the "mindless-stage" *(Amanee-Bhav)*. When the mind has thus totally ended, then there is *(Param-Artha-Darshanam)*, the experience *(Darshanam)* of the Supreme *(Param)* significance *(Artha)* of the world and our life in it.

When the Self is well-experienced, the sense of limitations experienced through identification with the body, mind and intellect, is ended. As a result of your withdrawal from the "vehicles", the concept of "outside" --gets eliminated. As long as the vehicles are there, so long we can say "outside" and "inside". When we have withdrawn from our body, mind, and intellect, there can be no more any *outer* world to be perceived, *outer* emotions to be felt, and *outer* thoughts to be entertained. Therefore, not to allow our attention to go out into the world-of-objects, but instead to revel in the "subject", the Infinite, the All-pervading, is to be in the State of Total Liberation.

A totally liberated Man's experience is that there is nothing other than *"the Brahman--everywhere"*. Even the world-of-plurality that we are seeing is nothing but the *"Brahman-Play"* in various forms. Not that the Man-of-Perfection will not have the experience of the world-of-objects, but the difference between an ignorant man and a wise man is that the ignorant man's mind runs after the sense-objects with sensuous hunger while the mind of the wise man never runs after the objects with sense-appetite. The objects will come to the mind but a wise man does not revel in them.[1] Shri Krishna says "I am not in them --they are in me".[2] He is not governed by the objects, but he rules over them as their Master. The objects are applicants to the wise man's mind begging for his special attention. In the ignorant man's case,

---

1. न तेषु रमते बुधः- Geeta V-22.
2. न त्वहं तेषु ते मयि– Geeta VII-12.

he runs after the objects and says, "Oh Objects! Recognise me. I am unhappy without your company!"

The liberation gained through self-withdrawal from the objects-emotions-thoughts, is permanent and total; it is not temporary or partial. Temporary liberation is the unconscious-state experienced under chloroform, or in deep-sleep. Temporarily the mind-intellect retires, and so objects-emotions-and-thoughts do not appear. From deep-sleep, or from swooning, when we wake up, the earlier sorrows faithfully reappear. In "total-liberation" *(Vi-mukti)*, never shall they return to persecute us. It is a total transmutation--a total resurrection of the personality.

Total Liberation is the State in which the mind does not at all go to the sense-objects for the gratification of its selfish and sensuous ends.

कः पण्डितः सन्सदसद्विवेकी
श्रुतिप्रमाणः परमार्थदर्शी ।
जानन्हि कुर्यादसतोऽवलम्बं
स्वपातहेतोः शिशुवन्मुमुक्षुः ॥३३७॥

337. Where is the man who being learned, able to discriminate between the Real and the unreal, believing the *Vedas* as authority, fixing his gaze upon the *Atman*, the Supreme Reality, and being a seeker after liberation, will, like a child, consciously run after the unreal, which will surely cause his fall?

Which wise man will take to foolish living? "No wise man will ever do so", is the import. *Pundit* means a "man-of-knowledge", who has deeply studied the *Upanishads*, an erudite scholar, an intellectual giant.

Not only is he a *Pundit* but he has also cultivated his intellect to discriminate bewteen the "Permanent" and the "impermanent". Also, he has accepted the logical and scientific statements of the scriptures as the only authority and he is constantly striving to experience the Supreme Reality *(Paramartha)*.

So, an individual who is an erudite scholar of the scriptures and who has the discriminative intellect, and who has convincingly accepted the *Upanishads* as the only authority, not because of the logic of it but because of his constant experience of the Divine Reality--will such an aspiring individual *(Mumukshu)* ever consciously hold on to the ephemeral things that constitute the fleeting joys of the world?

Is there a fool who, having woken up from the dream will consider that the wife and children of his dream are his life-long responsibility, and take out an Insurance Policy in the names of his dream-wife and dream-children? None will do such a foolish things, since dream projections have no existence away from the dream-state.

Again, such an action as holding on to an unreal things is not only meaningless, but is also the cause for his own downfall *(Swa-paata-Hetu)*. A realised person, an individual of the calibre as explained above, will never hold on to 'unreal' things--will not return to the terrible agonising experience of identifying again with the equipments.

Will a seeker after liberation ever go down and hug the terrible hosts of sorrows--woo and court this world of shadows? If he does, he will be foolish like a 'child'.

"As a child" --Supposing a mother, leaving her child alone at home has gone to the neighbour's porch for a chat. The child playfully crawls on its belly, and at that time if a snake appears near the child, without any hesitation, it will crawl forward to catch the snake--not knowing the deadly nature of the snake and not realising that its one bite would mean death. The child is an example of an utterly ignorant one who not knowing the venomous nature of objects, goes and courts them until at last they bite and pour their venom into him-

which then proves quite fatal. Similarly, you and I, in our infinite incompetency to think correctly with our mind and intellect might crawl forward to hug the sense-objects, which "inject" into us the venom of lust, greed, avarice, jealousy etc. As a result of that venom, we suffer the endless pangs of our life. Peace and tranquility die for ever in our bosom.

The child, while playing, goes directly and catches the candle-flame and gets his hand burnt. A wise man having been burnt once by the world-of-object, will he ever, even by mistake, catch the flame?

Total liberation is that state having reached which a man is totally withdrawn from the world-of-objects.*

देहादिसंसक्तिमतो न मुक्ति -
र्मुक्तस्य देहाद्यभिमत्यभावः ।
सुप्तस्य नो जागरणं न जाग्रतः
स्वप्नस्तयोर्भिन्नगुणाश्रयत्वात् ॥३३८॥

338. There is no liberation for him who is attached to the body etc., and the liberated man has no identification with his body etc. The sleeping-man is not awake, nor is the waking-man asleep --for, these two states are contradictory in nature.

He who is completely identified with the flesh, who thinks for certain "I am the body ", and caters to it all the time, filling it with some better food, washing it with a better soap, wrapping it with better clothes etc. --cannot gain liberation at all. He is nothing but a mass of flesh. He, who is liberated from the entanglements of the body, mind and intellect, in him such a total and abject body-identification can never be seen. Those who are identified with the body have no experience of the "Higher", and those who have experienced the "Higher" are not identified with the body. Thus, they

---

* बहिर्निरोधः पदवी विमुक्तेः - *Ibid. Verse 336.*

belong to two different worlds-of-experiences; where the one is, the other cannot be.

The waking and dreaming conditions are not available in deep-sleep. The deep-sleep is not there in the waking or dream conditions. In one State-of-Consciousness, the other two are not present. Similarly, when I am conscious of the body, through my body I become conscious only of the outer world and I cannot have the experience of the Infinite. In the State of the Supreme Self, while having the experience of the "Higher", in the Forth-Plane of Consciousness --in the state of God Consciouness--there cannot be the the experience of the other three states of waking, dream, or deep-sleep.

When I am working through the gross-body, I am the "waker". When I have withdrawn myself from the *gross-body*, and I am functioning through my *subtle-body*, I am the "dreamer". When I rest in my *causal-body*, I become the "deep-sleeper". Thus, these are the three different "states", forged by the three different identifications, either with the equipments of the 'gross', or the 'subtle' or the 'causal' bodies. When all these three bodies are transcended, then the experience of the Infinitude descends upon us. To a man, who is thus experiencing the Peace of Infinitude, how can there be the experience of "I am the body", which generates and sprouts the vitriol of burning desires for sense-objects?

Enjoyment of the sense-objects is demanded by the flesh. When one is identified with the flesh, the sense-objects can provide some pleasure. But when he is withdrawn, not only from the *gross-body*, but also from the *subtle-body* he can never seek, even come to think of the sense-objects. When withdrawn even from the *causal-body*, meaning, when the very causes for the desires are also transcended, then the true experience of the "Higher" dawns.

Therefore, "the condition of liberation" and "sensuous passions" cannot be expressed at once---in one and the same individual, at one and the same time.

60. Spiritual Growth---the Secret. (339-348)

अन्तर्बहिः स्वं स्थिरजङ्गमेषु
ज्ञात्वाऽऽत्मनाधारतयाविलोक्य ।
त्यक्ताखिलोपाधिरखण्डरूपः
पूर्णात्मना यः स्थित एष मुक्तः ॥३३९॥

339. That man is free who, knowing the Self through his mind in all moving and unmoving objects and observing It as their substratum, renounces all superimpositions and remains as the Absolute and the Infinite Self.

This verse gives us a very comprehensive narration of the experience of the liberated-man.

Looking at things from the standpoint of the Self, and recognising the entire-world-of-pluraltiy within, without, and everywhere, both the sentient and insentient, as one's own Self, is the state of *"total-liberation"*.

Through the *physical* body, we can see only the physical bodies, and recognise their individual sizes, shapes and colours. When my mind contacts another's mind, I understand the *emotional* contents of kindness, mercy, and goodness in his heart. When I come in contact with another person's ideas, I understand his *intellectual* qualities. When I shake hands with another, I will not thereby understand his intellectual capabilities. By a hand-shake all that I understand is, perhaps, the strength of his physical grip.

Similarly, in order to recognise the *Atman* in me, "as the Self present everywhere", I must look at It from my *spiritual* standpoint. Only when I withdraw myself into my spiritual-personality, and then look out, shall I recognise the entire world as the Spiritual Reality, the Self. Therefore, one who has transcended the body, mind, and intellect, meaning all the "conditionings", alone can come to experience the Nature-of-the-Self, as the Unbroken, Immutable, One-homogenous, Reality.

He who thus comes to experience this Infinite Consciousness---where there is no longer any separateness "within" and "without"---when there is no longer a perceived world-of-plurality, as all of them have now dissolved into this One-experience of Infinitude---is said to be "liberated" from all the natural limitations of his body, mind and intellect.

सर्वात्मता बन्धविमुक्तिहेतुः
सर्वात्मभावान्न परोऽस्ति कश्चित् ।
दृश्याग्रहे सत्युपपद्यतेऽसौ
सर्वात्मभावोऽस्य सदात्मनिष्ठया ॥३४०॥

340. To recognise "the entire-universe-as-the-Self" is the means of release from all sense of bondage. There is nothing Higher than realising the "universe-as-the-Self". One realises this state by excluding the objective world through steadfastness in the Eternal *Atman*.

To expand oneself in spiritual-vision and experience the totality as one's own Self is *Sarvatma-Bhava*, the recognition of the "Universe-as-the-Self". At present, our personality is extremely ego-centric. We fail to recognize or to identify with our country or state or community or even beyond our own terrible attachments to our body and possessions. In fact, beyond these attachments we have no other personality. From this self-centred, extremely limited, supremely circumscribed, frog-in-the-well-experience, we have to grow, expand and gain the vision of "the entire Universe-as-the-Self in us".

Expand to realise that "all is the Self". Try to find accommodation for everyone in your compassion, and in your love for the world around you. Recognise that all things are creation of Narayana. Then recognise that things are only Narayana Himself, His various Divine forms. As such they are all the moving temples of the Lord. Therefore, Lord alone exists. Ultimately when you come to experience that the "Self-in-me" is the "Self-everywhere", then alone there is total *liberation* from the bondage of the mortal. There is nothing superior to this experience of the Oneness in everything; this is the highest experience: *(Na-Paro-asti-Kaschit)*.

When once this experience is gained, we get completely rooted in the Spiritual Experience of the Supreme. The perception of plurality ceases, meaning, no more do we see the objects as distinctly separate, but in that new Light-of-wisdom, all of them coalesce to be the One, shining in their new garment of Beauty-Peace-Truth. The names and forms are there, but in and through them all, we come to see the Truth, the Reality, everywhere.

In our spiritual *sadhana* a stage comes, when nothing of the outer world is experienced---neither the objects, emotions, thoughts, nor the body, mind, intellect. Within and without, there is nothing but the blinding flash of Reality. that State, in which there is nothing but Consciousness, and, perceptions of the body, mind and intellect have totally ended, is the experience of the "whole-universe-as-the-Self" *(Sarva-Atma-Bhava)*.

The spiritual "apprehension" is in fact, entirely different from all the intellectual and logical conclusions arrived at by our sages. That pure spiritual "experience" is indicated here as *Sarvatma-Bhava*---the vision of the "Universe-as-the-Self"

दृश्यस्याग्रहणं कथं नु घटते देहात्मना तिष्ठतो
बाह्यार्थानुभवप्रसक्तमनसस्तत्तत्क्रियाः कुर्वतः ।
संन्यस्ताखिलधर्मकर्मविषयैर्नित्यात्मनिष्ठापरे -
स्तत्त्वज्ञैः करणीयमात्मनि सदानन्देच्छुभिर्यत्नतः ॥३४१॥

341. How is the exclusion of the objective-world possible for him who lives identified with the body, whose mind is attached to the perception of external-objects, and who performs various acts for that end? This exclusion should be carefully practised by sages who have renounced all kinds of duties and actions and objects, who are passionately devoted to the Eternal *Atman*, and who with to possess undying Absolute Bliss.

In order to attain total liberation, perception of the world-of-plurality has to cease. How can this be brought about? How the non-perception of the world-of-objects is possible under certain conditions, and how the same, under a different set of unfavourable conditions, is rendered impossible, are discussed in this verse.

First Sankara discusses how and why it is *not* possible for the many to gain this "State" of perfect "Vision of Oneness".

The state of *not*-perceiving the delusory world of objects-emotions-thoughts *(Drisya-sya-Agrahanam)* is not possible for an individual who has the idea "I am the body". Looking through the body, objects must be perceived. Where can they go? To a dreamer the dream is inescapable all along his dream-state: to the ego, the world-of-objects is inescapable as long as he has the idea: "body am I".

The body, mind and intellect equipments cannot realise the One. To a person of body-sense*(Deha-Atma-Bhava)* how can there be the experience of "the One Self in All" *(Parama-Atma-Bhava)?* How can he gain the concept of the *One ness* of the Infinite Reality? The non-apprehension *(Agrahanam)* of all "misapprehensions" cannot be, to an individual who is identified with and looking through the equipments. The State of Object less-Awareness cannot be experienced by an individual who is turned outward.

Not only is he identified with his physical body, but his mind is constantly contemplating upon the sensuous objects of the world outside. It is always engaged in the unholy experience of the plurality of worldly objects. Therefore, his actions get ordered by his own sensuous thoughts.

An individual, who is thus constantly associated with his body and so fully engaged and preoccupied with his sensuous thoughts that his hands and legs constantly sweat to fulfil his endless desires and accomplish his imposible thoughts---how can he ever have the non-apprhension

(Agrahana) of the world-of-objects? He is at all times turned towards them. He is deliberately nourishing delusory fanscies. He insists on recognising the world-of-plurality, which he hugs on to as his life's greatest fulfilment.

In utter love where the *Sadhak* merges into the Infinite Lord, there end all his responsibilities to duties, to activities, and to objects, and there he comes to That Experience Supreme.

The attachments to one's duties *(Dharma)* to worldly activities *(Karma)* and to the sensuous objects *(Vishaya)* have all to be renounced, and in their place we must cultivate the attachment to and contemplation upon the Self. When we are striving in meditation to propel ourselves and land into the Higher Consciousness, then all the ego-prompted secular and sacred activities of the lower planes must stop.

Whatever activities I might have done in my dream, however sacred and auspicious they might have been, the moment I wake up, the dream-work grinds to a stop. Not because I do not want to continue it, but the "dreamer" who was doing the work is no more available in his waking-state. The entire field of activity and equipments of action available in the dream have, now, merged into me the "waker". They are no more available in my waking-condition.

Similarly, the secular and the sacred activities, that we undertake and the various objects that we court, are all transcended by those, who are constantly living in the contemplation of the *Atman*, the *Brahman*. As a result of it, they become Knowers-of-*Brahman*, nay, they become *Brahman*. In the Brahmic-Consciousness, the world-of-plurality is not available.

सर्वात्मसिद्धये भिक्षोः कृतश्रवणकर्मणः ।
समाधिं विदधात्येषा शान्तो दान्त इति श्रुतिः ॥३४२॥

342. To the Sannyasin who has listened to the discourses upon the scriptures and who has cultivated "Calmness, Self-control" etc. to him the *Sruti* prescribes *samadhi* for realising that "the whole-universe-is-the-Self" *(Sarva-Atma-Siddhi).*

A very famous statement of *Brihadaranyakopanishad* is referred to in this verse. In one line it indicates what a seeker must do in order to make himself fit for the final spiritual experience. Six qualities are mentioned, and they are all to be diligently cultivated. Keep this six-fold "wealth" in your pocket, and start upon the pilgrimage to Perfection.

If you have these six adjustments in yourself, then you shall reach to see the Reality in your own Self *(Atmani)*.

These personality disciplines are (1) Calmness *(Sama)*, (2) Self-control *(Dama)*, (3) Mind withdrawn from all objects-emotions-thoughts *(Uparati)*, (4) capacity to suffer silently and nobly the little pin-pricks of life *(Titeeksha)*, (5) faith in youself, in the *Sastra* and in Reality *(Sraddha)* and (6) contentment with what you have been blessed with *(Samadhan)*.

Equipped with these, the seeker will find that Spiritual Realisation is very simple. He can now readily turn his entire attention upon his own Self, and realise It directly *(Atmani-Eva-Atmanam-Pasyet)*.

The two supplementary qualities necessary in an individual, who wants to experience "the One-Self, present everywhere", are that he must be a "renouncer" *(Bhikshu)* and has listened to the discourses upon the scriptures *(Krita-Sravana-Karmanah)*.

A Sannyasi *(Bhikshu)* is one who has renounced everything and lives on the bare minimum of objects that he may accidentally come across by sheer chance and is not running hungrily after them. Such an indivudual, if he has done sufficient "listening" to the Teacher, and has performed enough self-less dedicated activities in order to rub off his existing *vasanas*, is fit to gain the experience of *Samadhi*.

Such an individual must practice *Samadhi*. It is thus prescribed by the *Brihadaranyakopanishad* in one of its well known Statements.*

आरूढशक्तेरहमो विनाशः
कर्तुन्न शक्यः सहसापि पण्डितैः ।
ये निर्विकल्पाख्यसमाधिनिश्चला -
स्तानन्तराऽनन्तभवा हि वासनाः ॥३४३॥

343. Even wise-men find it impossible to suddenly destroy the ego, once it has become strong---except for those who have become perfectly calm through *Nirvikalpa Samadhi*. Indeed, desires are the effects of innumerable births.

The attitude of the individuality---"the perceiver-feeler-thinker-I-am-sense"---arises as a result of one's ignorance of the Self. It has been maintained by each one of us over a long period of time, during our slow scrambling up the ladder of evolution from the beginning of time. Hence this ego cannot be annihilated immediately; nor is it, at any time, easy.

Except those who have become steadfast in the experience of *Nirvikalpa Samadhi*, even great learned and wise men, cannot end their ego suddenly. *Nirvikalpa Samadhi* is the "State-of-mindlessness", where all thoughts have been consciously eliminated and blissfully transcended. At this stage, merger with the Reality becomes complete. When the ego goes deeper and deeper into the contemplation upon the purpose-of-existence, it totally disappears to become the Consciousness.

That State of hushed-Bliss is called *Nirvikalpa Samadhi*.

अहंबुद्ध्यैव मोहिन्या योजयित्वाऽऽवृतेर्बलात् ।
विक्षेपशक्तिः पुरुषं विक्षेपयति तद्गुणैः ॥३४४॥

---

* शान्तो दान्त उपरति तितीक्षुः समाहित ॥
श्रद्धावित्तो भूत्वाऽत्मन्येवऽऽत्मानं पश्येत्॥ Brihadaranyakopanishad, IV, iv,23.

344. The "projecting-power", through the aid of the "veiling-power" confuses the man with storms of egoistic-ideas, and distracts him through the attributes of that agitation.

The "power-of-veilling" renders the intellect incapable of apprehending Reality. Therefore, the mind gets agitated. Whenever the intellect gets clouded, the mind "projects" and "imagines". This is the natural trick of the mind-and-intellect at all times. The individual comes to suffer the endless sorrows because of the agitations created in the mind.

Thus, every one in this world is unhappy in his own way.

The quality and quantity of unhappiness in each individual is in accordance with the type of his manifesting *vasanas.*

विक्षेपशक्तिविजयो विषमो विधातुं
निःशेषमावरणशक्तिनिवृत्त्यभावे ।
दृग्दृश्ययोः स्फुटपयोजलवद्विभागे
नश्येत्तदावरणमात्मनि च स्वभावात् ।
निःसंशयेन भवति प्रतिबन्धशून्यो
विक्षेपणां नहि तदा यदि चेन्मृषार्थे ॥३४५॥

345. It is extremely difficult to conquer the "projecting-power" unless the "veiling-power" is perfectly rooted out. And that covering over the *Atman* naturally vanishes when the Subject is perfectly distinguished from the objects, like milk from water. But the victory is undoubtedly complete, and it becomes free from all obstacles, when there is no oscillation of the mind due to the false sense-objects.

Ordinarily a man cannot control his mind. He may conquer the whole world but conquering his own mind is no easy job. As long as the "veiling-power" *(Avarana-sakti)* is not completely removed, so long the "projecting-power" *(Vikshepa-sakti)* will naturally make the individual dance. As long as there is "non-apprehension" of the Reality, the "mis-apprehensions" will continue. Until the Reality is experienced, the *vasanas* will remain, and under their compelling urges, the body-mind-intellect equipment will gush out to gather their experiences among the world of object-emotions-thoughts. Nobody can stop this. Until the "Higher" awakening is experienced, the attractions and enchantments of the "lower" planes-of-consciousness will be natural. There is no escape. Only on the "apprehension" of the Supreme, can all this tragic gushing out truly come to an end.

So, to gain a total mastery over the agitations of the mind is not all that easy. It takes time. As long as the cause of the disease exists, the symptoms of the disease cannot end. Similarly, as long as the "Higher" is not apprehended, the flesh will crave for flesh, the mind will crave for emotional satisfaction, the intellect will gurgle out in a thousand desires. Hence a novice finds it impossible to give up his enchantments for sense-objects.

This "non-apprehension"-of-Reality can be ended only by those who have the capacity to analyse, understand, and discriminate, between the "subject" and the "object", and who have the heroism to reject the "lower" and live the "higher". This is as subtle and as difficult as separating water and milk from a mixture of the two. The capacity to distil away the milk from a mixture of milk and water is the special function attributed to the mythological bird the *Hamsa*.

When the intellect starts vividly discriminating between the "subject" *(Drik)* and the "object" *(Drisya)*, and when it has got the capacity of removing the *subject* away from the world-of-*objects*, the Subject, by Itself, rediscovers the Supreme Essence in Its own Nature Divine. Then, the "non-apprehension-of-Reality" *(Avarana)* automatically ends. When an intellect persists in its habit of continuously analysing and constantly understanding the Self and the not-self---when

---

* In Sanskrit, Hamsa, denoting this bird, has a pertinent etymological meaning. "I am" *(Aham)*, "He" *(Sah)* is Hamsa. To realise "I am He" is the "Bird" *Hamsa*.

it becomes brilliant in its function of discrimination between the "subject" and the "objects"---the "misapprehensions" of the "subject" caused by the "non-apprehensions" end by themselves without any extra effort *(Ayatnatah)*. When you start realising that you are the "subject", the "one who is *aware*", and that these "objects" are all in you, and when they are removed, you are the "objectless-Awareness" and are no more really involved in them, you become, as it were *distilled away* from them and their deluding confusions. As a result of this, the Pure Self is revealed without any "special effort"

In that experience of the Self there can be no trace of any doubt at all. I may doubt every thing; but about myself there will be no doubt at all. This Self, being the "subject", is the very core in each one of us. Realising that the Self in "Me" is the Self everywhere , there is nothing which is other than "Me". Hence, there are no mental agitations---so then, who will doubt? And how?

Having woken up from a dream, will the waker any more yearn for the embrace of the dreamer's wife? The dreamer's wife was loved by the dream-body, which on waking, is no more available to the waker. Similarly, when the individual "wakes up" to the "Higher" plane-of-Consciousness, he will have no more oscillations of the mind *(Prati-Bandha-Soonyah)*.

Even if tempting objects-of-pleasure are around him, he knows that they are all false *(Mrisha)*.

सम्यग्विवेकः स्फुटबोधजन्यो
विभज्य दृग्दृश्यपदार्थतत्त्वम् ।
छिनत्ति मायाकृतमोहबन्धं
यस्माद्विमुक्तस्य पुनर्न संसृतिः ॥३४६॥

346. Perfect discrimination arising from direct realisation distinguishes the true nature of the "subject" from that of the "object", and snaps the bond of delusion created by *Maya*. There is no more transmigration for one who has liberated himself from this.

How to discriminate between and understand the "subject" and the "object" is a theme exhaustively dealt with in the Bhagawat Geeta. Due to "right" knowledge, arising out of clear discrimination, the understanding of the "subject" as distinctly different from the "object", becomes deep and all doubts get completely clearned up.

"The Seer and the Seen" *(Drik-Drishya)*---this is a typical phraseology used in *Vedanta.* It is a comprehensive phrase; it indicates not only "the seer and the seen" but it includes "the hearer and the heard", "the smeller and the smelt", "the taster and the tasted", "the toucher and the touched" and thus "the knower and known"---in short the idiom denotes all known "subject-object" relationships.

Those who have thus, as a result of clear discrimination, Pure Knowledge of the "subject" and the "object", comprehend the Reality, which by Itself plays as both the "subject" and "object" everywhere. It is the substratum, the essential support, of both the "subject" and the "object". The "subject" and the "object" are different expressions of the same Reality.....just as the waker's mind is the only essence *(Tattwa)* in the dreamer and all that he had dreamt.

When this apprehension of Reality comes, it banishes all the effects created by the "non-apprehension-of-Reality." It destroys all *vasanas.* It cuts down the *Avidya* along with all its effects. The effects of *"non-apprehension*-of-Reality", *(Avidya)* are delusions or mis-apprehensions, and because of them, there is bondage--the strong sense of identification with one's body-mind-intellect equipment.

Hence, an individual is liberated totally, when all his sense of limitation, created by delusory misconceptions, arising from the *"non-apprehension*-of-Reality", has been ended because of his vivid and direct "apprehension-of-Reality".

---

* Bhagawat Geeta Chap. XIII.

To such an individual, there cannot be again any *Samsar*, as *Maya*,[1] the cause for it, has ended in him.

परावरैकत्वविवेकवह्नि -
र्दहत्यविद्यागहनं ह्यशेषम् ।
किं स्यात्पुनः संसरणस्य बीज -
मद्वैतभावं समुपेयुषोऽस्य ॥३४७॥

347. The fire of knowledge that the *jeeva*-is-the-Brahman, entirely consumes the impenetrable forest of *Avidya* or Nescience. For him who has realised the State of One ness, is there any "seed" left for future transmigration?

Out of one's discrimination, between the transcendental and the terrestrial, between the "Higher" and the "lower", *right*-knowledge arises. One should contemplate upon God *(Iswara)*, ego *(Jeeva)* and the world *(Jagat)*. What constitutes this Universe? What is this I? What is the Reality behind both these? What is that which plays as the world and as me? One alone plays as the "Higher" *(Para)* and the "lower" *(A-para)*. This fire-of-knowledge kindled by discriminative contemplation upon Reality, can burn down the entire *Avidya*[2]---Ignorance---leaving not even a flimsy streak of it to cloud the Vision Divine.

Will such an individual ever tumble again into the enchantments of the world[3] within and without? One who has that *Adwaita-Bhava*--he, who is the experiencer of the One Reality has no transmigration at all: no more *Samsar*.[4]

To him, who has fully realised the *Adwaita-Bhava*, there is no cause for repeatedly falling into the state of misconceptions. Should you once realise that you are the

---

1. Maya: "Non-apprehension-of-Reality"-- the cause, *PLUS* "Mis-apprehensions" ---the effects.

1. The "Non-apprehension-of-Reality".
2. The B.M.I., P.F.T., and O.E.T.
3. Samsar is देहादावात्म भ्रमः The delusion that I am the body.

Supreme Self, then you will not fall any more into the "misconception" that you are the body, mind, and intellect; even though all the time you may continue to function through your body, mind and intellect.

The king, dressed as a begger, sitting down and begging in the bazaar, does so only as a *recreation* for himself---a sport. He will never misunderstand that he has been born as a begger. He knows that he is the royal lord of the enitre kingdom. Under the begger's garments are the gold-embroidered silken robes from his royal wardrobe. He knows fully well that he is the king. So too, a Man of Perfection, having gained the experience of the Infinitude in himself, may move about in his physical body and experience the vicissitudes and sorrows of life, as a sport, yet, the tragedies of the body can no longer affect him in his newly gained Higher Perception. He never gets involved in them.

आवरणस्य निवृत्तिर्भवति हि सम्यक्पदार्थदर्शनतः ।
मिथ्याज्ञानविनाशस्तद्विक्षेपजनितदुःखनिवृत्तिः ॥३४८॥

348. The veil that hides Truth gets lifted, indeed, when Reality is fully experienced. Soon follows the destruction of false understanding, and the cessation of misery---brought about by agitations, created by the false-knowledge.

All misconceptions about an object end only when it is clearly seen. A post may be misunderstood as a ghost, a rope as a snake, or Ramu may be mistaken for Krishna. You may misunderstand thus, only when the post is seen in partial darkness, or the rope is seen in dim light or Ramu is seen from a distance. When our knowledge of a thing is not complete, the consequent "non-apprehension-of-Reality" breeds delusory mis-conceptions about it. This is a fundamental universal law. The non-apprehension ends only when I actually "apprehend" the Reality. When I see the post, the ghost is gone; when I recognise the rope, the serpent is gone; and when I see and recognise that he is Ramu, the misconception that he is Krishna has ended. When the misapprehension *(Avarana)* has ended, all sorrows created by the agitations *(Vikshepa)* will also end.

The "non-apprehension" of the post *veils* the post. In its place, then, I see "mis-apprehensions"---the post as a ghost. The misapprehension gives me fear and sorrow. The post has not directly caused me any sorrow. The post was not recognised as a post. When the post is veiled by the "non-apprehensions" I thought it was a ghost. This "misconceived knowledge" *(Mithya-gyana)* breeds for us our sorrows. The sorrows can end when the "ghost" is no more. Therefore, "false-knowledge" should be ended in order to annihilate the sorrow-experience.

At this moment, the *Atman*, the Self, is not realised. It is veiled by our "ignorance" of the Self. The "ignorance" of the Self is creating the misconception, "I am the body, mind, and intellect". The concept that I am a limited creature gives me the sorrows of life. When I "apprehend" the Consciousness, the Spiritual "non-apprehension" in me naturally ends. Therefore, there is no more the demeaning feeling, "I am a *Jeeva*". Thus the sorrows arising out of the ego-sense *(Jivattwa-Bhavana)* are all ended. This is more clearly brought out in the following verse.

61. Cause---Effect---False. (349-353)

एतत्त्रितयं दृष्टं सम्यग्रज्जुस्वरूपविज्ञानात् ।
तस्माद्वस्तुसतत्त्वं ज्ञातव्यं बन्धमुक्तये विदुषा ॥ ३४९॥

349. These three are observed in the rope when its true nature is fully apprehended. Hence, the wise man should know the true nature of things in order to break his bonds.

When the knowledge of a rope is veiled from one's cognition, three conditions are experienced---(1) the veiling or ignorance of the rope; (2) projecting a snake in its place and (3) the fear arising from the snake.

These three are always there whenever one sees a snake in a rope. Had the rope been seen as a rope, there would have been no sorrows. But when it is mistaken for a snake, the snake produces the sorrow. Therefore, it is absolutely essential for a man of true spiritual hunger to experience this great Reality and to know the nature of the Self, in order to end the non-apprehension of the Self and the consequent misconceptions---the identification with the BMI and the resulting unavoidable sorrows.

अयोऽग्नियोगादिव सत्समन्वया-
न्मात्रादिरूपेण विजृम्भते धीः ।
तत्कार्यमेतद्द्वितयं यतो मृषा
दृष्टं भ्रमस्वप्नमनोरथेषु ॥३५०॥

ततो विकाराः प्रकृतेरहंमुखा
देहावसाना विषयाश्च सर्वे ।
क्षणेऽन्यथाभावितया ह्यमीषा-
मसत्त्वमात्मा तु कदापि नान्यथा ॥३५१॥

350-351. Just as a piece of iron through contact with fire manifests as fire, the intellect manifests itself as the *knower* and the *known* through the immanence of *Brahman*. These two---the effects of the intellect---are observed to be unreal as in delusion, dream and imagination; so too, the modifications of *Prakriti*, from the ego down to the gross body and all the sense-objects are also unreal. Their unreality is, indeed, due to their being subject to change every moment. And the *Atman* never changes.

When an iron piece is in contact with fire, it absorbs the heat and the luminosity of the fire, and after a sufficiently long time, it will be difficult to tell which is the glowing iron piece and which the burning piece of charcoal. They both become of the same nature. Similarly, when the not-Self, the matter, is in contact with the Self, the Consciousness, it acquires the *semblance* of Consciousness. If the iron piece is removed from the fire and for a time kept away from it, the "fire" of the iron drains away to the elemental fire and the iron reverts to its own nature. Iron, by nature, is heavy, black in colour, and cold to touch. A glowing piece of charcoal is light in weight, golden in colour and hot to touch. Both have distinctly opposite characteristics. A piece of iron can never be mistaken for a burning piece of charcoal. Yet, if the iron is kept in the fire for a sufficiently long time, the qualities of the fire are transferred to the iron piece, and the iron's *own* qualities are temporarily not available at all.

The body, mind and intellect are inert and insentient by themselves. But when they are in contact with the Self, It lends Its glory to them and they seem to be divine by themselves. The BMI are brilliant only as long as they are "alive". Once removed from life, they lose their capacities for perceiving, feeling and thinking.

The Knowing Principle behind the intellect, when It suffuses the thoughts, It becomes the *knower*.Conscious thoughts of the intellect constitute the *knower* but there cannot be any *knower* unless there is something to be *known*. Thus, the *Atman* functioning through the intellect, not only becomes the *knower* but also the world to be *known*. The subject and the objects of the world are both the play of the Consciousness through the intellect. When the intellect is hushed up with chloroform or when it has folded up in deep sleep, the subject-object game ends. When thrilled by the Self, it is this intellect itself which manifests as the subject and the object. Both are the effects of the Light of Consciousness functioning through the intellect equipment.

In fact, the subject-object relationship is false and unreal. Dream, delusion and imagination are examples. It is I myself who becomes the experiencer and the objects experienced in my day to day life. The subject, the object and their play are all in me, myself. In my mental wool-gathering, the subject and the objects are my own projections. Similarly, all that I see at this moment are the delusory creations of my own intellect which has its capacity to project them from the Self. The *Atman* has not done anything by Itself, It never does. The intellect which is made up of matter, comes to shine in the Light of Consciousness. The Spirit suffuses it, and thereafter the mind-intellect equipment becomes thrilled with this capacity to project. Thus the entire world with its subject-object relationship gets projected. The intellect, gathering the semblance of Consciousness from the Self, becomes the subject, the objects and their relationship.

The subjective world---consisting of the ego (PFT), the *vasanas*, the equipments of experience: the gross, the subtle and the causal bodies, and the world of objects---consisting of the objects perceived, the emotions felt and the thoughts entertained---are all projected by the mind fired by Consciousness. The very nature of the entire creation is such that it never remains the same. Moment to moment it transforms into something else *(Annyatha-bhava)*. Never permanent, it is ever-changing and therefore unreal.

The changeless is the Real. The *Atman* is something other than the intellect and It never becomes anything other than Itself. It knows no change. It is of Its own nature at all times. It is Immutable.

This verse gives a beautiful example to show how from the Infinite the finite has emerged. But nothing finite has ever come out of the Infinite Self. "Then how is it that we are experiencing them?" Such questions would normally arise. "The answer is", Sankara asserts, "like an iron piece appearing to be a fire piece when in contact with fire *(ayo-agni-yogad-eva)*."

The superimposition can only reflect the qualities of the sub-stratum. On a rope we cannot have the delusory misconception of a cow. And superimposition is *always mutual*. It cannot be one way only. Sankara enquires into this phenomenon of superimposition and says, "It is mutual superimposition *(annyonya-adhyasa)*". This is the techincal term used by Sankara.

Not only does the rope gain the properties of the snake, but the snake also borrows some properties from the rope. The snake is spotted, slimy, long, and has a hood. These snake properties are not in the rope--but they *cover* the rope. And the rope lends its *existence* to the fancied snake. The rope exists. The snake exists-not. The non-existent snake *exists* for the deluded man. The imaginary snake has borrowed its existence from the rope. To the rope the snake has lent its spotted, slimy appearance. Together, we see the rope as "non-existent" and the snake as "existent". The snake properties *we see* and the rope properties *we do not see*. So, in delusion our conclusion is, "The snake *is*, the rope *is not*."

Today we *see* the BMI, the ego and its sorrows and say, "These exist". But the Reality of God, the Consciousness exists not for us.

When I apprehend the pure Consciousness in myself, all the *dharamas* of the BMI retire. The BMI, PFT and OET disappear. Alone, *Reality exists.*

This above described process is called mutual superimposition *(annyonya-adhyasa)*. Hence we attribute a reality to the world perceived. What we see in the world around is the glaring expression of the Infinite Truth which is the Substratum everywhere. Names and forms are merely projections of our minds.

नित्याद्वयाखण्डचिदेकरूपो
बुद्ध्यादिसाक्षी सदसद्विलक्षणः ।
अहंपदप्रत्ययलक्षितार्थः
प्रत्यक्सदानन्दघनः परात्मा ॥३५२॥

352. Eternal, non-dual, unbroken Knowledge, of One form, the Witness of the intellect etc., neither gross nor subtle, indicated by the term "I", the embodiment of subjective eternal Bliss, is the nature of the Supreme Self.

* For a fuller explanation of "indicated by the term "I", refer commentary on verse 248. For explanation of other indicative terms used here, refer commentaries on verses 221, 222, 238 and 239.

This verse gives an exhaustive definition of the *Atman* as far as words can express it.

"Eternal": *(Nitya)*--without beginning and end; "Non-dual": *(A-dwaya)*--there is nothing other than It in It; "Un-broken" *(A-khanda)*--Un-conditioned by time, place or objects; meaning that which is All-pervading; "Consciousness": *(Chit)*; "Of One form": *(Ekaroopah)*--The Consciousness that knows no modifications.

The Reality is the "Witness" of the functionings of body, mind and intellect: *(Buddhyadi sakshi)*; It is "neither gross nor subtle": *(Sad-asad-vilakshanah)*--meaning, It is something other than both, something unique.

That a thing is gross or subtle, that it exists or does not exist--these are the judgements of the intellect. With certain standards of understanding, we classify things as existing or non-existing, as good or bad, as subtle or gross etc. All these are intellectual estimates which one is conscious of. However, the Consciousness that illumines the gross and the subtle is in Itself something other than them. Hence, in terms of intellectual and emotional classifications, all that can be said about the Self, is, "It is beyond all such classification."

The Atman is indicated by the subject "I" *(Aham-pada)*, in the famous Vedantic maxims. It is the "I" in "I am Brahman" --*Aham Brahma Asmi.* This "I" is not the PFT, nor has It anything to do with the BMI and the OET. The "I" the Consciousness, illumines all my thoughts emotions and actions. That Consciousness is the true "I" which is present everywhere; the indicative meaning of "I" in the *Mahavakya* is the Self. To experience this Supreme Self *(Para-atma)*, we will have to go into the very subject *(Pratyak)*, of our beings.

At all times, the Self is a totality of Bliss *(Sada-anandaghana)*; this is so, because there is no sorrow in It, which can be weighed against any measure of happiness. The causes for these sorrows are the BMI, PFT, and OET. When these are transcended, all agitations end. Where there is agitation, there is sorrow. Therefore, in terms of our present experiences of the mind and the intellect, the *Atman* is described as *Ananda-ghana.*

इत्थंविपश्चित्सदसद्विभज्य
निश्चित्य तत्त्वं निजबोधदृष्ट्या ।
ज्ञात्वा स्वमात्मानमखण्डबोधं
तेभ्यो विमुक्तः स्वयमेव शाम्यति ॥३५३॥

353. Thus the wise man, discriminating between the Real and the unreal, establishing the Truth by the insight of his Knowledge and realising his own Self to be unbroken Knowlege, becomes free and himself attains Peace.

Sankara first explained that which constitutes things unreal.[1] Then he explained that which constitutes the Real.[2] A wise man should discriminate between the Real and the unreal in the manner already explained. By rational thinking and close observation, he determines the Truth by a process of discrimination. Through the vision of the Higher, he ultimately comes to experience the Consciousness in all Its purity.

When one realise one's own Self to be pure Knowledge, one gets liberated from the ignorance of spirituality, the veiling *(avarana)* gets lifted and the idetification with the non-spiritual and its consequent agitations *(vikshepa)* end. When these obstacles, "veiling" and "projection", are removed the individual comes to experience quietude-Divine.

All obstacles are completely eliminated when an individual apprehends his spiritual nature, (1) through intelligent discrimination between the Self and the not-Self; (2) through detachment from the not-Self; and (3) by complete identification with the Self.

---

1. Refer verses 350, 351.
2. Refer verse 352.

62. Samadhi--Its Nature. (354-372)

अज्ञानहृदयग्रन्थेर्निःशेषविलयस्तदा ॥
समाधिनाऽविकल्पेन यदाऽद्वैतात्मदर्शनम् ॥३५४॥

354. When the non-dual Atman is realised in *Nirvikalpa Samadhi*, the heart's "knots of ignorance" are completely destroyed.

As a result of a constant practice of quietening the mind, when one enters "absolute quietude" *(Nirvikalpa Samadhi)*, one gains the experience of the non-dual, universal Reality. When the mind is completely quiet, one is shot up into new dimensions of experience. This is the experience of the Infinitude. With this experience, the personality becomes free from all its encrustations.

In *Vedanta*, the personality-bondages are called "the knots of the heart". They are, (1) spiritual ignorance *(avidya)*; as a consequence of it, (2) desires *(kama)*, that create agitations of the intellect; and consequently at the body level, (3) activity *(karma)*.

Spiritual ignorance, intellectual desires, mental agitations and physical activities form a basic sequence of cause and effect, each succeeding one being the effect caused by the previous one.

The Conciousness that I am the ever-full Bliss, the Self, not being there, we are persecuted by an annoying sense of imperfections in ourselves. The intellect plans to gain perfection and completeness through its *desires*. Because of desires there are *thoughts* in the mind. The thoughts in the mind prompt us to act in the world, which is *work*.

This triple bondage of spiritual ignorance, desires and action which limits the human personality ends when the individual successfully trains himself to quieten his mind completely and gets ushered into the experience of the Infinite Consciousness --his own Real Nature. Then the "knots of the heart" are cut asunder.

त्वमहमिदमितीयं कल्पना बुद्धिदोषात्
प्रभवति परमात्मन्यद्वये निर्विशेषे ।
प्रविलसति समाधावस्य सर्वो विकल्पो
विलयनमुपगच्छेद्वस्तुतत्त्वावधृत्या ॥३५५॥

355. "You", "I", "this", "that" --these concepts are fancied in the Supreme Self which is Absolute and non-dual, due to inherent defects of the intellect. When the Real Nature of *Brahman* is realised in *Samadhi*, all these concepts are dissolved.

The imperfections of the intellect are the *vasanas*, due to which the mind imagines the perceived world of plurality where we constantly live with a sense of "you", "I", "this" and "that". Such a world of plurality manifests and yields to us our sorrows and agitation. This entire delusion takes place in the supreme, non-dual Self.

When the Real Nature of the Self is experienced, all these distrubances are completely dissolved. So, through the state of complete mental equipoise, when the thoughts have ceased to flow and dance about, the Infinite is experienced, wherein one understands the Real Nature of the Self and at such a time all distrubances created by the imaginations of our intellect due to its imperfections cease entirely.

"This" indicates an object very near to us. "That" indicates an object further away. The play of "this" and "that" creates the concept of time and space. It is in this field that all objects are imagined. When there are objects perceived, then "I" enters the field as the subject, the perceiver. The subject-object play is the mind in agitation. When the Self, which is the substratum for both the subject and its field, is realised, all mental turbulence comes to a halt. When the mind is thus quietened, the perception of the pluralistic phenomenal world will also end.

शान्तो दान्तः परमुपरतः क्षान्तियुक्तः समाधिं
कुर्वन्नित्यं कलयति यतिः स्वस्य सर्वात्मभावम् ।
तेनाविद्यातिमिरजनितान्साधु दग्ध्वा विकल्पान्
ब्रह्माकृत्या निवसति सुखं निष्क्रियो निर्विकल्पः ॥३५६॥

356. Serene, self-controlled, perfectly withdrawn from sense-objects, steadfast in silently enduring, struggling to attain *Samadhi*, the seeker always contemplates on his own Self as the Self in the universe. Destroying, by these means, all imginations which arise from the blindness of ignorance, he lives blissfully as *Brahman*, free from egocentric actions and oscillations of the mind.

An aspirant, in order to be successful in his meditation, should have the following fundamental qualities,[1] --

1. Serenity *(santi)*: his mind is trained not to run after sense-objects with the false notion that there is happiness in them.
2. Control of the sense-organs *(dantah)*: so that the sense objects may not enter his mind from the world outside and disturb him.
3. Total withdrawal from mental preoccupations *(parama uparatah)* : this is to be practised and perfected so that the mind, by itself, may not dash out to remember sense-enjoyments of the past, nor weave a tapestry of sense-indulgences in fancied imaginaions.
4. Forbearance *(kshanti yuktah)* : this trait in a seeker is essential so that the little pinpricks of life may not cause agitations in him.

Such a seeker at his meditation seat struggles to lift himself to the vision of the one Self everywhere *(Samadhi)*.

When he realises that the Self in him is the Self everywhere, the bondages born out of spiritual blindness are all burnt down. Thereafter, that *Mahatma* lives ever content

1. This is a very important verse which indicates all the essential adjustments a seeker must make in himself before he becomes fit for higher meditations. Those who ignore these values and disciplines suffer endless disturbances on the path and rarely achieve any enduring success.

and blissful. He lifts himself up to the state of *Brahman* and verily becomes Brahman.

समाहिता ये प्रविलाप्य बाह्यं
श्रोत्रादि चेतः स्वमहं चिदात्मनि ।
त एव मुक्ता भवपाशबन्धैः
नान्ये तु पारोक्ष्यकथाभिधायिनः ॥३५७॥

357. They alone are free from the bondage of birth and death who, having attained *Samadhi*, merge the objective world, the sense-organs, the mind, nay, the very ego, in the *Atman*, the Knowledge Absolute, --and none else; who blabber their *indirect* Knowledge.

Only then can one end forever the sorrows of births and deaths, when one has experienced the total merger of the experiencer and the world of objects experienced in the one Self in *Samadhi*. Till this experience of *Samadhi*[1], one will function in the field of time and space with the BMI and continue to experience constant change. Only on awakening to the vivid state of pure, infinite Consciousness can we be released from our binding identifications with the BMI and so be free from the swirl of time and its changes.

Till we thus subjectively gain a *direct* experience of the Self, all scriptural declarations are but empty noises and noisy emptiness produced for the sake of the students. Whatever we discuss upon the scriptures, whatever discourses we hear or give, are at best, indirect knowledge, a mere blabber, no matter how eloquent the talks may be.

उपाधिभेदात्स्वयमेव भिद्यते
चोपाध्यपोहे स्वयमेव केवलः ।
तस्मादुपाधेर्विलयाय विद्वान्
वसेत्सदाऽकल्पसमाधिनिष्ठया ॥३५८॥

1. The ideas in verses 354 and 356 are repeated here for emphasis.

358. Through the many "conditionings", a man is apt to think of his own Self as full of diversity; but by removing these he gains his own Immutable Self. Hence, for the dissolution of his conditionings, the wise man must devote himself to the practice of *Nirvikalpa Samadhi.*

If there is only One, Infinite, Eternal Truth, why is diversity seen? Because of the "conditionings"[1] and their differences, the Self by Itself is experienced *as though* differentiated into the pluralistic phenomenal world. Due to the BMI prism, the One ray of the Light of *Brahman* gets dispersed to form the many-- the world of objects, emotions and thoughts of endless varieties. When the conditionings *(upadhis)* are removed, meaning, when the identification with the *upadhis* ends, the pure Consciousness *(Kevala)*, is realised as only One, both within and without.

Therefore, the wise student of philosophy, in order to end his false identifications with the conditionings, in order to withdraw from the *upadhis*, must constantly practise *Nirvikalpa Samadhi.* He must try to bring the mind completely and absolutely to silence. Once or twice a day he should struggle hard to bring the mind into perfect quietude. The rest of the time, even while experiencing the various phenomena of the outer world, he should cultivate the habit of turning his mind into inner quietude. This is "practice of *Samadhi*" --*Samadhi Nishtha.*[2]

Nirvikalpa Samadhi indicates the state where one has negated all disturbances or agitations in the mind. Continuously live this. This is the only method.

सति सक्तो नरो याति सद्भावं ह्येकनिष्ठया
कीटको भ्रमरं ध्यायन् भ्रमरत्वाय कल्पते ॥३५९॥

359. One who is attached to the Real becomes the Real through single-pointed devotion, just as the "worm" contemplating intently upon the wasp *(bhramara)*, is transformed to become a wasp.

---

1. उपाधि = मायापञ्चकोशरूपोपाधि । – --The conditionings are the *Maya*-created, delusory, personality layers such as the five sheaths or the three bodies.

2. निष्ठा = नितरां स्थितिः- -continuous, consistent, steady, self-detention in any state is nishtha in that state--firmly established in the practice.

The man who is extremely attached to the Infinite Reality reaches It by constantly devoting his mind to It. This is achieved by his single-pointed meditation upon the Self *(Eka-nishtha)*.

To illustrate the above idea, a famous example is given here: a pupa meditating upon a wasp *(bhramara)*, becomes a wasp.

The wasp makes its nest generally in the crevices of the ceiling or at the corners of tables which are not disturbed. The queen wasp brings a wormlike pupa and keeps it inside the mud-nest, the mouth of which it closes but for a tiny little opening. The wasp sits outside the cage looking into the hole. The pupa can see nothing at all save this tiny opening guarded zealously by this terrible monster. The poor pupa continuously looks and "meditates" upon the wasp. Whenever the pupa's attention is diverted and it tries to get away, the wasp stings it. If ever you have been stung by a wasp, you will understand what it is like. The entire 250 lbs. of you will be rolling in pain. If the poison of one sting disturbs the peace and tranquility of a man six-feet tall, with chest 38 inches, you can understand the agony of the little pupa. Thus, tormented by the pain, it continuously "meditates" upon the terrible wasp. Its "meditation" is single-pointed. Due to this pain-driven "meditation", the pupa either dies inside the cage if it is a weakling, or comes out transformed as a wasp. When the pupa metamorphoses to become a wasp, it develops the capacity to break the very mouth of the nest and emerge out all by itself. As it comes out it kills the mother wasp, because all along it had developed an inconsolable anger towards the stinging mother wasp.

The "worm" which the wasp brings, is really a potential wasp in its pupa stage. Zoological observations prove that after the egg of the wasp develops into a larva and moults into a pupa, the mother wasp brings it to the prepared nest for protection and under its watchfulness, the pupa slowly *grows* to become a full-fledged wasp.

In their poetic vision, Vedantic scholars take this as an example for the limited pupa-like, insignificant PFT* transforming itself into the Unlimited, All-pervading, Omniscient Reality. This is achieved through single-pointed meditation. Those who are extremely attached to Reality *(Sati-saktah)* with single-pointed concentration, meditate upon *Brahman* and become *Brahman*. Here it must be clearly understood that it is not a becoming in the sense of any marked obvious transformation. But the Self of the individual expands to become the Self pervading the entire universe.

Just as every pupa is a potential wasp, so too, every man is potentially divine. But a great deal of discipline and *sadhana* has to be put in before the efforts bear the fruits of spiritual maturity. Every pupa does not become a wasp. Yet it is capable, of, it has the capacity for becoming a wasp.

The pupa metamorphoses into a wasp by virtue of its being a potential wasp and by its long period of wait--during its "meditation" it is constantly *growing* towards becoming a wasp. The human-pupa moults into a Divine Personality by virtue of its being essentially divine and, by its constant single-pointed meditation upon the Divine, it *grows* in spiritual dimensions to become the Divine.

At the pupa-stage, the shapeless larva does not promise us a wasp, yet it is a wasp. Similarly, the limited, mortal, pain-ridden individuality of man does not look at all, its Real Divine Nature. But when the PFT*(jeeva)* ends, its identifications with the BMI and OET through steady meditations upon the Self, the PFT, the limited individuality metamorphoses into Infinite *Sat-chit-ananda*.

When the pupa stops being a pupa, it becomes a wasp; when a man stops being a *jeeva*, he becomes the Supreme.

क्रियान्तरासक्तिमपास्य कीटको
ध्यायन्यथालिं ह्यलिभावमृच्छति ॥

* Cf. f.n. verse 124.

तथैव योगी परमात्मतत्त्वं
ध्यात्वा समायाति तदेकनिष्ठया ॥३६०॥

360. Just as the "insect", renouncing attachment to all other activities thinks intently upon the wasp and metamorphoses into one, so too, a *Yogi* meditating upon the nature of *Paramatman*, attains It through his single-pointed devotion to It.

The idea of the previous verse is continued here and the example is applied to the *Yogin's* life. Having left all anxiety for all other kinds of activity, the insignificant pupa constantly maintains the one "thought" of the wasp in its mind. Not crawling, not moving about, it is not even conscious of its own breathing, but with its attention held continuously upon the wasp *(ali)*, it becomes a wasp after a perfect metapmorphosis.

Similarly, when the PFT withdraws its attention from the world of OET, and turns the M & I towards Reality, it is transformed into the Infinite. Withdrawing one's expression through the sense-organs, when one continuously meditates upon the nature of the Infinite as indicated in the Upanishads, one reaches the ultimate state of evolution. At present, the PFT in us is meditating upon the OET through the BMI. This identification with the BMI has to be withdrawn, and our attention is to be redirected towards the *Atman* in order to realise the Self.

The example given here is very appropriate. In the pupa stage, the wasp behaves exactly like an ordinary worm. It looks like a worm, it crawls like a worm. This is one of the stages of its evolution but ultimately it has to grow into a wasp. This insignificant pupa has all the qualities of a wasp stage is the culmination of its fulfilment, which it becomes, given the time to grow in its "meditations". Similarly, the *jeeva* is potentially divine but, at this moment, this divinity is not manifest. By constant, single-pointed concentration upon the divine Self, however, it can glide into the Infinitude which is the state of ultimate human evolution. It is then that the ego dissolves into the *Vision-Divine*.

अतीव सूक्ष्मं परमात्मतत्त्वं
न स्थूलदृष्ट्या प्रतिपत्तुमर्हति ।
समाधिनाऽत्यन्तसुसूक्ष्मवृत्त्या
ज्ञातव्यमार्यैरतिशुद्धबुद्धिभिः ॥३६१॥

361. The Real Nature of *Paramatman* is extremely subtle and cannot be reached by the gross out-going tendency of the mind. It is accessible to noble ones with extremely pure intellects, through *Samadhi*, brought about by an extra-ordinary subtlety of the mind.

Reality cannot be recognised by the gross process of perception. The gross objects of the world can be seen and recognised if you have a pair of healthy eyes. If you go to the pond you may see a lotus; but the lotus reveals its subtle beauty only to a poet; he sees a beauty, a special charm and an unearthly attractiveness in it. Unless you too can feel like a poet, you will not be able to appreciate this subtler vision of the lotus in the pond. A philosopher will divine a subtler meaning in the picture. The deep message of the lotus growing in the pond is understood by him. To understand that message one needs a subtler intellect. We are told that the Einsteinian theory is, today, fully understood by only half a dozen people in the whole world. Only a highly developed and specialised intellect can grasp the subtle imports of the theory.

The *Atman* is subtler than the subtlest thought-possibility of the intellect, because it transcends the intellect itself. Hence, with the gross instruments of knowledge one cannot apprehend It. Then what is the instrument in whose focal length the subtle Truth is brought for our recognition and experience?

When the thoughts have become subtle in the hushed moments of deep meditation, the mind is tuned up for the higher transcendental experience divine. It can be known only by the best among men *(Arya)*, who have perfectly purified intellects. Those who have lifted the veilings and reduced the agitations in the mind are said to have "purified intellect". This is the stage when the *vasanas* have been reduced, when the desire for sense-objects no more agitates the intellect.

The intellect which has stopped wandering into the fields of sense gratification, which is not involved in the mesh of sense-objects around and which is steady in its comtemplation, such an intellect is capable of understanding this great *Brahman*.

There is only one method, therefore, to realise the Truth--subtilise the vision by eliminating desire-created agitations and the non-apprehension of Reality created by the *vasana*-veils.

यथा सुवर्णं पुटपाकशोधितं
त्यक्त्वा मलं स्वात्मगुणं समृच्छति ।
तथा मनः सत्त्वरजस्तमोमलं
ध्यानेन सन्त्यज्य समेति तत्त्वम् ॥३६२॥

362. Just as gold, by thorough heating in fire, gives up its impurities and gains its own lustre, so too, the mind through meditation, sheds its impurities of *Sattwa*, *Rajas* and *Tamas* and attains the nature of *Brahman*.

The purification of the mind through meditation is explained by the example of gold-purification.

In the smelting of gold, the ore from the mines is powdered and seived. The gold thus collected contains many baser metal impurities. the mixture is then heated and smelted. In the molten mixture, the different metals from different layers. All the gold comes together. The dross is removed and the pure gold gains its own essential quality of yellow lustre. Thus, by smelting, gold is purified. The same process is applicable to mental purification also.

Our minds are now impure because of the dross of *Sattwa*, *Rajas* and *Tamas*. When such a mind is kept under the heat of meditation, the dross in the mind drops off and the pure Sattwic mind emerges. *Sattwa* cannot remain in its pure nature so it sublimates to merge with the Inifinite. When *Sattwa, Rajas* and *Tamas* are removed from the mind, it dissolves into the vision of Reality. The great Infinite, homogenous Conscuiousness is experienced as One-without-a-second, both within and without.

निरन्तराभ्यासवशात्तदित्थं
पक्वं मनो ब्रह्मणि लीयते यदा ।
तदा समाधिः सविकल्पवर्जितः
स्वतोऽद्वयानन्दरसानुभावकः ॥३६३॥

363. Thus purified by constant practice when the mind merges with *Brahman*, then *Samadhi* passes from the *Savikalpa* to the *Nirvikalpa* stage, leading directly to the experience of the Bliss of *Brahman*, the Non-dual.

The mind matures in its purification by the constant practice of the removal of the dirt of *Sattwa, Rajas* and *Tamas* from it. Such a mind when it dissolves into *Brahman*, meaning when it is not separate from It, it attains the state of *Nirvikalpa Samadhi*.

When a mature mind is exposed to meditation for a long period of time, it becomes fit for total dissolution in *Brahman*. When the meditation becomes deeper, the mind leaves its negative tendencies and all its confusions and doubts are eliminated. When the intellect becomes quiet without even a single disturbance, it, by itself, with no special effort, reaches the state of *Nirvikalpa Samadhi*. When the mind has ended there is nothing else to do.*

The quietended mind enters the state of *Samadhi*. The mind is quietened when *Rajas* and *Tamas* are removed by meditation. In the heat of meditation all agitations are removed. Then there is the experience of the non-dual *Brahman*.

---

* As the doer himself disappears at that stage from one's bosom.

The experience is non-dual because of the absence of anything other than It, at all times and at all places.

Bliss *(Ananda)*--because of the absence of the mind, there is no sorrow whatsoever. It is "the *joy* in the joyous" *(Ananda-rasa):* the *essence* of joy. There is no other way of describing the Objectless-Awareness by Its mindless-Bliss-Infinite.

Therefore, miditate, meditate and meditate.

समाधिनाऽनेन समस्तवासना
ग्रन्थेर्विनाशोऽखिलकर्मनाशः ।
अन्तर्बहिः सर्वत एव सर्वदा
स्वरूपविस्फूर्तिरयत्नतःस्यात् ॥ ३६४ ॥

364. By this *Samadhi*, all desires which are like "knots" are destroyed. All work comes to an end. And within and without, everywhere and always, takes place a spontaneous manifestation of one's own Real Nature.

Samadhi cannot be achieved by digging a hole in the earth and going underground. Whenever and wherever you are trying to quieten your mind, you are in the practice of *Samadhi*. Detaching the mind from disturbances within and without, and directing it to rest in Brahman is *Samadhi*. When *Samadhi* is practised, all bondages created by the *vasanas* are destroyed.

Vasanas create desires in the mind. Desires create agitations. Agitations create ego-prompted selfish activities, and thus you are bound to the objects of the world. So then, when you act in the world without ego and egocentric desires, naturally, the mind becomes quiet. When you try to quieten the mind more and more, the *vasanas* must get exhausted. *Vasanas* are exhausted and bondages loosened in our constant and deliberate attempts at keeping the mind in peaceful silence.

The unmanifested *vasanas*[1] are destroyed in the practice of *Samadhi.* The entire *Sanchit-karma* which has been accumulated in millions of our past lives *(akhila-karma)*, both manifest and unmanifest, is destroyed when we experience *Samadhi.*

The *vasanas* that have come to fruition---meaning, the already manifested *vasanas*---can be destroyed by selfless dedicated activity.[2] The accumulated *vasana (Sanchit)*, which have no yet come to fruition---meaning, the unmanifested *vasanas*, are burnt down in the fire of right knowledge. The bondage of activity and that of enjoying the fruits of actions does not belong to that individual who has directly reached the state of *Samadhi.* On experiencing *Samadhi*, the PFT who is the "doer" of activities *(karta)* and the "enjoyer" of the fruits of actions *(bhokta)*, ends. When the criminal is dead, whom can the law arrest? The file is closed. One who performed the action alone can enjoy the fruit of the action. When the ego has ended, who is to suffer? Hence of entire past *karmas* end when the ego ends, on Realisation of the Infinite.

When all the *vasanas* and their consequent bondages are annihilated through the practice of constant meditation, the seeker, seeking himself, ends in the total exhaustion of his entire *karma.* At this stage, what is the experience? Is it an empty zero? When the PFT, the causal-body and the *vasanas* have ended, what can remain?

The Teacher says, "At that time you will have a clear subjective experience of your own Self. That experience requires no special effort. Nothing need be done for it---either to reach it or to preserve it in us."

When the waking and dream states have been transcended, no special effort is necessary to reach and preserve the state of sleep. There is no question then of "reaching" sleep. We are then already in deep-sleep. In fact,

---

1. *Sanchit-prarabdha.*
2. *Nishkama-karma-yoga.*

if we start any effort, we are sure to wake up from sleep. The state of this absolute quietude within when the individual meditation is transformed into realms of inexpressible Bliss is the final subjective experience. It is complete Realisation of the Self, by the Self, in the Self. Without any effort *(a-yatnatah)**, we shall realise our own Self.

श्रुतेः शतगुणं विद्यान्मननं मननादपि ।
निदिध्यासं लक्षगुणमनन्तं निर्विकल्पकम् ॥३६५॥

365. "Reflection" should be considered a hundred times superior to "listening" and "meditation" a hundred thousand times superior to reflection; but *Nirvikalpa Samadhi* is infinitely more sacred.

Knowledge can be obtained by "listening" to a Teacher. Reading books is also a method of "listening" to acquire knowledge. But when one sits down and reflects upon the ideas gathered from a Teacher or from a book and makes them one's own, that understanding is hundred times more powerful than what can be gained by merely "listening" to a Teacher, or reading books.

If the seeker starts meditating upon the knowledge thus acquired through reflection, the sharpness of his understanding becomes a hundred thousand times more effective, that is, when one starts hushing up one's mind, the clarity of knowledge that one gains becomes a hundred thousand times greater than what one had gathered through reflection.

As you start practising meditation, after some time, a stage comes when you are in a dynamic state of thoughtless-

---

*The Upanishad declares that at this experience.
भिद्यते हृदयग्रन्थिः छिद्यन्ते सर्वसंशयाः ।
क्षीयन्ते चास्य कर्माणि तस्मिन्दृष्टे परावरे ॥

In short, as Sankara so musically puts it:
अन्तर्बहिः सर्वत एव सर्वदा ।
स्वरूपविस्फुर्तिरयत्नतः स्यात् ॥

stillness---in the *Nirvikalpa* condition---and your knowledge becomes infinite. This is a result of your continuous meditation when you dissolve your ego into complete silence---into the plane of pure, infinite, Consciousness Divine.

निर्विकल्पसमाधिना स्फुटं
ब्रह्मतत्त्वमवगम्यते ध्रुवम् ।
नान्यथा चलतया मनोगतेः
प्रत्ययान्तरविमिश्रितं भवेत् ॥३६६॥

366. By *Nirvikalpa Samadhi*, the true nature of *Brahman* is clearly and definitely manifest, never otherwise, for then, the mind being unsteady, is apt to be mixed with other perceptions.

In the condition of *Nirvikalpa Samadhi* alone can this great Reality be apprehended with certainty. With cent-per-cent certainty you apprehend the Truth when all the waves and ripples in your mind have ended. Sankara is positive and declares, "Never by any other method"---bringing the mind to quietude is the *only* method.

To quieten the mind there are many methods. You may quieten your mind through devotion, or through knowledge, or through *Karma-yoga* or through *Pranayama*. Whether standing on the head or sitting down, whether by going to the Himalayas or by living in your own home---you have the freedom to choose these---but your mind you must quieten.

The mind's nature is to be constantly active. "Thought flow", it is called. Therefore, it is impossible to realise the changeless Self with the mind, which, by its very nature is unstable. Whenever you try to grasp anything through the mind and intellect, the object of knowledge gets entangled in your own thought-patterns. Pure Self can never be *understood*. so all that you understand about the *Atman* through the mind and intellect, is *Saguna Brahman* and not *Nirguna Brahman*. The Unconditioned Absolute is never understood, you just *become* It when the mind ends. As long as you look at It through the mind, It is only the conditioned, the limited *(Saguna)* version of the eternal Absolute Self.

अतः समाधत्स्व यतेन्द्रियः सन्
निरन्तरं शान्तमनाः प्रतीचि ।
विध्वंसय ध्वान्तमनाद्यविद्यया
कृतं सदेकत्वविलोकनेन ॥३६७॥

367. Therefore, with a serene mind and the senses controlled, ever drown the mind in the subjective supreme Self, and by realising your identity with that Reality, destroy the darkness created by the beginningless Nescience *(avidya)*.

When the mind is controlled, the sense-organs are automatically controlled. Then the mind becomes tranquil. The mind is subjected to two types of disturbances---subjective and objective. At this moment our mind is subjected to both these disturbances and hence it is in a state of flux. Objective disturbances are brought into the mind by the sense-organs. When the sense-organs are controlled, objective disturbance will not reach us. Subjective disturbances are created by the *vasanas* in the intellect. When the intellect is re-educated to think in the right direction, the subjective disturbances also will not agitate the mind. When both these types of disturbances are not affecting the mind, it is quiet. With this quiet mind, retreat into the chambers of sheer quietude and remain there alert to experience therein the dynamic silence. The divinity is recognised there, at that time, within oneself.

When the Reality is thus apprehended, the darkness of ignorance created by Nescience *(avidya)* gets totally annihilated. Destroy the "non-apprehension" by directly apprehending the Reality. The non-apprehension of the post can be destroyed only by the apprehension of the post---then the ghost apparition disappears completely, forever.

Therefore, start controlling the mind and the sense-organs.

योगस्य प्रथमद्वारं वाङ्निरोधोऽपरिग्रहः ।
निराशा च निरीहा च नित्यमेकान्तशीलता ॥३६८॥

368. The first gateway of *Yoga* consists of : (1) control of speech, (2) non-acceptance of possessions, (3) non-entertainment of expectations, (4) freedom from activity and (5) living always in a retired mood.

In the previous verse, control of sense-organs and mind have been advised. Some more hints are given here as steps to control the wild sense-organs and the restless mind.

To enter into the palace of *Yoga*, the very first gateway is "control of speech". Speech does not only mean speaking; it includes the functions of all the organs of action. All these are represented by the term "speech" *(vak)*.

Non-acceptance of possessions *(a-parigraha)*. The idea that one will be happier by posessing the objects of the outer world, has to be entirely eradicated. There is no harm if things and beings are around us, but mentally we should not hug them with a sense of ownership. Eliminate all sense of possessiveness.

Without any expectations *(nir-asha)*. Thoughts of the enjoyments of the fruits of our actions in a future period of time have to be given up.

Giving up of all ego-centric activity is *nireeha*.

With the above qualities of no excitement arising from expectations of future enjoyment, and no ego-prompted selfish activity, cultivate the habit of "being alone" constantly, *(nityam-ekanta-seelata)*.

"Aloneness" is different from "loneliness". By remaining *lonely*, at a place where there is nobody else, realisation is not guaranteed. Even in the midst of a crowd you can be "alone"---all alone is *Brahman*, the One-without-a-second.

* सकाम अहंकारयुक्त कर्मभ्य उपरतिःच निरीहा ॥

Aloneness" is not in the surroundings but it is in one's attitude within the bosom---to remain with one end or goal *(eka-antam)*---to remain with all attention fixed upon that One Goal. The habit of constantly remaining alone, even in a busy market-place, is to be cultivated.

Therefore, in order to reach *Samadhi*, lern to sit down at least ten minutes every day without any activity, physical and mental. Let us sit down, without any expectations of possible enjoyments, with the firm understanding that the objects around us can never give us happiness. Constantly keep up the habit of remaining "alone", remembering Him. With nothing else in the mind, the mind is alone. The alone-mind alone can move to Truth which is always alone.

एकान्तस्थितिरिन्द्रियोपरमणे हेतुर्दमश्चेतसः
संरोधे करणं शमेन विलयं यायादहंवासना ।
तेनानन्दरसानुभूतिरचला ब्राह्मी सदा योगिनः
तस्माच्चित्तनिरोध एव सततं कार्यः प्रयत्नान्मुनेः ॥३६९॥

369. Living in solitude helps to control the sense-organs, control of the senses serves to control the mind, and by controlling the mind the ego is destroyed; this gives the *Yogin* an Absolute Realisation of the Bliss of *Brahman*. Hence the man of reflection should always strive to quieten his mind alone.

Control of the mind leads to Self-realisation by stages. It will not happen all of a sudden as though by some strange and inexplicable magic. The progress is stage by stage, each one leading to a higher one, until at last he reaches in time, the final stage of Self-realisation. These various stages are explained in this verse.

When you practise keeping your mind in "continuous contemplation upon the Reality" *(ekanta-sthiti)*, the sense-organs will slowly retire *(indriyo-paramanam)* from their preoccupations with the sense-objects. They will stop running after them because the mind is now constantly dedicated to the contemplation of a much more satisfying, joyous state.

Control of the sense-organs and control of the mind are mutual---control of the one leads to control of the other. Thus is the mind *(chetas)* controllled. An uncontrolled mind is always in a state of agitation caused by the sense-organs and the ego *(ahamkara)*. When the sense-organs are not bringing in any stimuli from the sense-objects because of the mind's pre-occupation with its continuous contemplation upon the Reality, the ego is well-controlled because of its dedication to the higher ideal, and the mind naturally becomes quiet. In a quiet mind, *vasanas* get destroyed. Control of the mind means reduction of desires. When the desires have been reduced, *vasanas* get annihilated. Thus, when the ego is surrendered at the altar of the Self, then Realisation of the Bliss of *Brahman* is at hand.

When the ego is annihilated, the experience of the Infinite must necessarily come. That state of Brahmic Consciousness is the real Essence of the unbroken Bliss Absolute.

Therefore, the man of reflection, who has already listened to a Master and reflected independently upon the ideas, must control his thought-flow, his mind.

वाचं नियच्छात्मनि तं नियच्छ
बुद्धौ धियं यच्छ च बुद्धिसाक्षिणि ॥
तं चापि पूर्णात्मनि निर्विकल्पे
विलाप्य शान्तिं परमां भजस्व ॥३७०॥

370. Restrain speech in the mind, and restrain the mind in the intellect; and this again restrain in the "Witness" of the intellect, and merging that too in the infinite Absolute Self, gain supreme Peace.

We know how to unfold ourselves. We are doing it all along. Thoughts erupt because of desire. Thoughts arrogantly express through the physical body in the world outside and we try to acquire and aggrandise in all our activities. After getting the objects of our desire, we indulge in them and fulfil our immediate desires. The moment the present desire is fulfilled another desire luxuriously sprouts up and again the entire tragedy is enacted, down to the exhausting convulsions of actions. Thus, though we search for *satisfaction*, we unintelligently run after sense gratification only. This method of unfolding and projecting ourselves, distorting ourselves into mere caricatures of the equanimous centre, is very well known to us.

From such conditions of extrovertedness, how are we to pull ourselves back to the Centre in us, the peaceful Self? The stages on this inward pilgrimage are described by *Acharya* Sankara as thoroughly as a road map.*

"Fold back the *speech* into the mind. Fold the *mind* into the intellect. Fold that *intellect* into the "Witness" of the intellect. After gaining perfectly the attitude of a Witness to one's own *thought processes*, this witnessing faculty also should be folded into the tranquil *Atman*, the Self supreme...." so instructs the Kathopanishad *mantra*.

Speech here stands for all external activity. Let all the activities be held back at the mental level, meaning, though thoughts will be gurgling in the mind, the seeker must refuse to act. This mental activity should be held in abeyance at the intellect level, meaning, keep the thoughts at desire-level only, not allowing them any expression outside. Thus, when the intellect has changed its values, the mind which is entertaining the thoughts of extrovertedness must necessarily become quiet. If the intellect is still having irrepressible built-in-pressures of desires of extrovertedness, merge that restless intellect in the uninterested Observer of the intellect. Make yourself only a witness to the various agitations of the intellect.

---

* The ideas declared here by Sankara are echoes of the instructions in thee Kathopanishad:

यच्छेद्वाङ्‌मनसी प्राज्ञः तद्यच्छेज्ज्ञानमात्मनि ।
ज्ञानमात्मनि महति नियच्छेत्तद्यच्छेच्छान्तमात्मनि ॥

When we thus refuse to identify with the thoughts, or the desires, no desire-prompted travail of activity can ever take place. The desires must naturally die away because we are no more leading our dynamism to it. By continuously remaining as the witness, we are withdrawing all our dynamism from the waves of our desires and so they become impotent.

The instruction of the *Acharya* here is to be a witness of the intellect *(buddhi-sakshi)*, this means,remaining as a witness to what is going on in one's own intellect. The witness-hood can be maintained only as long as things are happening. When we are detached from what is happening, and when we cease to lend our vitality to the intellect, thoughts must get slowly reduced. When the intellect is thus merged in the witness, it gets quietly hushed up, until at last when the last thought is also ended, the witness can no longer be a witness. A witness is one who is *witnessing* something. When the last thought is also ended, there is no object for the witness to watch and, therefore, the witness-hood of the witness ends. Thus, the witness entity, the ego, merges with the pure infinite Consciousness.

This pure infinite Consciousness, while witnessing the intellect, meaning, in Its identification with the intellect and its thoughts had become the witness, the ego. This witness, identifying with its desires, becomes the desirer, the ego. The desirer, thereafter, thinks upon his desires and comes to play as the thinker, the ego. The *active*- "thinker" becomes the "doer". That doer is the final objective expression of the pure infinite Consciousness as the ego. Therefore, retrace the path of fall and rise again to attain the supreme Peace and Quietude, which is the true spiritual status of man. Thus, fold back the ego into the state of the Peaceful Self *(Santa-atma)*.

देहप्राणेन्द्रियमनोबुद्ध्यादिभिरुपाधिभिः ।
यैर्यैर्वृत्तेः समायोगस्तत्तद्भावोऽस्य योगिनः ॥३७१॥

371. The body, *Pranas*, sense-organs, mind, intellect, etc., with whichever of these conditionings the mind gets associated, the *Yogin* also gets transformed, as it were, into that.

According to his identification with the functions of his various equipments, the *Yogin* gets temporarily transformed. When we identify with any pain in our body, we become the sufferers of that pain. When we are detached from that pain as in deep-sleep, we do not suffer any longer. Through our identifications we come to experience exactly the condition of the equipment.

The word, *"Yogi"* here, is used in a peculiar sense. Ordinarily, *"Yogi"* means, one who is identifying with the higher. Here Sankara uses it in its etymological meaning. *"Yoga"* means "to join", "to get yoked with". *"Yogi"* means "one who is yoked". When we yoke ourselves to our physical passions, or emotional agitations, or intellectual perturbances, we, at least temporarily, become that only. When we identify with the anger in our minds, we come to behave in rapport with that anger. When we identify with the lust in us, we become, for the time being, the manifestation of lust.

Generally, Yoga with the world of objects is called Bhoga. Sankara here, however, deliberately uses the word "Yoga" so that it becomes easier for us to understand the following verse.

तन्निवृत्त्या मुनेः सम्यक् सर्वोपरमणं सुखम् ।
संदृश्यते सदानन्दरसानुभवविप्लवः ॥३७२॥

372. When this is completely removed, a man of reflection is found to detach easily from everything, and to get into the riotous revelry of the Essence of Bliss.

When the man of reflection, with correct understanding, gets divorced from his meaningless embrace with the flesh, he naturally comes to experience the "joy of total withdrawal" *(sarvo-paramanam-sukham)*, from all pains and sorrows.*

Ordinarily, in the world we are joyous when we acquire something. Here you gain the supreme joy of total withdrawal from every disturbance, by giving up your hold on objects. It is the joy of our Real Nature, where we come to experience the riotous revelry of the infinite Bliss.

63. Fully Detached---Samadhi Easy. (373-378)

अन्तस्त्यागो बहिस्त्यागो विरक्तस्यैव युज्यते ।
त्यजत्यन्तर्बहिःसङ्गं विरक्तस्तु मुमुक्षया ॥३७३॥

373. A man of dispassison alone is fit for this internal and external renunciation; for the man of dispassion, out of his desire to be free, readily renounces both internal and external attachments.

In essence, renunciation means "giving up". Giving up of the external world of objects is *external* renunciation. Giving up of sensuous thoughts of indulgences is *internal* renunciation. Renunciation, external and internal, can be successfully achieved only by such an individual who has developed dispassion towards worldly things. As a result of sufficient study, listening to a Master and deep reflection, having understood the hollowness of the world of objects, when one develops a sense of renunciation towards them, then alone does one become fit for renunciation, external as well as internal. In fact, it is very easy to give up the external objects. Just walk out. But if you have an attachment for them, wherever you may go, you will create a world of similar objects around you. A man of total dispassion *(viraktah)*, alone can effectively give up his attachments towards the objects, because his entire attention has turned towards a greater goal. He alone, who has developed irresistible passion for

---

*सर्वोपरमणं सुखं - सर्वेषां दुःखात्मकानां अनात्मनां उपरमणं अभानं यत्र सुखे तत्सर्वोपरमणं सुखम् ।

When we have withdrawn from the world of all pain-ridden not-Self, meaning, where we are not perceiving and experiencing the not-Self, there is infinite Bliss---which is here termed, "the joy of total withdrawal".

liberation and total detachment from the world of objects, is fit for a complete internal and external renunciation.

Incidentally, the word "dispassion" (vairagya), has two etymological derivations. One is "total absence of desire",* and the other is "special attachment".** The former implies a sense of detachment from the world of objects and the latter, a sense of attachment to the desire for liberation. Renouncing our present preoccupation, let us march towards the Higher. Ultimately, our ego-sense can end only through our own inner growth. Grow, we must.

बहिस्तु विषयैः सङ्गं तथान्तरहमादिभिः ।
विरक्त एव शक्नोति त्यक्तुं ब्रह्मणि निष्ठितः ॥३७४॥

374. Only the man of dispassion who is thoroughly established in *Brahman*, can give up his external attachment for objects and internal attachment to the ego, etc.

One who is capable of true renunciation, both internal and external, is vividly described in this verse.

Giving up attachment to sense-objects of the world outside is called external renunciation *(bahih-tyaga)*. External attachment is constituted of egocentric desires for an object. Running away from objects is not renunciation. Renouncing the wrong relationship with the world of objects is true renunciation. Objects by themselves cannot give anyone any sorrow. The moment one has the idea, "I want them", the objects cling on to him.

Giving up the ideas of "I", "my", "mine" etc., in short, the renunciation of the ego and ego-prompted thoughts, is internal renunciation *(antah-tyaga)*.

Renunciation, external, is possible only for one who has no desire for the sense-objects, that is, one who is a *viraktah*

---

* विगतः रागः विरागः । विरागस्य भावः वैराग्यम् ॥
** विशेषण रागः विरागः । विरागसय भावः वैराग्यम् ॥

He who has desires for the sense-objects and has a clinging attachment to them, can never give up hunting after sense-objects.

A dispassionate man can easily give up his pre-occupations with objects both external and internal, because his identification is rooted in *Brahman*. Only he can renounce who is holding on firmly to the feet of the Lord. He who has given a new direction to his mind towards an inspiring and noble goal, can give up all ignoble thoughts and actions as he has no attachment towards them. This is positive renunciation. Just trying to give up things, with no goal to aspire to, is negative renunciation and will not last long when one is faced with the irresistible tides of enchanting sense-objects.

वैराग्यबोधौ पुरुषस्य पक्षिवत्
पक्षौ विजानीहि विचक्षण त्वम् ।
विमुक्तिसौधाग्रलताधिरोहणं
ताभ्यां विना नान्यतरेण सिध्यति ॥३७५॥

375. Please understand, O wise one, that dispassion and discrimination in an aspirant are like the two wings of a bird; unless both are active, no one can take the help of just one and fly to the creeper of liberation which grows, as it were, atop a bungalow.

Vairagya is detachment from the world of objects and their tantalising enchanments. *Bodha* is subjective knowledge of the higher Reality. These two are essential to a spiritual aspirant. They function just like the two wings of a bird in flight. For a man of meditation who wants to soar into the higher planes of Consciousness, the two effective wings necessary are *vairagya* and *bodha*.

If these two are not there, the *sadhak* will not reach anywhere. He may be an erudite scholar, a recognised professor of philosophy, yet for direct spiritual experience he will need both these. Without even one of these two, no progress is possible. A bird cannot fly with one wing. Both wings are of equal importance. Both must be equal in length and strength. If *viveka* and *vairagya* are not fully developed in a man, such a man cannot meditate successfully for long.

Sri Sankaracharya was not only a great philosopher but also an equally great poet. In his commentaries upon the Geeta, the *Upanishads* and the *Brahman Sutras*, Sankara the philosopher was at his best. Because of the rigidity of the literary norms that he had, perforce, to follow in *Bhashya* writing, and the exactness of the ideas to be communicated, every word used was of great consequence and, therefore, it had to be perfect and precise. Hence, Sankara could not exhibit his poetic skill in his commentaries. But he fully quenched his poetic thirst in his works like Bhaja Govindam, Dakshinamoorthy Stotram and Vivekachoodamani. The subject matter remaining the same, Sankara revelled in poetry in these works. These books underscore the twin aspects of Sankara's personality---the poet and the philosopher. In some of the verses, where the ideas are of supreme importance, he expresses them clearly, sometimes compromising his poetry even to the detriment of the metre. While in others, there is an exuberance of poetry without any loss of clarity and vividness of the theme. At some places he lavishly employs more than one verse to indicate the same idea, painting it repeatedly with different examples. Sankara revelled in poetry in almost all the verses of his introductory text-books *(Prakriya grantha)*. This verse is an example of Sankara's invocation of Vedantic ideas, dressed in his resplendent poetry.

For a bird to reach the creepers on the roof of a tall edifice, there is no other method than to fly high, with a pair of wings spread out in grace and held in strength.

Similarly, to soar high into meditation, and to land successfully on the sequestered arbours set on the pinnacles of libration, we shall need the two wings of *viveka* and *vairagya*. There is no other way to reach the Peak.

Therefore, let us try to develop *viveka* and *vairagya* and equip ourselves fully for the flight to the Infinite.

अत्यन्तवैराग्यवतः समाधिः
समाहितस्यैव दृढप्रबोधः ।
प्रबुद्धतत्त्वस्य हि बन्धमुक्ति -
र्मुक्तात्मनो नित्यसुखानुभूतिः ॥३७६॥

376. A man of extreme dispassion alone experiences *Samadhi*; a man of *Samadhi* alone has steady Realisation; a man who has realised Truth alone is free from bondage and the free personality alone has the experience of eternal Bliss.

When a person is not disturbed by the objects, emotions and thoughts around him, he is said to have supreme detachment. When the objects within and without, can no longer tantalise one's thoughts, then alone can one reach the state of *Samadhi*. Transcendental experience is possible only to those who have cultivated complete *vairagya*.

Realisation is possible only in the state of *Samadhi*. One who has thus awakened to the supreme state of *Brahman*, to him alone, there is total linberation from all the bondages of *samsar*. The persecutions of a dream end only when the dreamer wakes up. The liberated one alone can have eternal Bliss. This Bliss experienced by a man of Realisation is not dependent upon the objects around. He revels in his own Self.*

वैराग्यान्न परं सुखस्य जनकं पश्यामि वश्यात्मन-
स्तच्चेच्छुद्धतरात्मबोधसहितं स्वाराज्यसाम्राज्यधुक् ।
एतद्द्वारमजस्त्रमुक्तियुवतेर्यस्मात्त्वमस्मात्परं
सर्वत्रास्पृहया सदात्मनि सदा प्रज्ञां कुरु श्रेयसे ॥३७७॥

* नन्दति नन्दति नन्दत्येव । Bhaja Govindam

377. For a self-controlled man, I find no better generator of happiness than dispassion and if that is coupled with a clear Realisation of the Self, it brings about absolute sovereignty, within and without. And since this is the gateway to the damsel of permanent liberation, so for your own well-being be dispassionate both within and without, always fixing your mind on the eternal Self.

Complete self-control is the stage when the mind is not running after sense-objects, though they may be crowding around and grinning at us all the time. When such a state of balance is attained, "I do not see", says Sri Sankara, "any other method by which the highest happiness can be gained, other than dispassion." One may develop in one self a temporary capacity to resist the temptation to indulge in the objects around. But unless a person changes his entire mental constitution, his entire values of life within, sufficiently, so as not to be tantalised any more by any new arrangement of objects, no enduring spiritual growth is ever possible. This changed attitude is called *vairagya.* There is, in a life of *vairagya*, not even a trace of pessimism. It is a sense of self-sufficiency, the inner richness experienced, a fabulous feeling of joy, compared with which the external world of objects is a petty, paltry, filthy, nothing. This is the only way by which a self-controlled man can yet increase his happiness by gaining the experience of Bliss.

Along with *vairagya*, if such an individual also discovers in himself the positive experience of the Bliss of the Self, his happiness becomes the greatest. He then becomes independent of the *inner* world of *thoughts (Swaa-rajya)* and the *outer* world of environments *(Saam-rajya)* as well, kingship within himself in the world of thoughts and sovereignty over the external world of objects.

Thus *vairagya* is the gateway to reach the damsel of liberation. Therefore, in all places, at all times and under all conditions, practise *vairagya* and reach the state of liberation. Liberation *(Moksha)* is the ultimate welfare *(Sreyas)*. Hence for your own welfare, constantly contemplate upon the Self. Sit in His lap and look at the world: Then where is sorrow? Where is inauspiciousness?---*Siva.......Siva!*

आशां छिन्द्धि विषोपमेषु विषयेष्वेषैव मृत्योः कृति-
स्त्यक्त्वा जातिकुलाश्रमेष्वभिमतिं मुञ्चातिदूरात्क्रियाः ।
देहादावसति त्यजात्मधिषणां प्रज्ञां कुरुष्वात्मनि
त्वं द्रष्टास्यमलोऽपि निर्द्वयपरं ब्रह्मासि यद्वस्तुतः ॥३७८॥

378. Cut asunder your craving for sense-objects which are like poison--- it is the very image of death; and giving up your pride of caste, family order of life, throw far away all selfish actions. Renounce your identification with such unreal things as the body and fix your mind upon the Self. For in reality, you are the Witness, Brahman, untainted by the mind, Non-dual, Supreme.

The sense-objects of pleasure are like poison. Those who desire them are sure to meet with annihilation. Death means "change". To be identified with the OET is to live in the realm of change, and therefore, in a continuous process of death. Hence renounce the desire for sense-objects which are full of mortal poison. Renounce also the vanity of caste, family and order of life. These blind your vision and you start seeing things distorted by vanity into a frightening, unreal caricature of the beautiful world.

Also, throw away all activities prompted by the ego, that is, all desire-prompted activity. Renounce the idea that you are the body, the mind and the intellect. Renounce this attitude, for the not-Self is impermanent.

Leaving all these, identify with the Self. Have the idea, "I am *Brahman*". Quieten the intellect in steady contemplation upon the *Atman**

You are the Witness. The on-looker of an activity, not getting involved in it, is a witness. You are not involved in any of the activities of the body, mind and intellect. Your are a mere on-looker. As a witness, you are ever-pure, never tainted. The things that are happening in the BMI are only

---

* Verses 377 and 378 may be learnt by heart. They are full of meaning for purposes of reflection and meditation.

the expressions of its *vasanas*. You are beyond the *vasanas*, and therefore,vasanas can never condition you. You are the nondual *Brahman*, with no otherness. That One, Infinite Narayana alone are you. In fact, "That Thou Art". Meditate upon this.

64. Meditation---the Technique. (379-383)

लक्ष्ये ब्रह्मणि मानसं दृढतरं संस्थाप्य बाह्येन्द्रियं
स्वस्थाने विनिवेश्य निश्चलतनुश्चोपेक्ष्य देहस्थितिम् ।
ब्रह्मात्मैक्यमुपेत्य तन्मयतया चाखण्डवृत्त्याऽनिशं
ब्रह्मानन्दरसं पिबात्मनि मुदा शून्यैः किमन्यैर्भृशम् ॥३७९॥

379. Fixing the mind firmly on *Brahman*, the point of concentration, restraining the sense-organs in their respective centres, holding the body steady and giving up all thought for its maintenance, attaining identity with *Brahman* and being One with It, continuously drink the Bliss of *Brahman* in your own Self. Of what use are other things? They are entirely false, empty!

Establishing the mind firmly in *Brahman*, the point of contemplation, persuade the sense-organs to stay quietly at their respective sense centres. Let not the sense centres in the intellect get excited and run after the sense-objects.

Keeping the body firm in a steady posture, give up all anxieties for it. Sit in a comfortable posture in which you can easily sit for about an hour without worrying over the limbs of the body.* Then meditate upon the Self and realise the Oneness of Its glory, within and without. Do not stand apart and try to understand It; you must strive to *become* It *(Tanmayata)*. Merge to be one with It, without any sense of separateness. Constinuously, without break, maintain the attitude, "I am *Brahman*" *(Aham-Brahma-Asmi)*.

Thus, revel in the Self, with the wisdom, "I am one with *Brahman*."

---

* स्थिरसुखमासनम् - Sthira-sukham-asanam-a firm and comfortable posture of sitting-Yoga Sutra.

Other than *Brahman*, everything is non-existent, totally unreal. When you wake up, the dream becomes false, non-existent. What is the use of the objects of the world? They can give you no happiness. Therefore, miditate and realise the Source of all happiness, deep within yourself.

अनात्मचिन्तनं त्यक्त्वा कश्मलं दुःखकारणम् ।
चिन्तयात्मानमानन्दरूपं यन्मुक्तिकारणम् ॥३८०॥

380. Having renounced all thought of the not-Self which is evil and productive of misery, think of the Self, the Bliss Absolute, which conduces to liberation.

Worry and anxiety over the not-Self is evil, full of pangs and pains and the cause for all sorrows and agitations. The not-Self is constituted of the BMI, PFT and OET. Hence renounce the pain-ridden anxiety about the not-Self. Renouncing thus, constantly contemplate upon the Blissful nature of the Self, which conduces to liberation from the thraldom of sorrows provided by the BMI, PFT, OET.

In the follwing verses, the ways of contemplation upon the Self during the early stages of meditation are advised by Adi Sankara.

एष स्वयंज्योतिरशेषसाक्षी
विज्ञानकोशे विलसत्यजस्त्रम् ।
लक्ष्यं विधायैनमसद्विलक्षण-
मखण्डवृत्त्याऽऽत्मतयाऽनुभावय ॥३८१॥

381. Eternally shines this *Atman*, the Self-effulgent Witness of all things, which has the intellect for Its seat. Making this *Atman* which is distinct from the unreal, your point of contemplation, meditate upon It as your own Self, eliminating all other thoughts.

The *Atman* is ever Self-effulgent. Nothing can illumine It. Shedding Its light over all our experiences, It illumines the thoughts and emotions in everyone. It is Light Itself. It is the Witness of everything, without any exception, just as the sun is the witness of everything that shines under its light.

Consciousness plays about in the intellect in endless varieties. All the functions of thoughts in the mind and intellect are illumined by It, just as the sunlight playing on the surface of the surging ocean illumines all waves, ripples, bubbles, foam etc. that are in it.

Establish your mind in this Self, which is other than the not-Self *(asad-vilakshanam)*. Contemplate upon this Consciousness constantly, without any break, *(akhanda-vritya)*, as your own Self *(atma-taya)*.

एतमच्छिन्नया वृत्त्या प्रत्ययान्तरशून्यया ।
उल्लेखयन्विजानीयात्स्वस्वरूपतया स्फुटम् ॥३८२॥

382. Contemplating continuously upon this *Atman*, with no intervention of any other thought, one must distinctly realise It as one's own Real Self.

Thus, through unbroken contemplation upon this Self, which is without any distinction within and without, you shall come to experience your own Real Nature-Divine very clearly.

When the dreamer wakes up he understands the waker as his own real nature, very clearly, beyond all traces of doubt. Realise this state clearly *(sphutam)*, as your own Self *(swa-swaroopa-taya)*.

अत्रात्मत्वं दृढीकुर्वन्नहमादिषु संत्यजन् ।
उदासीनतया तेषु तिष्ठेत्स्फुटघटादिवत् ॥३८३॥

383. By strengthening one's identification with this Self, and by renouncing all identifications with the ego etc. One must live with no concern for them, as if they were trifles like a broken pot or the like.

Constantly establish your firm identification with the experience of the Higher. As you move slowly into the higher plane of Consciousness, constantly try to leave behind the concepts of the individualised ego etc. Egoism, *Chitta*, intellect mind and body are the different attitudes, the sum total of which is the individualised entity. Leave egocentric attitudes behind and move towards the higher plane of Consciousness and get yourself more and more firmly established in It.

A similar thing happens when you go to sleep. The waking personality slowly gets eliminated and you get more and more established in the deep-sleep condition. When you get established in Truth, live uninvolved in the things that are happening around. If you participate actively in the happenings around, you will again tumble down into agitations. Therefore, remain in the world; let the thoughts in you dance about, but never get involved with them.

If you pour oil or water in a broken pot,* nothing will remain in it after some time. If the pot is not broken, the contents can remain in it for a long time. When it is broken few will come and take it away, as there is nothing in it. Remain like a broken pot. If you cannot eliminate the mind, at least make a few holes in it. This is how Kuchela (Sudama) lived in complete detachment. When his wife, in her exasperation gave him a talking-to, he ardently listened to her and deeply sympathised with her. But the moment she stopped, he started his *japa*-- *"OM NAMO BHAGAVATE VASUDEVAYA."* This is called "things going out of the mind" --the leaking mind. In this way, ever remain empty because, "Empty thyself, I shall fill thee", is the eternal promise of all prophets.

65. Continuous Attention to Self. (384-397)

विशुद्धमन्तःकरणं स्वरूपे ।
निवेश्य साक्षिण्यवबोधमात्रे ।

---

* There is another reading of the last *pada* of this verse:
तिष्ठेद्घटपदादिवत् ----here the meaning is direct and very elementary. "One must live as unconcerned for the objects perceived around." When we see a pot, we know the pot is an object and we do not generally misunderstand it to be ourselves. Similarly, let us not identify with the ego.

शनैः शनैर्निश्चलतामुपानयन्
पूर्णं स्वमेवानुविलोकयेत्ततः ॥३८४॥

384. By fixing the purified inner equipment upon the Self which is the Witness and Knowledge Absolute, and little by little making it quiet, one must try to realise one's inisinite Self.

A purified mind is that from which the *Rajas* and *Tamas* have been removed. A pure mind is free from its preoccupations with OET. These extrovert preoccupations can end only when the *vasana*-forces have slowed down. "Bring such a mind to contemplate upon the pure *Atman*, which is the Witness of all the movements of the body, mind and intellect" --this is the instruction here. When the Witness, the Consciousness, illumines our thoughts, we become conscious of our thoughts. Consciousness illumines the OET but the OET are not in the Consciousness. The sun is the witness of the world of objects, but the objects are not in the sun. The sun is light alone; the Self is Consciousness alone (Bodha-matra). In that Consciousness fix your mind which has been fully weaned away from all agitations. Slowly, slowly, bring those disturbances into quietude and rest the quiet mind in contemplation upon the Self.

As the mind becomes quiet, you come to experience the full, the eternal Self continuously and initimately.

देहेन्द्रिय प्राणमनोहरमादिभिः
स्वाज्ञानक्लृप्तैरखिलैरुपाधिभिः ।
विमुक्तमात्मानमखण्डरूपं
पूर्णं महाकाशमिवावलोकयेत् ॥ ३८५ ॥

385. Free from all limitations like the body, sense-organs, *Pranas*, mind and ego which are the projections of one's ignorance, let one come to realise the Atman, the Indivisible and Infinite, like the great endless sky.

The body, mind and intellect are false projections of one's *avidya*. When these limiting adjuncts are transcended, the

Self is experienced "like the great, limitless sky" *(Maha-akasam-iva).*

The outer space is unconditioned and all-pervading. It allows all other things to remain in it, without itself getting conditioned by them. Transcending all things exists space.

Similarly, when the body is transcended, I am not limited by any physical object. When the M & I are also hushed, there can be nothing but pure Consciousness. There is no other example by which we can indicate this great Consciousness which is All-pervading and Eternal. It can only be *compared* with space. Space itself is not the ultimate Reality. It is the nearest illustration which can indicate It, in as much as, it is the subtlest of all elements. Very often space is taken as an example for Conciousness. Since it has the property of sound it becomes a substance. Things which have properties and are substances are objects, finite--ever-changing. Since it is an object, it has a beginning and an end. *Atman* is not space but is *like* space; it is comparable with the subtlest element, space, for the purpose of intellectual understanding. In short, Sankara wants us to meditate upon and experience *Brahman*, the All-pervading and Eternal.

Elaborating upon the simile "like the infinite space" used here, he continues in the following verse.

घटकलशकुसूलसूचिमुख्यै-
र्गगनमुपाधिशतैर्विमुक्तमेकम् ।
भवति न विविधं तथैव शुद्धं
परमहमादिविमुक्तमेकमेव ॥३८६॥

386. Having dropped hundreds of its limitations such as a pot, a pitcher, a barn or the eye of a needle, space is recognised as one an not many. So too, *Brahman* is indeed one, when denuded of the ego etc.

The example of space given in the above verse is expanded in this one.

A pot, jar, barn[1] or the eye of a needle are the conditionings for space. Pot-space, jar-space, barn-space and needle's-eye-space are all parts of the same space and are so called because of their respective conditionings. Space is one, with no limiting adjuncts *(upadhis)*. When the upadhis are all removed the one space remains all by itself. There can be no differences in it. The apparent differences are all due to its conditionings. Similarly, Consciousness is one, ever free from the concept of PFT. The Self is free from all encrustrations of BMI and OET.[2]

The conditionings around the Self, made up of the ego and the body-mind-intellect equipment are only delusory projections of the mind, for the Supreme is ever Immaculate.

This is further explained in the following verse.

ब्रह्मादिस्तम्बपर्यन्ता मृषामात्रा उपाधयः ।
ततः पूर्णं स्वमात्मानं पश्येदेकात्मना स्थितम् ॥३८७॥

387. Right from Brahma to the most insignificant unicellular organism, all conditionings are quite unreal. Therefore, One should realise one's Self as the only existent Principle.

Stamba-paryantah[3]--From the Creator down to the most insignificant thing created --all are delusory appearances, they being limiting adjuncts *(upadhis)*. They are all unreal and belong to the realm of matter. From the stand-point of the Infinite, the realm of matter exists not. For the waker, the dream has no real existence. The call of *Acharya* Sankara to *sadhaks* in this verse is, "Come to experience *(pasyeth)*, your own Atman, which ever remains as the one Self in all (Eka-atmanaa-sthitam)."

---

1. कुसूलः = यत्र धान्यराशिः संश्रीयतेसः महापरिमाणः the ample bosom of a barn in which large quantiites of grain are stored

2. For the terms BMI, PFT, OET see foot-note verse 124.

3. स्तंबः अणीयान् जन्तुः, स पर्यन्तः अवधिः येषां ते = स्तंबपर्यन्ता : *Stamba* means an insignificant unicellular organism; upto this lowest expression of life in the scale of evolution -Stamba-paryantah.

In the following verse we have a conclusive and quite a persuastive analogy to drive home the idea that apart from Brahman there is nothing real in the world of plurality.

यत्र भ्रान्त्या कल्पितं तद्विवेके
तत्तन्मात्रं नैव तस्माद्विभिन्नम् ।
भ्रान्तेर्नाशे भ्रान्ति दृष्टाहितत्त्वं
रज्जुस्तद्वद्विश्वमात्मस्वरूपम् ॥३८८॥

388. Where, by mistake, something is imagined to exist, there, on right discrimination, the Real itself is re-cognised--there is nothing other than it. With the error removed, the falsely perceived snake itself becomes the rope. So too, the entire universe is, in truth, only the *Atman.*

When the delusory misconceptions have ended, the substratum is clearly seen. The post is not seen when the ghost is *seen.* The ghost is *seen* only in delusion. When the discriminative intellect comes into action, the delusion ends and the ghost is no more *seen.* Then the substratum of the ghost, the post alone is visible. The post alone exists.

When the delusions of the BMI, PFT and OET are ended, then Reality manifests and is fully recognised. When the delusion has ended, the serpent is not seen any more, but the reality behind the serpent-- the rope-- is seen. Similarly, the world of plurality is, in reality, *Brahman* only. The world is the projection of the mind and the intellect. When they are transcended, the apprehension of the *Atman* is automatic.

स्वयं ब्रह्मा स्वयं विष्णुः स्वयमिन्द्रः स्वयं शिवः ।
स्वयं विश्वमिदं सर्वं स्वस्मादन्यन्न किञ्चन ॥३८९॥

389. The Self is Brahma, the Self is Vishnu, the Self is Indra, the Self is Siva; the Self is this entire univers. Indeed, nothing exists except the Self.

When the ghost was seen, I was threatend by its long hands, its burning eyes and its bleeding mouth. But when I discovered the post, I recognised that the burning eyes are but the post, the long hands are nothing but the post, and the bleeding mouth is also the post. In the post, there are neither the long hands, nor the burning eyes nor the bleeding mouth.

Similarly, when the mind and the intellect are transcended, and the Infinitude is experienced, one realises that the pure Self is the Creator *(Brahma)*, that the same Self appears as the Sustainer *(Vishnu)*. All the deities of the Vedic period *(Indra, Varuna* etc.) are also nothing other than the One Self. *Parameswara* is also nothing but *Brahman*. The changeable, variable world, the field of objects and beings experienced as "this-this-this", is also none other than the Self. Except the Self, no one has any existence. When you see the post, the ghost is not available. Thus, everything is, in fact, nothing but *Brahman*.

अन्तः स्वयं चापि बहिः स्वयं च
स्वयं पुरस्तात् स्वयमेव पश्चात् ।
स्वयं ह्यवाच्यां स्वयमप्युदीच्यां
तथोपरिष्टात्स्वयमप्यधस्तात् ॥३९०॥

390. The Self is within, the Self is without; the Self is in front, the Self in behind; the Self is to the south, the Self is to the north; so too It is above and below.

Everywhere there is nothing but the Self. In fact, up and down, north and south, inside and outside, front and back, etc. are all possible only with reference to the body. In reality, they are not there. Even in the experience of deep-sleep, they are not with us. Sankara is compromising to a great extent and explaining here to the intellectual student, what exactly will be the condition of the Self in experience. The idea is not* original: we hear in this verse the echo of Mundakopanishad.

---

* Mundakopanishad II-ii-11
ब्रह्मैवेदं सर्वं पुरस्ताद् ब्रह्मपश्चात् ब्रह्मदक्षिण श्चोत्तरेण च ।

तरङ्गफेनभ्रमबुद्‌बुदादि
सर्वं स्वरूपेण जलं यथा तथा
चिदेव देहाद्यहमन्तमेतत्
सर्वं चिदेवैकरसं विशुद्धम् ॥३९१॥

391. Just as the wave, the surf, the whirlpool, the bubbles etc. are all in essence nothing but water, so too, the *Chit* is everything from the body etc. to the ego. Truly, everthing is the homogenous, pure *Chit* only.

The waves, the foam, the whirlpools and the bubbles etc. are all, in reality water. Similarly, the BMI, PFT and OET are all nothing but the essence of Consciousness *(Chit-ekarasam)*. The essence of Consciousness is objectless Consciousness. The world "Consciousness" can be used only with reference to objects. The essence of Consciousness is pure and uncontaminated by the BMI, PFT and OET.* All these are only illumined by the light of Consciousness.

सदेवेदं सर्वं जगदवगतं वाङ्मनसयोः
सतोऽन्यन्नास्त्येव प्रकृतिपरसीम्नि स्थितवतः ।
पृथक् किं मृत्स्नायाः कलशघटकुम्भाद्यवगतं
वदत्येष भ्रान्तस्त्वमहमिति मायामदिरया ॥३९२॥

392. The entire universe known through speech and mind is nothing but *Brahman*. There is nothing but *Brahman*, which exists even beyond the pale of *Prakriti*. Can the pitcher, jug, pot etc. ever be anything other than the mud of which they are made? As an effect of the wine of *Maya*, the deluded man talks of "you" and "me".

Whatever exists is *Brahman*, the pure Infinite Consciousness. All that is known through the sense-organs and the mind is nothing but misinterpreted Existence. The objects of the world are known by the sense-organs; those

---

** Mundakopanishad II-ii-10.

तमेव भान्तमनुभाति सर्वं तसय भासा सर्वमिदं विभाति ।

Verily everything shines after Him who shines. This whole world is illuminated by His light.

within i.e. the emotions and thoughts are known by the mind. All of them are nothing but pure Existence *(Sat)*. The OET are nothing but the Self. Those who have transcended *Prakriti*, can apprehend the Reality. *Prakriti* is constituted of the BMI, PFT and OET. The essential Reality is beyond all these and, in the final analysis, the BMI, PFT and OET are also nothing but Reality.

Different articles made of clay are nothing but clay. Whatever is perceived as a jar, pot, bowl etc. in a potter's house is nothing but clay. No doubt they are seen as separate from each other: the jar is not the pot; the pot is not the bowl; the bowl is not the jar: but when one looks at them from the stand-point of the substratum, they are all mud and mud alone. A deluded man alone will say that they are separate. The wise man understands that they are nothing but mud in different forms.

The *Sruti* says that all are nothing but the expressions of *Brahman*. Yet we say, "I" have got a separate existence from "you", because we are, at present, drunk with the "wine of *Maya" (Maya-madiraya)*. In the drunken hallucination of the *vasanas*, we assume that we are separate from each other. We are able to recognise the pluralistic world because we do not now experience the one Narayana present everywhere. When I look through a green glass, I see everything green. In reality there is no green-ness. When one looks through one's mind-intellect equipment, one sees the world of plurality. In Narayana, there is no plurality at all.

क्रियासमभिहारेण यत्र नान्यदिति श्रुतिः ।
ब्रवीति द्वैतराहित्यं मिथ्याध्यासनिवृत्तये ॥३९३॥

393. With many predicates, *Sruti* declares the absence of duality in the phrase, "where there is nothing else" etc., in order to remove all false superimpositions.

What has been said so far is not Sankara's own opinion. In order to establish that, *Acharya* Ṣankara is quoting this verse from the relevant Upanishad.*

With such statements the scriptures, at many palces, have indicated the absence of all duality in the Ultimate Truth. It all amounts to an assertion that *Brahman* is the only Reality. We have projected this pluralistic OET because of our BMI. To remove from our minds this misconception of the reality of OET, *Sruti* uses many predicates or verbs in her statement, as in the example given here.

Sankara means that the objects *perceived*, the emotions *felt*, and the thoughts *conceived* are all superimpositions upon the Reality, which alone is ever-present, everywhere.

In order to remove these superimpositions and to unveil the Reaity behind them, the scripture gives us various indications of what exactly constitutes the Infinite Truth. "There where we see nothing; hear nothing", meaning, where perception has no objects to perceive, where the mind has nothing to feel, where the intellect has nothing to think about, in those still moments of meditation, when one is neither in a condition of sleep-consciousness nor dream-consciousness, but where one is aware of the Transcendental --that State-Divine is the experience of the Infinite. In short, where the body-mind-intellect perceptions have ceased--meaning , where the ego has vanished--there Reality comes into vision. The state of spiritual awakening is indivated as the Truth. This is the ultimate goal of all seekers, wherein the individual ego *disappears into the vision* of the trascendental Reality.

आकाशवन्निर्मलनिर्विकल्पं
निःसीमनिःस्पन्दननिर्विकारम् ।

---

* यत्रनान्यत्पश्यति नान्यत्श्रुणोति नान्यद्विजानाति तद् भूमा ।
"Where one sees nothing else, hears nothing else, knows nothing else, -that is the Infinite". - Chhandogya VII-xxiv-i.

अन्तर्बहिःशून्यमनन्यमद्वयं
स्वयं परं ब्रह्म किमस्ति बोध्यम् ॥३९४॥

394. Like the sky, the supreme *Brahman* is untainted absolute, limitless, motionless and without modifications; it has neither an inside nor an outside; it is One Existence and Non-dual and is one's own Self. Is there any other "thing to be known?"

Hereafter, for more than a couple of verses, Sankara tries to give us the technique by which the mind can be brought into this State of Divine quietude, when the Highest can be achieved. A mere theoretical explanation of such a possibility would become a mere Utopian idea. The Aryans have no patience with such dreams. So everywhere in the scriptures, after such deep and subtle statements of Truth, the Teacher invariably gives elaborate guideliness on the know-how and technique by which such a high state can be gained in experience.

Here too, the Truth that has been indicated in the previous verse is too incomprehensible for the human intellect. Therefore, Sankara tries to give the exact methods by which a quietened mind, through contemplation, can come to experience this great State. To contemplate upon this great Truth is called *Nididhyasana.* Very rarely we find in the Upanishadic lore, a complete and exhaustive explanation of "contemplation and meditation" *(nididhyasana)*, though the Rishis invariably give us elaborate explanations of "listening to the scriptures" *(sravana)*, and "reflection upon them" *(manana)*.

Whenever they expound the technique of meditation, however, they only expound the external adjustments necessary at the body and the environmental levels. But how actually to apply the single-pointed mind in contemplation upon that which is indicated by the scriptures, is a technique which is very rarely dealt with by them. It is not because the Teacher wants to keep them a secret, but because it is impossible to communicate what exactly is to be done at the mental and intellectual levels in the seat of meditation. It is extremely subjective. Here, Sankara with his poetry and dramatisation has, to a very large extent brought out what exactly should be the line of contemplation in the seat of meditation.

Here the nature of Brahman has been depicted. This is not for mere reading, nor for continuous repetition. It is to help us lift our minds to the experience.

This great Reality is, like space, without any impurities or disturbances. In your mind, imagine yourself as the pure state, where there is nothing to limit you .... unlimited ....illimitable.......infinite space, where there is no other object to condition you ....infinite in dimension ....without activity......without any change *(nirvikaram)* The changes that take place in* the relative world are birth, growth, decay, and dissolution. These changes can take place only in the realm of time to limited objects only. In the Infinite, no changes is ever possible.

Again, in It there cannot be any modification within or without. The concepts of "within" and "without" are only with relation to the body. When we have transcended the body, there can only be one homogenous experience of the non-dual Reality. It is without any of those things of the world which we can point out as objects. It is an objectless state of pure Awareness. It is Self-evident. It is the supreme *Brahman.* Having known this, what else is there to know?

वक्तव्यं किमु विद्यतेऽत्र बहुधा ब्रह्मैव जीवः स्वयं
ब्रह्मैतज्जगदाततं नु सकलं ब्रह्माद्वितीयं श्रुतिः ।
ब्रह्मैवाहमिति प्रबुद्धमतयः संत्यक्तबाह्याः स्फुटं
ब्रह्मीभूय वसन्ति सन्ततचिदानन्दात्मनैतद्ध्रुवम् ॥३९५॥

* Brith *(utpatti)*; growth; *(vriddhi)*; decay *(nase)*; and dissolution *(vilaya)*......these are the common modifications through which all living creatures constantly pass, one of them has its own store of sorrow and tears to give to the creatures.

395. What is the use of enlarging upon this subject? The *jeeva* is nothing but *Brahman;* the whole expanse of this universe is nothing but *Brahman. Sruti* points out *Brahman* as being non-dual; and it is an undeniable fact that those who are enlightened, who have established their identity with *Brahman* and who have given up their associations with the outside world, live ever in union with *Brahman*, Eternal Knowledge and Bliss.

Acharya Sankara himself has given us the quintessence of the *Adwaita* philosophy in half a verse.* In the State of pure Awareness when the Infinite is experience, at that "moment of awakening", the experiences that we have had at the body, mind and intellect levels, should necessarily be looked upon as illusions when we functioned through those equipments. The world of plurality *is not unreal.* But, interpreted through our equipments at that moment, it *is not Real.* At such a moment, the egocentric entity disowns itself and therefore, the ego is experienced as nothing but *Brahman;* just as the dreamer re-discovers himself to be the waker.

In this Great Infinte Experience, what more remains to be said? Meaning, there is nothing more to express. No other discussion is possible in That which is Non-dual. At that moment the meditator awakens to understand that he is none other than the pure, infinite Consciousness. This *Bhrahman* alone is the essence of which the world of plurality is constituted, just as the waking mind itself is the material cause for all the objects of the dream cosmos. *Sruti* herself has so often repeated that *Brahman* is non-dual and One-without-a-second.**

For that wise man who has awakened through study and reflection to this great Truth expounded in the *Upanishads*-- " I am *Brahman*"-- there is nothing more to discuss. All

---

*श्लोकार्धेन प्रवक्ष्यामि यदुक्तं ग्रंथकोटिभिः।
ब्रह्मसत्यं जगन्मिथ्या जीवो ब्रह्मैव नापरः ।

That which is described by millions of books, I shall explain in half a verse; ; "*Brahman* alone is Real. the phenomenal world is an illusion; the individual ego is nothing other than Brahman."

** "तत्वमसि" - "अयमात्मा ब्रह्म" - "इदं सर्वं यदयमात्मा" - "आत्मैवेदं सर्वं" - "एकमेवाद्वितीयं" --etc. etc.

discussions are only in the relative field. When the wise man through discrimination and renunciation has transcended the world of plurality --has already rejected the perceptions, emotions and thoughts--and when he has entered this unique experience--what is there for him to talk about? Such a wise man therafter lives, becoming one with Brahman, *(Brahmabhooya)*. Awakened to the plane of supreme Consciousness, indeed, he remains ever steadfast in this great Truth. He has awakened and understood that he himself is *Brahman*.

जहि मलमयकोशेऽहंधियोत्थापिताशां
प्रसभमनिलकल्पे लिङ्गदेहेऽपि पश्चात् ।
निगमगदितकीर्तिं नित्यमानन्दमूर्तिं ।
स्वयमिति परिचीय ब्रह्मरूपेण तिष्ठ ॥३९६॥

396. Annihilate the hopes raised by the ego in the gross body, a bundle of filth; then, with force, do the same with the air-like subtle body. Realising *Brahman*--the personification of eternal Bliss, which the scriptures eulogise--as your own Self, live as *Brahman*.

Leave the idea of "I am......" in this body which is a bundle of faecal matter, so beautifully and enchantingly packed.* Leave the vulgar sensuous desires arising from this bundle of filth. Then go beyond the air-like subtle-body. The mind and intellect are said to be air-like because the thoughts are ever flying all over. Transcend the mind and the intellect. Realise that your nature is that of the eternal Bliss which has been glorified in the scriptures. Understand that you are nothing but *Brahman*. Come to the study of *Vedanta*, determined to experience that you are That. Thus remain and revel in the world as *Brahman*. Thereafter, let the body act and fulfill its own destiny-scheme, *parabdha*.

---

* In an earlier verse (289), Sankara has already said,
पिण्डाण्डं त्यज्यतां मलभाण्डवत् ॥

शवाकारं यावद्भजति मनुजस्तावदशुचिः
परेभ्यः स्यात्क्लेशो जननमरणव्याधिनिलयः ।
यदात्मानं शुद्धं कलयति शिवाकारमचलम्
तदा तेभ्यो मुक्तो भवति हि तदाह श्रुतिरपि ॥३९७॥

397. As long as man worships his corpse-like body, he is impure and suffers from "others" and from birth, death and disease. But when he thinks of himself as the Pure, the Auspicious, the Immovable, certainly he becomes free from them--the *Srutis* also testify to this.

As long as man identifies with his physical body, composed entirely of matter and so, lifeless in itself *(shavakara)*, he is impure. Even after taking a bath and applying powder and perfume to the body it remains impure. As long as you identify with it by doing its "pooja" --washing it, powdering it, dressing it,--you too are impure. A scavenger you are, as long as you carry this filth and polish this body-bucket*. Naturally, therefore, when you identify with it, you will suffer a thousand clashes from "others", and you suffer from yourself too. Objectively you suffer because of the clashes with other objects and subjectively you suffer from the sequence of the sorrows produced by birth, growth, disease, decay and death. These five pain-ridden stages of unavoidable modifications must come to every physical body.

You will be rid of these sorrows only when you realise the Truth. When the Truth is realised, you become the immovable substratum that stays behind all moveable, changeable and variable substances. You become "the embodiment of auspiciousness" *(Shivakara)*. Then alone are you liberated from all sufferings. This is the unanimous declaration of the Upanishads.**

---

* This does not mean that one should not keep the body clean. Regular cleanliness is a must. But let not its beautification be your sole preoccupation--do not, ever, *equate* yourself with this contemptible, dross, producer of foul matter.

** तरतिशोकं आत्मवित्" ।

"आनन्दं ब्रह्मणोविद्वान् न बिभेति कुतश्चन ॥

"One who has come to know the *Atman*, crosses over all sorrows."
"One who has experienced the *Brahman* as Bliss Itself, knows no fear."

66. No Diversity in Reality. (398-406)

स्वात्मन्यारोपिताशेषाभासवस्तुनिरासतः ।
स्वयमेव परं ब्रह्म पूर्णमद्वयमक्रियम् ॥३९८॥

398. When the apparent existences super-imposed on the Self are removed, then what remains is the supreme *Brahman*, the Infinite, Non-dual, that which is beyond all activities, alone, all by itself.

When all the delusory projections--the BMI, PFT and OET --have been negated, what remains is the Self. When these have been transcended, the realisation is, "I am the supreme *Brahman*". This realisation is the awakening to the higher plane of Consciousness, the *Atman*.

When the "ghost" and the details of the "ghost" have been negated, what remains is the the post in all its original splendour. *Brahman* is realised as one's own Self. It is non-dual, with no other-ness in It. There is no activity ever possible in It because It is All-pervading.

These ideas are very often repeated by Sankara, so that the student may catch them and their total effect, which ends in the comprehension of the Transcendental Reality, the Light of Life.

समाहितायां सति चित्तवृत्तौ
परात्मनि ब्रह्मणि निर्विकल्पे ।
न दृश्यते कश्चिदयं विकल्पः
प्रजल्पमात्रः परिशिष्यते यतः ॥३९९॥

399. When the functions of the mind, the thoughts, have merged in the *Paramatman*, the *Brahman*, the Absolute, then this phenomenal world is not perceived. Then all becomes mere talk.

When the thought-flow is quietened in the contemplation of *Brahman*, the pluralistic phenomenal world cannot be perceived even a little. The world of turbulation is in the mind.

When the mind is transcended, it is not available at all. From the watchtower of the supreme Reality, the varieties of imaginations are all mere talk *(prajalpa-matrah)*, a meaningless prattle of words.

While dreaming, a man shouts in his dream-fear "Oh, Oh.....save me .....please save ...." But those who are sitting in the room have no fear at all. They say, "Save you? From what? You save yourself". Sometimes when you are thus shouting in your dream, you wake up. You hear your-self crying out, then you stop. For you the cry then is a mere meaningless sound. Similarly, the pluralistic phenomenal world will not be experienced in the plane of pure Consciousness. All talk is the prattle of an ignorant man-- ignorant of his true, divine spiritual nature.

All that was said till then, including *Vedanta*, becomes a mad twaddle to cure the madness of others. Stop the mental processes and functions and "see" the divine Essence as your own Self-this is the incessant cry of Sankara.

Now Acharya Sankara, in a few verses, is advising and indicating to us the total non-existence (Atyanta-asatwam) of plurality.

असत्कल्पो विकल्पोऽयं विश्वमित्येकवस्तुनि ।
निर्विकारे निराकारे निर्विशेषे भिदा कुतः ॥४००॥

400. In the One Reality, the conception of the universe is a mere fancy. How can there be any diversity in the Changeless, the Formless, the Absolute?

Anubhava, yukti, drishtant and *sruti* are the four methods of teaching *Vedanta*. Through all the four methods *Acharya* Sankara is indicating to us that duality does not exist at all.*

---

* सकलवेदान्त तात्पर्यविषयं अनुभवयुक्ति दृष्टान्तश्रुतिभिः
द्वैतस्य अत्यन्त असत्वं उपदिशति आचार्यः ॥
Through direct experience *(anubhava)*, logical reasoning *(yukti)*, examples *(drishanta)* and scriptural statements *(sruti)*, *Acharya* Sankara points here the utter falsity of duality - the essential conclusion of all Vedanta.

The endless varieties of fancied names and forms and their mutual quarrels are all non-existent. That One Reality is without change *(nirvikara)*, without from *(nirakara)*, and Absolute *(nirvisesha)*. In such a Divine Entity how can there be any diversity? Since there cannot be any plurality, this entire phenomenal world is non-existent, at best an illusion of the mind in trumoil.

द्रष्टृदर्शनदृश्यादि भावशून्यैकवस्तुनि ।
निर्विकारे निराकारे निर्विशेषे भिदा कुतः ॥४०१॥

401. In the One Reality which is without the seer, the seeing and the seen etc., which is the Changeless, Formless, Absolute, how can there be any diversity?

For the terms "seer"*(drashta)*,"seeing"*(darṣana)*, and "seen " *(drishya)*, the synonyms often used in Vedanta are, "seer" *(pramata)*, seeing" *(pramiti)*, "seen" *(prameya)*, and "the instrument of seeing *(pramana)*.

There where there is no distinction between these, in that which is the substratum of all these seeming distinctions, in that Changeless, Formless, Absolute Reality, how can there be any plurality?

कल्पार्णव इवात्यन्तपरिपूर्णैकवस्तुनि ।
निर्विकारे निराकारे निर्विशेषे भिदा कुतः ॥४०२॥

402. In that One Reality which is All-pervading and Motionless, like the ocean after the dissolution of the universe, which is the Changeless, Formless, Absolute, how can there be any diversity?

In a deluge, when there is water everywhere, how can can there be any distinction? The waters of the Atlantic, the waters of the Pacific, the waters of the river and the tank, the waters of the well and the tumbler--these difference cannot exist where there is only water everywhere-unlimited, unconditioned.

In that supreme All pervading Reality which is without change, without form, which is Absolute, how can there be any diversity?

In the state of sleep, though there is no perception of plurality *(bheda-abhavam)*, yet there the cause for pluralistic perception, the spiritual non-apprehension *(avidya)* exists. In the moments of full apprehension of Reality there is a total annihilation of *avidya*.

This is brought out in the following verse.

तेजसीव तमो यत्र प्रलीनं भ्रान्तिकारणम् ।
अद्वितीये परे तत्त्वे निर्विशेषे भिदा कुतः ॥४०३॥

403. How can there be any diversity in the supreme Reality which is Non-dual and Absolute, where the very root of delusion dissolves, like darkness into light?

How can there be plurality in the Infinite? How can there be differences in the Changeless? How can there be distinctions in the Formless? How can there be diversity in the Absolute? They are all impossible dreams.

In the Absolute, all names and forms which constitute the world of plurality are absorbed: just as the dream objects are absorbed in the waking consciousness. It is impossible for the waker to continue to see the dream *also*. In the infinite Consciousness, there is neither the perceiver, nor the feeler nor the thinker. Therefore, there are no such distinctions as objects, emotions and thoughts. The very ego is not there to perceive the plurality. Where the ego has ended, the perception of plurality must also end. It merges into the infinite Experience, which is present everywhere, at all times.

Once there is light, the darkness is completely lifted. Similarly, when ignorance has lifted, Reality must rise in our experience. *Avidya*, is removed with the apprehension of Truth How can there be any plurality at any time in that Supreme, Non-dual, Absolute Reality?

एकात्मके परे तत्त्वे भेदवार्ता कथं वसेत् ।
सुषुप्तौ सुखमात्रायां भेदः केनावलोकितः ॥४०४॥

404. In the One, the Supreme Reality, how can there be any talk of diversity? Who can ever observe any diversity in the total bliss of deep-sleep?

That state is pure which has no other thing in it but itself. In the state of supreme Consciousness, there are no equipments of experience and, therefore, there cannot be an experiencer of the objects. All these merge to be the One Infinite Consciousness. There the "field" *(kshetra)*, and the "knower of the field" *(kshetrajna)*, become one.

In deep-sleep, there is only one experience, sheer bliss. That experience is One-without-a-second. In deep-sleep the mind and intellect are temporarily not functioning. Therefore, no distinctions can be made, no differences recognised. All is Bliss. In it there is no *other-ness*. How then, can there be any plurality in the infinite Reality, where the mind and intellect have been transcended, once and for all? The world of OET is interpreted by the equipments of our BMI. Where the BMI are not. there the OET can never be.

न ह्यस्ति विश्वं परतत्त्वबोधात्
सदात्मनि ब्रह्मणि निर्विकल्पे ।
कालत्रये नाप्यहिरीक्षितो गुणे
न ह्यम्बुबिंदुर्मृगतृष्णिकायाम् ॥४०५॥

405. Even before realisation of the supreme Truth, the universe does not exist in the Absolute *Brahman*, the quintessence of Existence. Never in the three periods of time is the snake in the rope, nor a drop of water in the mirage.

The BMI, PFT and OET, all put together constitute the universe *(viswam)*. Once the supreme Truth is gained, this world can never be . The confusing equipments of the BMI are not in the transcendental Reality. The world of OET cannot be in the highest plane of Consciousness. When one has awakened to that Reality, *avidya* cannot be there.

The serpent was never actually there in the rope in the past, nor is it there in the present nor shall it ever be there in the future. The rope is ever a rope; never has it been a serpent at any time. If you see a serpent in a rope, it is only because of your ignorance of the rope. Never can there be even a tiny drop of water in the mirage. Similarly, in Brahman, there can never actually be a universe of names and forms *(viswam)*.

मायामात्रमिदं द्वैतमद्वैतं परमार्थतः ।
इति ब्रूते श्रुतिः साक्षात्सुषुप्तावनुभूयते ॥४०६॥

406. The scriptures directly declare* that all duality is nothing but *Maya*, the Reality alone is the Absolute Truth. Such also is the experience in deep-sleep.

The pluralistic phenomena that we recognise is only an illusion *(Maya-matram-idam-dwaitam)*. The ultimate Reality is One without-a-second *(Adwaitam-paramaarthatah)*.

Brahman alone is. The perceived world of plurality is only a projection. This is the declaration of the *Upanishads*. It is also the direct experience of everybody. In deep-sleep, you experience the absence of plurality. If the world is true, it should be available at all times. That which is available at all times is called "Truth". That which has a beginning and an end cannot be Real.

A delusory nothingness is the world of plurality.

67. Atma-vichara: Contemplation. (407-413)

अनन्यत्वमधिष्ठानादारोप्यस्य निरीक्षितम् ।
पण्डिते रज्जुसर्पादौ विकल्पो भ्रान्तिजीवनः ॥४०७॥

---

* Kathopanishad IV-11.
Brihadaranyakopanishad II-iv-14.
Mundakopanishad II-ii-11.
Chhandogyopanishad VI-xiv.
Maṇḍukya-Karika I-i.

407. The wise have observed that the superimposition is identical with its sub-stratum--just as the rope and the snake. The difference exists only because of delusion.

A projection upon a substratum has no existence apart form the substratum. The superimposed snake is not separate form the rope. The ghost and the post, the silver in the mother-of-pearl, are examples. The silvery shine has no existence apart from the shell. It is not different at all *(ananya)*. The chain cannot exist apart from the gold. The pot has no existence independent of the mud.

The world of phenomena too, cannot exist apart from Brahman. You look at God all the time and ask, "Where is God?"

The wise man never sees any distinctions in the world, for it is world, for it is but *Brahman (Brahma-mayam-jagat)* The serpent in the rope is only a product of delusion.

Truly, this world is great lunatic asylum without walls.

The way out of it is explained in the following verse.

In three verses--408, 409 and 410--the Teacher is trying to express the Inexpressible by communicating to us the ecstasy of his own lived experiences--the mad revelry of his Bliss.

चित्तमूलो विकल्पोयं चित्ताभावे न कश्चन ।
अतश्चित्तं समाधेहि प्रत्यग्रूपे परात्मनि ॥४०८॥

408. The apparent universe has its root in the mind and cannot exist once the mind is annihilated. Therefore, dissolve the mind by fixing it on the most subjective supreme Self.

At present, all of us are suffering because of the vagaries of the mind. We want to get out of this mental turmoil. The mind turned outwards and gushing out is the *Chitta.* The manifestation of this world is from the *Chitta* only. Whenever the mind is not running out, there is no pluralistic world. To get out of this madness, the mind that is constantly running out has to be quietened. Do not allow it to sprout out. If it does, the world is, of course, real. It will give you on a silver plate, in a golden cup all its poisonous sorrows. If you want the pure Bliss and Beatitude of *Brahman*, you have to end this world. In order to do so, quieten the mind in the contemplation of the supreme Self which is your innermost core.

Thus, turn inward---this is the only method by which you can get out of this mad world. Sit down and consciously withdraw your mind as though in sleep and experience that stage where there is no object, emotion or thought. That conscious sleep is called *Samadhi* In sleep, though there is no perception of the outer world, and hence no misapprehension, there is neverthless, a blinding non-apprehension. When you *consciously* sleep, there is no non-apprehension either, only a complete apprehension of Reality.

किमपि सततबोधं केवलानन्दरूपं
निरुपममतिवेलं नित्यमुक्तं निरीहम् ।
निरवधिगगनाभं निष्कलं निर्विकल्पं
हृदि कलयति विद्वान् ब्रह्म पूर्णं समाधौ ॥४०९॥

409. Through *Samadhi*, the wise man realised the infinite *Brahman* in his heart as something (inexplicably) of the essence of eternal Knowledge and complete Bliss, which is unparalleled, which is beyond all limitations, which is ever free, which has no activity and which is indivisible and absolute like the limitless sky.

During *Samadhi*, the wise man realises in his heart, eternal knowledge which is of the nature of pure Bliss. We cannot explain It, because It is indescribable. *Sruti* says, "There is nothing like It" *(na-tatra-pratima-asti)*, anywhere in the range of our experiences today. Therefore, it is incomparable *(nirupamam)*.It transcends all limits *(ativelam)*. It is a state which is everfree. Never has It ever been limited.

It is a state where there are no activities, physical, mental, or intellectual. Such a state is called *niriham*. It is a state unconditioned by place, time or other things *(kalatah, deshatah, vastutah, antah soonyam)*. It is a limitless state *(niravadhi)* like space. A factor which is unconditioned by* time, place or objects can only be compared with space. Therefore, Sankara uses the simile- "like space", *(gaganabham)*.

That which has no parts : Nishkalam, *niravyayam*.

Not only has It no limbs, but It also has no thought-disturbances: *(nirvikalpam)*. In *Samadhi*, a wise man comes to experience this state of complete and full Reality *(Brahma-poornam)*.

प्रकृतिविकृतिशून्यं भावनातीतभावं
समरसमसमानं मानसम्बन्धदूरम् ।
निगमवचनसिद्धं नित्यमस्मत्प्रसिद्धं
हृदि कलयति विद्वान् ब्रह्म पूर्णं समाधौ ॥४१०॥

410. Through *Samadhi*, the wise man realises the infinite *Brahman* in his heart, as devoid of the concepts of cause and effect, as the Reality beyond all fancy, as homogenous and matchless, beyond all proofs, established by the declarations of the scriptures, always ingrained in us as the ego.

Having expressed what is inexpressible in the previous verse, the Teacher feels that he has not fully and efficiently communicated his experiences to the student. So he continues, moulding it in yet another brilliant set of words.

Matter *(Prakriti)*. Its various modifications *(vikriti)*. *Prakriti-vikriti-soonyam* is the state where there is neither matter (BMI), nor its various modifications (OET). So it is a state transcending all the equipments and their experiences. It is beyond all intellection *(bhavanateeta-bhavam)*, meaning, a state which lies beyond the comprehension of the intellect.

---

* Vide verses 384, 385.

The experience of Infinitude in the past, Its experience in the present and Its experience to come in the future, is the same for all periods of time. Therefore it is called, *samarasam.* Whether It is experienced by a Brahmin or a non-Brahmin, by a sinner or a saint, it is at all times and under all conditions, the same.

Nothing comparable to it: *(A-samanam)*--- It is without any contact with anything. It is a state which is without exemplar. It is beyond all proofs *(A-prameyam).* If there be a Truth which is beyond the comprehension of the intellect, which cannot be understood by logic, which cannot be percieved by the body, which is beyond description, how can one come to understand It? Sankara says, "It is established by the declaration of the Vedas." The Upanishadic declarations are the only stars which will help the student on his voyage.

Still the student may doubt whether it is possible for an individual to strive on, with a blind belief arising from his reverence to the *Upanishads.* Here the Teacher confirms with the heroism and courage of his own conviction that this is the Truth which has been experienced by all wise men. This is an experience that is lived constantly by "people like us", *(asmat-prasiddham).* It is experienced by the wise in *Samadhi.* In the state of *Samadhi,* the ego merges into the Infinite; the intellect *(dheeh),* of the meditator becomes "equal" *(sama),* where thought currents completely dry up.

Having explained this inexpressible state in these two verses, Sankara feels choked and dissatisfied and therefore, out of his infinite love for the disciple, he tries to indicate in yet another verse, what exactly is the state of Knowledge in which the man of Perfection lives, when he is plunged in utter meditation.

अजरममरमस्ताभाववस्तुस्वरूपं
स्तिमितसलिलराशिप्रख्यमाख्याविहीनम् ।

शमितगुणविकारं शाश्वतं शान्तमेकं
हृदि कलयति विद्वान् ब्रह्म पूर्ण समाधौ ॥४११॥

411. Through *Samadhi*, the wise man realises the infinite *Brahman* in his heart as undecaying and immortal, as the positive Entity which debars all negations, which is like a calm ocean, which has no name, in which there are neither merits nor demerits, which is eternal, tranquil and One.

This great Truth is undecaying *(apakshaya-soonyam)* and immortal *(nasha-rahitam)*. In that state where all thoughts have set *(astaabhava)*,* the student lives vitally the experience of Reality *(Vastu)*. All words used in wordly parlance are of no use there, hence It is the nameless state. It has no properties and cannot be indicated by name or word. This state which is indescribable in terms of words, the Teacher can indicate only by giving us an analogy. Each student will understand it only according to his capacity. If the student has the necessary mental tranquility and the intellectual purity to fly to the heights that Sankara is indicating, if he has the courage to take the plunge, it is impossible for such a student ever to fail to "understand" this great state.

The example given is, *stimita-salila-rasi-prakhyam*---it is as though all the waves of the ocean have suddenly stopped at the magic wave of a wand, as though they have been stunned into freezing.

This cannot be understood unless you are imaginative enough to visualise yourself on one of those solitary, uninhabited little islands in the Pacific, where, up to the horizon, all you can see is the seething, dancing, rolling, jumping, frisking waves. The clamour of their enthusiasm is noisily pulsating in all directions. When you have sufficiently imagined such a condition of dreadful awe and magnitude, imagine that all the waves have suddenly stopped. Likewise, when the meditating seeker has quietened his mind, intellect

---

* There is another reading where अस्ताभाव is read as अस्ताभास (Astaa-bhasa) which means "where all illusions have ended."

and sense agitations, all the pulsations caused by his *vasanas* come to a quiescence. And in that inner quiet, he comes to experience the Consciousness wherein all expression of thought *(vikara)* is quietened. *Gunas* qualify the *vasanas*. *Vasanas* manifesting at the mental level are called thoughts.

That which is beyond thought is naturally permanent since It is not conditioned by time as Time itself is a concept of the intellect. Since all that can be conceived by the intellect alone can be conditioned by time, that which transcends the intellect is unconditioned by time---It has to be Permanent.

Restlessness *(a-shantam)* is because of the disturbances in our inner Peace. The Self transcends the mind and so Its condition is devoid of the turmoil of the mind. It is therefore indicated here as *shantam*.

The One *(Ekam)*---this great Truth which is the state of pure infinite Consciousness, is experienced by the wise man.

When the second reading, *astabhasa*, is taken, it will mean "when all illusory perceptions have ended". When it is read as *astabhava*, it means "there where all *abhavas* have ended". According to the Nyaya philosophy, two kinds of *abhavas* are possible. *Abhava* means, "non-existence". The existence of a pot is only when it actually exists. But before its creation the pot was not there. The non-existence of the pot before it manifested is known as *prakabhava*. When the pot is destroyed, thereafter, again there is non-existence of the pot. This non-existence of the pot after it has been destroyed is called *pradhvamsabhava*. In Brahman, there is neither *prak-abhava*, nor *pradhvamsabhava*, meaning there was no time when the Self was not (when the ego arose), nor will a time ever come when the Self will not be (even after the ego has "set"). The ego is only a play of illusion upon the Reality which is the essential Truth. Truth was, is and shall ever be.

Both readings are acceptable and both have their significance.

In the three inimitable verses given above, having enumerated the exact experiences of a man in Samadhi, the author has given us the method of meditation. He has given a scheme where the mind is instructed as to what it should contemplate upon, and how. Now the Teacher continues.

समाहितान्तःकरणः स्वरूपे
विलोकयात्मानखण्डवैभवम् ।
विच्छिन्द्धि बन्धं भवगन्धगन्धितं
यत्नेन पुंस्त्वं सफलीकुरुष्व ॥४१२॥

412. With a controlled mind, in *Samadhi*, see in you own Self, the *Atman* of undying splendour. Cut off your bondages which have been strengthened by the impressions of your previous births and successfully strive to realise the fulfilment of a human birth.

Having quietened the mind and the intellect, (inner equipment : *antahkarana)*, come to experience the endless glory of this Self. In order to experience this, destroy all your contacts with the obnoxious odour of worldly contact, meaning, withdraw yourself from all your identifications with the objects, the body, the mind and the intellect, all of which are created as a result of the *vasanas*. So then, *bhava-gandha-gandhitam* means, *samsar-vasana-vasitam* i.e., *agyana.* Detach yourself completely from worldly life, stinking with the foul odour of change and sensuality. This cannot be done easily. A lot of effort has to be made. Hence the Teacher says, *yatnena*, by striving. Constantly be at it until you are redeemed from all the attachments with the world around. Thus fulfil your man-hood, your human birth, your goal of life. Fulfil the very programme of evolution.

This verse has a strong flavour of the thoughts expressed in the Bhavavad Geeta.* "Not only must it be intellectually understood, but thereafter it must become your very own".

* एतद् बुध्वा बुद्धिमान्स्यात् कृतकृत्यश्च भारत ।
--Bhagavad Geeta XV-20.

You must get involved, nay, even committed to this way of life. The same insistence of the Geeta is echoed in this verse without losing its emphasis.

सर्वोपाधिविनिर्मुक्तं सच्चिदानन्दमद्वयम् ।
भावयात्मानमात्मस्थं न भूयः कल्पसेऽध्वने ॥४१३॥

413. Meditate upon that *Atman* which is your Self, which is beyond all limitations, which is Existence-Knowledge-Bliss-Absolute, and Non-dual. Never will you come under the sway of births and deaths.

Liberating yourself from all the equipments (the BMI, or the gross, subtle and causal bodies), meditate upon the non-dual Existence-Knowledge-Bliss which is your own Self. Meditation, thus, consists of two aspects; 1) a total withdrawal from the equipments and their interpretations, and 2) turning the entire quietened mind to the contemplation of the Self which is of the nature of pure Bliss. As a result of such deep and serene contemplation in the hushed silence of the mind, you awake to the Higher. Such an individual will never return to the realm of births and deaths. No more will he be crushed by the wheel of change. In all the *Upanishads* we find the insistence that having awakened to the Infinite there is no return, there is no change ever again possible.

It is evident that this verse echoes the thoughts which were already there in the *Upanishads* and the Bhagavad Geeta.*

68. Give Up Perceptions. (414-418)

छायेव पुंसः परिदृश्यमान-
माभासरूपेण फलानुभूत्या ।

---

* नसःपुनरावर्तते (Upanishad)
मामुपेत्यतु कौन्तेय पुनर्जन्म न विद्यते । (Bhagavad Geeta).

शरीरमाराच्छववन्निरस्तं
पुनर्न संधत्त इदं महात्मा ॥४१४॥

414. Once the body has been cast off like a corpse, the wise man does not attach himself to it, though, like man's shadow, it is still visible, owing to the effects of past actions.

A man of Realisation has a metal attitude towards the world and himself which is almost an antithesis of our estimate of the world and himself which is almost an antithesis of our estimate of the world and our body. We consider that beyond the body we have no existence at all and in this plane of consciousness we have no field of experience other than the world of OET. So the world and the equipments are the only reality we know. At the moment, the nature of Reality is, to us, most unreal. This is an antithesis of the experience of the man of Realisation. Sankara brings this into relief in this verse.

This physical body which is apparent *(pari-drisya-manam)*, is negated by the man of Realisation. He ignores it as he would his own shadow. We do not consider our shadow as anything sacred. What does it matter if it is dragged along on the stones and over ponds? Even if the head of my shadow is in the ditcn, I do not feel suffocated, nor do I become dirty. Similarly, my body is something other than me and it is as much related to me as the shadow is to my body. No doubt, the shadow arises from the body. If there is no body there cannot be a shadow. We can safely say that the shadow is caused by the body. Similarly, we can say that this body is caused by the Self, the *Atman*. But the relationship between the *Atman* and the body is only as intimate as that between the human body and its shadow. So, to a good meditator who contemplates deeply and who has learnt the art of withdrawing his Consciousness totally from his physical body, his physical body is, as it were, a shadow of the Self. It is nothing but a dream-form, an illusion which has arisen in his Consciousness that he may experience the reactions of his past actions, including his state of *Samadhi*.

Such a man of Realisation considers his body as a disgusting corpse. Like a dead body he rejects it as something unholy, to be discarded and destroyed. Having rejected the body which is an illusion, as disgusting, awful and unholy, the *Mahatma* who has realised the Self, no more comes back to identify with it.

सततविमलबोधानन्दरूपं समेत्य
त्यज जडमलरूपोपाधिमेतं सुदूरे ।
अथ पुनरपि नैष स्मर्यतां वान्तवस्तु
स्मरणविषयभूतं कल्पते कुत्सनाय ॥४१५॥

415. Eternal, unsullied, Knowledge-Bliss- thus realising the *Atman*, fling far away this body which is inert and filthy. Then think of it no more, for a thing vomited brings disgust to the mind when remembered.

Having reached this ever-pure Knowledge, this Bliss-nature of yours, throw far away this inert and filthy body. Do not identify with it any more, nor cater to its sense-gratificational urges. Thereafter, do not ever remember the existence of this body. If at all, at acertain moments due to the pressure of your past *vasanas*, the body comes back to your cognition, with its satisfactions or passions, Sankara details what should be the attitude of a man of Perfection towards these flashes of recognition of the physical body. He says, "Like something you have vomited out *(Vanta-vastu)*", --let this remembrance bring but revulsion to the mind. Nobody likes to see what he has vomited. Similarly, once the body, mind and intellect have been rejected, do not ever remember them again. If at all the remembrance comes to you, let it be accompanied by a feeling of extreme revulsion.

In the last two verses, Sankara was exphasising the idea that the man of Perfection never cares for his body. He has nothing but abhorrence for the body-concept whenever it appears in his cognition. The same idea is extended in the next two verses, and Sankara tries to give the logic behind it. Why a man of Perfection develops an attitude of utter negligence and supreme indifference towards his physical existence has been explained in this verse.

समूलमेतत्परिदह्य वन्हौ
सदात्मनि ब्रह्मणि निर्विकल्पे ।
ततः स्वयं नित्यविशुद्धबोधा-
नन्दात्मना तिष्ठति विद्वरिष्ठः ॥४१६॥

416. Burning all this, root and all, in the fire of *Brahman*, the Eternal, Absolute Self, he who is truly wise remains alone, established as the pure *Atman*, Eternal Knowledge-Bliss.

Having destroyed in the fire of Knowledge the entire body-concept along with its very roots *(vasanas)*, the man of Perfection remains alone, as the Very Self. He destroys his gross-body-identification in the ecstatic and inspiring experience of awakening to the spot-less state of the inifinite Reality.

Thereafter, * the best among the men of Perfection, *(Vidvarishthah)* himself remains as the very essence of the Self. He becomes one with the Infinite which is ever pure Knowledge-Bliss. The knower of the Self *becomes* the Self. From the peaks of pure Bliss, he is no more aware of his physical body and if at all the body comes to his cognition, he has nothing but a sense of revulsion towards it, as one ould naturally have towards a disgorged thing.

प्रारब्धसूत्रग्रथितं शरीरं
प्रयातु वा तिष्ठतु गोरिव स्त्रक्
न तत्पुनः पश्यति तत्त्ववेत्ता-
ऽऽनन्दात्मनि ब्रह्मणि लीनवृत्तिः ॥४१७॥

---

* विदन्ति इति विदः। तेषां वरिष्ठः विद्वरिष्ठः।

417. This body is woven from the fibre of *prarabdha*, and the Knower of Truth is not concerned whether it drops off or remains--as the garland around the cow's neck, for his thoughts are reposed in *Brahman*, the quintessence of Bliss.

The man of Perfection considers his physical body only as something woven out of its *prarabdha*.

The body and its experiences are according to its existing *vasanas*. *Vasanas* are the foot-prints of past actions and thoughts. They determine the condition of the body, the beauty of the mind and the keenness of the intellect. It is again the *vasanas* that determine the type of environment we are in and the type of experiences we gather from the world. From the view-point of the man of Realisation, his body is a continuation of the body he had in the past, and one that has been taken up as ordered or determined by its *vasanas*. Now that he has transcended the equipments, he is content to remain in his experience of the infinite Consiciousness. Thereafter, the body may cling to him, it being a product of the past, but he cares not for it. The body is no more a source of fulfilment for him. He considers it as an excretion or like a discarded old dress and is least concerned whether it falls or remains. An individual is least concerned with the destiny of his own excretion, once it has left him. This unconcern towards the body is being described here by Sankara, by using a very powerful simile.

On the Gopashtami day, Hindus generally bathe their cow and adore and worship it. They put a garland around its neck. The garland is of no concern to the cow. It is not even conscious of it. If, because of the garland more people are looking at it, is unconcerned. If the garland breaks and falls down on the road, it is still unconcerned. Similarly, the man of Perfection strides the path of his existence considering his body as an unnecessary decoration upon him. Whether it falls or exists, it is a matter of no importance to him. He does not care. He has realised the Infinitude. He is in that awakened state. For us, the body is the only source of happiness, hence we care for its security. The man of Perfection is one who has merged himself with *Brahman*, the Infinite Bliss. Since he is always experiencing It, to him the little joys the sense-organs can bring through the body from the world outside are of no significance at all. Therefore, in that supreme state of fabulous richness that he is, he has no concern for his body.

अखण्डानन्दमात्मानं विज्ञाय स्वस्वरूपतः ।
किमिच्छन् कस्य वा हेतोर्देहं पुष्णाति तत्त्ववित् ॥४१८॥

418. Having known the *Atman* which is unbroken Bliss, to be his very own Self, with what motive or for whom is the body to be cherished by the Knower of Truth.

Continuing the same arguments for the rejection of the physical body, Sankara says, "Having realised his own essential Self to be of the nature of unbroken and infinite Bliss, then desiring what, or for what purpose should a man of Realisation fatten his body?" We fatten the body because it is the only source for our sense gratification. Seeking these little joys of life we preserve the body and try to maintain it as well as we can. But a man of Realisation who has awakened from his egocentric existence into the greater ambit of the Self and is continually experiencing the absoulte Bliss, for what purpose should he maintain the body? Or for fulfilment of which desire should he maintain it?

The term, "desiring what" *(kimichhan)*, echoes the words of the Brihadaranyaka Upanishad, where Yagnavalkya asks the same question,

आत्मानम् चेद्विजानीयाद् विजानीयाद् अयमस्मीतिपूरुषः ।
किमिच्छन कस्यकामाय शरीरमनुषज्जरेत ॥

"When one has realised one's Self to be nothing other than this great *Purusha*, this infinite *Satchidananda*, then desiring what, (or for the fulfilment of which desire), should he thereafter nurse, nourish and fatten his physical body?"

69. The Science of Reality--Its Benefits.
(419-425)

संसिद्धस्य फलं त्वेतज्जीवन्मुक्तस्य योगिनः ।
बहिरन्तः सदानन्दरसांस्वादनमात्मनि ॥४१९॥

419. The perfected *yogi* who is a *jivanmuktah*,* gets this as a result--within and without he enjoys eternal Bliss.

One who is fulfilled in life, one who has cut asunder the shackles of his finite existence as the ego, one who is no more bound by the chains of his physical passions, or mental pangs or intellectual agitations, what will he gain in life by such an experience? Sankara insists that such an individual then, constantly experiences the Bliss which is the nature of the Self, within and without. All exertions in life are only to discover happiness. Once the highest happiness is gained, other lesser objects of happiness are of no concern. Thus, through meditation, when an individual rises above the realms of disturbances and agitations and enters a realm of sweet Bliss, which manifests because of its own essential nature, he cannot then precipitate into any of the activities that we ordinarily engage in our day to day existence.

वैराग्यस्य फलं बोधो बोधस्योपरतिःफलम् ।
स्वानन्दानुभवाच्छान्तिरेषैवोपरतेःफलम् ॥४२०॥

420. The fruit of dispassion is Knowledge, that of Knowledge is withdrawal from sense pleasures. The fruit of this withdrawal is the experience of the Blissful Self, and peace is the result of this experience.

The results that will accrue to the personality as an individual starts his *sadhana* are enumerated in a logical sequence.

When an individual analyses the finite nature of the joys of the world, he comes to reject these lesser fields of

---

* Liberated-while-living.

gratification in order to gain a foot-hold in the higher realms of permanent satisfation. This detachment from the unreal is called *vairagya*. The individual then drifts away from the world of acquisition and pleasure. When the mind is released from the load of its engagements with the world of sense-objects, it becomes relatively quiet.

A quiet mind produces a more brilliant intellect. With this brilliance the student discovers a greater depth of understanding of the scriptures. Therefore, his knowledge of the true nature of the Self becomes fuller and more productive of results. Thus, *vairagya* gives *bodha* (knowledge), --a clear and full understanding of the nature of the Self. When this knowledge enters the level of our understanding then gratification in the old fields of sense indulgences automatically stops. This self-withdrawal is called *uparati*.*

With this Knowledge it is easy to withdraw our attention from our usual fields of mental dissipation. When as a result of the Knowledge of the Higher, the mind withdraws itself from the fields of agitations, it becomes more and more calm. Calmer the mind, greater the happiness. Happiness is a subjective condition wherein the mind is not over-agitated. When there is the experience of the Self within, there is peace--"the peace that passeth all understanding". And this great peace felt within, not because of any objects outside but because of the very essential nature of the Self in us, is the reward of Self-withdrawal.

यद्युत्तरोत्तराभावः पूर्वपूर्वन्तु निष्फलम् ।
निवृत्तिः परमा तृप्तिरानन्दोऽनुपमः स्वतः ॥४२१॥

421. When there are no succeeding stages, the preceding ones are useless. (In a perfect series), automatic cessation of the objective world, supreme satisfation and unequalled Bliss follow as a matter of course.

---

* बाह्यानालम्बनं वृत्तेः एषोपरतिरुत्तमा ॥

Verse 24 Ibid.

In the preceding verse a chain of cause and effect seen in the life of a true seeker, has been given.

Now in this verse, the Teacher says, if there is an absence of the succeeding stages, then the preceding ones are futile. If you have objective Knowledge but no *vairagya*, that knowledge is of no use. If you are practising self-withdrawal but if it does not lead to subjective knowledge of the Higher, the self-withdrawal is only escapism. It will never be creative. Each suceeding stage can be fruitful only if you have cultivated the noble qualities of the earlier. When an individual has, through withdrawal from sense-pleasures, cultivated the true Knowledge as it is expounded in the scriptures, then as a result of the knowledge, slowly and steadily, he grows in his healthy attitude of detachment from the fields of sence gratifications. When the seeker has, as a result of intelligent self-withdrawal, come to experience peace and happiness flooding his bosom, he becomes the true savant at the temple-gates of Reality. Such a prepared personality alone can get admission into the transcendental state of God-consciousness. It is only as a result of all these developments in oneself that one comes to a point of complete renunciation *(nivritti)*, from all worldly activities.

Because of a quarrel with his wife or due to the ingratitude of his children or because of failure in the market if a foolish young man rejects the world and runs to the Ganges banks and colours his cloth, he does not become fit for the highest experience. He is still an outcaste from the temple of Reality. Escapists from life cannot claim an entrance to religion. Religion in its highest realms is reserved only for evolved persons, who have cultivated, through sustained self-effort, the necessary perfection. Evolution is not an accident. It is a logical development and has its stages. Every evolute will have to go through all the preceding stages before he can climb to the final stage of evolution.

Thus, only an individual who has gone through all the disciplines indicated in the previous verse, will really come to live a life of complete detachment form the world outside. He alone, will experience a contentment that is unique and a bliss that is incomparable *(anupamah)*.

"When will it come? How will it come?" Sankara answers, "This state of complete Bliss and satisfaction comes naturallv *(swatah)*, as a result of all the previous disciplines. This is the final reward to the spiritual seeker".

Sankara continues, enumerating the result of this great experience.

दृष्टदुःखेष्वनुद्वेगो विद्यायाः प्रस्तुतं फलम् ।
यत्कृतं भ्रान्तिवेलायां नाना कर्म जुगुप्सितम् ।
पश्चान्नरो विवेकेन तत्कथं कर्तुमर्हति ॥४२२॥

422. The result of Knowledge is, non-chalance towards worldly sorrows. How can he who performs vile deeds in delusion, perform them again when he possesses discrimination?

When the final Beatitude is experienced, man is unruffled by the painful experiences that he may have to live thereafter in the world. The pinpricks that he is conscious of at the physical, mental and intellectual levels, all the jerks of life, subjective and objective, never disturb him. This is indeed the effect of the Knowledge that has come to him as a result of *sadhana*.

Not only is he unaffected by the sorrows of the body, mind and intellect, but he no more pursues the disgusting and repulsive actions that he may have performed when he was in a state of delusion, when he was bundle of misconceptions about himself.

Considering ourselves to be the body, in order to bring more comforts to it, we stride out into the world of competition and by means fair and foul, try to fulfil all our desires. We become slaves to our sense-organs and their demands.

How can a man who has regained his discriminative powers to the full, continue with the vile deeds that he might have perpetrated during his days of confusion and misunderstanding?

In a drunken mood, when the intellect is veiled by the fumes of drink, a drunk might behave and act in many a disgusting manner. When the effects of drink have worn off and the mind has emerged from the delusory fumes, then, in the saner moments, how can the drunk of the night before, repeat his mischiefs in the clear light of the morning after? In the same way, drunk with the *vasanas* and passions of the body, the individual, during his days of ignorance, might have perpetrated many shameful acts of viciousness. He cannot continue them after Realisation because by then he has come to experience his spiritual unfoldment and as a consequence, has realised the demeaning grossness of his lower personality.

विद्याफलं स्यादसतो निवृत्तिः
प्रवृत्तिरज्ञानफलं तदीक्षितम् ।
तज्ज्ञाज्ञयोर्यन्मृगतृष्णिकादौ
नोचेद्विदां दृष्टफलं किमस्मात् ॥४२३॥

423. Turning away from the unreal should be the result of Knowledge; attachment to the unreal is the result of "ignorance". Such is seen to be the case of one who knows a mirage etc. and one who does not. Else, what palpable result do the Knowers-of-reality gain?

What do you gain by experiencing the Supreme? The vision of the world from the spiritual watch-tower is explained in this verse. At the moment we are looking at it from the material stand-point--from the stand-point of the BMI. As a* result, the world is giving us the experience of the OET.

What would be the vision of the world when it is looked at without *ahamkara* in the body, mind, and intellect? How

* Refer foot-note on verse 124 Ibid.

does such an individual react at his physical, emotional, and intellectual levels?

Knowledge of the ghost is *avidya*, nescience --misapprehension. When we investigate into it and try to understand its real nature, we acquire the knowledge of the post--the right knowledge or *vidya*.

The result of right knowledge is the removal of nescience. When you have transcended the intellect, you have got away from the persecutions of matter. When you experience the spiritual centre and understand that you are not the body, mind, of intellect, you move away from the *An-atman*. That which is perceived as different from Brahman is An-atman.*

When you have the knowledge of the *Real*, you turn away from the *unreal*. You retire from the "not-Self". Right now, we are completely engaged and employed in the world as the body, mind, and intellect. We are identified with the *an-atman*. When the spiritual experience comes, there is no identification with matter. There is complete retirement from the concept, "I am body, I am the mind, I am the intellect": *(Asato-nivrittih)* just as, in the waker, there is a total retirement *(nivritti)*, from the experiences of the dream-world.

The result of "ignorance" *(agyana)* is action *(pravritti)*. Ego-motivated actions are called *pravritti*. Ego and desire-prompted activities are possible in *avidya* alone. When I identify with my outer vestures of matter, the ego-centric idea of my individuality crystallises. Motivated by my *vasanas*, I act in the world. The result of *agyana* is ego-centric activity and its consequent sorrows. But when there is Knowledge, there is complete detachment from the false world projected by "ignorance"--*non-apprehension* of Reality and the consequent *mis-apprehensions*.

---

* ब्रह्माभिन्नं सर्वमनात्मा । = All that is experienced as other than *Brahman* is "not-self" - *An-atman*..

These effects are observed in a man-of-Knowledge and in a man-of-ignorance. It can be seen in the reactions of men seeing a mirage. The man who does not know it is a mirage, runs after it, only to get disappointed, again and again. He who recognises it as a mirage does not move at all, though he sees the delusory appearance of water. He knows that it is an illusion and he enjoys it. The illusion cannot prompt him to activity.

He has already come to apprehend his own Real Nature and hence, will no more get identified with the BMI and run after the OET. He lives in peace and tranquility within himself, away from the persecutions of all *vasanas* and desires. What else will the man-fo-Realisation gain?

अज्ञानहृदयग्रन्थेर्विनाशो यद्यशेषतः ।
अनिच्छोर्विषयः किं नु प्रवृत्तेः कारणं स्वतः ॥४२४॥

424. When the knots of ignorance in the heart have been totally destroyed, what natural cause can prompt a man who is averse to sense-pleasures, to ego-centric action?

"Ignorance" *(avidya)*, "desire" *(kama)*, and "action" *(karma)*, are the hindrances in our attempt to gain the experience of our Real Nature. They are considered in *Vedanta Sastra*, as the "knots" on the heart of man. "Heart", here, does not mean the organ pumping blood, but the "personality" of man. The essential "personality" of man is always tied down by these three knots. When they are completly cut asunder the knowledge of the Self is easily gained. Partial destruction of them we find in deep-sleep also; but deep-sleep leads to no Realisation. The annihilation of these knots should be total.

When an individual gains the knowledge of the Real, the Infinite, the "ignorance" of the Self ends. Where ignorance has ended, there desires cannot arise. Where desires are not, there actions cannot be. When the knots of the heart have been cut, why should the individual entertain the OET? You and I do not run after toys because we have no desire for them. But in order to entertain children around us, we may play with them. When we thus play with the toys, that play will be entirely different from how we played when we were children. Then we lived life with ego and ego-centric desires. Now there is no ego nor ego-centric desires to corrupt our play.

In the same way, having gained the knowledge of the Self, an individual may play in the world outside, never involved with the ego and its desires.

Since the man-of-Realisation has no desires, he does not undertake any ego-prompted or desire-promted activity. "Ignorance" of Reality *(Avidya)* at the intellectual level is called *desire*, at the mental level, *thoughts*, and at the physical level, *actions*.

The man-of-Realisation has no *pravritti*, as all the possible "impulses" for actions are dried up in him.

वासनानुदयो भोग्ये वैराग्यस्य तदावधिः ।
अहंभावोदयाभावो बोधस्य परमावधिः ।
लीनवृत्तेरनुत्पत्तिर्मर्यादोपरतेस्तु सा ॥ ४२५॥

425. The culmination of dispassion is when the sense-objects do not excite any more desire. Supreme perfection of Knowledge is when there is no egoistic feeling. The peak of self-withdrawal is reached when the thoughts which have been merged manifest no more.

The states of total attainment of detachment *(vairagya)*,* Knowledge *(bodha)*, and withdrawal *(uparati)*, which have been already explained are now elaborated upon.

The summit of *vairagya* is the total absence of desire to seek any enjoyment in the world of objects. *Vairagya* finds

---

* प्रयोजनं अनुदिश्य न मन्दोऽपि प्रवर्तते
Without an idea upon the result, even an idiot does not act.

its fulfilment when there are no *vasanas* in the inner equipment. Annihilation of all *samskaras* is the non-manifestation of *vasanas* and *samkalpas*. In the exciting dance of the objects around, the absence of thoughts of enjoyment is the culmination of *vairagya*.

The climax of Knowledge *(bodha)*, is the absence of "I-ness" and "my-ness". The fulfilment of Knowledge is when one is completely established in the Reality having torn asunder the veil of ignorance. The veil of ignorance drops when the PFT has been transcended. Total annihilation of the ego is the limit of Knowledge.

Supreme peace attained as a result of complete renunciation of the OET is the state of total withdrawal *(uparati)*. When all agitations are quietened and there is no thought disturbance rising in the bosom, understand that to be the state of *parama-uparati*. When all the misapprehensions have ended and there is endless peace and tranquility in the bosom, understand that state to be the state of *uparati* at its best, the zenith of effort and attainment. The sublime height of wisdom is reached with the total withdrawal from the BMI.

When these three are gained, you come to experience the unbroken Knowledge of infinite Bliss.

70. Signs of a Realised Seer. (426-445)

ब्रह्माकारतया सदा स्थिततया निर्मुक्तबाह्यार्थधी-
रन्यावेदितभोग्यभोगकलनो निद्रालुवद्बालवत् ।
स्वप्नालोकितलोकवज्जगदिदं पश्यन्क्वचिल्लब्धधी-
रास्ते कश्चिदनन्तपुण्यफलभुग्धन्यः स मान्यो भुवि ॥४२६॥

426. On account of constant absorption in *Brahman*, freed from the sense of reality of external objects, only seemingly enjoying them when offered by others, like one sleepy or like a baby, perceiving the world as one seen in a dream and recognising it only now and then, such a man is indeed rare.

He is the enjoyer of the fruits of untold merit and is truly held blessed and revered on earth.

In this verse Sankara tries to indicate the matchless joy experienced by a man of Realisation in the supreme moments of meditation and even during his hours of contact with the world around.

He has cleansed his intellect from all disturbing objects of perception of the outer world because his mind is completely identified with Brahmic consciousness and so no thought distrubances can be there. How will an individual who has risen totally above the lower planes of awareness and has awakened to the higher state, live? Will he thereafter, have the anxiety of an ordinary mortal to acquire the necessary things of life? Sankara answers, "He will, thereafter, enjoy things given to him by others. He himself will no more be anxious to get anything. Whatever is given to him--sometimes forced upon him--by others, objects of utter necessaity, he will accept and use." His way of enjoying these objects supplied to him by others unasked, is also clearly brought out when the Acharya says that he is like one who is sleeping *(nidralu)*, or like a baby *(bala)*.

When, for instance, you sleep in winter and others seeing the blanket off your back put it back on you, no doubt the sleeping body is warmer than before, but you the sleeper are not even conscious of it. Similarly, a child is fed by the mother. The child is not conscious that it is being fed regularly and properly, it just takes the feed for granted.

There is yet another significance concealed in the choice of these examples. In a sleeping man, there is total cessation of any awareness of the outer world.* Similar is the case of a man of Realisation. He is unconscious of the outer world and at that time if others help his physical existence, he remains totally unconcious of the solicitude he has received.

---

* बहिर्मुख अभावात् ।

The example of a child indicates, in its depths, that like a child, a man of Realisation also has no self-consciousness or vanity.* A child is not at all aware of itself or its hunger, nor is it aware of the mother feeding it. It has no *abhimana* of itself. A man of Realisation is much the same.

Now the question is, does such a man of Perfection experience the outer world at all? Yes, he does. Now and then. At certain moments he vaguely recognises the existence of the world around. Sankara here indicates that the percevied world for the man of Perfection is like the world seen in a dream. Thus, the man of steady wisdom does recognise the world around, but at all such moments, he is conscious of the non-existent illusory nature of the world interpreted by him through the play of his mind and intellect due to his *prarabdha.*

Rare indeed, are such men of Realisation. Such a rare one sits ever merged in the Self, extremely relaxed and completely happy as a result of the infinite merits acquired in many many lives in the past *(ananta-punya-phala-bhuk).* When he thus lives established in his divine Self, he is most revered one on the surface of the earth.

The last two lines remind us of Sankara's own verse elsewhere, where he says, "By such an individual whose mind has melted into the supreme *Brahman* which is the ocean of limitless Consciousness by the very existence of the individual, his tribe has become blessed, his family purified, his mother fulfilled and the entire world rendered blessed".

From the next verse onwards for about sixteen verses, Sankara attempts to give us the hall-marks of a man of Perfection.

स्थितप्रज्ञो यतिरयं यः सदानन्दमश्नुते ।
ब्रह्मण्येव विलीनात्मा निर्विकारो विनिष्क्रियः ॥४२७॥

---

* निराभिमानिता ।

427. That man of steady wisdom, having merged himself in *Brahman* enjoys everlasting Bliss, without modification or activity.

Sankara imitates the literary technique adopted by Vyasa in the Bhagawad Geeta, Chapter II, where the last eighteen verses gives us the picture of a man of Perfection. He even uses the same term as Vyasa --*"Sthitaprajna"* --the man of steady wisdom.

That great one who has got steady illumination of Knowledge and who has merged his entire inner equipment in the infinite *Brahman*, enjoys eternal Bliss. Such a one is ever changeless and free from all ego-prompted selfish activities. He who has the firm Knowledge, meaning, steady wisdom or understanding, of the true nature of the Self, reaches the state of perfect tranquility only when his inner equipment has totally dissolved in the pure infinite awareness of the Self. Since he is no more identified with his body, mind and intellect, he is no more sufferer of the destinies of these matter vestures. Therefore, he goes beyond the realm of change and strives to serve all, at all times, without any trace of selfishness.

ब्रह्मात्मनोः शोधितयोरेकभावावगाहिनी ।
निर्विकल्पा च चिन्मात्रा वृत्तिः प्रज्ञेति कथ्यते ।
सुस्थिता सा भवेद्यस्य स्थितप्रज्ञः स उच्यते ॥४२८॥

428. The sort of mental activity which admits only the identity of the Self and *Brahman*, free from all limitations and devoid of duality, which is only concerned with pure Knowledge, is called the illumination. One who has this steady illumination is known as a man of steady wisdom.

The mind should be purified through steady discrimination, realising the oneness of the Self within and the Consciousness that is the substraum for the whole world.* In short, the inner equipment should be purified through meditation upon the great statements of the Vedas--

* तत्पदार्थार्थं शोधितम् ।

the *Mahavakyas.* With such a purified mind when an individual experiences nothing but pure Intelligence, free from all other distracting throughts, that pure mind revelling in total contemplation upon the infinite Self is called a mind emblazoned with illumination. This is the mind that has ended, the mind that has been stilled.

He who experiences this condition of mental illumination steadily is called a man of steady wisdom.

Inspired moments of wisdom are possible in rare moments of life--during study or when listening to a Master, etc. At such moments an individual gets a glimmer of the higher possibility of the greater Consciousness. But rare indeed is the man who is completely established in his identity with the Higher. Such men who are established in the higher Consciousness are called *"Sthitaprajna"* --"rooted in Consciousness".

Numerous doubts may arise about the mental attitude of such an individual and his relationship with the world around. The ideas enumerated in Geeta, Chapter II, give the picture of a man of Perfection. In order to encourage us to undertake the pilgrimage, the Teacher gives his post-Realisation relationship with the objective world around him. He gives us the resurrected view, the re-orientation in the Higher, when one is refitted with wisdom and better understanding.

All the following fifteen verses of the section are meditation verses. They are not a mere repetition of the Geeta-verses. The Acharya, as usual, adds a few more strokes, unique in themselves, to the picture of the man of Perfection.

यस्य स्थिता भवेत्प्रज्ञा यस्यानन्दो निरन्तरः।
प्रपञ्चो विस्मृतप्रायः स जीवन्मुक्त इष्यते ॥४२९॥

429. He who has steady wisdom, who experiences endless Bliss, who has forgotten the phenomenal world, he is considered a *jeevan-mukta.*

We are all living now in the realm of the PFT, the *jeeva*, identified with the BMI. *Jeevan-mukti* is liberation from the concept of *jeeva-hood.* He who is liberated from the concept of the PFT, he who has no identification with his BMI, he is called the liberated one. He is liberated from the lower because of his awakening to the Higher.*

The *jeevan-mukta's* understanding is firm and steady. His experience of the Higher is not temporary or accidental. His Realisation is not because of any external prop. It is independent of time and place. It is constantly with him *(sahaja).*

His experience of the Bliss and peace within is unbroken *(nirantara)* because his mind has been transcended and therefore, the sorrows created by the mind are not there. In that condition, the world is exactly like things forgotten *(vismritaprayah)* and forgotten things cannot disturb him. Established in *Brahman* he lives in a state of continuous experience of joy.

Such an individual is considered a *jeevan-mukta.*

लीनधीरपि जागर्ति जाग्रद्धर्मविवर्जितः ।
बोधो निर्वासनो यस्य स जीवन्मुक्त इष्यते ॥४३०॥

430. He who has merged himself in *Brahman*, yet is alert, but without the characteristics of wakefulness, whose Knowledge is free from desire, he is considered a *jeevan-mukta.*

He is a *jeevan-mukta* whose intellect is merged in *Om*, the Reality. Even the thoughts are thus merged, he is brightly awake. In sleep, when the mind and intellect have become quiet, we are not conscious of the world. On awakening to the Higher Reality, the mind is *as though* asleep, but the individual is *as though*, awake: "Wakeful sleep". "Sleepless sleep". Consciousness bright and vigilant but not

---

* See foot note on Verse 124 Ibid.

apprehending any object. Therefore, this state is called objectless-Awareness.

Waking to the Reality is the state of waking without its properties. Properties of the waking condition are perceptions and actions. These are not there in Realisation. It is waking unlike the waking condition. It is pure Awareness alone. It is knowledge, but not the knowledge of things. It is Knowledge without any *vasana*, any urge or passion.

He who is alive to this state, he is called a *jeeva-mukta*.

शान्तसंसारकलनः कलावानपि निष्कलः ।
यस्य चित्तं विनिश्चिन्तं स जीवन्मुक्त इष्यते ॥४३१॥

431. He whose concern about the world has been stilled, who has a body consisting of parts yet is without parts, whose mind is free from anxiety, he is considered a *jeevan-mukta*.

Thought disturbances create the perception of plurality. Cares, sorrows, worries and anxieties of the pluralistic phenomenal world are perceived by an agitated mind. When the mind is quietened, all these sorrows are also quietened.

When we look at a *jeevan-mukta*, we see his body as made up of parts--heads, limbs, trunk etc., but he is at all times in the experience of the one homogeneous Infinite. Though he is living with his equipments, in and through their experiences, he is constantly living the One-ness.

His thoughts are without any worry *(chinta)*. He is never persecuted by uncontrollable agitations and sorrows. Such an individual is a *jeevan-mukta*.

वर्तमानेऽपि देहेऽस्मिञ्छायावदनुवर्तिनि ।
अहन्ताममताऽभावो जीवन्मुक्तस्य लक्षणम् ॥४३२॥

432. The absence of the "I" and "mine" concepts even in this body which persists like a shadow--this is the indication in a *jeevan-mukta*.

An object is distinguished from others because of its properties. Understanding an object through its properties is called "intellection". The sun is understood by its light and heat. Sugar is understood by its sweetness. The characteristics of a *jeevan-mukta* are given in the following verses.

Even though a liberated man lives in his physical, mortal, finite, material body, he has no "I-ness" and "my-ness". He does not consider himself to be the body, nor does he consider the objects belonging to the body as his. Though he expresses through the body, he has no subjective or objective ego-centric idea. The body just follows him like a shadow. No one can have ego-centric identification with his own shadow. Such too, is the man of Perfection's relationship with his body.

While doing *surya-namaskaras*, it is advised that one should look at the sun and then look at one's shadow after every *suryanamaskar*. It is traditionally believed in India that by doing so, there will be no evil effects of the planets upon one. This ritual is a dramatisation of a greater philosophical implication.

On realising the great light of Consciousness, your relationship with the body will be the same as that with its shadow. The persecutions of your shadow have no effect upon you. The planetary organisation may affect the physical frame and its relationship with the world, but if you have awakened to the supreme Reality it has no effect on you whatsoever. Thus, the relationship of the man of Perfection with his body is exactly like your relationship with your shadow

अतीताननुसन्धानं भविष्यदविचारणम् ।
औदासीन्यमपि प्राप्ते जीवन्मुक्तस्य लक्षणम् ॥४३३॥

433. No thought for the enjoyments of the past, no thought for the future and indifference even for the present--this is the indication of a *jeevan-mukta*.

A man of Realisation refuses to think of the failures and regrets of the past. He does not worry about the future and is totally indifferent to the cares of the present.

He who has experienced the Higher refuses to remember and relive the past. Even a street dog will not eat its own disgorging. What has already been lived in the past, the *jeevan-mukta* does not live again, nor does he get anxious about the future. And in the present, never is he excited.

गुणदोषविशिष्टेऽस्मिन्स्वभावेन विलक्षणे ।
सर्वत्र समदर्शित्वं जीवन्मुक्तस्य लक्षणम् ॥४३४॥

434. Looking everywhere with an equal eye on this world riddled with elements possessing merit and demerit, characteristically different one from the other--this is the indication of a *jeevan-mukta*.

On this level of consiousness, everything is experienced without the mind and the intellect. We cannot experience anything unless it is in the world of plurality. Relative experiences alone are available for the M & I. Pure Consciousness is that where there is no mind and intellect accompanied by their disturbances. All the experiences of the M & I are an admixture of good and bad, *(guna-dosha-visishta)*.

This world is full of properties --god and bad, merit and demerit, happiness and sorrow. It is, by its very nature, different from *Brahman*. In the Infinitude there is no pluralistic world. It is the state where the mind and intellect are transcended. Those who experience this Reality look upon the world with an equal eye *(samadarsitwam)*.

Naturally, when one has experienced the Absolute, in which the entire pluralistic world has merged, and when one looks back at the world, one must necessarily become a *samadarsi*--a man of equal vision in all situations.

The dreamer while dreaming, experiences the dream world. In waking up, he understands that the dream has merged in the waking knowledge.Supposing,with that knowle--dge he is introduced into that dream, how will he react to the dream world?

In a similar fashion, a man who has realised the Highest lives in the world. With his equipments he also suffers his joys and sorrows. But he has an extra smile on his face seeing which the world is tempted to put him on the cross. He understands the trick of the mind which gives him hallucinations, so glorious in their beauty and ugliness. His equanimity cannot be broken by any happenings around.

इष्टानिष्टार्थसम्प्राप्तौ समदर्शितय ऽऽत्मनि ।
उभयत्राविकारित्वं जीवन्मुक्तस्य लक्षणम् ॥४३५॥

435. When confronted with things pleasing or painful, to be unperturbed in both cases, by maintaining an equal attitude--this is the idication of a *jeevan-mukta*.

Liberated in life is he who lives in the body yet is not of the body. When happenings good, bad or indifferent reach him, he maintains an equanimous attitude towards them all since he experiences the *Atman* in all of them. In all such situations he sees the substratum only. He is not interested in the matter vestures the body, mind and intellect of individuals. He has the "X-ray vision" to look through the BMI and their convulsions and to recognise the play of Consciousness in every bosom. The man of Perfection sees his own Self in the Consciousness which is playing through all bodies.

In circumstances pleasant or otherwise, he is an *a-vikari*. *A vikari* is one who reacts and brings about modifications in his own mind. In our case, when pleasant things come, we are pleased; when things are unpleasant, we become cross. Our mind is turned and ruffled by the circumstances and happenings around. Unruffled, the man of Perfection watches the passing parade of the world.

ब्रह्मानन्दरसास्वादासक्तचित्ततया यतेः ।
अन्तर्बहिरविज्ञानं जीवन्मुक्तस्य लक्षणम् ॥४३६॥

436. Constantly engaged in tasting the Bliss of *Brahman*,a *Sanysin* entertains no distinctions of within and without---this is the indication of a *jeevan-mukta*.

He is the liberated one who is engrossed in the enjoyment of that Brahmic consciousness which is the experience of Bliss *(ananda)*. There is Bliss because the mind has been trascended. Mind is a cancerous ulcer which bleeds out sorrows. As long as you work through the mind you will suffer.

Sanskrit is a language known for the subtlety of its expression. The term *Brahmaanda-rasa*, is an example. The man of Perfection is extermely addicted to *Brahmaananda-rasa*. The Infinite : *Brahma*. Infinite Bliss : *Brahmaananda*. The essence of Infinite Bliss : *Brahmaananda-rasa*. The liberated one is addicted to the experience of this Essence. He strives to get that experience always. One who is striving to realise is a *yati*.

At such moments of experience of the Essence of infinite Bliss which is homogeneous and whole, one knows no inside nor outside. He does not know the outer world of objects nor does he know the inner world of emotions and thoughts.

देहेन्द्रियादौ कर्तव्ये ममाहंभाववर्जितः ।
औदासीन्येन यस्तिष्ठेत्स जीवनमुक्तलक्षणः ॥४३७॥

437. Having no idea of "I" and "mine" with regard to the body, sense-organs etc. nor to duties, living with an attitude of indifference ---this is the indication of a *jeevan-mukta*.

The *jeevan-mukta* is rid of the ideas of "I" and "mine in the equipments. With regard to the body, mind and intellect he does not feel, "I am these". Nor has he the idea that they belong to him. Just as the waker does not have the ego-centric feeling, "I am the dream body and the dream-objects are all mine". In the dream, of course, the dream body is "me", and the dream wife and children are "mine". After waking up, the I-ness of the dream body and the my-ness of the dream-objects vanish. Similarly, the individuality and its possensiveness vanish when one has awakened to the higher plane of Consciousness.

He thereafter, lives indifferent to tragedies and comedies that visit the flesh and its mind and intellect. Such an attitude towards his own equipments is the sign of a *jeevan-mukta.*

विज्ञात आत्मनो यस्य ब्रह्मभावः श्रुतेर्बलात् ।
भवबन्धविनिर्मुक्तः स जीवन्मुक्तलक्षणः ॥४३८॥

438. Deep-rooted Knowledge that the Self is *Brahman*, affirmed by the scriptures, and free from the bondage of transmigration---this is the indication of a *jeevan-mukta.*

He who has understood that the Self in him is the Self everywhere, aided by the study of the *Upanishads*, is the liberated one. By a method of systematic analysis he, who has come to experience that the one Matrix upon which the entire world is playing about is his very own Self, is the realised sage. When the identification with the BMI is completely dropped, and when he has risen to the higher plane of Consciousness, he suddenly realises that not only is he the pure Consciousness, but the whole universe too is nothing else but the supreme Self.

One who has experienced thus, becomes completely liberated from all "becoming" (transmigration).*

He is not affected by the changes that take place outside him and subjectively within him.

देहेन्द्रियेष्वहंभाव इदंभावस्तदन्यके ।
यस्य नो भवतः क्वापि स जीवनमुक्त इष्यते ॥४३९॥

439. He who has no ego with regard to body, sense-organs etc., nor the concept of "this" with regard to other things, he is considered a *jeevan-mukta.*

All these verses indicating the *jeevan-mukta* are not for judging others. Others can never be judged by you, for you will judge them with your mind and intellect and so you will

---

* सकल अविद्याभ्रान्तिनिर्मुक्तः भवबन्धविनिर्मुक्त : ।
totally liberated from all changes.

see things which are not there. All these verses are for self-observation.

Ordinarily, the common experience of each of us is that we consider ourselves to be the body, the sense-organs, the mind and the intellect. Our individuality-concept and I-ness are conditioned by our body, our mind and our intellect. "My body convulsions are my convulsions. I am not separate from them"---this is our attitude.

Our attitude towards things outside the skin is that they are either "this" or "that". Things other than our body, mind and intellect are all "others".

He in whom the idea, "I---the *subject*", and "this---the *object*", never comes, is a *jeevan-mukta*. Instead of the distinctions of "I" and "this", he who sees the play of the one Consciousness everywhere, is the man of Realisation.

न प्रत्यग्ब्रह्मणोर्भेदं कदापि ब्रह्मसर्गयोः ।
प्रज्ञया यो विजानाति स जीवन्मुक्तलक्षणः ॥४४०॥

440. Through Knowledge, he who never distinguishes between the *jeeva* and *Brahman* and between the universe and *Brahman*, is indicated as a *jeevan-mukta*.

He never recognise any distinction between his subjective personality and the essential "substance" behind the objective world. Not only that, but within himself too, he sees no distinction whatsoever.

He sees no distinction between the Lord behind the whole cosmos called *Iswara*, and the Lord functioning through the body called *jeeva*. *Jeeva-Iswara-eka-bhava* is the identity between the individual *jeeva* and the universal Self.

Patterns are woven into a cloth with coloured thread. Flowers, plants, houses, trees, animals---all are woven into paterns. It becomes a world of its own. When a child starts pulling the thread from one end, slowly it comes out and the entire *jagat* is liquidated into yards and yards of thread. In the thread, the entire world has become one.

Similarly, the whole world is a "Conscious" world, the material of which is this Consciousness. He who has unwound all this knows the Reality behind the entire cosmos. "That Reality alone am I", he realises. To him there are no more distinctions perceivable.

Never is there any more a difference between *pratyagatma* and Brahman. Nothing is ever there which is not *Brahman*. We do not make proper investigation into It, that is all. Thought is the father for all you sorrows, joys and sufferings. All of them have sprung from the non-apprehensions. One who apprehends Reality ends all misapprehensions.

Never did any difference exist between Brahman and the world which has emerged out of Brahman. He who know this, is liberated in life.

साधुभिः पूज्यमानेऽस्मिन्पीड्यमानेऽपि दुर्जनैः ।
समभावो भवेद्यस्य स जीवन्मुक्तलक्षणः ॥४४१॥

441. He who feels the same when his body is worshipped by the virtuous or tortured by the wicked, is considered a jeevan-mukta.

The man of Realisation does not react either positively or negatively to the external world. If the waking man with his waking consciousness enters the dream, he surely will not react to the dream experiences. He simply enjoys it whether it be pleasurable or painful in the dream. He knows that it is all himself. So does the man of Realisation when he lives in the world.

Good people worship him with flowers and adore him with prostrations. The wicked persecute him. Under both circumstances, the man of Realisation maintains the same attitude *(sama-bhava)*. He knows that the world outside is but he himself.

The glories of the liberated man are endless. How can we enumerate them all? Here Sankara concludes the theme.

यत्र प्रविष्टा विषयाः परेरिता
नदीप्रवाहा इव वारिराशौ ।
लिनन्ति सन्मात्रतया न विक्रिया -
मुत्पादयन्त्येष यतिर्विमुक्तः ॥४४२॥

442. The *Sanyasin* in whom the sense-objects chanelled by others are received like flowing rivers into the ocean producing no change because of his absorption in Existence Absolute, is truly liberated.

A realised man never courts the objects of pleasure. However, when they are thrust upon him by others, they enter and merge into him. They do not add even an iota of happiness, nor do they cause him the least sorrow.

Thousands of rivers bring millions and millions of gallons of water to the ocean, day in and day out. Yet the ocean does not rise even a centrimetre. It swallows them all.

Similarly, when into the unfathomable depths of the perfected man's wisdom, objects are thrust by the virtuous and the wicked, his mind never emerges into the world to hug them.*

When the objects and expriences reach him, what happens to them?

Threats, punishments, persecutions, censures and worships, commendations, adorations and praises---they all merge into his bosom and disappear. Infinite consciousness alone remains. They cannot create any activity, for his mind never jumps out. Such an individual is totally liberated from the thraldom of matter. Whatever comes within his knowledge only strengthens his identity with *Brahman.*

---

* आपूर्यमाणमचलप्रतिष्ठं समुद्रमापः प्रविशन्ति: यद्वत् ।
तद्वत्कामा यं प्रविशन्ति सर्वे स शान्तिमाप्नोति न कामकामी ॥
--Bhagavad Geeta II-70.

The following verse-re-emphasises the thoughts in the previous verse by negative argument.

विज्ञातब्रह्मतत्त्वस्य यथापूर्वं न संसृतिः ।
अस्ति चेन्न स विज्ञातब्रह्मभावो बहिर्मुखः ॥४४३॥

443. For him who has realised the Essence of *Brahman*, there is no reaching out for sense-objects as before. If there is, then he has not realised *Brahman*. His senses still have an outgoing tendency.

For one who has experienced the Reality, there is no *samsar*. *Samsar* is the phenomenon of going and coming* of reapeated births and deaths. If any avenues for ego-centric activity have opened up, then the man has not experienced *Brahman*. Entering *samsar* is possible only when the mind is turned outward. When the mind is turned outward, Reality cannot be experienced.

Mind and intellect turn towards objects emotions and thoughts only when there are *vasanas*. One who has realised *Brahman* has no *vasanas*. When the mind and intellect are completly turned inward and they discover therein the greatest of all happiness, then there is no *samsar* for the individual. But in case the seeker is tempted to run after the ever-changing sense-fields of experiences, it is a clear indication that he has *not* realised the Self fully. Extrovertedness is the sign of "ignorance".

प्राचीनवासनावेगादसौ संसरतीति चेत् ।
न सदेकत्वविज्ञानान्मन्दी भवति वासना ॥४४४॥

444. If it is asserted that still there is attachment for sense-objects because of the momentum of past *vasanas*, the reply is, "NO". For the *vasanas* get weakened when there is realisation of oneness with *Brahman*.

On Realisation the *vasanas* become weak and are not able to manifest and produce any activity. They become like

---

* संसरति इति संसारः

roasted seeds. Roasted seeds look like seeds, but they will bot sprout even under extremely favourable conditions.

The opponent to the Vedantic thoughts who is against the Vedantic theory, that a man of Perfection will have no more *vasanas* is now raising his cudgel against *Acharya* Sankara. Sankara answers in this verse. "If your argument is that a man of Perfection also will fall into the clutches of sense-objects due to the momentum of his old ways of living, we reply that this is impossible. The moment of enlightenment reduces the old *vasanas* to impotency. Even one who had been the greatest sinner before will not continue sinning after the extraordinary and unique experience of the one Self every where."

To reinforce his argument with a striking illustration Sankara employs the following verse.

अत्यन्त कामुकस्यापि वृत्तिः कुण्ठति मातरि ।
तथैव ब्रह्मणि ज्ञाते पूर्णानन्दे मनीषिणः ॥४४५॥

445. The propensities of even a downright rake are checked in the presence of his mother. So too, ther are no more any worldly propensities in one who has realised the Knowledge of *Brahman*, the Bliss Absolute.

The *vasanas* of a man of Realisation can never express themselves. Sankara gives an example to illustrate how this can be so.

A libertine who is an extremely uncontrollable super-sensualist cannot indulge in his sensuous actions in the presence of his mother. If, when on the point of committing an immoral act, his father, mother or Teacher were to walk in, then, for the time being at least, he will desist from committing the act.

If you have once tasted the infinite Bliss of *Brahman*, then in the presence of that experiece in you, the *vasanas*, even though they are there, will never manifest.

Supposing a man is frustrated with life, so much so, that he decides to hang himself, when all preparations have been made and he is about to tighten the noose around his neck, if his mother were to call to him affectionately, he stops in the very attempt which probably is forever thwarted. In the presence of his mother, all his determination is checked *(kunthi-bhavati)*.

A *sadhak* trying to lead a noble way of life should mentally have the presence of his ideal or his Teacher always before him so that his baser tendencies get weaker and he is always inspired to live the ideal way of life.

71. Prarabdha for a Saint? (446-464)

निदिध्यासनशीलस्य बाह्यप्रत्यय ईक्ष्यते ।
ब्रवीति श्रुतिरेतस्य प्रारब्धं फलदर्शनात् ॥४४६॥

446. He who is an adept at meditation is yet seen to have external perceptions. *Sruti* says, this is prarabdha at work. This can be inferred from actual results seen.

Earlier in two verses it was said that to a man of Perfection the *vasanas* created by his past actions cannot be powerful promptings because he has awakened from his ego-centric misconceptions. If thus, through meditation and Realisation his *vasanas* have been completely exhausted, an inteligent student would naturally ask a pertinent question. How is it that such an individual is seen to have his experiences in the world? We see that such a *Mahayogi* still has transactions with the world around him. He eats. He sleeps. He walks. He talks. He enjoys a cool bath in summer and a warm bath in winter. Therefore, if he has no *vasanas*, why should he continue to exist and gather experiences in contact with the world outside?

In answer to this pertinent question, Sankara Says

He who constantly practises meditation is certainly observed to have outer perceptions and experiences. This is explained by *Sruti* as being the result of his *Prarabdha.* It can only be *prarabdha* for we observe the man of Perfection to have his quota of joys and sorrows when he comes in contact with the world.*

सुखाद्यनुभवो यावत्तावत्प्रारब्धमिष्यते ।
फलोदयः क्रियापूर्वो निष्क्रियो न हि कुत्रचित् ॥४४७॥

447. As long as there is the experience of happiness etc., the work of *prarabdha* is seen to persist. Every result is seen to have a preceding action; there can be no result independent of action.

Why is this so? Why have the *Upanishads* indicated that the man of Perfection gains the experience of nothing that is not the expression of his *prarabdha?* This is explained by the *Acharya.*

As long as there is perception of happiness, sorrow, etc. *Sruti* acknowledges that *prarabdha* persists. The logical reason for this is that without a cause an effect is impossible. We see the Master experiencing joys and sorrows. Therefore, there must have been causes for them in the past. If all *prarabdha* ends at the moment of Realisation, there cannot be any experience of joy or sorrow. Since we see men of Realisation also experiencing joy and sorrow, there must be previous cause for these experiences. Every result is preceded by an action and nowhere is a result seen accruing independently of aciton. Naturally, therefore, the conclusion is, that when there are expreiences of joys and sorrows for the wise man, they must have arisen from his own past actions. This is the declaration of *Sruti.*

अहं ब्रह्मेति विज्ञानात्कल्पकोटिशतार्जितम् ।
सञ्चितं विलयं याति प्रबोधात्स्वप्नकर्मवत् ॥४४८॥

448. "I am *Brahman*"---with this Realisation, the actions of a hundred crore cycles come to nought, like the actions in the dream on waking up.

---

* सुखदुःखानुभवदर्शनात् सतस्यकारणं प्रारब्धमिति श्रुतिः ।

The idea is emphaissed that there is total destruction of all *vasanas* that have been hoarded from the past *(sanchita)*, in the knowledge arising from deep contemplation upon, "I am *Brahman*". By this subjective Realisation that I am the supreme Consciousness all the imprints of past actions left on our personality get totally eradicated, completely erased. No more can the *vasanas* accumulated in millions of lives ever grow potent and manifest their influences on the personality of the individual who has realised Truth.

Thus, the accumulated *vasanas (sanchita)*, get completely destroyed, just as the results of the activities done in a dream. On waking up, the results of all activities of the dream-state completely cease to act upon the awakened individual. Similarly, for one who has awakened to the higher plane of consciousness in the knowledge, "I am *Brahman*", all the *vasanas* that have been gathered by him through the play of the ego in the entire past become null and void.

The *Upanishads* also cry out the same.* In the *Upanishad*, the *Rishi* says that all the *vasanas* of the man of Perfection are completely fried in the fire of Knowledge. Sankara interprets here that the *Rishi* could have meant only *vasanas* other than *prarabdha*. In short, the man of Realisation has to live no more the effects of his past actions.

To illustrate this idea vividly for the comprehension of the student, Sankara gives the example of the dream in the follwing verse.

यत्कृतं स्वप्नवेलायां पुण्यं वा पापमुल्बणम् ।
सुप्तोत्थितस्य किंतत्स्यात्स्वर्गाय नरकाय वा ॥४४९॥

449. Can the meritorious acts or sinful deeds that a man has imagined doing in a dream take him to heaven or hell when he has awakened?

---

* भिद्यते हृदयग्रन्थि छिद्यन्ते सर्वसंशयाः ।
क्षीयन्ते चास्य कर्माणि तस्मिन्दृष्टे परावरे ॥ Mundakopnishad II-ii-8.

In the previous verse Sankara asserted that on waking to the higher plane of consciousness, all the *vasanas* that have been created in the past are totally wiped out. Meaning, they become impotent and can no longer yield any results. All the results of actions done in the past, accrued to the personality through the endless lives that have already been lived are called *sachita karma.* In order to drive home the point, an example is given which amplifies Vedantic contentions. The illustration given in this verse is very effective indeed.

Whatever activities have been done during the dream-state of consciousness *(swapna-velayam)*, irrespective of their merits or demerits, cannot have any reaction after the individual has woken up. The good actions of the dream cannot give one extra happiness on awakening. Nor can the crimes perpetrated in the dream give one consequent sorrows in his state of awakening.

In short, between the two states of consciousness there cannot be any transaction. For the subjects that experience the two states of consciousness totally different, meaning, the waker *as the waker* is not available in the dream and the dreamer *as the dreamer* is not there to experience the waking.

In the same way the egocentric individuality must have performed innumerable actions in his pilgrimage from one from to another. Yet, now that the ego has ended, in his new-found experience of the infinite consciousness as his own true nature, none of these fruits of actions *(karma-phala)*, can ever affect him, because the doer of those actions is not available any more.

स्वमसङ्गमुदासीनं परिज्ञाय नभो यथा ।
न श्लिष्यति च यत्किञ्चित्कदाचिद्भाविकर्मभिः ॥४५०॥

450. Being unattached and indifferent like sky, one who is realised is never concerned in the least about actions yet to be performed.

Here the Teacher wants to emphasise that the *vasanas* accumulated in the past are destroyed. Not only that, but as a result of Realisation, all the *vasanas* that are to mature in the future and yield their results in terms of joys and sorrows *(agami karma)*, are also totally destroyed. On realising the Self which is unattached and indifferent *(udaseena)* to the activities taking place around, the seeker's contact with the past is so completely annihilated that even the immature *vasanas* waiting for expression get totally roasted in the fire of Knowledge, newly kindled by the seeker's Realisation.

The *Atman*, unattached and actionless, has been again compared with space.*

The *Atman* is described as being indifferent *(udaseena)*. This is to indicate that in Its presence all the activities take place but in none of the activities is It involved. In It's presence the matter vestures gather dynamism to act, but the vehicles always act according to their *vasanas*.

When a man of Realisation acts, he is not affected at all at any time *(yatkinchit-kadachit)*, by the *vasanas* yet to mature in the future---the *agami*. Sankara calls it *bhavi-karma*---actions that are yet to yield their fruits in future periods of time. In short, *karma* is done by the ego and the ego alone can get its reward or punishment. When the doer of the actions, the vain ego, has been totally sublimated, who is to receive the results? When the ego is no more, the results of the *karma* done by the ego cannot take effect and therefore no *agami* can function.

However, the karmas that have taken effect already, for the experience of which the man of Realisation has taken this embodiment, i.e. the prarabdha, will contunue to function and this is the topic that Sankara hereafter takes up for elaboration.

---

* *Vide verse 386.*

न नभो घटयोगेन सुरागन्धेन लिप्यते ।
तथात्मोपाधियोगेन तद्धर्मैर्नैव लिप्यते ॥४५१॥

451. The sky, because of its contact with the jar, is not affected by the smell of the liquor in it. So too, the *Atman* is not affected by the properties, the conditionings because of Its contact with them.

All our activities are called *karma. Karma* is of three types. It is classified with reference to the past, present and future. The total impressions gained by an individual through his activities and thoughts accumulated at the unconscious level of the mind are called *sanchitam*---acquired. The large number of *vasanas* within are all *sanchita karma.* Of them a few become fructified *(phalon-mukha)* and surge forth to express. They are called *prarabdha karma , that which has started yielding fruits. There are yet other vasanas* which are awaiting maturity. They are yet to become effective. Such *vasanas* are called *agami*---yet to come.

The *sanchita* which is acquired in the past and the *agami* which is yet to come, both are destroyed at the moment of Realisation. They can no longer affect the individual because he has transcended his little identification and has experienced the Bliss beyond. The individuality which is to be accused for the past *karmas* is no more in that equipment. It has dissolved itself in the transcendental experience of the Infinitude.

In order to explain to us how the *karmas* do not affect the realised one, the Teacher gives this example.

Space is present everywhere. The contents in space can never contaminate it. A toddy pot may contaminate the surrounding atmosphere, the air, but not the space. The space in the pot cannot be conditioned by the contents of the pot. Similarly, even though a realised man lives in the body, the body cannot condition him. At all times he is conscious

---

* प्रकर्षेण आरब्धं इति प्रारब्धम् ।

of his oneness with the Infinitude. He being subtler than the subtlest, he cannot be conditioned by the *vasanas* of his past actions.

But this body being *prarabdha* that which is the result of past actions which have already started yielding fruits, has to continue existing till it exhausts itself by itself.

ज्ञानोदयात्पुरारब्धं कर्मज्ञानान्न नश्यति ।
अदत्वा स्वफलं लक्ष्यमुद्दिश्योत्सृष्टबाणवत् ॥ ४५२ ॥

452. That work which was performed before the dawn of Knowledge and because of which this body is conjured up, is not destroyed, by the Self-Knowledge with out yielding its fruits.....just like and arrow shot at an object.

The *vasanas* which have started yielding fruits before the auspicious hour of Realisation, will not cease to yield fruit after Realisation. At a particular stage in his pilgrimage of life an individual realises the Truth. Sankaracharya at the age of twelve, Vivekananda at twenty-four and Buddha at forty-two are some of the examples. But before Realisation, the individual had already been conceived in his mother's womb and had started his earthly career. The great pilgrimage that has started is, in itself, an expression of the past *vasanas*. The *karma* that has started manifesting does not end because of *jnana*. Because of its *prarabdha*, the body continues to exist even after Realisation. The body has to go through all its experiences because of its past *karmas*.

From the stand-point of the realised man, it is *prarabdha* of the body and so it has to live through it. In our case, it is our *prarabdha* and hence we suffer through life whether we like it or not. The realised man is not involved in the experiences of the body. It is only others around him who get involved with it.

Irrespective of the involvements of the subject, the *prarabdha* will not end without yielding its dues. The arrow that has left the bow must reach its target. After leaving the bow it cannot be stopped. You may change your mind only before it leaves. Once it has left it shall certainly reach its target.

The *agami karmas* are the total arrows in your quiver. Out of them you have taken one, fitted it to the bow and pulled the string. Even at that point you can stop it. But having pulled it up to the ear and shot it, you cannot bring it back. It has to pant and exhaust itself. Nothing can be done about it.

This body is the arrow which has already started from the mother's womb and has been aimed at the tomb. From womb to tomb is its journey. In that flight, having started its career, nobody can stop it.

To elucidate clearly the subtle distinction indicated here, Sankara gives in the following verse an unforgettable illustration.

व्याघ्रबुद्ध्या विनिर्मुक्तो बाणः पश्चात्तु गोमतौ ।
न तिष्ठति छिनत्त्येव लक्ष्यं वेगेन निर्भरम् ॥४५३॥

453. Thinking it to be a tiger if an arrow is shot at an object, it does not then stop because it turns out to be a cow. It still pierces it with full force.

A hunter thinking that there was a tiger, aimed an arrow at it and shot it. As the arrow whizzed towards the target the hunter recognised it to be a cow. Now what could he do? By his revised knowledge the arrow does not stop in its flight. Certainly it strikes its target with full force. The knowledge that it is a cow does not change or modify the direction of the arrow.

In the past, thinking that you are the body, you let loose many arrows of thoughts and desires. In the midst of this suffering you realise the Truth. Still you are the son of you father, the father of your children and the husband of your wife or perhaps the wife of your husband. Once the thoughts have been wished and willed in a particualr direction, they have to take their course and come to manifestation in the given body. The body has to go through the convulsions of enjoyments and sufferings. No one can stop this.

The *agami* and the *sanchita* can be eliminated, but not the *prarabdha* i.e., the *prarabdha* of the body, not of the realised individual, for he who lives in It has no more identification with his body.

From verse 454 onwards, Sankara discusses prarabdha and how it works for the man of Realisation.

प्रारब्धं बलवत्तरं खलु विदां भोगेन तस्य क्षयः
सम्यग्ज्ञानहुताशनेन विलयः प्राक्संचितागामिनाम् ।
ब्रह्मात्मैक्यमवेक्ष्य तन्मयतया ये सर्वदा संस्थिता -
स्तेषां तन्त्रितयं नहि क्वचिदपि ब्रह्मैव ते निर्गुणम् ॥४५४॥

454. *Prarabdha* is very powerful for the realised man and becomes nought only through the exhaustion of its fruits; while the *sanchita* and *agami* are destroyed in the fire of perfect Knowledge. But none of these three affects them who have realised *Brahman* and always live identified with It. They are, truly, the Transcendental *Brahman*.

Prarabdha karma is very strong even for those who have known Reality. The *agami* and the *sanchita* can end by the experience of the Higher, but *prarabdha* will end only when it has been lived through. Then whether a person is a *Jnani* or an *anjani*, he has to live through it. There is no escape. A *Jnani* may have a luxurious smile on his face, since he knows that he is not the equipments. An *Anjani*, unfortunately, will make a long face for he will not have the strength to grin and bear his lot.

The fire of Knowledge kindled by the experience of Reality burns the *vasanas* that have been stored from the past and the *vasanas* that are yet to manifest in future births.

That for the *jnanis, praralbdha* is still powerful has to be carefully understood, for the statement has subtle points which should not be missed in a hasty reading.

When *Brahman* and *Atman* are understood to be one and the same, the individual remains in that experience only. When I realise that the Self in me is the Self present everywhere, I remain absorbed in it, *(tanmayataya)*. No more do I identify with the BMI but I remain There and There alone. Those who have lifted themselves from their identification with the BMI and are identified with the Reality and remain there, then in those moments, to such individuals there is no *prarabdha* also.

Naturally, when I am not conscious of the body, mind and intellect, whatever the equipments might do in the world outside, whatever they may perceive or get as reactions, they do not affect me. Because I am my own Self and fully engaged in It. My attention is totally turned towards the infinite.

None of the three categories of *karmas* affect such individuals. At such moments of experience they are *Brahman* alone. That *Brahman* is Absolute and being absolute, It has no properties.

Thus the three karmas---*sanchita, agami* and *prarabdha* leave us only when the ego is completely dead. *Vasanas can affect only the ego.* The ego is liquidated in the transporting experience of the Infinite.

A man of Realisation becomes himself that *Brahman* whcih has no qualities.

उपाधितादात्म्यविहीनकेवल -
ब्रह्मात्मनैवात्मनि तिष्ठतो मुनेः ।
प्रारब्धसद्भावकथा न युक्ता
स्वप्नार्थसंबन्धकथेव जाग्रतः ॥४५५॥

455. The sage who is ever absorbed in his own Self as *Brahman*, Non-dual, and free from limitations---the question of the existence of *prarabdha* is meaningless, just as the question of a man having anything to do with dream-objects is meaningless when he has awakened.

The man who has awakened to the higher plane of Consciousness has no more body, mind and intellect conditionings. The feeling that "I am the body, the mind and the intellect" is not in him. Ego-centric individuality cannot maintain itself when the identification with the body, mind and intellect is withdrawn. When the individuality becomes unconditioned by the equipments, it becomes "the alone"---*kevala.** "The alone" expressing through the BMI is the personality, the ego. As an ego when I look into the world outside, I find a world of endless objects, emotions and thoughts. The multiplicity is perceived only when I look out through the equipments of the body, mind and intellect.

The man who is capable of analysing life in the world and also his own experiences is a man of reflection. When such an individual lives in his own Self as *Brahman*, he is not affected by his *prarabdha*. Enjoyment of *prarabdha* and experience of the Infinite are on two different planes of consciousness. The wealth of the king cannot help him when he dreams of himself as a begger. The king of the waking state cannot help the begger of the dream, though they are essentially one and the same person. How can the individual who has withdrawn from the BMI be molested by the OET?**

न हि प्रबुद्धः प्रतिभासदेहे
देहोपयोगिन्यपि च प्रपञ्चे ।
करोत्यहन्तां ममतामिदन्तां
किन्तु स्वयं तिष्ठति जागरेण ॥४५६॥

456. He who has awakened from sleep has no idea of "I" and "mine" with respect to the dream-body, nor for the dream-objects relcated to it. He lives ever awake as his own Self.

---

* त्रिविधपरिच्छेदशून्य वस्तु is केवलः । "The alone".
** Ibid footnote Verse 124.

The same idea of the previous verse is being elaborated for vivid picturisation in the student's mind. On waking up no one considers himself to be the dream-body. In the delusory dream-body the I-ness is not there for the waker. The things that pertain to the dream-body and the dream-objects will not be considered as "mine" by the waker.

I-ness : *(ahamta)*---The feeling of I-ness in the body will not be there when the individual has awakened to the higher plane of consciousness. On waking up, the feeling of I-ness towards the dream-body will vanish.

My-ness: *(mamata)* --The feeling of my-ness towards the objects around will not be there on waking to the higher plane of Consciousness. The dream house, the dream wife, the dream wealth and the experiences that have been lived through in the dream will not cause the feeling of my-ness to the waker.

This-ness: *(idamta)*--The world around that is cognised and declared as "this-this-this" will not have any sense of reality on waking to the higher plane of consciousness. On waking up, the dream world loses all its reality.

On waking to the higher plane of Consciousness, I shall no longer consider my dream-body to be me, the dream-belongings as mine and the dream-world as something that really exists. While I was dreaming, to the dreamer in me, my dream-body, my dream-belongings and my dream-world were real. When I wake up, I do not have *ahamta* in my dream body, nor *mamata* in the dream possessions nor *idamta* in my dream world of contacts. In them there is no reality any more. The *prarabdha* of the dream world does not affect the waker.

Similarly, *prarabdha* cannot affect the man who is rooted in the higher Experience.

न तस्य मिथ्यार्थसमर्थनेच्छा
न संग्रहस्तज्जगतोऽपि दृष्टः ।

तत्रानुवृत्तिर्यदि चेन्मृषार्थे
न निद्रया मुक्त इतीष्यते ध्रुवम् ॥४५७॥

457. He does not wish to prove the unreal objects to be real, nor is it observed that he maintains the dream-world. If he still holds on to the unreal objects, he is exphatically declared to be not yet free from sleep.

In the dream, to the dreamer, the dream experiences are vivid, true and real. After waking up, the individual will not have any desire to maintain the dream-world, to acquire the dream-objects and to protect the dream-wealth. Having woken up, you are not ashamed to leave the dream. You do not strive to take up the dream again. On waking up you realise that the dream is false. In case you have any anxiety or excitement for the dream, then, it is clear that you have not woken up from it. If you have woken up, the dream-objects will hold no fascination for you.

Similarly, on Realisation, the objects of our waking world have as much significance as the dream-objects have for the waker.

तद्वत्परे ब्रह्मणि वर्तमानः
सदात्मना तिष्ठति नान्यदीक्षते ।
स्मृतिर्यथा स्वप्नविलोकितार्थे
तथा विदः प्राशनमोचनादौ ॥४५८॥

458. So too, the man who remains identified with the Eternal Realisty does not perceive anything else. Just as one remembers having seen the objects in the dream, the Realised man remembers his day to day acts of eating etc.

The relationship of the individual who is living in the higher plane of Consciousness with the world of OET is similar to that of the waker with his dream-world. In moments of Realisation, he sees nothing except Consciousness. In my waking state, I do not see anything of the dream-world. The dream-world has rolled away and has dissolved into my Self in another plane of consciousness--the waking.

In case you possess memory of the dream, you remember it as non-existent and as of no consequence. That is, you remember things which were never actually there, but which were only imagined by you in your dream. Similarly, the man of Realisation goes through the world. His activities such as eating, breathing, sleeping, etc. take place even though he is not involved in them. The man of Perfection goes through the activities of maintaining the body exactly like going through his dream experiences.

कर्मणा निर्मितो देहः प्रारब्धं तस्य कल्प्यताम् ।
नानादेरात्मनो युक्तं नैवात्मा कर्मनिर्मितः ॥४५९॥

459. The body has been fashioned by *prarabdha* so one accept that relates to the body. But it is not reasonable to attribute it to the Self, for the *Atman* is never the result of any earlier work.

A man who has realised the Truth is one who has sought and discovered successfully his identity with the Self. Having thus awakened to the higher plane of Consciousness, he can no longer be involved in any way with the world of OET which belongs to the lower plane of Consciousness. In the two preceding verses, the *Acharya* laboured to point out the truth of this statement by comparing it with the experiences of a waker with reference to the dreamer that he was before. Having quoted that *prarabdha* cannot be for the man of Realisation the fact still remains that even after *Samadhi*, he is found to be a member of society, going through the various joys and sorrows of his existence. A Ramakrishna suffers from cancer, a Christ suffers on his cross; one *Acharya* is claimed and proclaimed as the greatest and the noblest and, therefore, he lives as a pontiff in luxurious circumstances on a golden throne under silken umbrellas, while yet another Master seems to live with nothing to clothe him and without assurance of his next supper. How is this explained?

Sankara in this verse gives us the clue. He says, the egocentric, desire-prompted deliberate activities of the past leave behind their impression, and prompted by these impressions *(vasanas)*, the individualised ego seeks a conducive physical environment where it can live and fulfil its residual *vasanas*. Hence he dons an appropriate body and manifests himself under the required environments. Thus the body stems forth from the actions of the past; and since *prarabdha* is a resultant of past actions, it can be conceded that the body is the product of *prarabdha*. Therefore, *prarabdha* belongs to the body alone. It is the destiny of the body, gross, subtle and causal, that it should suffer or enjoy; that it should be in conducive environments or otherwise.

When the Teacher says that *prarabdha* is not for the man of Realisation, he means, that there is no *prarabdha* for the Self, as the Self is not created by past acctions. The Self was, is and shall ever be. All actions take place in the Self, with the Self, by the Self and for the Self. Since the man of Realisation is one who has discovered his perfect identity with this supreme infinite Self, to him indeed, there cannot be any *prarabdha*. The same idea is expressed so vividly in the Bhagavad Geeta when Krishna declares the Self to be "Unborn, Eternal, Permanent, the most ancient, It gets not killed when the body is killed"*. In Kathopanishad also the same idea is expressed. The *Atman* is Beginningless *(anadi)*, Endless *(ananta)*. Everything springs forth into birth an disappears in its death in the medium of Consciousness only. Destiny can only pertain to that which has birth and death and not to the Eternal Substratum upon which the illusion of birth and death is taking place from time to time.

अजो नित्यः शाश्वत इति ब्रूते श्रुतिरमोघवाक् ।
तदात्मना तिष्ठतोऽस्य कुतः प्रारब्धकल्पना ॥४६०॥

460. The *Atman* is "Birthless, Eternal and Undecaying" --such is the absolute declaration of *Sruti*. How can *prarabdha* be attributed to him who lives ever-identified with That?

---

* अजो नित्यः शाश्वतोऽयंपुराणो ।
न हन्यते हन्यमाने शरीरे ॥ Bhagavad Geeta II-20.

Having given in the previous verse the logical reason why the *Atman* has no *prarabdha*, here Sankara supports his rational argument by quoting the scriptures.

In *Vedanta*, conclusion arrived at by mere reasoning are not in themselves acceptable since the intellect, itself a product of delusion, can get more and more confused by its own illusory perceptions. Therefore, in the science of Reality as conceived by the great Rishis of yore, the rational conclusions, arrived at logically by an intellect, when supported by similar conclusions declared by the scriptures, become doubly guaranteed and, therefore, totally acceptable to the students. In the verse under commentary, the Teacher gives the authority of the scriptures *(Sruit pramana)*. Here, a verse from the Kathopanishad* is quoted--" Birthless, Eternal and Changless --is the nature of the Self", says the *Upanishad* and** the words of the scriptures are infallible-- *amoghavak*.

प्रारब्धं सिध्यति तदा यदा देहात्मना स्थितिः ।
देहात्मभावो नैवेष्टः प्रारब्धं त्यज्यतामतः ॥४६१॥

461. Only as long as one lives identified with one's body, can one accept *prarabdha* work. But no one accepts that a man of Realisation ever identifies himself with his body. Hence, in his case, *prarabdha* world should be rejected.

The scriptural Truth quoted in verse 460 is thus sandwiched between logical reasons.

Since the body is a product of past actions, it should continue enjoying and suffering its fruits and those who identify with their bodies naturally continue to suffer.

A man of Perfection is one who has ended his misconceptions and is therefore, not identifying with his physical body, the tragedies and comedies of the body will not

---

* Kathopanishad I-ii-18.

** अबाधितअर्थ । --the meaning of which can never be proved false.

affect him. Sankara concludes here and commands us "give up the concept of all *prarabdha* working in the case of a man of Perfection."

शरीरस्यापि प्रारब्धकल्पना भ्रान्तिरेव हि ।
अध्यस्तस्य कुतः सत्त्वमसत्यस्य कुतो जनिः ।
अजातस्य कुतो नाशः प्रारब्धमसतः कुतः ॥४६२॥

462. To attribute *prarabdha* even to the body is decidedly an illusion How can a superimposition have any existence? How can the unreal have a birth? And that which is never born, how can it die? So how can *prarabdha* function for something unreal?

More precise and authoritative, more eloquent and impressive than an international constitutional lawyer is *Adi* Sankara here cascading an irresistible logical thinking. Not only can there be no *prarabdha* for the Self, but for a man of Perfection, even his body can have no *prarabdha*. To gain say this would be ridiculous, for he, in his absolute state of realisation, does not perceive or recognise the existence of the physical body. When you start pondering deeply, says Sankara, you cannot accept that there is *prarabdha* even for the physical body* of a man of Perfection.

This assertion is now explained in detail.

The superimposed snake is apparently visible only to a deluded observer. It is very well known that it has no reality. The play of the three bodies is but an illusion superimposed upon the Self; so where is reality for the body? Again that which is unreal can never be born; the snake in the rope has no birthday. The body that is superimposed upon *Brahman* cannot be said to have been born "due to *prarabdha*". The ghost on the post was never born, so it can never die; the unborn is undying. The body that is never born has no death or decay; birth and death of the body are both

---

* विचार्यमाणे शरीरस्यापि प्रारब्धं कल्पनामात्रम् ।

superimpositions on the Self. Summing up his arguments, Sankara, with biting ridicule asks, "How can there be *prarabdha* for the unreal, which naturally is unborn and, consequently, non-existing?"

In short, the witty *Acharya* indicates that *prarabdha* cannot be either for the Self or for the body which is the not-Self. It can only be in the imagination of the deluded perceiver.

ज्ञानेनाज्ञानकार्यस्य समूलस्य लयो यदि ।
तिष्ठत्ययं कथं देह इति शङ्कावतो जडान्* ।
समाधातुं बाह्यदृष्ट्या प्रारब्धं वदति श्रुतिः ॥४६३॥

463. If the effects of ignorance are destroyed, root and all, by Knowledge, how does the body continue to live? *Sruti*, from a relative stand-point, hypothesises the work of *prarabdha* for those fools who entertain such doubts.

In this verse the *Acharya* tries to explain why even the *Upanishads* discuss this great concept of *prarabdha* working upon all bodies including that of the man of Perection. This is done only from a relative stand-point, to quieten the foolish doubt of an ignorant student. The student sees the body of the Master continuously functioning in the world and naturally, therefore, he feels that the Master continues living because of his *prarabdha*. Little does he understand that from the lofty panoramic vision of the Master, there is no body, that he is but the pure Self, the Witness of all.

Thus the *Upanishads* compromise and condescend to accept the concept of *prarabdha* for the man of Realisation only to help the dull ones who are still living in the relams of plurality. This is given out only from a relative aspect *(vyavahara-reetya)*. From the absolute point of view, there is no *prarabdha* for the perfected man, for he is one with *Brahman*.

* प्राकृतान् or मन्दान् ।

न तु देहादिसत्यत्वबोधनाय विपश्चिताम् ।
यतः श्रुतेरभिप्रायः परमार्थैक गोचरः ॥४६४॥

464. The idea of *prarabdha* has been expounded by the Upanishads not for proving the reality of the body etc., for the man of Realisation--because the *Upanishads* are without exception striving to point out the one supreme Reality.

Sankara concludes his discussion and says that the perceivers of plurality *(the dwaitins)*, quote Upanishadic passages that sanction the *prarabdha* theory, to prove that even the man of Realisation has body-consciousness and therefore, there exists a world of matter, other than *Brahman*. *Sankara, here, takes away the very plank from under the feet of the dwaitins*. He says that the *Upanishads* condesend to recognise the play of *prarabdha* only out of their infinite grace to accomodate fools in their early stages of unpreparedness, that they may later accept the total vision of the Absolute One. The *Acharya* says that any student of the *Upanishads* can easily understand that, by and large, the anxiety of the scriptures is to communicate to him the one Reality, the *Brahman*.

Now follows a team of seven verses, all of them repeatedly declaring the nature of the Atman to be the one, immutable, undecaying, infinite, eternal Substratum for the universe. Sankara, when he talks of the supreme Reality, forgets the audience he is addressing and gets irresistably carried forward by the impulsive joy of the Infinitude. He waxes eloquent upon the nature of the Self that he himself is living vitally in his own heart.

---

* The Mandukya Karika in the final analysis--
असंगोऽहं असंगोऽहं असंगोऽहं पुनः पुनः ।
सच्चिदानंदरूपोऽहं अहमेवाहमव्ययः ॥
Gaudapada also comes to declare this universal Truth --
न निरोधो न चोत्पत्तिर्न बद्धो न च साधकः ।
न मुमुक्षुर्न वै मुक्त इत्येषा परमार्थता ॥ Mandukya II-32.

72. There is No Plurality. (465-471)

परिपूर्णमनाद्यन्तमप्रमेयमविक्रियम् ।
एकमेवाद्वयं ब्रह्म नेह नानास्ति किञ्चन ॥४६५॥

465. Only *Brahman* there is, Non-dual, with no beginning or end, Incomparable and Changeless; in It there is no duality whatsoever.

That which is ever full with nothing else in It: *(Paripoorna)* --therefore, the One-without-a-second.

Without beginning or end: *(anadi-antam)*--means, without birth and death.

Incomparable: *(a-prameya)*--There is nothing that can compare with it, because It is beyond the realm of the BMI and their OET. Since It is unique, It cannot be compared with any of the experiences in the lower planes of Consciousness. Briefly speaking, It is transcendental. Similarly, It is changless in-as much as, It never undergoes any modifications *(a-parinami)*. *Brahman* is non-dual *(adwayam)*, meaning, *sajatiya-vijatiya-bhedarahita-vastu.* To remove any lingering doubt that there may be an exception, the most powerful word, *kinchana (kinchidapi)*, is used by Sankara. It has the full force of the English word, "whatsoever".

सद्घनं चिद्घनं नित्यमानन्दघनमक्रियम् ।
एकमेवाद्वयं ब्रह्म नेह नानास्ति किञ्चन ॥४६६॥

466. The essence of Existence, the essence of Knowledge, the essence of Eternal Bliss, Non-dual, devoid of any activity, there is only Brahman; in It there is no duality whatsoever.

The nature of *Brahman* is discussed here since its is the theme for the next few verses. The nature of the Self cannot be defined, but it can be indicated in terms of Its expression in the gross, subtle and causal bodies during Its corresponding waking, dream and deep-sleep conditions. In the gross body it can be said to be That which expresses as its Existence, in the subtle body That which expresses as

Intelligence or Knowledge, and in the causal body That which expresses as Bliss, *(Sat-chitananda)*--This is a famous term used in the *Upanishads* to indicate *Brahman.*

The Self is a mass of Existence: *(sat-ghana)*--We generally know only the existence of things and beings. But really speaking, when we say that a tree exists, we refer to the Existence in the tree. The existence in the tree is the Existence in the stone, in the animal, in the human. This Existence which is the common factor in all things that exist is called *sat.* The mass of Existence is *Brahman.*

That which is essence of pure Intelligence: *(chit-ghana)*--by which an intelligent man expresses himself, his intelligence, is the Self, the Consciousness, the Life. Where Life exists, there is intelligence; where life is extinct, there is no intelligence. This principle of Intelligence is the same in the scientist and in the artist, in the saint and in the sinner, in the criminal and in the animal, nay, even in the plant and the unicellular organism. That which expresses as Intelligence everywhere is indicated here as a mass of Intelligence *(chit-ghana).*

That which is of the nature of eternal Bliss: *(ananda-ghana). Ananda* is bliss. When the mind is not agitated there is the experience of joy. Lesser the agitations, greater the joy. Naturally, therefore, when you have trascended the mind the state should be, in terms of the mind, supreme happiness. On the mind-intellect level, there is the concept of time and therefore, every experience is changeable and variable. This Bliss, Supreme, since it is experienced beyond the mind, cannot be conditioned by time. Therefore, It is eternal Bliss *(nitya-ananda).*

Without activity: *(a-kriyam)*--In the presence of the Self activities take place, but in these activities It is not involved.*

---

* आत्मचैतन्यमाश्रित्य देहेन्द्रिय मनोधियः ।
स्वक्रियार्थेषु वर्तन्ते सूर्यलोकं यथा जनाः ॥

Depending upon the energy or vitalty of Consciousness the body, senses; mind and intellect engage themselves in their respective activities, just as men work depending upon the light of the sun.
--Atma-bodha-20.

The sun illumines the world, the dynamic activities of which go on unmolested, but the sun is not involved in them in any way. So too, this mass of Existence-Knowledge-Bliss, the Self, is not involved in any of the activites of the cosmos.[1]

This Self alone is Real. Indeed there is no duality in It whatsoever.

प्रत्यगेकरसं पूर्णमनन्तं सर्वतोमुखम् ।
एकमेवाद्वयं ब्रह्म नेह नानास्ति किञ्चन ॥४६७॥

467. The subject within all. Non-dual, homogeneous, endless, all-pervading, there is one *Brahman;* in It there is no duality whatsoever.

This *Brahman* is not an object but is the very subjective core, the essence in each individual *(pratyak)*. It knows no change and so ever remanis in the same nature *(eka-rasa)*, meaning, It is without any change or modification and knows no destruction.[2]

All-full: *(poornam)*--There is nothing in It except Itself. So no distinction in It is ever possible.[3] It is endless, in-as-much as It is unborn and therefore, undying. That which is birthless and deathless is not only changeless, but also Infinite.

Whose face is everywhere: *(sarvatomukham)*--It is All-pervading and therefore, never can we reach a point in the cosmos where It is not, It being the very Consciousness and the Life in each one of us. This *Brahman*, the Self alone is. Indeed, in It there can be no duality whatsoever.

अहेयमनुपादेयमनादेयमनाश्रयम् ।
एकमेवाद्वयं ब्रह्म नेह नानास्ति किञ्चन ॥४६८॥

---

1. Therefore, commentators interpret अक्रियम् as सृष्ट्यादि क्रिया शून्यम्॥

2 एकरसम् is equal to नाशरहितम् ।

3 सजातीय विजातीय स्वगत भेदरहित वस्तु पूर्णम् ॥

468. That which is to be neither shunned nor taken up nor accepted, that which is Non-dual and without support--there is one *Brahman;* in It there is no duality whatsoever.

The very essence in all can never be rejected. Nor can It be "accepted". You can only accept or reject a thing which is other than you. It is one's own Real Nature and hence can neither be rejected nor accepted. You cannot say, "I have met me"; nor can you say, "I have not met me". "I am", that is all. The Self is the ultimate subject, one's own nature *(atmaswaroopatwat)*. How can I jump on to my own shoulders?

That which has no superimposition: *(an-aadeyam)*--In this *Brahman* there is no non-apprehension and consequently, no super-impositions. Reality is pure and is untouched by the vehicles of matter and their projections.

With no support: *(an-ashrayam)*[1]--*What is the abode of Brahman?* It is Its abode.

There is only one *Brahman* with no duality in It.

निर्गुणं निष्कलं सूक्ष्मं निर्विकल्पं निरंजनम् ।
एकमेवाद्वयं ब्रह्म नेह नानास्ति किञ्चन ॥४६९॥

469. With no qualities or parts, It is subtle without disturbances and taintless-- there is one *Brahman;* in it there is no duality whatsoever.

Without any qualities or properties: *(nirguna)*--Anything that has properties is perishable. All finite things have properties. If there be an infinite Reality which is imperishable, It cannot be a substance. If It is not a substance, It cannot have properties.

Without parts: *(nishkala)*--It is One-without-a-second. It is Infinite. In the Infinite there cannot be any parts. If there are parts, there should be something other than the Infinite which conditions It. No more then is it Infinite.

---

1. न आश्रयो यस्य ।

Subtle: *(sookshma)* --because of Its all-pervasiveness.*

Without any thoughts and agitations. *(nirvikalpa)* --because the mind and intellect have been transcended.

Taintless: *(niranjanah)* --because there are no *vasanas* in It. This great Reality is one alone, without any plurality.

अनिरूप्यस्वरूपं यन्मनोवाचामगोचरम् ।
एकमेवाद्वयं ब्रह्म नेह नानास्ति किञ्चन ॥४७०॥

470. The Real Nature of which is incomprehensible, which is beyond mind and speech and Non-dual, there is only *Brahman;* in It there is no duality whatsoever.

Incomprehensible: *(aniroopya)*--Brahman has an incomprehensible nature. It is imperceptible. Through the organs of perception and comprehension you can have only mediate knowledge. It is not an object, so it cannot be perceived by the sense-organs.

There are very many things in the world which we cannot perceive through our sense-organs,--love, mathematical formulae, the veracity of scientific truths etc. They are comprehended by our mind and intellect. But the Self is that, where even mind and speech cannot reach *(mano-vacham-agocharam)***

The supreme Reality is that which cannot be perceived through the mediation of the instruments of sense-organs nor

---

* सर्वव्यापकत्वा ।

** यन्मनसा न मनुते येनाहुर्मनो मतम् ।
तदेव ब्रह्मत्वं विद्धि नेदं यदिदमुपासते ॥
यद्वचानभ्युदितं येनवागभ्युद्यते ।
तदेव ब्रह्म त्वं विद्धि नेदं यदिदमुपासते ॥

This great Truth is that, which the mind cannot feel but because of which the mind feels, that which speech cannot explain but because of which speech is; understand That to be Brahman.--

--Kenopanishad. Ch. I. 5 & 4.

through the mediation of the mind and the intellect. It is not a *mediate* knowledge. It is *immediate* knowledge. It is subjective Realisation.

Truth is the non-dual *Brahman.* There is truly, no plurality in It.

सत्समृद्धं स्वतःसिद्धं शुद्धं बुद्धमनीद्दशम् ।
एकमेवाद्वयं ब्रह्म नेह नानास्ति किञ्चन ॥४७१॥

471. Self-existing, Self-evident, pure Intelligence, unlike anything finite. Non-dual, there is only one *Brahman;* in It there is no plurality whatsoever.

This great Reality is full of *sat*--pure Existence. It is not gained by th intervention of any equipment. It is Self-existing. It is Self-evident. It is not an object which can be established by any proo. Your existence need not be proved. You are. Everything else you can prove or disprove, but that "you are" needs no proof.

Pure : *(suddham)*--because there is nothing other than It, in It.

Intelligence: *(buddham)*--is the very nature of Truth --It is Knowledge Absolute.

Not like "these" : *(aneedrisham)*--"These" means, the experiences that we live at these moments in the finite realms. It is not like the objects, emotions and thoughts. This great Truth is something Unique. It is *vilakshana*--not like any of the things we know.

This *Brahman* is verily One-without-a-second. In It there is no pluralistic phenomenon.

73. Experience of Self-hood. (472-479)

निरस्तरागा विनिरस्तभोगाः
शान्ताः सुदान्ता यतयो महान्तः ।

विज्ञाय तत्त्वं परमेतदन्ते
प्राप्ताः परां निर्वृतिमात्मयोगात् ॥४७२॥

472. Noble-hearted renunciated who are rid of attachments, who have given up all sense-enjoyments, who are calm and controlled, realise this supreme Truth and at the end, they gain Bliss supreme as a result of their Self-realisation.

Having explained the nature of Reality, the Teacher gives some practical suggestions for students who are trying to experience the Supreme. Here, practical methods for *sadhana* are being advised.

Those in whom all desires are withdrawn: *(nirastaragah)*

All desires for sense-indulgences set: *(vinirastabhogah)*--The idea of indulging and seeking a fulfilment in the world outside is completely set *(asta)* in his mind.

Whose mind has become serene: *(santah)*--Whose mind is no more rushing into the world of objects since it is established in the contemplation of the Lord.

Those who are not allowing their minds to enter into the remembrances of past indulgences: *(sudantah)*.

Those high-souled people: *(mahantah)*.

Those who are putting forth the efforts: *(yatah)*.

Those who have completely controlled their sense-organs and mind and have apprehended Reality within themselves, reach supreme Peace and contentment at the end of their *prarabdha karma*. There will be such all-enveloping Bliss Absolute into which they merge that there are no more *vasanas* to excite their minds to run towards the OET in order to seek fulfilment.

भवानपीदं परतत्त्वमात्मनः
स्वरूपमानन्दघनं विचार्य ।

विधूय मोहं स्वमनःप्रकल्पितं
मुक्तः कृतार्थो भवतु प्रबुद्धः ॥४७३॥

473. You too, discriminate thus, (be established in) this surpassing Truth, the real nature of the *Atman* which is Bliss Absolute, and shaking off the delusion created by your own mind, be liberated and illumined and reach the fulfilment of your life..

In the early part of the text,* the *Guru* had promised the student who had surrendered at his feet, by saying, "Fear not, O intelligent boy! There is no danger for you. For crossing the ocean of *samsar*, there is a method. I shall prescribe to you that path by which all others have crossed this *samsar* in the past." By the time Sankara came to verse 471, he finished prescribing the path to the disciple. Now he says, "Thou too, O learned one, having directly experienced this supreme Self which is of the nature of Bliss Absolute, go completely beyond the pluralistic world which is a projection of thy own mind."

The BMI, PFT and OET are not the Self. We have the idea that we are them. This is a delusion. Having removed this delusion, he who has awakened to the higher plane of Consciousness is liberated from all weaknesses of mortals, *(adhyasa-roopa-bandha-mukta)*. May you too, become fulfilled--fully awakened--to the higher plane of Consciousness.

समाधिना साधुविनिश्चलात्मना
पश्यात्मतत्त्वं स्फुटबोधचक्षुषा ।
निःसंशयं सम्यगवेक्षितश्चे-
च्छ्रुतः पदार्थो न पुनर्विकल्प्यते ॥४७४॥

474. Perceive the nature of the Self with the eye of perfect Knowledge through *Samadhi*, where the mind has been brought to complete quietude. If the declarations of *Sruti* (heard from the Teacher) are perfectly understood without a trace of doubt, it can lead to no more scepticism.

---

* Ibid verse 43.

A steady mind is one which does not oscillate under the fascination of objects, emotions and thoughts. The mind which is steadily trained to withdraw from the storms of passions of the OET, and which has come to rest quietly in single-pointed comtemplation of the non-dual *Brahman*, sees the Reality. "Seeing" here does not mean seeing with the eyes. When you see a thing with your eyes, you have no doubt about its existence. A quietened mind apprehends Reality beyond all doubt and hence it is said, it "sees". The mind sees this great Self with the clear eye of Knowledge. "Clear eye of Knowledge" means, "with steady mind and intellect". The contemplative mind develops intuitive power by which it comes to apprehend the Reality.

Till there is such an experience, there will be doubts. All traces of doubt are dispelled only when one apprehends this great Truth. If you have understood the theme of the scriptures *(srutipadartha)*, i.e. the meaning of the *Mahavakyas*, you have an intellectual appreciation of the Self. Thereafter, when you experience Reality, your knowledge of the scriptures will be confirmed.

स्वस्याविद्याबन्धसम्बन्धमोक्षा-
त्सत्यज्ञानानन्दरूपात्मलब्धौ ।
शास्त्रं युक्तिर्देशिकोक्तिः प्रमाणं
चान्तःसिद्धा स्वानुभूतिः प्रमाणम् ॥४७५॥

475. When the Self, the Existence-Knowledge-Bliss, is realised, through liberation from one's bondage of ignorance, then the scriptures, logical reasoning, the words of the Teacher--these are proofs; the subjective experience of one's own concentrated mind is yet another proof.

Liberation is defined as "Liberation from the bondage of one's contact with the non-apprehension", *(avidya-bandha-sambandha-mokshah)*--When there are misapprehensions, one is bound to identify with them. This is the sorrowful condition of the *jeeva*. To be free from this conditions is to be liberated. *Avidya* can be ended only on the apprehension of Reality, the *Atman*, which is of the nature of *satyam-jnanam-anantam.*

Truth: *(satyam)*--is that which remains the same in all the three periods of time.

Pure Knowledge: *(jnanam)* --in the light of which all other kinds of knowledge are possible.

Endless, Infinite: *(anantam)*.

The authorities from which Knowledge of the Self is gained are, (1) The Sastras : (Sruti)--the *Upanishads* which are the recorded declarations of men of Realisations: (2) Argumentation and logical thinking : *(yukti);* and (3) Words of the learned Master: *(desikoktih).* By reading books and by logic, to some extent, one can understand, but the words of the learned Teacher help us to grasp the theme thoroughly.

If, what you have read and understood by logical thinking and what has been told to you by the Teacher, are all in one line, then, you have caught the plane. But even these are not quite sufficient. The final take-off is one's experience of Reality.

बन्धो मोक्षश्च तृप्तिश्च चिन्ताऽऽरोग्यक्षुधादयः ।
स्वेनैव वेद्या यज्ज्ञानं परेषामानुमानिकम् ॥४७६॥

476. Bondage and liberation, contentment and anxiety, health, hunger, etc. are known only by the person concerned; others have knowledge of these by mere inference.

Our experiences of boundage, liberation, and contentment are just like our worries, health, hunger etc. These are to be experienced by each individual himself. My hunger you cannot experience. My worries you can never understand. For your ill-health I will not take medicine. Others can only infer; but they cannot live my experiences. Every one has to live his own.

This is a supporting verse for the term *swanu-bhootih* in the previous verse.

Just as physical pains and hungers can be known only through subjective experience, so too, Reality has to be experienced by each one, individually. As long as others tell us about It, we can only imagine what It could be like. But Knowledge will come only through a direct experience.

तटस्थिता बोधयन्ति गुरवः श्रुतयो यथा ।
प्रज्ञयैव तरेद्विद्वानीश्वरानुगृहीतया ॥४७७॥

477. Standing apart, the Teachers and the scriptures instruct the disciple; the man of Realisation crosses over *(Avidya)* by illumination and the Grace of God.

The *Upanishads* and the Teachers, standing apart, can only indicate the Truth. They do not stand apart from Truth; they stand apart from us, the disciples. When the Teacher advises the disciple, it is indirect knowledge for the student *(anumana)*. The Teacher declares it. The *Upanishads* declare It. But It is not the disciple's own experience.

Taking these as an authority or guidance, the intelligent disciples go beyond because of their own illumination, and with the Grace of the Lord. *Anugraha* means Grace. Hence the spiritual *vasanas* must be cultivated. Spiritual practices must be undertaken for many years.

One who controls, regulates and orders everything in the cosmos is called *Iswara*, the Lord. He is the Lord in each one of us. Our own *vasanas* determine, order, regulate and control our lives. Hence our *vasanas* are our Lord.

Thus, Truth can be experienced only by the student who has done *sadhana* for a sufficiently long time. He who has created spiritual *vasanas* can bless himself. Such an individual crosses *samsar* by his own illumination, when he studies and thinks independently and is helped by his Teacher from time to time.

स्वानुभूत्या स्वयं ज्ञात्वा स्वमात्मानमखण्डितम् ।
संसिद्धः सम्मुखं तिष्ठेन्निर्विकल्पात्मनाऽऽत्मनि ॥४७८॥

478. Knowing his own Absolute Self through Realisation, becoming perfect, a man should stand face to face before the *Atman*, with mind free from all concepts of dualism.

The Self is apprehended in yourself, by yourself. When the unagitated intellect is rendered steady, one can sit face to face with one's Self, in one's Self, by one's Self.

"To sit fact to face" is to become one with. When you have moved away from sleep and dream, you are face to face with the waker. When you have away from the BMI, PFT, OET, you are face to face with *Brahman*.

वेदान्तसिद्धान्तनिरुक्तिरेषा,
ब्रह्मैव जीवः सकलं जगच्च ।
अखण्डरूपस्थितिरेव मोक्षो
ब्रह्माद्वितीये श्रुतयः प्रमाणम् ॥४७९॥

479. The final opinion of all Vedantic discussion is, that the *jeeva* as well as the entire universe are *Brahman* alone, that liberation means to be rooted in *Brahman*, the indivisible Entity: (The statement) that *Brahman* is non-dual has its authority is *Sruti*.

The *Upanishads* from the essence of the teachings of the *Vedas*, of which they are the concluding portions. Hence the *Upanishads* are known by the term, *"Vedanta"*. Concluding the address, the Teacher summarises his instructions to the disciple in this verse. The conclusions arrived at in the *Upanishads* briefly are, (1) *jeeva*, the individuality is *Brahman* alone; (2) *Jagat*, the world of plurality is also *Brahman;* and (3) the state of experience of this one Reality where there is no duality, is liberation.

When the dreamer merges with the waker, the dream world also merges into the waking world. That is the liberation of the dreamer. Similarly, the seeker, by his *sadhana,* merges with the Infinitude. The absence of plurality is the experience of Reality.

The authority for the above conclusions is *Sruti,* the *Upanishads* themselves.

74. Practice of Knowledge--Disciple. (480-520)

इति गुरुवचनाच्छ्रुतिप्रमाणा-
त्परमवगम्य सतत्त्वमात्मयुक्त्या ।
प्रशमितकरणः समाहितात्मा
क्वचिदचलाकृतिरात्मनिष्ठितोऽभूत् ॥४८०॥

480. Through the words of the Teachers, the pronouncements of the scriptures and by his own reasoning with senses controlled and mind fixed, at an auspicious moment realising the supreme Truth, he becomes motionless in form and perfectly established in the Self.

Earlier, in the first quarter of the text,* the disciple asked, "When I reject the *pancha-kosas* I find that there is nothing. What is there to be experienced and with what? It is all a big Zero." The *Guru* started his answer from verse 213 and concluded his arguments in verse 478, summarising the conclusions of the *Upanishads.*

So far, with what has been said by the Teacher compared with Upanishadic declarations and one's own independent logical thinking, one indirect knowledge of the Self. Now, having gained this indirect knowledge, if he quietens his sense-organs and also quietens his mind and intellect in comtemplation of Narayana, he gains direct experience of the Realisty.

Thus, the disciple becomes immovable established in the nature of the Self. A rare student thus BECOMES.

* Ibid verse 212.

किञ्चित्कालं समाधाय परे ब्रह्मणि मानसम् ।
उत्थाय परमानन्दादिदं वचनमब्रवीत् ॥४८१॥

481. After concentrating his mind on the supreme *Brahman* for some time, he rose, and out of supreme Bliss, he sopke as follows.

When one transports oneself into the experience of Infinitude, nobody can say how long the experience will last. There is not count of time. It all depends upon the individual. Time is relative, and its standards cannot be exchanged in the different planes of Consciousness. To reach There is your *purushartha;* but having reached no *purushartha* is involved.

Having lived in that state of *Samadhi* for an immeasurable period of time, the disciple rose form his seat of meditation. He could not contain his joy within the web of his body-min-intellect equipment. So he cried out and declared in exquisite ecstasy the infinite Bliss of his experience.

बुद्धिर्विनष्टा गलिता प्रवृत्ति-
र्ब्रह्मात्मनोरेकतयाऽधिगत्या ।
इदं न जानेऽप्यनिदं न जाने
किं वा कियद्वा सुखमस्त्यपारम् ॥४८२॥

482. My intellect is completely razed and all activities have dropped off by realising the oneness of *Atman* and *Brahman;* I understand neither "this" nor "not-this", nor do I know what or of what measure is this endless Bliss.

My intellect is gone: *(Buddhir-vinashta)*--The intellect which was asking a thousand questions, Why? How? When? Where? What? --that intellect, even if I serach for it now I cannot find it there is no trace of agitation.

My activity at all levels of personality is completely dissolved: *(galita-pravrittih)*-- The activity and the intellect are not destroyed because of Tamas; but they are dissolved at the alter of the experience that the Self in me is the Self everywhere-- *Brahma-atmanoreka-taya-adhigatya.* Having awakened to the plane of Consciouness, the present intellect is no more and so, the various egocentric activities cannot be pursued.

The function of the intellect is to discriminate. Now a stage has come where I do not understand anything as this-this-this, nor do I understand anything as not-this, not-this, not-this. I do not see anything other than *Brahman*. I see only one *Brahman*, everywhere, at all times. That experience cannot be explained. I cannot, in terms of measure, say what It is or how much It is.

"What" and "how much" are the methods of explaining a thing, they being the questions asked during a qualitative and quantitative analysis. The experience of infinitude can not be subjected to such analysis. To explain a thing the intellect is necessary. The intellect cannot explain an experience that trascends it. All that I can say is, *"Brahman* alone is, all that is". It is endless Bliss.

With that experience when I look around all things get destroyed, in the sense, all names and forms disappear and only pure Consciousness remains. The meditator without getting up from his seat jumps up and dances without legs, in the ecstatic joy where there is no mind to enjoy and thunders forth where there is no mouth to talk.

वाचा वक्तुमशक्यमेव मनसा मन्तुं न वा शक्यते
स्वानन्दामृतपूरपूरितपरब्रह्माम्बुधेर्वैभवम् ।
अम्भोराशिविशीर्णवार्षिकशिलाभावं भजन्मे मनो
यस्यांशांशलवे विलीनमधुनाऽऽनन्दात्मना निर्वृतम् ॥४८३॥

483. Impossible for speech to express, impossible for the mind to conceive is the splendour of the ocean of the supreme *Brahman*, replete with the swell of the nectarine Bliss of the Self. In an infinitesimal part of It my mind merged like a hailstone in the ocean is now content with the essence of that Bliss.

A change of metre is adopted here to suit the song of Ecstasy.

It is impossible to express in words the experience of Infinitude. It is not possible to think of that experience with the mind. It is the glory of the ocean of the supreme Self which is Immortal Joy. This glory is the unending infinite Bliss of my own Real Nature.

Overflowing Bliss, Eternal and Immortal, is the ocean of the infinite Self, whose glory can neither be expressed nor thought of. When I go there, "I" cannot exist; when I come back, "I" cannot explain.

"What happens to you at that time?"

"Ambhorashi-vishirnavarshikashilabhavam bhajanme mano."

My mind becomes exactly like the hailstone fallen in the ocean."*

A hailstone is essentially water. When it falls into the vast expanse of water, the ocean, it may sink in and reach a few yards below the surface, then, there is no more going or coming. It becomes the ocean. Similarly, the mind in meditation can take you thus far and no further..... All that I can say is that It is *Ananda*. In It there is a completer sense of fulfilment. It is the joy in which there is no trace of the fear of ever losing It. When the mind meditates on *Brahman*, since it is of the nature of *Brahman*, it itself becomes *Brahman*.

क्व गतं केन वा नीतं कुत्र लीनमिदं जगत् ।
अधुनैव मया दृष्टं नास्ति किं महदद्भूतम् ॥४८४॥

484. Where has it gone, who has removed it, where has the universe merged? Just now it was seen by me, has it now ceased to be? Wonder of wonders!

---

* Here one remembers Sri Ramkrishana's parable of the salt doll entering the ocean to measure its depth and beocming the ocean, itself being essentially of the nature of the ocean.

The experience of Infinitude is being dramatised on the stage of the finite. The disciple asks, "Where has the pluralistic world gone? By whom was it removed? I saw a world before, which I do not see now. Into what has it dissolved? Is it, that all these years I was suffering in a non-existing world?

"A wonder of wonders it is! The world I saw was a wonder. Greater still is the wonder that it has all disappeared now. The wonder of wonders is what I am experiencing now."

किं हेयं किमुपादेयं किमन्यत्किं विलक्षणम् ।
अखण्डानन्दपीयूषपूर्णे ब्रह्ममहार्णवे ॥४८५॥

485. What is to be accepted and what rejected, what is different and what dissimilar, in the mighty ocean of *Brahman* filled with the nectar of absolute Bliss?

The ocean of *Brahman*, is the limitless nectar of Bliss. In that boundless, overflowing, unbroken Bliss, what is to be shunned or accepted? There is nothing other than It. It alone is.

You cannot say,"that" because in It there is not "this". "This" you cannot say because there is no "that". There is no "this-ness" or "that-ness". It is IS-NESS. Even this is a compromise. It is endless Bliss.

न किञ्चिदत्र पश्यामि न श्रृणोमि न वेद्म्यहम् ।
स्वात्मनेव सदानन्दरूपेणास्मि विलक्षणः ॥४८६॥

486 In this I neither see nor hear nor know anything. I exist as the *Atman*, Bliss Eternal, distinct from everything else.

In the culmination of meditation, where the meditator has merged into the meditation, there are no objects other than "me", nor are there any equipments of experience. There is neither mind nor intellect. I simply exist as myself *(swatnanaiva)*. It is the total annihilation of the individuality at the altar of the Absolute. In my own Self, I revel as my Self, with my Self, which is of the nature of unbroken Bliss at all times. Unique It is, something totally different from all that is known.

नमो नमस्ते गुरवे महात्मने
विमुक्तसङ्गाय सदुत्तमाय ।
नित्याद्वयानन्दरसस्वरूपिणे
भूम्ने सदाऽपारदयाम्बुधाम्ने ॥४८७॥

487. Salutations to thee, O noble *Guru*, who art free from attachments, best among the noble ones, the embodiment of the essence of Eternal, Non-dual Bliss, who art endless, ever the limitless ocean of mercy.

The student remembers his Teacher who has showed him the path, and is grateful to him.

"O large-hearted one", *(Mahatmane)*, he exclaims. Large hearted because, in spite of our weaknesses and animal tendencies, he, with his infinite kindness, lifts us from our present limitations to the vision of this Great Goal.

The salutations are not offered to the form, the physical frame of the Teacher. For, he who is best among realised ones, who has segregated himself from his physical, emotional, and intellectual layers, from egocentric attitudes and from the sense of fulfilment arising out of objects, emotions and thoughts, is the *GURU*.

The Teacher is of the nature of *Brahman* Itself. He is addressed here as "best among the realised ones", because there are a number of realised ones in the world, but it is this Master who has helped the student and guided him to the realisation of the Self. The discription of the Teacher given in this verse is that of *Brahman* Itself---*Nitya, Adwaya* and *Ananda-Swaroopa*.*

The Teacher is that shoreless ocean of kindness, which is external, Non-dual, and the All-prevading Bliss-Form.

* For elaboration refer verses 220,221 and 222.

To that Teacher, my *namaskaras.*

यत्कटाक्षशशिसान्द्रचन्द्रिकापातधूतभवतापजश्रमः ।
प्राप्तवानहमखण्डवैभवानन्दमात्मपदमक्षयं क्षणात् ॥४८८॥

488. Whose glance, like a cascade of moon-beams, has removed my fatigue caused by the miseries of the word, and taken me to the indestrictible Bliss of infinite splendour, the Atman, in but a moment.

As the moon cools the earth which has been backed by the sun during the day, the sorrows arising in one's bosom because of worldly tensions are lifted by the compassionate glance of the Teacher. The personality which has been feeling the tensions of *samsaric* sorrows is cooled and comforted and the disciple rises to the State of Self-hood, the glory of which is unbroken Bliss, blessed by the Grace of the *Guru.* The *samsaric* exhaustions gathered during one's "lifetime" are all lifted from the personality in a twinkle of the eye by the *Guru's* Grace.

The example of the moonlight cooling the earth is taken because the moon does not actually come in contact with the earth to remove its heat. In the presence of the moon, the earth by itself gives up the heat gathered during the day. Similarly, the student, in the presence of the Teacher, guided by his Knowledge, himself reaches the cool comfort of the blissful state of the Self and leaves all the tensions and stresses of life created by the ego and the endless avarices of the flesh. All this happens in the flash of a moment, by just one look.

To that great *Guru* my *namaskaras.*

धन्योऽहं कृतकृत्योऽहं विमुक्तोऽहं भवग्रहात् ।
नित्यानन्दस्वरूपोऽहं पूर्णोऽहं त्वदनुग्रहात् ॥४८९॥

489. Blessed am I, I have reached the fulfilment of my life and am free from the "shark" of transmigration. I am the embodiment of eternal Bliss, I am the Infinite, all by your Grace.

Blessed am I. I have attained the fulfilment of my life. I am completely liberated from the clutches of the shark of *samsar*.

Samsar is compared to a shark because the shark will not eat you up limb by limb. It will swalow you whole---suit and boot. The digestion takes place without your knowledge, even when you are living inside. In the chambers of the belly you can walk about. You can go to office, you can eat, sleep and breed and the digestive secretions will slowly work upon you and reduce you to a deplorable state. Are we not living this living-death in the belly of *samsar?*

Having realised the Self-hood, I am liberated from this death and hence am indeed blessed. As the Self, I am of the nature of eternal Bliss. I am full. there is no sense of deficiency and consequently, there is no desire to supply it.

All this is gained by thy Grace, O Teacher! To thee, my *namaskara.*

असङ्गोहमनङ्गोऽहमलिङ्गोऽहमभङ्गुरः ।
प्रशान्तोऽहमनन्तोऽहममलोऽहं चिरन्तनः ॥४९०॥

490. Unattached am I, disembodied am I, free from the subtle body am I and undecaying; serence am I, Infinite am I, unsullied am I, and endless too.

The teacher has been advising and guiding the student up to verse 478. From verse 482 onwards, it is the student who is talking. Having realised this Self-hood, the student talks about his experience of Infinitude. From 482 to 489 he was talking as the PFT.

Now the entire vision has changed. Having reached the *Paramatman*, the individual who has become the Self, cries out in the ecstasy of his identification with *Brahman*.

These verses help the *sadhaks* in their contemplation. Unattached am I: *asangoham*---It is only the BMI that get attached to the world of OET and in their self-identification they conjure up the miserable PFT attitude themselves. Attachment is the function of the M-&-I and the state of Self-hood being beyond the M-&-I, there cannot be any sense of attachment. In the one Infinite mass of Consciousness, who can get attached to what? disembodied am I; *anangoham*--- In the homogeneous mass of consciousness which is the nature of the Self there can never be any separate part, with different structures and funtions. As the Self is a realm transcending the physical, mental and intellectual bodies, there are no "limbs"---in the Self.

Free from the subtle body am I---*alingoham*---The instruments of feeling and thinking together constitute the subtle body which is otherwise called in *Vedanta* as *Linga-sarira*. The term *alinga* means one devoid of the M-&-I, and therefore, of their agitations. Undecaying am I--- *abhangurah*--the term also can mean "without sprout".* In the context here it means that there will be no *vasanas* sprouting into thoughts and actions. The meaning and the ideas conveyed by the rest of the terms are given elsewhere.** Contemplate upon them.

अकर्ताहमभोक्ताहमविकारोऽहमक्रियः ।
शुद्धबोधस्वरूपोऽहं केवलोऽहं सदाशिवः ॥४९१॥

491. I am not the doer, I am not the experiencer, I am without modification and without activity; I am the embodiment of pure Knowledge, I am Absolute, and eternal Auspiciousness am I.

The *Atman* functioning through the mind is the doer and expressing through the intellect is the enjoyer. Since the mind and the intellect have been transcended, what remains is the Self. Enjoyment of one's own Self *(swaroopa-ananda)*, then becomes possible and the enjoyment of other objects

* ankura---sprout.
an-ankura---without sprout.

** Verses 220, 221 and 222.

(vishaya-ananda or dwaita-ananda or bhoga-ananda), is not possible.

Activities take place in me. But I have no activity. I am pure Knowledge---the objectless-Awareness. I am That in whose presence all knowledge is possible. I am "knowledge of a thing minus the thing". Absolute and ever Auspicious, Immaculate and without imperfections am I.

द्रष्टुः श्रोतुर्वक्तुः कर्तुर्भोक्तुर्विभिन्न एवाहम् ।
नित्यनिरन्तरनिष्क्रियनिःसीमासङ्गपूर्णबोधात्मा ॥४९२॥

492. Indeed, I am other than the seer, hearer, speaker, doer and experiencer. I am eternal and unbroken, beyond activity, boundless, unattached and Infinite, the essence of Knowledge.

Trying to express in words that which is beyond the reach of words, he feels, as it were, choked. Hence the choking metre. The incapacity to express the Inexpressible is indicated in this stammering verse.

Seer, hearer, speaker, doer and enjoyer, all put together form the individuality. When the individuality is transcended, one reaches the state of Self-hood.

There is the negation of the PFT in the first half and the assertion of OM in the latter half of the verse. Upon this. CONTEMPLATE.

नाहमिदं नाहमदोऽप्युभयोरवभासकं परं शुद्धम् ।
बाह्याभ्यन्तरशून्यं पूर्णं ब्रह्माद्वितीयमेवाहम् ॥४९३॥

493. I am neither *this* nor *that* but the supreme Illuminator of both; I am pure. I have neither an exterior nor an interior. I am Infinite; verily, I am the non-dual *Brahman*.

The student, while experiencing the pure Consciousness, feels, "I am neither this which I considered myself to be through *avidya*, nor am I that, which the Teacher made me understand through *vidya*. I am the Illuminator of both these

---*avidya* and *vidya* which are but aspects of my intellect. I am the supreme Self."

"This" means the body. With reference to the body we generally say, inside and outside. Inside the body are matters subjective and outside the body are matters objective. If the body itself is not, then what is inside or what is outside? Inside and outside of what? In deep-sleep when the body is not available there is no inside and outside. In that condition, is the darkness inside or outside the body? It is *poornam*, all-full.

I am the non-dual *Brahman*, other than which there is nothing at all.

निरुपममनादितत्त्वं त्वमहमिदमद इति कल्पनादूरम् ।
नित्यानन्दैकरसं सत्यं ब्रह्माद्वितीयमेवाहम् ॥४९४॥

494. I am unparalleled, the originless Reality, beyond such imaginations as you and I, this and that. The essence of Bliss eternal, the Truth, non-dual *Brahman* am I.

Reality is unequalled and is without beginning. Time itself is a concept projected on *Brahman*. Egocentric attachment with my body (gross, subtle and causal), is "I"; egocentric projection on your body is "you". Thus, "you" and "I" can only be at the egocentric BMI level. With reference to my body, that which is nearer to it is "this" and that which is further away is "that". "This" and "that" are just another set of superimpositions at the gross level. These concepts imply conditioning in space. The Self is beyond time, space and causation, eternal and nor-dual.

That *Brahman* am I.

नारायणोऽहं नरकान्तकोऽहं
पुरान्तकोऽहं पुरुषोहमीशः ।
अखण्डबोधोऽहमशेषसाक्षी
निरीश्वरोऽहं निरहं च निर्ममः ॥४९५॥

495. I am Narayana, I am the slayer of Naraka. I am the destroyer of Tripura; I am the supreme Being, the Lord. I am unbroken Knowledge, I am the Witness of everything; I have no othere Lord and I am devoid of "I" and "mine".

Who makes these statements? It is not the one who is the son/daughter of one's parents. It is the one who is established *(aaroodha)*, in the Self who cries out.

Nara is Brahman; *ayana* is the "glory". *"Narayana"* is one whose glory is the whole universe. *Narka* is hell. *Narakantaka* is one who has ended his hell; one in whom there is no trace of sorrow. Living at the body level is to be in *naraka.* The criminal, the devil who creates hell for one is the PFT. One's own, not somebody else's *Narakosura*, the ugly devil with horns and tail is the inflated ego. When he is destroyed, the Atman is attained.

In mythology, Lord Shiva is *Purantaka*, the destroyer of the demon Tripurasura. The deeper implication of the term is this. *Puri* means, a town in which people live. Individual live in the three states of waking, dream and deep-sleep. When these three worlds are transcended, one enters the state of Self-hood, also called the *Turiya* state. It is the fourth plane of Cionsciousness and hence he is the destroyer of the three *puris.* At every moment in our lives, we live in one *puri* destroying the other two. We are not able to destroy all the three at the same time. Lord Shiva, the embodiment of Auspiciousness Absolute is the One who has accomplished this feat. he is the supreme meditator. He am I. shiva am I *(Sivoham)*, I am purusha, the Atman, "who dwells in this equipment"*.

I am *Isa*, the Lord, the controller, the ruler, the Regulator. But for me, the body would not have worked. But for *me*, none of the experiences of waking, dream and deep-sleep would have been possible. Because of me everything is possible. Without me nothing can be. Naturally, therefore *Isa* am I, the Lord of all experiences.

---

* पुरिशयनात् - पुरुषः ।

I am objectless-Knowledge, the Witness of everything, without exception. When I myself have become *Iswara*, how can there be any other *Iswara* for me? I am the Self, without I-ness and my-ness.

सर्वेषु भूतेष्वहमेव संस्थितो
ज्ञानात्मनाऽन्तर्बहिराश्रयः सन् ।
भोक्ता च भोग्यं स्वयमेव सर्वं
यद्यत्पृथग्दृष्टमिदन्तया पुरा ॥४९६॥

496. I alone reside as Knowledge in all beings and am their external and internal support. I myself am the experiencer and the experienced; I am all that was experienced by me separately as "this" and "not-this" before.

"I alone revel in all creatures as their Knowledge".---When a scientist discovers what is in outer space and a bird understands what is edible---in both cases, the understanding Principle is I alone. The discriminative intellect in the scientist and that in the bird could not have functioned without me. I am the Light in which all subjects know their objects. The subject and the object, the enjoyer and the enjoyed are all nothing but me.

On waking, one realises that the mind itself had become the dreamer and the dream-world. So too, all that was declared as this-this-this before awakening to one's Self-hood is now realised as one's own Self.

मय्यखण्डसुखाम्भोधौ बहुधा विश्ववीचयः ।
उत्पद्यन्ते विलीयन्ते मायामारुतविभ्रमात् ॥४९७॥

497. In me the ocean of unbroken Bliss, endles waves of the universe are created and destroyed by the play of the storm of *Maya*.

The infinite varieties of the names and forms in the world around are but ripples and waves in me, the ocean of infinite Bliss. The world of plurality rises from Truth, exists in Truth and dies away in Truth.

That Truth am I.

The waves rise in the ocean because of the breeze, the winds and the storms. *Maya*, the non-apprehension of Reality, is the cause because of which the waves of misapprehension rise, exist and subside in me, who am the ocean of Bliss.*

स्थूलादिभावा मयि कल्पिता भ्रमा -
दारोपितानुस्फुरणेन लोकैः ।
काले यथा कल्पकवत्सरायण -
नर्त्वादयो निष्कलनिर्विकल्पे ॥४९८॥

498. Concepts of gross etc. are wrongly imagined in me by people because of the manifestation of superimpositions---just as in the indivisible and absolute time, cycles, years, half-years, seasons etc. are imagined.

Concepts of gross, subtle and causal bodies are created by the non-apprehension of Reality. These attitudes are all super-impositions upon me, the Self.

Time is indivisible and absolute. It is not possible to divide it into parts. Yet, for the comprehension of the human mind, units of time have been conceived. Cycles, years, half-years, seasons, months, fortnights, weeks, days, hours, minutes and seconds are all imaginary projections in the absolute Time. A minute is also time, a month is also time, years are also time. All these distinctions are in time.

Similarly, in the undivided hush and quiescence of the mind---in that absolute Reality---there is neither anything subtle nor anything gross. All these are but superimpositions.

In these verses, Sankara pointedly tells us that for the man of Realisation, there is no *sanchita, agami* or *prarabdha*.

---

* The misapprehension of the snake rises in the rope, exists in the rope and dies in the rope.

When I have no gross or subtle bodies how can I have *prarabdha? Prarabdha* is for him who sees the body.

आरोपितं नाश्रयदूषकं भवेत्
कदापि मूढैरतिदोषदूषितैः ।
नार्द्रीकरोत्यूषरभूमिभागं
मरीचिकावारिमहाप्रवाहः ॥ ४९९॥

499. That which is superimposed by supremely ignorant fools, can never sully the substratum; the great onrush of waters perceived in a mirage can never wet the desert tract.

By the fancy of my mind if I project something upon an object, it, in fact, can never have the qualities of my projection. Because of my delusory projection of a bleeding, ugly ghost upon a post, the post can never have the qualities of the ghost. The ghost can never contaminate the post, *(aaropitam na-ashrayam-dooshakam bhavet)*.* The superimpositions can never contaminate the substratum. Even if the ghost seen by me vomits blood, the post will not be sullied by a single drop of blood.

The causal, subtle and gross bodies are but superimpositions upon me. How then can their *karmas* ever affect me? I am Immaculate.

The desert land cannot get wet even by floods of water seen in the mirage.

Because of non-apprehension, I misapprehended myself to be the body. Thereafterwards, whatever I did was followed by its results. The results were accrued according to the quality of my work, *(karma-anusara phala)*. Thus *prarabdha, agami* and *sanchita*, were conceived. Now that I have realised the substratum, the delusory projections have ended and hence the *karma-phala* will not affect me at all.

---

* आरोपितम् नाश्रयदूषकं भवेत् । --is an axiom in Vedanta. "The superimpositions can never contaminate the sustratum."

आकाशवल्लेपविदूरगोऽह-
मादित्यवद्भास्यविलक्षणोऽहम्
अहार्यवन्नित्यविनिश्चलोऽह-
मम्भोधिवत्पारविवर्जितोऽहम् ॥५००॥

500. Like space, I am beyond contamination, like the sun I am distinct from things illumined, like the mountain I am always mortionless, like the ocean I am limitless.

Like space I can never be contaminated. I am not involved, even an iota, in the activities and experiences of the body. Like the sun, I am other than all that is illumined. The sun is not the world, though everything in the world is illumined by it. My body and its activities, my mind and its emotions and my intellect and its thoughts are all things illumined by ME, the Consciousness. I am something different from them all.

Like the mountain, immovable am I and limitless like the ocean. All these terms extol the infinite Reality, which is beyond them all. These 'pointers to Truth' are to be used in one's contemplation and deep meditations.

न मे देहेन सम्बन्धो मेघेनेव विहायसः ।
अतः कुतो मे तद्धर्मा जाग्रत्स्वप्नसुषुप्तयः ॥५०१॥

501. I have no relationship with the body just as the clouds (have no connection) with the sky. so how can the waking, dream and deep-sleep states---attributes of the body---ever affect me?

I am not in the body; nor am I the body. The body is in me. I am other than the body. the relationship between it and me is similar to that between the sky and the clouds. The sky has nothing to do with the clouds. In its vast accomodation, it allows the clouds to remain. The properties of the clouds are not in the sky. When the clouds move, we do not say, "The sky is moving."

Similarly, the nature and *dharmas* of the body can never affect me. I am consciousness. I am not the gross, subtle and causal bodies whose *dharmas* are the waking, dream anddeep-sleep states. Since they are not me, how can their *dharmas* be mine? In short, in Vedantic idiom the last line indicates that in me there is neither non-apprehension of Reality (sleep) nor misapprehensions (dream and waking).

उपाधिरायाति स एव गच्छति
स एव कर्माणि करोति भुङ्क्ते ।
स एव जीर्यन् म्रियते सदाहं
कुलाद्रिवन्निश्चल एव संस्थितः ॥५०२॥

502. It is the conditioning which comes and that alone which goes; it performs actions and experiences (their results); it alone decays and dies--- I remain immovable like the Kula mountain.

The coming into the body and going out of it is done by the mind and the intellect. It is the function of the subtle body. This coming and going happens in me, the pure Consciousness. The *upadhi*, the BMI alone performs all actions, good, bad or indifferent, It is the BMI which enjoys the fruits of actions. All these things happen in me. But I am like the Meru mountain* without movement or chnage.

न मे प्रवृत्तिर्न च मे निवृत्तिः
सदैकरूपस्य निरंशकस्य ।
एकात्मको यो निबिडो निरन्तरो
व्योमेव पूर्णः स कथं नु चेष्टते ॥५०३॥

503. There is neither 'engaging-in-work' nor 'abstaining-from-it' for me who am always the same and without parts. How can that which is One, unbroken and infinite like the sky, ever strive?

---

* It is a mythological concept repeatedly endorsed in the Vedas that the Meru mountain is the centre of the universe around which all the solar systems revolve rhythmically. Thus Meru is the motionless centre around which all movements take place.

Engaging in work and cessation from it are both egocentric ideas. They are the engagements of the equipments. Since I am not, in any way, connected with the equipments, I am not doing anything good, nor am I doing anything bad, being totally uninvolved in everything.

Existence alone is my nature. All things borrow my existence and dance around in me. I am "Existence" in everything. Their differences are due to names and forms. Names and forms constitute the world. The world *has* existence; the world *is not* existence. Just as you *have* health; you *are not* health. Health is a condition of the body. The world minus names and forms is Existence. This existence alone am I. Existence has no parts in it. It is homogenous and uniform. It is *eka-rasa.* That alone am I.

I am one homogenous mass of Consciousness without any differences. Like space, I am infinite. For such an entity, how can there be any activity?

Activity and retirement are possible only when there are parts to do the work and there is a field for activity. In space what can Mr. Space do? It cannot move even an inch, since it is all-prevading. If at all you see any work being done by me, you are not looking at me, but the movements of my equipments..... for, in my Infinitude I am like the sky, all-prevading.

पुण्यानि पापानि निरिन्द्रियस्य
निश्चेतसो निर्विकृतेर्निराकृतेः ।
कुतो ममाखण्डसुखानुभूते -
र्ब्रूते ह्यनन्वागतमित्यपि श्रुतिः ॥५०४॥

504. How can there be merits and demirits for me who have no sense-organs, no mind, who am without modification and form---who am the realisation of Absolute Bliss? In the passage, "not touched" etc., *Sruti* also mentions this.

How can I have *punya* and *papa?* Neither have I commission nor any ommission. I am pure Consciousness.

How can one who has no sense-organs and no mind, who is without modification and form, have merits and demerits? A blind man lying totally paralysed cannot be accused of having kicked me on my nose.

The first line of the verse is in the language of negation and explains what I am not and what I have not. My nature is positively the essence of unbroken Bliss. How can I be accused of having merits and demerits? In support of his statement, Sankara quotes from *Sruti,* "Untouched by merit, untouched by sin, he is then in deep-sleep, gone beyond all mental agitations."* This is the description of the individual who is in the deep-sleep-state. In Brihadaranyakopanishad, Yajnavalkya the Teacher, says so while explaining the sleeper.

In sleep, the individual is in deep ignorance *(moola-anjana).* On waking up, his desires will sprout again; so will his thoughts and actions, faithfully, as the same speices of his *vasanas*.When you are in the causal body there is no sorrow. It is only in the realm of effect that there is sorrow. How can there be sorrow for the individual who has gone beyond his *vasanas.* to OM? When you are in *avidya* you are a potential *punyavan or papi.* But once you have gone beyond *avidya* into *vidya,* how can there be any merit or demerit? When the non-apprehension of Reality has ended in Its apprehension, how can there be any misapprehension?

छायया स्पृष्टमुष्णं वा शीतं वा सुष्ठु दुःष्ठु वा ।
न स्पृशत्येव यत्किञ्चित्पुरुषं तद्विलक्षणम् ॥५०५॥

505. If the shadow of a man is touched by heat or cold, good or evil, it does not in the least affect the man who is other than his shadow.

---

* अनन्वागतम् पुण्येन अनन्वागतम् पापेन तिर्णोहि तदा सर्वान् शोकान् हृदयस्य भवति ।
--**Brihadaranyaka Upanishad.* IV-iii-22.

Heat or cold touching my shadow will not give me any sensation. When the shadow was being dragged along the road it fell into the gutter, then it came on to the road and was run over by a car. The fate of my shadow is not my fate. Let the shadow be run over, crushed, bruised and distorted. How shall it ever affect me? Not an iota of its tragedies and destinies will even touch me, for I am totally different from my shadow.

Thus the man of Realisation is untouched in his awakened Consciousness by the experiences of the world that he apparently gathers during his waking, dream and deep sleep states.

न साक्षिणं साक्ष्यधर्माः संस्पृशन्ति विलक्षणम् ।
अविकारमुदासीनं गृहधर्माः प्रदीपवत् ॥५०६॥

506. The witness is not affected by the properties of things observed, for it is distinct from them; it is without modification and indifferent just as the properties of a room (do not affect) the lamp (that illumines it).

The properties of objects observed cannot affect the observer. If I observe a waterfall, I need not have a back-ache. The observer is other than the observed.

The nature of the Witness *(sakshi)*, is changeless and indifferent *(avikaram-udasinam)*,* He is not involved in the activities. The nature and properties of the house do not affect the lamp which illumines them. In this house of flesh I am the Consciousness which illumines all its objects, emotions and thoughts without being involved in any of their activities.

The light in the house illumines all that is happening in the house. Bereavement or marrige, the fight between husband and wife, birth and death, the light illumines them faithfully. It is not affected by any of them. Similarly, the nature of the body, the sense-organs, the mind etc. can never affect the *Atman* who is the One illuminator.

---

* अविकारमुदासीनं गृहधर्मप्रदीपवत् ।
देहेन्द्रियमनोधर्माः नैवात्मानं स्पृशत्यहो ॥

रवेर्यथा कर्मणि साक्षिभावो
वन्हेर्यथा दाहनियामकत्वम् ।
रज्जोर्यथाऽऽरोपितवस्तुसङ्ग -
स्तथैव कूटस्थचिदात्मनो मे ॥५०७॥

507. Just as the sun is the witness of all men's actions, just as fire burns everything without distinction, just as the rope is connected with a superimposition, so too am I, the unchangeable Self, the essence of Intelligence.

You say, "How bright and cheerful the sun looks today!" Actually the sun is the same every day. Today you saw it as bright and cheerful because of the happy state of your mind.

In the light of the sun all activities take place. Therefore, the sun is said to be the witness of all activities. But it has no attachment with what it illumines. Unattached, it witnesses everything that happens.

Unattached, fire burns all things that come in contact with it. If you know the law of fire---avoid; Ignorance of the law is no excuse! The rope has no attachment with the snake that you see.

Immutable, changeless, *chidatma* am I. You may project anything upon me. I am unaffected by your projections. I am the pure Conscious-self.

कर्तापि वा कारयितापि नाहं
भोक्तापि वा भोजयितापि नाहं ।
द्रष्टापि वा दर्शयितापि नाहं
सोऽहं स्वयंज्योतिरनीदृगात्मा ॥५०८॥

508. I am neither the doer nor do I make others do anything, I am neither the experiencer nor do I make others experience, I am neither the seer nor do I make others see. The Self am I, self-luminous and transcendent.

Just now,* it was pointed out that the shadow is not affected by heat, or cold, good or evil. Even if the shadow is on a block of ice, one does not freeze. From the stand-point of the *Atman*, the transcendent Reality is as independent of the individual as the individual is of his shadow. Therefore, the Self can never get involved in the experiences of the world either directly or indirectly. To indicate that It is not involved in nor responsible for any of the activities of the world, the verse under commentary is given by Sankara.

I perform no action, nor do I enjoy nor do I see. Not only do these functions of the ego not belong to me, but I, the Self, do not prompt others to act, enjoy or see either.

Denying any direct involvement in the activities of the little ego, Sankara asserts the positive nature of the Self and cries out, "I am the self-effulgent, the transcendental Self."

Self-effulgent: *(swayam-jyoti)*--The Self illumines everything alike--the objects, the sense-organs, the mind and the intelltect. The question does not arise, "Who illumines the Self?" Because as pure Consciousness It is the source of all Light. It is unborrowed Light!

Transcendental: *(anidrigatma)*--Something which cannot be explained by comparison with things known, i.e. Transcendental.

चलत्युपाधौ प्रतिबिम्बलोल्य-
मौपाधिकं मूढधियो नयन्ति ।
स्वबिम्बभूतं रविवद्विनिष्क्रियं
कर्तास्मि भोक्तास्मि हतोऽस्मि हेति ॥५०९॥

509. When the conditioning moves, fools attribute the resulting movement of the reflection to the object reflected, like the sun which is devoid of activity; and they cry out, "I am the doer, I am the enjoyer, I am being killed, Alas!"

*** In verse 505.**

When the reflecting medium is disturbed, the reflection gets disturbed. If the sun is reflected in a bucket of water and the water is disturbed, the image is also disturbed. The sun is not disturbed. If anyone thinks the sun is moving, he is indeed a fool. If a child sees the image broken he cries out, "The sun is broken."

When the child cries out for the moon, the mother generally gives him a mirror. He sees the moon relfected in it and is happy because he thinks he has the moon. He plays awhile with the mirror and then drops it. It breaks, and the child cries thinking the moon has broken.

This is exactly our condition. When the body is ill, we say, "I am ill". When the mind is a little agitated, we say, "I am agitated". When the intellect is worried, we say, "I am worried". I, the *Atman*, like the sun, am never involved in any of these activities. Fools, not knowing that all these are the play of the equipments, cry out, "I am the doer, I am the enjoyer, I am the sufferer, I am dying. Oh! Alas.

जले वापि स्थले वापि लुठत्वेष जडात्मकः ।
नाहं विलिप्ये तद्धर्मैर्घटधर्मैर्नभो यथा ॥५१०॥

510. Whether in water or on land, let this intert body drop down; I am untouched by its properties like the sky (is untouched) by the properities of the jar.

This unnecessary weight of 75 kilos that I am carrying around with me, let it drop down anywhere. I am not involved or contaminated by its *dharmas*. Let it fall wherever or whenever it likes. The quicker the better.

Just as the space is not contaminated by the properties of the pot, I am not conditioned by the *dharmas* of the physical body I am the infinite Reality.

कर्तृत्वभोक्तृत्वखलत्वमत्तता-
जडत्वबद्धत्वविमुक्ततादयः ।

बुद्धेर्विकल्पा न तु सन्ति वस्तुतः
स्वस्मिन्परे ब्रह्मणि केवलेऽद्वये ॥५११॥

511. Doership, enjoyership, cunning, drunkenness, dullness, bondage and freedom-- these passing states of the intellect are, in reality, never in the Self, which is the supreme *Brahman*, Absolute and Non-dual.

I am the illuminator of all intellectual concepts which are nothing but thought waves in me. Intellectual judgements, wise or otherwise, are all in me; I am but their illuminator. In point of fact, none of them really exist, for the nature of Reality is pure infinite consciousness. Awake as I am to that Reality, no intellectual concepts and judgements have any significance at all.

सन्तु विकाराः प्रकृतेर्दशधा शतधा सहस्त्रधा वापि ।
किं मेऽसङ्गचित्तस्तैर्न घनः क्वचिदम्बरं स्पृशति ॥५१२॥

512. Let there be modifications in *Prakriti* in ten, hundred or thousand ways. What have I, unattached, Knowledge Absolute, got to do with them? The clouds can never touch the sky!

Prakriti is the realm of matter which undergoes modifications at every moment. There are modifications at the physical, mental and intellecutal levels which do not affect me, for I am the substratum of all of them.

Let there be changes in tens, hundreds and thousands; I have nothing to do with them. I, the Self, am unattached to the matter envelopments, so their changes do not affect me. As long as I am attached to the body, its changes are my changes, and so I suffer the consequent sorrows. When I am unattached, I am not affected by the changes taking place in that realm. For instance, as long as I am attached to the Bombay office, the worries of the Bombay office are my worries. The moment I am transferred to Poona and I hand over charge at Bombay, then the Bombay problems are no longer my problems.

Similarly, before Realisation I was attached to the body and so I suffered the persecutions of the body. When I detach from it, its sorrows no longer affect me. Just as clouds come and go but space is never affected by them.

The pure Consciousness in which, among other things, this body also exists, that Consciousness am I, so I have nothing to do with the body.

This is the sort of complete detachment and positive experience of the infinite eternal Consciousness, the state of Perfection to which the student has risen.

अव्यक्तादिस्थूलपर्यन्तमेतत्
विश्वं यत्राभासमात्रं प्रतीतम् ।
व्योमप्रख्यं सूक्ष्ममाद्यन्तहीनं
ब्रह्माद्वैतं यत्तदेवाहमस्मि ॥५१३॥

513. That in which the entire universe from the unmanifest down to the gross, appears as but a shadow, which is like the sky, subtle and without beginning and end, indeed, that non-dual *Brahman* am I.

Till, now the student was talking in terms of what he is not, in the negative language of our familiar experiences. By such statements we understand only half his views.

Standing in the "known", we can stretch our intellect into the "Unknown",. So a few verses are now given in positive language in which the student tries to say what he is. The wisdom of Reality, not known to us at the moment, is pointed out, where our intellect can make at least an attempt to stretch itself.

Suppose I introduce myself to you and say, "I am not my younger brother. I am not my sister either", etc. I cannot be satisfied with such an introduction, because I have not said who I really am. But if I mention the name of a common acquaintance, you will perhaps know who I am. "I am the nephew of Gopalakrishan's wife's cousin's uncle."

Similarly, the student is somehow hooking his experience of the Infinite to our known experiences.

Whatever It is, That I am: *(Yat-tat-eva-aham-asmi)*--That nature which is now explained, that I am.

From the Unmanifest down to the grossest OET, everything is called *viswa*. The universe consists of the entire world, the equipments of experience and the objects of experiences. This universe is only a projection rising out of imagination *(abhasamatram)*. *Brahman*, the Reality, is the substratum upon which all these imaginations are projected. That Reality am I.

That Reality is infinite and all-pervading. It is without beginning and end. Like space it is extremely subtle. That great Reality, that non-dual *Brahman*, am I.

सर्वाधारं सर्ववस्तुप्रकाशं
सर्वाकारं सर्वगं सर्वशून्यम् ।
नित्यं शुद्धं निश्चलं निर्विकल्पं
ब्रह्माद्वैतं यत्तदेवाहमस्मि ॥५१४॥

514. That which is the supprot of all, which is the Illuminator of all things, which is of all forms, which is omnipresent, devoid of multiplicity, eternal, pure, motionless and Absolute, indeed, that non-dual Brahman am I.

Adhara means, substratum; that without which things have no existence. The substratum for cloth is cotton; for the pot it is mud; for the chain it is gold; for the universe it is *Brahman*. Verily, It is *Sarva-adhara*.

The illuminator of all: *(sarva-vastu-prakasam)*--It illumines forms through the eyes; sounds through ears; smells through the nose; taste through the tongue; touch through the skin; feelings through the mind; and thoughts through the intellect.

All forms are Its own. It is the cause for this entire universe. The Infinite in Its grossification, has become the stone life, the plant life, the animal life and the human life. All forms that constitute the universe are Its forms alone.

It is all-pervading, devoid of plurality. All these are but Its expressions. It is eternal unconditioned by time. It is pure, uncontaminated by the BMI, PFT, OET. It is motionless. Everything moves in It; It has no movement. It is Absolute and is beyond all modification.

This Absolute Factor, whatever It Be, That am I.

यत्प्रत्यस्ताशेषमायाविशेषं
प्रत्यग्रूपं प्रत्ययागम्यमानम् ।
सत्यज्ञानानन्तमानन्दरूपं
ब्रह्माद्वैतं यत्तदेवाहमस्मि ॥५१५॥

515. That which transcends the endless differentiations of *Maya*, which is the subjective essence in all, which is beyond the range of Consciousness, which is of the nature of Truth, Knowledge and endless Bliss, indeed, that non-dual *Brahman* am I.

All pluralistic misconceptions are the creations of *Maya* *(Maya-prateeta-dwaita-bhavana.)** When Reality is experienced subjectively, all these misconceptions end.

Reality cannot be understood by properties. That which has properties can be understood through the BMI. If Atman is perceivable it becomes an object of our cognition; *Atman* is the Subject because of which we are able to cognise things. The essence in me because of which I know everything I know, can never be an object.

Eternal Pure Consciousness, which is endless bliss is my nature. This non-dual *Brahman* alone am I.

---

* मायाकल्पित देशकालकलना वैचित्र्यचित्रीकृतम्। -*Dakshinamoorthy stotram.*

निष्क्रियोऽस्म्यविकारोऽस्मि
निष्कलोऽस्मि निराकृतिः ॥
निर्विकल्पोऽस्मि नित्योऽस्मि
निरालम्बोऽस्मि निर्द्वयः ॥५१६॥

516. I am devoid of activity, modifications, parts and forms. I am absolute and eternal, with no other support, and non-dual am I.

Till now, because of my identification with the BMI, the nature of the BMI was my nature. Now that I have realised the Self, I have become of the nature of the Self

My identification with *Brahman*, has ended my identification with the matter vestures. I am the Self from which they draw their nurture and nourishment, and perform actions in the world.* The Self never acts.

That non-dual *Brahman* alone am I.

सर्वात्मकोऽहं सर्वोऽहं सर्वातीतोऽहमद्वयः ।
केवलाखण्डबोधोऽहमानन्दोऽहं निरन्तरः ॥५१७॥

517. I am the Universal, I am all in all, I am trascendent and non-dual I am absolute, unbroken knowledge, I am Bliss and eternal am I.

I am the one Self everywhere. The Universal I am, Names and forms are nothing but me. At the same time, as the Absolute, I transcend them all.

Unbroken objectless-Awareness am I. There are no distinctions in me.

The happiness that we know today is only an interval between consecutive sorrows. The bliss that we know is broken by the sequence of sorrows. Since there is no sorrow

---

* सूर्यलोकं यथा जनाः- *Suryalokam yatha janah -- (Atma Bodha).*
The explanation or the terms *Avikari, Nishkala* and *Nirakriti* is given elsewhere.

in that realm of experience, It is absolute, unbroken Bliss. That Bliss is not within the ambit of relative experiences but is beyond them.

That *Brahman* alone am I.

स्वाराज्यसाम्राज्यविभूतिरेषा
भवत्कृपाश्रीमहिमप्रसादात् ।
प्राप्ता मया श्रीगुरवे महात्मने
नमो नमस्तेऽस्तु पुनर्नमोऽस्तु ॥५१८॥

518. By the supreme majesty of your Grace, I have gained the grandeur of the sovereignty of Self-effulgence. O noble Teacher, salutations to thee, again and again.

Sovereignty within one's own Self is called *swarajya* in Vedanta; *samrajya* is mastery over the external world of objects. Freedom from inner persecutions is *swarajya.* When the BMI are not under the control of the individual, he becomes, as it were, persecuted by himself. When the objects of the world tempt him, they make him run after them. He who is free from such persecutions is a *samrat.*

The glory of mastery over one's Self and that over the world around me, has been gained by me by the Grace of my Teacher. By the sheer brilliance of his Grace, I have gained the glory of *swarajya* and *samrajya.*

O *Guru !* O great *Mahatman !* To thee my prostrations, again and again.

After pointing out his experience in the language of negation, the student asserts his absolute nature. Here he expresses his gratitude towards the Teacher who guided him.

महास्वप्ने मायाकृतजनिजरामृत्युगहने
भ्रमन्तं क्लिश्यन्तं बहुलतरतापैरनुदिनम् ।

अहंकारव्याघ्रव्यथितमिममत्यन्तकृपया
प्रबोध्य प्रस्वापात्परमवितवान्मामसि गुरो ॥५१९॥

519. Out of sheer Grace, O Teacher, you have awakened me from "sleep" and saved me, who was roaming in a never-ending "dream", in the forest of birth, decay and death created by illusion, and was tormented day after day by innumerable tribulations and greatly persecuted by the tiger of the ego.

In the deepest caverns of this mighty dream called life, the concepts of birth, growth, decay, disease, old age and death created by *Maya* afflict me day in and day out. I am confused, confounded and deluded. I am choked by various persecutions Thus I pass day after day.

Let us take a typical expample. I was born to my parents. I spent my childhood in my backyard. I went to school. In school I was told I was no good at grammar. So I worked hard at grammar. Then they told me to study Shakespeare and Keats. When I started quoting Shakespeare and Keats, they told me I was only repeating and had no original thinking. Finally, I landed up as a clerk in a government office. Parents got me married. In no time at all, there were two or three children. Government started family planning campaign. But there was one more by sheer accident. I was in Bombay where both ends never meet. Wife wanted the saree she had seen on the boss's wife at the party. Elder son wants college fees. Second son is doing Class V for the third time. Third child always sick. Doctor bills soaring high. Baby milk available only in black market. House has become a hell impossible to live in. All this is prompted by a ferocious tiger called Ego, sitting at the door. There seems no escape from this terrible agonising dream...............

From all such dreams, you have woken me up, O *Guro!* To you my prostrations, again and again.

नमस्तस्मै सदैकस्मै कस्मैचिन्महसे नमः ।
यदेतद्विश्वरूपेण राजते गुरुराज ते ॥५२०॥

520. Salutations to you O prince among Teachers, who are indefinable greatness, who are ever the same, who manifest as this entire universe. To you my salutations.

That one infinite Reality which is the same everywhere, which has come in the form of the *Guru*, to That my *namaskara*. To you, O Teacher, who revel in the form of the BMI,OET,*(viswa-roopena)*, my prostrations.

With this benediction, the student expresses his adoration to the Teacher who has initiated him into the science of Reality and Its unforgettable experience.

75. Final Words of Advice (521-575)

इति नतमवलोक्य शिष्यवर्यं
समधिगतात्मसुखं प्रबुद्धतत्त्वम् ।
प्रमुदितहृदयः स देशिकेन्द्रः
पुनरिदमाह वचः परं महात्मा ॥५२१॥

521. Seeing that the worthy student has gained the Bliss of the *Atman*, is enlightened, and is prostrating, the noble Teacher being glad at heart again spoke these supreme words:

To the best of disciples who has realised his Self and is standing before him in all humility, with head bowed in gratitude; to him who has quietened his mind completely and has awakened to the essence of the Bliss of the Self, to him, whose heart has become light and happy, the Teacher addressed the following words

The *Guru* now advises the disciple how a man of Realisation should work in the world and what his relationship with it should be.

ब्रह्मप्रत्ययसन्ततिर्जगदतो ब्रह्मैव तत्सर्वतः ।
पश्याध्यात्मदृशा प्रशान्तमनसा सर्वास्ववस्थास्वपि ।

रूपादन्यदवेक्षितं किमभितश्चक्षुष्मतां विद्यते ।
तद्वद्ब्रह्मविदः सतः किमपरं बुद्धेर्विहारास्पदम् ॥५२२॥

522. An unbroken series of perceptions of *Brahman* is this universe; so in every respect it is nothing but *Brahman*. In all conditions see this with the vision of illumination and a serene mind. Is it ever possible that he who has eyes can see anything other than forms all around? So too, what is there to engage the intellect of a realised man, save *Brahman*?

This entire universe is *Brahman* seen through the mind. *Brahman* experienced through thoughts and perceptions is the world of plurality. See this *Atman* with the inner or spiritual eye i.e. with a contemplative mind.

Those who have a pair of eyes, will they ever see anything other than forms? Those who have quiet minds, will they ever see anything other than *Brahman*?

Nevertheless, the man of Realisation has to go through the tragedies and comedies of life. He cannot avoid them. But in and through them, he never loses sight of the idea that the objects, emotions and thoughts are, in reality, nothing but *Brahman*.

कस्तां परानन्दरसानुभूति -
मुत्सृज्य शून्येषु रमेत विद्वान् ।
चन्द्रे महाह्लादिनि दीप्यमाने
चित्रेन्दुमालोकयितुं क इच्छेत् ॥५२३॥

523. Which wise man would relinquish revelling in supreme Bliss for the enjoyment of paltry things? When the greatly enchanting moon is shining, who would wish to gaze upon a painted moon?

Which intelligent man, leaving the supreme state of the Bliss of *Paramatman*, would wish to revel in the empty things of the world? The moon, shedding its mellow light, makes the four quarters of the earth cool and brings relief to one and all from the oppressive heat of the day. Leaving this aside who will desire to see a painted picture of the moon? Who would rather miss the beauty of the moon rising over the horizon to gaze upon the dead canvas of an arrested moment of reported beauty?

When the source of all happiness is within the bosom, who will court the impermanent joy of objects?

The realised man, having experienced the supreme state of infinite Bliss, will not throw even a backward glance upon sense-objects.

असत्पदार्थानुभवेन किञ्चि
न्न ह्यस्ति तृप्तिर्न च दुःखहानिः ।
तदद्वयानन्दरसानुभूत्या
तृप्तः सुखं तिष्ठ सदात्मनिष्ठया ॥५२४॥

524. In the perception of objects unreal, there is neither the slightest contentment nor the cessation of misery. Therefore, content in the realisation of the essence of non-dual Bliss, remain happy, ever identified with the Self.

Sense demands give us sorrow. In order to end this sorrow we run towards sense objects. By courting the objects, the desire to indulge in them multiplies. This makes us run after sense objects again and again.

The world of objects, emotions and thoughts is unreal, and so the experience of objects never brings enduring satisfaction or contentment.

Endless satisfaction can be gained only by the experience or the essence of the joy of the Self. *Atma-nishtha* alone can give us absolute contentment.

At this, moment, we are estalished in the not-Self *(anatma-nishtha)*. Get established in the Self *(atma-nishtha)*, and come to live this Bliss.

स्वमेव सर्वथा पश्यन्मन्यमानः स्वमद्वयम् ।
स्वानन्दमनुभुञ्जानः कालं नय महामते ॥५२५॥

525. O noble one, beholding the Self always contemplating upon the Self which is non-dual and enjoying the Bliss of the Self, you should spend your time.

The Teacher addresses the student as "noble one" because he has realised the Truth.

Sarvatha, means, *sarvatra*, *sarva-bhavena*, *sarva-prakarena* --at all times, in all circumstances, at all places.

The *Guru* advises the disciple to spend his life seeing in all beings, at all times, in all conditions, the play of his own Self and contemplating upon his non-dual Real Nature.

When your sense-organs feel the objects around, may that perception be accompanied by a close understanding that all the objects are but different froms of the one Self. When the mind is withdrawn from the objects, instead of being plagued by lust, anger, greed, delusion, passion and jealousy, may it constantly reflect upon the non-dual Self. Enjoying the Bliss of the Self, O noble One, spend your time.

When you are extrovert, see the play of the Self alone in the world. Maintain the thought that the world is nothing but *Brahman*. When you are introvert, in the hushed silence of the mind, may you constantly feel that the inner world is also *Brahman*. Since thus there is nothing but Brahman everywhere, may you enjoy the Bliss of your own Self.

अखण्डबोधात्मनि निर्विकल्पे
विकल्पनं व्योम्नि पुरप्रकल्पनम् ।
तदद्वयानन्दमयात्मना सदा
शान्तिं परामेत्य भजस्व मौनम् ॥५२६॥

526. In the unbroken Knowledge, the Absolute, the *Atman*, dualistic conceptions are like castles in the air. Therefore, attaining supreme Peace, live in silence, identifying yourself with the non-dual Bliss Absolute.

Projecting the world upon *Brahman* is like buliding castles in the air. In the *Atman* which is Indivisible and non-dual, you see the *pancha-kosas*, the three bodies, the "I" and "mine", the world of objects. All this is like imagining a city in the sky *(vyomni-puraprakalpanam)*. It has no existence at all.

Renouncing this fancy and keeping the mind and the intellect quiet, enjoy supreme Peace. Let not your mind rush outside. This is real *mounam*. Let not your mind worry over the dead, the unborn and the living. They are all mere figments of the imagination and as fanciful as castles in the air.

तूष्णीमवस्था परमोपशान्ति -
र्बुद्धेरसत्कल्पविकल्पहेतोः ।
ब्रह्मात्मना ब्रह्मविदो महात्मनो
यत्राद्वयानन्दसुखं निरन्तरम् ।५२७॥

527. The cause of all fancies, the mind, becomes perfectly serene to the sage who has *known Brahman*. Indeed, this is the state of quiescene in which, ever identified with *Brahman*, he constantly enjoys the non-dual Bliss Absolute.

A *Brahmatman* in one whose Atman has become one with *Brahman;* one who has found his identity with the Self everywhere. He is called *Brahma-vid*, the knower of *Brahman*. He has realised that he is divine and knows that the divinity in him is the divinity everywhere. Only he who has realised this Truth can keep his mind quiet.

Objects, emotions and thoughts cause us to be agitated. The cause for their projection and the consequent agitations in the mind. It is the cause for the non-existent imaginations and agitations *(asat-kalpa vikalpa hetoh)*.

When the mind, which always plays dirty tricks is quietened, there is total peace. When the mind which is responsible for the flights of fancy and chaotic emotions walks the path of *sadhana* the realises the Self, it becomes completely quiet. This quietitude of the mind is not because of deep-sleep or stupor but because of the experience of the objectless unbroken Bliss *(adwaya-ananda-sukham nirantaram).*

नास्ति निर्वासनान्मौनात्परं सुखकृदुत्तमम् ।
विज्ञातात्मस्वरूपस्य स्वानन्दरसपायिनः ॥५२८॥

528. There is nothing more exhilarating than the quiescence which comes form being free of *vasanas*, to him who has known his own nature and who drinks the Bliss of the Self.

The joy that we are familiar with is the joy arising from sense enjoyments. This temporary quietude arising from the fulfilment of a desire is accompanied by intense agitation for the repetition of the sense-fulfilment in order to re-live the moment of happiness. Compared with the Bliss of the Self, this ephemeral happiness is nothing but sorrow.The Bliss of the Self is an unbroken experience arising out of desirelessness. The state of desirelessness itself is supreme Bliss *(nirvasanamounat param-sukham nasti).*

He who has known the Self, and has drunk the essence of Its Bliss, can never be satisfied with the happiness arising from sense indulgences.

गच्छंस्तिष्ठन्नुपविशञ्छयानो वाऽन्यथापि वा ।
यथेच्छया वसेद्विद्वानात्मारामः सदा मुनिः ॥५२९॥

529. Whether going or staying, sitting or lying down, or in any other state, the enlightened sage whose sole pleasure is in the *Atman*, lives ever at ease.

A man of Realisation always lives in absolute freedom, as he desires *(swa-iccha)*. He does nothing prompted by the dictates of others *(anya-iccha)*. *Anya* includes everything which is the not-Self. The BMI are also *anya*. Their demands are not prompted by the Self. They are *paraechha.* He who lives as the Self, acts as the Self and exists by *swa-iccha.*

A wise man who ever revels in the Self as the Self, is a man of steady reflection.

न देशकालासनदिग्यमादि -
लक्षाद्यपेक्षाऽप्रतिबद्धवृत्तेः ।
संसिद्धतत्त्वस्य महात्मनोऽस्ति
स्ववेदने का नियमाद्यवस्था ॥५३०॥

530. The sage who has perfect Realization of Truth and whose mind, therefore, encounters no obstruction, no more relies upon conditions of place, time, posture, direction, moral discipline, objects of meditation etc. What formulae can there be for recognising one's own Self?

When spiritual practises are undertaken, certain instructions are given to beginners, according to the demands of the *sadhak.* In the initial stages, strict adherence to the instructions will help the *sadhak* in his spiritual progress. So long as a patient is suffering, medicines are prescribed. Once he regains his health, who can prescribe medicines for him and for what? The normal demands and the usual prescriptions are given here.*

Place : *(desa)* :-The Lord is all-pervading. He is present everywhere. But the *sadhak*, in the beginning, cannot think noble thoughts in all places.

In order to create a divine atmosphere, it has been suggested that a clean place be set aside as the *pooja* room. Going to the temple for congregational prayers etc., are all to help the student.

* The difficulty with the majority of believers is that they consider the means as the very end. They practise *bhakti, karma* or *Jnana* and in their dull and unintelligent preoccupation with their path they overlook the fact that these are only means to an end. Sankara brings out this idea very clearly here.

Time: *(kala)*--The student is psychologically available for prayer only at certain times of the day-early in the morning or at dusk in the evening. The rest of the time he is generally extrovert. So these two relatively quiet periods during the day are considered conducive to meditation.

Posture: *(asana)*--Physical posture greatly helps to maintain a particular pattern of thought during the initial stages. With the hands raised in an ardent attitude of prayer, you cannot have sensuous thoughts. Hence the scriptures prescribed a posture for meditation-- a sitting position with legs folded, with vertebral column erect and hands placed lightly in the lap with fingers interlocked.* Relaxed in this posture, you can maintain a chosen thought for a comparatively longer period of time.

Direction: *(dik)*--In every religion there are instructions regarding the direction to be faced while praying. Various reasons are given for the particular direction. If facing east (in the morning), one is said to face the Lord Sun who will bestow his blessing upon the meditator. In the evening facing north is advisable, since the Himalayas, where the Mahatmas live, are to the north. In Islam one is told to face the direction of Mecca. Association of ideas create an atmosphere of prayer in the bosom.All these regulations are to be observed by the *sadhak* in the nebulous stages of his *sadhana*. Once Truth is realised, they are of no consequence.

They story goes, a great *Mahatma* went to Mecca on pilgrimage. After reaching the shrine, he felt tired and fell asleep. After some time, he was woken up rudely by a priest who shouted at him.

"*Kafir!* Do you know that while sleeping you should not have your legs pointing towards the holy Kaaba? Get up and turn around."

---

* Refer Swamiji's Meditation and Life.

The *Mahatma* replied, "Brother! Why do you get angry for a simple thing like this? You may turn my legs wherever you think the Lord is not."

The prist turned the *Mahatma's* legs in the opposite direction and was surprised to find that the Kaaba too had turned with the feet of the Master. He tried another direction. The Kaaba too, turned again.

Verily, the Lord is enshrined everywhere, in all directions. There is no place where Mecca is not. All these prescriptions are to be followed only in the infancy of the *sadhana.*

Similarly, *yama, niyama,* etc., all have to be strictly followed to start with. They help you to achieve the Goal. Having reached the Goal, they are not necessary. What rules can there be for one who has realised the Self? Means are only to reach the Goal. In the Goal there are no means.

Wherever the man of Perfection lives, that becomes a pilgrim centre for spiritual instruction and solace.

घटोऽयमिति विज्ञातुं नियमः कोऽन्वपेक्षते ।
विना प्रमाणसुष्ठुत्वं यस्मिन्सति पदार्थधीः ॥५३१॥

531. "This is a jar" --to know this what condition is necessary save that the means of knowledge be without any defects, which alone ensures a cognition of the object?

To know an object which is in front of you, you need a healthy sense organ without defects, To know a form, you need a healthy pair of eyes. The instrument of knowledge is all that is required. Beyond this nothing else is necessary. To make you understand a thing which is not within the range of your sense organs, I will have to draw upon all kinds of information and proofs. But with an object already in front of you, what other proof is required of its existence?

अयमात्मा नित्यसिद्धः प्रमाणे सति भासते ।
न देशं नापि वा कालं न शुद्धिं वाप्यपेक्षते ॥५३२॥

532. This *Atman* which is an eternal Truth, manifests Itself in the presence of the right means of knowledge. It is dependent neither on place nor time nor (outward) purity.

Even while making a negative statement of the awareness of the *Atman*, "I do not konw", the *Atman* is present.

"How do you know that you do not know?"

"I just know".

This "I" which knows and also knows that it does no know is the "I" we are talking about. It is because of this "I" that one is able to say, "I do not know". To know it, nothing more than a quiet mind is required.

If the means of knowledge are there, there is no difficulty at all. Place, time, direction, taking bath, posture, rules etc. are not required at all, for the ever-present Reality does not depend upon them in the least. These are only the externals advised to quieten the mind.

To konw that I am what I am, no special time or pose or occasion is necessary. Even if in pitch darkness somebody calls out to you, "Are you there"? you do not say, "Wait. I cannot see. Let me bring a lamp.",Absurd.

So too, knowledge of your own Self is independent of external aid.

देवदत्तोऽहमित्येतद्विज्ञानं निरपेक्षकम् ।
तद्वद्ब्रह्मविदोऽप्यस्य ब्रह्माहमिति वेदनम् ॥५३३॥

533. "I am Devadatta", this knowledge is independent of conditions. Similarly, the knower of *Brahman* realises that he is *Brahman*.

If somebody says, "I am Mr. So-and-so", will you ask him, "How do you know? What instrument did you employ this morning to know that you are really you?"

"Did you see yourself"

"No."

"Did you hear yourslef?"

"No."

"Did you taste yourself?"

"No"

"Did you feel yourself"

"No."

"Did you think of yourslef?"

"No."

"Then how do you know you are you"?

"My dear sir! To know myself I do not need any instrument. *I am me.* To know a thing other than me I need instruments."

The subjective knowledge that I am So-and-so is independent of any intermediation. Just as intimately then, the knower of *Brahman* knows himself to be *Brahman*. Nobody need tell him this, nor does he need any instrument* to interpret this knowledge.

भानुनेव जगत्सर्वं भासते यस्य तेजसा ।
अनात्मकमसत्तुच्छं किं नु तस्यावभासकम् ॥५३४॥

534. What indeed can manifest That whose effulgence, like the sun, cause the entire fallacious, unreal and unimportant universe to appear at all?

The objects of the world borrow the light of the sun and reflect it. The universe of the OET and the equipments of the BMI all exist and shine forth borrowing their existence from

* न दीपस्यान्यदीपेच्छा यथा स्वात्मप्रकाशने ॥

--*Atma Bodha,* 29.

the brilliance of conciousness; for if Consciousness does not function through the equipment, that equipment is considered dead.

To know the sun no illuminator is necessary. To known whether the sun has risen or not, there is no need to light a match. To know Consciousness, you do not need an instrument. It is an immediate knowledge.

वेदशास्त्रपुराणानि भूतानि सकलान्यपि ।
येनार्थवन्ति तं किन्नु विज्ञातारं प्रकाशयेत् ॥५३५॥

535. That by which all Vedas, *Sastras* and Puranas and all other beings are endowed with meaning, verily, what can illumimine That Eternal Subject?

All the great scriptural texts are meaningful and purposesful only becasue of this great Reality. Whatever was expounded by the mighty Masters, was because of this Consciousness which is the theme of the scriptures.

All beings have Existence. If this Existence is removed, nothing exists. The Self is the material cause for all the objects that we see, just as the waking mind is the material cause for the entire dream world. Infinite Consciousness illumines this universe. Because of It everything exists. What other illuminator is necessary to illumine this mighty Truth which lends existence and life to every living creature?

Therefore, at the time of *Samadhi*, it is meaningless to discuss, "What is That because of which I am experiencing this Infinite Consciousness."

एष स्वयंज्योतिरनन्तशक्ति -
रात्माऽप्रमेयः सकलानुभूतिः ।

---

[1] तमेव भान्तमनुभाति सर्वं तस्यभासा सर्वमिदं विभाति ।

(Svetasvatara Upanishad, VI. 14).

यमेव विज्ञाय विमुक्तबन्धो
जयत्ययं ब्रह्मविदुत्तमोत्तमः ॥५३६॥

536. Here is the Self-effulgent *Atman*, of endless power, beyond all conditioned knowledge yet the direct experience of all. Freed from bondage, realising this alone, the best among the knowers of *Brahman* lives his life of victory.

The *Atman* is Self-effulgent and is infinite Power. The power of the universe is its capacity to produce, nourish and dostroy. This capacity is because of the Infinite, the Omnipotent. Indeed It is All-powerful.

The Self is indefinable *(a-prameya).* That which is conditioned (finite) can be defined. Finite things are substances which have properties that can be defined. When a thing has no properties, it cannot be defined. It is not a substance, therefore, It is Eternal, Immutable, Infinte. Who can talk about That? It is beyond all definition, meaning, beyond all conditioned knowledge. It is the universal experience of all living creatures hence It is not a void. Everyone has Consciousness. Though It is within the experience of everybody, nobody can describe It. By realising the Infinte, one is liberated from all bondage. Thereafter, one lives gloriously and victoriously. He is the best among the best since he has realised That which exalts men and makes them rise above their imperfections.

न खिद्यते नो विषयैः प्रमोदते
न सज्जते नापि विरज्यते च ।
स्वस्मिन्सदा क्रीडति नन्दति स्वयं
निरन्तरानन्दरसेन तृप्तः ॥५३७॥

537. Neither grieved nor elated, neither attached nor averse to sense-objects, but content with the endless essence of Bliss, he sports and revels in the Self.

Never does the man of Realisation grieve, nor does he get thrilled. Even when he comes in contact with sense-objects, he does not get attached to them.

Grief: *(kheda)*--is the state of mind created by the absence of objects of one's liking. Ecstasy *(pramoda)*, is the state of mind where the objects are in one's possession unrestrictedly available for indulgence. He who has no likes and dislikes knows no grief nor elation. The man of Realisation is above likes and dislikes, and knows fully the evanescent joy of sense-objects. He knows it to be short-lived and a forerunner of sorrow. He is unaffected by the presence or absence of the objects. They do not produce any disturbance in him.

We are so attached to them because we know no realm of greater happiness. The man of Realisation is detached from them because he sports and revels in his own Self. He is well-balanced at all personality levels because he has drunk at the fountain of infinite Joy and satisfaction which springs from within himself.

Nandana and *kreeda* are two words used to denote the expression of joy. When he revels *(nandana)*, he needs nothing other than himself to entertain himself. He enjoys himself in himself by himself. This democratic joy is called *nandana*.

Sport: *(kreeda)*--is when he needs something other than himself to entertain himself.

A man of Perfection coming in contact with the objects outside, sports in the divine Presence everywhere. When he embraces objects it is not flesh embracing flesh, but it is hunging the Lord who is present everywhere. When he withdraws himself in mediation, he enjoys and revels within. Such an individual is always well-content. His contentment is born of the experience of the unbroken Bliss of the Self.

क्षुधां देहव्यथां त्यक्त्वा बालः क्रीडति वस्तुनि ।
तथैव विद्वान् रमते निर्ममो निरहं सुखी ॥५३८॥

538. Forgetting his hunger and physical pains a child palys with toys. In the same way the wise man is happy and revels without the ideas of "I" and "mine".

Without recognising hunger and pain, forgetting exhaustion and fatigue, a child plays with the objects of his liking. Similarly, the wise man revels, forgetting his exhaustion and hunger at all levels of his personality. Without the ideas "I" and "mine", very happily he revels, just like a child.

The analogy is very important here. Exhaustion and hunger are present in the child. Because of the joy of the play, the child refuses to recognise them. Similarly, in a man of Perfection, the "I" and "mine" are there. But because he is constantly revelling in the Bliss of the Self, he does not recognise them, and his *ahamkara* and *mamata* rest unnoticed. Whether you do not have a thing or have quite forgotten its existence, it matters not, for you are oblivious to it.

It is interesting to note the careful and masterly technique of Sankara's poetry. The words "hunger" and "pain" are balanced against the terms "my" and "I" in the second line. The my-ness *(mamata)*, creates 'hunger' for more and more objects, while I-ness is equated here with the endless pains. One who has eliminated both the sense of I-ness and my-ness is one in whom there are no more 'hungers' for sense objects nor egocentric pains. Such an individual alone is happy *(sukhi)* in the world.

चिन्ताशून्यमदैन्यभैक्षमशनं पानं सरिद्वारिषु
स्वातन्त्र्येण निरंकुशा स्थितिरभीर्निद्रा श्मशाने वने ।
वस्त्रं क्षालनशोषणादिरहितं दिग्वास्तु शय्या मही
संचारो निगमान्तवीथिषु विदां क्रीडा परे ब्रह्मणि ॥५३९॥

539. Without the anxiety and humiliation of begging, men of Perfection have their food, and drink the waters of rivers; they live, free and independant,

sleeping without fear in cremation grounds or in forest; their clothing is the "quarters", which need no washing or drying, or some bark etc, the earth is their bed and they roam in the avenues of *Vedanta* while they revel in the supreme *Brahman*.

Food, clothing and shelter are the basic needs of a human being. The company he keeps and the type of activity he delights in indicate his cultural evolution. These conditionings of the man of Realisation are described in this verse. The man who has awakened to the higher plane of Consciousness lives in perfect independence in this world.

Without worry: *(chinta-shoonyam)*--No thought comes to his mind which will disturb and destroy him. Worry cannot reach him who refuses to worry.

Without any sense of humiliation: *(adainyam)*--He is ready to meet anybody, at any time on any level, without the least hesitation.

Food obtained by begging: *(bhaikshya-ashanam)*--He eats whatever anybody gives him.

Drink river water: *(panam-saridwarisu)*--Rivers do not belong to anybody in particular. Anyone can drink as much water as he wants.

Without any fear: *(abhih)*--He is not afraid of anyone or of anything.

Sleeping in a cremation ground or in a forest: *(nidra smasane-vane)*--He is perfectly at home in both places. It makes no difference to him where he sleeps.

Vastram means cloth. It also means the bark of any tree. A man of Realisation wears any cloth. If cloth is not available, the bark of any tree suffices.

The clothes which need no washing or drying: *(kshalan soshana-adi rahitam)*--It is not drip-dry. Nor is it wash and wear. If no cloth is available he clothes himself in the four quarters.

Thus he lives, totally independent of all external conditions, for he is least affected by them.

विमानमालम्ब्य शरीरमेतद्
भुनक्त्यशेषान्विषयानुपस्थितान् ।
परेच्छया बालवदात्मवेत्ता
योऽव्यक्तलिङ्गोऽननुषक्तबाह्यः ॥५४०॥

540. He wears no insignia and is unattached to sense-objects; he remains in this body without identifying with it and experiences sense-objects as they come, by the wish of others; the knower of *Atman* is like a child.

Holding on to total non-identification with the body, the man of Realisation enjoys the entire range of objects. Ordinarily, we are all identified with the body. The perfected man enjoys the world of objects without identification with his body. He never runs after them but they come to him unasked, by the desire or instrumentation of others *(para-iccha)*.

His relationship with objects is like that of a child. The child does not know how and when to take milk. If you give him an object to play with, he will play. If it falls from his hands he does not know how to pick it up. Somebody has to do that and put it back into his hand.

Like a child, a man of Realisation, by the desire of others "enjoys" the objects around. With no outward mark: *(avyaktalingam)*--He lives with no external symbols to set him apart from others......yet he outshines all in a crowd by his mere *presence*.

दिगम्बरो वापि च साम्बरो वा
त्वगम्बरो वापि चिदम्बरस्थः ।

उन्मत्तवद्वापि च बालवद्वा
पिशाचवद्वापि चरत्यवन्याम् ॥५४१॥

541. Sometimes wearing no clothes except the quarters, sometimes with clothes, sometimes wearing skins, established in the ethereal plane of Knowledge Absolute, he roams about in the world, sometimes like one insane, sometimes like a child and sometimes like a ghost.

Irrespective of what he wears, he always remains in an atmosphere of pure Consciousness. His behaviour in the world is also indeterminable.

He may act like a drunk who sees not the world as it is. A man of Perfection sees in and through the varieties of objects of the world, the common presence of the one Reality and hence his attitude towards the world is peculiar when compared with our norms.

He may behave like a child, yet without being childish. A child never drags his past into the present, nor does he live in the future. Anxieties of the past and worries of the future never affect him. He just lives in the present. But the child lives in ignorance while the man of Perfection lives in his Knowledge of Reality.

A man of Realisation may live like a ghost. Renouncing society he may live all alone in a dark cave. If anyone happens to enter the cave he will suddenly come out and disappear behind the tress in the jungle. Everybody is afraid of a ghost, but no ghost is known to have been afraid of anyone.

He thus moves about in the world unaffected by anything around.

कामान्निष्कामरूपी संश्चरत्येकचरो मुनिः ।
स्वात्मनैव सदा तुष्टः स्वयं सर्वात्मना स्थितः ॥५४२॥

542. Being of the nature of desirelessness, the sage 'enjoys' sense-objects but lives alone. He is ever-satisfied with his own Self, and exists as everything everywhere.

A man of Perfection also entertains desire but with a difference--he entertains "desireless-desires." From our standpoint he may be working with a goal, a purpose, but from his standpoint there is no desire-prompted activity. It is only we who superimpose upon him the desires, for the work undertaken by him is done as sincerely, exhaustively and completely as though prompted by desires. All his actions are spontaneous.

He moves about alone, with no companions. Though he lives in our midst, we can never share his thoughts and emotions. He is all alone in his unique experience. Ever revelling in the Self as the Self of the whole universe, he entertains desires which are desireless. This way of life he cannot share with us since neither has he the vocabulary to explain nor we the wisdom to understand the plane of Consciousness in which he revels.

क्वचिन्मूढो विद्वान् क्वचिदपि महाराजविभवः
क्वचिद्भ्रान्तः सौम्यः क्वचिदजगराचारकलितः ।
क्वचित्पात्रीभूतः क्वचिदवमतः क्वाप्यविदित -
श्चरत्येवं प्राज्ञः सततपरमानन्दसुखितः ॥५४३॥

543. Ever enjoying the Blissful state of wisdom the realised man lives, sometimes a fool, sometimes a sage, sometimes with royal grandeur; sometimes roaming, sometimes like a motionless python; sometimes with a benignant expression, sometimes respected, sometimes insulted and sometimes unknown.

How will a man of Perfection live in this world after his final Realisation? No rules can be laid down for his behaviour. This verse tells us of some of the ways in which he lives.

Sometimes he behaves like a fool; sometimes as a man with brilliant intellect. The same man who was a rank idiot yesterday may be a formidable intellectual today. Sometimes he lives in regal glories with royal dignity; at other times he may wander like a mad man. All these outward judgements of him are from the standpoint of the world.

At times he may be very quiet, lying down still like a python. The python is the biggest snake of the jungle which lies down quietly in one place, sometimes for six months at a stretch. It never goes out of its way for good. If anything by chance passes its way, it just draws it in and eats it. Else it goes without food. The man of Perfection may behave in a similar manner sometimes. If you go and ask him, "*Maharaj*, have you taken your food?"

"Nothing has come to me yet."

"Will you eat something?"

"Why are you asking this question?"

"How much do you want?"

"Whatever you can give."

"An elephant?"

"Doesn't matter!"

"A rat?"

"Doesn't matter."

This sort of *ajagara-vritti* he may adopt sometimes. Sometimes he may be available for honour and recognition. At other times people may call him a rascal or a devil. He may be insulted or even remain completely unknown to the world.

Thus a man of Realisation moves about, always enjoying the supreme Bliss of the Infinite. He is so engrossed in the bliss of the Supreme, that others will have to remind him that he has a body. He gets reports about his body. In the Infinite, the body is indeed the minutest dust particle.

---

* Food here need not necessarily mean the food that he takes by month but embraces in its meaning all sense objects which are the "food" for the sense organs.

निर्धनोऽपि सदा तुष्टोऽप्यसहायो महाबलः ।
नित्यतृप्तोऽप्यभुञ्जानोऽप्यसमः समदर्शनः ॥५४४॥

544. Though without wealth, he is ever-satisfied, though without help he is very powerful, though he does not enjoy sense-objects, he is eternally content, and though without, exemplar, he has equal vision.

A man of Realisation may have no wealth at all to call his own. Even then, he is ever content and happy, unlike worldly men who, with all their possessions, are yet generally found miserable.

He has nobody to help him, he is all alone in the world. Yet he is very powerful. He fears none and so, nothing can threaten him. He is always content, and so, never indulges in sense-enjoyments. We run after the world of objects because we have the desire to enjoy them. He has none, for, he is ever-content. Naturally, the passions and the consequent pantings of sensuous life are not for him, the ever-peaceful, the ever-joyous *Mahatma*.

Therefore, he is incomparable *(Asamah)* yet the man of Realisation, in all cicumstances, is a "man of equal vision" *(samadarshi)*. In this wisdom he is an exemplar; yet he is humble enough to maintain an equal vision for all; none is too low for him. Viewed with his eye of wisdom, he recognises all as his own Self.

अपि कुर्वन्नकुर्वाणश्चाभोक्ता फलभोग्यपि ।
शरीर्यप्यशरीर्येष परिच्छिन्नोऽपि सर्वगः ॥५४५॥

545. Though acting he is inactive, though he experiences the fruits of past actions he is untouched by them, though he has a body he is not identified with it and though limited he is Omnipresent.

From our standpoint he is performing actions. From his standpoint he is not doing anything. The BMI are doing their work because of their *prarabdha*. What can "I" do? I am the witness of their activity. In my presence they are all acting. It is immaterial to me whether the matter vastures are acting or not. The man of Realisation has the attitude, "though doing, I am not the doer."

Doing and enjoying are for the mind and the intellect to indulge in. They are in me; I am not in them. Though he has a body the man of Realisation *is not* the body. Though he is apparently a limited individual, his identification is with the Self in all.

अशरीरं सदा सन्तमिमं ब्रह्मविदं क्वचित् ।
प्रियाप्रिये न स्पृशतस्तथैव च शुभाशुभे ॥५४६॥

546. This knower of *Brahman* lives without the body idea, and neither pleasure nor pain, neither good nor evil ever touch him.

To a man of Realisation, the body canot give any joy or sorrow because he lives without any poignant body-consciousness. He is not involved in the body-experiences as we are. Conducive happenings around us give us happiness and unconducive happenings give us sorrow. The perfected man, having woken to the higher plane of Consciousness, is not affected by the happenings at the lower plane. The subjective and objective environments at the lower plane of Consciousness can never affect him who has awakened to a higher one. He dwells, ever steeped in Brahmic Consciousness.

स्थूलादिसम्बन्धवतोऽभिमानिनः
सुखं च दुःखं च शुभाशुभे च ।
विध्वस्तबन्धस्य सदात्मनो मुनेः
कुतः शुभं वाऽप्यशुभं फलं वा ॥५४७॥

547. Only he who has connections with the gross body etc., and is identified with them is affected by happiness and sorrow, good and evil. How can any good or evil or their effects affect the sage who has severed his bondage and is identified with Reality?

This verse is an elaboration of the previous one. In the previous verse we were told that no circumstances, whether subjective or objective, can affect the man of Realisation. Here it is explained why they do not affect him.

When you are attached to the body (gross, subtle and causal), you contact the world outside and derive joys and sorrows from it. Those set of circumstances which give you joy are considered auspicious by you and those which give you sorrow, inauspicious. It may be otherwise for others.

If you are attached to the three bodies and also have the vanity, "I am the body", you become the waker, the dreamer and the deep-sleeper in accordance with your vain identification to enjoy the waking, the dream or the deep-sleep world. All the experiences of the three worlds you put under two heads: auspicious and inauspicious, depending upon your feelings of joy and sorrow.

Thus, whenever there is identification, it gives rise to the PFT,* and the PFT alone experiences joys and sorrows.

To the individual who has done sufficient reflection, and as a result of his awakening to the higher plane of Consciousness where he has realised the eternal Self *(Sadatma)*, how can there be anything "auspicious" *(subha)*, or "inauspicious" *(a-subha)*,** as we label it to be? From the standpoint of the Self there are no environments at all. After waking from the dream, how can the conditionings of the dream affect the waker?

तमसा ग्रस्तवद्भानादग्रस्तोऽपि रविर्जनैः ।
ग्रस्त इत्युच्यते भ्रान्त्या ह्यज्ञात्वा वस्तुलक्षणम् ॥५४८॥

---

* Ibid verse 129.

** There cannot be *subha* for him because in his continuous experience of the Infinite divine there is no trace of *a-subha:* and without comparing with inauspiciousness how can there be auspiciousness? Auspiciousness and inauspiciousness are relative terms and *Brahman* the Absolute is beyond both.

548. The sun which appears to be swallowed by Raahu is not actually so. People who know not the real nature of the sun, in their delusion, say that it has been swallowed.

An example from the solar eclipse is employed here.

From the observer's standpoint, the sun is eclipsed. Those who say that the sun has been covered by darkness say so because of their lack of correct knowledge. How can darkness cover the source of light? To say so would be a contradiction in terms. But we do "see" it happen. Even though we see the phenomenon, we know that the darkness has never covered the sun, which at all times, is fully effulgent. The illusion takes place because of an obstruction (the moon), coming between the observer and the sun. In fact, the moon can never throw its shadow upon the sun The shadow falls upon the observer. Even when the eclipse is total at that very time the sun in its solar domain shines as brilliantly as ever.

तद्वद्देहादिबन्धेभ्यो विमुक्तं ब्रह्मवित्तमम् ।
पश्यन्ति देहिवन्मूढाः शरीराभासदर्शनात् ॥५४९॥

549. So too, the perfect knower of *Brahman*, liberated from the bondages of his body, etc. is looked upon by foolish people as possessing a body; they but see an appearance of it.

The knower of *Brahman* is totally liberated from the bondages of the BMI. Foolish people consider him to be embodied. From his standpoint he is not the body, just as from the sun's standpoint no shadow can ever fall upon it. We have no knowledge of the Self because of our mental agitations (the shadow of the moon).*

अहिनिर्ल्वयनीवायं मुक्तदेहस्तु तिष्ठति ।
इतस्ततश्चाल्यमानो यत्किञ्चित्प्राणवायुना ॥५५०॥

550. The body of the liberated man remains like the slough of the snake. Here and there, it is moved about by the force of *Prana*, the way it pleases.

* The moon is the presiding deity of the mind.

When a serpent becomes old, its skin is slowly sloughed off. At that time the serpent lies in a motionless condition. It does not move about or eat anything. When the skin dries up completely, the snake moves out through the slough and becomes rejuvenated. The slough left behind is exactly like the snake---it is of the same pattern, length and design. But the snake has no connection with the slough. Whatever might happen to the slough, it does not affect the snake. It is its own slough, yet it has no identification with it.

Similar is the relationship of the man of Realisation with his body. Having awakened to the higher plane of Consciousnes, he leaves his identification with his body. He has nothing to do with its destinies. The body moves about as long as the *Prana* functions through it.

He is not responsible for the merits and demerits acquired by the body. By the grace of life and the dictates of *prarabdha*, it moves up and down. He does not care a hoot whether the slough (body), is preserved or destroyed, consecrated, adored or insulted. It matters not to him.

स्रोतसा नीयते दारु यथा निम्नोन्नतस्थलम् ।
दैवेन नीयते देहो यथाकालोपभुक्तिषु ॥५५१॥

551. Just as a piece of wood is carried by the current to a high ground or low ground, so too his body is carried by the momentum of its past actions to their fruits, as and when they appear.

Timber is carried by the water current as it floats down a river. You may say that the timber is floating down fast or slow, to the right or to the left. In fact, the wood does no move of its own accord. It is being carried by the current. It has no intention of going anywhere. It is the current which determines the directions, position, speed and destiny of the timber it carries.

Similarly, the body of a man of Perfection is led and guided by the general stream of life *(daiva)*. The directions of his actions are determined by the total *vasanas*, which are the *upadhis* of God, the Creator, the Controller of everything. So his body moves in accordance with the time as the *prarabdha karma* manifests.

प्रारब्धकर्मपरिकल्पित वासनाभिः
संसारिवच्चरति भुक्तिषु मुक्तदेहः ।
सिद्धः स्वयं वसति साक्षिवदत्र तूष्णीं
चक्रस्य मूलमिव कल्पविकल्पशून्यः ॥५५२॥

552. Through desires produced by *prarabdha karma*, the man of Perfection, bereft of the body-idea, moves in the midst of sense-enjoyments like one subject to transmigration. He, however, lives unmoved in the body, like a witness, free from mental agitations, like the pivot of a potter's wheel.

A liberated man also lives amongst sense-objects like any other man in the world. As long as the body is living, it moves about in the same world. The world is created by the sum total of fructifying *vasanas*.* The ordinary man gets involved in the activity of this world, but not the man of Perfection. He is the one who has gained *(siddha)* that which was to be gained, *(saddhya)*. He has awakened to the higher plane of Consciousness where he lives, as the Self. In the body he lives as a witness. The BMI function according to the unexhausted *vasanas*---the *vasanas* to exhaust which he has taken the gross, subtle and causal equipments. In their midst, the realised one identifies himself with the Consciousness which is the witness of all their activities. Uninvolved, the maintains the *tooshnibhava*, the quietude.

Sankara, true to his style, gives an example here. Just as the pivot on which the potter's wheel rotates,---though all the movements of the wheel are conducted on the pivot, the pointed base which in itself does not move at all,---the attitude of the man of Perfection is of non-involvement in all movements that may be taking place around him.

---

* *Prarabdha karma* has been described in verses 453-463.

Whatever be the shape and size of the pots made on the wheel, the pivot of the wheel is unaffected. The finished product may be round or crooked, tall or short, symmetrical or otherwise; yet, neither the nature nor the shape nor the use of the pots spun on that wheel have anything to do with the motionless pivot on which the wheel is continuously rotating.

Similarly the man of Perfection remains unaffected with all that happens to his body, mind, intellect---ever established in the experience of the Self. In short, he too has *prarabdha* but he is not involved in it.

नैवेन्द्रियाणि विषयेषु नियुक्तं एष
नैवापयुक्तं उपदर्शनलक्षणस्थः ।
नैव क्रियाफलमपीषदवेक्षते स
स्वानन्दसान्द्ररसपानसुमत्तचित्तः ॥५५३॥

553. He does not direct the sense-organs to their objects, nor does he detach them from these, but he remains like an indifferent onlooker. His mind being drunk with "wine" of Bliss of the Self, he holds not the least regard for the fruits of action.

The attitude of the man of Perfection in his transctions with the world is indicated in this verse.

He is never at pains to guide his sense-organs into sense-indulgences. Ordinarily, you and I run after sense-objects. Objects are around the man of Perfection also. Neither does he run after them, nor does he deliberately take himself away from them. He is not affected either way.

If you are sleeping, you are not consciously responsible for kicking or not kicking the fellow by your side, because when asleep, you are not in the equipment at all. You are on a different plane of Consciousness altogether. The man who has gone into a higher plane of Consciousness has no body at all, Yet you and I see the body of the Master moving about.

He stays in the body as an unconcerned onlooker *(upa-darsana-lakshanasthah)*.

The man of Perfection has least concern for fruits of action. We generally act because we want something, or that we may get some joy out of the act. His dispassion towards joys arising from sense-contacts is because he is full of the esctatic joy of the Self. He is full of the undiluted elixir of the Bliss of the Self *(swananda-sandra-rasapana sumatta-chittah)*

लक्ष्यालक्ष्यगतिं त्यक्त्वा यस्तिष्ठेत्केवलात्मना ।
शिव एव स्वयं साक्षादयं ब्रह्मविदुत्तमः ॥५५४॥

554. He who has renounced the anxiety to reach the Goal and never to deviate from it, and lives as the Absolute *Atman*, indeed, he is Siva himself, the best among the knowers of *Brahman*.

Having renounced the anxiety to reach the Goal, and the anxiety never to deviate from the Goal *(lakshya-alakshya gatim tyaktva)*---i.e., "I must move towards the Self, I must not move towards the not-Self, I am slipping away from the Goal", etc.---in him there is no more this anxiety. The anxiety to reach the Goal will leave when the Goal is reached. Such an individual whose mind is free from all worry and dissipation is Lord Siva himself, the very embodiment of auspiciousness. He who has thus reached this *Siva-pada* is the best among the knowers of *Brahman*.

जीवन्नेव सदा मुक्तः कृतार्थो ब्रह्मवित्तमः ।
उपाधिनाशाद्ब्रह्मैव सन् ब्रह्माप्येति निर्द्वयम् ॥५५५॥

555. The perfect knower of *Brahman* becomes eternally free, even in this life and is fulfilled; he merges with the nondual *Brahman*---which he had been all along---through the destruction of his limitations.

The man of Perfection, even while living in the physical body attains the Infinitude, though he may be a PFT from the stand-point of others. He who attains thus is said to be fulfilled *(kritartha)*, having gained what is to be gained.

In our bosoms there is always the sense of unfulfilment or discontent. But he is always content, ever-fulfillled. There is nothing more to be gained by him at any level of personality. When the equipments are transcended he becomes the non-dual *Brahman.* He does not experience the pluralistic phenomenal world. He does not find himself separate from *Brahman.* He experiences the entire significance of *tvamevatad* etc. *(tvamevatad tadtvameva).*

शैलूषो वेषसद्भावाभावयोश्च यथा पुमान् ।
तथैव ब्रह्मविच्छ्रेष्ठः सदा ब्रह्मैव नापरः ॥५५६॥

556. Just as an actor, whether he wears the dress of his role or not, is always a man, so too, the perfect knower of *Brahman* is always *Brahman* and nothing else.

The actor, when on stage, is called king, soldier, hero etc. according to the part he plays. When the make-up is removed he is just an ordinary man, Mr. So-and-so. He was Mr. So-and-so even while he was playing his part on the stage. In both cases, with or without make-up, he is Mr. So-and-so.

If a husband is playing the part of Duryodhana, and mace in hand, meets his wife near the green room, will his attitude towards her be that of duryodhana? He will only be her husband. When the play is over, the make-up removed, and the mace changes hands, he is still her husband. Similarly, the best among the knowers of *Brahman,* who has realised the Infinitude, is always *Brahman,* even while living in the world and playing his part on the stage of life. Never does he identify with the role of the flesh.

यत्र क्वापि विशीर्णं सत्पर्णमिव तरोर्वपुः पतनात् ।
ब्रह्मीभूतस्य यतेः प्रागेव तच्चिदग्निना दग्धम् ॥५५७॥

557. The body of a *Sanyasin* who has realised *Brahman* may wither and fall anywhere like the leaf of a tree; (it matters not) for it has already been burnt in the fire of Knowledge.

The tree is found to have no identification with the leaves that have fallen off. The man of Perfection has as much identification with his body as a tree has with a fallen leaf.

Even before a leaf falls off it becomes useless to the tree, for it has already yellowed and dried up. It still clings to the tree because it has no energy to fall off. When the strong autumn breeze carries it away, the tree is not worried about it or its destiny, for long ago it had ceased to be of any use to it.

Similarly, the Man of Perfection, even before realisation, has burnt down his identification with the body in the fire kindled by Knowledge. It is of no consequence if such a body which no more serves any useful purpose falls off. Good riddance of bad rubbish.

सदात्मनि ब्रह्मणि तिष्ठतो मुनेः
पूर्णाऽद्वयानन्दमयात्मना सदा ।
न देशकालाद्युचितप्रतीक्षा
त्वङ्मांसविट्पिण्डविसर्जनाय ॥५५८॥

558. The sage who is firmly established in the eternal Reality, *Brahman*, as Infinite, non-dual Bliss, depends not on the usual consideration of place, time etc. for giving up this bundle of skin, flesh and filth.

An individual who has a reflective mind and who remains in the experience of *Brahman*, the Self everywhere, enjoys unbroken Bliss. Such an individual who has become one with *Brahman* even while living, will not wait for an appropriate time and place for dying (leaving the body). He does not anticipate *(prateeksha)*, all these things.*

---

* A devote cries--
कृष्ण त्वदीयपदपंकजपित्र्जरान्ते अद्यैव मे विषतु मानसराजहंसः ।
प्राणप्रयाण समये कफवातपित्तैः कण्ठावरोधनविथौ स्मरणं कुतस्ते ॥
O Lord" Let me enter the presence of Thy lotus feet right now because at the time of death when phlegm has come into the mouth and breathing itself is difficult, where can I get the remembrance of Thee ?

The realised man's attitude is जलेवापि स्थलेवापि .... verse 510.
"This unnecessary bucket of filth that I have carried all the while has been taken off. Thank you God."

He does not depend upon the time, place, circumstances etc. He has no problem like, "This bundle of flesh and faecal matter, packed in a sack of skin, where should I throw? At what time should I throw it? who should be the witnesses when I throw it? etc. Really speaking, the decent thing to do is, to throw away the filthy thing when nobody is looking your way.

देहस्य मोक्षो नो मोक्षो न दण्डस्य न कमण्डलोः ।
अविद्याहृदयग्रन्थिमोक्षो मोक्षो यतस्ततः ॥५५९॥

559. For, giving up the body or the staff or the water bowl is not liberation; liberation is the sundering of the heart's knots which are constituted of ignorance.

Liberation from the body is no liberation. If the destruction of the body is liberation, it would be easiest to employ alength of rope, or to fling it into a river or under an oncoming train. Why struggle at all? Nature will one day take it away. To free oneself from the physical body is not liberation for one will continue to exist in the subtle and causal bodies.

The staff *(danta)*, and the water bowl *(kamandalu)*, are a *Sanyasin's* accoutrements. These he throws away when he becomes a *Parivrajaka Sannyasin*. A *Parivrajaka* is one who moves about from place to place. Liberation from the *danta* and the *kamandalu* is not liberation, just as by throwing away the physical body one does not become spiritual.

True liberation consists of freedom from the knots of the heart *(hridaya-granthih)*, i.e. ignorance *(avidya)*, desire *(kama)* and action *(karma)*. These three knots must be cut asunder. Then it* matters not whether one has a body and possession or not.

कुल्यायामथ नद्यां वा शिवक्षेत्रेऽपि चत्वरे ।
पर्णं पतति चेत्तेन तरोः किं नु शुभाशुभम् ॥५६०॥

*Earlier elsewhere ***avidya, kama, karma*** have been described.

560. If a leaf falls in a stream or a river, in a place consecrated to Siva or at a crossroad, what good or evil will it bestow upon the tree?

The leaves of a tree fall off in autumn. One leaf may fall into a gutter, one into a river, one at a cross-road, a fourth into the Ganges and yet another may fly, drift in breese and land in a Siva temple---what has the tree got to do with them?

Let the body fall down anywhere, whenever its *prarabdha* ends. If the people around want a little more satisfaction, let them burn it. Else let it rot and stink. What have I got to do with it?

पत्रस्य पुष्पस्य फलस्य नाशवद् -
देहेन्द्रियप्राणधियां विनाशः ।
नैवात्मनः स्वस्य सदात्मकस्या -
नन्दाकृतेवृक्षवदस्ति चैषः ॥५६१॥

561. Like the destruction of a leaf, flower or fruit (to a tree), is the destruction of the body, sense-organs, *pranas* and intellect; the Atman, the eternal Reality, is never affected. It is the embodiment of Bliss which is one's Real Nature and exists like the tree.

When the leaf, the flower and the fruit fall off, nothing happens to the tree. They are all its fulfilment; but the tree is separate from all these. Similar is the *vinasa* of the body, the sense-organs, the vitality and the intellect. When they all die and fall away, I still exist.

Just as the tree survives after the fallen leaves, the fallen flowers and the fallen fruits, the pure, eternal, infinite Consciousness which knows no destruction, survives the body and the intellect.

प्रज्ञानघन इत्यात्मलक्षणं सत्यसूचकम् ।
अनूद्यौपाधिकस्यैव कथयन्ति विनाशनम् ॥५६२॥

562. "The embodiment of consciousness"--- in these words the scriptures indicate the nature of the Self, establish Its Reality, and voice the destruction of apparent conditionings only.

Pragnana-ghana is the world used by Yajnavalya in Brihadaranyaka Upanishad.* He indicates the nature of Reality by using this word.

Pragnana-ghana means, a homogeneous mass of consciousness, where there is nothing other than It. It points out the eternal Reality that survives all destructions. It is that which was, is and shall ever be *(satyam)*. That Reality is the Self in the individual which is the Self in the whole universe.

Pragnana-ghana also indicates that infinite, eternal Reality which is all-pervading within and without, which survives the destruction of all other things in the universe consisting of names and forms, emotions and thoughts. The state of existence transcending all the equipments is pointed out as *Pragana-ghana*. The vision of the world that we have today ends with the experience of the Reality.

अविनाशी वा अरेऽयमात्मेति श्रुतिरात्मनः ।
प्रब्रवीत्यविनाशित्वं विनश्यत्सु विकारिषु ॥५६३॥

563. "Immortal is this Atman, my dear"---this passage from the scriptures speaks of the Immortal in the midst of things finite and subject to modification.

In the same *Upanishad***, Yajnavalkya advises his wife Maitreyi, by saying, "That which is indestructible, that Immutable Reality is the Self, my dear."

By so saying, the *Upanishad* indicates the immutability of the *Atman*. Destruction can only come to *an-atman*. In the midst of change It is the Changeless. It is the light of consciousness in which all changes take place. That consciousness has no involvement in the destruction.

पाषाणवृक्षतृणधान्यकडङ्कराद्या
दग्धा भवन्ति हि मृदेव यथा तथैव ।

---

* Brihadaranyaka Upanishad, IV-V- 13.
** Brihadaranyaka Upanishad, IV-v-14.

देहेन्द्रियासुमनआदि समस्तदृश्यं
ज्ञानाग्निदग्धमुपयाति परात्मभावम् ॥५६४॥

564. Just as stone, tree, straw, grain, husk, etc. are reduced to ashes when burnt, so too, the whole objective universe comprising the body, sense-organs, *Pranas*, mind etc. are reduced to the supreme Self when burnt in the fire of Knowledge.

As long as it exists, a stone is a stone, a tree is a tree, a leaf is a leaf, etc., but when they are burnt, they all become nothing but ahses. The tongue of fire scorches the name, the shape, the quality, etc. of whatever it licks. What is left is only ahses.

Similarly, the whole world of objects, the body, sense-organs, mind etc. which are seen, felf and thought of, when enquired into, are found to be nothing but the Self. If the entire world of perceptions *(the kshetra)*, is burnt in the fire of understanding and awakening *(gyanaagni dagdha karmani)*, what remains is the Self alone. When the identification with the BMI is burnt down, the OET are no more felt. When all this world consisting of names and forms is burnt in the fire of Realisation, the Self alone remains.

विलक्षणं यथा ध्वान्तं लीयते भानुतेजसि ।
तथैव सकलं दृश्यं ब्रह्मणि प्रविलीयते ॥५६५॥

565. Just as darkness---which is distinctly different from sunlight---vanishes in the sun's effulgence, so too, this entire objective universe vanishes into *Brahman*.

This dissolution of the phenomenal world into the Self is a unique experience. It cannot be explained.

The world of perception being the product of ignorance *(Tamas)* must necessarily disappear at the rise of knowledge. In the fourth plane of Consciousness there will be no other experience than the pure Infinite Consciousness itself.

Sadhaks who are not fully initiated might find it difficult to conveive this idea as their intellect can never think of the state of existence where there are no names and forms. Usually, Vedantic Teacher glide over this by saying, "the world of plurality gets *merged* in the state of pure Awareness."

What exactly is this merger? How does it take place? Such doubts are being answered here by an example.

Before sunrise there is massive darkness all around, grining its horrors and frightening all weak minds. As the sunrises, in the blazing light of the Lord of the day, the darkness gets completely wiped out. When one awakenens from dream, the dream gets merged in the waker's mind. In the same way, ignorance *(avidya)*, and its consequent misapprehensions *(jagat)*, disappear in the effulgent light of Infinite Truth.

घटे नष्टे यथा व्योम व्योमैव भवति स्फुटम् ।
तथैवोपाधिविलये ब्रह्मैव ब्रह्मवित्स्वयम् ॥५६६॥

566. Just as when a pot is broken the pot-space becomes the limitless space, so too, when the conditionings are destroyed, the knower of *Brahman* becomes *Brahman* Itself.

When the body, mind and intellect are transcended, the knower of *Brahman* becomes Brahman, i.e., what was till now an intellectual understanding becomes a direct subjective experience *(Brahmavid Brahmaiva bhavati)*.

When the dreamer is no more in the dream, the dream-world objects can no more exist. When the subjective "I" in the dreamer rises above the dream mind and intellect, the dream world is no longer perveived.

When the dreamer and dream world are ended the individual awakes to a positive state of experience as the waker and naturally, in the waking world.

Following the same argument, if the waker awakes from the waking BMI, the waking OET are no more perveived by him, but he awakes, not to a "non-existent nothingness", "an empty vacuum", "a stupid zero," but he becomes the pure Infinite consciousness. When the dream ends the dreamer *becomes* the waker i,e, *becomes Brahman.*

क्षीरं क्षीरे यथा क्षिप्तं तैलं तैले जलं जले ।
संयुक्तमेकतां याति तथाऽऽत्मन्यात्मविन्मुनिः ॥५६७॥

567. Just as milk poured into milk, oil into oil and water into water each becomes united and one so too, he who has relised the *Atman* becomes one with the *Atman.*

In order to illustrate the subtle idea described in the previous verse Sankara, the Teacher, brings out yet another beautiful example. It is impossible for the human intellect to understand that at the moment of realisation his entire, separative, egocentric sense will end and that he shall become the pure Self. This unique experience gained on transcending the intellect is being communicated here with worldly examples for the struggling intellect of the student.

Just as when oil is mixed with oil, they merge to become one homogeneous mass of oil, similarly the Consciousness in the bosom, till now playing as an individual, when it transcends the BMI during moments of deepest contemplation and meditation, it merges with the Self to become one with the Self.

So long as the dreamer lives the dream the Teacher in the dream can never make the dreamer understand that on awakening from the dream, the dreamer will become the waker.

---

* Cf. जलें जले वियद्व्योम्नितेजस्तेजसि वा यथा । Atma Bodha 53.
The idea in the verse can be profitably compared with Katho IV-15. and Mundako III-ii-8.

एवं विदेहकैवल्यं सन्मात्रत्वमखण्डितम्
ब्रह्मभावं प्रपद्यैष यतिर्नावर्तते पुनः ॥५६८॥

568. He does not suffer transmigration having experienced seclusion as a result of being disembodied, and becoming ever identified with the one Reality, *Brahman*.

The state of Oneness *(Kevalah)* is called *Kaivalya*. It is the state in which there are no distinctions of time, space, etc.

Disembodiedness, some say, is phenomenal death. But according to Sankara, it is non-attachment with the body (gross, subtle or causal).

The non-dual condition *(Kailvalya)* is pure unbroken Existence alone *(sanmatratvam-akhanditam)*.

Experience of *Kaivalya* is *Brahma-bhava*. Having attained this, the seeker never comes back into the realm of change. The individual who has lifted himself from his identification with the BMI and has realised Om, never returns to the realm of bondage.

सदात्मैकत्वविज्ञानदग्धाविद्यादिवर्ष्मणः ।
अमुष्य ब्रह्मभूतत्वाद ब्रह्मणः कुत उद्भवः ॥५६९॥

569. By realising the oneness of the *Jeeva* and *Brahman*, his bodies (gross, subtle and causal), consisting of ignorance etc. are burnt and he becomes *Brahman* Itself; how can *Brahman* (the unborn), ever have rebirth?

The apprehension of Reality burns down the entire series of complications from *avidya* upto the gross body. The individual who has apprehended Reality becomes *Brahman*. Having become *Brahman*, how can there be any more becoming for him? The birth of a thing is the destruction of its previous condition. *Brahman* is indestructible. How can It have birth?

Now you may ask, "But Swamiji, how was It first born?"

"It never was!"*

"Then what am I now?"

"Nothing. *Maya.*"

"Then why should I struggle to realise?"

"Don't struggle. Just be It. If you think you are other than It, then struggle, by all means. But we know that you are not, for you are nothing but *Brahman* alone."

मायाक्लृप्तौ बन्धमोक्षौ न स्तः स्वात्मनि वस्तुतः ।
यथा रज्जौ निष्क्रियायां सर्पाभासविनिर्गमौ ॥५७०॥

570. *Maya*-conjured up bondage and liberation do not really exist in the Reality, one's Self, just as the appearance and disappearance of the snake are not in the rope which undergoes no change.

The concepts of bondage and liberation are in the realm of non-apprehension. They do not exist in the Self. When somebody superimposes the idea of the snake in the rope, the rope does not change. The appearance and disapperance of the delusory serpent will never change the rope.

Similarly the *Atman* the Self the Infinite *Brahman* is not affected by the stupid plurality that individualised egos in their hallucination have come to experience.

आवृत्तेः सदसत्त्वाभ्यां वक्तव्ये बन्धमोक्षणे ।
नावृतिर्ब्रह्मणः काचिदन्याभावादनावृतम् ।
यद्यस्त्यद्वैतहानिः स्याद् द्वैतं नो सहते श्रुतिः ॥५७१॥

571. When there is the presence or absence of veiling, bondage and liberation can be spoken of. There can be no veiling for *Brahman* as It is

* Mandukya Karika न चोत्पत्ति .... नचसाधकः ।
(Vide Verse 575 and translation)

obvious, there being no second thing besides It. If there is, it will contradict the non-duality of *Brahman;* the scriptures will never suffer duality.

Bondage lies in the non-apprehension of Reality. when It is veiled *(avarana)*, there is bondage. Having withdrawn from the equipments, *sravana, manana* and *nididhyasana* reduce the *Rajoguna* and *Tamoguna* in the mind. As the agitations become less, *Sattvaguna* becomes predominant. The mind becomes calmer. Calmer the mind, greater the contemplativeness. With a contemplative intellect one apprehends Reality, and says, "Till now I did not know *Brahman*. Now I know what Brahman is."

In fact, never can there be any veiling on *Brahman*. How can *Brahman* be veiled? With what will It be veiled? In *Brahman* there is a total absence of any otherness *(anya-bhava)*. In the Self there is nothing but the Self. How can there be *avidya* in *Vidya? Brahman* is never veiled, so It can never be revealed.

If you say there is veilling, it will be the destruction of the idea that *Brahman* Is One-without-a-second. the Infinite can only be One. If It is conditioned even by 0.00001, It becomes finite. The Infinite has no parts. *Brahman* is non-dual and the scriptures will brook no idea of duality.

From the stand-point of the Self there is no *an-atman;* Sankara talks from the highest standpoint when he is trying to talk to us of the nature of Absolute *Brahman*.

बन्धश्च मोक्षश्च मृषेव मूढा
बुद्धेर्गुणं वस्तुनि कल्पयन्ति ।
दृगावृतिं मेघकृतां यथा रवौ
यतोऽद्वयाऽसङ्गचिदेतदक्षरम् ॥५७२॥

572. Bondage and liberation are attributes of the intellect which the foolish superimpose upon the Reality, as the veiling of the eyes by clouds is superimposed upon the sun. In fact, this Immutable Reality is Absolute Knowledge, non-dual and unattached.

The ideas of bondage and liberation are the conditionings of the intellect. It is the intellect that judges whethere one is bound or linberated. They are nothing but intellectual concepts formed under the influence of "delusion". *Brahman*, the Reality, is never bound and hence can never be liberated. It has never been anything other than Itself.

You put your hands over your eyes and say that the whole world is darkned. If your vision was covered by a cloud, you say that the sun has come out again. In point of fact, the sun never went away nor came back. It always was. it is only the clouds which cames and went. The clouds are neither in the sun nor in the eye; they are somewhere in between.

How can you then say that Brahman, which is non-dual unattached and Absolute has become the *jeeva?* It is imposible.

From OM when you look at the world (OM is not a place but a state of experience), all the declarations of the scriptures are mere blabberings.* Yet an illusory tiger of the dram can frighten the dreamer into wakefulness. Like the dream tiger the scriptures, the *Guru*,the *sadhana* can accomplish an awakening of a person. The scriptures, the Teachers and the philosophies are all meant for the egocentric PFT to turn his attention in the direction of the Reality. When he realises the Truth he finds that all else was a bold bluff.

अस्तीति प्रत्ययो यश्चयश्च नास्तीति वस्तुनि ।
बुद्धेरेव गुणावेतौ न तु नित्यस्य वस्तुनः ॥५७३॥

573. The concept that bondage is and the concept that it is not, are, with reference to the Reality, only attributes of the intellect. Never do they belong to *Brahman*, the eternal Reality.

---

* यावानर्थ उदपाने सर्वतः संप्लुतोदके ।
तावान्सर्वेषु वेदेषु ब्राह्मणस्य विजानतः ॥ --Bhagavad Geeta, II-46.
To the Brahmana who has known the Self, all the Vedas are of so much use as a reservoir is, when there is a flood everywhere.
विज्ञानेपि परे तत्वे शास्त्राधीतिस्तु निष्फला ॥ --Ibid, verse 59.

"There is", and "there is not", these are the two concepts of the intellect. They are intellectual judgements. Consciousness is the light in which you arrive at these conclusions. It is not touched by your judgements. You are conscious of these concepts.

The illuminator can never be the illumined. The sun illumines the world but the world of objects are not in the sun.

As far as the Consciousness is concerned we cannot say that It exists, or that it exists not; for these two are intellectual expressions arrived at by the rational faculty in us. In short, the language of the intellect can never express the nature of the Absolute.

The absolute can never have any qualities; that which has a quality is a substance and all substances are finite and perishable. Therefore the Infinite must be that which has no qualities, we cannot define It in terms of Its existence or non-existence.

अतस्तौ मायया क्लृप्तौ बन्धमोक्षौ न चात्मनि ।
निष्कले निष्क्रिये शान्ते निरवद्ये निरञ्जने ।
अद्वितीये परे तत्त्वे व्योमवत्कल्पना कुतः ॥५७४॥

574. Therefore, bondage and liberation are conjured up by *Maya* ane are not in the *Atman*. As there can be no limitation regarding the infinite space, how can there be any limitation regarding the supreme Reality which is devoid of parts, devoid of activity, serene, unimpeacheable, untainted and non-dual?

Hence, bondage and liberation are the creations of the non-apprehension of Reality. In the Self they do not exist. How can there be any idea of limitation in That which is without parts, without activity, calm, unimpeachable, taintless, One-without-a-second and all-pervading like space?

न निरोधो न चोत्पत्तिर्न बद्धो न च साधकः ।
न मुमुक्षुर्न वै मुक्त इत्येषा परमार्थता ॥५७५॥

575. Neither is there birth nor death, neither a bound nor a struggling one, neigher a seeker nor a liberated one---this is the ultimate Truth.

In Reality, you are *Brahman* Itself. There is nothing whatsoever other than *Brahman*. There is never any birth nor death. There is neither a seeker in *Brahman* nor one who has the burning desire for liberation, nor even one who is liberated.

So, then, even liberation is not an occasion for glorification. That is your Real Nature. In fact you have no gained anything at all. All that you say is, "What a fool I was! I never knew my own nature." There is nothing to be realised. You are That. This is the supreme Truth---at the moment of Realisation, to the realised.

76. Blessed Disciple Liberated (576-578)

सकलनिगमचूडास्वान्तसिद्धान्तरूपं
परमिदमतिगुह्यं दर्शितं ते मयाद्य ।
अपगतकलिदोषं कामनिर्मुक्तबुद्धिं
स्वसुतवदसकृत्त्वां भावयित्वा मुमुक्षुम् ॥५७६॥

576. Considering you to be a seeker after liberation, as one purged of the taints of this Dark Age, with mind free from desires, I have today revealed to you, again and again, as I would to my own son, the supreme and profound secret, the innermost essence of *Vedanta*, the crest of the Vedas.

The crest of the thoughts in the Vedas, the deepest purport of Upanishadic literature, the most secret Knowledge has been given out to you by me, that you may achieve purification from the impurities of *vasanas (kali)*, and that you may make you intellect fully free from desires.

Thus, the *Guru* in Vivekachoodamani concludes his exposition addressing a student who had approached him in utter reverence and asked him the questions.

इति श्रुत्वा गुरोर्वाक्यं प्रश्रयेण कृतानतिः ।
स तेन समनुज्ञातो ययौ निर्मुक्तबन्धनः ॥५७७॥

577. Hearing the words of the Teacher, the disciple prostrated to him with reverence, and obtaining his permission, went his way, freed from bondage.

With the previous verse, the main thesis on *Vedanta* is concluded and Sankara is, in the few concluding verses, trying to wind up the drama of the Teacher-taught relationship. In the opening verses we had the enumeration of the qualities of a true student and were told of the nobility and grandeur of the Teacher's personality. Then such a perfect student was made to surrender to an ideal Teacher. When the student raised intellectual questions regarding his spiritual problems the questions were exhaustively answered and the discourse has concluded in verse 576.

In these few following verses Sankara is pointing out the reactions upon the student on intelligently listening to and dynamically pursuing the wisdom of this text book.

Freed from all personality encumbrances, the student, on full Realisation, takes leave of his Teacher and goes his way to revel in his own subjective experience, ever after ....

To the student who has thus realised, from his view, there is no difference between himself and the Teacher, both are experiences of the One-Infinite Self. Yet the student prostrates at the feet of the teacher "Out of reverence". Inspite of his Realisation the student cannot overlook his sense of utter gratitude to the Master who has awakened him from the dark dreary misconception of the ego and introduced him into the amphitheatre of the Self.

गुरुरेव सदानन्दसिन्धौ निर्मग्नमानसः ।
पावयन्वसुधां सर्वां विचचार निरन्तरः ॥५७८॥

578. And the Teacher, his mind immersed in the Ocean of eternal Bliss, for ever wandered about, indeed blessing the whole world.

When the disciple had gone, the *Guru* did not sit back with a sign of relief.

The *Guru* also, with his mind fully steeped in the Ocean of eternal Bliss, moved about blessing the whole world, ever ready to explain and guide seekers who might approach him.

77. The glory of the text-book (579-581)

इत्याचार्यस्य शिष्यस्य संवादेनात्मलक्षणम् ।
निरूपितं मुमूक्षूणां सुखबोधोपपत्तये ॥५७९॥

579. Thus, by means of a dialogue between the Teacher and the disciple, the *Atman* has been indicated for the easy comprehension of seekers after liberation.

Here in this verse we have Sankara's own declaration of the motive with which the poet-philosopher had industriously laboured through the 578 verses so far. The verse also indicates that Sankara had no philosophy of his own. It is only in recent times we find that every philosopher has got his own philosophy.

In Vivekachoodamani all that we have is a logical thought development of the entire theory of Vedanta given out in a style and language most fit for the easy comprehension of even the dull-witted. With this aim in view Sankara had woven this poetic tapestry, most successfully indeed.

Just as the great scripture the Bhagwad Geeta is presented to the public in a conversational style, here we find *Acharya* Sankara employing a Teacher-Taught dialogue. The entire theme discussed is the nature of the Self and how best the seeker can be trained and helped to come to apprehend the Truth.

हितमिदमुपदेशमाद्रियन्तां
विहितनिरस्तसमस्तचित्तदोषाः ।
भवसुखविरताः प्रशान्तचित्ताः
श्रुतिरसिका यतयो मुमुक्षवो ये ॥५८०॥

580. May those men appreciate this salutory teaching, who are seekers after liberation, who have cleansed themselves of the taints of the mind by observing the prescribed methods, who have a distaste for worldly enjoyments, who have serene minds and who take a delght in the scriptures.

Listening to or reading vivekachoodamani is no gurantee of understanding. Sankara could see that after reading the whole thing some will surely say, "All this is a big bluff." "Hence", he says, "I have written this only for those who have the following six qualifications---

1. Those who have completely purged the impurities of the mind *(vihita-nirasta-samasta-chitta-doshah)*, by following the prescribed methods--- *sama, dama, uparati, titiksha, sraddha, samadhana.*

2. Those who are averse to the pleasures of the world which are ever-changing *(bhava-sukha-viratah)*.

3. Those whose minds are quiet and calm, because of the reduction of *vasanas (prasanta-chittah)*.

4. Those who take delight in the study of the scriptures i.e., those who have the mental attitude to understand the *Upanishads (sruti-rasikah)*.

5. Those who are putting forth the effort, those who are striving to realise what they have understood *(yatayah)*.

6. Those who have a burning desire for liberation *(mumukshavah)*."

Such people, when they read Vivekachoodamani, will understand and appreciate it.

संसाराध्वनि तापभानुकिरणप्रोद्भूतदाहव्यथा -
खिन्नानां जलकांक्षया मरुभुवि भ्रान्त्या परिभ्राम्यताम् ।
अत्यासन्नसुधाम्बुधिं सुखकरं ब्रह्माद्वयं दर्शय-
त्येषा शङ्करभारती विजयते निर्वाणसंदायिनी ॥५८१॥

581. For those who are affilicted in this *samsar* by the burning pains caused by the scorching sun rays of the three-fold sorrows *(Adhyatmika, adhidaivika,* and *adhibhautika)*, and those who, in delusion, roam in a desert in search of water, for them here is the glorious message of Sankara pointing out the Ocean of Nectar, the non-dual Brahman, within easy reach, in order to lead them to liberation.

This wide and ample meter is generally employed by Sankara when he wants to pack a library of suggestive meanings into the band of a single verse. To a student who has seriously gone through the text, the terms employed in the verse need no commentary, and we are afraid that an exhaustive commentary would spoil the enchantment of its voiceless poetry.

To those who are in vain searching in a desert, thirsty and exhausted, to them, Sankara points out, with his confident message, an ocean of Nectar---the *Brahman* which is *Satchidananda.*

The final result of such a spiritual Self rediscovery is a total liberation of the mortal individuality from all its physical mental and intellectual entanglements. This is called Liberation, Self-Realisation or God Realisation,

HARIH OM
